WORKERS ACROSS THE AMERICAS

WORKERS ACROSS THE AMERICAS

The Transnational Turn in Labor History

Edited by Leon Fink

UNIVERSITY PRESS

Oxford University Press, Inc., publishes works that further
Oxford University's objective of excellence
in research, scholarship, and education.

Oxford   New York
Auckland   Cape Town   Dar es Salaam   Hong Kong   Karachi
Kuala Lumpur   Madrid   Melbourne   Mexico City   Nairobi
New Delhi   Shanghai   Taipei   Toronto

With offices in
Argentina   Austria   Brazil   Chile   Czech Republic   France   Greece
Guatemala   Hungary   Italy   Japan   Poland   Portugal   Singapore
South Korea   Switzerland   Thailand   Turkey   Ukraine   Vietnam

Copyright © 2011 by Oxford University Press

Published by Oxford University Press, Inc.
198 Madison Avenue, New York, New York 10016

www.oup.com

Oxford is a registered trademark of Oxford University Press

All rights reserved. No part of this publication may be reproduced,
stored in a retrieval system, or transmitted, in any form or by any means,
electronic, mechanical, photocopying, recording, or otherwise,
without the prior permission of Oxford University Press.

Library of Congress Cataloging-in-Publication Data
Fink, Leon, 1948–
Workers across the Americas : the transnational turn in labor history / edited by Leon Fink.
p. cm.
Includes index.
ISBN 978-0-19-973163-3; 978-0-19-977855-3 (pbk.)
1. Labor—America—History.
2. Transnationalism. I. Title.
HD8045.F56   2011
331.097—dc22   2010019005

1 3 5 7 9 8 6 4 2

Printed in the United States of America
on acid-free paper

To a new, cross-border geography of labor history

CONTENTS

Preface—LEON FINK   xi
Acknowledgments   xvii

PART ONE: *Overview: The Challenge of Transnational Labor History*

1. Another *World* History Is Possible: Reflections on the Translocal, Transnational, and Global—JOHN D. FRENCH   3
2. Historians of the World: Transnational Forces, Nation-States, and the Practice of U.S. History—JULIE GREENE   12
3. Transnational Labor History: Promise and Perils—NEVILLE KIRK   18
4. Labor History as World History: Linking Regions over Time—AVIVA CHOMSKY   23
5. Overlapping Spaces: Transregional and Transcultural—DIRK HOERDER   33
6. Transnational Migration: A New Historical Phenomenon?—VIC SATZEWICH   39

PART TWO: *Labor and Empire*

Introduction—ALEX LICHTENSTEIN   49

7. "black service ... white money": The Peculiar Institution of Military Labor in the British Army during the Seven Years' War—PETER WAY   57
8. "We Speak the Same Language in the New World": Capital, Class, and Community in Mexico's "American Century"—STEVEN J. BACHELOR   81

PART THREE: *Indigenous Peoples and Labor Systems*

Introduction—COLLEEN O'NEILL   103

9. Indigenous Labor in Mid-Nineteenth-Century British North America: The Mi'kmaq of Cape Breton and Squamish of British Columbia in Comparative Perspective—ANDREW PARNABY   109

10. "De Facto Mexicans": Coffee Workers and Nationality on the Guatemalan-Mexican Border, 1931–1941— CATHERINE NOLAN-FERRELL   136

PART FOUR: *International Feminism and Reproductive Labor*

Introduction—PREMILLA NADASEN   163

11. "No Right to Layettes or Nursing Time": Maternity Leave and the Question of U.S. Exceptionalism—EILEEN BORIS   171

12. The Battle within the Home: Development Strategies and the Commodification of Caring Labors at the 1975 International Women's Year Conference—JOCELYN OLCOTT   194

PART FIVE: *Labor Recruitment and Immigration Control*

Introduction—CAMILLE GUÉRIN-GONZALES   215

13. Feminizing White Slavery in the United States: Marcus Braun and the Transnational Traffic in White Bodies, 1890–1910— GUNTHER PECK   221

14. Patronage and Progress: The Bracero Program from the Perspective of Mexico—MICHAEL SNODGRASS   245

15. Unspoken Exclusions: Race, Nation, and Empire in the Immigration Restrictions of the 1920s in North America and the Greater Caribbean—LARA PUTNAM   267

PART SIX: *Transnational Labor Politics*

    Introduction—BRYAN D. PALMER   295

16. Claiming Political Space: Workers, Municipal Socialism, and the Reconstruction of Local Democracy in Transnational Perspective—SHELTON STROMQUIST   303

17. A Migrating Revolution: Mexican Political Organizers and Their Rejection of American Assimilation, 1920–1940—JOHN H. FLORES   329

PART SEVEN: *Labor Internationalism*

    Introduction—NELSON LICHTENSTEIN   355

18. Fugitive Slaves across North America—JEFFREY R. KERR-RITCHIE   363

19. Movable Type: Toronto's Transnational Printers, 1866–1872—JACOB REMES   384

20. Global Sea or National Backwater?: The International Labor Organization and the Quixotic Quest for Maritime Standards, 1919–1945—LEON FINK   409

Contributors   431

Index   437

PREFACE

Like those in other fields, labor historians are challenged to rethink their work in light of the ubiquitous border-crossings of people, money, and ideas taken for granted in the current era of globalization. This book is the first broad intellectual response by labor and working-class historians to what we might call the "transnational turn" in historical studies. Not only will one find here gleanings from a wide variety of research projects leading outward from a U.S. focus but also readers will encounter important work from Canadianists, Caribbeanists, and Latin American specialists, all following historical developments that cross national boundaries. As distinct from comparative histories built around the integrity of their nation-state subjects (a tradition boasting distinguished examples within labor studies), transnational works emphasize the supranational or subnational aspect of their subjects.

Yet, rather than deny the power of nation-states or national cultures, the transnational approach offers an additional angle of approach as we interrogate the origins and authority of nation-states, as well as their contradictions. As the *La Pietra Report* (2000), prepared by the Organization of American Historians' Project on Internationalizing the Study of American History, defined the current imperative, "If historians have often treated the nation as self-contained and undifferentiated, it is increasingly clear that this assumption is true in neither the present nor the past." This published collection began as an intellectual event. Befitting its own hemispheric aspirations, the journal *Labor: Studies in Working-Class History of the Americas* organized an international conference at the Newberry Library in Chicago in September 2008 on "Workers, the Nation-State, and Beyond: The Newberry Conference on Labor History across the Americas." Across two-and-a-half intense days, some one hundred scholars arrayed in twenty panels digested dozens of precirculated papers; to provoke discussion, the panels regularly matched a U.S.-centered presentation with a Canada- or Latin America–based counterpart, as well as a senior scholarly commentator. The call for papers for the Newberry conference provided the initial framing ideas for this volume. As the organizers declared.

We understand global processes, historically conceived, to be fundamental to labor's history, be it capital and labor mobility, imperial and neo-imperial political economies, or the mobilization of labor internationally and/or across borders.... The transnational also opens new avenues for understanding—over time and space—changes in the concepts, policies and practice of states, their interactions with each other and their populations, and the ways in which the popular classes resist, react, and use both the nation-state and the non-state entities to advance their interests.

Like M. Jourdain in Molière's *Le Bourgeois Gentilhomme*—who belatedly but happily discovered that he had been speaking prose all his life—we U.S. labor historians have long been practicing transnational history. The only problem is that we've been doing it rather haphazardly. In particular, much of the work in the early decades of the "new labor history" shadowboxed with the concept of American (i.e., U.S.) exceptionalism, an internationally comparative construct, to be sure, but one with distinctly limited reach. To illustrate the problem, let me quote from a typical elaboration (in this case, my own) on the theme:

> One of the favorite tasks of American historians has been to explain why the United States, alone among the nations of the western world, passed through the industrial revolution without the establishment of a class consciousness and an independent working-class political movement. Cheap land, the cult of individualism, a heterogeneous labor force, social mobility, and the federal separation of powers comprise several of the numerous explanations that have been offered. While not directly denying the importance of any of the factors listed above, this study implicitly suggests a different approach to the problem of American exceptionalism.[1]

The context for studies of workers' movements has been "global" since the nineteenth century. However, while pretending to reach out to a comparative framework—superseding a mere national or ethnocentric narrative—both the American-exceptionalist framework and anti-American-exceptionalist framework (as in the example) remained largely imprisoned in national historiographies. Worker subjects continued to be *defined* by their national affiliations, as well as rootedness in local working-class communities. And the coherency with which they acted—or failed to act—was chalked up to *factors within their national context*. Too often, American exceptionalist arguments comparing worker organizations and political movements were satisfied with quick generalizations, treating "straw" men and women, rather than wrestling with a rich and complicated international context. We rarely engaged people or concepts as truly transnational subjects that moved across borders. Indeed, even our treatment of immigrant workers too often drew on superficial characterization of "Irish" canal workers, "German" bakers, "Polish" steelworkers, and "Mexican" farmworkers—people defined by their economic function once in the United States. The problem in this case was not only that our interest in transnational subjects (be they people or ideas) often began *only when they entered U.S. territory* but also that we regularly affixed national signifiers to the outside world, giving nation-states outsized influence as both historical agents and sources of identity. In this respect, immigration historians, using a "village-outward" approach, as Donna Gabaccia called it, were often better able than labor historians to connect immigrant family, community, and work behavior across the divides of time and space.

As so often happens with scholarly rethinking, it was less any inherent weakness or perceived flaw in logic or evidence that precipitated a revised orientation to historical subject matter. The transformation of viewpoint stemmed from the contemporary processes of globalization in the 1990s, which woke us up and took us in new directions. It became clear that one could not think about contemporary labor without accounting for the drastic international reordering that encompassed flows of investment capital and deindustrialization, as well as heightened labor emigration and recruitment across national lines. The problem of the "global sweatshop"—as enhanced by NAFTA, the World Trade Organization, and the even more recent worldwide economic downturn—dramatically challenged the organized labor movement and its allies in every country. Moreover, the source of the problems inevitably took one beyond the borders of any single nation-state, as did most visions for their redress. Even more important, however, it changed the direction and framework of studies trained on the more distant past of workers and their struggles. Sensitized to the new, our antennae increasingly drew us to themes that were transnational, international, translocal, transcultural, and comparative—themes that had been there before but whose significance was not adequately recognized.

What understandings are encompassed by the transnational turn? And what are its likely perils as well as promise as a framework for research and analysis? To address these questions, we have asked six accomplished scholars to lead off the volume with their own critical commentaries on the project of transnational labor history. Their responses effectively offer a tour of explanations, tensions, and cautions in the evolution of a new arena of research and writing. John French acknowledges the hesitation among historians who have heretofore concentrated on the "local [community-centered] knowledge" of the working class to embrace a "global" perspective that may appear to deny the significance of their chosen subjects. Julie Greene stresses that the policies of nation-states themselves still require close attention, while Neville Kirk suggests that greater awareness of past connections across countries, and even continents, will inevitably transform our understanding of the politics of labor movements. Aviva Chomsky further draws our attention to the lessons of an earlier school of Caribbean political economists, who constructed a framework for world history emphasizing the continuing cycle of subsistence workers pulled into the capitalist orbit. Dirk Hoerder warns against a fetishization of the "nation" as *the* defining historical agent, pointing instead (especially within immigration studies) to transregional and transcultural influences that regularly cut across national boundaries. Finally, Vic Satzewich cautions—on both analytic and political grounds—against exaggerating the differences between today's transnational migrants and the various classes of migrants who preceded them.

Unfortunately, any attempt to size up the project of transnational historical practice—especially at this early stage of development—is itself likely to fall under the sway of the "sponsoring" national historiographical tradition. As Julie Greene warns, "Transnational approaches might constitute simply another form of U.S. intellectual hegemony." Thus, even our own conceptual effort is likely to privilege a U.S. labor history practice (in both its strengths and weaknesses) over that of Latin Americanists, Caribbeanists, and Canadianists. Needless to say, the latter rarely partake of the cult of U.S. exceptionalism, even if, as the guardians of other national stories, they may insist on their own distinctiveness. Moreover, as Jesse Hoffnung-Garskof has argued, "Outside the United States there is nothing new about attention to international contexts in the practice of national and local histories."[2]

Forced to recognize the hemisphere's force majeure, Canadian and Latin American historians, in particular, have regularly practiced a form of transnationalism in documenting the pervasive impact of the United States on their own societies. And of course, by definition those hired to teach and research as "Latin Americanists" are likely to have already accepted the challenge of deep acquaintance with more than one national history. Still, as Aviva Chomsky notes, dependency theory, which heavily influenced Latin American historical analyses, "privileged the story of how the core shaped the periphery, rather than its converse." May a more active dialogue among historians crossing borders from different directions, physically as well as intellectually, help redress this intellectual imbalance.

We invite readers now to dig into what they will surely discover is a rich historical feast. Following the initial methodological arguments, they will encounter fourteen original chapters, grouped in six thematic parts, with each of the latter introduced by a prominent scholar in the field. Two chapters on "Labor and Empire" feature explanations of the "contractual unfree labor" of eighteenth-century British colonial soldiers and the contradictions of "development" ideology for Mexican autoworkers employed by U.S. firms in the post–World War II era. "Indigenous Peoples and Labor Systems" at once emphasizes the persistent effect of European colonialism on native economies and the race-making and race-marking roles of the New World states. The political issues raised by both chapters in "International Feminism and Reproductive Labor" offer a special case of the centrality of subsistence workers—in this case, the unpaid or low-wage "care work" of women inside and outside the home—for the rights within as well as basic social provision of working-class communities. Each of the three chapters grouped under "Labor Recruitment and Immigration Control" brings our attention to unanticipated historical agents. A single immigration officer redirects anticontract labor law toward the pursuit of sex traffickers. Mexican state authorities and braceros play an important role in a contract labor program often denigrated as mere exploitation. Early-twentieth-century exclusionary immigration laws in the United States and across Central America ironically help foster a radical West Indian intelligentsia. The part on "Transnational Labor Politics" highlights contrasting possibilities across a diverse communicative sphere. Whereas a study of early-twentieth-century municipal socialist centers indicates, as Bryan Palmer suggests, that "the transnational coexists comfortably with the local," Chicago's liberal and radical Mexican activists brought a determinedly national zeal, as well as identity, to their work in the diaspora. Finally, three chapters on "Labor Internationalism" illustrate the differences in the capacity of labor reform (here encompassing slaves, printers, and seafarers), depending on a context of what Nelson Lichtenstein calls thin states or thick states.

Across a century, more or less, of specialized practice, labor history has enjoyed several significant and defining turns. From its institutional-political beginnings through the social history emphasis of the "new labor history" charted in the 1960s, scholars have drawn inspiration and instruction from the temper of their times, as well as the insights of surrounding intellectual inquiries. If the transnational turn in labor history is to sustain itself, it will no doubt have to pay close attention to both impulses. This book, we hope, is an early step in the right direction.

NOTES

1. *Workingmen's Democracy: The Knights of Labor and American Politics* (Urbana: University of Illinois Press, 1983) 229.
2. Jesse Hoffnung-Garskof, *A Tale of Two Cities: Santo Domingo and New York after 1950* (Princeton N.J.: Princeton University Press, 2008), xii.

ACKNOWLEDGMENTS

The contributions to this book date to an initiating conference at the Newberry Library, Chicago, in September 2008 on "Workers, the Nation-State, and Beyond." The conference, and therefore this book, is indebted to support from the Newberry Library (and especially its Vice President for Research and Education, James R. Grossman), the Colleges of Liberal Arts and Sciences and Departments of History at both the University of Illinois at Chicago and the University of Illinois at Urbana-Champaign, and Roosevelt University. A stellar team of conference organizers—Eileen Boris, John French, Julie Greene, Joan Sangster, and Shelton Stromquist—agreed to join me in organizing and editing the current volume, a task accomplished only with continuous coordinating assistance from early conference planning to final manuscript submission by Emily LaBarbera-Twarog. Finally, the manuscript benefitted from the wisdom and commitment of editor Nancy Toff of Oxford University Press as well as the expert ministrations of Sonia Tycko and Jaimee Biggins.

OVERVIEW: THE CHALLENGE OF TRANSNATIONAL LABOR HISTORY

1

ANOTHER *WORLD* HISTORY IS POSSIBLE

REFLECTIONS ON THE TRANSLOCAL, TRANSNATIONAL, AND GLOBAL

John D. French

Under the rubric of the global and transnational, contemporary historians are striving for a new type of history that links subnational specificities with supranational processes, extranational connections, and international institutions. In doing so, we are grappling with the viability and conceptual, epistemological, and empirical challenges of writing a truly international or global history self-consciously situated outside strictly national narratives. My engagement with transnational and global history originated as a venture into public policy terrain at the height of the debate over NAFTA (North American Free Trade Agreement) in the early 1990s, a time when the word *globalization* was virtually unknown.[1] By 2000, when I had completed the draft of my manuscript's first four chapters, U.S., German, and Italian newspapers used the word *globalization* up to nine times more frequently than five years earlier.[2] Nor was its use restricted to journalists. The word now appeared regularly in scholarly monographs, specialized textbooks, and an array of edited collections; by 2005, the word (not its cognates) turned up in the titles or subtitles of sixty-eight English-language books, all but seven published after 2000. Based on abstracts in a Web-based index of scholarly articles, Fred Cooper discovered that the word *globalization* occured nineteen times more often in 2002 than it had in 1993, a sure sign of its popularity and scholarly respectability.[3]

This article examines how globalization in the 1990s affected established scholarly conceptualizations, although only belatedly among historians. It clarifies key terminological debates while offering guidelines for a historically grounded approach to the global and transnational. In conceptualizing linkages and connections across boundaries, I argue that *translocal and transnational approaches* offer the best avenue to create "another world history," something not only possible but within reach as we enter a postneoliberal world.[4]

The impetus for a new transnational or global history sprang up in the aftermath of the "death of another world" in 1989–1991 when, with the fall of the Soviet Union, many were quick to proclaim "an end to history" and to celebrate or lament the unchallenged hegemony of liberal capitalist ideology. The abolition of a geopolitical framework that had lasted since 1945 ushered in a decade of unparalleled U.S. predominance, accompanied by a destabilization of entrenched intellectual, political, and even geographic understandings of the world. The same period also saw the culmination of debates within the North Atlantic intellectual sphere about a postmodern transition that many thought ended a modernist historical epoch that had begun in the early twentieth century. Antiquated institutions and old ways of thinking, it was suggested, were being swept away by historical transformations so profound that some even proclaimed the withering away of the nation-state, whether to lament its passage or to celebrate its demise. It was a global moment characterized, in Fred Cooper's words, by the "Banker's Boast" and the "Social Democrat's Lament."[5]

The debate about the local and the global, the particular and the universal, stood at the heart of this intellectual and political clash, with much of the journalistic and academic marketing of globalization presenting the local as "contained within, and thus defined fundamentally by the global," in the words of anthropologist Carla Freeman.[6] Such an "implicit but powerful, dichotomous model," according to Freeman, codes the Global masculine and the Local as feminine, which explains the gendered metaphors of globalization as rape and its associated orientalist metaphor of globalization as juggernaut.[7] The heightened prominence accorded universalistic theories, such as a neoliberal economics and an increasingly visible rational choice and game theory, compounded the sense of being besieged. These developments seemingly marked the definitive marginalization of those who specialized in "local knowledge" or a working class approached almost exclusively at the level of the community, region, and nation. Until the last five years, historians in almost all fields of history were reluctant to grapple with the contemporary challenge of the global, even as social scientists had opened up this debate in the 1990s.[8] After all, this powerful discourse of globalization directly challenged the preeminence of the very narrative framework, the nation, that provides the primary if not exclusive domain of recognized disciplinary expertise. It is likely, as well, that this response reflects a tendency to hold our noses when confronted with fashionable buzzwords, although lamenting faddishness is an entirely inadequate stance on contemporary globalization, however defined.

The truth is that nonhistorians, whether from the social sciences or the avant-garde humanities, have produced the most provocative and generative studies to date. Yet historians in the United States would have benefited—even if only to boost our disciplinary self-esteem—from engagement with the nonhistorical "history" debates that swirled around these varied and peculiarly U.S. interdisciplinary fields of postcolonial, cultural, women and gender, Black, Latino, Native American, Asian-Pacific, and "American" studies. Although historians may indeed be "distrustful of or indifferent to work done in other disciplines,"[9] I suspect that they are even more hostile when scholars from other disciplines fabricate their own stylized and emblematic "histories," which inevitably fail to meet our professional standards of evidence, proof, and argument. In our misguided insistence on rigor, we have failed to contend with the impulse behind such projects, which speak to vital contemporary events, anxieties, and perceived needs from which we have maintained a fussy professional distance.

To recognize the fruitfulness of dialogue with other intellectual currents does not by any means require that we abandon our disciplinary moorings. It may be that the history profession was behind the times in the 1980s and 1990s, when the locus of intellectual innovation lay in fields beyond history that were better equipped to translate the contemporary into compelling intellectual quests. This was certainly the judgment of Africanist historian Fred Cooper, who over the past decades has tied developments within the discipline, such as the new imperial history, to broader interdisciplinary debates related to postcolonialism.[10] As he noted in 2005, the cultural turn of the 1980s and 1990s produced "excellent research and valuable reflections," while correcting "the excesses of a previous turn, toward social history and political economy in the 1970s." But this was followed by a declining yield as "once provocative constructs" have now been impoverished by age and a tendency toward "conformism, gatekeeping," a following of fashion, and a predictable politics of citation.

Grappling with globalization, the imperial, and the transnational in his 2005 book, *Colonialism in Question*, Cooper made a powerful case that "only a *more precise historical practice* will get us out of the involuted framing" of too many current debates regarding colonialism and postcolonial legacies (emphasis added). In a richly suggestive 2002 article on the colonial archive, anthropologist Anne Stoler already had called for a more uncompromising historicization if the ethnography of colonialism is to move beyond well-worn postcolonial gestures.[11] Michel-Rolph Trouillot, another influential anthropologist, has rebuked even more directly the academic politics of marketing the new, here the global, in ways that speak to history as well as his own discipline. "While empirical data can never speak for themselves, anthropologists cannot speak without data. Even when couched in the most interpretive terms, anthropology requires observation—indeed, often field observation—and relies on empirical data in ways and to degrees that distinguish it as an academic practice from both literary and Cultural Studies."[12]

To advance our understanding, Cooper suggests, now requires an exacting focus on "specific conceptual and methodological issues" as we "develop a [far more] precise and incisive vocabulary for analyzing affinity, connections, and change" across space and through time.[13] In coming to terms with key concepts, the path forward depends upon "assessing the work they do, the blind spots as well as insights they entail, and the difficulties of using them to examine change over time." Above all, we must stop a practice of operating with "vaguely specified temporalities" and avoid giving "explanatory weight to agent-less abstractions."[14] So what are the conceptual and methodological tools that are required if we are to historicize the contemporary?

My work on global phenomena, going back to the early twentieth century, suggests a renewed focus on the definitional and terminological issues that impinge so centrally upon this booming arena of scholarly investigation and political praxis. As is characteristic of rapidly developing frontiers of knowledge, historians who now grapple with the transnational and global have tended toward a plurality of vocabularies and conceptualizations whose rationales are seldom made fully explicit. Choosing from a broad circulating universe of terms, they make ad hoc choices based on pragmatic judgments as to whether a given term "works" in a particular context, for a specific subject, and in the sense intended by a particular author (even if not defined). The result of such an idiosyncratic approach is a certain analytical slackness in our thinking, since terms are treated as "more or less" the same based on "good enough equivalences" and a belief that "we all know what we mean" (or are gesturing toward) with the words we use.

Any project for a transnational or global history must puzzle directly over how we are to meaningfully conceptualize the enmeshment of the local, national, and global. Globally engaged scholars rightly reject the juxtaposition of the local and global; as Hopkins notes, such "dualisms are at best inadequate and at worst misleading," even when factoring in the "asymmetrical relationships of size, structure and power."[15] Freeman also attacks this "binary logic of dichotomies,"[16] although simple negation does not advance our cause, and we too often fall back on formulaic statements that things are "mutually constituted" (a problem with the term *glocal*, or *glocalization*). This gesture fails to gain analytical traction because it does not tell us how, in what ways or proportions, with what consequences, and at which point in time. As Cooper notes, these are the fundamental questions we face as historians, in addition to the further challenge specific to our craft: how to produce a compelling narrative capable of expressing these dialectical relations between the local, the national, and the global.

To a far larger degree than desirable, the term *global* (even more so than the flatter *world*)[17] begins with the disadvantage, in English at least, of automatically suggesting its antonym (the local or national). This is precisely the reason the term *transnational* has certain advantages because of the ambiguities of the prefix ("on the other side of, over or across" and "above and beyond, transcending") and the fact that the term *nation* is not erased but qualified. Yet the term *transnational* does suffer from historical anachronism, since nations and nation-states are a very recent historical development that quickly became, as Trouillot notes, "one of the most powerful and pervasive fictions of modernity, an essential part of the North Atlantic narratives of world history." In a very real sense, the current vogue for things global originates in the anxieties occasioned by our realization, in the core of the world system, that this fiction had "become suddenly less persuasive, though we are not entirely sure what, if anything, should replace it . . . [And if] changes in the functions and boundaries of national states generate confusion even among social scientists," this is precisely "because globalization now produces spatialities—and identities—that cut through national boundaries more obviously than before."[18]

In addition to decrying linear and teleological narratives of the nation-state, Trouillot denies exaggerated claims about its weakness, much less its demise (especially in the case of the world's great powers and hegemonic regions). From there, he goes on to suggest that scholars need to give up their inherited illusions by recognizing that "the national state was never as closed and as unavoidable a container—economically, politically, or culturally—as politicians and academics have claimed since the nineteenth century."[19] Yet Trouillot's sound and stimulating observations do not go far enough in terms of the critique being offered, in part because, as a critic of contemporary globalization, he is committed in effect to a foreshortened chronology that treats capitalism as synonymous with the global over the past five hundred years.[20]

Yet there is a price to be paid for treating the two as coterminous. While the critic can thus repudiate globalization and its associated forms of transnationalism as a return to untrammeled capitalist greed, colonial rapacity, and imperialist diktat, it ignores the fact that processes similar to transnationalism long have characterized world history. In the words of anthropologist Lorand Matory, we not only should reject this facile equation of transnationalism with the recent but can do so through elaborating on the concept of the translocal. Like Trouillot, he, too, doubts scholarly prophecies that treat transnationalism as inevitable, while observing that such claims minimize "the enormous power of certain territorial nations over their residents' lives by pointing out clearly demonstrable gaps in any territorial nation's ability to monopolize the loyalty of and control over its residents." Like Cooper, Matory also observes that even modern transnationalism neither is shapeless nor does it embrace "all regions equally or simultaneously."[21]

More important, Matory moves beyond these established criticisms through emphasizing the hierarchy implied by the term *transnational*. He argues for an alternative formulation of history in which "the isolation of local cultural units has long been the exception rather than the rule, and territorially bounded social groups have never monopolized the loyalty of their members." Such territorial jurisdictions—whether nation-states, "kingdoms, empires, religions, acephalous republics, ... [or] fiefdoms"—never existed as "the sole fonts of authority and agents of constraint in such people's lives." Our modern conceptual blinders instead lead us to ignore or diminish the "translocalisms that preceded the nation-state," as well as to neglect momentous developments "structured by forces other than 'capitalism'—such as Islam and international socialism—[that] are cast outside of this new monocausal grand narrative" of capitalism and the nation-state.[22]

Matory's sketch of the implications of the translocal does more than resolve the anachronism of the term *transnational*. Our neglect of "translocal forces should not be mistaken," he suggests, as proof for the following propositions: (1) that "before the late 20th-century, most societies functioned in an entirely local field," (2) "that every present-day society is equally enmeshed in transnational forces," or (3) "that the entire world is becoming a boundary free whole." Matory ends with an even broader and more daring hypothesis: that translocalism, "far from emerging from the death throes of the nation-state ... long predated nationalism everywhere in the world. Indeed, translocalism was a founding condition of nationalism," as well as a multitude of other cross-cutting forms of identity and identification.[23]

The historian of China Arif Dirlik, a prolific theorist regarding contemporary globalization, also stresses the looming importance of the translocal for our discussions of global processes and connections. His paring of meaning suggests what we might gain from a translocal *and* transnational approach to global (worldwide) history.

> Transnational is not the same as worldwide.... What makes transnational radical in its implications is its emphasis on processes over settled units. More importantly, perhaps, the other side of challenging national history from supranational perspectives is to bring to the surface subnational histories of various kinds. The radical challenge of transnational history itself lies in its conjoining of the supranational and the subnational (or intranational), which calls forth an understanding of transnational as translocal, with all its subversive implications historiographically and politically. If national history serves as an ideological "strategy of containment," the containment of the translocal—as process or structure—is of immediate and strategic importance as it bears directly on the determination and consolidation of national boundaries.[24]

Latin American historian Heidi Tinsman and anthropologist of the United States Sandhya Shukla make a forceful appeal that "the paradoxes of globalization and power—the 'accelerated migration of goods and peoples' alongside deepening inequalities—compel us to rethink conventional categories of knowledge."[25] As they observe, the twenty-first century is marked by both a "more profound sense of global connection and a more acute experience of national and regional division." These "twinned imperatives" should challenge historians to craft an adequate response to the challenges of today: "to contend with contemporary globalization's intensity and to understand globality's historical depth."[26] In recognizing "how 'local' and 'global' dynamics thoroughly inform one another," they insist, we will find new and "innovative ways of telling stories from multiple perspectives: comparative, transnational, and global histories that transcend conventional boundaries of region and nation."[27]

As we survey the contemporary world politics of the last decade,[28] it is clear that the labor question occupies a central position, in new and more complicated global ways. The cycle that began with the Seattle World Trade Organization (WTO) protests of late 1999, climaxing during the July 2001 Group of 8 (G8) summit meeting in Genoa, Italy, dramatized the social and democratic deficit in the world economy and polity. Whether in China or the United States, the problems facing working- and middle-class people in a global political economy will never be resolved on a purely national basis. Even in the best of circumstances, enhanced trade union organization within a given country, even with new political and legislative conquests, is not enough unless one addresses the governance of the global political economy.[29] Intermestic (*inter*national/do*mestic*) problems demand international as well as domestic solutions, and the challenge of the new millennium is to integrate these very different praxes in response to the ever deepening integration of the domestic, the transnational, and the international. Our labor histories in the future will gain relevance precisely to the degree that we place them more consciously within the context of a transnationalized world economy and a lopsided world geopolitical structure characterized by complex economic, political, and ideological conflicts and cross-currents. There is much to be done.

NOTES

1. For more information on this 1991–1994 project dealing with labor in both NAFTA and the Common Market of the South (Mercosur), see Russell E. Smith and John D. French. "Labor, Free Trade, and Economic Integration in the Americas: A Conference Report," *Latin American Labor News*, nos. 12–13 (1995): 3–4; Smith and French, *Labor, Free Trade, and Economic Integration in the Americas: National Labor Union Responses to a Transnational World (a Conceptualization and Agenda for Future Research)*, Latin American Labor Occasional Paper #21 (Miami: CLRS, Florida International University, 1995).

2. See the tables on usage in the *New York Times*, the *Frankfurter Allgemeine Zeitung*, and *La Repubblica* in Neil Smith, *The Endgame of Globalization* (New York: Routledge, 2005), 125. On appearance of the word *globalizzazione* in an

Italian and German newspaper in the 1990s, see table 1.1 in Massimiliano Andretta et al., *Global, Noglobal, New Global: La Protesta Contro Il G8 a Genova* (Roma: GLF editori Laterza, 2002).
3. Frederick Cooper, *Colonialism in Question: Theory, Knowledge, History* (Berkeley: University of California Press, 2005), 7–8, 244.
4. The title of the paper, "Another World (History) Is Possible," consciously echoes the slogan of World Social Forum (WSF), an annual civil society gathering that began in Porto Alegre, Brazil, in 2001; in 2004, it was held in Mumbai, India, and in 2009 in the Amazon. José Corrêa Leite and Carolina Gil, *World Social Forum: Strategies of Resistance*, trans. Traci Romine (Chicago: Haymarket Books, 2005); Boaventura de Sousa Santos, *The Rise of the Global Left: The World Social Forum and Beyond* (London: Zed Books, 2006). I would like to thank my Duke colleague Jocelyn Olcott, who suggested the title during a brainstorming session in December 2007.
5. Cooper, *Colonialism in Question*, 93–94.
6. Carla Freeman, "Is Local: Global as Feminine: Masculine? Rethinking the Gender of Globalization," *Signs* 26, no. 4 (2001): 1008–9.
7. Ibid., 1012, 1015; Cooper, *Colonialism in Question*, 92.
8. Georg G. Iggers, Q. Edward Wang, and Supriya Mukherjee, *A Global History of Modern Historiography* (Harlow, England: Pearson Longman, 2008), 391.
9. Bruce Mazlish, "Comparing Global History to World History," *Journal of Interdisciplinary History* 28 (1998): 394.
10. Frederick Cooper and Ann Laura Stoler, *Tensions of Empire: Colonial Cultures in a Bourgeois World* (Berkeley: University of California Press, 1997).
11. Ann Laura Stoler, "Colonial Archives and the Arts of Governance," *Archival Science* 2 (2002): 87–109.
12. Michel-Rolph Trouillot, *Global Transformations: Anthropology and the Modern World* (New York: Palgrave Macmillan, 2003), 118, 128.
13. Cooper, *Colonialism in Question*, 6, 11.
14. Ibid., 12, 17.
15. A. G. Hopkins, "Introduction," in *Global History: Interactions between the Universal and the Local* (New York: Palgrave Macmillan, 2006), 2.
16. Freeman, "Is Local: Global," 1008–9.
17. Mazlish, "Comparing," 389.
18. Trouillot, *Global Transformations*, 84–85.
19. Ibid.
20. Janet Abu-Lughod's 1989 book on precapitalist circuits and nodes within multiple world systems that antedated the rise of Europe was a direct challenge to this conflation of world systems theory with capitalism. She offers a pioneering exploration of what would now be glossed under the terms *translocal* or *transnational*; as she observed in her introduction, she was interested in "looking at the *connections between* geographic entities that are usually treated by separate sets of specialists" in the hope that it might "yield enough to compensate for the hubris

of taking so global a view." See Janet L. Abu-Lughod, *Before European Hegemony: The World System* A.D. *1250–1350* (New York: Oxford University Press, 1989), ix.
21. James Lorand Matory, *Black Atlantic Religion: Tradition, Transnationalism, and Matriarchy in the Afro-Brazilian Candomblé* (Princeton, NJ: Princeton University Press, 2005), 3, 271, 268. A similar observation is offered by Abu-Lughod, *Before European Hegemony*, 32, where she observes that "no world system is global, in the sense that all parts articulate evenly with one another, regardless of whether the role they play is central or peripheral. Even today, the world, more globally integrated than ever before in history, is broken up into important subspheres or subsystems.... And each of these subsystems may have its own core."
22. Matory, *Black Atlantic Religion*, 4, 8.
23. Ibid., 9.
24. Arif Dirlik, "Performing the World: Representation in the Making of World Histor(Ies)," *Journal of World History* 16, no. 4 (2007): 33.
25. Sandhya Rajendra Shukla and Heidi Tinsman, eds. *Imagining Our Americas: Toward a Transnational Frame* (Durham, NC: Duke University Press, 2007), viii. That only a single contributor, coeditor Heidi Tinsman (a Latin Americanist), is in a history department reinforces my point about the discipline's reluctance to embrace these challenges. In the case of this volume, the overwhelming preponderance of contributors are from literary, American, and ethnic studies programs.
26. Ibid., 1, 3.
27. Ibid., 18, vii. See also the thoughtful reflections on transnationalism research offered by two young Latin Americanist scholars: Micol Seigel, "Beyond Compare: Comparative Method after the Transnational Turn" *Radical History Review* 2005, no. 91: 62–90; and Lara Putnam, "To Study the Fragments/Whole: Microhistory and the Atlantic World," *Journal of Social History* 39, no. 3 (2006): 615–30. For an annual seminar dedicated to this U.S.–Latin Americanist configuration of discussion of the transnational, see Pamela Voekel and Elliott Young, "The Tepoztlán Institute for the Transnational History of the Americas," *Social Text* 25, no. 3 (2007): 9–18; David Kazanjian and María Josefina Saldana-Portillo, "The Traffic in History," *Social Text* 25, no. 3 (2007): 1–7.
28. John D. French, "From the Suites to the Streets of Seattle: The Unexpected Re-Emergence of the 'Labor Question,' 1994–1999," *Labor History* 43, no. 3 (2002): 285–304.
29. John D. French and Kristin Wintersteen, "Crafting an International Legal Regime for Worker Rights: Assessing the Literature since the 1999 Seattle WTO Protests," *International Labor and Working-Class History* 2009, no. 75: 145–68.

2 HISTORIANS OF THE WORLD

TRANSNATIONAL FORCES, NATION-STATES, AND THE PRACTICE OF U.S. HISTORY

Julie Greene

Movement across nation-state boundaries stands as a central dynamic in labor history. Working-class men and women's need for international activism and broad global solidarities provides a powerful theme, as does the intense impact on their lives of globalization and the international flow of capital. These factors help make recent efforts to internationalize historical research and teaching of special interest to scholars of labor and the working class. Conversations about how to reach beyond traditional nation-state territorial boundaries in our studies abound in historical journals, and important works have appeared that rely on a transnational methodology.[1] Nonetheless, significant challenges remain. Some historians find the term *transnational* to be unclear. Others are confused about its meaning. Some see transnational historians as wishing to deny the importance of the nation-state, and they feel troubled by that. Others, whose scholarly agenda remains focused within the traditional geography of nation-states, feel that the transnational discussion potentially threatens the intellectual respectability of their work. In short, there remain important issues to consider if transnational labor history is to build a strong intellectual foundation.

How we approach these issues often owes a great deal to our individual training, intellectual background, and area of specialization. I come to questions of transnational labor history after originally studying European and British history. My first significant exposure to the history of the working class began with a thesis on Welsh miners during the 1930s. For the PhD, I jumped from European to U.S. history, and my training from that point onward was entirely on the United States. My early research focused on U.S. labor politics in the era of Samuel Gompers. The nation-state was a given; I accepted it as setting the boundaries of my work rather than seeing it as an entity worthy of investigation. More recently, I have grown interested in the relationship between the working class and imperialism, particularly in terms of the construction of the Panama Canal. This project involves a world where actors from many different nation-states intermingled, shared ideas, and sometimes contested one another's authority. Three issues related to transnational labor history have emerged from my experience as a U.S. historian increasingly focused on the relationship between the United States and the world: the meaning of the term *transnational* as applied to historical methodology, the role of the nation-state in transnational history, and the special challenges transnational methods pose for those of us trained as U.S. historians.

What do we mean by *transnational*? The term is in dialogue with and influenced by many other approaches—global and world history, international history, and efforts to examine more fully the connections between the United States and the world (especially as associated with the Organization of American Historians' LaPietra report).[2] At the most straightforward level, transnational history looks at processes and actors that move across territorial boundaries of diverse nation-states. Those processes are themselves extremely diverse: They may include economies, demographic movements, capital flows, ideas, cultures, and commodities. Transnational history sees this flow and movement itself as constructive of change, as causally significant, and thus as producing history.[3]

These ideas are central to transnational history, but I think we can state its goals somewhat more broadly. Although transnational historians warmly embrace the need for more studies of singular nation-states, our interests lie elsewhere. Transnational historians seek to move beyond approaches that see any nation-state as discrete and distinct or that study it unproblematically as a self-contained unit, essentialized or ahistorical. As Heidi Tinsman and Sandyha Shukla argued in a call for writing a history of the Americas, transnational approaches seek to go beyond dichotomies that oppose a developed United States and Canada to an undeveloped Latin America and Caribbean, or that pose a stark North versus South opposition.[4]

There are many ways to pursue this project, and diversity of strategies is an intellectual strength. The broadest, most ecumenical approach will generate the most work and the most vibrant dialogue among us. The important impulse here involves connecting hemispheric or global processes to one another and to the interrogation of nation-state boundaries and powers. This connection can take the form of studies of borderlands, empires, economic ties, diasporas, commodity chains, working-class formation, or international organizations, to mention just a few areas of study.

This approach raises a second issue: the place of the nation-state in transnational history. It is sometimes said that transnational historians ignore or neglect the nation-state or that they naively think that history transcends the nation-state. Such claims mischaracterize the way most transnational historians think about the role of the nation. It is certainly possible to study subjects in which nation-states play little role: Studies of diasporas or international solidarity movements, for example, may stress continuities across different national environments and traditions. Scholarship anchored chronologically before the rise of nation-states is therefore more accurately characterized as translocal. Yet for many—perhaps most—transnational scholars, nation-states are key components. Historicizing our understanding of the nation-state, exploring its role in new ways and with greater precision, and placing it in interaction with other nation-states and with other actors and historical forces—these approaches are all central to the transnational project. Consider Ian Tyrell's definition of the *transnational*. It seeks, he said, "to focus on the relationship between nation and factors beyond the nation."[5] A central claim of transnational scholars is that precisely by examining the nation-state in relation to other forces we will generate new insights into the workings of the nation-state and into the workings of the world.

In this view, a complex and dynamic relationship exists between nation-states and transnational forces. Consider, for example, the thousands of white U.S. and black Caribbean women who traveled to the Panama Canal Zone in the early twentieth century. They went sometimes to work at jobs as nurses or clerical employees (if they were white U.S. citizens) or as domestic servants (if they were West Indians). Most often, however, they went to maintain households for their men who were building the canal. The world of the Canal Zone was created through actions of the U.S. government most importantly, but the Panamanian, British, French, and Spanish governments played a role as well. The women who shopped at commissaries, who cleaned, and who went into Panama City on the weekends for pleasure all lived in a world shaped by these various governments. Yet they also dwelled amid the diverse cultures and life strategies of a working class that came to the Zone from all over the world. To improve their lives, women needed to push not only against various nation-states (making their grievances known, for example, to U.S. government officials as well as to diplomatic representatives from Britain or France) but also against working men and women from many different countries. Women from the United States and from the Caribbean interacted most often in private households where the former employed the latter. That space became a crucial fulcrum in which they negotiated the tensions of U.S. empire building and sought to maximize circumstances to their own benefit. But government officials had structured to a significant degree the character of that private space and the possibilities for negotiating within it. A similar mix of transnational and nation-state forces shaped working-class mobilizations in a very different setting, one explored by Samuel Truett in *Fugitive Landscapes: The Forgotten History of the U.S.-Mexico Borderlands*. Truett demonstrates how working people moved amid a diverse array of forces, from state actors to elite employers to an international workforce that itself moved back and forth across national boundaries. Not only does the crossing of boundaries make history, we learn, but the interaction between nation-states and transnational forces also emerges as a central causal agent.[6]

These examples suggest that the relationship between nations and the transnational involves an uneven, complex, back-and-forth kind of history—some spheres moving beyond the control of nation-states even as other spheres become more tightly contained. The nation and the transnational are often juxtaposed, interrelated, and interdependent. As Saskia Sassen discusses, for example, the globalization of capital has recently resulted in a denationalization as global capital has penetrated and literally denationalized national territory. But this has taken place even as the nation-state has gained more power in regard to people, as rising anti-immigrant sentiment in the United States has led to a renationalizing of politics.[7]

Finally, it is important to consider the special challenges and opportunities that transnational methods pose for U.S. historians. There is a paradox here. Although trained as U.S. historians, we seek to engage in a dialogue with world history. We need to be self-aware of the role of the United States historically and today, its capacity for cultural and intellectual as well as economic and political hegemony. The power of the United States is in part what makes the transnational project necessary and exciting—it promises great rewards by historicizing the United States and moving the field of U.S. history toward a broader outlook. Yet we also need to be mindful of the capacity of the United States to construct a triumphalist narrative of its own history and absorb the world's history into that narrative. To phrase the problem more bluntly, transnational approaches might constitute simply another form of U.S. intellectual hegemony.[8]

Aims McGuinness, a world historian whose scholarship explores the intersections of U.S. and Panamanian history, once expressed his concerns about U.S. historians in the form of a joke. When I think of a U.S. transnational historian, he said, I imagine someone at a cocktail party filled with historians from all over the world. The U.S. historian walks into the party and says, "Hi! I'm so happy to be here! I want to learn from all of you and I ESPECIALLY want to learn what you all think about … ME!"[9]

McGuinness's metaphor underscores the unsettling potential of the transnational project, particularly for U.S. historians. When I was teaching an undergraduate seminar on transnational labor history recently, I shared this image of the U.S. historian at a cocktail party with my students and asked if there was any way they could imagine changing the metaphor so the U.S. historian wouldn't seem like such an ass. They started asking a number of interesting questions: Who paid for the party? What language is being spoken? One student suggested (perhaps medicalizing the problem unnecessarily) that everyone at the party should take quaaludes and chill out a bit. Others said the U.S. historian should focus on learning from all the others about their historical traditions. But the best answer came from a student who asked: Who is doing the labor? Who cleans up when the party is over? The historian, my student declared, should focus on those people, sit down with them and talk and learn their stories, and figure out how historical research can help them.

This metaphor and the students' reactions suggest the importance of listening to and learning about discrete national histories, even as we examine global processes that connect them. They suggest the importance of multiarchival research in diverse nations and serious engagement with the historiographies of those nations. As transnational historians, we need to open a broader dialogue with scholars trained in different national traditions, with world historians, and with our colleagues in U.S. history whose work may not take them in a transnational direction. All sorts of work are needed, and all kinds of dialogue. Writing histories of the world requires precisely this sort of expanded conversation and explorations of more diverse and complex global interactions. Let's go to the cocktail parties filled with historians from all over the world and to the working people who make the parties possible; just don't ask them what they think about . . . us!

NOTES

1. For useful discussions of transnational history, see "*AHR* Conversation: On Transnational History," *American Historical Review* 111, no. 5 (2006); Michael P. Hanagan, "An Agenda for Transnational Labor History," *International Review of Social History* 49 (2004): 455–74; David Thelen, "The Nation and Beyond: Transnational Perspectives on United States History," *Journal of American History* 86 (December 1999). Books that employ transnational methodology include Eiichiro Azuma, *Between Two Empires: Race, History, and Transnationalism in Japanese America* (New York: Oxford University Press, 2005); Linda Basch, Nina Glick Schiller, and Cristina Stanton Blanc, *Nations Unbound: Transational Projects, Postcolonial Predicaments, and Deterritorialized Nation-States* (New York: Bordon and Breach, 1994); Jana Lipman, *Guantánamo: A Working-Class History between Empire and Revolution* (Berkeley: University of California Press, 2008); Aims McGuinness, *Path of Empire: Panama and the California Gold Rush* (Ithaca, NY: Cornell University Press, 2008).
2. Thomas Bender and the Organization of American Historians, "La Pietra Report: A Report to the Profession," http://www.oah.org/activities/lapietra/index.html, provided an important early influence in favor of internationalizing U.S. history.
3. Isabel Hofmeyr makes this point eloquently in "*AHR* Conversation: On Transnational History," 1444.
4. Heidi Tinsman and Sandhya Shukla, "Introduction: Across the Americas," in Shukla and Tinsman, eds., *Imagining Our Americas: Toward a Transnational Frame* (Durham, NC: Duke University Press, 2007), 1–33.

5. Ian Tyrell, "What Is Transnational History?" http://iantyrrell.wordpress.com/what-is-transnational-history/ (accessed July 1, 2009).
6. On women's work and nation-states in the Canal Zone, see Julie Greene, *The Canal Builders: Making America's Empire at the Panama Canal* (New York: Penguin Press, 2009. Samuel Truett's book *Fugitive Landscapes* was published by Yale University Press in 2006.
7. Saskia Sassen, "Introduction," from *Globalization and Its Discontents*, reprinted in Sanjeev Khagram and Peggy Levitt, eds., *The Transnational Studies Reader: Intersections and Innovations* (New York: Routledge, 2008), 74.
8. Louis Perez, "We Are the World: Internationalizing the National, Nationalizing the International," *Journal of American History* 89, no. 2 (2002): 558–66.
9. This anecdote was communicated by Aims McGuinness in a private conversation with the author. My thanks to him for allowing me to recount it here.

3

TRANSNATIONAL LABOR HISTORY

PROMISE AND PERILS

Neville Kirk

In this "postmodern" world with its focus on the present, to subject the term *transnational labor history* to historical scrutiny goes against the contemporary grain. But to do so is to show that the current "turn" to transnationalism, as with the relatively recent "turn" to language, is far less novel than often claimed. Depending on how we define *transnationalism*, historians in general have long practiced this branch of their craft. Certainly we have a long history of such analysis if we use the double-pronged definition of John French: extranational connections—movements, encounters, exchanges, and mutual influences of people, institutions, ideas, cultures, goods, and services beyond national boundaries—and supernational processes, such as capitalism, imperialism, and industrialization.[1] A robust scholarship by some labor historians explores worker and labor movement connections, exchanges, and influences beyond national boundaries and the effects of processes such as capitalist development on a variety of people, places, and spaces across the globe.[2]

To be sure, such study of the transnational has for the most part been a minority concern among both historians in general and labor historians in particular. Not only the hegemonic national paradigm but also subsidiary concerns with international labor history, internationalism, and cross-national comparison have overshadowed such analysis.[3] Yet interest in transnational labor history, especially among new and younger scholars, is now at a much higher level than at any time in the past.[4] This is to be warmly welcomed in a subdiscipline that since the 1980s has all too often been written off as in being in a permanent state of crisis or even dead. It is also fitting and by no means accidental that the transnational turn is taking place at a time when the forces of globalization, capitalist instability, and systemic crisis are once again of paramount importance to people's lives.

The study of transnational labor history holds both great promise and potential pitfalls for the future development of historical studies and the revitalization of labor history. In terms of promise, it provides us, above all, with an excellent opportunity to widen our frameworks of reference, knowledge, and understanding beyond the study of the national picture and its regional and local aspects. In integrating transnational and cross-national comparative history, we are well placed to rigorously interrogate notions of national and subnational labor movement and worker uniqueness, peculiarities, and exceptions. Perhaps more important, we can move beyond these largely tired notions to pose more interesting and potentially fruitful questions about worker and labor movement connections, influences, similarities, and differences in various global spaces and places that both include and transcend their national and subnational components.

We might, for instance, develop further labor historians' past and present interests in the effects of the massive transnational, transcontinental, and transhemispheric migrations of people during the late nineteenth and early twentieth centuries on the development of labor movements and worker consciousness.

For example, with reference to current interest in the notion of a British world, there is scope to more extensively and intensively explore the influences exerted by labor movement migrants from Old World Britain on the character and ideologies of labor movements in the New World contexts of Australia, New Zealand, the United States, Canada, and South Africa.

At the level of individual and collective biography, to what extent, if at all, did that considerable late-nineteenth- and early-twentieth-century radical transnational traffic of labor movement leaders—including Sam Gompers, Tom Mann, Keir Hardie, Dora Montefiore, Margaret MacDonald, H. M. Hyndman, Andrew Fisher, Ben Tillett, and Henry Hyde Champion—influence both the labor movements and countries visited? How did these visits and in some instances periods of residence abroad (such as Britain's Tom Mann in Australia and South Africa) affect the leaders' notions of place and the *mutual* connections and influences between their domestic movements and those visited overseas?[5]

Beyond the ranks of labor leaders, what links did considerable numbers of ordinary labor-movement migrants maintain with their friends and families back home, and in which ways and to what extent did they influence developments in their adopted countries? In turn, what effects did New World experiences have on labor movements in the Old World? By the time of World War I, we know that the very young Australian labor movement had become the most successful in the world. Not only did the Australian Labor Party, established as recently as 1901, dominate federal and much of state politics but also the strength and density of the trade union movement were already renowned. Australian labor movement activists, including significant numbers of British-born veterans, now held up their movement as a beacon to the rest of the world and claimed that the old British pioneer could learn much from their example. Did the British heed Australian lessons, and did the Australian example influence workers in other New World countries?[6]

The promise of transnationalism, then, pushes us to address new issues and rethink more traditional concerns. Let me provide four brief examples.

First, the very scale of population movement during the period of the second Industrial Revolution, of which the extensive transnational travels of labor leaders and the migrations of rank-and-file workers were a part, means that the labor historian's traditional emphasis on the overriding importance of "the local" to working-class people needs both rethinking and engaging with working people's attachments to other spaces, places, and people, including transnational ones. Second, we must seriously question conservative core-periphery and top-down models, still so influential in the mainstream British imperial literature and scholarship on U.S. influence in the Americas and the world outside. These works frequently and misleadingly assume that influences and ideas pass largely, or even entirely, and with little opposition from the elite or establishment in the metropolitan core to the colonial or subordinate periphery. Such an approach, of course, underestimates pressures and influences from below, from periphery to core, and the complex, contested, reciprocal, and multidimensional aspects of transnational encounters, exchanges. and influences. Third, in view of the importance of notions of whiteness, manliness, and separate spheres to many labor movements across the globe and their complex and shifting interplay with the forces of class solidarity and gender-based and racial and ethnic mutuality, if rarely equality, we must pay due and careful attention to the ways in which transnational connections and processes are racialized, gendered, and classed. Fourth, it is high time that the material and politico-economic aspects of transnationalism are afforded their due significance. Recent works on imperial, postcolonial, and transnational representations of workers and their worlds frequently undervalue or ignore the social in favor of the cultural. We need to reconnect, in a nonreductionist manner, material, political, and cultural structures and experiences.[7]

Despite its promise to reenergize labor history, transnationalism also carries with it potential pitfalls. Transnational scholars must be well versed in the history of not simply one but many places and spaces and immerse themselves in a multitude of secondary and primary sources. They should be attentive to the relevant conceptual, methodological, and substantive issues. In some instances, they must possess a range of language skills. They must be fully alive to the importance of change, continuity, context, nuance, and complexity and to the very real danger of presenting thin, simplistic, largely one-dimensional accounts. For example, some of the literature on transnational and even global whiteness is too sweeping and uniform and lacks proper attention to historical context, to change over time, complexity, diversity, and contestation. We would do well to remember that the whiteness historically imputed to whites by subsequent generations of scholars has to be *demonstrated* rather than merely asserted as a form of identity, that historical subjects possess multiple and shifting identities and attachments, and that whiteness is constructed and reconstructed rather than naturally given and in some cases contested, sometimes successfully so.[8] Finally, the transnational labor historian who is also to utilize the comparative method must take care to compare like with like and, I would suggest, to tease out and explain cross-national similarities and differences rather than simply present a number of additive or parallel national case studies in which the explicit process of comparison is left largely to the wit of the reader.[9]

Provided that we abide by and continue to have confidence in the well-tried and trusted rules of historical method, the opportunities presented by transnationalism greatly outstrip the potential weaknesses. Transnationalism opens up a treasure trove of new questions, subject areas, largely untapped sources, and last and by no means least, unprecedented opportunities for collaborative labor history projects both within and across national boundaries. Given the often centrality of solidarity and cooperation in labor movements, how fitting that we as their historians would practice our own form of collective labor.

NOTES

I am grateful to Eileen Boris for her very constructive comments and suggestions on my essay.

1. See John French's comments in the introduction of this book.
2. See, for example, Eric Hobsbawm, *Worlds of Labour: Further Studies in the History of Labour* (London: Weidenfeld and Nicolson, 1984); Jan Lucassen, ed., *Global Labour History: A State of the Art* (Bern: Peter Lang, 2006).
3. See, for example, Mary Hilson, *Political Change and the Rise of Labour in Comparative Perspective: Britain and Sweden 1890–1920* (Lund: Nordic Academic Press, 2006); Neville Kirk, *Comrades and Cousins: Globalization Workers and Labour Movements in Britain, the USA and Australia from the 1880s to 1914* (London: Merlin Press, 2003).
4. This is reflected, for example, in the success of not only the Newberry Conference on Labor History across the Americas but also the transnational labor history conferences held recently in Ulster and South Africa.
5. See, for example, Kirk, *Comrades and Cousins*, 8, 70–78, 82–91, 108–16, 123; John Barnes, *Socialist Champion: Portrait of the Gentleman as Crusader* (Melbourne: Australian Scholarly Publishing, 2006); Jacqueline Dickenson, *Renegades and Rats: Betrayal and the Remaking of Radical Organisations in Britain and Australia* (Carlton: Melbourne University Press, 2006); Melanie Nolan, "The

Reality and Myth of New Zealand Egalitarianism: Explaining the Pattern of a Labour Historiography at the Edge of Empires," *Labour History Review* 72 (August 2007): 113–34; Samuel Gompers, *Labor in Europe and America* (New York: Harper and Brothers, 1910). Karen Hunt is currently writing a book-length study of Dora Montefiore.

6. See Kirk, *Comrades and Cousins*, chapter 2. See also the articles in Ray Markey and Kerry Taylor, eds., "Trans-Tasman Labour History," *Labour History* no. 95 (November 2008): 1–167. These articles offer comparative perspectives on gender, class, trade unionism, labor parties, consumer cooperatives, and the roles of the police and the state in New Zealand and Australia. For the various influences of the regulatory social laboratories of New Zealand and Australia, complete with their high labor and living standards, on the thinking of U.S. trade unionists and radicals such as Gompers and Henry Demarest Lloyd, see, for example, Kirk, *Comrades and Cousins*, 66; Alun Munslow and Owen R. Ashton, eds., *Henry Demarest Lloyd's Critiques of American Capitalism 1881–1903* (Lampeter, Wales: Edwin Mellen Press, 1995), xxxii–xxxiii, xxxvi (note 1).

7. For an elaboration of these four examples, see Neville Kirk, *Labour and the Politics of Empire: Australia and Britain from 1900 to the Present Day* (Manchester, England: Manchester University Press, forthcoming), Introduction. For useful critiques of recent imperial, postcolonial, and transnational culturalist works, see Richard Price, "One Big Thing: Britain, Its Empire and Their Imperial Culture," *Journal of British Studies* 45 (July 2006): 602–27; Bernard Porter, "Further Thoughts on Imperial Absent-Mindedness," *Journal of Imperial and Commonwealth History* 36 (March 2008): 102, 106–10. For convincing statements in favor of the importance of culture to imperial history, see the essays in Catherine Hall, ed., *Cultures of Empire: A Reader* (Manchester, England: Manchester University Press, 2000).

8. See Kirk, *Comrades and Cousins*, chapter 3; Laura Tabili, "Race Is a Relationship, and Not a Thing," *Journal of Social History* 37 (Fall 2003): 125–30. For an ambitious but too sweeping, one-dimensional, and insufficiently contextualized transnational study of whiteness, see Marilyn Lake and Henry Reynolds, *Drawing the Global Colour Line: White Men's Countries and the Question of Racial Equality* (Carlton: Melbourne University Press, 2008). For the importance of context and contestation, see, for example, Andrew Gyory, *Closing the Gate: Race Politics and the Chinese Exclusion Act* (Chapel Hill: University of North Carolina Press, 1998).

9. I argued this point and provided examples of the additive approach in my *Labour and Society in Britain and the USA*, vol. 1, *Capitalism, Custom and Protest 1780–1850* (Aldershot, England: Scolar Press, 1994), 2. I continue to stand by it. For a typically constructive response to the additive criticism directed at some of the "comparative" projects organized by the International Institute of Social History in Amsterdam, see Marcel van der Linden, "The Globalization of Labour and Working-Class History and Its Consequences," in Lucassen, ed., *Global Labour History*, 35–36.

4 LABOR HISTORY AS WORLD HISTORY

LINKING REGIONS OVER TIME

Aviva Chomsky

This essay explores some of the ways that a global approach can reshape how we think about labor history and how a labor history focus suggests new ways of understanding world history. It invokes an earlier generation of Third World historians who placed the conditions and struggles of working people at the center of a global analysis. While the discipline of world history dates from the 1980s, revolutionary labor historians like C. L. R. James, Eric Williams, and Walter Rodney began looking at labor history from a global perspective, and at world history from the perspective of labor, significantly earlier. Perhaps nobody was as well situated as the descendants of enslaved Africans in the Caribbean to see how colonialism fundamentally shaped the modern world and understand colonialism as a process of the transnational movement and exploitation of labor.

James's *The Black Jacobins* (1938) asked readers to view African working people in Saint-Domingue not only as transnationally transplanted workers in a global capitalist system but also as protagonists in the global age of revolution. Eric Williams's *Capitalism and Slavery* (1944) argued that profits from the slave and sugar trades laid the groundwork for England's industrial revolution. Walter Rodney's *How Europe Underdeveloped Africa* (1972) became a classic in the annals of dependency theory (another early form of world history), and his *A History of the Guyanese Working People 1881–1905* (1981) in some ways mirrored James's earlier claim that the ideas and issues that historians were studying in a European context—like E. P. Thompson in *The Making of the English Working Class* (1963)— could also be looked at in a global sphere. Thompson paved the way for modern labor history by putting worker consciousness, rather than institutions, at center stage. Rodney's less celebrated work reminded us that consciousness, institutions, and structures exist globally as well as locally and that the colonial system was fundamental to the "making" of working classes in the peripheries. Postcolonial pioneers like Edward Said, with *Orientalism* (1978), took James's, Williams's, and Rodney's ideas into the cultural realm, showing how colonialism shaped Europe culturally as much as economically. Reflecting on these building blocks can help transnational labor historians illuminate how colonial, neocolonial, and postcolonial relationships "made" the working classes, in both structural and cultural terms, throughout the Americas.

Although the study of the periphery was globalized practically from the outset, it has taken longer for historians to globalize the study of the core, much less of labor history in the core. As Steve Stern, Barbara Weinstein, and others have pointed out, one of the weaknesses of a *dependencia* approach was that it privileged the story of how the core shaped the periphery, rather than its converse.[1] Yet as authors like Williams and Said argued decades ago, people and events in what we once called the periphery shaped the core and its projects, as well as being shaped by them. Recent works by Thomas Bender and others have begun to decenter the national narrative of U.S. history.[2] Although workers and labor history in the core are also, if less immediately visibly, embedded in global patterns and global changes over time, historians of labor in the United States are only beginning to map out the ways a global or transnational approach can enrich their own work. They draw on insights mapped out by Williams, about how global structures shaped the core (and its workers), and Said, about how colonialism shaped the cultures of the core.

Most U.S. labor historians focus on the industrial era or, in U.S. periodization, the national period. The structural and ideological developments in this era were clearly more globally integrated than ever before in human history, although they built on the previous 300 years of global connections. The Americas, of course, were peopled through the largest forced labor migration the world had yet seen. By 1820, some 8 million Africans and some 2 million Europeans had migrated to the Americas; arrivals of enslaved Africans continued to outnumber those of Europeans until 1840, and not until the 1880s did people of European origin become the majority in the Americas.[3]

The majority of enslaved Africans went to Brazil and the Caribbean. Charles Bergquist has convincingly argued that the different forms of coerced and free labor that developed in different regions of the Americas during the colonial period played a key role in the emergence of the contrasting socioeconomic and political structures of, say, Haiti (or even Alabama) and New England. The colonies that produced the most wealth ended up the poorest. While Terry Karl looks at the impact of natural resources, primarily on states, Bergquist places labor systems at the center of the analysis: exploitable resources led to exploitative labor systems, which structured long-standing inequalities in the distribution of land, wealth, and power.[4] Exploitative labor systems also, of course, shaped cultural constructions of race throughout the Americas.

The main subjects of labor history in the Americas, though, have been free workers. The general pattern in the system of free labor as it emerged in the nineteenth century has been toward proletarianization, or separation of workers from the means of production in which peasants and artisans become wage workers. Although in some ways apparently unidirectional, the process has in fact been more complex. The capitalist sector has always relied on a subsistence sector, because this ongoing relationship compensates for wages too low to fully sustain the reproduction of a labor force. When workers become fully proletarianized, employers continually reach out to new sources of labor that still retain the subsistence tie. Part of the dynamism of capitalism has been its ongoing incorporation of new subsistence workers. And individual workers' ties to the subsistence sector have sometimes proved quite durable over the course of generations.

In the Caribbean, slaves "reconstituted" themselves into peasantries after emancipation.[5] Florencia Mallon reminds us of the usefulness of the Marxist concept of the "articulation of modes of production" for understanding the process of proletarianization in the Peruvian Andes, where subsistence villages provided the labor force for foreign-owned mines.[6] In Guatemala, highland Mayan villagers have engaged in seasonal migration to work for others in export crops since colonial times. Today's Mayan communities in Providence, Rhode Island, argues Patricia Foxen, are merely continuing long-term patterns for community and ethnic preservation in a culture where temporary migration has served as a source of cultural resistance and identity.[7] All of these workers are engaged in different types of transnational labor systems, and their histories reveal the extent to which global capitalist projects depend on subsistence sectors and subsistence workers are linked to global capitalist projects.

The industrial system in the United States also drew its labor force from subsistence economies. The most obvious way has come through the recruitment and migration of workers. In the nineteenth century, as David Eltis provocatively suggests, it was "the victim of economic development who became the vanguard of American immigration." The immigrant-sending peripheries expanded southward through the twentieth century.[8] Michael Piore shows how generations of immigrants have "cycled through" the lower regions of Boston's labor market—as each generation became more proletarianized, it sought better employment opportunities. Thus employers sought new sources of immigrants with stronger links to subsistence economies.[9] Several studies trace this chain, in which migrants take jobs rejected by residents, that has sent Haitians to the Dominican Republic, Dominicans to Puerto Rico, and Puerto Ricans to New York City. In each case, a more marginal subsistence economy contributed to the reproduction of workers for whom poverty at home and the slightly higher wages in the host country made migration an attractive option.[10]

The wages paid in the capitalist sector went further in the poorer, more heavily subsistence-based regions that supplied migrants or immigrants to industry. Because their frame of reference was the home country (or region) and their initial goal was to support a family or a living standard at home, migrant workers were willing to accept wages and conditions that were clearly below the subsistence level in the host society. This pattern applied as much to the nineteenth-century European immigrants studied by Michael Piore as to the Latin Americans whose remittances undergird the economies of Mexico, El Salvador, and other Latin American countries today.[11]

In some ways, these structural factors inhibited migrant worker organization. Yet the experiences and identities that migrant workers brought from their homes, as well as the lives and communities that they built in their new contexts, could also contribute to organizing. Italian factory workers in nineteenth-century Milford, Massachusetts, brought traditions of anarchism and peasant uprising from Foggia; Mayan Guatemalan poultry workers in Morganton, North Carolina, and New Bedford, Massachusetts, at the end of the twentieth century came from "one of the hemisphere's oldest cultures," but their historical memory of collective resistance included not only opposition to the Spanish conquerors but also union organizing on the coastal coffee plantations in Guatemala, exposure to Liberation Theology and Christian Base Communities, and knowledge of Marxist guerrillas in their "traditional" homeland.[12]

Just as the slippage of workers between subsistence and capitalist economies has characterized the industrial system throughout its history, so has the mobility of capital. The New England textile and banana industries were among the earliest to experiment with both immigration and capital mobility to maintain access to a consistent supply of new, subsistence-reared workers. They also learned early the advantages of maintaining multiple sites of production. By the beginning of the twentieth century, they were experts at playing local, regional, and national governments against each other in their search for the most favorable investment conditions. Multiple production sites also helped with labor discipline, as they were able to easily shift production among sites if workers raised unwelcome demands.

In *Capital Moves*, Jefferson Cowie shows how an industrial employer (RCA) shifted its site of production over the course of the twentieth century, first within the United States and then to Mexico, in search of workers who were "cheap" in part because a subsistence economy subsidized their reproduction. As worker militancy increased over time in each location, the company set its sights on young, female workers in a new location. As RCA was moving to Mexico, the U.S. meatpacking industry was also busy shifting to a Mexican labor force, shutting down urban, unionized packing plants and reopening in the rural South and Midwest, taking advantage of the new mobility many Mexican immigrants acquired when the Immigrant Reform Control Act (IRCA) legalized their status in 1986.[13]

In some cases, manufacturers disarticulated the production process, relocating labor-intensive components to lower cost regions. Industrial producers began to experiment with off-shoring in the early twentieth century. Textile and garment producers sent handkerchiefs to Puerto Rico and to Swatow, China, in the 1920s to take advantage of workers there who were "reproduced" in their home societies. The maquiladoras of the late twentieth century were building on patterns established decades earlier.[14]

Some foreign employers deliberately sited factories in areas characterized by high out-migration and reliance on remittances because they could pay lower wages there, counting on the fact that families had multiple sources of income.[15] Even when factories did not actively seek to locate in regions characterized by out-migration, the coming of a factory often spurred out-migration, as it introduced industrial labor and consumption patterns but denied First World wages and benefits. In addition, industrial restructuring in the United States created a new low-wage labor market there, not only in moribund industries and those that had succeeded in breaking unions but also in the cleaning and caring sectors that were increasingly outsourced from middle-class homes.[16] Thus the economies of the advanced industrial regions depend on multiple, ongoing relationships with subsistence economies, just as subsistence regions increasingly depend on remittances from the industrialized regions to sustain their own reproduction.

The nation-state, of course, plays a role in transnational and global histories, even if decentered or demoted. National borders codified differences in legal rights and economic access. State institutions competed for worker loyalty and shaped worker identities. Rooted in place, they nevertheless contributed to the reproduction of a mobile labor force. National tariffs and trade agreements between governments structured jobs and investment, as well as the movement of people and products. National armies and police patrolled the borders that limited labor migration and supervised the fulfillment of contracts that enabled it. They also enforced labor discipline, with varying degrees of violence.[17]

Local, national, and transnational, as well as internationalist, identities shaped worker organization, often through extraordinarily complex dynamics. In Lawrence, Massachusetts, Ardis Cameron shows how the internationalist IWW succeeded in organizing workers through preexisting national and ethnic communities in the 1912 Bread and Roses strike. Gary Gerstle looks at how French Canadian ethnic identity and socialism contributed to a "working class Americanism" among textile workers in Woonsocket, Rhode Island. David Roediger asks us to examine how race-making shaped working-class identities and divisions in the United States as the New Deal, industrial unionism, and housing policies opened the door to whiteness for European immigrants.[18]

On U.S.-owned plantations in Costa Rica and Cuba, Jamaican migrant workers asserted their British identities while also mobilizing pan-Africanism. Revolutionary anti-imperialism, both communist and nationalist, flourished among Chilean mine workers and Colombian oil workers employed by U.S. companies. Nicaragua's Augusto César Sandino led a movement to drive the U.S. marines from his country after working in U.S.-owned oil fields in Mexico. These examples may not add up to a single, overarching interpretive approach, but they do suggest the limitations of imposing local or national boundaries on histories of worker consciousness and identity.[19]

A closer engagement with the ideas of Williams and Said can also lead us to ask in what ways a U.S.-American location in a global economic system has influenced U.S. workers' identities, organizations, cultures, and goals. Several historians have looked at the ways that the U.S. labor movement came to identify with U.S. imperialism, and white immigrant U.S. workers with U.S. racial ideologies. But we also need to explore the ways in which the American Dream depended structurally on the labor and resources of poorer regions, and working-class patriotism on an unspoken commitment to global inequality.[20]

As the twentieth century drew to a close, deindustrialization overtook the old industrial centers, as heavy industries followed the path southward blazed by the textile industry a century earlier, seeking to escape the very First World conditions that industrialization—and worker and government action—had helped to create. Today's unions are only beginning to explore ways to respond to this challenge.[21]

Even as labor organizations and the welfare state crumbled in the First World, high levels of consumption continued to characterize it. Third World labor—both at home and abroad—continued to fund extravagant lifestyles in the First World. The U.S. labor movement finally noticed in the 1990s that its Cold War alliance with the U.S. government in enforcing labor-repressive policies in the Third World had set the stage for the capital flight that was decimating jobs in the United States. Yet both the AFL-CIO and Change to Win remained committed to the American standard of living that required a continuing, massive influx of artificially cheap labor and products from the Third World. Their attempts to revive actual solidarity with Third World workers sometimes veer uncomfortably close to economic nationalism tinged with racism ("Buy American!"), while their wholehearted commitment to capitalist economic growth augurs a collision course with unions in the global south that understand that a decent standard of living for all—and the environmental survival of the planet—means that the global north will have to drastically lower its levels of consumption. A transnational labor history that acknowledges the unequal links among workers of the Americas over the past centuries will contribute to helping us understand, and transcend, the differences that continue to divide them.

NOTES

1. Steve J. Stern, "Feudalism, Capitalism, and the World-System in the Perspective of Latin America and the Caribbean," *American Historical Review* 93, no. 4 (October 1988): 829–72; Barbara Weinstein, "Presidential Address: Developing Inequality," *American Historical Review* 113, no. 1 (February 2008): 1–18.
2. Patricia Nelson Limerick, *The Legacy of Conquest: The Unbroken Past of the American West* (New York: W. W. Norton, 1987); Thomas Bender, *A Nation among Nations: America's Place in World History* (New York: Hill and Wang, 2006).
3. David Eltis, "Free and Coerced Transatlantic Migrations: Some Comparisons," *American Historical Review* 88, no. 2 (1983): 251–80.
4. Charles Bergquist, *Labor and the Course of American Democracy: U.S. History in Latin American Perspective* (London: Verso, 1996); Terry Lynn Karl, *The Paradox of Plenty: Oil Booms and Petro-States* (Berkeley: University of California Press, 1997).
5. Sidney W. Mintz, "From Plantations to Peasantries in the Caribbean," in *Caribbean Contours*, ed. Sidney W. Mintz and Sally Price, 127–53 (Baltimore: Johns Hopkins University Press, 1985); Mintz, *Caribbean Transformations* (Chicago: Aldine, 1974); Mintz, "The Rural Proletariat and the Problem of Rural Proletarian Consciousness," *Journal of Peasant Studies* 1, no. 3 (1974): 291–325.
6. Florencia E. Mallon, *The Defense of Community in Peru's Central Highlands: Peasant Struggle and Capitalist Transition, 1860–1940* (Princeton, NJ: Princeton University Press, 1983).
7. Patricia Foxen, *In Search of Providence: Transnational Mayan Identities.* (Nashville, TN: Vanderbilt University Press, 2007).
8. Eltis, "Free and Coerced Transatlantic Migrations," 257.
9. See Víctor Q. García, "Mexican Enclaves in the U.S. Northeast: Immigrant and Migrant Mushroom Workers in Southern Chester County, Pennsylvania", JSRI Research Report #27, The Julian Samora Research Institute, Michigan State University, East Lansing, Michigan, 1997. Available at http://www.jsri.msu.edu/RandS/research/irr/rr27.pdf.
10. David Griffith compared several studies that trace the cycling backward: "Sherri Grasmuck (1982) found Haitians filling jobs in the Dominican Republic that Dominicans either wouldn't or couldn't fill, Jorge Duany (1990) found Dominicans filling jobs in Puerto Rico that Puerto Ricans either wouldn't or couldn't fill, and David Griffith and Manuel Valdés Pizzini (2002) found Puerto Ricans filling jobs in New York that New Yorkers either wouldn't or couldn't fill." See David C. Griffith, "Rural Industry and Mexican Immigration and Settlement in North Carolina," in *New Destinations: Mexican Immigration in the United States*, ed. Víctor Zúñiga and Rubén Hernández-León, 53–54 (New York: Russell Sage Foundation, 2005).

11. Michael Piore, *Birds of Passage: Migrant Labor in Industrial Societies* (Cambridge: Cambridge University Press, 1980). There is a vast literature on the role of remittances in today's global economy; see, for example, Rodolfo O. de la Garza and Bryant Lindsay Lowell, eds., *Sending Money Home: Hispanic Remittances and Community Development* (Lanham, MD: Rowman and Littlefield, 2002), and for a comparison between past and current systems, Aviva Chomsky, *Linked Labor Histories: New England, Colombia, and the Making of a Global Working Class* (Durham, NC: Duke University Press, 2008).
12. For Milford, see Aviva Chomsky, *Linked Labor Histories*; for Guatemala, see Leon Fink, *The Maya of Morganton: Work and Community in the Nuevo New South* (Chapel Hill: University of North Carolina Press, 2003); Lisa Maya Knauer, "Maya in New Bedford: Politics, Community and Identity in the Wake of ICE," paper presented at the Boston Immigration and Urban History Seminar, October 30, 2008.
13. Jefferson Cowie, *Capital Moves: RCA's Seventy-Year Quest for Cheap Labor* (New York: New Press, 2001; Ithaca, NY: Cornell University Press, 1999); Lance Compa, "Blood, Sweat and Fear: Workers' Rights in U.S. Meat and Poultry Plants," Human Rights Watch, January 2005. Available at http://www.hrw.org/reports/2005/usa0105/.
14. See Chomsky, *Linked Labor Histories*.
15. Jane Collins, *Threads: Gender, Label, and Power in the Global Apparel Industry* (Chicago: University of Chicago Press, 2003); Humberto Juárez Núñez, *Rebelión en el Greenfield* (Puebla, Mexico: Benemérita Universidad Autónoma de Puebla, 2002).
16. Articulation and disarticulation were often gendered: the productive or capitalist economy depended on the reproduction of a labor force by the unpaid work of women. Women's labor in the home unpaid, and generally not acknowledged to be part of the economy at all. Economist Nancy Folbre noted that the "invisible hand" of the market economy could function only thanks to "the invisible heart"—the labor of caring that did not follow any of the so-called laws of the economy. See Nancy Folbre, *The Invisible Heart: Economics and Family Values* (New York: New Press, 2001). Barbara Ehrenreich and Arlie Russell Hochschild take the story to a global level in their anthology, *Global Woman: Nannies, Maids, and Sex Workers in the New Economy* (New York: Henry Holt/Metropolitan Books, 2002), which looks at how women migrant workers from the Third World take on the reproductive jobs that are increasingly commodified in the First World.
17. From the slave trade through the importation of contract workers and systems of debt peonage, vagrancy, and prison labor in the nineteenth century, through the bracero program and subsequent guest worker programs in the twentieth, as well as immigration quotas and the creation and enforcement of the legal category of "illegal immigrants" deprived of labor rights, state institutions have played a major role in guaranteeing an exploitable labor force in the Americas. This role has

continued in the era of so-called globalization, as has the use of violence. For a wide-ranging discussion of the ways states have increased their strength in the context of globalization, see Saskia Sassen, "The Nation-State as a Global Project," *Internationale Politik Global Edition* [*Journal of the German Council on Foreign Relations*] 9 (Fall 2008); and *Territory, Authority, Rights: From Medieval to Global Assemblages* (Princeton, NJ: Princeton University Press, 2006, updated ed. 2008). On the postmodern use of state violence to impose labor discipline, see Chomsky, *Linked Labor Histories*, chapter 5.

18. Ardis Cameron, *Radicals of the Worst Sort: Laboring Women in Lawrence, Massachusetts, 1860–1912* (Champaign: University of Illinois Press, 1995); Gary Gerstle, *Working Class Americanism: The Politics of Labor in a Textile City, 1914–1960* (Princeton, NJ: Princeton University Press, 2002); David Roediger, *The Wages of Whiteness: Race and the Making of the American Working Class* (London: Verso Books, 1999) and *Working toward Whiteness: How America's Immigrants Became White: The Strange Journey from Ellis Island to the Suburbs* (New York: Basic Books, 2005).

19. For Costa Rica, see Aviva Chomsky, *West Indian Workers and the United Fruit Company in Costa Rica, 1870–1940* (Baton Rouge: Louisiana State University Press, 1996) and Lara Putnam, *The Company They Kept: Migrants and the Politics of Gender in Caribbean Costa Rica* (Chapel Hill: University of North Carolina Press, 2002). For Cuba, see Barry Carr, "Identity, Class and Nation: Black Immigrant Workers, Cuban Communism and Sugar Insurgency, 1925–34," in *Marginal Migrations: The Circulation of Cultures within the Caribbean*, ed. Shalini Puri (London: Macmillan Caribbean, 2003). On Latin American revolutionary nationalism among workers at foreign-owned industries, see Charles Bergquist, *Labor in Latin America: Comparative Essays on Chile, Argentina, Venezuela, and Colombia* (Stanford, CA: Stanford University Press, 1986). For Sandino, see Donald Clark Hodges, *Intellectual Foundations of the Nicaraguan Revolution* (Austin: University of Texas Press, 1986).

20. There is a small literature on labor movement foreign policy, beginning with Philip S. Foner, *U.S. Labor Movement and Latin America*, Vol. 1, 1846–1919 (South Hadley, MA: Bergin and Garvey, 1988). See also Robert Armstrong, Hank Frundt, Hobart Spalding, and Sean Sweeney, *Working against Us: The American Institute for Free Labor Development and the International Policy of the AFL-CIO* (New York: North American Congress on Latin America, n.d.); Tom Barry and Deb Preusch, *AIFLD in Central America: Agents as Organizers* (Albuquerque, NM: Inter-Hemispheric Education Resource Center, 1986); Andrew Battista, "Unions and Cold War Foreign Policy in the 1980s: The National Labor Committee, the AFL-CIO, and Central America," *Diplomatic History* 26, no. 3 (2002): 419–51; Paul G. Buchanan, "'Useful Fools' as Diplomatic Tools: Organized Labor as an Instrument of U.S. Foreign Policy in Latin America," in *Exporting Democracy: The United States and Latin America*, ed. A. Lowenthal, 174–206 (Baltimore: Johns Hopkins University Press, 1992);

Daniel Cantor and Juliet Schor, *Tunnel Vision: Labor, the World Economy, and Central America* (Boston: South End Press, 1987); Beth Sims, *Workers of the World Undermined: American Labor's Role in U.S. Foreign Policy* (Boston: South End Press, 1992). One particularly interesting attempt to explore the nature and implications of labor nationalism for the U.S. working class and its organizations is Dana Frank's *Buy American: The Untold Story of Economic Nationalism* (Boston: Beacon Press, 1999).

21. The case studies in Kate Bronfenbrenner's *Global Unions: Challenging Transnational Capital through Cross-Border Campaigns* (Ithaca, NY: ILR/Cornell University Press, 2007) look primarily at examples of unions collaborating across national borders in campaigns against common employers or in particular sectors. In *Solidarity Divided: The Crisis in Organized Labor and a New Path toward Social Justice*, Bill Fletcher Jr. and Fernando Gapasin call for a more profound shift in thinking toward global and social justice unionism that challenges U.S. foreign policy and empire (Berkeley: University of California Press, 2008).

5

OVERLAPPING SPACES

TRANSREGIONAL AND TRANSCULTURAL

Dirk Hoerder

Transnational has become an academic catchword. Political criteria, like bordered nation-states and empires, fail to capture the experiences of labor migrants, who, like nonmigrants, were socialized in localities and regions, which did not always begin or end at imposed borderlines. Thus, I argue for superimposing on political-legal frameworks worldwide economic spaces, including sectoral linkages across borders: Specific forms of work and specific sectors rather than national economies per se attracted working men and women to change locales. But to fully capture the meaning of such processes requires moving from state and economy to the agency of migrants and the spaces they created through migration systems that developed on the individual, community, and regional levels of social life. Trans*cultural* spaces need to be determined empirically from labor market options and cultural insertion or exclusion and cannot be considered as emanating from states and nations, as implied by the term *transnational*.

If material culture, work space, and reproduction patterns interact with cultural capabilities, language knowledge, and everyday culture, as well as with stateside exit and entry rules, *transcultural* is a most useful generic term. Culture in this approach encompasses all aspects of human lives. In myriad individual and family decisions, we thus observe men and women establishing transcultural migration spaces, sometimes coalescing into migration systems that permit income-generating labor, ideally in secure political circumstances.

In 1997, sociologist Nancy Foner asked, "What is new about transnationalism?"[1] The term *transnational* migrants, introduced in the early 1990s, *conceptualized* what historians long had *described*.[2] Indeed, the term itself has a robust history, with commentators like Randolph

Bourne, in 1916, speaking of the United States as a "trans-nationality" and Fernando Ortiz, in the 1940s, discussing transculturation in Cuba. Ortiz discussed a mixing—*métissage, mestizaje*—or fusion of elements of one culture in the context of another rather than "in-between" bordered cultures or specific intercultural relationships between a bordered culture of origin and an equally bordered receiving culture.[3] The reintroduction of the term *transnational* in the early 1990s reflected specific scholars' concerns: They studied Latin American migrants arriving from nation-states with dictatorial right-wing regimes that were producing refugees with the help of U.S. state agencies.[4] Thus stateside politics and international relations—rather than cultural or economic factors—forced people into refugee migrations. Political refugees do look back to their polity (nation-state) of origin because they intend to change the oppressive regime and, then, return. *Transnational* or *transpolity* is a useful term only for refugee movements and those other connections that are based in at least two nation-states as distinct from regions within states or suprastate economic sectors.[5]

The 1990s catchword falls victim to contradictions within the very working of the nation-state: Under liberal political theory, the republican *state* was to treat each and every citizen as equal before the law, while the *nation* divided the state's inhabitants into unequal, hierarchized slots of nationals, minorities, and immigrants. Neither women nor the working classes became members of either nation or state with voting rights and equal access to societal-cultural resources.

Over the centuries, European states developed arbitrarily from dynastic territorial realms that fluctuated because of warfare and marriage alliances. In North America, neither geographic nor cultural logic explains the borders along the Rio Grande or the 49th parallel. Within such borders and under existing power relations, people are born, socialized, and live in particular local and regional cultures, Sussex or London, New York or New Orleans. When they decide to migrate, they carry with them their specific regional socialization. Thus the scope, or scape, of "trans" requires empirical documentation. For example, around 1900, migrating Slovaks came to the United States from three major cultural regions with distinct linguistic patterns; Chinese migrants traveled from four specific regions in two southern provinces and spoke several mutually unintelligible dialects. Today's migrating Filipinas leave Manila's metropolitan culture, the island of Luzon, or economically marginal smaller islands. No migrants are generic nationals, even though they carry the passport of a particular state.

Within the Atlantic world, some 50 to 55 million men and women departed from their "nation" of origin between the 1820s and the 1930s—and then "were departed" from nation-state historiography since their life-course decisions did not fit concepts of national identity and duty to the nation. In principle, the state was to serve the people, and its staff were the civil *servants*; in practice, however, they elevated themselves to gatekeepers. Rather than one single culturally uniform people, states usually were a conglomerate of a (presumed) national core, colonized societies of other ethnocultures, and from the later nineteenth century on, imperialist realms. An unholy alliance of administrators and bureaucrats (i.e., document/source producers) and historians (i.e., narration and memory producers) has obscured the fluid character of bordered polities.[6]

Before and parallel to the nation-state, regional, continent-wide, and global economic sectors emerged. Though *globalization* also recently has entered scholarship as a catchword, such processes are historical. The seventeenth-century fur trade was global, extending from Alaska via Labrador and Scandinavia to Siberia, and capitalized from London, Paris, Amsterdam, and Moscow. It involved migrations of traders and producers. Its gendered work processes involved men and women. Nineteenth-century colonialism and imperialism were global, as was the plantation regime in subtropical and tropical zones. In a transpolity and transsociety, people easily marked by color of skin or other outward physical traits became classified as inferior, segregated, and force-migrated as slaves or indentured servants and later found themselves in industrial agriculture or in low-wage industries. Scholars never conceptualized this globalization, which affected peoples *outside* the North Atlantic core, in the same frame as they have its more recent form affecting the *inside* of the industrialized world.[7]

The textile sector best illuminates global economic connections and their gendered patterns. Steel and heavy industry privileges the northern Atlantic world and men's over women's work. Textile production and its capitalization involved family economies as well as individuals. Fiber production, whether wool, cotton, or other, was local, macroregional, and global. Specific regional cotton strains, like specific qualities of wool, competed in macroregions and, since the establishment of transcontinental and transoceanic trading networks, globally. In the eighteenth century, calicoes from "India" (i.e., from specific regions and socioeconomic spaces on the subcontinent) competed with British manufactures; nineteenth-century factory production in some English shires reversed the direction of the trade. Entrepreneurs and workers in Lanarkshire (not in "Britain") depended on fleece from specific regions in Australia, light alpaca from the Peruvian Andes, or mohair from specific regions of Turkey. Manchester factories competed with those in Bombay and Lodz and, if processing cotton, linked to plantations in the U.S. South, India, Egypt, or Uganda.

Many of the aspects and forces shaping movements of capital and labor within and between empires, nation-states and other states, and larger or smaller intrastate regions are best understood in terms of sectoral, macroregional economic developments, including the growth or decline of transregional and often global multisectoral economies. Migrants to the textile factories of Lowell, Manchester, Cairo, or Kyoto wove yarns produced elsewhere in the global economy with machines, the steel, iron, rubber, and palm oil for which originated again in other segments of the global economy. Technological expertise to turn metals into machines and political expertise to impose class hierarchies came from other social groups and often different regions. To some workers, wage advantages might accrue because of a particular state's protectionist policies in the *inter*national competition for economic power, although ruling elites turned to protection usually for accumulation of capital and, perhaps, to prevent "disruptive" working-class discontent. Others experienced disadvantages from the international global division of power under late-nineteenth-century imperial rule or similar terms of trade during the late twentieth century.[8]

Workers, whether resident or migrant, joined middle classes and elites in becoming dependent on food resources produced by migrants in yet other regions, for example, by migrants "who opened the cattle and wheat fields of North America, the rice paddies of Southeast Asia, and the soy bean fields of Manchuria, not to mention those recruited to work the sugar plantations of Cuba, the tea plantations of Assam and Sri Lanka, and the coffee plantations of Brazil."[9] To gather, store, and transport raw materials, foodstuffs, craft products, and semifinished products, local men and women connected regions, producing spaces through littorals and ports to consuming hinterlands. Unskilled earthworks in developing regions and skilled rail production in industrialized regions, which usually coexisted in the same nation-state, generated jobs filled by migrants from differing regional origins both within and outside a given state. An "economic glue," to use Adam McKeown's term, was more important than political borders, constructed national cultures, or international relations.[10]

Migrants focus not on a whole polity but a specific location about which they have *information*, where they may rely on *networks* of earlier migrants, and where they are able to insert themselves into *a segment of the labor market*. Just after 1900, the U.S. Senate's Dillingham Commission studied the "immigrants" in the Atlantic World—actually "migrants," since many returned to their region of origin—and found that 94 percent of them headed for family and friends rather than believing in a nation-state providing "unlimited opportunities"—a slogan that for them referred to the economy rather than the nation-state. As working people moved to and between localities in the plantation belt of the Indian Ocean societies, and from specific places of origin in northern China to specific places in Manchuria and beyond, they joined family members, fellow villagers, and comigrants from earlier trajectories in economic sectors with internationalized access to particular labor markets. They came from regions within empires rather than nations and moved to regions in which residents and newcomers from many cultures interacted conflictually or cooperatively.[11]

Migrants move "glocally." Rather than pursue trans*national* strategies, they move across transregional, transcontinental, or transoceanic spaces and evaluate *life chances* in terms of *family economies* or *individual life-course projects and prospects* in shifting macroregional or global economic frames. They move translocally or transregionally within the economic sectors in which their skills, whether in productive or reproductive work, provide access to an internationalized segment of a labor market and where, culturally, difference of language is of little importance. Around 1900, cigar makers could move between work spaces in northern Europe, Havana, and Manila. Agricultural laborers, whether Chinese, East European, or Mexican, could move into earthworks for canal, railroad, or road building nearby or on a different continent.[12] Economic linkages and migrant connectivity establish transregional spaces of production and reproduction. Economic and migration spaces overlap, and both overlap with bordered polities in which *métissage* is more common than national monocultures. In the present, some 190 million transregionally mobile migrants in the People's Republic of China attempt to return to their localities of origin for the New Year, where they remain locally rooted. The Filipinas' *balikbayan* gift boxes are sent back to specific social *spaces*, even though the *state* provides the framework for duty-free import. Migrants in sub-Saharan Africa form village or neighborhood organizations to channel remittances and support from their spaces of arrival back to where families and friends live.[13]

In this chapter, I have questioned the easy use of the term *transnational* to understand the history of working people who have migrated from one place to another. It appears that both as regards space and connectivity, the nation-state does not provide the frame of reference for migrant decision making, though, in a process evolving from the 1880s to the 1920s, it does frame migration by laws concerning entry and, sometimes, exit. Migrant experience emerges in regions mediated by labor markets that provide access to another society and economy. The transcultural concept better describes the data emanating from overlapping economic, societal, cultural, and political regions.[14]

NOTES

1. Nancy Foner, "What's So New about Transnationalism? New York Immigrants Today and at the End of the Century," *Diaspora* 6, no. 3 (1997): 354–75.
2. Nina Glick Schiller, Linda Basch, and Cristina Blanc-Szanton, eds., *Towards a Transnational Perspective on Migration: Race, Class, Ethnicity and Nationalism Reconsidered* (New York: New York Academy of Sciences, 1992), esp. 1–24.
3. Randolph S. Bourne, "Trans-National America," *Atlantic Monthly* 118 (1916): 86–97, esp. 96, reprinted in Carl Resek, ed., *War and Intellectuals: Essays by Randolph S. Bourne, 1915–1919* (New York: HarperTorch, 1964), 107–23; Fernando Ortiz, "Del fenómeno de la transculturación y su importancia en Cuba" (1940), in *Cuban Counterpoint: Tobacco and Sugar*, trans. Harriet de Onís (New York: Knopf, 1947; reprinted Durham, NC: Duke University Press, 1995).
4. Glick Schiller, Basch, and Blanc-Szanton, *Towards a Transnational Perspective on Migration*. The term has been adopted by researchers dealing with Mexican and other Latino/a migrations, esp. Alejandro Portes and cooperating scholars. See Portes, Luis E. Guarnizo, and Patricia Landolt, "The Study of Transnationalism:

Pitfalls and Promise of an Emergent Research Field," *Ethnic and Racial Studies* 22 (1999): 217–37. For an early critique, see Peter Kivisto, "Theorizing Transnational Immigration: A Critical Review of Current Efforts," *Ethnic and Racial Studies* 24, no. 4 (July 2001): 549–77; and Kivisto, "Social Spaces, Transnational Immigrant Communities, and the Politics of Incorporation," *Ethnicities* (Bristol) 3, no. 1 (2003): 5–28.

5. Christiane Harzig and Dirk Hoerder with Donna Gabaccia, *What Is Migration History?* (Cambridge, England: Polity, 2009), chapters 3 and 4; Dirk Hoerder, "From Interest-Driven National Discourse to Transcultural Societal Studies," in Dirk Hoerder, *"To Know Our Many Selves Changing across Time and Space": From the Study of Canada to Canadian Studies* (Edmonton: Athabasca Univ. Press, 2010), Chapter 14, 316–26.
6. Dirk Hoerder, "Historians and Their Data: The Complex Shift from Nation-State Approaches to the Study of People's Transcultural Lives," *Journal of American Ethnic History* 25, no. 4 (Summer 2006): 85–96.
7. Rather than use a globalization approach, scholars studied economies in an imperial frame, in particular British, or divided economic sectors by region and color of skin as in dividing transatlantic from Indian Ocean migrations.
8. Dirk Hoerder, *Cultures in Contact: World Migrations in the Second Millennium* (Durham, NC: Duke University Press, 2002).
9. Adam McKeown, "A World Made Many: Integration and Segregation in Global Migration, 1840–940," in *Connecting Seas and Connected Ocean Rims: Indian, Atlantic, and Pacific Oceans and China Seas Migrations from the 1830s to the 1930s*, ed. Donna Gabaccia and Dirk Hoerder (Leiden: Brill, forthcoming, 2011).
10. Thomas Faist, *The Volume and Dynamics of International Migration and Transnational Social Spaces* (Oxford: Oxford University Press, 2000); Adam McKeown, "A World Made Many: Integration and Segregation in Global Migration, 1840–1940," in *Connecting Seas and Connected Ocean Rims: Indian, Atlantic, and Pacific Oceans and China Seas Migrations from the 1830s to the 1930s*, ed. Dirk Hoerder and Donna Gabaccia (Leiden: Brill, forthcoming).
11. Dillingham Commission (U.S. Senate, Immigration Commission), *Reports of the Immigration Commission*, 41 vols. (Washington, DC, 1911–1912).
12. Hoerder, *Cultures in Contact*, chapter 14.
13. Ibid., chapter 19.
14. Harzig and Hoerder with Gabaccia, *What Is Migration History?* 53–114; Hoerder, "From Interest-Driven National Discourse to Transcultural Societal Studies," in Hoerder, *"To Know Our Many Selves,"* 361–90."

6

TRANSNATIONAL MIGRATION

A NEW HISTORICAL PHENOMENON?

Vic Satzewich

In their 1994 book, *Nations Unbound*, anthropologists Linda Basch, Nina Glick Schiller, and Christina Szanton Blanc called for a new transnational perspective on migration and settlement. They argued that traditional approaches social scientists used to understand individuals who moved and settled abroad were no longer suitable for an increasingly complex world. In their view, "the word 'immigrant' evokes images of permanent rupture, of the abandonment of old patterns of life and the painful learning of a new culture and often a new language." These people become the "uprooted," who leave the homeland to "pledge allegiance" to the new. Migrants, in contrast, are temporary sojourners, "transients who have come only to work." Representations derived from past immigrations, they assert, "no longer suffice. Today, immigrants develop networks, activities, patterns of living, and ideologies that span their home and host society."[1] These social scientists are not the only ones who claim that nations and states no longer serve as adequate units of analysis, that transnational ties and identities are the defining features of immigrant and ethnic community life, and that the concepts of assimilation and integration are no longer relevant to understanding immigrants.[2]

Much of my own work is sympathetic to a transnational perspective,[3] but significant aspects of the literature on contemporary migration and settlement demand historical correction: An interdisciplinary dialogue might help us historicize general hypotheses, creating a more nuanced understanding of workers' local, national, and transnational lives. A labor history that pays attention to both the local and the transnational can help to temper certain social science claims about the unprecedented nature of contemporary transnationalism, particularly as it relates to understanding immigrant lives. Furthermore, a renewed emphasis on immigrants as workers instead of immigrants as simply carriers of certain transnational identities and practices will help establish a more complete picture of the lives of those who cross national boundaries in search of work, business opportunities, and better lives.

First, the traditional distinctions between immigrants, migrants, refugees, and other categories of people who cross international borders are relevant not only to histories of migration[4] but also to contemporary patterns of labor. It is tempting to dismiss these distinctions on the grounds that many people who move across national boundaries do so many times and often move back and forth between their place of origin and their place of settlement. However, sociolegal distinctions between categories of migrants mattered in the past, and they still matter, particularly at the level of state immigration policies and citizenship rights. In many countries, the distinction between migrants (those who have the right of only temporary entry and settlement), immigrants (those who have the right of permanent residence), and illegal immigrants was and remains an important point of differentiation in access to public resources, such as health care, employment insurance, and social assistance.[5] Moreover, such state-defined categories shape processes of community formation and associated transnational practices. Displaced persons who traveled to Canada after World War II to work on farms as "unfree immigrant labor" faced severe state restrictions on their ability to circulate freely in the labor market, though this proved temporary.[6] Migrant farm workers who now come every year to Canada from Mexico are granted the right of temporary entry and also face restrictions over their ability to circulate in the labor market. However, in that they are forced to return to Mexico after their labor contracts expire, state immigration laws make their transnationalism compulsory.[7] Historically changing definitions of employer "need" and categories of racial preference shape these laws and regulations.[8] Those people who enter Canada with the right to permanent settlement may engage in transnational practices and have transnational identities, but the state does not enforce these forms of transnationalism in the same manner.

Second, are nation-states really less important in a supposedly transnational world, as some who advance a transnational perspective suggest? One way to measure the importance of the nation-state derives from looking at the relative importance of national as opposed to international norms and conventions in shaping the rights of migrants and immigrants over time.[9] In the post–World War II world order, and probably earlier, geography mattered in this regard. Sociologist Christian Joppke argues that within liberal democracies, the main source of immigrant rights tends to be domestic in nature. While not discounting the increasing salience of international human rights norms, Joppke argues that states with liberal infrastructures and traditions have little interest in resorting to international norms to define migrant and immigrant rights within their national boundaries.[10] In contrast, international human rights norms affect mostly "illiberal or newly liberalizing states" and migrant-sending countries. The United Nations Convention on the Protection of the Rights of Migrant Workers, which came into force in July 2003, has generated far more interest in "liberalizing states" than in the "developed world." As of January 1, 2004, thirty-two states adopted this convention, but no major immigrant-receiving states, like Australia, Canada, the United States, and the European Community, did so.[11] The rights claims of migrant and immigrant workers in migrant- and immigrant-receiving states continue to be based mainly on state-based charters, legislation, judicial decisions, and human rights codes.

Moreover, states and nations still weigh heavily on immigrant and ethnic community politics and identity. Diaspora communities may finance various kinds of national struggles and projects, and nation-states see their respective diasporas as political and economic resources and use bonds of ethnicity to secure capital, financial aid, and political influence. As sociologists James Kennedy and L. Riga note in their study of the formation of the state of Czechoslovakia in 1918, Czech and Slovak immigrants in the United States voted in a referendum to support a united Czech and Slovak state. Tomás Masaryk, the future first president of Czechoslovakia, used the support of Czech and Slovak immigrants in the United States to convince Woodrow Wilson to support the formation of the new country.[12] States and borders mattered, and they still matter, as Sarah Carter's historical work on indigenous women's varying rights and roles across the 49th parallel makes clear.[13]

Third, the focus within transnational studies on documenting multiple identities and the ways that individuals and groups maintain ties to ancestral homelands offers important insights into immigrant and ethnic community life, whether that involves early-twentieth-century Ukrainian Canadian workers' political and cultural bonds (and battles) across borders[14] or more recent studies of Croatians in Canada and their support of the independent Croatian state in the 1990s.[15] However, in searching for evidence of transnational practices and identities, we cannot slight the importance of productive and reproductive work—waged labor, unpaid labor, and entrepreneurial work—of immigrants and members of ethnic communities in their country of settlement, as Franca Iacovetta, among others, notes.[16] Immigrants, we know, vote, run for office, join trade unions or business associations, send their children to school, watch television, buy groceries, and take visiting relatives to see Niagara Falls. In other words, at the same time that people maintain transnational identities and practices, they also reproduce their conditions of existence within territorially bounded states. These productive and reproductive activities shape and solidify emergent identities; they also point to the continued importance of class relations and class differences in our understanding of immigrant and ethnic community life. "Old" models of immigrant settlement, including political economy perspectives that explored, for instance, the relationship between the nature of work and ethnic working-class cultures, or the interconnections between gender, class, ethnic identity, and class consciousness, may be able to offer important insights into how members of transnational communities reproduce their conditions of existence in their country of settlement.[17] Tomas Almaguer's work on the Oxnard sugar beet workers' strike of 1903, for example, shows how Mexican and Japanese farmworkers drew on traditions of labor radicalism in their countries of origin to forge the first major agricultural workers' union in California comprised of different groups of minority workers.[18] Ruth Frager shows how patriarchal traditions among Jewish immigrants from Eastern Europe shaped, and were modified by, Jewish immigrant women workers in their course of union organizing in Toronto.[19] And Franca Iacovetta's recent study of immigration gatekeepers in Canada points to the important role that state and social service agencies in Canada played in attempting to transform immigrant foodways, family relationships, and sexual mores.[20] The organization of both productive and reproductive activities is arguably as important to understand as voting in an election back home or sending money to support causes in countries of origin.

Fourth, while scholars like Basch may have been correct that "the popular" image of immigrants in the 1970s and 1980s was one of "uprootedness" and "permanent rupture from their ancestral homelands," earlier research on immigrant and migrant incorporation did in fact recognize the complexity of migratory flows, the fluidity of international boundaries, and the complicated attachments and relationships that migrants had with their ancestral homelands. Some authors were silent on transnationalism and the significance of homeland ties and identities, but others did pay attention to "transnationalism," although they may not necessarily have named the activities, behaviors, and identities as such.[21] Marcus Lee Hansen, for one, was well aware of transnational connections, the fluidity of international boundaries, and the influence of "home countries" on the lives, experiences, and practices of immigrants in North America. In "A Resume of the History of Canadian-American Relations" published in 1937, Hansen argued that "no population study of historical interest is complete if it ignores the fact that the Canadian-American boundary, which meant so much to the diplomat, legislator and tradesman, was non-existent in the consciousness of the unnumbered hundreds of thousands who were doing the principal jobs of the century—turning the wilderness into farms and homes."[22]

Hansen's early recognition of the fluidity of international borders and the importance of multiple identities was not just relevant to his analysis of migration between Canada and the United States. In his 1926 overview of the field, Hansen was aware that European immigrants to the United States had complicated identities and relationships with their ancestral homelands. Immigrants and their descendants, according to Hansen, have on occasion, ... been more interested in fighting the battles of the old country than in participating in the affairs of the new.... Research will probably reveal that the emergence of the new nations of Eastern and Central Europe in consequence of the World War was possible only because there had existed in America, for a generation or two, active colonies of those nationalities, which had kept alive the ideal of independence and could offer financial support and political pressure at the critical moment.[23]

Clearly, earlier work in the field did recognize the fluidity of boundaries and borders, the transitory nature of identity, and the impact of the "homeland" on the lives, consciousness, and social and political organization of immigrants and members of ethnic communities.[24] This is not surprising, given the large and dramatic flows of migrations in the twentieth century—some voluntary, some forced. The extent to which scholars have attended to these transnational connections has ebbed and shifted over time. Our current attentiveness to their importance has been shaped in part by specific historical conditions of new economic and political forms of globalization, along with immense public discussion of globalization. As Donna Gabaccia points out, while the forms and intensity of transnationalism may have become more complex, immigrants have always had transnational orientations.[25]

To this long scholarly recognition of transnationalism's importance as a key characteristic of earlier immigration comes the rejoinder by current researchers that new communications and transportation technologies have made transnational practices and identities more intense, more immediate, and more systematic than in the past. According to Alejandro Portes and his collaborators, while previous generations of immigrants engaged in behaviors that reinforced bonds between their country of origin and their country of settlement, these lacked the "regularity, routine involvement, and critical mass characterizing contemporary examples of transnationalism." Although such researchers admit that there are some legitimate examples of transnationalism in past migrations, they see these as largely exceptional cases that are not relevant for the vast majority of Europeans who left their ancestral homelands in the first half of the twentieth century. In their view, "contemporary transnationalism corresponds to a different period in the evolution of the world economy and to a different set of responses and strategies by people in a condition of disadvantage to its dominant logic. Herein lies the import of its emergence."[26]

This argument is not entirely convincing, since few have *systematically* compared the similarities and differences between the "old" ways that immigrants maintained ties with their homelands that were based on letters, telexes, trains, and ships and the new forms of transnationalism that are facilitated by e-mail, Facebook, and fast airplanes. While it is obvious that communications and transportation technologies have changed, it is not obvious that these technologies have produced *qualitatively* different kinds of communities or patterns of settlement and adjustment. Nor is it obvious that disadvantage and social exclusion from the modern world economy drives contemporary transnationalism.[27] Differences between the migrant and immigrant communities of yesterday and today have tended to be asserted rather than demonstrated with empirical and comparative case studies.

The transnational history of migrant and immigrant communities may be able to temper some of the more suspect claims advanced by social scientists who study present-day transnational migration.[28] The assumption that new immigrants are more transnational in their orientation than previous waves of immigrants may unwittingly feed commonsense stereotypes about the presumed dual identities of today's immigrants and the threats they pose to the stability of immigrant-receiving states. Much of current anti-immigrant discourse in Canada and the United States focuses on the presumed unhealthy transnationalism of such recent immigrants. Common to this discourse is that borders are being breached at will, that security is being threatened by immigrants who don't have real loyalties to the countries that graciously accept them, that immigrants have too much influence over foreign policy, that they are not integrating and pay too much attention to events in their homelands, and that they have dual political loyalties.[29]

This "then and now" distinction unwittingly reifies distinctions between earlier European immigrants and current immigrants from Asia, Africa, Latin America, and the Middle East. The distinction is also racialized insofar as the latter groups are also represented as a new racial other that poses new problems for Canadian society. To put it probably too crudely, it reinforces the idea that the old European immigrants were good immigrants because they were not truly transnational; they had interests in homelands, but in the end they integrated and assimilated. The new transnational immigrants are not like the good immigrants of before because their transnational identities and loyalties are more significant and permanent. And now that the old immigrants have become white, shedding their racial distinctions in the minds of detractors, the newest groups represent racial threats.

My concern is that those who argue that there is something historically unprecedented about present-day transnationalism may lend weight to these anti-immigrant sentiments. After all, one person's celebrated dual loyalty is another person's threat to the state. As argued by sociologist Rogers Brubaker: "The purported prevalence of transnationalism gives those already thinking that the national community is under threat additional reason to worry and insist that boundaries get rolled back"[30] Until we have more comparative and historical studies that engage with social science hypotheses about an unprecedented growth and change in transnationalism, we will be unable to map, judge, and explain changes over time. Transnational labor history can play a role in this endeavor and also in reminding social scientists that immigrants also work for their livings. Such work necessarily entails paying attention to both the local and the transnational.

NOTES

1. Linda Basch, Nina Glick Schiller, and Christina Szanton Blanc, *Nations Unbound: Transnational Projects, Postcolonial Predicaments, and Deterritorialized Nation-States* (Amsterdam: Gordon and Breach, 1994), 3–4.
2. Alejandro Portes, Luis Guarnizo, and Patricia Landolt, "The Study of Transnationalism: Pitfalls and Promise of an Emergent Research Field," *Ethnic and Racial Studies* 22, no. 2 (1999): 217–37.
3. Vic Satzewich, *The Ukrainian Diaspora* (London: Routledge, 2002); Vic Satzewich and Lloyd Wong, eds., *Transnational Communities in Canada* (Vancouver: University of British Columbia Press, 2006).
4. Donna Gabbacia, "Is Everywhere Nowhere? Nomads, Nations, and the Immigrant Paradigm of United States History," *Journal of American History* 86, no. 3 (1999): 1115–34.
5. Satzewich and Wong, *Transnational Communities in Canada*.
6. Vic Satzewich, *Racism and the Incorporation of Foreign Labour: Farm Labour Migration to Canada since 1945* (London: Routledge, 1991), 85–98.
7. Tanya Basok, *Tortillas and Tomatoes: Transmigrant Mexican Harvesters in Canada* (Montreal: McGill-Queen's University Press, 2002).
8. Satzewich, *Racism and the Incorporation of Foreign Labour*.
9. Yasmeen N. Soysal, "Citizenship and Identity: Living in Diasporas in Post-War Europe?" *Ethnic and Racial Studies* 23, no. 1 (2000): 1–15.
10. Christian Joppke, "How Immigration Is Changing Citizenship: A Comparative View," *Ethnic and Racial Studies* 22, no. 4 (1999): 629–52.
11. Satzewich and Wong, *Transnational Communities in Canada*; David Weissbrodt, "Comprehensive Examination of Thematic Issues Relating to the Elimination of Racial Discrimination," *Working Paper, Sub-commission on Prevention of Discrimination and Protection of Minorities* (Geneva: Office of the United Nations High Commissioner for Refugees, 1999). The reasons for the reluctance of European Union states to ratify the convention are analyzed by Euan Macdonald and Ryszard Cholowenski, *The Migrant Workers Convention in Europe: Obstacles to the Ratification of the International Convention on the Protection of the Rights of All Migrant Workers and Members of Their Families* (Paris: UNESCO, 2007). Reluctance in the United States is similarly complex since the country rarely signs anything, given congressional conflict with executive branch and other aspects of foreign policy. The United States is also reluctant to expand rights to noncitizens and working people.

12. James Kennedy and L. Riga, "Mitteleuropa as Middle America? The Inquiry and the Mapping of East Central Europe in 1919," *Ab Imperio* 4 (2006).
13. Sarah Carter, "Transnational Perspectives on the History of Great Plains Women: Gender, Race, Nations, and the Forty Ninth Parallel," *American Review of Canadian Studies* 33, no. 4 (2003): 565–596. See also Joan Sangster, "Historia Social," *Historia Social* 60, no. 1 (2008): 213–24.
14. Donald Avery, "Divided Loyalties: The Ukrainian Canadian Left and the Canadian State," in *Canada's Ukrainians: Negotiating an Identity*, ed. Lubomyr Luciuk and Stella Hryniuk (Toronto: University of Toronto Press, 1991).
15. Daphne Winland, "Raising the Iron Curtain: Transnationalism and the Croatian Diaspora since the Collapse of 1989," in *Transnational Identities and Practices in Canada*, ed. Vic Satzewich and Lloyd Wong.
16. Franca Iacovetta, *Such Hardworking People: Italian Immigrants in Postwar Toronto* (Toronto: McGill-Queen's University Press, 1992). See also Sangster, "Historia Social"; and Brian Palmer, "Fin-de-Siecle Labour History in Canada and the United States: A Case for Tradition," in *Global Labour History*, ed. Jan Lucassen (Bern: Peter Lang, 2008).
17. Stephen Castles and Godula Kosack, *Immigrant Workers and Class Structure in Western Europe* (London: Oxford University Press, 1973); Stephen Castles and Mark Miller, *The Age of Migration: International Population Movements in the Modern World*, 3rd ed. (New York: Guilford Press, 2003); Ivan Light, *Ethnic Enterprise in America* (Los Angeles: University of California Press, 1972); and Elizabeth Ewen, *Immigrant Women in the Land of Dollars* (New York: Monthly Review Press, 1985).
18. Tomas Almaguer, "Racial Domination and Class Conflict in Capitalist Agriculture: The Oxnard Sugar Beet Workers Strike of 1903," *Labor History* 35 (1989): 328.
19. Ruth Frager, "Class and Ethnic Barriers to Feminist Perspectives in Toronto's Jewish Labour Movement, 1919–39," *Studies in Political Economy* 30 (1989): 146.
20. Franca Iacovetta, *Gatekeepers: Reshaping Immigrant Lives in Cold War Canada* (Toronto: Between the Lines Press, 2006).
21. Daphne Winland, "Our Home and Native Land? Canadian Ethnic Scholarship and the Challenge of Transnationalism," *Canadian Review of Sociology and Anthropology* 35, no. 4 (1998): 555–77.
22. M. L. Hansen, "A Resume of the History of Canadian-American Population Relations," *Proceedings of the Conference on Canadian-American Relations*, Kingston, Ontario (September 14–18, 1937): 95–106. Reprinted in *The Immigrant in American History* (New York: Harper & Row, 1940), 177.
23. M. L. Hansen, "The History of American Immigration as a Field for Research," *American Historical Review*, XXXII (1926–1927): 500–518. Reprinted in *The Immigrant in American History* (New York: Harper & Row, 1940), 212.
24. Rogers Brubaker, "The 'Diaspora' Diaspora," *Ethnic and Racial Studies* 28, no. 1 (2005): 1–19.

25. Donna Gabaccia, *Italy's Many Diasporas* (Seattle: University of Washington Press, 2000).
26. Portes, Guarnizo, and Landolt, "The Study of Transnationalism," 227.
27. Kim Matthews and Vic Satzewich, "The Invisible Transnationals: American Immigrants in Canada," in Vic Satzewich and Lloyd Wong, eds. *Transnational Identities and Practices in Canada.*
28. Marcel van der Linden, "Transnationalizing American Labor History," *Journal of American History* 86, no. 3 (1999): 1078–92.
29. See, for example, Jack Granastein, *Whose War Is It: How Canada Can Survive in the Post-9/11 World* (Toronto: HarperCollins, 2007).
30. Brubaker, "The 'Diaspora' Diaspora."

LABOR AND EMPIRE

INTRODUCTION

Alex Lichtenstein

Despite the best of intentions, many studies of "transnational" labor still remain bound to nationalist or at best regional paradigms, as historians of necessity continue to talk about labor migration across single borders, and consider global or cross-border emancipatory labor struggles within the context of national states or in combat with national bourgeoisies. Yet, as the two chapters in this section suggest, a more "imperial" approach to these questions may be fruitful. After all, between the seventeenth and twentieth centuries, rapid capitalist accumulation depended heavily on the efficient transfer of labor across enormous distances and far-flung imperial domains, whether in the bodies of slaves, convicts, forced laborers, soldiers, seamen, indentured workers, temporary migrants (guestworkers), immigrants, or refugees.[1] As ships crisscrossed the globe during the age of empire, much of their cargo was human: Indian contract workers to Natal, to Trinidad, to Guyana; Irish convicts to New South Wales; Chinese indentures to Cuba or, later, to the South African gold fields; Batavian and Malagasy slaves to the Cape of Good Hope or the island of Mauritius; "recaptured" and freed slaves to Sierra Leone and Trinidad; and, not least, diverse African peoples dispersed all across the Atlantic world in the slave trade. Land-based labor migration—and transport—also proved instrumental to territorial expansion and economic growth: Workers from Portuguese colonial Africa traveled to the South African Rand; colonial states and powerful corporations alike subjected rubber tappers to forced labor, whether in Amazonia or the Belgian Congo; Stalin's Gulag sent millions of workers to incorporate the USSR's eastern reaches.[2] Whether voluntary, coerced, or (more often) something in between, much of this extraordinary traffic of labor around the globe was organized by imperial networks, sometimes in rivalry with one another and sometimes in concert. The constantly evolving international proletariat forged by this process appears strikingly multinational in its composition—think, for example, of the slaves who made the Haitian Revolution, the lascars who manned British sailing vessels, or the vast assemblage of Caribbean workers who dug the Panama Canal, to name but three examples across time and space.[3]

As the bibliography that follows conveys, there is no shortage of existing studies of labor in various specific imperial contexts, from Sydney to San José. With the important exception of the vast literature on the Atlantic slave trade, however, labor historians, in contrast to scholars who focus on gender and race, have yet to fully develop analytical paradigms that sufficiently take into account the peculiar dynamics of empire as a broader category of analysis.[4] Tellingly, the eight volumes of the Oxford History of the British Empire Companion Series published so far include thematic editions on environment, missions, gender, the black experience, and most recently, migration, but not, as of yet, labor.

The following chapters, while still rooted in very particular times and places, offer a glimpse of what kind of issues such a "labor and empire" paradigm might begin to take up. First, imperial labor forms seem to be inherently hybrid in character, and this on multiple levels. As anthropologist Sidney Mintz showed long ago in his studies of sugar, it is in empires that the most advanced forms of production, accumulation, and consumption often collide with the most primitive and coercive ones.[5] Such hybridity might be considered diachronic as well, since in imperial encounters evolving "traditional" forms of labor collided with newly emergent ones, remaking both in the process. As Ravi Ahuja remarks in a study of colonial Madras, historians of imperial labor should strive to "identify *ancién regime* forms of subordinating labour that proved to be compatible with colonial conditions and to distinguish them from forms that did not survive or were newly created."[6]

Studying imperial labor and its myriad forms also compels us to confront the inherent instability of the free-unfree labor dyad. This overly teleological and increasingly unsatisfying model tends to obscure many of the most crucial aspects of long-distance imperial labor recruitment, such as indenture and contract, which do not fit either category very well. The cost and difficulty of transporting labor meant that even when workers were ostensibly free, employers demanded a means with which to bind them to service as tightly as possible. Such hybrid "contractual unfree labor" defined the employment relationship for soldiers, sailors, indentured laborers, contract workers, and many other workers central to the imperial labor process.[7]

Finally, in terms of historical development, imperial labor can be regarded as dialectical. Imperial laborers often struggled against their situation in such a way as to force to the surface systemic tensions and contradictions—between competing empires, between national states and multinational capital, and between sectors of capital itself. For instance, even while encouraging tightly bound forms of labor migration at one moment, at another an imperial state might step in to "protect" its subjects from maltreatment by corporate entities or by other states, rightless though these imperial "citizens" may have been in their home territory.

Whether such interventions were motivated by noblesse oblige, economic or political rivalries, or larger imperial and military ambitions, if historians want to go looking for cracks in the facade of global capitalism at any particular conjuncture, the experience of imperial laborers is often a good place to start.

I think many of these general observations can be gleaned from a close reading of the following chapters. Still, at first glance, the paired contributions to this part, "Labor and Empire," appear to make a rather disparate whole. They jump from eighteenth-century British imperial military labor to the struggle of Mexican autoworkers in American subsidiaries in the post–World War II era. On closer examination, however, they offer from quite different angles of vision an account of the imperial project at two crucial points in its historical trajectory: at a moment of formation and consolidation and during its neocolonial reconstitution under the signs of development and modernization.

One of the first works of labor history to employ an imperial perspective, even if only implicitly, was Marcus Rediker's *Between the Devil and the Deep Blue Sea*.[8] Rediker's book demonstrated that eighteenth-century Anglo-American seamen constituted the Atlantic capitalist world's first proletariat; undeniably, these rootless workers proved central actors in an early global economy shaped by imperial trade, labor recruitment, power, and juridical forms. Yet oddly, until recently very few if any labor historians have applied a similar approach to the hundreds of thousands of men under arms who journeyed around the globe in the imperial age to secure, police, and patrol new colonial possessions on behalf of the metropole, against indigenous inhabitants, unruly slaves, restless colonists, and competing empires. Like sailors, soldiers represented a mobile, proletarianized mass, both drawn from many corners of the empire and sent to work beyond its current borders. As Peter Way notes in his groundbreaking chapter, "Soldiers were both instruments and objects of imperial authority." And like sailors, they (usually) volunteered their labor but in doing so entered into an employment relationship more akin to coerced than free labor—"contractual unfree labor"—as the "black service" they complained of implied.

Employing a supple Marxian approach, Way's chapter rightly posits "warfare as a central engine of the process of capital and state formation," especially in an imperial setting. His consideration of the "peculiar institution" of eighteenth-century British military labor provides a useful framework for grasping the connections among imperial ambition, capital accumulation, the production of commodities, and the deployment of human labor across enormous distances by the consolidating national state. Way asks us to take seriously the military garrison as a key site of large-scale eighteenth-century production every bit as significant as the plantation, the ship, the household, or the expanding workshop. We must, he argues convincingly, "reconceptualize soldiers as transnational laborers whose martial toil around the globe proved integral to the development of international capitalism."

Most provocatively, drawing creatively on the existing (but decidedly non-Marxist) historiography of the "military revolution" of the seventeenth and eighteenth centuries, Way unveils the dialectical relationship between proletarianization and the ongoing availability of surplus labor necessary for the recruitment of a large military force. This available labor was, in turn, an absolute necessity for empire building and thus for securing the material conditions for further proletarianization of masses of dispossessed labor. It is worth noting, for example, that the growth of imperial armies seems to parallel the growing proletarianization of soldiering itself, as the military revolution supplanted the "artisanal" labor of mercenaries with the "professional soldier who voluntarily enlisted or was coerced to serve in the army of a particular nation-state." Moreover, drawing on the important work of legal historian Robert Steinfeld, Way also insists that we regard even enlisted military service as a form of semicoerced labor and that we see soldiers as a constituent part of early British America's working class, serving in "bondage to the state and its imperial ambitions." Finally, he suggests the social means by which this entire process was mystified. Soldiering, Way reminds us, was "embedded in militarist and nationalist discourses that vaunt the soldier's patriotic duty, valor, and manliness," a fact that has served to disguise its status as proletarianized labor and a central site of imperial "production."

Strictly speaking, Steven Bachelor's treatment of Ford Motor Company operations in post–World War II Mexico does not touch on "empire" at all: After all, unlike the West Indies and even Cuba (which was dominated by the United States), mid-twentieth-century Mexico was decidedly a sovereign country with a powerful sense of nationalism forged in the immediately preceding revolutionary era, a nationalism shared by the working class. Nevertheless, incorporated into a hemispheric political economy underwritten by the ideology of the "American century," Mexican national development depended heavily on multinational investment emanating from north of the border. Bachelor reminds us that Mexican "underdevelopment," as posited by the Truman administration's Point Four international program of economic uplift and multinational penetration of the country's political economy, can be understood only when counterpoised to the exceptionalist hubris of the colossus to the north.

Ford Motor Company seems an appropriate point of focus within this dynamic because, as Bachelor observes, "The automobile industry figured as the foremost industrial arena through which U.S. unions and U.S. state agencies sought to extend their influence in Mexico." With the construction of modern industrial plants around Mexico City, the Fordist model of political economy extended its hegemony into a transnational project of Latin American modernization. But as with most imperial projects, this one, too, proved open to modification by the "colonized." In this case, Mexican autoworkers laid claim to some of the same benefits of Fordism enjoyed by their northern counterparts, including economic security and new levels of consumption. These expectations could breed militancy as well as complacency, not least because the corporatist industrial relations regime in Mexico so stifled rank-and-file initiatives that even the Reuther brothers practically came to resemble syndicalists. Faced with restructuring of production in the 1960s, Mexican autoworkers generated shop-floor movements, at times in league with the United Automobile Workers (UAW), to challenge the corrupt corporatist model of industrial relations overseen by the Mexican state.

Of course, these chapters offer a mere taste of what an imperial labor history might look like. Confined mostly to the Anglo-American imperial ambit and entirely to the Western Hemisphere, they leave out the vast majority of the colonial world and the rich potentialities of comparative imperial histories.[9] Historians may pursue studies of imperial labor by organizing research around competing imperial pathways, networks, and territorialities; by types of labor recruitment, control, and resistance; or even by the global commodity chains that remain so central to the projection of neoimperial power in today's globalized economy. A transimperial study of rubber—stretching from Henry Ford's utopian Fordlandia Amazonia to Firestone's forced labor enclaves in Liberia to the Indochinese British and French rubber plantations planted with seeds taken from South America—comes to mind. "Black Indians armed with heavy blades will slash down their one-time haunts to make way for future windshield wipers, floor mats, balloon tires," reported *Time* magazine breathlessly in 1927, upon the founding of Fordlandia. "A fleet of steamships will make regular trips from the U.S. to Brazil. In time, a fleet of airplanes will do likewise."[10] In this instance, Ford's dream never came to pass. Nevertheless, Bachelor's conclusion that "capitalism structured a pattern of resource extraction and division of labor (international, regional, and workplace) that privileged certain workers as more valuable than the other" strikes me as an excellent starting point for future efforts to integrate an imperial perspective into our studies of transnational and global labor history.

NOTES

1. For some interesting interpretations of this phenomenon, see John Torpey, *The Invention of the Passport: Surveillance, Citizenship, and the State* (New York: Cambridge University Press, 2000); Adam McKeown, *Melancholy Order: Asian Migration and the Globalization of Borders* (New York: Cambridge University Press, 2008).
2. Patrick Harries, *Work Culture and Identity: Migrant Laborers in Mozambique and South Africa, 1860–1910* (Portsmouth, NH: Heinemann, 1994); Jordan Goodman, *The Devil and Mr. Casement: One Man's Battle for Human Rights in South America's Heart of Darkness* (New York: Farrar, Strauss and Geroux, 2009); Adam Hochschild, *King Leopold's Ghost: A Story of Greed, Terror, and Heroism in Colonial Africa* (Boston: Houghton Mifflin, 1998); Stanislaw Swianewicz, *Forced*

Labour and Economic Development: An Enquiry into the Experience of Soviet Industrialization (New York: Oxford University Press, 1965).

3. Laurent Dubois, *Avengers of the New World: The Story of the Haitian Revolution* (Cambridge: Harvard University Press, 2004); Rana Behal and Marcel van der Linden, eds., *Coolies, Capital, and Colonialism: Studies in Indian Labour History* (New York: Cambridge University Press, 2006); Julie Greene, *The Canal Builders: Making America's Empire at the Panama Canal* (New York: Penguin, 2009).
4. Angela Woolacott, *Gender and Empire* (New York: Palgrave Macmillan, 2006); Marilyn Lake and Henry Reynolds, *Drawing the Global Colour Line: White Man's Countries and the International Challenge of Racial Equality* (New York: Cambridge University Press, 2008).
5. Sidney Mintz, *Sweetness and Power: The Place of Sugar in Modern History* (New York: Penguin, 1985).
6. Ravi Ahuja, "Labour Relations in an Early Colonial Context: Madras, c. 1750–1800," *Modern Asian Studies* 36 (December 2002): 793–826.
7. Douglas Hay and Paul Craven, eds., *Masters, Servants, and Magistrates in Britain and the Empire, 1562–1955* (Chapel Hill: University of North Carolina Press, 2004).
8. Marcus Rediker, *Between the Devil and the Deep Blue Sea: Merchant Seamen, Pirates, and the Anglo-American Maritime World* (New York: Cambridge University Press, 1987).
9. For an excellent example of a comparative history of labor and empire, see Frederick Cooper, *Decolonization and African Society: The Labor Question in French and British Africa* (New York: Cambridge University Press, 1996).
10. "Ford Rubber," *Time*, October 24, 1927. See also Eduardo Sguglia's fine novel, *Fordlandia*, trans. Patricia J. Duncan (New York: St. Martin's Press, 2000); Greg Grandin, *Fordlandia: The Rise and Fall of Henry Ford's Forgotten Jungle City* (New York: Metropolitan Books, 2009).

FURTHER READING

Ahuja, Ravi. "Labour Relations in an Early Colonial Context: Madras, c. 1750–1800." *Modern Asian Studies* 36, no. 4 (2002): 793–826.

Arrighi, Giovanni. "The Political Economy of Rhodesia." *New Left Review* no. 39 (September–October 1966).

Ayala, César. *American Sugar Kingdom: The Plantation Economy of the Spanish Caribbean, 1898–1934.* Chapel Hill: University of North Carolina Press, 1999.

Behal, Rana, and Marcel van der Linden, eds. *Coolies, Capital, and Colonialism: Studies in Indian Labour History.* New York: Cambridge University Press, 2006.

Bieber, Judy, ed. *Plantation Societies in the Era of European Expansion.* Aldershot, England: Variorum, 1997.

Bolland, O. Nigel. *The Politics of Labour in the British Caribbean: The Social Origins of Authoritarianism and Democracy in the Labour Movement*. Princeton, NJ: Markus Weiner, 2001.

Bourgois, Phillipe. *Ethnicity at Work: Divided Labor on a Central American Banana Plantation*. Baltimore: Johns Hopkins University Press, 1989.

Chomsky, Aviva. *West Indian Workers and the United Fruit Company in Costa Rica, 1870–1940*. Baton Rouge: Louisiana State University Press, 1996.

Christopher, Emma, Cassandra Pybus, and Marcus Rediker, eds. *Many Middle Passages: Forced Migration and the Making of the Modern World*. Berkeley: University of California Press, 2007.

Cooper, Frederick. *Decolonization and African Society: The Labor Question in French and British Africa*. New York: Cambridge University Press, 1996.

Cooper, Frederick, Thomas Holt, and Rebecca Scott. *Beyond Slavery: Explorations of Race, Labor, and Citizenship in Postemancipation Societies*. Chapel Hill: University of North Carolina Press, 2000.

Cooper, Frederick, Florencia Mallon, Allen Isaacman, and Steve Stern, eds. *Confronting Historical Paradigms: Peasants, Labor, and the Capitalist World System in Africa and Latin America*. Madison: University of Wisconsin Press, 1993.

Eltis, David, ed. *Coerced and Free Migration: Global Perspectives*. Palo Alto, CA: Stanford University Press, 2002.

Gonzalez, Gilbert, ed. *Labor versus Empire: Race, Gender and Migration*. New York: Routledge, 2004.

Grandin, Greg. *Fordlandia: The Rise and Fall of Henry Ford's Forgotten Jungle City*. New York: Metropolitan Books, 2009.

Greene, Julie. *The Canal Builders: Making America's Empire at the Panama Canal*. New York: Penguin, 2009.

Guterl, Matthew Pratt, and Christine Skwiot. "Atlantic and Pacific Crossings: Race, Empire, and the 'Labor Problem' in the Nineteenth Century." *Radical History Review* (Winter 2005): 40–61.

Hay, Douglas, and Paul Craven, eds. *Masters, Servants, and Magistrates in Britain and the Empire, 1562–1955*. Chapel Hill: University of North Carolina Press, 2004.

Isaacman, Allen. *Cotton Is the Mother of Poverty: Peasants, Work, and Rural Struggle in Colonial Mozambique, 1938–1961*. Portsmouth, NH: Heinemann, 1996.

Kale, Madhavi. *Fragments of Empire: Capital, Slavery, and Indian Indentured Labor to the British Caribbean*. Philadelphia: University of Pennsylvania Press, 1998.

Keegan, Timothy. *Colonial South Africa and the Origins of the Racial Order*. Charlottesville: University Press of Virginia, 1996.

Lai, Walton Look. *Indentured Labor, Caribbean Sugar: Chinese and Indian Migrants to the British West Indies, 1838–1918*. Baltimore: Johns Hopkins University Press, 1993.

Linebaugh, Peter, and Marcus Rediker. *The Many-Headed Hydra: Sailors, Slaves, Commoners, and the Hidden History of the Revolutionary Atlantic*. Boston: Beacon Press, 2000.

McKeown, Adam. *Melancholy Order: Asian Migration and the Globalization of Borders*. New York: Cambridge University Press, 2008.

Post, Ken. *Arise Ye Starvelings: The Jamaican Labour Rebellion of 1938 and its Aftermath*. The Hague: Martinus Nijhoff, 1978.

Reid, Kirsty. *Gender, Crime and Empire: Convicts, Settlers and the State in Early Colonial Australia*. Manchester, England: Manchester University Press, 2007.

Rodney, Walter. *A History of the Guyanese Working People, 1881–1905*. Baltimore: Johns Hopkins University Press, 1981.

Salman, Michael. *The Embarrassment of Slavery: Controversies over Bondage and Nationalism in the American Colonial Philippines*. Berkeley: University of California Press, 2001.

Stanfield, Michael. *Red Rubber, Bleeding Trees: Violence, Slavery, and Empire in Northwest Amazonia, 1850–1933*. Albuquerque: University of New Mexico Press, 1998.

Steinfeld, Robert. *The Invention of Free Labor: The Employment Relation in English and American Law and Culture, 1350–1870*. Chapel Hill: University of North Carolina Press, 1991.

Stoler, Ann. *Capitalism and Confrontation in Sumatra's Plantation Belt, 1870–1979*, 2nd ed. Ann Arbor: University of Michigan Press, 1995.

Striffler, Steve, and Mark Moberg, eds. *Banana Wars: Power, Production, and History in the Americas*. Durham, NC: Duke University Press, 2003.

Tabili, Laura *"We Ask for British Justice": Workers and Racial Difference in Late Imperial Britain*. Ithaca, NY: Cornell University Press, 1994.

Tomlins, Christopher. "Reconsidering Indentured Servitude: European Migration and the Early American Labor Force, 1600–1775." *Labor History* 42, no. 1 (2001): 1–43.

Ward, Kerry. *Networks of Empire: Forced Migration in the Dutch East India Company*. (New York: Cambridge University Press, 2008).

7

"BLACK SERVICE . . . WHITE MONEY"

THE PECULIAR INSTITUTION OF MILITARY LABOR IN THE BRITISH ARMY DURING THE SEVEN YEARS' WAR

Peter Way

A general court-martial held at Albany, New York, on May 19, 1756, tried fifteen soldiers of the 44th and 48th regiments, all on the capital offense of desertion. Thirteen received death penalties; the other two suffered 1,000 lashes.[1] Such a meting out of military justice regularly occurred in the British army in the Seven Years' War (1756–1763), barely receiving comment in other than official court records and officers' order books. More broadly, harsh punishment for a litany of infractions pervaded eighteenth-century society, practiced in the home, in the workshop, and by the church, while civil law hung and whipped with abandon. But not to the degree of severity witnessed at Albany for the crime committed. The law operates to maintain social order, but that order is not some abstraction, being rather the construction of dominant social groups. Just as historians have exposed the class politics within the courts of justice in English society at that time, these cases of military justice can serve as a departure point for an exploration of labor relations within the army.[2]

John Baptist Freyder and Hendrick King of the 44th regiment deserted because they had been promised to be clothed upon enlistment but had not been. John Owens of the 48th deserted when lured away by his former master. Peter Storts of the 44th deserted when offered other work at significantly more than the six pence per day a soldier earned.[3] All of these men died for their actions, making the cases more than simple instances of military infractions and summary justice. The soldiers articulated their desertion in labor terms. Whether from the belief that the labor contract had not been fulfilled, the pull of a prior occupation, or the lure of economic betterment, they sought to escape military employ. And the army, like all masters at this time, sought legal recourse for the loss of their labor. Yet, military justice operated differently from civil courts. The Crown derived the power to form courts-martial from the Mutiny Act, which Parliament passed annually. This act combined with the Articles of War that laid out the crimes and punishments covered by military law. The system operated at two levels. Regimental courts-martial tried minor offenses such as insubordination or neglect of duty in ways that allowed officers to exercise wide discretion and often did not offer "due process" to soldiers. General courts-martial tried all offenses that in civil society constituted capital offenses, for example, robbery, rape, and murder, but also desertion. The civil equivalent, flight from a labor contract, fell under various statutes of laborers and artificers, which imposed penalties of mild corporal punishment or imprisonment and enforced completion of the labor contract. In the military, desertion constituted a capital offense, and soldiers gambled their lives when leaving their employment.[4]

These cases lay bare the army's implicit assumption of complete control over the lives and bodies of the defendants, indicating that soldiers were conceived of as existing outside civil society and its norms and as subject to extraordinary punishment in a way that evoked slavery (but not indentured servitude). For these and other reasons, military labor constituted a peculiar institution straddling the axis of free and unfree. This chapter examines the British regular army and its labor force in the Seven Years' War as a means of exploring this seeming contradiction.[5]

The Seven Years' War has received much attention recently. This is partly explained by the 250th anniversary of the conflict but is also due to the convergence of developments in the writing of colonial American, British imperial, and Native American history, which has led to a reappraisal of the conflict. Coming out of the shadow of the American Revolution, the Seven Years' War has been cast by historians as the war that made America (not to mention English Canada) and as central to the making of the modern British Empire.[6] To this list of consequences of the Seven Years' War should be added the globalization of merchant capital. The war also raged in Europe, Africa, India, and the Far East. But the tinder first caught alight in America and primarily amounted to the standoff of British and French imperial interests. From the end of King George's War in 1748, the French and British vied from Nova Scotia to the Ohio Valley, sending expeditions to and building forts in these disputed territories in an attempt to assert their territorial claims. Matters came to a head in 1754, when a Virginian force led by George Washington clashed with and ultimately surrendered Fort Necessity to the French. French incursions into the Ohio Valley prompted Britain to reply with armed force, justification for which was expressed in clearly commercial terms. George II informed Parliament, in the King's Speech of November 1754, that the ministry's proposals for expenditures to support the expanding army presence in the colonies for the coming year was aimed at "promoting the trade of My good Subjects, and protecting those Possessions which make One great Source of Our Commerce and Wealth." And in the ensuing debate, Horace Walpole, senior, made this point more explicit: "It is to them [the colonies] that we owe our wealth and our naval strength. Our trade thither is the chief nursery of our seamen: and the imports from thence by being again exported, is what alone keeps the general balance of trade in our favour."[7] General Braddock was dispatched with two regular army regiments to take Fort Duquesne at present-day Pittsburgh. The ambush and rout of Braddock's expedition by the French and Indians initiated (excepting British victory in Nova Scotia in 1755) three years of British defeats: Fort Oswego (1756), Fort William Henry (1757), and Fort Ticonderoga (1758). But from 1758, Britain strung together a series of victories—in particular, Louisbourg (1758), Quebec (1759), and Montreal (1760)—that evicted the French from the continent. It then turned its sights on the Caribbean, taking Martinique, St. Lucia, Grenada, and St. Vincent from the French (1761–1762) and Cuba from Spain (1762). Seven Years' War made Britain the dominant power in the New World.

This recitation of victories is the stuff of military history, but it should also constitute the material of labor history. Soldiers fight wars, and the soldiers in this instance were paid professionals who marched and fought from Fort Duquesne to Havana and yielded up the prize of empire. The troops of the 15th regiment, for example, sailed from England in time to participate in the siege of Louisbourg in 1758. Thereafter, they participated in the siege of Quebec in 1759, its defense against a French counterattack the following year, the surrender of Montreal that same year, and the French Caribbean campaign. The true test of the soldiers' mettle, however, came after Spain entered the war and the fleet sailed for Cuba. Havana fell in mid-August 1762, yielding booty worth £368,000 to the army.[8] But it came at a cost. The hard labor of the siege under the equatorial sun and the tropical diseases decimated the ranks more so than enemy fire.[9] To make matters worse for the 15th, the British commanders designated the regiment for garrison duty in plaguey Havana. When peace finally came in the spring of 1763, instead of returning to England as they had hoped, the star-crossed 15th received orders to return to Canada. They then retraced their steps, sailing for New York, boating up the Hudson to Albany, and setting out on the long march to Quebec. The military governor of Quebec, James Murray, met the regiment at his farm outside the city. "He order'd each man a pint of wine, and expressed himself to one of the Grenadiers, of whom he used to take notice.... I did not know you, you look so black! the soldier replied, we have been on black service, and have got very little white money for it!"[10]

The words of that one disgruntled grenadier to the governor and commanding officer require closer attention. On first blush, it appears a play on the tanned features of the trooper, but his riposte suggests more depth than a play on the eternal opposites of black and white. The very little white money that the unnamed grenadier mentioned probably referred to the grossly unequal distribution of the booty money from Havana. Private soldiers who participated in the siege each received just over £4 as their share: a tidy sum, but a pittance when compared with the princely £122,697 Lord Albemarle earned for his generalship.[11] The black labor he mentioned probably referred to the hard work of the siege of Havana. As a soldier in the 15th recalled, "The fatigues of this Siege pass description, the foundation, being a solid rock, and no earth to cover us, part of the army, were employed in bringing sand bags, two miles distance, amidst showers of grape shot. The soldiers, named this road bloody lane!"[12] But the fact that soldiers performed this labor alongside slaves the army had hired or purchased in the Caribbean made this service so *black*. The high command justified using slaves by claiming it would spare the troops much hard labor. General Jeffery Amherst advocated: "It would be a great Saving to the Troops, and help to the ... Service, as well as that it will Answer many other Labouring Works, if a Number of Negroes could be got." The Earl of Albemarle, military commander for the Havana siege, desired slaves, "as this is an Article of the most serious nature upon which (considering the violent Heats) the Health of the Soldiery and even the Success of the Expedition may greatly depend."[13] One officer purchased 403 slaves at Antigua in May 1762 alone. That same month, Robert Monckton, leader of the victorious Martinique expedition, reported that the army paid £30,820.8.3 sterling for slaves, while also expending £7,574.10.3 for hired slaves accumulated from across the British Caribbean. The owners of hired slaves received 2s. 3d. per day for each slave, significantly more than the 6d. soldier's wage.[14] Not only did the army value slaves more highly than its troops but also it defaulted on the original justification for their acquisition. Slaves did perform much of the manual labor, but soldiers worked side by side with them. While siege work was part and parcel of a soldier's responsibility, having slaves engaged in the same labor seemed to sully the art of war, leading to soldier discontent.

The soldiering that had defeated the French and the Spanish, winning an empire for Britain, at once had been devalued by poor wages and denigrated by its approximation to slave labor, which produced a certain confusion as to exactly what form of labor it was. Did soldiering constitute a service to one's king and country voluntarily entered into by free individuals in return for the king's shilling or "white money," as recruiting officers and some later historians would have it? Or did the term of service, ostensibly for life but typically for the duration of the war, and the nature of the labor, not only laying one's life on the line but hauling sandbags through enemy fire while yoked to slaves, make it a form of bondage, or "black service"? At this particular place and point in time, in the British American army at the end of the Seven Years' War, the answer would appear to be yes to the latter interrogative, which contributed to soldiers' sense of alienation from the imperial enterprise.[15] This current of subaltern discontent manifested itself shortly after the return of the 15th and those other regiments from Havana when a general mutiny erupted in the army, infecting nearly every unit in America, lasting in some outposts until the late spring of 1764.[16]

While the amalgamation of white and black military labor in the Caribbean campaign stands outside the norm of experience in the Seven Years' War—being a rare time that soldiers and slaves joined ranks in a military campaign—it does point to the peculiar nature of military labor. At once free and unfree, soldiers occupied a marchland of labor relations that, while not that unusual in the eighteenth-century Anglo-American world, were exaggerated in the military because of the unusual nature of "production" in warfare. Early modern historians have given much attention to the slave factory, plantation, merchant ship, craft shop, and household as significant sites where labor forms were produced and reproduced by Janus-faced merchant capital, but the military garrison has largely been ignored by other than military historians. Yet, the army was a central player in the making of capitalism. The triangle trade may have coursed around the Atlantic on the sails of merchant and naval ships, but a military presence grounded it in every colonial setting. The military revolution that has received so much attention from military historians intertwined with the process of primitive accumulation, together making for the "bloody lane" that led to modern industrial capitalism, a broad pathway of human toil and suffering trodden by slaves, servants, laborers, and artisans alike with soldiers and sailors, every mile in this forced march marked by a resistive act, with the stocks, the whipping post, and the gallows that met this resistance being the mileposts.

Primitive Accumulation and the Military Option

"Force is the midwife of every old society pregnant with a new one," Karl Marx avowed in *Capital*. "It is itself an economic power." He referred in particular to the actions taken by the state that contributed to the process he termed "the so-called primitive accumulation," in which capital and labor initially formed. In Britain, he addressed the conversion of feudal lands to private property, the enclosure of the commons, the vagrancy and poor law acts, and wage and anticombination measures, the whole coercive apparatus that constituted the infrastructure of capitalism and freed workers from feudal relations for participation in the market. Such "methods of primitive accumulation . . . conquered the field for capitalistic agriculture, made the soil part and parcel of capital, and created for the town industries the necessary supply of a 'free' and outlawed proletariat." In the colonies, the expropriation of native lands and of indigenous peoples, the extraction of staple commodities, and the enslavement and transshipment of Africans received his attention. "These idyllic proceedings are the chief momenta of primitive accumulation. On their heels treads the commercial war of the European nations, with the globe for a theatre."[17]

The army played a central role in the transition to capitalism. State-sponsored armed conflict fostered imperial aggrandizement in the interests of merchant capital, which led directly to modern colonialism and the social formation of capitalism. If force is necessary to change and itself economic in nature, the courts, customs collectors, and colonial officials embodied but implied threats. Ultimate force came in the form of military action, which flowed from and proved essential to the process of primitive accumulation at home and abroad. Further, if the military is central to—in fact, productive of—these profound economic changes, it is necessary to reconceptualize soldiers as war workers, indeed, as transnational laborers whose martial toil around the globe proved integral to the development of international capitalism.

The early modern era witnessed what historians of warfare have called a military revolution, involving relatively swift technological and organizational innovation and marked growth in the scale and intensity of armed conflict, developments that had profound implications for both state and society. Often discussed in curiously bloodless terms of military innovation or state formation, military revolution actually was part and parcel of the very bloody enterprise of primitive accumulation through the pacification of a nation's general populace, the subordination of feudal or regional opponents to state power, state formation, and the creation of fiscal structures to support the military. Empire comprised the larger theater of military revolution, involving the conquest of formerly autonomous states or prestate polities, as well as the subjugation of indigenous peoples. The war machine provided the means necessary to the creation of international capital and its protection within the imperial sphere, the soldiers the requisite force. Historians thus need to liberate warfare from nationalist discourses of diplomacy, nation building, and the formation of national identities to reveal the fundamental role of state-sponsored warfare in the accumulation of capital, and our understanding of the state and state power needs to expand beyond confining national boundaries at a time when commerce defined the accessible globe, but the state, through its transnational projection of military and naval power, secured the domains, trading routes, and human labor upon which merchant capital depended. State, capital, and armed forces formed a triad, a military-commercial complex, that lay at the heart of the international process of primitive accumulation.

That understanding alone proves insufficient, however. War is not some abstract process; it is work—sometimes hellish, other times banal—performed by a peculiar type of worker. Viewed on his own, it is hard to see a soldier as a worker whose hands produce tangible value. But conceived as a collectivity, an army, cogs in the war machine, soldiers acquire power to wrought fundamental political, economic, and social change. The paid labor of soldiers aggregated contributed directly to the political economic project of the imperial state. Soldiers' Herculean labors must be understood in relation to the experiences of other laborers, that is, in terms of proletarianization, work discipline, class formation, and class conflict.[18] At the same time, military labor departed from more traditional forms of labor in its normative separation from civil society because of its engagement in bloodletting, work at once taboo and naturally deemed destructive rather than productive. Soldiers have been made to stand aside from the working class, but their labor in the service of the state forms no less a part of capitalism than other "service" industries and, in the context of the early modern era, one more central to the entire enterprise.

To engage fully with these ideas, we must move beyond a narrow reading of class rooted in an age of industrial machinofacture. First, our understanding of the transition to capitalism should be expanded beyond the economic and legalistic means by which capital accumulated to incorporate warfare as a central engine of the process of capital and state formation, as well as of the related phenomenon of colonization. Second, production needs to be less narrowly construed as the generation of a commodity for market consumption. While actively engaged in a destructive enterprise, the military labor process also created social and political formations and produced infrastructure as essential to the emergence and operation of the international market as the sugar and tobacco produced by slaves or indentured servants on plantations. Third, the worker needs to be reimagined so that military labor is understood in terms of proletarian labor. Wage workers, but bound by their oath to serve ostensibly for life, subject to work discipline far more punitive than in civil society, the blood they purged in performing their duties became the currency of commercial empire. This chapter focuses on the British experience in the Seven Years' War, but the military history of merchant capital was not peculiar to the British, nor confined to the Atlantic. Wherever European nations fought for territory and access to trade across the globe, the labor of soldiers and sailors comprised crucial components to empire building.

Military Revolution and the Fiscal-Military State

Michael Duffy observed, "The governments of Ancien Régime Europe were really giant war-making machines devoting their main efforts to the maintenance of large armed forces."[19] This situation arose as the result of a military revolution, which according to the originator of the concept, Michael Roberts, occurred between 1560 and 1660. Geoffrey Parker updated and globalized the concept, arguing that fortification, firepower, and swelling numbers of armies were the three key elements to the revolution, allowing western powers to dominate the world. The intensification of warfare required greater coordination, training, and discipline.[20] By the eighteenth century, soldiers rarely were mercenaries fighting for a fee and booty but more commonly the paid employees of the state, subject to its disciplines and instruments of its political economic objectives. The era of the Seven Years' War marked the culmination of the military revolution for Parker.[21]

The expansion of military power proved integral to state formation. One of the central strands of the military revolution and of modern state formation entailed the nation-state's appropriation of the right to exercise armed force.[22] The struggle for monopoly rights to military force and the concomitant engagement in increasingly intensive armed conflict caused political changes leading to the development of the modern state. The growth in the size and professionalism of standing armies in the sixteenth and seventeenth centuries, increasing tenfold in just 200 years,[23] necessitated an expansion in the state apparatus to maintain and finance the military. This incestuous relationship in most cases led to absolutist rule and the privileging of a military caste (particularly so in Prussia).

While most argue that England departed from this trajectory, managing both to maintain powerful combined military and naval forces and to develop the most liberal of governing systems of its time, John Brewer maintained that the military was a dominant force in British society. He proposed the model of "the fiscal-military state," by which he meant a state with the main function of waging war and a fiscal policy and administrative apparatus geared to that end.[24] From the late seventeenth through the eighteenth centuries, Britain waged war repeatedly with France and its allies, and the scale of war grew exponentially; between 1689 and 1780, Britain's army and navy grew by 300 percent. In addition, the state constructed a support infrastructure of tax collectors, contractors, makers of armaments, dockyard workers, and paymasters. Consequently, the fiscal-military state "dwarfed any civilian enterprise."[25] Needless to say, it entailed great expense. Military expenditure during the major wars of 1688 through 1783 amounted to 61 to 74 percent of public spending, and when costs of servicing debt are included, 75 to 85 percent of annual expenditures went to fund Britain's war-making capabilities.[26]

England was able to wage war on this scale because of its wealth, and the state was able to raise this money because of its fiscal acumen. Government powers expanded in the late seventeenth and early eighteenth centuries to enhance the nation's war-making abilities. It was able to fund its expanding military commitments by sharply increasing taxation, engaging in "public deficit finance (a national debt)" in an unprecedented fashion, and creating an administrative structure for military and fiscal needs.[27] The Treasury emerged after the Restoration as the controlling body over government expenditure and tax collection, particularly of customs, excise, and the land taxes. Public debt in this period transformed from short-term to long-term borrowing in the form of interest-bearing stocks to be paid for from indirect taxes (i.e., customs, excise, and stamp duties).[28] The British state transformed into a fiscal-military state with elevated taxation, sophisticated government administration, a standing army, and the desire to be a major European power.

The literature on military revolution and state building, for all its differences, agrees on the central role of war in the formation of states. But a strong tendency exists to treat warfare as a closed loop of advances in military technique and technology and corollary state development that operates at a level divorced from the main historical actors—the soldiers—and in some instances from the social and economic transformations making Europe modern. Even in its most fully realized form, Brewer's fiscal-military state, there is little acknowledgment that what is actually being documented is the emergence of the capitalist state with its instruments of wealth accumulation and the development of the associated fiscal infrastructure of banks and insurers populated by a burgeoning bourgeoisie. The very things that Brewer denotes as marking the formation of Britain's fiscal-military state at the turn of the eighteenth century—the expansion of a system of taxation, public credit and creation of a national debt, and the founding of the Bank of England in 1694—Marx argued marks the era as one of the consolidation of capital. He traced these developments back to the "colonial system with its maritime trade and commercial wars."[29]

The imperial setting receives little attention from most historians of the military revolution. Yet the fiscal-military state derived in large part from colonial sources—in the need to extend and protect commerce, to keep the colonies free of threats from other colonizers, and to ensure the flow of commodities that, through customs payments and the spur they provided to the domestic economy, fueled the war machine. England's exploration and settlement of new territories necessitated military support, fueling growth in armies and navies that required unprecedented amounts of capital, which colonial trade provided through customs collection and taxation of the wealth generated, while the state apparatus grew in size and activity as a means of managing the military, trade, and colonies. Not only did the fiscal-military state have its roots in the colonies but also it would reach its logical fulfillment there in the form of militarily dominated dependencies productive of the economic resources requisite to the perpetuation of the fiscal-military state at home. A supranational accumulative structure developed—funding military expeditions, manufacturing trade goods, building ships to wage sea battle or ply trade routes, producing textiles for soldiers' uniforms, engrossing lands, freeing people from their cultural roots and reallocating them to where their labor was needed, colonizing new territories, and engaging in wars to protect the whole structure—a whirlpool of economic activity that spun and spun. Hardly apart from civil concerns or the hellbent pursuit of profit, the military under the guise of national interests helped propel merchant capital's vortex.

> In England at the end of the 17th century, they [the different momenta of primitive accumulation] arrive at a systematical combination, embracing the colonies, the national debt, the modern mode of taxation, and the protectionist system. These methods depend in part on brute force, e.g., the colonial system. But they all employ the power of the State, the concentrated and organized force of society, to hasten, in hothouse fashion, the

process of transformation of the feudal mode of production into the capitalist mode, and to shorten the transition.[30]

The army was the most visceral embodiment of the brutish power of the state, its muscles and sinews the essential apparatus of the colonial system.

The conjoining of militarism and colonialism entered a new era when Britain exported the military revolution to the New World in the Seven Years' War. Historians have characterized the empire in the seventeenth and eighteenth centuries as commercial in nature, a broad and loosely connected mercantile market ultimately made more systematic by what Daniel Baugh calls Britain's "blue-water" policy.[31] Valuing colonies primarily for their exports, Britain largely left them to fend for themselves in times of war, instead concentrating its resources on the Royal Navy to protect the British Isles and keep seas open for commerce. Militias and armies raised by the colonies, crisis by crisis, waged the land war in North America. By the mid-eighteenth century, however, the causes of war shifted from issues of succession and alliance in Europe to the acquisition and defense of territories abroad. Just as at home, lands were being enclosed, their former inhabitants removed, and their perimeters fenced and protected by an increasingly punitive and violent legal system; foreign lands came to be seen as the personal property of the British people, as embodied by the king, to be forcibly taken from those who formerly used them and ringed by a chain of forts manned by the king's troops. The army occupied the center of this empire-building process.

The Seven Years' War constituted an important catalyst to these processes. The war marked a significant turning point in the nature of empire, from being distinctly commercial to being increasingly territorial.[32] The army was an essential player in the winning of this territorial empire, and the empire was increasingly dependent on the army for its defense. The military revolution that had transformed European warfare and the nature of the state was exported to the New World. From Braddock's failed expedition to the Ohio Valley in 1755 to the British capture of Havana in 1762, tens of thousands of men labored to make Britain the preeminent imperial power in the New World. To ignore their efforts, to shroud their work by the red coat, is to buy into the nationalist mystification of military life and the concomitant conjuring of death as the lifeblood of the fatherland.

Freeing the War Worker

Manpower constituted the sine qua non for warfare in the era of the military revolution. Technology and strategy might propel, but flesh and blood bore the brunt of the assault. And soldiers, like workers, had to be created, either uprooted from the soil or exiled from the workshop, but certainly severed from the means of production. Military labor itself did not remain static in nature, in fact undergoing a transformation as part of the military revolution that paralleled primitive accumulation's "freeing" of the worker. In general terms, the labor of soldiers evolved (in a messily overlapping fashion) from a serf's military service owed a feudal lord to the selling of labor power by a mercenary to a captain who contracted it to a general or state to the professional soldier who volunteered or was coerced to serve in a national army. The growing control of the state over armed conflict witnessed a transition from local militias and "feudal and quasi-feudal" forces, to professional armies largely manned by mercenaries and officered by military enterprisers, to standing armies raised and administered by the nation-state. Even within state-based armies, soldiers occupied various labor relations, ranging from the coerced military labor in wartime of, for example, Frederick the Great's Prussia, to the more voluntary enlistment of France.[33] In every instance, however, an army had to be raised; labor had to be extracted from the civil economy and fed into the war industry as armies became engines of primitive accumulation's freeing of the worker.

The connection between proletarianization and military mobilization can be seen at work in the Seven Years' War. The strength of the British army in America rose from about 3,000 men in 1754 to a peak of 25,000 to 30,000 troops in 1761 (exclusive of tens of thousands of provincial troops raised by the colonies). When high rates of attrition as a result of incapacitation, death, and desertion are taken into consideration, the army's labor needs probably figured in the 50,000 to 75,000 range for the American theater alone over the course of the war, the largest concentration of European military resources in North America up to that time. The army met these labor requirements in a number of ways. Coercion offered one obvious solution. The press gang and the crimp (a private individual contracted by a regiment to perform recruiting) resonated in contemporary popular culture, but the naval service more often pursued these methods of mobilization. The legacy of the army's role in the Civil War made the English leery of soldiers practicing strong-arm tactics on the populace. Thus while the state routinely adopted impressment for the army during wartime, it functioned in a more limited fashion than did the naval press gang. It targeted those on the margins of society, "such able-bodied men, as have not any lawful employment or calling, or visible means for their maintenance and livelihood," in the words of the first Press Act of 1704, and local civic officials administered the press, not the military. Even so, when the government adopted a press act for the Seven Years' War, popular resistance meant that it operated for only two years (1756–1758); only a very small minority of those who served in the army during the war had been pressed into service.[34] As a result, Britain primarily relied on volunteers to man its army.[35]

Men volunteered for various reasons. Military historians typically point to recruits enlisting out of a sense of adventure and a desire to escape the humdrum of laboring life or the clutches of local legal authorities for some indiscretion as motivation. As well, one should not underestimate the power of patriotism in this era. It has been observed that the eighteenth century witnessed the emergence of strong nationalist and imperialist currents in British culture and that the Seven Years' War may have been the first to produce recognizably modern forms of war jingoism.[36] People no doubt could be caught up in the anti-French, anti-Catholic fervor and enlist to defend English liberties and the Protestant faith, especially when duty was wedded to the promise of adventure.

Britain proved able to wage war according to the principles of the military revolution, and to do so primarily with a voluntary army, not as a result of youthful exuberance or patriotism's siren call but for the very same reasons that necessitated such military operations: the economic changes associated with the primitive accumulation of capital. E. A. Wrigley asserted that "the acid test of the strength of an economy is its ability to mobilize sufficient resources to conduct warfare successfully." As warfare grew in scale and duration, and as taxation became the basis for military expansion, a nation's economic strength became more important as a factor in military success. The amount of national income that could be mobilized effectively proved equally important as the absolute wealth available. Peasant-type economies based largely on subsistence produced less mobile resources that were more easily taxed than did numerically smaller populations operating within a commercial economy. But equally important to the equation was a society's ability to harvest fighting bodies in abundance without unduly harming the economy's productivity. The English economy differed from those on the continent in the smaller proportion of the labor force occupied in agriculture. Roughly a third of males worked the land (compared with two-thirds and above on the continent) and were productive enough to feed the rest of the population. "The release of labor from the agricultural sector was such a prominent and unusual feature of modern England," affirmed Wrigley. Those freed from the land were available to work in commerce, manufacturing, service, or transportation.[37] This highly mobile society also made England ripe for military mobilization. While Wrigley broadly accepted the "progressive" nature of the English agricultural economy and its "release" of labor power, a more traditional Marxian perspective suggests that primitive accumulation created a proletariat that could not be fully absorbed by industry. Merchant capital required armed forces to secure its interests, and the changes initiated by capital accumulation, in the freeing of labor power, generated its own martial labor force. The fact that Britain rose to the status of most advanced economic power and dominant military power in the mid-eighteenth century derived from no mere coincidence.

We can get a clearer idea of exactly what lay behind that mobility by looking at the timing and character of mobilization for the war, as well as the composition of the army. British soldiers of the eighteenth century were commonly referred to as "the scum of the earth." But as I have reported elsewhere, data drawn from the

Chelsea Hospital Out-Pension Books suggests that the British army in America during the Seven Years' War came from a more skilled occupational background than implied by that sobriquet. While those who had been unskilled laborers, the classic proletariat, accounted for more than 41.5 percent of the sample, 49 percent unexpectedly came from skilled craft backgrounds. Within the gross skilled category, three occupations predominated: textile workers (15 percent of the total sample), shoemakers (7 percent), and tailors (4 percent).[38] These data reflect the mobile nature of the English labor market, as Wrigley would have it, but also points to an underlying current. Those individuals who already had been "freed" from the means of production by primitive accumulation, laborers, and the crafts most affected by the organizational changes in the relations of production (deskilling, piecework, casualization of labor)—weaving, shoemaking, and tailoring—comprised the vanguard of military labor. The unexpected higher representation of men with skill among recruits for military service can be explained by specific economic factors at work in the English economy. The years when army recruitment spiked, 1756 and 1757, were years of depression with high prices and stagnant wages accompanied by food riots and strikes, most significantly in the 1756 bread riots cum wage disputes in the Gloucester textile trades.[39] Economic change, both in the long-term proletarianization of the laboring classes and in the short-term swings of an increasingly capitalistic economy, directed thousands into martial wage work. But for what form of employment exactly did recruits sign on?

Artisans of War

"The starting point of the development that gave rise to the wage-labourer as well as to the capitalist, was the servitude of the labourer," wrote Marx. "The so-called primitive accumulation, therefore, is nothing else than the historical process of divorcing the producer from the means of production."[40] The teleology embedded in this formulation, canted as it is to industrial capitalism and the reified free worker, obscures the long drawn-out process of proletarianization, as well as the varying forms of "unfreedom" that arose along the way. Partial freedom proved more common than free labor, arguably until the nineteenth century. At the same time, using unfree labor as a catchall to ensnare slaves as well as servants and soldiers only reinforces how broad and cumbersome a concept this is unless it is used in a carefully measured fashion.

The modern distinction drawn between free and unfree labor is far too rigid. Thus, engaging in a more nuanced reading of free and unfree labor would be productive. While slavery occupied one pole and proletarian labor another, a variety of labor forms inhabited the rest of the continuum between. If anything, the kaleidoscope of labor forms that inhabited the early modern world reminds us how the nature of labor exploitation in its finer workings was situational and contingent upon relations of power in specific contexts, including both the power of those who controlled labor and the undeniable agency of those very same laborers. Robert Steinfeld contested the assumption that free labor constituted the norm in Anglo America once feudal villeinage had disappeared in England, instead arguing unfree labor proved the norm in early modern England and its colonies. Free labor, at least as defined in its modern sense as "labor undertaken under legal rules that did not give employers either the right to invoke criminal penalties for departure or the right to specific performance," first emerged in America in the early eighteenth century, but as "a special rather than universal form of contractual labor."[41] Laborers and artificers, as well as servants, were subject to punishment and imprisonment for violating the labor contract by early departure, and most labor law concerned the legal control exercised by masters over their workers.

The law conceived of that control in two ways: "as a kind of jurisdiction or personal government that one person exercised over another" or "as a kind of property that employers enjoyed in the services of their workers, a legal right to the exclusive use and enjoyment of their workers' energies for the period or purposes specified in the agreement."[42] Patriarchal logic underpinned the personal jurisdiction perspective. Servants were like members of a family, dependents subject to the governance of the head of household. The proprietarian model was rooted in medieval and early modern law, which recognized a spectrum of property rights in persons, not of their body but of elements of their services. The English preferred to view the labor relationship in terms of personal jurisdiction rather than ownership, but from the mid-seventeenth century, the proprietarian model emerged as the dominant interpretation within what was a developing market society increasingly driven by "English possessive individualism."[43] As a result "contractual unfree labor" came to be seen as voluntary. An emerging legal notion prevailed that individuals owned themselves and could transfer ownership in their labor power on the market, a transaction essentially the same for both free and unfree labor (barring slavery) as both were contractual in nature. Labor in England remained primarily unfree in that it was subject to legal restriction; free labor developed in the colonies but alongside servitude and sharing the same intellectual understanding of the meaning of labor as a commercial entity. While indentured servitude is viewed today as unfree, a form of slavery in that it involved legal compulsion, this view ignores the voluntary aspect of the contract shared with free labor.[44] Regardless of its logical framework, the jurisdiction of proprietarian, master-servant law clearly placed and intended to keep the servant in a subordinate position. In fact, agreeing to work for someone else in early modern England implicitly entailed yielding up one's liberty to a greater or lesser extent, depending on the nature of the agreement.

Looking more closely at the different iterations of the unequal labor relationship will help to situate military labor in the broader spectrum of working relationships. Laborers and artificers most closely approached a modern understanding of free labor. They worked casually, by the day, week, or other term, or by the task, but were still subject to the legal restrictions obligating them to fulfill their contracts just as did those who contracted for longer terms. Both types tended to be married and to head a household, which entailed leasing a cottage and small parcel of land or acquiring a right to common land. This access to land gave them the ability to exercise more control over the selling of their labor power.[45] The ubiquitous servant was another labor form. The term *servant* typically applied to household servants who resided with their master and served for a contractual amount of time, normally a year. Servants tended to be unmarried and to leave service around age twenty-six for men and twenty-four for women, after they had accumulated sufficient wages to marry and establish a household, though some labored into their thirties.[46] Apprentices were another labor form, youths contracted to masters for a number of years in return for being taught a trade. An apprentice by law had to obey his master, who could "correct" him if he did not perform his duties properly, although he could not beat him without going to civil authorities to make his case. If the apprentice was found wanting in his duty, these authorities would have him punished. Apprentices differed from servants in that theirs was an educative relationship; they received no wages for their labor, and they served multiyear terms.[47] The statutes of laborers and Statute of Artificers compelled service from artificers, laborers, servants, and apprentices alike. If they left before their term expired, they could be forcibly brought back to their master.[48] The prohibition against leaving a position before the contract was fulfilled in fact was tightened in eighteenth-century English law and, in particular, applied to those occupations that had been most commercialized, like tailors and shoemakers, so as to ensure the labor supply.[49]

Colonial American practices and labor law essentially followed English patterns, with the exception of indentured servitude, although English precedent existed for this form of labor. Indentures in the colonies were for longer terms and the servants subject to harsher discipline, and servants also could be sold in colonies. The intensification of indentured labor resulted from the nature of the colonial labor market, where scarcity prevailed and relatively easy access to the land existed. Over time, the harshness of indentured servitude led to its differentiation from regular household service, but it still only amounted to a variation of other forms of voluntary wage labor.[50] By the eighteenth century, Americans viewed indentured servitude in terms of property, a commercial model that at its extreme posited a relationship between a person and a thing untempered by other than market forces, the indentured servant being but "the dehumanized instrument of the other."[51]

How does our reading of Steinfeld inform an understanding of military labor, a group that is never addressed in his book? First, in terms of its logical framing, the state or the military never really directly confronted soldiering as a form of labor, at least not in the way that labor law would. War work is embedded in militarist and nationalist discourses that vaunt the soldier's patriotic duty, valor, and manliness in ways that bleed out its labor quotient, making it selfless sacrifice rather than work performed for wages. These discourses effect a normative severance between the reality of soldiering and the soldier's ability to understand his experience. At the same time, in the fact that soldiers were laborers who had to be controlled by their masters (i.e., officers), the same models for labor control that operated in civilian life were at play in the army, albeit policed by military law rather than master-servant law. Of the two, the personal jurisdiction model most closely approximates practice in the army. Premised on a patriarchal framework for family governance that subsumed the laborer within the family under the authority of the master, this model perfectly fit the needs of the military. Dressing the military chain of command in a patriarchal guise and subordinating the soldier in a lineage of authority, it naturalized the work performed by the soldier as what a son would perform for the family and his parents, in this instance, his country and king. As for the paternalism often associated with the patriarch and ideally practiced by a master to his servant, military officers could be heard expressing concern for the well-being and health of their "boys" and characterizing their supply of food and clothing to soldiers as paternal benevolence rather than the exchange of labor for wages, which was actually the case. The proprietarian model fits less neatly with military labor, at least on an ideological level. Asserting ownership of the labor of its soldiers would be seen to devalue the selfless sacrifice for country to which patriotic rhetoric equated enlistment, making it too nakedly a commercial exchange of money for labor. At the same time, officers in practice certainly tended to treat soldiers as if they owned their labor, setting them to work whenever and to whichever task they deemed necessary, unalloyed by any sense of noblesse oblige, not to mention willingly spending their lives for the military cause. That said, the personal governance model appears to come closest to the military experience of labor. Soldiers were seen as part of a larger institution that approximated the family, and the lines of dominance and dependence paralleled those of patriarch and offspring. In joining this "family," the soldier owed obedience and his productive abilities to his "father," and in return, he received paternal care for his welfare and a wage.[52]

Where does military labor fit within the spectrum of labor types drawn by Steinfeld? Soldiers were least like artificers and laborers. They did not work casually by day, week, or task but served for a long term, technically for life but for a majority just for the duration of the war. They did not tend to be married and were not the heads of independent households. Unlike adult artificers and laborers from the beginning of the eighteenth century, soldiers could be corporally punished by officers for not following orders. Like these workers, however, soldiers were compelled to complete the term of their contract or face legal punishment, although in the American colonies from the beginning of the eighteenth century, this seemed to be no longer the case for civilian workers. Military laborers did share a number of features with servants. They resided with their masters, they could not depart their employ for the duration of the labor contract, and they were unlikely to marry. Soldiers, like servants, would be deemed adults but certainly not independent adults. Servants, however, escaped this status by leaving service by their mid-twenties as a prelude to getting married and setting up a household. While some soldiers, particularly noncommissioned officers, were allowed to marry and, less frequently, set up a home, it was at the sufferance of their commanding officer. Most soldiers were not so favored. If they stayed in the military, they did so without a wife, family, or house to call their own, making them adults but in perpetual servitude. Military labor would seemingly have the least to do with apprenticeship, which after all was for educating youth in a particular trade without other remuneration. Soldiers were, for the most part, adults who worked for a wage. But there are rough correlations between the two labor forms. Soldiers, like apprentices, served multiyear terms and remained subject to corporal punishment throughout that term. And many soldiers entered service as youths, and all those in the army were trained in the skills of warfare. But apprenticeship was seen as a stage in one's work life, to be left behind by one's early twenties, whereas soldiering led nowhere but to more soldiering and prolonged dependence, or to work in a totally unrelated type of labor once out of the army. War work offered soldiers a form of perennial youth, but in its unemancipated sense.

Military labor shared a number of features with indentured servitude. Indentured servants voluntarily exchanged a number of years of their labor in return for the costs of their transportation to the American colonies, care, food, and clothing. They were wholly under the authority of their masters, subject to corporal punishment, and increasingly seen as a commodity that could be traded in a labor market. Most British soldiers voluntarily enlisted, nominally for life, but except for a core of professional soldiers, typically for war's duration. For their military service, they received a wage, minus deductions to pay for clothing, equipment, food, and health care. Soldiers also were subject to physical punishment—and punishment that proved far more brutal than that applied in civilian service, with punishments of 1,000 lashes being not unusual and loss of life regularly being exacted as penalty for flight from work. While soldiers were not viewed by the military as commodities to be acquired or exchanged with economic profit, they were transferable or expendable components of the war machine that could be drafted from one regiment to another.

Martial labor emerges from this analysis as an occupation in the early modern Anglo-American world exhibiting less freedom relative to others, with the possible exception of indentured servitude. The unfree nature of soldiers' work constituted the central feature it shared with all these other forms of labor. And martial labor's unfreedom was compounded by the fact that it was likely to last longer than these other forms, rendering soldiers subordinate for an indeterminate period, subject to the fortunes of war and the whims of their officers. While all the other forms of labor, even indentured servitude, seemed to offer a way out, a means of advancement, soldiering seemed to promise only more of the same, death, or perhaps life as a crippled beggar. Military servitude appears more galling in that it threatened to consume one's life in a way that approached too close to slavery. Human capital to be accumulated and expended in the state interests, even more so than indentured servants, soldiers were "the dehumanized instrument" of their masters,[53] although their dehumanization did not result from their commodification but from their amalgamation with national interests. Soldiers constituted both instruments and objects of imperial authority. As soldiers (excepting those pressed), they freely enlisted in an occupation that involved taking from others their lands, their freedom, and their very lives. As workers in the war industry, they were regimented and rendered unfree for the duration of their enlistment, subordinated as laborers, and subjected to a cruel work discipline, their alienated labor producing value by accumulating land and subordinating others. Unless we confront the elements of bondage in military service, we can never fully comprehend the soldier's experience, or recognize yet another stream of unfreedom in merchant capital's imperial project.

Empire Building

Youths did not enlist to become bonded servants to perform the routinized rounds of common labor, drill, and drudgery that soldiers' work involved. For them (as well as for most military historians), military labor meant combat. But when a recruit took the king's shilling, he effectively sold his labor power to the army. Officers controlled soldiers as workers and warriors, issuing orders, overseeing work, and disciplining the recalcitrant, just as masters would in civil society. Soldiers spent little of their time engaged in armed conflict but nearly all of their waking hours making war, for war was more than fighting. Training to fight absorbed more of their energy: marching, performing maneuvers, learning to wield bayonets and fire muskets. Soldiers also stood guard for a prescribed number of hours, often on a daily basis. A matter of course most of the time, in times of military action picket duty secured the fort or camp against enemy attacks, while troops also went scouting to ensure no enemy approached too closely or to identify the best lines of approach to that enemy. More mundane labor came in the form of maintenance of the garrison, policing the grounds of refuse, digging or emptying latrine pits, and erecting fences. On a grander scale of infrastructural labor, troops engaged in constructing permanent forts, laying roads through the wilderness, or building bateaux to be used in the campaigns. As well as these more easily identifiable military duties, soldiers performed many tasks auxiliary to the war effort. Chopping firewood, hauling water, felling trees for use in defensive emplacements, and hunting and fishing for fresh meat not only served the military but also could bring additional wages to the men. Furthermore, those with civilian skills such as tailoring, weaving, shoemaking, or blacksmithing often continued to practice their craft in the military, earning artisanal wages in the process.[54] The army owned the sum of a soldier's labor and deployed it to a variety of tasks. The fact that military law prescribed obedience to an officer's orders meant that almost any task could be considered soldiers' work, although custom intruded, as in the case of additional pay for work not normally deemed to fall within normal expectations. Still, fighting men also dug trenches, laid roads, and erected stockades. But precisely such productive activities, where a soldier dirtied his hands rather than drenched them in blood, contributed to the making of the empire in North America, constituting part of the production process of warfare.

The building of forts and garrisons, such as Fort Pitt in Pennsylvania or Crown Point in New York, both acted as defensive military positions and marked out the expanding perimeter of state imperium, making safe new lands for settlement and ultimately conversion to commercial agriculture, while demonstrating to indigenous peoples that the land had changed hands and they had been reduced to client status. Likewise, the building of roads, such as Braddock's Road heading west from Cumberland, Maryland, and Forbes's Road establishing connections between Philadelphia and Fort Pitt, laid the infrastructure of commercial growth, allowing the movement of troops and agricultural produce in one direction and consumer goods in another. These are but two examples of the more material products of soldiers' labor. On a more exalted height, one usually occupied by military historians, one can see how the true art of war, fighting, in the acquisition of territories, key cities, and trade routes led directly to the advancement of the British state and produced its superpower status in the colonies. In the Seven Years' War, several key victories achieved exactly this objective of evicting the French from North America: Louisbourg, Quebec, and Montreal. With the continent secure, Albion shifted its military might to the Caribbean. Martinique fell, followed by the capitulations of St. Lucia, Grenada, and St. Vincent. Next, with Spain now in the war, came the siege and fall of Havana. With the Treaty of Paris, these islands were exchanged for title to Canada and Florida, making North America British east of the Mississippi.

The Americas were but one theater of the Seven Years' War, albeit the most hotly contested. As well as the war in Europe, conflict transited the globe to West Africa, India, and the Far East. In 1758, England attacked the French stations on the west coast of Africa, the center of its trade in slaves, gold dust, ivory, and, particularly, gum arabic (essential to silk production). A small naval squadron manned with marines took Fort Louis on the Senegal River in April, and a second expedition later in the year took Fort St. Michaels on the island of Gorée and a slave-trading factory on the Gambia River. At war's end, Britain returned Gorée to the French but held onto the Senegal base for its African trade, securing direct access to the gum arabic for its textile manufacturers and cementing its preeminent position in the trade of human flesh.[55] The Indian subcontinent would prove even more central to the British imperial project. The East India Company served British interests in India rather than a colonial government, but the British transformed themselves from traders to rulers of densely populated provinces during the eighteenth century as state involvement increased. The shift began with the Seven Years' War and, for the first time to any extent, a larger commitment of state military and naval resources to the subcontinent. Regular soldiers and a naval squadron went with Robert Clive to India in 1754. In 1757, Clive retook Calcutta from the nawab of Bengal, captured the French *Compagnie des Indes* factory at Chandernagore, and established control in Bengal. In January 1760, the British victory at the Battle of Wandiwash ended the influence of the French in India. At the peace, France surrendered all fortifications and territories settled since 1749. British dominance of the East Indian trade was secured.[56] Britain next used India as a base to project its interests to the Far East. When Spain entered the war belatedly, Whitehall decided to target Manila in the Philippines, the center of Spanish trade in the region. An expedition left Madras in 1762, reaching Manila in September, and soon took the city and fort. The Spanish withdrew across Manila Bay, however, established a base for a provisional government, and continued to harry the British forces until the end of war, when Manila was returned to Spain.[57]

The global scale of the Seven Years' War made clear the extent of Britain's imperial ambitions and might of arms, but it should also illuminate for the historian that the nation of shopkeepers meant to bring as much of the world as possible within the embrace of British merchant capital. Soldiers and sailors constituted the instruments of this engrossment, and while they could take pride in their martial achievements, they were not unaware of the price they paid for the advancement of the interests of others. The general mutiny of 1763 and 1764 attests to this fact. In standing up to the army's alteration of the labor contract, soldiers made a case for the free nature of their labor. The fact they had to, after all their sacrifices on the battlefield, underlines the military's presumption of absolute command over their labor power.

Martial labor did not equate to slavery, being for many a voluntary occupation, but it was a form of servitude, a bondage to the state and its imperial ambitions, as well as to the merchant capital that permeated the entire enterprise. Martial labor was coerced, cruelly corrected, and put to that most loathsome of human professions, bloodletting. Bondage was necessary for such labor. Only bondage by law, bondage by force, or bondage of the mind could compel such bloodwork. Bondage legimitized pushing slaves to the extreme of human labor even unto death in black service for the profit of the master. A soldier's bondage enabled his deployment on the periphery of acceptable human conduct, on the killing fields to perform the black service of spilling blood in the interests of the state in return for white money. The two, slave and soldier—despite the grenadier's objection to the pairing—amounted to similar commodities in the international marketplace of merchant capital, to be exchanged and expended according to the logic of the immoral economy that cared not what body it consumed, slave, servant or free, in its pursuit of gain.

NOTES

1. Judge Advocate General's Office, Court Martial Proceedings, Part 43, pp. 136–50, Series 71, War Office Papers, British National Archives, Kew, London [hereafter in form WO71/43/136–50].
2. Douglas Hay, Peter Linebaugh, John G. Rule, E. P. Thompson, and Cal Winslow, *Albion's Fatal Tree: Crime and Society in Eighteenth Century England* (New York: Pantheon, 1975); Peter Linebaugh, *The London Hanged: Crime and Civil Society in the Eighteenth Century* (London: Penguin, 1993).
3. WO71/43/137–44.
4. Stephen Payne Adye, *A Treatise on Courts Martial* (New York: H. Gaine, 1769); Sylvia R. Frey, "Courts and Cats: British Military Justice in the Eighteenth Century," *Military Affairs* 43 (February 1979): 5–11; Robert J. Steinfeld, *The Invention of Free Labor: The Employment Relation in English and American Law and Culture, 1350–1870* (Chapel Hill: University of North Carolina Press, 1991), 3–4, 8, 22–24, 40–41.
5. Fred Anderson, *A People's Army: Massachusetts Soldiers and Society in the Seven Years' War* (Chapel Hill: University of North Carolina Press, 1984); Harold E. Selesky, *War and Society in Colonial Connecticut* (New Haven, CT: Yale University Press, 1990); James Titus, *The Old Dominion at War: Society, Politics, and Warfare in Late Colonial Virginia* (Columbia: University of South Carolina Press, 1991).
6. P. J. Marshall, *The Making and Unmaking of Empires: Britain, India, and America, c. 1750–1783* (Oxford: Oxford University Press, 2005); Fred Anderson, *The War That Made America: A Short History of the French and Indian War* (London: Penguin, 2006).
7. R. C. Simmons and P. D. G. Thomas, eds., *Proceedings and Debates of the British Parliaments Respecting North America 1754–1783*, vol. 1, *1754–1764* (London: Kraus, 1982), 1, 19.
8. A. J. Guy, *Oeconomy and Discipline: Officership and Administration in the British Army 1714–1763* (Manchester, England: Manchester University Press, 1985), 107; Julian S. Corbett, *England in the Seven Years' War: A Study in Combined Strategy* (London: Longmans, Green, 1907), vol. 2, 283; James Miller, Memoirs

of an Invalid, 769–70, Amherst Papers, U1350 Z9A, Centre for Kentish Studies, Maidstone, England.

9. In the end, the taking of Havana led to the deaths of 40 percent of the 14,000 soldiers involved, most likely to a combination of yellow fever and malaria. See John R. McNeill, "The Ecological Basis of Warfare in the Caribbean, 1700–1804," in *Adapting to Conditions: War and Society in the Eighteenth Century*, ed. Maarten Ultee (Tuscaloosa: University of Alabama Press, 1986), 36.

10. Miller, Memoirs of an Invalid, 76–78.

11. Guy, *Oeconomy and Discipline*, 107; Corbett, *England in the Seven Years' War*, vol. 2, 283.

12. Memoirs of an Invalid, pp. 64–65. See also David Syrett, ed., *The Siege and Capture of Havana 1762*, vol. 114 of *Publications of the Navy Records Society* (London: Spottiswoode, Ballantyne, 1970), 200, 210, 323–24; Corbett, *England in the Seven Years' War*, vol. 2, 270ff.

13. Amherst to Gov. Dalrymple, October 9, 1761, vol. 44, Monckton Papers, Northcliffe Collection, MG18 M, Library and Archives Canada, Ottawa [hereafter LAC]; Albemarle, April 6, 1762, Monckton Papers, vol. 50, Martinque, vol. 7.

14. James Grant to Monckton, May 7, 1762, Monckton Papers, vol. 50, Martinque, vol. 7; [Monckton to] Lords of the Treasury, May 24, 1762, ibid.; Monckton's Accounts with St. Christophers, 1762, Monckton Papers, vol. 51, Martinque, vol. 8; Mackenzie Order Book, vol. 2, 22, 25, 27, 30, Jan., 3, 4 July, 7 Aug. 1762, pp. 26, 29, 31–33, 94, 110, Frederick Mackenzie Collection. MG 23, K 34, LAC.

15. Slaves served in the British army during the Revolution and later in the West Indies. Peter M. Voelz, *Slave and Soldier: The Military Impact of Blacks in the Colonial Americas* (New York: Garland, 1993), 181–84, 187, 195–96, 231–44, 250–56; chapters 11 and 23 generally. See also McNeill, "Ecological Basis of Warfare in the Caribbean," 40.

16. For a fuller treatment of this mutiny, see my "Rebellion of the Regulars: Working Soldiers and the Mutiny of 1763–1764," *William and Mary Quarterly*, 3rd Ser., 57, no. 4 (October 2000): 761–92.

17. Marx, *Capital: A Critique of Political Economy*, trans. from 3rd German edition by Samuel Moore and Edward Aveling (New York: Random House, 1906), 805, 823–24, 784–848 passim.

18. Russell L. Johnson, *Warriors into Workers: The Civil War and the Formation of Urban-Industrial Society in a Northern City* (New York: Fordham University Press, 2003).

19. Michael Duffy, "Introduction," in Michael Duffy, ed., *The Military Revolution and the State 1500–1800* (Exeter, England: University of Exeter, 1980), 4.

20. M. Roberts, *The Military Revolution, 1560–1660* (Belfast: M. Boyd, 1956), 1–2; Geoffrey Parker, *The Military Revolution: Military Innovation and the Rise of the West, 1500–1800* (Cambridge: Cambridge University Press, 1988; 2nd ed. 1996), 3–4, 10–11, 19–20, 24, 43.

21. Parker, *Military Revolution*, 149–51.

22. Peter H. Wilson, *German Armies: War and German Politics, 1648–1806* (London: University College London Press, 1998), 7; M. S. Anderson, *War and Society in the Old Regime 1618–1789* (Leicester, England: Leicester University Press, 1988), 29–30.
23. John Brewer, *The Sinews of Power: War, Money and the English State, 1688–1783* (London: Routledge, 1989), 8.
24. Ibid., xi, xv, xvii, xx.
25. Ibid., 29, 34.
26. Ibid., 27, 40–41.
27. Ibid., xi, xv, 42, 65.
28. Ibid., 91–98, 128–29, 91, 117–19.
29. Marx, *Capital*, 827–28.
30. Ibid., 823–24.
31. Daniel A. Baugh, "Great Britain's 'Blue-Water' Policy, 1689–1815," *International History Review* 10, no. 1 (February 1988): 40–41; Baugh, "Maritime Strength and Atlantic Commerce: The Uses of 'a Grand Marine Empire,'" in Lawrence Stone, ed., *An Imperial State at War: Britain from 1689 to 1815* (London: Routledge, 1994), 185–88.
32. P. J. Marshall, "Introduction," *The Oxford History of the British Empire*, vol. 2, *The Eighteenth Century* (Oxford: Oxford University Press, 1998), 1.
33. Anderson, *War and Society*, 16–32; Wilson, *German Armies*, 277; Andre Corvisier, *Armies and Societies in Europe, 1474–1789*, trans. Abigail T. Siddall (orig. ed. 1976; Indianapolis: Indiana University Press, 1979).
34. Arthur N. Gilbert, "An Analysis of Some Eighteenth Century Army Recruiting Records," *Journal of the Society of Army Historical Register* 54, no. 217 (Spring 1976): 39; Arthur N. Gilbert, "Charles Jenkinson and the Last Army Press, 1779," *Military Affairs* 42 (1978): 7; Arthur N. Gilbert, "Army Impressment during the War of the Spanish Succession," *Historian* 35 (August 1976): 705.
35. Anderson, *A People's Army*, 41–42; Selesky, *War and Society*, 155–62; Titus, *Old Dominion at War*, 59, 63–65, 79–80, 98–100, 145–48.
36. Linda Colley, *Britons: Forging the Nation, 1707–1737* (London: Vintage, 1996); Kathleen Wilson, "Empire of Virtue: The Imperial Project and Hanoverian Culture c. 1720–1785," in Stone, ed., *An Imperial State at War*, 128–64.
37. E. A. Wrigley, "Society and the Economy in the Eighteenth Century," in Stone, ed., *An Imperial State at War*, 72–73, 76–81, 89–91 (quotations on pp. 72, 83); Marx, *Capital*, 805–6.
38. This analysis is based on the records of 845 soldiers granted pensions in March 1757 through December 1760 from regiments that had served in North America. See Way, "Rebellion of the Regulars, 761–92. The skill quotient of the provincial forces did not depart too far from this profile: 33.4 percent of Massachusetts natives in the provincials had been artisans (and 32.7 percent of British immigrants) as had 39 percent of Virginia troops. See Anderson, *A People's Army*, 236, Table 18; Titus, *Old Dominion at War*, 85–87.

39. John Rule, *The Vital Century: England's Developing Economy, 1714–1815* (London: Longman, 1992), 102–104, 110, 147–48; Rule, *The Labouring Classes in Early Industrial England, 1750–1850* (London: Longman, 1986), 256–59; Robert W. Malcolmson, *Life and Labour in England 1700–1780* (London: Hutchinson, 1981), 113, 125.
40. Marx, *Capital*, 787, 786.
41. Steinfeld, *Invention of Free Labor*, 3–4.
42. Ibid., 4.
43. Ibid., 55–60, 66–73, 76–78, 80–81.
44. Ibid., 4–10.
45. Ibid., 34–41.
46. Ibid., 17–21, 34.
47. Ibid., 25–27.
48. Ibid., 22–24.
49. Ibid., 113–14, 121.
50. Ibid., 40–54.
51. Ibid., 87–93; quote on p. 91. For other studies of indentured servitude, see David W. Galenson, *White Servitude in Colonial America: An Economic Analysis* (New York: Cambridge University Press, 1981); Sharon V. Salinger, *"To Serve Well and Faithfully": Labor and Indentured Servants in Pennsylvania, 1682–1800* (Cambridge: Cambridge University Press, 1987); Aaron S. Fogleman, *Hopeful Journeys: German Immigration, Settlement, and Political Culture in Colonial America, 1717–1775* (Philadelphia: University of Pennsylvania Press, 1996); Christopher Tomlins, "Reconsidering Indentured Servitude: European Migration and the Early American Labor Force, 1600–1775," *Labor History* 42, no. 1 (2001): 1–43.
52. That this understanding of labor relations is at one and the same time a class and gendered discourse is something that Steinfeld did not consider, but it is of significance to a broader understanding of martial labor and a theme I am pursuing elsewhere in the larger project.
53. Steinfeld, *Invention of Free Labor*, 91.
54. For a fuller examination of the military labor process, see Way, "Class and the Common Soldier in the Seven Years' War," *Labor History* 44, no. 4 (December 2003): 455–81.
55. Anderson, *Crucible of War*, 306.
56. Ibid., 417–18.
57. Ibid., 490, 515–17.

Parts of this essay previously appeared in *Über Marx hinaus. Arbeitsgeschichte und Arbeitsbegriff in der Konfrontation mit den globalen Arbeitsverhältnissen des 21 Jahrhunderts*, eds. Marcel van der Linden and Karl Heinz Roth (Berlin and Hamburg: Association A, 2009).

8

"WE SPEAK THE SAME LANGUAGE IN THE NEW WORLD"

CAPITAL, CLASS, AND COMMUNITY IN MEXICO'S "AMERICAN CENTURY"

Steven J. Bachelor

At a lavish banquet held in Mexico City's University Club in February 1948, Ernest R. Breech, the recently named executive vice president of Ford Motor Company, hired to help revitalize the flagging firm, laid out the his employer's postwar plan for Latin America[1]. Entitled "We Speak the Same Language in the New World," Breech's address called on leaders of the region to put aside past differences, embrace U.S. investment, and enter the "American Century."[2] Coined seven years earlier by publishing magnate Henry Luce, the term referred to what Luce and others saw as the U.S. moral imperative to spread worldwide democracy and free-enterprise capitalism.[3] "Unprecedented material abundance, a higher standard of living for all, and the dawn of a new era of peace, harmony, and prosperity" would surely follow, Breech told the assembled dignitaries, among them business-minded Miguel Alemán, Mexico's first civilian president since the revolution.

A new era, in fact, had already begun. Three years earlier, Henry Ford II, the maverick thirty-year-old grandson of Henry I, had taken over the company's reins and begun a far-reaching, global reorganization the *New York Times* termed a "palace revolution."[4] "The chaos [of Ford's international operations] has to be cleaned up and order made of it. . . . This is an American company and it's going to be run from America," declared the new chief.[5] Ford's international restructuring put an end to the relative autonomy and lax oversight that local officers had enjoyed since the company began expanding internationally before World War I.[6] Corporate policy would now emanate from Detroit and be closely overseen by Breech, whose main charge was to conform the company's vast international enterprises to a single, unified business strategy. Breech's visit to Mexico, the first stop on a lengthy tour that took him to all of Ford's Latin American facilities, served not only to unveil the company's blueprint for the region but also to signal sweeping changes for the company's Mexican branch. For one thing, Breech took the opportunity to announce the retirement of Benjamin Kopf, an Argentine who previously ran a small Ford branch in Uruguay, and the appointment of Fraine Rhuberry, a highly touted General Motors man with more than twenty years of experience in Detroit. Breech also used the occasion to formally celebrate a multimillion-dollar expansion of Ford's Mexico City factory, La Villa, so named because of its location in the neighborhood of La Villa de Guadalupe, two blocks from the Basílica de Guadalupe. The ambitious project would transform La Villa, built sixteen years earlier largely with secondhand material from Detroit-area plants, into Latin America's most technologically sophisticated automobile factory. Executives deemed the expansion a critical first step in Ford's long-range strategy to nurture and dominate Latin America's burgeoning automobile market.

A watershed for Ford, Breech's visit coincided with a number of pivotal events in international affairs. Less than a year before Breech's trip, Harry Truman became the first U.S. president to make an official visit to Mexico. While there, he laid a wreath at the monument honoring six young military cadets killed a hundred years earlier defending Mexico City from invading U.S. forces and delivered an important speech that praised the "friendly cooperation and mutual respect" that the countries of the Americas had established. "Here in the Western Hemisphere we have already achieved in substantial measure what the world as a whole must achieve."[7] Heralding peace and security as universal human goals, the speech presaged themes embodied in the Truman Doctrine, unveiled a few days after his return from Mexico, and even more in his famed 1949 inaugural address. A landmark in international relations, Truman's inaugural address is considered by many to mark the birth of the "age of development."[8] It outlined a "bold new program for making the benefits of [U.S.] scientific advances and industrial progress available for the improvement and growth of underdeveloped areas" and committed the "imponderable resources" of the United States to help the world's "least fortunate ... achieve the decent, satisfying life that is the right of all people." "Greater production," concluded Truman, "is the key to prosperity and peace."[9]

This new age was characterized as well by a novel framework and discourse that fundamentally changed the way humankind would be organized and construed. Development discourse, which Truman's address both embodied and propelled, bifurcated humanity into two distinct discursive realms: the developed and underdeveloped worlds. It also rendered as natural a number of normative concepts like growth, progress, and modernity and legitimated an imperial project of resource extraction and capital accumulation through which only capital investments from "developed" countries like the United States could lift "underdeveloped" countries from their putative condition of "primitiveness," "stagnation," and "limited productive capacity."[10]

Delivered at the dawn of this new age of development, Breech's 1948 address proved prophetic. Much of the "New World"—by which Breech meant both the Western Hemisphere and the new postwar order over which the United States presided—did come to speak the same language. Indeed, development discourse became the postwar era's new common sense, embraced as much by audiences in the so-called underdeveloped world as by those in the so-called developed world. And perhaps nowhere within the "underdeveloped" world was this more the case than in Mexico, where state officials and industrial workers, in particular those at U.S. multinational corporations like Ford, embraced development discourse. Granted, this process was not without conflict or contention; decades after the nationalization and mass mobilizations of the Cárdenas presidency (1934–1940), industrial workers and state authorities in Mexico continued to frame much of their political discourse in the language of the 1910 revolution. These nationalist claims, however, tended to be part of a broader, shared commitment to "development." Indeed, in the years following World War II, state officials, industrialists, and working people on both sides of the U.S.-Mexico border united in a manner never before seen in Mexico, embarking on a historic and, in many ways, still ongoing project to remake aspects of Mexico in the image of the developed world's archetype, the United States. Together, these actors provided a level of political and industrial stability unprecedented in postwar Latin America. Encouraged by this stability, U.S. capitalists, especially Big Three automakers, poured massive amounts of direct investment into Mexico. Their investments not only fueled Mexico's modernizing "miracle" but also, by providing outlets for the U.S. economy's greatly expanded productive capacity, helped overcome a looming crisis in postwar capitalism and thereby safeguard the "American way of life."[11] These two phenomena—Mexican development and the American way of life—remained inextricably linked. Rarely, however, are the two phenomena studied together. Scholars of Mexico have tended to confine themselves to nationally bounded lines of inquiry and rely on dichotomous, state-centered formulations of nationalism and imperialism.[12] Notions of U.S. exceptionalism within American studies meanwhile have tended to elide the imperial relations that helped give rise to and underwrote the American way of life.[13] This has particularly been the case in countries like Mexico, where U.S. authorities so vigorously promoted both the image of and Mexico's own prospects for the American way of life.

Using the case of the automobile industry, this chapter situates Mexican development and the American way of life within a shared social field. It argues that both phenomena were constituted through a mutual—though certainly contradictory and asymmetrical—process of transculturation and capital accumulation. More than any other, the automobile industry helped create the

American way of life. It also spearheaded the Mexican government's postwar economic growth strategy, which promoted domestic manufacturing as a means to spark Mexico's own Fordist revolution. By the end of the 1960s, Mexico's automobile industry had become the country's largest manufacturing industry, and its workforce had become one of Mexico's most industrially strategic. Initially upheld as exemplars for Mexico's "modernizing" working class and "official" union movement, autoworkers embraced development discourse, particularly its universalist claims to democracy, modernity, and security. These claims figured prominently in challenges autoworkers increasingly waged in the 1970s against authoritarian rule and corporate efforts to uproot the modicum of working-class power that "collaborative capitalism" helped beget. These rank-and-file challenges culminated in *la insurgencia obrera* of the 1970s, the largest union democratization movement in Mexican history, in which autoworkers took a central role. Yet, as autoworkers militated for their own version of the American way of life, state and corporate authorities—long accustomed to labor stability—turned to coercion and repression to combat working-class mobilization. Faced with labor insurgence and a plateauing consumer market within Mexico and declining rates of profit at home, Big Three automakers steadily relocated production from Mexico City to areas closer to the U.S. border, where they could take advantage of low-wage, nonunionized workers and close proximity to the still expanding U.S. market. This transformation not only marked an end to the automakers' experiment with bringing the American way of life to Mexico but also represented automakers' abandonment of their earlier model of Fordism and collaborative capitalism for one based on deterritorialized markets, low wages, and flexible modes of accumulation. This shift in capitalist production, which took root in Mexico in the late 1960s and 1970s, made possible the epochal transformation that played out in the United States in subsequent decades, whereby automakers shuttered their U.S. factories in favor of new sites in northern Mexico. Such was the irony of "developing" Mexico. As much as development bolstered the American way of life in the United States by providing outlets for capitalism's ever-expanding productive capacity, it also set in motion a process that ultimately undermined opportunities for industrial workers on both sides of the U.S.-Mexico border to secure what they considered to be the American way of life.

La Villa, Via Detroit

When Ernest Breech delivered his auspicious address at the University Club in 1948, conspicuously absent from the crowd were members of Ford's workforce. The absence of even token representatives of the workforce was surprising, given the importance laborers would have in the company's expansion plans, which looked to double the size of the workforce and triple its productivity. It also seemed odd, given all the fanfare the company produced leading up to Breech's visit. Trips by Ford de México executives to Detroit were common, but rare were those by Detroit executives to La Villa. For several months prior to Breech's arrival, Ford de México publicized his upcoming visit in both the company newsletter and Ford's monthly magazine, *Ruedas*, which boasted a 30,000-copy run and was distributed freely to workers and managers at neighboring factories and businesses. In particular, the articles spoke of the growing importance Ford de México had in Ford Motor Company's global operations and the confidence executives in Detroit had in the benefits that would come to Mexico through a partnership of U.S. capital and Mexican labor, a sentiment that the latter's absence from the celebration seemed to betray.

Perhaps officials considered working people, even those employed by one of the world's most vaunted corporations, ill suited for a formal affair at the tony University Club, founded before the 1910 revolution by wealthy scions of the ancien régime. More likely, their absence derived from the mounting discord between workers and managers at La Villa. When production resumed at the factory in November 1946, after a lengthy hiatus prompted by the war, autoworkers demanded that managers bargain in good faith with legitimate representatives of the workforce, not the "strangers and crooks who purport to speak on our behalf."[14] These strangers and crooks were the leaders of the Alianza de Trabajadores de Ford, the *sindicato blanco* (literally "white union," the term is comparable to "yellow union") to which all Ford workers belonged.

As a collective bargaining agent, the Alianza had a dubious history. It formed not long after La Villa opened in 1932. Its leaders were members of management who, in cahoots with officials from the labor department, created the organization and secured government certification as a union and a collective contract, all without the participation of the workforce. Since Ford de México's founding in 1925, its workers had militated for a union and a collective contract. Their activism seemed to fly in the face of the plans Henry Ford initially had for his Mexican workforce. Of the company's first cohort of forty workers in 1925, thirty of them came via Ford facilities in Detroit. All Mexican nationals, they had traveled to Detroit, where they were enrolled in a special training program for Mexican autoworkers. As part of the program, the men voluntarily returned to Mexico, where, in Henry Ford's words, they would "form the nucleus of a native force to whom they will be an example and an inspiration." And indeed they were, for not only did they bring skills they learned on the job but also they brought their experiences living in Detroit's *colonia mexicana*, which was a hotbed of mutual aid associations and labor activism in the mid-1920s. Thousands more returned to Mexico in 1931 and 1932, when, bowing to Anglo fears that laid-off Mexican workers would fill up relief rolls in Detroit, Henry Ford arranged with the Mexican consulate to pay for their repatriation. Of these thousands, fifty of them secured employment at La Villa, which began production in September 1932.[15]

These workers proved more combative than their predecessors. A number of them had been active in the Liga de Obreros y Campesinos, which several hundred Ford workers in Detroit formed with Diego Rivera while he was painting his famed fresco, *Detroit Industry*. Within weeks of La Villa's opening, workers had organized the Sindicato Rojo de Trabajadores de Ford and petitioned the Calles government for certification. The labor department instead recognized the Alianza, which Ford managers had hastily created in response. Workers, however, continued their protests against the Alianza, and after Lázaro Cárdenas took over the presidency from Calles in 1934, the organization became a bone of contention between the two men. After visiting personally with Ford workers in his first week of office, Cárdenas encouraged them to continue their mobilizations, joining with tens of thousands of other wage earners in Mexico City demanding union representation. Calles officials within the labor department, however, continued to ignore workers' petitions. Ultimately, the conflict came to a head in the summer of 1935, when Calles accused Cárdenas of treason for inciting working-class mobilizations like those that continued at Ford. Cárdenas responded by sending Calles into exile in the United States and removing Callista supporters from the government. Within months, the Sindicato Rojo had won union recognition and a collective contract.

The union, however, dissolved during World War II. Owing to Detroit's conversion to war production, Ford de México was forced to close its doors and lay off its workers. When production resumed in 1946, many of the same workers returned, but the rank-and-file union they helped organize did not. In its place, managers reconstituted the Alianza, naming the same production chief from years earlier as its head. The government promptly certified it. In 1947, Ford workers filed an *emplazamiento* (strike petition), arguing that both the Alianza and the collective contract its leaders signed were illegitimate. The Alemán administration denied their petition. Undeterred, workers staged a walkout a few days after Breech's visit. Other than media attention and calls from labor leaders for moral support, little came of the walkout, and employees returned to work the next day. That same month they joined 60,000 other wage earners in a protest against Alemán's antistrike policies. They also allied themselves with the dissident groups under the leadership of Vicente Lombardo Toledano, a Marxist intellectual and longtime labor activist whose ties to Ford workers stretched back to the founding of the Sindicato Rojo. A month earlier, Lombardo Toledano had been expelled from the Confederación de Trabajadores de México (CTM), the country's largest labor confederation, whose leaders were closely allied with Alemán. Lombardo Toledano considered the workforce at La Villa a critical element in forging an independent labor movement. Despite its small size (roughly 500 workers in 1948), the workforce, held up by company and government alike as a model of progress, had symbolic importance. Accordingly, Lombardo Toledano put Ford workers in the forefront of his broader campaign to challenge the CTM and its support of the Alemán administration.[16]

The protests at Ford reflected larger complaints industrial workers made against Alemán's policies. By mid-1948, dissidents had organized themselves into a rival labor confederation and claimed to represent the bulk of organized labor, particularly in strategic industries like mining and railroads. Launching a series of protests and strikes, they posed a serious challenge to Alemán's industrialization policies, which were predicated on foreign investment and firm control over industrial labor. Alemán maneuvered aggressively to establish an environment conducive to U.S. investments. Even before taking office, Alemán met with U.S. embassy officials and allayed any fears they may have had about his administration. "The industrialization of Mexico," he asserted, "would come from the United States, not from Great Britain and much less from Russia."[17] Once in office, he denounced nationalization, halted land reform, and replaced several prolabor officials with business executives as heads of Mexico's labor arbitration boards. He also invited Donald Nelson, a former Sears, Roebuck chief who had chaired the War Production Board, to design an industrialization plan for Mexico. It emphasized expanding domestic production and imports from the United States.[18] In the wake of the passage of the Taft-Hartley Act, whose developments the Mexican government closely followed, Alemán passed his own legislation that outlawed wildcat strikes, then happening with great frequency. Alemán considered the move "one of the most important things that had to be done before Mexico could progress."[19] Alemán's strongest thrust came in October 1948, when he used armed force to crush an insurgent movement within the national railway workers union, the most industrially strategic union of those that belonged to a dissident coalition that was challenging the CTM. Mobilizing state security forces, Alemán forcibly removed the union's head and replaced him with a government stooge.

This episode, known as the *charrazo* because of the progovernment replacement's fondness for Mexican rodeo (*charrería*), was a watershed in Mexican labor history. It severely weakened union independence by reining in one of the country's most militant and industrially strategic unions. Its new leaders quickly severed all ties to dissident labor groups, which weakened the labor movement in general. The *charrazo*, however, did not stall Ford workers' efforts to oust the Alianza. If anything, it strengthened their resolve. In the months that followed it, wage earners continued to stage brief work stoppages, disturbing production schedules. The company operated under a strict quota of vehicles it was permitted to assemble, a number executives considered inadequate for full efficiency; thus, any interruption in production threatened company profitability. In February 1949, workers filed another strike petition, claiming again that the company union and its collective contract violated federal labor law. Lombardo Toledano again lent his assistance, hoping the rank-and-file campaign would draw national attention to his newly formed Unión General de Obreros y Campesinos. The organization brought together the remnants of dissident groups ousted from the CTM. Government officials refused to rule on the petition, claiming that the group of workers did not hold legal title to the collective contract in place at Ford. In other words, their complaints were ignored. Nonetheless, workers continued their protests, joining with several other organizations that continued to oppose the government's economic policies. By the end of March, their protests convinced the head of the company union, the same production chief who presided over the Alianza in the early 1930s, to step down. In his place, he named Benjamin Téllez Girón, who in the words of wage earners was "unknown to entire workforce." Brought in from outside the company, Téllez Girón had spent the last few years as a CTM functionary. He quickly signed a new collective contract with Ford, which workers immediately branded "apocryphal" and "signed by people whose names we've never heard."[20]

Managers must have considered the matter resolved. In April, speaking privately to U.S. State Department officials, Fraine Rhuberry enthused that, more than any Latin American country, Mexico "gives the most facilities and guarantees to private investment."[21] He must have been pleased, for soon thereafter he relaunched the company expansion plans, which he had put on hold during the earlier unrest. New machinery began to arrive from Detroit, replacing the antiquated material that made up much of La Villa. The company also started construction on two new wings for the factory and put out word that they would soon be looking to hire a couple of hundred new workers. For workers, however, the matter was hardly resolved. Knowing that the new hires would automatically be enrolled in the company union, workers filed another strike petition. Again, the officials charged with investigating the claims, at least one of whom had for two years enjoyed the use of a luxury vehicle compliments of Ford, denied the petition.[22] Workers responded by staging a wildcat strike. It was the industry's first strike, illicit or otherwise, in more than ten years. Answering appeals from Rhuberry, Alemán dispatched security forces to the plant to intimidate workers and break up the strike. The actions succeeded, as the strike lasted but one day. The next day Rhuberry wired the president, telling him that "now all is calm" and that managers had "fired all the undisciplined ones." These undisciplined ones numbered nearly 150 workers, many of whom had been with the company since La Villa opened in 1932.[23]

The episode at Ford resembled the *charrazo*, but it marked a different type of turning point at Ford and within Mexico's automobile industry more broadly. Scholars point to the *charrazo* as *the* defining moment in postwar Mexican labor history. In one leading authority's words, it "constituted Mexico's Thermidor" and "led to organized labor falling under the domination of a small camarilla of trade union leaders."[24] Subsequently, scholars deduced from the *charrazo* a model of authoritarian union control, known as *charrismo*, which they have used to explain working-class acquiescence across a variety of industries. Unfortunately, *charrismo* is all too often presented instrumentally as an explanation of working-class politics rather than as the result of broader transformations going on within working-class political culture. This is particularly the case within Mexico's automobile industry. As we shall see, following the suppression of the rank-and-file insurgency at Ford in 1949, automakers turned to other methods to win working-class loyalty. They were joined by others, like the United Auto Workers, who similarly sought to gain working-class support in a larger bid to combat Communism and promote the American way of life.

Making Mexico's "American Way"

As in the United States, where constructing the American way of life was a political-economic project, nurturing it in Mexico demanded more than mere rhetoric. It required, first, delivering unprecedented benefits, unmatched by contemporary Mexican firms. Like their counterparts in the United States, autoworkers in Mexico were among the best paid industrial workers (only wage earners in the state-owned oil industry on average earned more per hour).[25] Even the least paid positions within the industry earned seven times Mexico City's minimum wage. After the famed Treaty of Detroit in 1950, automakers in Mexico followed suit, offering contracts that linked wage increases to rising productivity and the cost of living. Automakers also provided unparalleled benefits, including paid vacations, pensions, annual bonuses, education subsidies, and scholarships for workers' children.

Company largesse reached beyond the factory walls as well. For instance, in 1954 General Motors (G.M.) began sponsoring English courses for their employees at the Instituto Cultural, which proved so popular that they continued the program for a number of years. Firms also sponsored trips for employees to Detroit, where they could see firsthand the types of industrial establishments to which the Mexican automakers aspired. Companies also funded several recreational sports leagues, which brought together Mexican wage earners and U.S. managers to "showcase U.S. sportsmanship and teamwork."[26] These included bowling leagues, tennis clubs, and baseball teams. Chrysler and G.M. joined forces in constructing a ballpark in the space between their two plants, separated by less than a mile, that drew large crowds from the surrounding neighborhood.

At first glance, Mexico City seems an odd locale for employers to offer such generous benefits. Mexico City had an enormous reserve army of the unemployed and one of the largest labor markets in the world. According to government-released figures, notorious for undercounting, the unemployment rate in 1950 was 20 percent.[27] Indeed, each day, prospective workers formed long lines around the factory gates, eager to land a job. The generous benefits seem especially counterintuitive, considering that Mexican automobile operations lacked the productivity rates and economies of scale that made "efficiency wages" possible within the United States. But like in the United States, these policies were meant to mold a class of stable, loyal, and productive workers.

Such welfare policies were especially meant to demonstrate the firms' "good corporate citizenship," a term they used with regularity in the 1950s.[28] Ford went so far in the 1950s as to appoint a manager of civic affairs, a Mexican national, whose job included carrying out activities that illustrated Ford's good corporate citizenship.[29] These programs included a national manual arts program for school-age children, meant to "offer routes to find one's vocation" and "diminish drop-out rates and juvenile delinquencies."[30] By far, Ford's largest civic project was the Escuelas Henry Ford initiative, begun in the 1950s. Through it, the company partnered with the Mexican government to "build primary schools in regions with Ford facilities and to make available the educational resources that will combat Mexico's deficiencies." Within a decade of its founding, the program had sponsored more than sixty schools, including five within greater Mexico City.[31]

Automakers also helped facilitate contact between Mexican and U.S. autoworkers. For instance, executives at G.M. and Ford joined with heads of the American Federation of Labor and Congress of Industrial Organizations (AFL-CIO) to provide leadership grants, which brought local labor leaders from Mexico to Detroit for training in union organizing. Automakers even encouraged contact with the UAW and its head, Walter Reuther, the era's most visible working-class spokesman for the American way of life.[32] Reuther's gospel of the "politics of productivity" and the "revolutionary power of economic abundance" closely jibed with the economic policies advocated by U.S. multinationals. "It is in our [the UAW's] self-interest in terms of providing a market for finished goods from American industries, a market for goods manufactured by American workers," he noted, "to see the living standards of others raised—to see their own indigenous economies developed and strengthened."[33] No doubt, too, automakers considered that the UAW's brand of unionism, which encouraged high wages and employment security, would appeal to Mexican workers. However, amid the rapidly changing workplace relations ushered in by Mexico's transition to full-scale automobile manufacturing, these transnational influences would have far-reaching consequences for Mexico's industrial working class.

Subterranean Shop-Floor Blues

Positioning the auto industry at the center of its import-substitution industrialization strategy, the Mexican government passed the Automotive Integration Decree in 1962. It mandated that by the end of 1964, all automobiles sold in

Mexico would need to be manufactured domestically.[34] When it was still in the proposal stage, U.S. automakers opposed the government's plan because it placed restrictions on the number of models and type of model changes they could make, key features in the firms' competitive business strategies. They also grimaced at the suggestion that motor vehicle manufacturing be done through joint ventures with Mexican-majority ownership, not the wholly owned U.S. subsidiaries then in operation. Before the decree's final passage, however, the U.S. firms had secured the help of Thomas Mann, U.S. ambassador to Mexico and soon-to-be head of the Automobile Manufacturers Association, who threatened to withdraw millions of dollars in U.S. investment should the automakers not maintain full and direct ownership of their operations and complete control over model changes. With these prerogatives in place, automakers welcomed the production increase and chance to expand in the burgeoning market. Though still small, the Mexican automobile market was growing rapidly and made up predominantly of first-time buyers. This was a promising counterpart to the U.S. market, where automakers were experiencing declining sales, as replacement-vehicle buyers supplanted first-time buyers, and, for the first time in decades, falling rates of profit.[35] In Mexico, by contrast, analysts predicted that future sales would increase by 5 to 10 percent each year for several decades to come.[36]

The Integration Decree gave automakers just twenty-nine months to convert from assembly operations to full-scale manufacturing. Needless to say, the industry underwent tremendous change swiftly. Between 1960 and 1965, the industry's workforce more than tripled in size, bringing more than 5,000 new wage earners into the factories. Between those same years, productivity jumped by more than 100 percent. Line speed increased from fifteen inches to twenty-five inches per minute, and workers went from assembling forty units to seventy units per shift.[37] With this came increased injuries and closer managerial scrutiny—an environment one veteran said was "more suited to a *burro*."[38] As employers recruited hundreds of new wage earners, they also began systematically terminating older men, with many years of service, and replacing them with younger, ostensibly hardier laborers. (By 1964, the average age among autoworkers had reached forty-one years.) Autoworkers saw these dismissals as an affront to a lifetime of loyalty to the firm and the industry's cherished ideal of job security. Employers also began restructuring the wage scale, introducing more minutely defined and lesser paid categories and job classifications. The firms also introduced new bosses, engineers from technical schools, to oversee departments, who, as one autoworker recalled, "would come over and bark orders at us . . . and with their titles and degrees still didn't know how to do the work."[39] The work itself was increasingly divided into more singular, repetitive tasks. For instance, only in 1964 did the engine block department at G.M.'s Mexico City factory acquire overhead conveyor belts linking it to the other assembly areas.[40] Previously, one worker did the various parts of chassis assembly; by the end of 1964, chassis assembly consisted of divided functions, now performed by a four-man team. The biggest change, however, came with the construction of new manufacturing facilities, which opened in January 1965. For these, automakers purchased huge tracts of land along Mexico City's industrial periphery, where they poured more than five billion pesos into their new operations, constructing Latin America's most technologically advanced automobile factories. In contrast to the assembly plants within Mexico City, which possessed antiquated machinery, the new sites boasted state-of-the-art equipment, equal to that in U.S. factories.

The UAW officials found these changes, and the thousands of new workers they would bring into the industry's fold, to be "fertile ground for trade union work."[41] In the 1950s, the UAW showed little interest in Mexico's automobile unions, content that they had "good organization and excellent leadership."[42] This attitude changed, however, following the passage of the 1962 Automotive Integration Decree. By then, UAW officials had grown concerned with both "wage dumping" and, in the wake of the Cuban Revolution, Communist influence within Mexican unionism. As Victor Reuther put it, "The Mexican situation is serious. Mexican trade unions are moving into a position of isolation even worse than neutralism."[43] In response, he called on the UAW to dramatically increase its activities in Mexico. He launched this effort in November 1962, when he traveled to Mexico City to meet personally with automobile union officials. He brought with him translated copies of a typical UAW contract, which he hoped they would use to guide their future contract negotiations.[44] That same year, Dan Benedict, the Mexico City–based assistant general secretary of the International Metalworkers' Federation (IMF), began working closely with the UAW. Together, they held several seminars for auto union members, training them in wage systems, time and motion studies, and wage incentive plans. They also disseminated among autoworkers a variety of informational material, including U.S. Information Agency–made films, translations of popular labor-related books and songs ("Solidaridad Para Siempre," for example), and photographs of a badly beaten Walter Reuther taken at the Battle of the Overpass. As part of this campaign, the UAW also put together a group of "opinion molders," made up of prominent journalists, creative writers, and scholars, who were tutored in and encouraged to publicize the benefits that could come to Mexican workers through international solidarity with the UAW.

Largely unconcerned with the Cold War motivation behind them, rank-and-file autoworkers found great inspiration in their contacts with the UAW and drew on them in their own efforts to refashion unionism in Mexico. Obviously, the labor activism that would mark the industry in the coming years was not directly caused by autoworkers' links to the UAW. Instead, the solidarity and resources they provided helped give meaning to the language of development being advanced by U.S. agents. This language, however, belied the sometimes harsh reality of changing work relations on the shop floor as the industry shifted to full-scale manufacturing. Indeed, the industry's long-standing paternalist strategies of labor control proved ineffective in mollifying the many grievances that rapid industrialization wrought.[45] Autoworkers, particularly those at G.M., where a rank-and-file movement to oust the reigning *charro* had begun to take shape, considered Victor Reuther's 1962 visit to be a special boon. Meeting with dissident G.M. workers, Reuther condemned the *charro*, Raúl Sánchez del Castillo, as a "company tool" and promised the support of the UAW in their attempts to "revive *sindicalismo*."[46] Critics of Sánchez del Castillo called for his resignation, claiming that "on the shop floor the consensus is that the union leaders haven't done anything for us. . . . They have no legitimacy and should immediately step down."[47] In a hotly contested union election that came a few months later, G.M. workers voted Sánchez del Castillo out of office and replaced his leadership team with five members of a militant faction of autoworkers that went by the name Grupo Democrático. Upon winning, the group's most vocal member, Clemente "El Negro" Zaldívar, declared, "Unions are for making demands, not supplicating. This union belongs to *you*; not the company." He also underscored the example of the UAW, which had representatives as well as "opinion molder" journalists on hand to observe the election.[48] "The UAW's success," which he upheld as a goal for Mexican autoworkers, "has come through lengthy union struggle and working-class *conquista*."[49]

In their first contract negotiations with G.M., *democratistas* made a host of new demands, all of which they stipulated their U.S. counterparts enjoyed. For one thing, they insisted on having real contract negotiations, in contrast to the typical closed-door talks presided over by entrenched *charros*. And the issues they wanted placed on the table reached further into managerial prerogatives than ever before. For instance, they demanded the right to decide how the transition to full-scale manufacturing would be carried out on the shop floor. They also asserted the right to participate in setting production quotas, the pace of production, and the percentage of workers employed in different wage categories. These last demands had been inspired directly by Reuther, who provided Mexican autoworkers with analyses of every contract G.M. had ever signed worldwide. Noting their production increases and high efficiency rates without commensurate wage increases, Mexican workers concluded that "the company is exploiting Mexican labor and taking all the profits to the 'other side.'"[50] As one journalist who covered the emerging movement similarly observed, G.M. was "not creating new industry but, rather, taking advantage of new labor in new places."[51]

For autoworkers, this became especially clear in Toluca, where G.M. and Chrysler had constructed new manufacturing facilities. Autoworkers at the two firms' Mexico City plants sought to organize these and their workforces into a single union. "Look at the power of the UAW," explained one G.M. worker. "We need a single union for the whole industry, like theirs. Only then can we expect to challenge the farce that is charrismo."[52] These efforts at Chrysler were aided in

July 1965 with the death of its long-ruling *charro*, in place since 1942, a man Victor Reuther acknowledged received a steady flow of "payola from the company" (plus his brother was the chief of personnel).[53] Employees quickly held union elections, bringing to power an insurgent group committed to "union democracy and social justice."[54] At both firms, workers claimed the right to organize the workforces, pointing to provisions in their collective contracts that stipulated the Mexico City unions had the right to organize at all facilities the companies might establish in the future. In both cases, however, well before the Toluca plants had hired a single worker, management had met with officials from Mexico's largest and notoriously corrupt labor confederation, the Confederación de Trabajadores de México (CTM), to create *sindicatos fantasmas* (phantom unions). Rumors had begun to circulate that all three automakers intended to shut down their Mexico City facilities and transfer all operations to the new plants along the industrial periphery, where wages were fully 70 percent less than what entry-level autoworkers earned in the capital. At G.M., this prompted the first labor strike in the company's thirty-year history in Mexico, a month-long walkout in 1965 that drew international attention. The G.M. workers requested and received considerable financial support from the UAW's Free World Labor Defense Fund. Victor Reuther recommended the grant because he recognized "it would set a bad precedent about factory relocations if G.M. succeeds in breaking the strike."[55] Nevertheless, G.M. did break the strike and put in place a phantom union, presided over by the brother of a regional political boss.

At Chrysler, the company's response to autoworkers' protests was more severe. In 1969, Chrysler workers staged the company's first walkout, a wildcat strike involving some 6,000 employees. Government and corporate authorities responded by opening fire on the protesters, leaving a half-dozen critically wounded. It was the first open strife at a U.S. firm in Mexico since the consolidation of revolutionary rule, and yet it went unnoticed by media on both sides of the border. Chrysler followed by terminating and blacklisting 500 of the most vocal participants, sending *guardias blancas* (terror squads) to patrol the factory floor, and imposing the firm's chief of production as the new union head (a post he would hold until 1994, when he passed it on to his son, its current occupant). Already considered a harsh production chief, Hugo Díaz established a "reign of terror" that included routine reprisals against insubordinates, frequent firings of "subversives," and constant threats of violence. Díaz established a police substation within the plant, made use of spies among the workforce, and turned the company soccer teams, which earlier had helped foster working-class solidarity, became "into armed shock forces for managers" to intimidate and terrorize employees.[56]

When, eighteen months after the first shootings at Chrysler, authorities formally commented on the ongoing strife, they did so by denouncing the dissidents as "Communists" who were "threatening the fiber of the Mexican nation."[57] Such claims only served to legitimize ongoing violence being unleashed on workers. In 1972, two more shootings occurred at Chrysler's Toluca plant, both of which authorities failed to acknowledge. Workers responded by mounting more protests, including numerous occupations of the headquarters of the nation's largest labor confederation. It is beyond the scope of this chapter to list the litany of examples of continued state and corporate repression against autoworkers. Every instance, however, came in response to workers' demands for legitimate union representation and contractually stipulated job security. And every instance included automakers quickly offering wage increases as an incentive for workers to return to work and resume production. But wage increases failed to resolve the industry's endemic class conflict, which revolved around issues more fundamental than remuneration. Instead, these disputes increasingly were settled through state repression and corporate chicanery. For instance, in 1980, G.M. launched what would become one of the longest strikes in Mexican history. As participants explained, "This strike movement is the direct result of difficult relations that began in 1965, when the company and the government assumed an intransigent attitude toward our civic rights."[58] As they did in 1965, autoworkers demanded the right to organize a democratic union at G.M.'s newest plant, this one in the northern state of Coahuila, where, once again, a corrupt union boss created a phantom union and signed a collective contract before a single employee had been hired. Following a protracted struggle, authorities succeeded in crushing the movement through intimidation and outright fraud. The movement's death knell came when company executives and state officials bribed a former union leader to sign doctored documents that acceded to management's requests. Similarly, Ford workers mobilized numerous times in support of union democracy, each time rebuffed by government and company security forces. In 1990, government agents killed one demonstrator, and several more were kidnapped and severely beaten. Ultimately, in January 1991, after firing hundreds of workers, state and corporate authorities held their own closed-door union elections, which human rights observers concluded denied "the fundamental rights of Ford workers to choose their union representatives." Even the Partido Acción Nacional, a right-wing party that is no friend of labor, squarely blamed the ongoing violence on Ford authorities.[59]

In mobilizing against state and corporate authorities, autoworkers joined with laborers in other strategic, mass-production industries, forming the largest, most extensive strike wave in Mexican history. Obviously, the growing influence of U.S. multinational corporations does not explain the era's labor insurgence, nor can it be explained simply by attending to changing workplace conditions in the wake of rapid industrialization, which would be succumbing to a type of technological determinism that obscures more than reveals. Most scholars have tended to understand the insurgence in connection with Mexican president Luís Echeverría's *apertura democrática* (democratic opening), crediting his change in presidential labor policy with the increased activism.[60] Echeverría projected an ostensibly populist image and welcomed the creation of "independent" unions while simultaneously repressing dissent. For instance, Echeverría repeatedly denounced multinational corporations as "voracious imperialists [who] foster national dependence" while simultaneously dispatching the army to help employers crush opposition.[61] Among the most violent of these episodes was his use of the army in 1976 to crush a nationwide strike launched by electrical power workers. Autoworkers discerned the apparent political contradiction, labeling the armed men "official assassins for Mexican 'progress'" who have "destroyed the companies' pretensions of bringing social advancement."[62]

The turn toward violence and repression by state and corporate authorities is best explained by the strategic power that autoworkers had come to exercise by the 1970s and their capacity to use this power to achieve what they believed to be the promise of modernization. Prior to the shift to full-scale manufacturing, autoworkers held little bargaining power, despite the seemingly advantageous structure of the industry's product market (i.e., a limited number of automakers producing a similar product and competing for the same workers and consumers).[63] Interestingly, during this period they received their most generous benefits. By the early 1970s, automakers had curtailed most of their welfare programs, and wages failed to keep pace with inflation. Workers' power derives from their location and position in the productive process, and autoworkers during this period lacked strategic power in the automobile market because they lacked a strategic position in automakers' productive operations. From its beginnings, Mexico's automobile industry was part of a North American operation; that is, automakers could weather any production stoppage Mexican autoworkers might launch. In fact, Mexican autoworkers were frequently put out of work owing to stoppages waged by workers in the United States. Following the shift to full-scale manufacturing, however, Mexican autoworkers exercised much greater strategic power. Not only was the industry the center of the government's import-substitution industrialization strategy but also it was the fulcrum in automakers' hemispheric plans. Although the industry was meant to industrialize Mexico, automakers also positioned Mexican operations to serve its entire American market. By 1970, Mexico was exporting domestically manufactured automobile parts to the United States. It had also become the largest supplier of engines to Peru, Venezuela, and Chile.[64] Of course, autoworkers' ties to the UAW offered them resources that few Mexican industrial workers enjoyed, but this paled in comparison to the strategic power they enjoyed in what increasingly (and decades before NAFTA) emerged as a hemispheric productive process. Mexican autoworkers recognized the changing division of labor this wrought, mobilizing around the fundamental issue of organizing workforces in lower wage areas. Speaking to a meeting of Latin American automobile union leaders in Venezuela in 1967, Victor Reuther made a similar conclusion, declaring that "the internationalization of the companies is a giant octopus reaching out with its tentacles to all corners of the globe and that the auto sector meeting should address itself to finding the sensitive nerve upon which to hit on in order to fight back."[65] However, at the very moment Latin American workers, particularly those in Mexico, were gaining strategic power, the UAW turned its back on Latin American workers. By the early 1970s, their participation with Mexican workers had abruptly ended, perhaps owing to the economic woes beginning in the United States, a belief in the frequent charges of Communist infiltration within Mexican automobile unions made by state and corporate authorities, or an aversion to the decidedly anti-imperialist turn that working-class denunciations had taken in the 1970s. Regardless, this proved to be a fatal error, as automakers succeeded in both undoing the strategic power and community that autoworkers in Mexico City had cultivated and, by doing so, crushing the community power that autoworkers on the U.S. side had amassed and bringing to an end the American dream that the automobile industry was said to have created.

Coda: Missed Modernity

Today, directly across from Mexico City's most opulent shopping mall, Antara Polanco, in the heart of the fashionable district locals call "*el Rodeo Drive mexicano*," stands an ironic but all too fitting symbol for Mexico in the so-called American century: a concrete bus shelter, emblazoned atop with the words "General Motors" in the automaker's classic block-letter font. Weathered and cracked and out of place amid the high-end retailers and tuxedo-clad parking valets, the bus shelter is all that remains from G.M.'s Mexico City factory. In 1995, as it was doing at sites across North America, G.M. shut down its flagship Mexico City plant and shifted operations to the *maquila* zone along the U.S.-Mexico border, where it could enjoy cheaper labor costs and proximity to the U.S. market. The factory was razed, and in its place was built the elegant Antara Polanco, which its developers said would rival "Paris's Champs-Elysées and New York's Fifth Avenue."[66] Less than a mile away stands a similarly extravagant complex, Parques Polanco, which boasts high-rise residential dwellings, ten parks, three corporate towers, and a bustling commercial corridor. It sits where, until the late 1990s, when the company closed its doors and transferred operations closer to the border, Chrysler's Mexico City factory. Finally, a few more miles away stands the former home of Ford La Villa, which after five decades of operation became the first to abandon the capital for the burgeoning border zone. The site—two blocks from Mexico's holiest site, where in 1530 the Virgin Mary is said to have appeared before an Indian peasant—is today a Wal-Mart.

Much of Mexico, it seems, is still speaking a language emanating from the United States, particularly in this current era of formalized economic integration.

And the so-called American century seems far from over in Mexico's capital, which over the past twenty years has experienced the sort of industrial relocation that has left Detroit and its surrounding environs a rust belt. It would be wrong, however, to think that Mexico has simply trailed after the United States, a teleology that betrays modernization theory. Rather, the two trajectories were joined in a shared dynamic of "creative destruction" that mutually, yet asymmetrically, constituted working-class communities on both sides of the border. Spatially, however, industrial capitalism structured a pattern of resource extraction and division of labor (international, regional, and workplace) that privileged certain workers as more valuable than others, regardless of whether they performed the same work at the same productivity and efficiency levels. And this value depended largely on the strategic and community power that specific working people possessed at any given time. While on the U.S. side, this process helped produce, and ultimately undo, the cherished notion of the American way of life, on the Mexican side it represented yet another example of that country's recurring aspiration to an unachieved modernity.

NOTES

1. I would like to thank Eric Arnesen and John French for their thoughtful comments on earlier drafts of this essay.
2. Breech's address is found in Archivo General de la Nación, Mexico City, Ramo Presidentes, Miguel Alemán Valdés [hereafter AGN-MAV], exp. 111/3752, February 19, 1948.
3. Henry Luce originally formulated the term "American Century" in an editorial of the same name in the February 7, 1941, issue of *Life*. He argued that the people of the United States "have failed to play their part as a world power—a failure which has had disastrous consequences for themselves and for all mankind." See Michael J. Hogan, *The Ambiguous Legacy: U.S. Foreign Relations in the "American Century"* (Cambridge: Cambridge University Press, 1999), 11–29.
4. *New York Times*, March 23, 1947.
5. Mira Wilkins and Frank Ernest Hill, *American Business Abroad: Ford on Six Continents* (Detroit, MI: Wayne State University Press, 1964), 370.
6. In 1904, Ford Motor Company opened its first international branch, a small workshop in Walkerville, Canada, just across the Detroit River from the company's rented factory on Detroit's Mack Avenue. Henry Ford hoped then to open a branch in Mexico City. In 1909, he began negotiations with Mexican president Porfirio Díaz. They could not reach agreement on tariff and freight terms, and negotiations soon stalled. The ensuing revolutionary turmoil put Ford's plans on hold, during which time the company opened plants in England, France, Denmark, and South Africa.

7. John T. Woolley and Gerhard Peters, "Harry S. Truman: Address in Mexico City," in *The American Presidency Project*, available at http://www.presidency.ucsb.edu/ws/?pid=12841.
8. Arturo Escobar, *Encountering Development: The Making and Unmaking of the Third World* (Princeton, NJ: Princeton University Press, 1995), 3.
9. Harry S Truman, "Inaugural Address, January 20, 1949," in *The Presidents Speak: The Inaugural Addresses of the American Presidents from Washington to Clinton*, ed. David Newton Lott (New York: Henry Holt, 1994), 292–98.
10. Ibid.
11. Susan George and Fabrizio Sabelli, *Faith and Credit: The World Bank's Secular Empire* (Boulder, CO: Westview, 1994), 23.
12. Gilbert M. Joseph, Anne Rubenstein, and Eric Zolov, eds., *Fragments of a Golden Age: The Politics of Culture in Mexico since 1940* (Durham, NC: Duke University Press, 2001); John D. French, "Latin American and International Working Class History on the Brink of the 21st Century: Points of Departure in Comparative Labor Studies," *Development and Society* 29, no. 2 (2000): 137–63.
13. Amy Kaplan and Donald E. Pease, *Cultures of United States Imperialism* (Durham, NC: Duke University Press, 1994); Robert Gregg, "Apropos Exceptionalism: Imperial Location and the Comparative Histories of the United States and South Africa," in *American Exceptionalism? U.S. Working Class Formation in an International Context*, ed. Rick Halpern and Jonathan Morris (London: Macmillan, 1997).
14. AGN-MAV, exp. 432/450, letter from Ford workers to Alemán, January 7, 1948.
15. Zaragoza Vargas, *Proletarians of the North: Mexican Industrial Workers in Detroit and the Midwest, 1917–1933* (Berkeley: University of California Press, 1999).
16. Luis Medina, *Civilismo y modernización del autoritarismo* (Mexico City: El Colegio de México, 1979), 173.
17. United States National Archives, Record Group (hereafter USNARG) 59, 812.00/3-2946. Notes from meeting with Alemán and U.S. Embassy officials, Mexico City, March 29, 1946.
18. Stephen R. Niblo, *Mexico in the 1940s: Modernity, Politics, and Corruption* (Wilmington, DE: Scholarly Resources, 2000), 174–75.
19. USNARG 59, 812.504/7-347, July 3, 1947.
20. AGN-MAV, exp. 432/450, Telegram from Ford workers to Alemán, March 11, 1949.
21. Niblo, *Mexico in the 1940s*, 207.
22. AGN-MAV, exp. 710.1/524, telegram to Robert Amézaga, September 11, 1946.
23. AGN-MAV, exp. 432/450, telegram from Rhuberry to Alemán, July 17, 1949.
24. Ian Roxborough, "Mexico," in *Latin America between the Second World War and the Cold War*, ed. Leslie Bethell (Cambridge: Cambridge University Press, 1997).
25. Jeffrey Bortz, *Los salarios industriales en la Ciudad de México, 1939–1975* (Mexico City: UNAM, 1984).
26. *Noticiero GM*, November 1956.

27. Estados Unidos Mexicanos, *VII censo de poblacion*, 1950.
28. See, for instance, *New York Times*, June 26, 1957.
29. Ford Industrial Archives, International File [hereafter FIA], Accension 67-6, box 2.
30. Ford de México, *Apuntes para una historia de la industria automotríz* (Mexico City: privately printed, 1977), 45.
31. Secretaría de Educación Pública, Box 54, exp. IV/161 (IV-120/4205), April 1973.
32. Nelson Lichtenstein, *The Most Dangerous Man: Walter Reuther and the Fate of American Labor* (New York: Basic Books, 1995), 334.
33. Jack Scott, *Yankee Unions Go Home: How the AFL helped the U.S. Build an Empire in Latin America* (Vancouver, BC: New Star Books, 1978), 197.
34. *Diario Oficial de la Federación*, August 25, 1962.
35. *New York Times*, "Auto Woes Cloud the Economy," October 17, 1961.
36. Ford Motor Company, "A Study of Automotive Manufacturing in Mexico" (privately printed by Ford, April 1960); D. D. Bennett and K. E. Sharpe, *Transnational Corporations versus the State: The Political Economy of the Mexican Auto Industry* (Princeton, NJ: Princeton University Press, 1985), 106.
37. Secretaría del Trabajo y Previsión Social, Registro de Asociaciones [hereafter STPSRA], exp. 10/6298, leg. 5, December 8, 1964; FIA, Accension 65–71, box 31.
38. STPSRA, exp. 10/6298, leg. 5, December 6, 1964.
39. Mario Reynoso, interview with the author, Mexico City, May 22, 1997.
40. STPSRA, exp. 10/6298, leg. 5, January 9, 1964.
41. United Auto Workers, International Affairs Department, Victor Reuther and Lewis Carliner Collection [hereafter UAW-IAD], box 112, folder 6, June 19, 1961.
42. UAW-IAD, box 110, folder 9, Arturo Jaureguí [secretary general of ORIT], "The Automobile Industry in Mexico," Sept. 1956.
43. UAW-IAD, Box 112, folder 6, memo to Walter Reuther, June 19, 1961.
44. UAW-IAD, box 110, folder 14, October 31, 1962, and November 14–16, 1962.
45. Kevin J. Middlebrook, *The Paradox of Revolution: Labor, the State, and Authoritarianism in Mexico* (Baltimore: Johns Hopkins University Press, 1995), 233.
46. UAW-IAD, Box 55, folder November 12, 1962; STPSRA, exp. 10/6298, leg. 3, December 8, 1962.
47. STPSRA, exp. 10/6298, leg. 3, December 11, 1962.
48. Sánchez del Castillo and his supporters walked out of the meeting hall when it became clear that the vote count went against them. The next day they petitioned the Secretaría del Trabajo y Previsión Social to nullify the election results, claiming fraud. An inspector individually questioned each worker and determined that Grupo Democrático's victory would stand. STPSRA, exp. 10/6298; leg. 4, August 8, 1963. Junta Central de Conciliación y Arbitraje, Sección de Asociaciones, exp. R.A. 312/1605/937 (902), September 25, 1965.

49. STPSRA, exp. 10/6298, leg. 4, August 8, 1963.
50. STPSRA, exp. 10/6298, leg. 5, January 5, 1965.
51. *Siempre* (Mexico City), February 1965.
52. STPSRA, exp. 10/6298, leg. 5, July 18, 1964.
53. UAW-IAD, Box 55, folder 12; Nov. 1962.
54. *Justicia Social* (Toluca, Mexico), August 1971.
55. UAW-IAD, box 48, folder 18, January 27, 1965.
56. *El Día* (Mexico City), March 17, 1971.
57. *El Universal* (Mexico City), January 4, 1971; STPSRA, exp. 10/5441, leg. January 3, 1971.
58. Quoted in Valentina Cerda de López, "Historia de una huelga: GM y la lucha de 106 días" (Licenciatura thesis, Universidad Nacional Autónoma de México, 1983), 16.
59. Quoted in Dan LaBotz, *Labor Suppression in Mexico Today* (Boston: South End Press, 1992), 158.
60. Jorge Basurto, *En el régimen de Echeverría: Rebelión e independencia* (Mexico City: Siglo Veintiuno Editores, 1983); Ilán Bizberg, *Estado y sindicalismo en México* (Mexico City: El Colegio de México, 1990). Two important exceptions are Middlebrook, *The Paradox of Revolution*, and Ian Roxborough, *Unions and Politics in Mexico: The Case of the Automobile Industry* (New York: Cambridge University Press, 2009).
61. *El Universal*, September 18, 1973.
62. *El Día*, November 22, 1976; *Uno Más Uno* (Mexico City), December 17, 1977.
63. John T. Dunlop and Benjamin Higgins, "'Bargaining Power' and Market Structures," *Journal of Political Economy* 50 (February 1942): 1–26.
64. UAW-IAD, box 55, folder 12, Nov. 1970.
65. UAW-IAD, box 57, folder 12, March 13, 1967.
66. *El Universal*, January 13, 2007.

INDIGENOUS PEOPLES AND LABOR SYSTEMS

INTRODUCTION

Colleen O'Neill

Labor historians writing about nonindigenous workers have explored varied aspects of class formation, including how workers experienced the transformation of artisanal crafts, the creation of industrial discipline, and how labor markets emerged, structured along racial and gendered lines in ways that often undermined collective resistance. We have also examined workers' communities and their cultures (as well as their amusements), looking for clues to how gender and race shaped individual and collective behavior and how those histories fit within our changing economic and political power structures. And of course, we have been telling "labor's story," chronicling workers' efforts to advance social, industrial, and political changes. In doing this work, we have learned a lot about the history of capitalism.

We also know a great deal about the impact of European colonialism on Native economies, cultures, and political structures in the Americas. Important and now classic works in Latin American history explore the fate of indigenous peoples in the Spanish silver mines, plantations, and mission economies. In the literature on French and English colonialism to the north, Native people remain significant actors in the history of fur-trading empires. We know much less about indigenous workers in the mid-nineteenth and twentieth centuries, as older forms of European control yielded to the development of new republican states and economic systems.[1]

But that gap in the literature is beginning to close, possibly as a response to indigenous people asserting greater economic and political power in the late-twentieth century. In the last twenty years, Canada's First Nations gained significant land and sovereignty rights, and American Indians in the United States began to wield greater political clout, thanks to their success in the gaming industry. Indigenous peoples in Latin America have become increasingly militant, mobilizing support for a variety of social movements from Bolivia to Mexico.

Whatever the inspiration, new studies examine the lives and labor of Native peoples as historical actors, working on railroads and on the Vancouver waterfront, in the canneries and hop fields in the Pacific Northwest, and in the mining districts in the North American Southwest.[2] These studies stress the resourcefulness of Native communities in adjusting to new economic challenges. Most important, this new work overturns previous assumptions, mired in dependency theory that associates cultural demise with indigenous peoples' venture into wage work and their participation in the capitalist marketplace.

Certainly, in the nineteenth century, indigenous peoples throughout the hemisphere suffered a great deal as new republican governments confiscated most of their lands (that which earlier colonists had not already claimed), undermined their communities' livelihoods, and repressed their cultural and political sovereignty. Even so, states such as Mexico, Canada, and the United States at times embraced, even encouraged, indigenous cultural expression. Facing a kind of double standard, some indigenous communities carved out niches within transnational labor systems as performers or producers of culture.

Yet, emerging scholarship emphasizes Native agency and resiliency, and it helps to explain why and how indigenous communities and their cultures persisted, despite the harsh assaults they endured in the last 500 years. Native peoples found ways to supplement their subsistence or wage work income by making and selling baskets, weavings, pottery, or other craft items that non-Native consumers wanted to buy. The cultural marketplace was (and is) rife with contradictions and fueled colonial expectations of indigenous exoticism. But recent histories reveal a much more complicated relationship between the Native producers, colonial consumers, and the cultural objects they were buying and selling. Making and selling baskets, pottery, and rugs or dancing for tourists may have helped to reinforce tribal cultural identities, rather than reducing them to meaningless commodities.[3]

This new literature is more than compensatory or celebratory history. Pioneering scholarship such as Rolf Knight's *Indians at Work* and Alice Littlefield and Martha Knack's anthology, *Native Americans and Wage Labor*, documented the historic role of American Indian workers in the twentieth-century industrial economy.[4] Telling those stories added previously silenced voices to the labor narrative and opened the door for later studies that stressed the agency and resiliency of indigenous peoples, their cultures, and their economies. Building on that research, Brian Hosmer, Paige Raibmon, and I, among a handful of other scholars, examined how wage work could fuel cultural innovation, not simply serve as an agent of assimilation. For Navajos in the mid-twentieth century, becoming wage workers or small mine operators did not mean turning their backs on pastoral traditions. Rather, they incorporated mining coal into their sheep-herding and kin-centered ways or followed the jobs rather than the herds along well-worn migration routes. Similarly, as Paige Raibmon demonstrated in her study of Native peoples in the Puget Sound, jobs provided Kwakwaka'wakw additional resources to give away at potlatch ceremonies.[5]

Authors in this section ask broader questions about indigenous workers and their transnational contexts. Andrew Parnaby and Catherine Nolan-Ferrell's chapters direct our attention to the margins to help us understand the historically specific dynamics that shape the global economy overall. Adjusting the focus on Native peoples encourages scholars to think about the persistence of colonial structures of power and their influence in shaping regionally specific racial categories within the global capitalist market. This is one place where scholars of indigenous working-class history have a lot to offer non-Native labor historians. Including Native workers in labor's story forces us to bend the black-white continuum for understanding race—and offers obvious places to think about the role of the state in maintaining racial categories. Catherine Nolan-Ferrell demonstrates, for example, how Mexican and Guatemalan states policed borders and defined categories of "national identity," sorting out who was "Guatemalan" and who was "Mexican" depending on certain cultural characteristics and the labor needs of coffee plantation owners. Yet, in the early twentieth century, many indigenous people living in this borderland, such as the Mam community, rejected both national designations, preferring to identify themselves in specific ethnic or tribal terms. Similarly, as Andrew Parnaby shows in this section, Mi'kmaq families continued their seasonal migrations that included hunting, fishing, wage work, gathering, and trading and defied reserve boundaries defined by Canadian officials.

Certainly, we can draw distinct parallels between indigenous communities living in different regions in the Western Hemisphere. Yet, as the chapters in this section so aptly demonstrate, Native peoples have occupied diverse places in transnational economies at varying historical moments. Parnaby encourages us to ask larger questions about "what is universal and what is particular about colonialism, capitalism, and indigenous peoples." Stressing the historical specificity of colonial systems, he shows how Native communities occupied different places within the colonial economy: the M'ikmaq on the fringes, while Squamish maintained a stronger position as lumbermen on the western coast. The indigenous workers in Nolan-Ferrell's study were well integrated into the world of commercial agriculture. Nevertheless, they remained on the margins, subject to coercive state measures that bound them to plantation labor. Such comparative thinking explains how historical and geographical contexts created distinct trajectories of indigenous experience.

Thinking about Native workers in comparative contexts highlights colonialism as a factor that shapes not only the histories of indigenous peoples but also the experience of non-Native workers. Like gender, which is relevant to men as well as women, and race, which is as much about white people as it is about people of color, colonialism ties Native and non-Native workers together in a larger political economy, where culture and ethnicity give rise to specific racial and gendered outcomes. Often left out of labor history altogether, indigenous workers did not simply recede to the margins of the industrial workplace. And as Parnaby's chapter demonstrates, Squamish lumbermen, for example, managed to carve a niche for themselves even in a labor market that defined work along rather rigid racial categories.[6]

As capital becomes more fluid and even less confined by nation-states and borders, historians are looking for ways to understand how workers fit into that changing economic landscape. Stronger states and tighter borders mean additional burdens for indigenous people, who after long struggles over land, culture, and political sovereignty find themselves colonized and on the margins of the broader economy, differentiated from other workers by race and culture. As Catherine Nolan-Ferrell explains in her chapter, they may have a lot in common with non-Native workers across the border (and at home), but their particular histories place them apart, in a racialized category, vulnerable to employers looking for cheap labor and still carrying the burden of colonial policies that displaced them centuries before. Like the First Nations workers in Parnaby's study, they navigated around colonial policies or even transcended state boundaries, refusing to abide by the physical restrictions or ethnic definitions imposed on them. But while they shared a great deal, their experiences under colonial systems were historically distinct, shaped by the particularities of culture and race from which transnational labor systems emerged.

NOTES

1. Karen Spaulding, *Huarochirí: A Colonial Province under Inca and Spanish Rule* (Stanford, CA: Stanford University Press, 1984); Eric Wolf, *Europe and the People without History* (Berkeley: University of California Press, 1982); Steve J. Stern, *Resistance, Rebellion, and Consciousness in the Andean Peasant World—18th to 20th Centuries* (Madison: University of Wisconsin Press, 1987); Richard White, *The Middle Ground: Indians, Empires, and Republics in the Great Lakes Region, 1650–1815* (New York: Cambridge University Press, 1991); Cynthia Radding, *Wandering Peoples: Colonialism, Ethnic Spaces and Ecological Frontiers in Northwestern Mexico, 1700–1850* (Durham, NC: Duke University Press, 1997); Sylvia Van Kirk, *Many Tender Ties: Women in Fur-Trade Society, 1670–1870* (Norman: University of Oklahoma Press, 1980). See Andrew Parnaby's chapter for his discussion of the Canadian literature on the fur trade.

2. Paige Raibmon, *Authentic Indians: Episodes of Encounter from the Late-Nineteenth-Century Northwest Coast* (Durham, NC: Duke University Press, 2005); Colleen O'Neill, *Working the Navajo Way: Labor and Culture in the Twentieth Century* (Lawrence: University Press of Kansas, 2005); Erik V. Meeks, *Border Citizens: The Making of Indians, Mexicans, and Anglos in Arizona* (Austin:

University of Texas Press, 2007); Andrew Parnaby, *Citizen Docker: Making a New Deal on the Vancouver Waterfront, 1919–1939* (Toronto, ON: University of Toronto Press, 2008).
3. Jessica R. Cattelino, *High Stakes: Florida Seminole Gaming and Sovereignty* (Durham, NC: Duke University Press, 2008); Kathy M'Closkey, *Swept under the Rug: A Hidden History of Navajo Weaving* (Albuquerque: University of New Mexico Press, 2008); Clyde Ellis, *A Dancing People: Powwow Culture on the Southern Plains* (Lawrence: University Press of Kansas, 2003); Paige Raibmon, *Authentic Indians: Episodes of Encounter from the Late-Nineteenth-Century Northwest Coast* (Durham, NC: Duke University Press, 2005); Erika Bsumek, *Indian-Made: Navajo Culture in the Marketplace, 1868–1940* (Lawrence: University Press of Kansas, 2008); Sarah H. Hill, *Weaving New Worlds: Southeastern Cherokee Women and Their Basketry* (Chapel Hill: University of North Carolina Press, 1997).
4. Rolf Knight, *Indians at Work: An Informal History of Native Indian Labour in British Columbia, 1858–1930* (Vancouver, BC: New Star Books, 1978); Alice Littlefield and Martha Knack, *Native Americans and Wage Labor: Ethnohistorical Perspectives* (Norman: University of Oklahoma Press, 1995).
5. Brian Hosmer, *Indians in the Marketplace: Persistence and Innovation among the Menominees and Metlakatlans, 1870–1920* (Lawrence: University Press of Kansas, 1999); O'Neill, *Working the Navajo Way*; Raibmon, *Authentic Indians*. See also William Bauer, Clyde Ellis, and David Arnold's chapters in *Native Pathways: American Indian Culture and Economic Development in the Twentieth Century*, ed. Brian Hosmer and Colleen O'Neill (Boulder: University Press of Colorado, 2004).
6. Notable studies that examine indigenous workers within a broader racial context include Eric V. Meeks, *Border Citizens: The Making of Indians, Mexicans and Anglos in Arizona* (Austin: University of Texas Press, 2007); and Samuel Truett, *Fugitive Landscapes: The Forgotten History of the U.S.–Mexico Borderlands* (New Haven, CT: Yale University Press, 2006).

FURTHER READING

Albers, Patricia. "Labor and Exchange in American Indian History." In *A Companion to American Indian History*, edited by Philip Deloria and Neal Salisbury, 269–86. Malden, MA: Wiley-Blackwell, 2004.

Bauer, William J., Jr. We Were All Like Migrant Workers Here: Work, Community, and Memory on California's Round Valley Reservation, 1850–1941. Chapel Hill: The University of North Carolina Press, 2009.

de la Cadena, Marisol. *Indigenous Mestizos: The Politics of Race and Culture in Cuzco, Peru, 1919–1991.* Durham, NC: Duke University Press, 2000.

Gould, Jeffrey. *To Die in This Way: Nicaraguan Indians and the Myth of Mestizaje, 1880–1965.* Durham, NC: Duke University Press, 1998.

Hosmer, Brian C. *American Indians in the Marketplace: Persistence and Innovation among the Menominees and Metlakatlans, 1870–1920*. Lawrence: University Press of Kansas, 1999.

Hosmer, Brian, and Colleen O'Neill. *Native Pathways: American Indian Culture and Economic Development in the Twentieth Century*. Boulder: University Press of Colorado, 2004.

Khouri, Emilio. *A Pueblo Divided: Business, Property, and Community in Papantla, Mexico*. Stanford, CA: Stanford University Press, 2004.

Knight, Rolf. *Indians at Work: An Informal History of Native American Labour in British Columbia, 1858–1930*. Vancouver, BC: New Star Books, 1978.

Larson, Brooke. *Cochabamba, 1550–1900: Colonialism and Agrarian Transformation in Bolivia*. Durham, NC: Duke University Press, 1998.

Littlefield, Alice, and Martha C. Knack. *Native Americans and Wage Labor: Ethnohistorical Perspectives*. Norman: University of Oklahoma Press, 1996.

Lutz, John Sutton. *Makuk: A New History of Aboriginal-White Relations*. Vancouver: University of British Columbia Press, 2008.

Mallon, Florencia. *The Defense of Community in Peru's Central Highland: Peasant Struggle and Capitalist Transition, 1860–1940*. Princeton, NJ: Princeton University Press, 1983.

Meeks, Erik V. *Border Citizens: The Making of Indians, Mexicans, and Anglos in Arizona*. Austin: University of Texas Press, 2007.

O'Neill, Colleen. *Working the Navajo Way: Labor and Culture in the Twentieth Century*. Lawrence: University Press of Kansas, 2005.

Palmer, Brian D., and Joan Sangster. *Labouring Canada: Class, Gender, and Race in Canadian Working-Class History*. Don Mills, ON: Oxford University Press – Canada, 2008.

Parnaby, Andrew. *Citizen Docker: Making a New Deal on the Vancouver Waterfront, 1919–1939*. Toronto, ON: University of Toronto Press, 2008.

Peloso, Vincent. *Peasants on Plantations: Subaltern Strategies of Labor and Resistance in the Pisco Valley, Peru*. Durham, NC: Duke University Press, 1999.

Raibmon, Paige. *Authentic Indians: Episodes of Encounter from the Late-Nineteenth-Century Northwest Coast*. Durham, NC: Duke University Press, 2005.

Stephen, Lynn. *Transborder Lives: Indigenous Oaxacans in Mexico, California, and Oregon*. Durham, NC: Duke University Press, 2007.

9 INDIGENOUS LABOR IN MID-NINETEENTH-CENTURY BRITISH NORTH AMERICA

THE MI'KMAQ OF CAPE BRETON AND SQUAMISH OF BRITISH COLUMBIA IN COMPARATIVE PERSPECTIVE

Andrew Parnaby

We begin with two photographs.[1] The first photograph was taken in Sydney, Cape Breton Island, Nova Scotia, in 1880 (figure 9.1). In it nine Mi'kmaw people—men, women, and children—pose before a photographer, whose identity and motivations are unknown. The left side of the image is dominated by a Mi'kmaw dwelling, against which six people stand. On the right side of the picture is a second group of people: an older man—who is identified as "chief" in a handwritten caption—and two small girls. Coniferous trees frame the image's background; cleared land fills its foreground, where a wooden barrel, washtub, bundle of poles, and a basket lie among the tree stumps. While the people—probably a family or extended family from the Eskasoni reserve—are the focus of this visual composition, the presence of wooden handiwork hints at why this group had settled on the fringes of Sydney, the island's administrative and commercial capital, beginning in the mid-nineteenth century: to sell these handmade items—for cash or trade—door-to-door to non-Natives. The second photograph was taken in North Vancouver, British Columbia, in 1889 (figure 9.2). It depicts a gang of longshoremen posing in front of several sailing vessels tied to a wharf on Burrard Inlet. Most, if not all, of the waterfront workers are Squamish from a nearby aboriginal reserve; a few others in the gang are Kanakas—indigenous Hawaiians. Above their heads, filling in the background of the image, is a skein of masts and rigging; ramps used for loading cargo slope down from ships' sterns and bows to the wharf, where the men are located. Three white men, probably the gang bosses or stevedores, stand off to the left of the group; an Asian laundry man and a young Asian boy—perhaps his son—appear alongside the longshoremen. Rough-hewn pieces of

FIGURE 9.1 Mi'kmaw people at the King's Road settlement, Sydney, Cape Breton, 1880
Beaton Institute-Cape Breton University, Harold Medjuick Collection, #78-712-2462

lumber, waiting to be stowed, lie in the foreground. Lumber handlers since 1863, when the first sawmill was constructed in the area, the Squamish men pictured here were part of the port's large, growing, and diverse laboring class.

Taken together, the images reveal much about aboriginal labor history in the mid-nineteenth century. Neither the Mi'kmaq nor the Squamish are presented pursuing their customary and seasonal rounds of resource gathering, suggesting a shared experience of economic adjustment on the Atlantic and Pacific coasts, as older sources and practices of material support became less viable by the 1880s and 1890s. Yet within this shared pattern of adaptation, some important differences are clearly evident. Whereas the Mi'kmaq are pictured in a family setting, bartering trade items on the margins of the non-Native economy, the Squamish are presented in an all-male, multicultural context, working for wages in an industry—the port—that was at the center of industrial life in the area. While neither group prioritized hunting, fishing, or gathering as they used to, they did insert themselves as families and as individuals into the more mainstream economy in different ways, from independent production to wage labor. The history and character of that participation is the primary concern of this chapter.[2]

Aboriginal people in North America, like indigenous peoples in Latin America and Africa, have been engaged in paid work for centuries. Yet despite a long and diverse history, this dimension of aboriginal life has been understudied by Canadian scholars, at least when compared with the voluminous and important work that has explored "traditional" native cultures; the impact of settlement, trade, disease, technology, warfare, and Christianity on indigenous life; and the coercive nature of colonial Indian policies.[3] This general orientation has been reinforced by much recent postcolonial scholarship, which emphasizes identity and discourse, not labor

FIGURE 9.2 Squamish longshoremen on Burrard Inlet, British Columbia, 1889
CVA, Charles S. Bailey Photograph, #Mi P2

and economics—producing what Robert Young has called a "dematerializing effect" in the literature as a whole.[4] Aboriginal workers have fared little better in the context of American and Canadian labor history, where the experiences of newcomers, not Natives, dominate the historiography concerned with race and ethnicity. But this is starting to change—and quickly.[5] In the Canadian context, for example, a handful of historians, building in no small way on a vibrant literature centered on the aboriginal laboring classes of British Columbia that emerged in the 1970s, have turned their attention to indigenous work experiences outside the fur trade, an area of scholarship where Native labor has been examined to a great degree.[6] Focusing on the nineteenth and early twentieth centuries, these writers, including Bill Parenteau, Robin Jarvis Brownlie, Frank Tough, and John Lutz, have drawn our attention to the variety of occupations undertaken by Native peoples, the skillful ways in which they moved between indigenous and colonizing economies, the influence of these varied remunerative experiences on their cultures and communities, and the role of capital and the state in enabling, constraining, or eliminating their economic choices.[7] All four of these themes, which are also present in the work of American scholars such as Richard White, Brian C. Hosmer, and Colleen O'Neill, have guided my present analysis in important ways.[8]

Yet as the juxtaposition of the two photographs suggests, there is a potentially rich comparative dimension to aboriginal labor history to be explored, making this analysis, in many important ways, an exercise in "transnational" history. Used to great effect in other colonial contexts to answer other questions, a comparative perspective helps to fence off narratives of nation building and thus refocus our attention on the characteristics of historically and geographically specific colonial cultures and political economies, in this instance on the east coast and the west coast of British North America in the mid-nineteenth century.[9] Specificity of this sort, which is made sharper through juxtaposition, is important because it helps to explain why aboriginal occupational experiences, for all the homogenizing pressures and clear determinations associated with class formation, were never everywhere and always the same—a notion illustrated well by the photographs that began this chapter. In a broad sense, then, this comparative analysis is transnational in character because it not only explores historical change in more than one politically bounded territory but also examines phenomena that cut *across* these political borders—namely, colonialism, capitalism, and movement of people. That final item, movement of people, is especially important to this comparative analysis. In mid-nineteenth-century Nova Scotia and British Columbia, where state formation was weak and indigenous definitions of place were strong, Indian peoples circulated routinely across the boundaries of culture, politics, and economics that defined native-newcomer relations in search of work opportunities, whether close to home or far away. They made their laboring lives largely in those spaces of movement; they changed both indigenous and European communities in the process. Shedding our "bordered" perspective—as transnational historians urge us to do—brings the full range of that motion, and its many and varied implications for Indian workers, into clear view.[10]

I have chosen the Mi'kmaq and the Squamish for comparison for two reasons. First, prior to European contact, both the Mi'kmaq and the Squamish were—and still are—coastal peoples, "living at the land/sea interface," for whom agriculture possessed little or no use.[11] Second, the Mi'kmaq and the Squamish possessed very different histories of encounter with Europeans and their economic systems. That incongruity is useful.[12] For the Mi'kmaq, interaction with non-Natives began in the late 1500s with Basque fishermen and deepened over subsequent centuries with the French and British through a wide range of avenues, including an extensive trade in furs. Conversely, the Squamish did not engage Europeans until the late 1700s, nor did they participate in the region's fur trade to any great extent. Thus by the mid-nineteenth century, the Mi'kmaq and the Squamish were not only positioned differently in their respective colonial societies—the former, after nearly 250 years of interaction with Europeans, comparatively weaker than the latter—but, as time went on, their work experiences diverged in important ways. This chapter is about these changing economic possibilities, their similarities and differences, and the ways in which indigenous peoples on the Atlantic and Pacific coasts sought to understand them, negotiate their pressures and promises, and blunt their negative effects.

No historian writing about the mid-1800s in Nova Scotia doubts that the Mi'kmaq were a marginalized population.[13] By no means inevitable, this precarious position emerged slowly and deepened after the collapse of the French imperial presence in the region in 1758, the arrival of the Planters and Loyalists from the American thirteen colonies between 1760 and 1784, and the massive influx of Scottish settlers—about 30,000 to Cape Breton Island alone between 1815 and 1838—following the end of the Napoleonic wars.[14] That the Mi'kmaq of Cape Breton, whose population in the mid-nineteenth century was thought to be around 500, were in a difficult economic position was particularly obvious when it came to the question of land. "These lands are eagerly coveted by the Scottish Presbyterian settlers. That the Micmac's fathers were sole possessors of these regions is a matter of no weight with the Scottish emigrants," the Commissioner of Indian Affairs reported in 1846. "They are by no means disposed to leave the aborigines a resting place on the Island of Cape Breton."[15] As a consequence, the island's indigenous people, like the Mi'kmaq on the Nova Scotia mainland, petitioned the colonial government for land grants or demanded licenses of occupation repeatedly and forcefully, prompting the government to finally conduct a survey of "Indian Reservations on Cape Breton Island" in 1832 and 1833.[16] In total, six reserves—located at Chapel Island, Eskasoni, Whycocomagh, Wagamatcook, Malagawatch, and "Indian Garden"—containing 12,205 acres were set aside. Within forty years, however, the total number of acres reserved for the island's Mi'kmaw people had contracted by approximately 20 percent, due principally to white encroachment.[17]

Yet loss of land did not mean loss of initiative. Indeed, a comprehensive government census of the Mi'kmaw people residing at the newly created Chapel Island reserve in 1841—completed by George Edward Jean, the Clerk of the Peace for the area—hints at the sophisticated blend of cultural tenacity and economic ingenuity that existed within Indian communities at this time. "After planting their few potatoes they wander about the Island," the document observed,

> many [c]amping for a season in the vicinity of Arichat—the men employed as labourers—the women selling their handy work, and others Birch rinds for covering and as dunnage for shipping dried cod fish—and when the digging season returns they come home to gather in their potatoes and settle themselves down for the remaining part of the winter.[18]

Flexible and mobile, Mi'kmaw families were engaged in a mixed economy, in which men and women deployed some of their labor power some of the time in new ways, while maintaining older practices of seasonal family migration and ties to an economically and culturally significant locale. Known to the Mi'kmaq as Potletek, Chapel Island was located by a short isthmus that linked the Atlantic Ocean to the Bras d'Or Lake—an inland saltwater lake around which the Mi'kmaq's subsistence economy was historically based.[19] A portage route and seasonal encampment, Chapel Island was, simultaneously, a site of deep spiritual attachments for the Mi'kmaq, both before and after the arrival of Europeans.[20]

That the Mi'kmaq still utilized that location at mid-century, and indeed held it in high esteem, suggests that a resilient, adaptive, internal logic unique to them persisted during this context of material deprivation and political weakness, providing part of the framework within which they pursued new economic activities.

Agriculture was one of those new pursuits. As early as 1783, the colonial government expressed its desire that the Mi'kmaq must abandon their "original roving practices" and become farmers; only in this way, so the argument went, could their wretched condition be arrested and the ascent from savagery to civilization begin.[21] Legitimized by settlement pressures, commercial self-interest, and the pervasive discourse of the "dying Indian," this desire to make Indians more sedentary manifested itself in the government's early reserve policy, adopted in 1819, and, thirty-four years later, in its "Act for the Instruction and Permanent Settlement of the Indians." That act authorized the Commissioner of Indian Affairs to "parcel out to each head of a family a portion of the reservations... and also to aid them in the purchase of implements and stock."[22] Probably nonexistent in precontact society and of marginal importance during the French regime, agriculture became more important to indigenous life, as pressures emanating from government policy and white settlement mounted.[23] By 1841, numerous Mi'kmaw families on at least four of the island's six reserves planted potatoes, wheat, barley, and hay—some in small garden-sized plots, others in fields as large as two acres. Pigs, cows, and sheep were kept on these reserves as well.[24] Subsistence farming was never easy, of course, for the land itself was contested terrain. Beginning in 1811, Scottish settlers began clearing land; building fences, houses, and barns; grazing animals; and planting crops along the Wagamatcook River valley and the Wagamatcook reserve; by 1837, at least thirteen immigrant families were squatting on hundreds of acres of reserve land.[25] For the local Mi'kmaw families, this encroachment not only removed "good upland" from their possession, thus depriving them of its potential benefits, but also produced friction between themselves and their unwanted neighbors.[26]

The challenges to farming posed by white encroachment were compounded further by land that was often difficult to clear, seeds and implements that were hard to acquire, and potato crops that, as the islandwide famine of 1845 to 1851 made painfully clear, often fell prey to disease.[27] Not surprisingly, then, Mi'kmaw families tended to view subsistence agriculture as only one economic option, opting to deploy their labor power in customary ways—seasonally and in family units—when the need arose, much to the government's dismay. This they often did when migrating from Chapel Island to Arichat, located on Isle Madame on Cape Breton's south coast, to participate in the commercial cod fishery. There, the Mi'kmaq joined a multiethnic assortment of workers—Channel Islanders, Acadians, and Irish—in a preindustrial enterprise calibrated to the seasonal movement of fish and connected to global networks of merchant capital and exchange.[28] As "laborers," Mi'kmaw men perhaps maintained fishing premises, helped build shallops and schooners, crewed fishing vessels, and constructed barrels for shipping dried fish—a craft that, according to one colonial official, they came to dominate by the 1850s.[29] For Mi'kmaw women, the seasonal migration to Arichat provided an opportunity to sell or trade baskets, earning them a meager income in cash or trade goods. The generosity of friends and family, who provided food, shelter, and company, was critical to the success of a woman's basket-selling sojourn; so, too, were repeat customers, who were purposely sought out in a given locale.[30]

In addition to laboring in the commercial fishery and craft production, hunting remained important to many Mi'kmaw families in the 1840s and 1850s, providing a source of food, clothing, and modest financial gain. Although the heyday of the region's fur trade was long over, small quantities of fur were still being exported from Cape Breton to Halifax (the colonial capital) and then on to Europe in the early decades of the nineteenth century.[31] No doubt dominated by poor white settlers, who faced dire material circumstances on the island, too, the early-nineteenth-century fur trade also included the Mi'kmaq of Cape Breton, but only in a limited way. Diminished though it was, the collection of "peltry" was still orchestrated through a "family hunting territory system"—a sophisticated method of regulating access to, and the dimensions of, specific hunting grounds that evolved from similar practices that predated contact with Europeans.[32] In a context shaped decisively by the presence of European settlers and colonial Indian policy, the Mi'kmaq organized themselves to hunt in a deeply familiar way, thereby eluding the encompassing and encaging geographies of the reserve system and the wider policy of assimilation of which they were a part.

Like hunting, fishing for personal and family consumption was still a viable component of the Mi'kmaq's seasonal rounds of resource gathering in the mid-1800s.[33] French missionaries and colonial officials on Cape Breton during the early to mid-eighteenth century understood the importance of rivers, lakes, and the ocean to indigenous life and thus located their missions near the Mi'kmaq's customary fishing sites, which ringed the Bras d'Or Lake. Critical to the Mi'kmaq's subsistence economy and imbued with deep spiritual and political import, fish and sea mammals played only a modest role in trade relations with the British and French.[34] Removed somewhat from the commercial incentives of mercantilism, fishing was thus a zone of relatively autonomous activity for the Mi'kmaq well into the middle-to-late 1700s—a status reinforced by the continued use of fishing materials derived largely from indigenous, as opposed to European, resources.[35] Yet as population pressures tied to the Planter, Loyalist, and Scottish migrations mounted, fishing, like hunting, became severely circumscribed. Occasionally, conflicts between natives and newcomers flared up around the Bras d'Or Lake and along the Margaree River system—"the Indians have been giving trouble to the new settlers"—as immigrants established farms and mills or sought access to spawning fish.[36] "You have put ships and steamboats upon the water and they scare away the fish," stated the "Chiefs and Captains of the Micmac Indians" in 1849. "As our game and fish are nearly gone and we cannot sell the articles we make, we have resolved to make farms."[37]

Many on the island, of course, did pursue agriculture, but others sought to insert themselves into the commercial fishery (as laborers or as fishermen in their own right); rent pieces of land to white tenants; sell wood "whenever they can find an opportunity"; act as guides for surveyors, hunters, and travelers; and petition government officials.[38] At least thirty-eight separate petitions arrived in Halifax between between 1819 and 1867.[39] Accustomed to, and masters of, the face-to-face diplomacy of the eighteenth century, in which their positions were set before the British and French orally, the Mi'kmaq's use of petitions, a written form, makes manifest not only the narrow range of political options available to them by the mid-nineteenth century but also, as in the realm of economics, a capacity to adapt older ways of doing things to new circumstances.[40] Several quite lengthy Mi'kmaw petitions deployed a discourse of deference, duty, and protection to underscore the obligations that the British had to the island's indigenous people.[41] Often such claims to legal status were followed by specific objections related to land and white settlement and specific demands for better seed, tools, coats, blankets, and rifles.[42]

When George Edward Jean, a Clerk of the Peace, arrived at Chapel Island in July 1841 to complete his investigation of the Mi'kmaq's economic "habits," he arrived on the occasion of St. Anne's Day, a celebration in honor of the Virgin Mary's mother in which hundreds of Mi'kmaw people gathered to socialize, discuss politics, and attend religious services. A blend of aboriginal spirituality and Catholicism, the annual ritual was not only enjoyable but also helped reaffirm the bonds between Mi'kmaw bands. A similar combination of the old and the new formed the material basis of Mi'kmaw society at mid-century as customary and intimately experienced routines of attaining resources were adapted to a newer and less understood context of occupational pluralism. That this transition was taking place at the same time that St. Anne's Day was assuming a new vitality is significant. The celebration—spiritual, political, and social in equal measure—helped to reaffirm their patterns of living and language and, in doing so, prepared Mi'kmaw families for the difficult economic choices that lay before them.[43] Moreover, that they were able to piece together a meager livelihood at all ensured that they were able to hold the celebration in the first place. Cultural *and* material resources—as displayed on that special day—were necessary to engage and deflect colonialism's heavy pressures. "For months before, they save all the money they can collect from the sale of baskets, tubs, and fancy work in order to display a little finery for this grand event of the year," John Bourinot, a journalist and government official from Sydney, recounted in 1867.[44]

Despite the government's opposition to their "wandering" way of life, the Mi'kmaq continued to move about the island, across the colony, and throughout the region, a landscape that remained for them the single, unified context of Mi'kma'ki. Mobility was key to their history; it remained vital to their future. Older cycles of migration tied to the availability of resources, and modulated by kin ties and identities, persisted, joined by new patterns of movement brought about, in part, by the influence of white settlement, economic change, and colonial policy. The route from the Eskasoni reserve to Sydney, for example, traveled to sell baskets or secure supplies from the government, was well-worn by the 1850s. In time, enough people would stay permanently in the city and create the King's Road settlement; an unknown photographer would capture that presence on film in 1890. Other individuals and families migrated farther and moved to the eastern shores of the Nova Scotia mainland or left the colony altogether, as some had done in the 1760s, when they migrated to western Newfoundland on a permanent basis. "We found Micmacs everywhere in these Provinces, and scattering ones all the way to Montreal," Protestant missionary Silas T. Rand wrote of his travels in 1858 and 1859. "A Micmac family reached that city by the same train by which we arrived. We met another company there one day in the streets who were from Cape Breton."[45]

Among nineteenth-century government officials in Nova Scotia, there was little doubt that the Indians were headed in one of two directions: extinction or assimilation. "When I take a impartial view of the Indians at Eskasonie, and thoroughly consider their customs, honesty, integrity, and their burning desire to serve their Maker," an Indian agent for Cape Breton County opined in 1876, "I am led naturally to conclude that the tide of time, the liberal support they receive from the government, together with a very close supervision, will eventually put the Micmacs of Eskasonie on par with other people of whiter and more tender complexions."[46] But these Indians, like indigenous people across the island, eschewed the stark set of choices laid out for them by the colonial (and later federal) state and European settlers and opted, instead, to farm, utilize their customs, and serve their maker at one and the same time. Indeed, within an evolving set of punishing circumstances, the Mi'kmaq understood that there was still room to maneuver and thus avoid utter despair.

Cheakamus Tom understood the history of native-newcomer relations in British Columbia very well. "For many years, . . . our people could and did gain a living suitable for our wants from the forest and the sea," he stated in a letter to the Royal Commission on Indian Affairs, which was holding hearings in the province from 1912 to 1916. "The different tribes or bands had their own territory in which they fished and hunted, and over which they had control," he continued. "But when the White man came he was allowed to go where he pleased to hunt, trap, or fish. Then our troubles began."[47] Pithy and succinct, Tom's assessment evokes an era prior to European settlement, when his people, the Squamish, a linguistic subdivision of the Coast Salish, utilized a swath of land between what would become Howe Sound and Burrard Inlet in southwestern British Columbia. Across this vast and varied geography, they harvested aquatic and terrestrial resources in groups of family or extended family members on a seasonal basis—joining other indigenous groups, like the nearby Cowichan, Musqueam, Tsawwassen, and Sto:lo, in a zone of complex political, economic, linguistic, and cultural exchange.[48] The food, tools, and other items derived from these rounds of collective gathering—salmon, in particular, was highly prized and possessed considerable spiritual importance—were utilized by Squamish families directly as part of their subsistence economy. Any surplus resources, especially canoes, weapons, and woven blankets, were circulated widely among families, extended families, and other indigenous communities through gift giving and feasting, drawing them all together in an elaborate prestige economy. Linking the two cycles of exchange together was the potlatch, a collection of ceremonies that reaffirmed the status of particular leaders, validated their stewardship of valuable resource sites, or marked significant events, like deaths and marriages, within their communities.[49]

Yet Cheakamus Tom's observations also bring to mind the Squamish's encounter with non-Native immigrants, which began in 1792 when George Vancouver sailed into Burrard Inlet.[50] The extent to which Squamish life changed in the aftermath of that first encounter is hard to judge, although preliminary evidence, including in some cases Squamish oral tradition, supports four general observations. First, the Squamish were affected deeply by the smallpox epidemic that swept through the region in the late 1770s and early 1780s prior to Vancouver's arrival.[51] Second, they were only marginal participants in the maritime and later land-based fur trade, which operated in the region between 1785 and 1825 and between 1793 and 1848, respectively; however, they surely traded for foreign items from aboriginal intermediaries or occasionally from non-Natives themselves, perhaps at Fort Victoria or Fort Langley.[52] Third, between 1827 and 1830, the Squamish and other Coast Salish groups faced numerous attacks by Lekwiltok, a Kwakwaka'wakw group from the north, which used war and pillage to gain access to the European goods they could not secure through direct trading; the raids diminished by the 1850s, only after the Squamish acquired firearms.[53] And fourth, the construction of a sawmill on Burrard Inlet in 1863 altered Squamish life in a considerable way, as families and extended families gravitated to the area on a more permanent basis to incorporate wage labor into their seasonal migrations. "[There is] a very mixed assemblage of people [here]. While Europeans or at least whites fill the responsible posts, Indians (Squa'mich), Chinamen, Negroes, and Mullattoes and half breeds and Mongrels of every pedigree abound," observed surveyor George Dawson in 1875.[54] "The Squamish Indians were sharp enough to see the advantage of being beside the white men employed at these mills," stated Gilbert Malcolm Sproat, a member of the Joint Indian Reserve Commission, a year later. "They, therefore, so far as I can make out, while retaining their claims to their old lands on the Squamish River in Howe Sound, began to frequent and settle upon the lands of Burrard Inlet in considerable numbers."[55]

Sewell Moody's mill on the north shore of the inlet, and then Edward Stamp's on the south shore, were portents of change as Burrard Inlet moved into the industrial age by the early twentieth century.[56] Squamish men and women were important, if unequal, actors in this changing economic context: Between 1863 and the early 1900s, they could be found stacking lumber in the mills, acting as guides for recreational hunters and fishers, building fences on farms, felling trees in the coastal forests, gutting fish in the canneries, piloting small boats in the salmon fishery, and loading and unloading cargo on the waterfront—usually combining a range of occupations to earn a modest livelihood. That all of the occupational pursuits undertaken by aboriginal workers were seasonal is important, reflecting not only the range of employment options that emerged as British Columbia industrialized but also the ways in which the temporal and spatial rhythms of a customary, kin-ordered way of life articulated with the logic of a burgeoning capitalist labor market.[57] The result was a mixed economy in which Squamish men and women activated some of their labor power some of the time in a new way—working for wages—while simultaneously maintaining older methods of regulating access to resources sites and affirming links between their families and larger aboriginal groups. "They [the Squamish] wanted to be permitted to continue to enjoy, in common with the white people, the right of moving about freely and seeking employment or occupation where they pleased," a government official observed in 1877. "They particularly asked if they would be allowed to hunt and fish as usual."[58]

There was a culturally specific logic in operation here that was internal to Coast Salish society: It is likely that Squamish men and women engaged in wage labor because their earnings could be used to purchase the goods necessary to hold a potlatch—a rationale shared by other Coast Salish groups, notably the Lekwammen and Kwakwaka'wakw of Vancouver Island. Fragmentary evidence reveals that the Squamish continued to hold potlatches throughout this period of economic adjustment. A report penned by Sproat in 1877 indicated that potlatching—"the foolish custom of giving away property to the other tribes for the sake of the praise such extravagance obtains"—was "rapidly falling into disuse" among the Squamish. Or so he hoped. Nineteen years later, in 1896, one Indian agent observed that the practice was still utilized on at least one Squamish reserve on Burrard Inlet, despite being banned by the federal government in 1885.[59] The impression left by Charles Hill-Tout, an English immigrant to the Pacific province, perceptive amateur anthropologist, and author of "Notes on the Skqomic [Squamish] of British Columbia" published in 1900, is that the potlatch remained vibrant and probably had expanded in the middle to late nineteenth century, as European goods purchased with wages now circulated within the indigenous prestige economy.[60] He describes "great gatherings" in which "whole tribes from long distances" were invited to the Squamish encampment of "Qoiqoi" on the south shore of Burrard Inlet. "Over two thousand in all sat down to the feast," he observed. "An immense quantity of property was distributed on this occasion."[61]

For some Squamish men, the resources needed to sponsor such "great gatherings" were derived, in part, from working as loggers and longshoremen, two occupations that dominated male employment from the middle to late nineteenth century well into the twentieth century. Talent and facility with an axe or saw in the coastal forests flowed in some measure from a long history of woodworking among the Squamish; "in bygone days my ancestors cut down many cedar trees in Stanley Park [on Burrard Inlet] for making canoes and other purposes," Andrew Paull, a Squamish leader and longshoreman, recalled in the 1930s. "[They used] nothing but stone chisels and a big stone for a hammer."[62] On the waterfront, where work was a casual affair and competition for available positions was fierce, the "Indian gangs" could usually be found handling logs and lumber—their specialty. While aboriginal dockers chose to work "the lumber" because they possessed the right skills, and specialization helped to bring some predictability to casual work, they did so in an occupational context in which their options, although not closed off entirely, were constrained. White waterfront workers tended to dominate general cargo, which, importantly, was less dangerous and more lucrative than working the lumber.[63]

Along Burrard Inlet, as in other ports, a longshoreman's success or failure in the competition for work was dependent on a wide range of factors, not the least of which was the ability of racial groupings to recruit other group members to work in their particular occupational niches, no matter how undesirable or difficult the work within that niche was.[64] It was not uncommon for the sons and nephews of aboriginal longshoremen to follow their fathers and uncles to the waterfront and, in the process, learn the arts and mysteries of "working the lumber." On other occasions, experienced aboriginal longshoremen could be found enticing "young fellows" from the Mission and other reserves to work on a specific lumber ship, a maneuver made easier by the extensive familial relationships—"Their cousinships are endless and even perplexing to themselves," Hill-Tout observed—that characterized aboriginal life on the north shore and elsewhere.[65] "Our legend began in the 1800s during the days of the sailing ships. They had one mill at the time on the North Shore. They hired all the Indians on the North Shore who were able to work," Simon Baker, a Squamish chief, observed in his autobiography. "Five generations of our family have worked on the waterfront."[66]

In addition to wage labor, many Squamish families added small-scale agriculture to their economic repertoire, but only in a limited way. "[There is] very little improvement [in the land]," James Lenihan, a superintendent with Indian Affairs, observed in 1877, after visiting several Squamish communities in the Lower Mainland. There were, however, some small "patches of vegetables," "fruit gardens," and "meadow[s]," where hay, some of it sold to local businesses, was growing. Writing fifteen years later, a Catholic missionary in the same area made a similar observation: "Some have a small garden attached to their dwellings on which they raise berries in season and sell them."[67] It was not uncommon—according to numerous government surveys conducted between 1876 and 1899—for families to grow potatoes and keep chickens and cows as well.[68] Geared toward personal consumption and modest financial gain, household cultivation and husbandry helped to insulate some indigenous families from the booms and busts of the industrializing economy. These practices did not, however, eclipse older pursuits (such as hunting and fishing) and customary dietary staples (such as dried salmon or cranberries) which were also used to weather periods of reduced earning ability and reduced material sustenance.[69] Fish and game were not only an important source of food but also a potential source of revenue: Both could be sold to the "ready markets" at the sawmills and logging camps and traded among other indigenous communities along the coast, a sophisticated network of exchange that existed long before sustained contact with non-Natives began and persisted well into the nineteenth century.[70]

Significantly, household gardens were typically, though by no means exclusively, the responsibility of Squamish women, who could be found peddling produce, as well as berries, clams, and crafts, in Vancouver and other locales.[71] When Squamish women were not tending to their gardens or participating in the "door-step" economy, they could often be found working for wages themselves—migrating on a seasonal basis to the hop fields of southern British Columbia and Washington State and the canneries that dotted the Fraser River and northern coastal areas, beginning in the late 1870s and early 1880s.[72] In both occupational contexts, family and kin ties, as well as prevailing assumptions about race, gender, and work, shaped Squamish women's experiences in important ways. To work in the hop fields, they sojourned in the context of their families, who were sometimes recruited at the behest of a local chief who acted as a labor broker.[73] Once on the job, however, each family member performed a different task: The women, young children, and older men did the picking, while younger men packed and baled the hops. Similar dynamics occurred in the canneries. Women—sometimes with their children strapped to their backs—cleaned and packed the fish, while men angled under license with the cannery owners. This gendered division of labor resembled the ways in which the Squamish had customarily organized themselves when fishing and hunting. Like longshoring, cannery work was a multiracial, multicultural, hierarchical affair, with indigenous peoples like the Squamish working alongside, and sometimes competing for opportunities against, Japanese and Chinese employees.[74]

Yet decisions about the utility of wage labor did not belong to the Squamish alone. With a gold rush on the Fraser River underway by 1858, thousands of fortune seekers poured into the colony; non-Natives' interest in permanent settlement, economic development, and state formation was subsequently heightened. That the balance of power in the colony-turned-province—British Columbia entered the Canadian federation in 1871—was just starting to turn against the Squamish was felt in the context of land and the fisheries. Not only were the Squamish confined to reserves, which were marked off in the Lower Mainland and at the Squamish River between 1863 and 1877, but that modest land base, with its household gardens and access to aquatic and terrestrial resources, was under pressure from non-Native settlers and entrepreneurs as the turn of the century approached.[75] "You must know that Squamish (that is up the Squamish River which empties into Howe Sound) is their native Place and where they wish to have their land assigned to them, several of them having cultivated potato patches up there for years and their fathers before them," two interlocutors, writing on behalf of the Squamish to the Indian Commissioner in 1875, observed. "What they naturally want is to have their land given them before the new whites interfere with them up there and I must say I think they have justice on their side."[76] In the salmon fishery, a similar dynamic of enclosure was starting to take place. Beginning in 1878, with the passage of provincial fisheries legislation, it was unlawful for indigenous peoples in British Columbia to fish for food unless they possessed the right permit, specific gear, and did so in specific locales; fishing for barter or sale was also banned under that same set of regulations.[77] "A long time ago, the Indians depended upon hunting and fishing as their only means of living," Mathias Joseph, a Squamish leader, observed in 1913. "Now things have changed."[78] Indeed, they had. While the Squamish were drawn into the capitalist labor market by a desire to continue potlatching, they continued to work for wages because, by the early 1900s, they possessed few other options, save for selling their labor power in the salmon canneries or on the waterfront.

During the mid-nineteenth century, the economic basis of Mi'kmaq and Squamish societies underwent an important series of changes, as customary and well-understood ways of supporting oneself, family, and community intersected with, and in many ways were eclipsed by, an economy built on work, wages, and market principles. Throughout this period of adjustment, the Mi'kmaq and the Squamish created new forms of material support that were similar in many ways. On reserves and off, life was still lived in and through ties of family and extended family; its rhythms were still influenced by seasonal changes, the desire and need to be mobile, and ties to spiritually significant places.[79] Occupational pluralism became the norm for most people. Among the Mi'kmaq and the Squamish, the pursuit of craft production, subsistence agriculture, or waged work did not obviate the need and desire to pursue more customary methods of support such as hunting and fishing. Nor did it negate the significance of particular culturally specific activities such as St. Anne's Day or the potlatch, which assisted both groups in navigating periods of adjustment or crisis.

To say this, however, is not to assert that St. Anne's Day and the potlatch were equivalent rituals or that they served the same function when performed by their respective indigenous communities. A vital linkage between subsistence and prestige economies, the potlatch provided the Squamish with a rationale to move into paid work among Europeans; from their perspective, the acquisition of cash and trade goods could strengthen, not weaken, their indigenous ways of being. For the Mi'kmaq, in contrast, necessity born out of marginality, not St. Anne's Day itself, decisively shaped their new economic decisions. The differences between East Coast and West Coast on this point are important, for they highlight the range of possible motivations on which indigenous peoples acted—from the "romantic" (cultural) to the "rationalistic" (profit and practicality) to borrow ethnohistorian Bruce Trigger's pithy summation.[80] The Squamish may have been drawn into the European economy by a desire to continue potlatching, but, as the Mi'kmaq experience suggests, it is important not to emphasize the role of indigenous cultural imperatives alone. To do so risks missing the similarities between Native and non-Native motivations, reducing all aboriginal choices to a simple pursuit of 'traditional' identities and practices, and eliding the importance that context makes—specifically the sequence of encounter, immigration, and economic change—in opening up or closing off specific work options.[81] The comparative analysis advanced here makes that final point especially visible.

Equally clear is the link between gender and work in native communities, which has been the subject of considerable debate since Eleanor Leacock published her influential analysis of Montagnais women and the Jesuits nearly thirty years ago. In that publication, Leacock argued that Montagnais women experienced a drastic reduction in power and influence as their exposure to patriarchal Western norms, embodied in the missionaries' "program for colonization," deepened over time.[82] Writing about the Mi'kmaq from the early 1600s to the late 1800s, Ellice Gonzalez, who was more interested in economic questions than Leacock, reached a similar conclusion: By 1850, she argued, the combined impact of "western technology, trade items, and religion" had undermined the Mi'kmaq's traditionally "interdependent" gender relations—a trend only hastened by the introduction of wage labor into Atlantic indigenous communities by the late nineteenth century.[83] Yet as this chapter maintains, the gendered division of labor among the Mi'kmaq of Cape Breton at mid-century was not so sharply or starkly drawn. In the fields, forests, and fisheries, entire families worked together, with some specialization dependent on sex, age, and geography; indeed, the nature and value of an individual's contribution in these years depended on the economic task being performed, and no singular task dominated Native life in the

1830s, 1840s, and 1850s. By the late 1860s and 1870s, however, this ambiguity appears to have lifted: In these decades, men worked primarily on the land or as woodworkers, earned the lion's share of family income, and received the bulk of direct aid from government officials, who prioritized the male heads of families. Importantly, these new patterns of employment varied greatly by reserve, with some locales more heavily invested in agriculture, which rested on more complementary gender relations, than others.[84] While this perspective does not overturn Gonzalez's basic argument, it does reveal with greater clarity the gendered complexity of Mi'kmaw occupational life at mid-century and suggests a later periodization—the late 1800s—for the onset of female economic subordination.

On the Pacific Coast, the ways in which gender shaped employment options among the Squamish is reasonably clear. Women, for example, did not work on the waterfront; they did, however, process fish in the canneries or maintain a household garden. To what extent the changed employment landscape diminished or strengthened the position of Squamish women within their own communities is not certain at this point and thus calls for additional archival work. In the absence of original research on this point, however, the work of John Lutz, who has studied work and gender relations among another Coast Salish group (the Lekwammen of Vancouver Island) is highly suggestive. Lutz begins his analysis by rejecting the "one-sided" picture of female subordination presented by Leacock, positing instead that the role and influence of Lekwammen women ebbed and flowed over time. During the early contact period of the 1840s, 1850s, and 1860s, he argues, women's contribution to the Lekwammen economy declined as hand-woven blankets—customarily their contribution to the potlatch—were replaced by factory-made blankets brought by Hudson Bay Company traders; importantly, though, this attenuation of female economic roles was "offset" by a heightened demand for Lekwammen women as potential spouses by European men. In the decades that followed, as the Fraser River gold rush gave way to industrialization, a similar set of fluctuations took place. Lutz maintains that while earnings accumulated in the salmon canneries or the hop fields "restored" the economic clout lost by Lekwammen women a generation before and opened up the possibility of potlatching to smaller and less wealthy families, the introduction of the federal Indian Act in 1876, which placed significant legal restrictions on female autonomy, undermined that new position.[85] So, too, perhaps did the daily on-the-job subordination of cannery workers demanded by cannery owners, who understood that their profitability was derived in no small measure from the availability of an efficient, cheap, and racially divided labor force—a point that Lutz does not examine directly.[86]

As the two photographs that began this analysis suggest, by the late nineteenth century, neither the Squamish nor the Mi'kmaq possessed the freedom to hunt, fish, and gather as they once had. Yet, importantly, they were not similarly situated within the new, colonizing capitalist economy. Preliminary analysis of Cape Breton's six native reserves between 1869 and 1901 reveals that agriculture and woodworking (barrels, laundry poles, pit supports) dominated Mi'kmaw economic activity, although there was considerable variation across reserves.[87] In this experience, Mi'kmaw life resembled that of many non-Native inland settlers who eked out a living on marginal lands and combined a range of activities to make ends meet. Significantly, however, there is no evidence (yet) that the Mi'kmaq found employment in the island's coal mines, steel mills, or lobster canneries, all of which emerged during the last quarter of the nineteenth century, expanded rapidly, and employed thousands of European workers—especially the "backlanders" with whom the Mi'kmaq competed for land, furs, and fish.[88] The Squamish experience is different in important ways. Between 1908 and 1916— years for which there is solid evidence—waged work, not farming, hunting, or fishing, was the most important economic activity on the Burrard Inlet reserves.[89] The persistence of aboriginal longshoremen captures this reality well: Indian lumber handlers first went to work on the waterfront in 1863; with the exception of a brief hiatus in the middle-to-late 1920s, they remained on the docks well into the twentieth century.[90]

How do we explain such divergent work experiences? Part of the answer can be found in the different patterns of Native-newcomer relations that emerged on both coasts. As John Reid and William Wicken have argued, the Mi'kmaq's autonomy was severely eroded by the cumulative impact of the Seven Years' War, American Revolution, and Napoleonic wars, which, combined, brought tens of thousands of non-Native refugees to Nova Scotia over an eighty-year period. This influx redirected patterns of settlement, the nature of political institutions, and the economic basis of Mi'kma'ki in significant and forceful ways. Between 1801 and 1881, the non-Native population on Cape Breton increased from 2,500 to 87,000, while the number of Mi'kmaq on the island was thought to be around 500 and falling. In this revised context, the Mi'kmaq were particularly vulnerable, as more and more land was cultivated by non-Natives, access to fish and game was steadily reduced, and reserve life became a reality for most. When Mi'kmaw men and women sought to insert themselves into the commercial fishery, construct European-style farms, or sell handicrafts in the 1840s, 1850s, and 1860s, they did so not because they wanted to, but because they *had* to. They also found that in most areas of economic activity—hunting for personal consumption and trade in furs or the cod fishery—they faced stiff competition from poor non-Natives, who faced difficult economic circumstances, too. Thus, when opportunities for waged work emerged in the late 1800s, the Mi'kmaq were on the outside looking in; not only were they politically weak and subjected to government Indian policies that prioritized farming but also they were massively outnumbered by non-Native workers who thronged to the new industries and successfully mobilized to protect their positions in informal (family relationships) and formal (unions) ways. As Bernd Christmas, the former chief executive officer of Cape Breton's Membertou First Nation, remarked in a recent documentary about the island's economic history: "Our people missed the industrial revolution."[91]

The difference between the East Coast and West Coast indigenous experiences on this specific point is stark. When the Squamish first started to incorporate waged work into their seasonal rounds of resource gathering, they did so from a position of strength, not marginality: They were demographically strong, occupied customary territories, pursued subsistence economies, and practiced culturally significant activities, with little destructive interference from missionaries, European settlers, or state officials until later in the century. In this context, they worked for wages initially not because their customary resources had failed them, but as a way to attain additional wealth and thus enrich existing and still vibrant cultural practices, specifically the potlatch. More important, they did so at a time when the local labor market was not yet dominated by non-Native workers. When sawmills were first constructed on Burrard Inlet in the early 1860s, for example, employers hired aboriginal men not only because they could do the work but also because there were few other people around; the Squamish were, as the Indian Reserve Commissioners reported in 1877, a "local source of labor constantly available."[92] Whereas the Mi'kmaq were vastly outnumbered by non-Natives at the time waged work became available and thus had limited access to those new remunerative options, the Squamish were not. Of the nearly 1,200 people enumerated in and around Burrard Inlet in 1881, about 500 (42 per cent) were Squamish.[93]

In sum, on Cape Breton, massive non-Native immigration and the marginalization of the Mi'kmaq preceded the island's (partial) transition to industrial capitalism; on British Columbia's lower mainland, the opposite appears to have occurred, with industrial employment emerging before Burrard Inlet had ceased being a Native place. For the Mi'kmaq and the Squamish, this made an enormous difference, shaping two divergent experiences of class formation—the former on the margins of the mainstream economy, the latter at its center.

NOTES

1. This essay draws extensively from material presented in two previous publications under different titles. See Parnaby, "'The Best Men That Ever Worked the Lumber': Aboriginal Longshoremen on Burrard Inlet, BC, 1863–1939," *Canadian Historical Review* 87, no. 1 (March 2006): 53–78; "The Cultural Economy of Survival: The Mi'kmaq of Cape Breton in the Mid-19th Century," *Labour/Le Travail* 61 (Spring 2008): 69–98. Thanks are due to both journals for generously granting permission to reproduce some of that material and for waiving the permission fees.

2. Beaton Institute–Cape Breton University (BI-CBU), Harold Medjuick Photo Collection, #78-712-2462; City of Vancouver Archives (CVA), Charles S. Bailey Photograph, #Mi P2. Both archives gave permission to reproduce these images.
3. On this point, see Parnaby, "'The Best Men That Ever Worked the Lumber,'" 53–78.
4. Robert J. C. Young, *Postcolonialism: An Historical Introduction* (Oxford: Blackwell Publishing, 2001), 340.
5. In the voluminous and ever-growing literature devoted to Canadian indigenous history, labor themes remain on the periphery. For example, see *Be of Good Mind: Essays on the Coast Salish* (Vancouver: University of British Columbia Press, 2007). The classic analysis of aboriginal labor history in Canada is Rolf Knight, *Indians at Work: An Informal History of Native Indian Labour in British Columbia, 1858–1930*, 2nd ed. (Vancouver: New Star Books, 1996). One of my favorites in this field is Henry Pennier, *"Call Me Hank": A Sto:lo Man's Reflections on Logging, Living, and Growing Old*, 2nd ed., ed. Keith Thor Carlson and Kristina Fagan (Toronto: University of Toronto Press, 2006).
6. Arthur J. Ray, *Indians in the Fur Trade: Their Role as Trappers, Hunters, and Middlemen in the Lands Southwest of Hudson Bay, 1660–1870* (Toronto: University of Toronto Press, 1974); Rennie Warburton and Stephen Scott, "The Fur Trade and Early Capitalist Development in British Columbia," *Canadian Journal of Native Studies* 5, no. 1 (1985): 27–46; Glen Makahonuk, "Wage Labour in the Northwest Fur Trade Economy 1760–1849," *Saskatchewan History* 41, no.1 (Winter 1988): 1–17.
7. Bill Parenteau, "'Care, Control, and Supervision': Native People in the Canadian Atlantic Salmon Fishery, 1867–1900," *Canadian Historical Review* 79, no. 1 (March 1998): 1–35; Parenteau and James Kenny, "Survival, Resistance, and the Canadian State: Transformation of New Brunswick's Native Economy, 1867–1930," *Journal of the CHA* new series, 13 (2002): 49–71; Robin Jarvis Brownlie, "'Living the Same as the White People': Mohawk and Anishinabe Women's Labour in Southern Ontario, 1920–40," *Labour/Le Travail* 61 (Spring 2008): 41–68; Frank Tough, *"As Their Natural Resources Fail": Native Peoples and the Economic History of Northern Manitoba, 1870–1930* (Vancouver: University of British Columbia Press, 1996); John Sutton Lutz, *Makuk: A New History of Aboriginal-White Relations* (Vancouver: University of British Columbia Press, 2008).
8. Richard White, *The Roots of Dependency: Subsistence, Environment, and Social Change among the Choctaws, Pawnees, and Navajos* (Lincoln: University of Nebraska Press, 1983); Brian C. Hosmer, *American Indians in the Marketplace: Persistence and Innovation among the Memominees and Metlakalans, 1870–1920* (Lawrence: University of Kansas Press, 1999); Colleen O'Neill, *Working the Navajo Way: Labor and Culture in the Twentieth Century* (Lawrence: University of Kansas Press, 2005). See also Alice Littlefield and Martha Knack, eds., *Native Americans and Wage Labor: Ethnohistorical Approaches* (Norman: University of Oklahoma Press, 1996)

9. See Ann Laura Stoler, "Tense and Tender Ties: The Politics of Comparison in North American and (Post) Colonial Studies," *Journal of American History* 88, no. 3 (December 2001): 829–65.
10. See "AHR Conversation: On Transnational History," *American Historical Review* 111, no. 5 (December 2006): 1441–64. *Be of Good Mind* presents a transnational (or "cross-border") focus of indigenous history.
11. Ronald J. Nash, *The Evolution of Maritime Cultures on the Northeast and the Northwest Coasts of America* (Burnaby, BC: Simon Fraser University, Department of Archaeology, 1983).
12. Robert Gregg, *Inside Out, Outside In: Essays in Comparative History* (New York: St. Martin's Press, 2000), ix–xiii.
13. See Olive P. Dickason, *Canada's First Nations: A History of Founding Peoples from Earliest Times*, 2nd ed. (Toronto: Oxford University Press, 1997), 202–3; Daniel N. Paul, *We Were Not Savages: A Micmac Perspective on the Collision of European and Aboriginal Civilization* (Halifax: Nimbus, 1993), 185; Harald E. L. Prins, *The Mi'kmaq: Resistance, Accommodation, and Cultural Survival* (Toronto: Harcourt Brace, 1996), 164–65.
14. According to D. C. Harvey, the population of Cape Breton increased from approximately 6,000 in 1815 to 35,420 in 1838; see his "Scottish Immigration to Cape Breton," in *Cape Breton Historical Essays*, ed. Don MacGillivray and Brian Tennyson (Sydney: Cape Breton University Press, 1980), 31. This section is informed by L. F. S. Upton, *Micmacs and Colonists: Indian-White Relations in the Maritimes, 1713–1867* (Vancouver: University of British Columbia Press, 1979), 81–95; John Reid, *Six Crucial Decades: Times of Change in the History of the Maritimes* (Halifax: Nimbus, 1987), 61–93; Bill Wicken, "Mi'kmaq Land in Southwestern Nova Scotia, 1771–1823," in *Making Adjustments: Change and Continuity in Planter Nova Scotia, 1759–1800*, ed. Margaret Conrad (Fredericton: Acadiensis Press, 1991), 113–46; William C. Wicken, *Mi'kmaq Treaties on Trial: History, Land, and Donald Marshall Junior* (Toronto: University of Toronto Press, 2002). In particular, John H. Reid, "*Pax Britanica* or *Pax Indigena*? Planter Nova Scotia (1760–1782) and Competing Strategies of Pacification," *Canadian Historical Review* 85, no. 4 (December 2004): 669–92.
15. Quoted in Richard H. Bartlett, *Indian Reserves in the Atlantic Provinces of Canada* (Saskatoon: University of Saskatchewan Native Law Centre, 1986), 22.
16. See Gary P. Gould and Alan J. Semple, *Our Land: The Maritimes: The Basis of the Indian Claim in the Maritime Provinces of Canada* (Fredericton: Saint Anne's Point Press, 1980), 48. As William Wicken has illustrated, it appears that in some cases aboriginal people called for a ticket of location/license of occupation as an interim step, with an eye to making a formal petition for a land grant at another time. See Wicken, "Mi'kmaq Land in Southwestern Nova Scotia," 115–18.
17. Bartlett, *Indian Reserves in the Atlantic Provinces*, 10–11.

18. Nova Scotia Archives and Records Management (NSARM), RG 5, Nova Scotia House of Assembly, Series P, Volume 8a, Number 14B, "An Account of the Indians living within the County of Richmond as taken on July 16th, 1841.
19. A. J. B. Johnston, *Storied Shores: St. Peter's, Isle Madame, and Chapel Island in the 17th and 18th Centuries* (Sydney: Cape Breton University Press, 2004), 15–24, 112–13.
20. Ibid., 23, 135; NSARM, Land Petitions, Cape Breton Island, 1787–1843, Number 2157, "Kavanagh, Lawrence & Others for the Indians in Bras d'Or Lake," 1819.
21. "Original roving practices" is from NSARM, RG1, Volume 431, Number 62.5, H. W. Crawley to Joseph Howe, February 13, 1852.
22. The emergence of agriculture in government policy is detailed in Prins, *The Mi'kmaq*, 168–69; Elizabeth Haigh, "They Must Cultivate the Land: Abraham Gesner as Indian Commissioner, 1847–53," *Journal of the Royal Nova Scotia Historical Society* 3 (2000): 54–71; NSARM, RG1, Volume 432, Joseph Howe Letterbooks, "An Act to Provide for the Instruction and Permanent Settlement of the Indians."
23. The extent to which the Mi'kmaq cultivated the soil prior to ongoing contact with Europeans has been the focus of debate. See, for example, Patricia Kathleen Linskey Nietfeld, "Determinants of Aboriginal Micmac Political Structure" (PhD thesis, University of New Mexico, 1981), 306–65.
24. NSARM, RG 5, Nova Scotia House of Assembly, Series P, Volume 8a, Number 14B, "An Account of the Indians Living within the County of Richmond as Taken on July 16th, 1841."
25. Rusty Bittermann, "The Hierarchy of the Soil: Land and Labour in a 19th Century Cape Breton Community," in *The Acadiensis Reader*, vol. 1, 3rd ed., ed. P. A. Buckner, Gail G. Campbell, and David Frank, (Fredericton: Acadiensis Press, 1998), 263, 266–67; NSARM, RG 1, Volume 432, Joseph Howe Letterbooks, "List of Trespassers on a Tract of Land Reserved for the Indians of Wagamatcook," July 8, 1837.
26. Harold Franklin McGee, "White Encroachment on Micmac Reserve Lands in Nova Scotia, 1830–67," *Man in the Northeast* 8 (1974), 57–64; Parnaby, "The Cultural Economy of Survival," 77–79.
27. On the famine, generally, see Robert Morgan, *Early Cape Breton* (Wreck Cove, Cape Breton: Breton Books, 2000), 136–52. The impact of potato rot on the island's Mi'kmaq is described in NSARM, MG 15 Volume 3, Number 111, "Year End Report from Cape Breton with a Strong Appeal for More Assistance from Dodds, Indian Commissioner, 1846."
28. Rosemary E. Ommer, *From Outpost to Outpor t: A Structural Analysis of the Jersey-Gaspe Cod Fishery, 1767–1886* (Montreal Kingston: McGill-Queen's University Press, 1991).
29. Olive Dickason highlights the Mi'kmaq's skills as mariners in *Louisbourg and the Indians: A Study in Imperial Race Relations, 1713–1760* (Ottawa: Parks Canada, 1976), 46, 75–77. There is no evidence that the Mi'kmaq participated

in the cod fishery centered at the French stronghold of Fortress Louisbourg between 1713 and 1758, although fish may have circulated between the two groups as part of the diplomacy of gift giving. See B. A. Balcolm, "The Cod Fishery of Ile Royale, 1713–1758," in *Aspects of Louisbourg*, ed. Eric Krause, Carol Corbin, and William O'Shea (Sydney: Cape Breton University Press, 1995), 169–97; A. J. B. Johnston, "The Fishermen of 18th Century Cape Breton: Numbers and Origins," *Nova Scotia Historical Review* 9, no. 1 (1989): 62–72. On barrel making, see NSARM, RG 1, Volume 431, Number 62.5, H. W. Crawley to Joseph Howe, February 13, 1852. According to Crawley, "They are expert workmen at the coopering business and supply all the trade in this part of the Island with fish casks. . . ."

30. Ronald Caplan, ed., "Annie and John Battiste: A Mi'kmaq Family History," in *Cape Breton Works* (Wreck Cove, Cape Breton: Breton Books, 1996), 163–84.

31. Julian Gwyn, "The Mi'kmaq, Poor Settlers, and the Nova Scotia Fur Trade, 1783–1853," paper presented at the 82nd meeting of the Canadian Historical Association, Dalhousie University, 2003. On the fur trade during the French regime on the island, see B. A. Balcolm and A. J. B Johnston, "Missions to the Mi'kmaq: Malagawatch and Chapel Island in the 18th Century," *Journal of the Royal Nova Scotia Historical Society* 9 (2006): 115–40.

32. Janet Chute, "Frank G. Speck's Contributions to the Understanding of Mi'kmaq Land Use, Leadership, and Land Management," *Ethnohistory* 46, no. 3 (1999): 481–539. Speck's contentions on this specific subject have been highly controversial; see, for example, Alfred G. Bailey's summary of the debate in *The Conflict of European and Eastern Algonkian Cultures, 1504–1700: A Study in Canadian Civilization* (Toronto: University of Toronto Press, 1969), xviii–xxii. Thanks to John Reid for bringing this source to my attention.

33. Janet E. Chute, "Mi'kmaq Fishing in the Maritimes: A Historical Overview," in *Earth, Water, Air, and Fire: Studies in Canadian Ethnohistory*, ed. David T. McNab (Waterloo: Wilfrid Laurier University Press, 1998), 100; Frances L. Stewart, "Seasonal Movements of Indians in Acadia as Evidenced by Historical Documents and Vertebrate Faunal Remains from Archaeological Sites," *Man in the Northeast* 38 (Fall 1989): 55–75.

34. In "Mi'kmaq Fishing in the Maritimes," 96, Chute stresses that "commercial incentives likely permeated Mi'kmaq fishing practices at a fairly early date." I don't doubt her basic point, only that this commercial activity appears—based on the evidence she presents—quite small compared with the fur trade.

35. Chute, "Mi'kmaq Fishing in the Maritimes," 96. This is not to say that Europeans were not involved in the Mi'kmaw fishery at all. See Balcolm, "The Mi'kmaq and Louisbourg," guide for interpreters at Fortress Louisbourg, revised edition, 2006, on file at Fortress Louisbourg.

36. NSARM, Land Petitions, Cape Breton Island, 1787–1843, Number 854, petition from Charles McNab, 1812; Number 624, petition from "Margaree Inhabitants," 1810.

37. NSARM, RG 5, Series P, Volume 45, Number 162, Petition of the "Chiefs and Captains of the Micmac Indians of Nova Scotia for aid to make farms," 1849.
38. For the commercial fishery see NSARM, RG 1, Volume 431, Number 75, petition from "Indians near St. Peter's in the County of Richmond," October 17, 1864; for renting of land see NSARM, RG 1, Volume 431, Number 99, Samuel Fairbanks to Provincial Secretary, August 12, 1858; for selling of wood, see Library and Archives Canada (LAC), RG 10, Volume 459, Number 6, Fairbanks to Secretary of State (Canada), April 3, 1868.
39. Gould and Semple (*Our Land*, 48) state that by 1821 the colonial government had received "no fewer than fourteen petitions for land on the Island from the Indians as well as demand for 15 tickets of location in the same area." To this total of 29, I have added an additional 9 petitions that were sent to the colonial government between 1819 and 1867. Some of these petitions—the additional 9—were sent by the Mi'kmaq of Cape Breton on their own or as part of a wider coalition that included the Mi'kmaq from the Nova Scotia mainland.
40. Micah A. Pawling, "Petitions, Kin, and Cultural Survival: The Maliseet and Passamaquoddy Peoples in the Nineteenth Century" (MA Thesis, University of Maine, 1999). On the orality of diplomacy in the eighteenth century, see Wicken, *Mi'kmaq Treaties on Trial*, 3–16.
41. NSARM, RG 5, Volume 3, Number 162, "Petition from Francis Tomma (Head Chief of the Micmacs) . . . concerning the Intrusions . . . ," July 12, 1860.
42. NSARM, RG1, Volume 431, Number 75, "Account of Great Coats, Blankets, and Muskets Issued to Indians in 1853."
43. Janet Chute, "Ceremony, Social Revitalization, and Change: Micmac Leadership and the Annual Festival of St. Anne," in *Papers of the 23rd Algonquin Conference*, ed. William Cowan (Ottawa: Carleton University, 1992), 45.
44. Quoted in Brian Tennyson, ed., *Impressions of Cape Breton* (Sydney: Cape Breton University Press, 1986), 161.
45. Chute, "Frank G. Speck's Contributions," 508; Dennis A. Bartels and Olaf Uwe Janzen, "Micmac Migration to Western Newfoundland," *Canadian Journal of Native Studies* 10, no. 1 (1990): 71–94. Rand is quoted in Thomas S. Abler, "Micmacs and Gypsies: Occupation of the Peripatetic Niche," in *Papers of the Twenty-First Algonquian Conference*, ed. William Cowan (Ottawa: Carleton University, 1990), 5.
46. Canada, *Sessional Papers* (Ottawa, 1877), Annual Report, Department of Indian Affairs, report by Indian Agent Alex F. McGillivray for District #8, Cape Breton County, October 24, 1876.
47. British Columbia Archives (BCA), Department of Indian Affairs (DIA), RG 10, V11021, File 520c, Chief Cheackmus (Tom) to "Honourable Gentlemen," undated, likely 1912 to 1916.
48. Cole Harris, "Voices of Smallpox around the Strait of Georgia," in *The Resettlement of British Columbia: Essays on Colonisation and Geographical Change*, ed. Cole Harris (Vancouver: University of British Columbia Press, 1997), 5, figure 1.1.

49. This paragraph is also informed by Wayne Suttles, *Coast Salish Essays* (Vancouver and Seattle: Talon Books, 1987); Harris, "The Making of the Lower Mainland," in *The Resettlement of British Columbia*, 68–102; and Homer Barnett, *The Coast Salish of British Columbia* (Westport, CT: Greenwood, 1975).

50. Jean Barman, *The West Beyond The West* (Toronto: University of Toronto Press, 1996), 26; J. S. Matthews, comp., *Conversations with Khahtsahlano, 1932–1954* (Vancouver: Vancouver City Archives, 1955), 47, 54A, 50. Other observations made by European seafarers about the Squamish can be found in Keith Thor Carlson, ed., *A Sto:lo-Coast Salish Historical Atlas* (Vancouver and Toronto: Douglas and McIntyre, 2001), plate 28B, "Perceptions and Perspectives of the 'Other.'"

51. On the epidemics, see Robert Boyd, "Smallpox in the Pacific Northwest: The First Epidemics," *BC Studies* 101 (Spring 1994): 5–35; Charles Hill-Tout, "Notes on the Cosmogony and History of the Squamish Indians of British Columbia," *The Salish of British Columbia* (Vancouver: Talon Books, 1978, 22; Matthews, *Conversations with Khahtsahlano*, 25.

52. Harris, "The Making of the Lower Mainland," 73; BCA, DIA, RG10, V3611, F3756-7, "New Westminster Agency, Commissioner Gilbert Malcolm Sproat's Report on the Squamish River Reserve, 1877." For more on J.M.Yale, see the *Dictionary of Canadian Biography Online* at: http://www.biographi.ca/EN/ShowBio.asp?BioId=39452.

53. Carlson, ed., *A Sto:lo-Coast Salish Historical Atlas*, plate 14, "Intercommunity Conflicts"; Hill-Tout, "Notes on the Cosmogony and History of the Squamish Indians of British Columbia," 49–50; Paige Raibmon, *Authentic Indians: Episodes of Encounter from the Late-Nineteenth-Century Northwest Coast* (Durham: Duke University Press, 2005, 17–18; Harris, "The Making of the Lower Mainland," 79.

54. Robert A. J. McDonald, *Making Vancouver: Class, Status, and Social Boundaries, 1863–1913* (Vancouver: University of British Columbia Press, 1996), 19.

55. BCA, DIA, RG10, V3611, F3756-7, "New Westminster Agency, Commissioner Gilbert Malcolm Sproat's Report on the Squamish River Reserve, 1877."

56. McDonald, *Making Vancouver*, xi.

57. This generalization is based on an analysis of the annual reports of the Department of Indians Affairs published by year as part of Canada, *Sessional Papers* (1877–1930). See Andrew Parnaby, "On the Hook: Welfare Capitalism on the Vancouver Waterfront, 1919–1939" (PhD Thesis, Memorial University of Newfoundland, 2001), 204–7, 453, 454.

58. BCA, DIA, RG10, V3611, F3756-7, "New Westminster Agency—Commissioner Gilbert Malcolm Sproat's report on the Squamish . . . 1877."

59. Douglas Cole and Ira Chaikin, *An Iron Hand upon the People: The Law against the Potlatch on the Northwest Coast* (Vancouver: Douglas and McIntyre, 1990); Tina Loo, "Dan Cranmer's Potlatch: Law as Coercion, Symbol and Rhetoric in British Columbia," *Canadian Historical Review* 73, no. 2 (June 1992): 125–65.

60. Writing about another Coast Salish group, the Lekwammen of southern Vancouver Island, John Lutz makes the same point; see *Makuk*, 80–82.
61. Evidence of continued potlatching among the Squamish is found in: BCA, DIA, RG10, V3611, F3756-11, "Gilbert Malcolm Sproat's Summarized Report of the Indian Reserve Commission in British Columbia 1877"; V3944, F121,698-53, Devlin, Indian Agent for New Westminster to Vowell, Indian Superintendent, July 16, 1896; V1479, Letterbook, Peter Byrne to Assistant Deputy and Secretary, DIA, February 3, 1914; Union of British Columbia Indian Chiefs (UBCIC), Add.Mss 1056, testimony of Chief Mathias Joseph and Chief Harry; Hill-Tout, "Notes on the Skqomic of British Columbia, A Branch of the Great Salish Stock of North America," in *The Salish of British Columbia*, 49; Matthews, comp., *Conversations with Khahtsahlano*, 23, 34–36, 41, 69.
62. Jean Barman, *Stanley Park's Secret: The Forgotten Families of Whoi Whoi, Kanaka Ranch, and Brockton Point* (Madeira Park, BC: Harbour Publishing, 2005), 20. Between 1899 and 1906, income derived from hand logging was more than double that secured from commercial fishing. See BCA, DIA, RG10, V1493, "Agricultural and Industrial Statistics, 1899–1919"; V1451, Letterbooks, New Westminster Agency, 1897–98, Devlin to Vowel, January 24, 1898.
63. CVA, Shipping Federation of British Columbia (SFBC), Add.Mss 279, Box 36, File 1, "Accidents for the 1st Half of 1925."
64. Bruce Nelson, "Ethnicity, Race, and the Logic of Solidarity: Dock Workers in International Perspective," in *Dock Workers: International Explorations in Comparative Labour History, 1790–1970*, 2 vols., ed. Colin J. Davis et al., 655–80 (Aldershot, England: Ashgate, 2000)
65. ILWU Pensioners, *Man along the Shore! The Story of the Vancouver Waterfront as Told by Longshoremen Themselves, 1860s–1975* (Vancouver: ILWU Pensioners, 1975), 56; Dorothy Irene Kennedy, "Looking for Tribes in All the Wrong Places: An Examination of the Central Coast Salish Social Network" (MA Thesis, University of Victoria, 1995), 122–26; Hill-Tout, "Notes," 33.
66. Simon Baker, *Khot-la-cha: The Autobiography of Chief Simon Baker*, ed. Verna L. Kirkness (Vancouver and Toronto: Douglas and McIntyre 1994), 2–4, 8–11, 36–37, 53–60, 76–78.
67. BCA, DIA, RG10, V3650, F8424, "New Westminster—Superintendent James Lenihan's Report and Census on the Indians of the Lower Fraser Country, 1877"; V3857, F80, 782, Paul Durieu, OMI to A.W. Vowell, Indian Superintendent, 1892; V 1451, Letterbooks, New Westminster Agency, 1897–98, Devlin to Chief [?], Squamish Mission, December 14, 1897.
68. LAC, DIA, RG 10, V1001, reel T-1455, "Burrard Inlet Indians" to Mr. Lenihan, September 2, 1875; BCA, RG 10, V3645, F7936, Report of the British Columbia Reserve Commission, 1877 (the census is attached and dated 1876); V3650, F8424, "New Westminster—Superintendent James Lenihan's Report and Census of the Indians of the Lower Fraser Country, 1877; V1493, "New Westminster Agency, Agricultural and Industrial Statistics, 1899–1919."

69. BCA, RG 10, V3664, F9916, W. F. Tolmie to Sir Alexander Campbell, August 21, 1883; BCA, British Columbia Colonial Correspondence, F778/38, reel B-1334, "1870 Petition of Fraser Valley Chiefs to Governor Musgrave Regarding the Sale of Cranberry Patches"; two Squamish chiefs signed this petition.
70. See BCA, DIA, RG 10, V3611, F3756-11, "Gilbert Malcolm Sproat's Summarized Report of the Indian Reserve Commission in British Columbia, 1877." Interaction among Coast Salish peoples is described by Harris in "Making of the Lower Mainland," 68–76; Lutz makes specific reference to the Squamish and Lekwammen in *Makuk*, 71. See also Wayne Suttles, "The Persistance of Intervillage Ties among the Coast Salish," in *Coast Salish Essays*, 210–22.
71. Simon Baker remembers his grandmother, Mary Agnes Capilano, paddling her "dugout canoe" from the Squamish's north shore Mission reserve, across Burrard Inlet, to Vancouver. See Baker, *Khot-La-Cha*, 2–4.
72. The phrase "door-step economy" is taken from Carol Williams, "Between Doorstep Barter Economy and Industrial Wages: Mobility and Adaptability of Coast Salish Female Laborers in Coastal British Columbia, 1858–90," in *Native Being, Being Native: Identity and Difference*, Proceedings of the Fifth Native American Symposium, ed. Mark B. Spencer and Lucretia Scoufos (Durant: Southeastern Oklahoma State University, 2005), 16–27. "At this season of the year all the Indians are employed at the canneries and earning good wages." See BCA, DIA, RG10, V1451, Letterbook, New Westminister Agency, 1897–98, Devlin to Bryan, May 7, 1897. See also Dianne Newell, *Tangled Webs of History: Indians and the Law in Canada's Pacific Coast Fishery* (Toronto: University of Toronto Press, 1993), 79–80; Alicja Muszynski, *Cheap Wage Labour: Race and Gender in the Fisheries in British Columbia* (Montreal and Kingston: McGill-Queen's University Press, 1996).
73. BCA, DIA, RG10, V1455, Letterbook, New Westminister Agency, 1900–01, Devlin to Vedder, August 18, 1900.
74. Carlson, ed., *A Sto:lo-Coast Salish Historical Atlas*, plate 25, "The Salmon Canneries: Making Room for Families."
75. Cole Harris, *Making Native Space: Colonialism, Resistance, and Reserves in British Columbia* (Vancouver: University of British Columbia Press, 2002), maps 3.6, 5.1, and 5.2 on pages 67, 110, and 111, respectively. See William John Zahoroff, "Success in Struggle: The Squamish People and Kitsilano Indian Reserve No. 6" (MA Thesis, Carleton University, 1978). On the loss of small-scale agriculture due to encroachment on aboriginal land, see BCA, UBCIC, Add.Mss 1056, Royal Commission on Indian Affairs, testimony of Samson Thomas, June 23, 1913; BCA, DIA, RG10, V3857, F80,782, Inspector of Indian Agencies to Secretary, Department of Indian Affairs, April 15, 1912; June 10, 1912; November 8, 1912; BCA, DIA, RG10, V4074, F441, 744.
76. LAC, DIA, RG 10, V1001, reel T-1455, Richard Alexander and S. Lenihan, on behalf of the "Burrard Inlet Indians," to Indian Commissioner, September 2, 1875.

77. See Newell, *Tangled Webs*; Douglas C. Harris, *Landing Native Fisheries: Indian Reserves and Fishing Rights in British Columbia, 1849–1925* (Vancouver: University of British Columbia Press, 2008).
78. BCA, UBCIC, Add.Mss 1056, Royal Commission on Indian Affairs, testimony of Mathias Joseph, 1913.
79. Paige Raibmon, "Meanings of Mobility on the Northwest Coast" in *New Histories for Old: Changing Perspectives on Canada's Native Pasts*, ed. Ted Binnema and Susan Neylan, 175–95 (Vancouver: University of British Columbia Press, 2007).
80. Bruce Trigger, "Early Native North American Responses to European Contact: Romantic versus Rationalistic Interpretations," *Journal of American History* 77 (March 1991): 1195–1215.
81. Frank Tough, "From the 'Original Affluent Society' to the 'Unjust Society': A Review Essay on Native Economic History," *Journal of Aboriginal Economic Development* 4, no. 3 (Fall 2005): 30–70.
82. Eleanor Leacock, "Montagnais Women and the Jesuit Program for Colonization," in *Women and Colonization: Anthropological Perspectives*, ed. Eleanor Leacock and Mona Etienne, 25–41 (New York: Praeger, 1980).
83. Ellice Gonzalez, "An Ethnohistorical Analysis of Micmac Male and Female Economic Roles," *Ethnohistory* 29, no. 2 (1982): 117–29.
84. Parnaby, "Cultural Economy of Survival," 92–94.
85. Lutz, "Gender and Work in Lekwammen Families, 1843 to 1970," in *Gendered Pasts*, ed. Kathryn McPherson, Cecilia Morgan, and Nancy Forestell, 80–105 (Toronto: Oxford University Press, 1999).
86. Muszynski, *Cheap Wage Labour*, 129–79.
87. Parnaby, "Cultural Economy of Survival," 94.
88. Stephen J. Hornsby, *Nineteenth Century Cape Breton: A Historical Geography* (Kingston and Montreal: McGill-Queen's University Press. 1992), 152–85, 201–10.
89. Carlson, ed., *A Sto:lo–Coast Salish Historical Atlas*, plate 22A, "Seasonal Rounds in an Industrial World"; Chris Roine, "The Squamish Aboriginal Economy, 1860–1940" (MA Thesis, Simon Fraser University, 1996).
90. Andrew Parnaby, *Citizen Docker: Making a New Deal on the Vancouver Waterfront, 1919–1939* (Toronto: University of Toronto Press, 2008), 75–99, 169–73.
91. Quoted in *Cottonland* (Directed by Nancy Ackerman. National Film Board, 2006).
92. McDonald, *Making Vancouver*, 9.
93. Ibid., 5, 13.

10 "DE FACTO MEXICANS"

COFFEE WORKERS AND NATIONALITY
ON THE GUATEMALAN-MEXICAN BORDER,
1931–1941

Catherine Nolan-Ferrell

In December 1935, seven men swam across the Suchiate River, the official dividing line between Mexico and Guatemala.[1] Shortly after they arrived on the shore, Guatemalan police arrested the men and charged them with smuggling. The ensuing court case sheds light on transnational labor migrations, governmental regulations of nationality, and workers' efforts to control their participation in labor markets. The men admitted to working on Finca Santo Domingo, on the Mexican side of the border. Each man carried personal items (clothing and coffee) that the police labeled as contraband, even though the smuggled goods had little value. In their defense, the men asserted that they had no intention to smuggle but that the tax cost more than the value of the goods. In subsequent questioning, court officials repeatedly challenged the men about their decision to work in Mexico. One man claimed that he fled to Mexico to escape the sorrow of his wife's death on the Guatemalan finca where he previously worked. Domingo and José López, brothers from the town of San Pablo, asserted that they went to work in Mexico because another brother invited them.[2] The ease with which these men crossed the border for work contrasts sharply with their treatment upon their return to Guatemala. Although local officials charged the men with smuggling contraband, the men also "smuggled" their labor, in effect, stealing from Guatemalan coffee plantations. The state-defined problem of smuggling along the Guatemalan-Mexican border illustrates the ways in which defining national boundaries reshaped social and economic practices.

Prior to the 1930s, people living along the Mexican-Guatemalan border rarely described themselves by nationality. Yet, by the 1940s, such descriptions became ubiquitous. Why did nationality seemingly become important between 1931 and 1941? The Mexican and Guatemalan governments increasingly classified people by nationality in order to assert economic and political control over workers, even though the rural poor often challenged these labels. Laborers and government officials shared various definitions of nationality through what Jesse Hoffnung-Garskof calls "transnational social fields." Hoffnung-Garskof argues that migrants and members of their home communities share ideas and symbols, including discourses of nationality and citizenship, across national boundaries through migration processes.[3] National governments, regional authorities, local elites, and ordinary workers continually create and interpret symbols of inclusion and exclusion, which fundamentally label members of a nation.

Recently, social theorists have questioned the all-inclusive term *identity* to explain both peoples' self-understanding and the external descriptions imposed on particular groups. Rogers Brubaker and Frederick Cooper argue that identity is not a reified condition that a person "has," but rather is a process of identification. The authors shift the discussion away from using identity markers such as ethnicity or nationality. Instead, they ask what historical conditions have defined people as group members, why have group labels crystallized at particular historical moments, and why do they erode? Brubaker and Cooper describe two main types of identification processes: categorical identification occurs when an external power, usually a national state (including government officials and bureaucracies), classifies people by assumed categories of "sameness." In this top-down process, people belong to a group only if they share particular state-defined characteristics. In contrast, relational identification develops horizontally. Group belonging depends on a person's relationships with others—their shared work and community experiences, shared interests, or kinship.[4] Along the Guatemalan-Mexican border, federal and local government officials relied on categorical identification to assign national identity. In contrast, workers themselves generally used relational identification to define nationality and citizenship. Relational and categorical identification processes continually interacted, creating variable meanings of citizenship.

The decade between 1931 and 1941 became a transitional period in which both the Mexican and Guatemalan governments developed particular definitions of nationality and citizenship. Nationality became increasingly important to local and federal authorities as they attempted to control rural labor. By the 1930s, the Mexican government restricted access to revolutionary land and labor reforms exclusively to Mexican citizens. Similarly, from 1931 to 1944, Guatemalan officials labeled indigenous workers as Guatemalans in order to enact vagrancy laws designed to secure workers for Guatemalan plantations. Government officials assigned citizenship to rural workers based on perceived differences in ethnicity, by dress, or even by the sound of a particular accent. Claims to nationality became increasingly important to each country because of their own concerns about the control of land, in the case of Mexico, and the control of labor in Guatemala.

At the same time that states sought to control claims on citizenship to meet their own needs, rural laborers challenged state power. For workers, using official definitions of nationality became a way for them to claim citizenship. Mexican and Guatemalan campesinos used changing definitions of citizenship both to gain access to Mexican revolutionary reforms and to combat the exploitation they experienced on the coffee plantations of the Soconusco. Other rural laborers built upon a Guatemalan identity that allowed them to preserve their indigenous and community practices. In Chiapas, campesinos also defied official categorizations by using relational identification to redefine national membership. Citizenship status included those who lived and worked together on the coffee fincas, regardless of a person's birthplace or official papers.

Recent historiography of state formation in the aftermath of the Mexican Revolution has explored the interactions between state institutions, local and regional officials, and peasant and working classes to show how various groups negotiated different meanings of the emerging Mexican state. What emerges is a regionally diverse image of federal power, local caciquismo, and some cases of grassroots peasant activism. In Chiapas, federal power gradually expanded from 1931 to 1934, and more rapidly from 1935 to 1941 during President Lázaro Cárdenas's administration. This era undermines images of a leviathan state and instead shows a federal government that bargained with elites and lower classes to implement government policies.[5] The indigenous highlands of Chiapas provide several case studies in which federal reforms resulted in new political strongmen, or caciques, who undermined Cárdenas's revolutionary programs. In contrast, the federal government exercised more power in Soconusco, though not enough to change unequal socioeconomic structures. Cultural studies of Soconusco highlight ways in which indigenous Mames used evolving revolutionary rhetoric to assert their own meanings of Mexican nationality.[6] Most scholars explore capitalist expansion and labor migration within Chiapas, minimizing connections between Soconusco, Chiapas, and San Marcos, Guatemala. The western Sierra Madres (which span the Pacific coast of Guatemala and Mexico) constitute a transnational social field, providing a case study of historical conditions that made national identity significant.

Officials Establish the (In)Effective Border, 1931–1934

Trading and migration along the Sierra Madre had existed since the colonial era. With the creation of a formal border in 1882, people and goods continued to move across the "artificial" boundary. By March 1926, Mexican President Plutarco Elías Calles signed a "New Law of Migration," hoping to solidify Mexico's borders through regularizing people's movements. The law stipulated that immigrants into Mexico pay an immigration tax of 20 pesos, plus 1 peso for vaccinations and 1 peso for paperwork tax. These taxes applied to all immigrants over fifteen years old, regardless of the amount of time they planned to spend in the country.[7] A different memo listed the costs as $10.30 for registration fee, $2.00 for photographs, and an additional $45.00 to have someone complete the forms correctly.[8] All Guatemalans were supposed to enter through official ports of entry, show an ID card granted by Mexican officials, and have proof of required vaccinations.[9] The New Law of Migration represented the emerging Mexican state's aspiration to control its territory and people.

Actual enforcement varied. Border enforcement often fell to local police because of limited federal funds. However, these officials expressed uneasiness about identity cards because they feared restricting labor supplies during coffee harvests. Workers had trouble acquiring required paperwork, struggling to pay the identity card fees. Most Guatemalans along the frontier who had settled in Mexico lacked official documents such as birth certificates. The government drafted regulations for birth certificates, identity cards, and passports in 1926, well after immigrant laborers established communities in Soconusco. Guatemalan officials complained that Mexican federal authorities failed to notify either local municipal presidents or Guatemalan workers in coffee-growing regions about the new legal requirements. Both Mexican and Guatemalan officials voiced concerns because the federal government decided to enforce registration requirements without providing adequate notice to the workers, the coffee plantation owners, or the local authorities.[10] Planters and local authorities worried that enforcing the new identity card laws might leave coffee cherries rotting unpicked in the groves.

Guatemalan government officials strenuously objected to this law, and for three years (1926–1930) they obtained concessions for twenty-four-hour temporary passes for workers.[11] For Guatemalan "natives," enforcing the law created significant blocks to local commerce. Typically, indigenous peoples on both sides of the border traded in foodstuffs and local consumer goods. However, because the Guatemalan government had less restrictive visa requirements, the Guatemalans argued that the Mexican law created unfair advantages for Mexican campesinos—who faced very few limitations when they entered Guatemala. The disrupted trade networks created hardships for campesinos and merchants in both Mexico and Guatemala.

The Mexican government's decision to restrict regional trading foreshadowed increasingly negative depictions of Guatemala. Mexican newspapers described Guatemalans as a threat to southern Mexico. A *La Prensa* article of August 4, 1932, described Guatemalans as "infiltrating" Mexican territory, displacing Mexican workers and landholders. However, Guatemalan officials and local Mexican authorities recognized that the 1926 migration laws affected impoverished, illiterate day laborers—not those who qualified as threats to landowning

Mexicans. The newspaper "urged that the invaders be eliminated, fraudulents, who have come to deceive and exploit us."[12] Although the documents did not detail the number of Guatemalans detained by Mexicans, newspapers and official reports show that perceptions of migration were a significant border issue in Chiapas.

In contrast to images of "invading Guatemalans," the U.S. chargé d'affaires described Guatemalans in Chiapas in this way: "The natives imprisoned and expelled are humble merchants or day laborers in search of work who, through ignorance, enter Mexican territory without an identity card." People detained by the Mexican authorities faced severe conditions. Guatemalan delegates charged local authorities in Tapachula of imprisoning Guatemalans and denying food to them while they awaited deportation. Mexican authorities confiscated merchandise and personal goods from merchants and laborers caught violating the law. Guatemalans who had settled (squatted) north of the Suchiate faced the loss of years of hard work improving the land, loss of farm animals, and personal property if they were denounced as Guatemalans.[13] Presumably, authorities could use or distribute the land and property as they saw fit. The negative stereotypes of Guatemalans contributed to a climate that encouraged the abuse of immigrant workers.

In August 1932, Mexican and Guatemalan delegations met to resolve the questions of workers' rights and nationality along the border. Guatemalans complained about Mexican labor laws that restricted foreign workers to only 10 percent of laborers in an industry, ID card expenses, and the $250 "security deposit" that was set aside for repatriation costs if Guatemalans overstayed their visas. The Mexican delegate dismissed Guatemala's concern, charging that the registration fee was only excessive to people who lacked appropriate documentation. He blamed workers because "they have been careless in obtaining the [the documents] from competent officials of their country." Guatemala's delegation leader disputed this characterization of workers as "careless." Instead, they wanted a special census to determine the citizenship of people living along the border. When the Mexicans refused, the Guatemalan envoy pointed out that many people "would be without definite nationality . . . without a country." He advocated that people be labeled as "de facto Mexicans" so that the Mexican government could not deport people to Guatemala as "undesirable foreigners." The Mexican delegate agreed that they shared the goal "to suppress that irregular state in which individuals without a definite nationality and lacking nationality are placed."[14] The meeting concluded with recommendations to conduct a census of the population in Chiapas, with representatives of both Mexico and Guatemala to decide people's nationality.

The decision to have government authorities set nationality seems particularly important because it ignored workers' efforts to determine their own nationality. Government representatives investigated the validity of people's documents used to establish nationality and had the power to reject citizenship claims. Additionally, government officials sought to develop procedures establishing nationality for those who could not provide absolute proof.[15] The desire to control laborers motivated both Mexican and Guatemalan officials in determining nationality. In the concluding statement, the delegates agreed that "the two governments will cooperate in preventing the emigration of their nationals who are laborers."[16] By having authorities determine nationality, the two nations attempted to assert more control over "their" workers.

Although Mexico set new requirements to register workers and to assert a stronger Mexican presence along the border, its limited ability to enforce the laws meant that ordinary workers experienced few concrete changes in labor and migration patterns. Formal border crossings between Mexico and Guatemala remained scarce. In 1908, the Pan American Railroad Bridge connected Mexico and Guatemala at Ciudad Hidalgo, Mexico, and Tecún Umán, Guatemala. A "temporary" wooden bridge also connected these two cities and remained the main official route between the two nations until a permanent bridge replaced it more fifty years later, in 1962. The state government had more success with bridge renovations at Talismán, a tiny border town in the heart of the coffee region. By 1932, engineers declared the bridge strong enough for vehicle traffic. Limited roads in the region meant that most people crossed the Suchiate River by wading or swimming, not on formal bridges. The 1926 migration law stipulated the need for border checkpoints, but limited resources for constructing and staffing the checkpoints made them a theoretical tool for controlling migration.[17] The state's inability to effectively control its borders highlights the differences between legal rhetoric and practical experiences.

Workers' Experience the Border

While governments debated border issues and set rules, official proclamations had little impact on ordinary campesinos' experience of the border. Labor migrations into Soconusco mixed settlers from multiple ethnic groups. Guatemalan and Mexican workers moved across the imperceptible border with relative ease. Since the intermingling of Guatemalan and Mexican campesinos had occurred over an extended time, the formal "nationality" of someone caused little notice. People often blanketed all community members under the same nationality, emphasizing relational identification as the dominant form of assigning group membership. Jacobo Galván, a campesino leader from ejido El Edén, claimed those who organized in his agrarian committee knew that several laborers came from Guatemala, but that their nationality had little impact for the vast majority of workers. Juan Velásquez corroborated this recollection: "Almost all of the workers were from here, well, they were born there [in Guatemala] but they have lived here for many years... they were 'natives.'" Felipe Robledo acknowledged that many people came to finca Santo Domingo from Guatemala, but that "nobody asked" about where people came from, in part because many leaders among the finca workers also came from Guatemala.[18] Living and working together seemed to determine campesinos' definition of belonging that trumped official declarations of nationality.

Government authorities disrupted migration and settlement patterns when enforcing boundary regulations. Rhetoric by Mexican authorities emphasized controlling labor migration, while Guatemalan officials focused on regulating commerce. Guatemalan workers initially seemed to view the border as an economic line that interrupted regional trade. Although cases of smuggling occurred during the 1920s, after the rise of Guatemalan President Jorge Ubico, enforcement of customs regulations appeared to increase.[19] In the department of San Marcos, Guatemala, charges of carrying contraband became ubiquitous in the early and mid-1930s. Cindy Forster explains the high number of cases of contraband as an example of growing resistance to the repressive policies of the Guatemalan government.[20] However, documents also suggest that carrying goods across the border was accepted practice for workers traveling home after working on fincas. Most court cases from San Marcos concerned people smuggling personal goods such as clothing, food, coffee, *aguardiente* or *comiteca* (alcohol or moonshine), and tobacco paper.

Given the extreme poverty that campesinos experienced in the region, transporting food and clothing for family and personal use supplemented meager wages and subsistence farming. For example, border officials arrested Francisca López for smuggling coffee, but she argued that it was for her family and so she did not pay customs fees. In a similar case, a prisoner argued that he carried coffee but that "he did not know if he had to pay the customs fee for coffee."[21] In other cases, people sold small amounts of smuggled goods to other campesinos. Cases of smuggling *aguardiente* filled the criminal court system in San Marcos. Selling *aguardiente* became a way for families, particularly female-headed households, to supplement their incomes.

Smuggling became increasingly risky as border enforcement tightened. Laborers attempted to avoid prosecution by arguing that crossing the border with personal goods did not constitute criminal behavior. Crisanto Hernández, an indigenous worker from Sibinal, San Marcos, worked on finca Mishcum [Mixcum], in Unión Juárez, Chiapas. After the 1935 harvest, he returned to Sibinal with one bottle of *aguardiente*, a hoe, white fabric, blue fabric, two towels, and a pair of pants, totaling Q$3.75. ($Q is the Guatemalan currency, the quetzal.) Guatemalan soldiers arrested Hernández for failure to pay import taxes of Q$4.79. The courts charged him with smuggling, fining him Q$300 in spite of Hernández's explanation that the items "were for his family, because of their poverty, and not for business purposes." He explained that he worked subsistence agriculture but to "meet urgent family needs, he had to go to work on the [Mexican] finca," but that it was his first time working in Mexico. Ultimately, Crisanto Hernández spent almost five months in prison and paid a fine for smuggling alcohol. When local authorities released Hernández, he owed the government the cost of prison food, as well as the cost of paper needed to record his case.[22] The fact that people often claimed ignorance or personal use shows that they thought it was a plausible excuse—regardless of whether they actually were ignorant of the law. Hernández's case also highlighted the authorities' limited resources for enforcing borders. Charging prisoners for prison costs occurred in many municipalities, according to court cases. Having official records of costs suggests that these were not simply local police bribes, but ways to offset government expenses.

Finqueros also allegedly ordered peasants to smuggle. In one case, Mexican authorities arrested seventeen Guatemalans for smuggling. In their defense, the campesinos argued they were "unaware of what they were doing" because they obeyed the plantation owner's orders to bring coffee across the Suchiate River. The Mexican court found the workers guilty, even after the Guatemalan consul in Tapachula proved that finca administrator, Ernesto Barrios, had ordered the smuggling. Local authorities in San Marcos, Guatemala, convicted Barrios for illegally instigating smuggling. The Guatemalan consul initially appealed but withdrew the request because the Mexican appellate court was in Meria [Mérida] Yucatán, making travel costs prohibitive.[23] Ultimately, the workers took the punishment.

Campesinos skirted laws restricting movement and trade between the two nations. Guatemalan soldiers claimed two men crossed the border illegally. One man admitted he was planning to sell corn to a Sr. Juan López, "who lives on the other side" of the Suchiate River. However, when he was questioned about migration requirements (a passport, crossing at an official bridge, etc.), the man replied, "Since we were going to the sand bar in the middle of the river, it didn't count as an official border crossing."[24] The rural poor claimed ignorance, poverty, and unfamiliarity with the formal entry ports as a way to avoid culpability for crossing the border. The documents suggest, however, that people knew about border regulations but refused to comply with them.

In spite of official border regulations, the coffee economy created an integrated economic system that transcended national boundaries. To ensure adequate laborers for the coffee harvest, planters on both sides of the border used *enganche* (debt servitude) to recruit workers. Workers received wage advances from the fincas, promising to work off debts during harvest. Some German growers owned coffee fincas on both sides of the border, actively recruiting Guatemalan laborers for their Mexican plantations. Coffee growers in San Marcos, Guatemala, owned "fincas de mozos" in the higher altitude regions in both San Marcos and Huehuetenango. *Finqueros* acquired land at high altitudes where indigenous campesinos grew subsistence crops. Villagers "paid rent" for land by picking coffee for the landowner.[25] Campesinos supplemented their income by participating in *enganche* among plantations in both nations during the harvest.

Historians debate *enganche*'s impact on indigenous communities. Some argue that during labor shortages, workers manipulated the system by obtaining multiple advances, fleeing oppressive conditions, and bargaining for better treatment. Others emphasize the repressiveness of debt servitude. In Guatemalan historiography, Forster argues that even though some people used the system to their own advantage, ultimately, planters and authorities successfully repressed workers. McCreery contends that abuses of the *enganche* system abounded; however, indigenous workers perceived it as less repressive than previous forced labor systems. In Mexico, Sarah Washbrook's comparison of *enganche* in Soconusco and Palenque highlights weaknesses of debt servitude in Soconusco.[26] *Enganche* constituted a coercive labor system, abusing workers' rights even though people bargained to lessen exploitation. More importantly, differences in state power to enforce labor contracts significantly affected workers' experiences of *enganche*. Documents suggest that Guatemalan officials enforced labor laws more effectively than Mexican authorities in Soconusco did. Because of this imbalance, Guatemalan campesinos routinely smuggled their most valuable commodity: their labor.

The 1934 Vagrancy Law in Guatemala officially ended debt servitude but replaced it with a similar forced labor system. Rural workers had to "contribute" labor to either the government or the coffee plantations for 150 days each year. Local police and federal Treasury Police enforced the new vagrancy law, often conducting sweeps prior to the start of the coffee harvest. The timing suggests that "vagrants" worked off their punishment for finca owners in the subsequent harvest season.[27] Landed elites also relied on local police or military to capture campesinos who failed to complete their work contracts. Reports from the department of San Marcos in March 1934 provided information on the number of workers detained for vagrancy: Malacatán, 5 *mozos*; Nuevo Progreso, 13 *mozos* (but crimes not labeled); San Marcos, "various *mozos de fincas* were detained for lack of work"; San Pablo, "15 *mozos* arrested, the majority were for lack of work." (*Mozos* broadly refers to rural day laborers). In Concepción Tutuapa, people resisted forced labor by charging the mayor, treasurer, and military commander with abuse of authority. The complaint stated: "These individuals detain people under the charge of vagrancy and bring them to work on the finca of Don José Longo." Those residents who requested an explanation of the charge were thrown into jail.[28] Workers did not meekly accept debt servitude, but openly defying forced labor rarely succeeded.

Mexico offered an escape for Guatemalan workers struggling with high debt and labor duties. Strict compliance with Guatemalan vagrancy laws made work in Mexico more appealing to many workers, while Mexican growers repeatedly complained about the authorities' inability to enforce labor contracts.[29] Simeona González and her son Eduardo Morales worked on the Finca Clarita in San Marcos, Guatemala. When Eduardo's father died, Eduardo inherited his debt. The finca *caporal* (work boss) soon came after Eduardo but found only Simeona home. She told the caporal that it was "not just that a son pays for the father." She sent her son "to the other side" (to Mexico) to look for work. Finca Clarita's owner charged *caporales* with finding *mozos fugos* (fugitive laborers) who had outstanding debts or who had fled work contracts. If fugitives failed to appear, the patrón ordered *caporales* to arrest family members to "guarantee" workers' return. The municipal judge found that the finca owner overstepped his power and convicted *caporales* of illegally detaining Simeona González. Court records do not show the outcome, but most likely Eduardo remained in Mexico to escape the unjust debt.[30] The case shows that Mexico became a refuge for those fleeing from perceived injustices on Guatemalan fincas. It also highlights that campesinos knew the border existed and demonstrated a willingness to switch nationality for protection.

Guatemalan and Mexican coffee plantation owners competed for scarce laborers and attempted to use the legal system to retain workers. Campesinos resisted coerced labor with mixed results. When Guatemalan officials accused two campesinos of vagrancy, they vehemently denied the charge. They argued that they lived in Concepción Tutuapa and grew corn and wheat. However, they received a thirty-day prison sentence and the following warning: "The accused were going to provide their agricultural services to the neighboring Mexican Republic, and they were denounced in order to protect Agriculture and occupy themselves in work for *this* nation."[31] Planters found more sympathy for coercion if they appealed to national needs for workers.

Finqueros saw any weakness in enforcing labor law as a threat to the entire system. When Florencio Gómez López was arrested for vagrancy in October 1934, the court records claimed that he "refused to complete, without justifiable cause, his promised work contract." Gómez López received thirty days in prison for his crime, yet the local justice of the peace in Malacatán, Joaquín Velasco R., freed him before he completed the full thirty days. The finca's lawyer, Lic. Vicente J. Rosal, complained to Velasco about the lax punishment and requested that Gómez López serve his entire sentence. The judge explained that he freed the *mozo* "in the spirit of justice . . . he is not a prisoner for a criminal act, but is a decrepit old man, and very sick." Velasco chided, "I find it very strange that a man like Lic. Rosal, with sufficient mental capacity, commits inhuman acts like this request against this worker . . . when it is almost impossible for him to work." Rosal apparently approached other judges to have Gómez López rearrested, which Rosal explained was based on his desire to act "within the letter of the law."[32] The case of Gómez López provides an example of how and why Guatemalan elites so forcefully sought to enact the laws. Any lapse in compulsory labor, even by an elderly, ill man, undermined the strength of the law.

To counteract the idea that Mexico provided refuge for Guatemalan workers, Guatemalan officials fomented ideas of Mexico as dangerous or a threat to Guatemala. Authorities welcomed negative claims about Mexican citizens, using them to cast Mexicans as "problems." Because border towns often mixed Mexican-Guatemalan identity, people labeled tensions between various factions as national differences. For example, in Ayutla, a village in San Marcos, Guatemala, Santiago Vargas and others requested a new municipal judge in order to "ensure material, moral, industrial and scientific progress." In response, regional authorities replied that "Mexicans" protested against the judge. As foreigners, they did not have the right to remove the judge.[33] The Mexican "troublemakers" lacked proper concern for Guatemalan citizens.

Charges against Mexican nationals also occurred partly because of their "outsider" status. Local authorities in Guatemalan border towns warned against outbreaks of malaria, dengue, smallpox, and measles, quarantining Mexicans because they "carried diseases." Healers or witches (*brujos/as*) were frequently labeled as Mexicans. In a more unusual case, Isabel Pérez and Marcelo López charged Bernardo Godínez with witchcraft against their daughter Tomasa. Godínez, called "el Brujo" in court documents, claimed he could cure Tomasa's worsening illness. Her parents complained to authorities after they paid Godínez four chickens, four bottles of *aguardiente*, and two *quintales* (bushels) of maize. After the last cure failed, Godínez promised that for the right price, he could cure Tomasa. He explained that witches from Huixtla, Tapachula, and in Medio Monte—all Mexican towns and villages—had sickened her. He claimed that witchcraft would eventually kill Tomasa. Court records stop at this point, so it is unclear why Mexican witches targeted Tomasa, or if these charges simply provided Godínez with opportunities to extort money from her desperate parents.[34] Court records circumvent identifying Godínez as a Mexican. However, his close connections with witchcraft in Mexico, as evidenced by his alleged knowledge of death threats by Mexican witches, shifted the tone of the case. Initially, documents cast Godínez as a charlatan, exploiting Tomasa's parents. When the documents end, he clearly is associated with foreign threats against a Guatemalan minor. This case highlights the perceived danger of Mexicans to ordinary Guatemalans. Authorities reinforced these negative depictions of Mexico but ultimately did little to stem the flow of Guatemalan labor across the border.

1934–1941: Mexico: Creating Nationalism through Revolution

Limited resources to enforce border regulations and ordinary campesinos' general noncompliance with migration laws made the 1932 agreements ineffective. The period from 1934 to 1941 marks a transitional stage in the process of inculcating Mexican national identity in Soconusco. As President Lázaro Cárdenas's government consolidated power, his administration advocated reform programs for workers and peasants. By 1936, President Cárdenas forced Victórico Grajales, Chiapas's counterrevolutionary governor, from power. Grajales's departure opened opportunities for improving labor conditions and land redistribution in Soconusco. Governor Efraín Gutiérrez, an ally of Cárdenas, sought to implement reforms in Soconusco, partly based on campesino demands for change and partly based on the governor's limited ability to challenge Chiapanecan elites in the center of the state. In Soconusco, foreign elites (primarily German immigrants, naturalized as Mexicans citizens) provided an opportune target for Cardenistas. *Finqueros* exploited campesinos for cheap labor, made tremendous wealth from Chiapas's natural resources, and had tenuous ties with power brokers in central Chiapas. By supporting campesinos' demands for rural programs in Soconusco, local Cardenista activists could undermine political opponents and cement popular support for the emerging postrevolutionary state.[35] The federal Agrarian Department envisioned *ejidos* (community-owned land that villagers either farmed collectively or parceled out into individual plots) as the cornerstone of rural improvements in postrevolutionary Mexico. Officially, only Mexican campesinos qualified for land reform and membership in state-authorized labor unions.[36] Because so many finca workers lacked proof of nationality, eligibility for Mexican citizenship became a significant issue for campesinos and reformers alike. Campesinos who "became Mexican" gained citizenship, access to postrevolutionary benefits, and the right to assert their interests to the Cárdenas government.

The challenge became defining "Mexican." Cardenista reformers, local officials, planters, and rural workers shared no consensus that defined *mexicanidad* or Mexicanness. Instead, Mexican authorities began defining criteria for citizenship—both inclusively, by creating an expansive "imagined community" of Mexicans, and exclusively, by disciplining those who did not behave in government-sanctioned ways. The federal government particularly struggled to classify workers who had established villages near the coffee fincas. Settlers in these communities came from diverse backgrounds, including people born on both sides of the border. Most campesinos lacked official documents to prove their country of origin. Impoverished finca laborers often registered their children in Guatemala's Civil Register because it was cheaper than registering them in Mexico. (It cost $4.00 pesos in Mexico and the equivalent of $1.50 pesos in Guatemala, a savings of $2.50 pesos per child.) Migrant workers and their families labeled themselves as mestizos, which allowed them to avoid repressive Guatemalan laws against the indigenous peoples. During the Mexican Revolution, many village archives in the districts of Soconusco and Mariscal burned, leaving no way to prove nationality for thousands of campesinos.[37] For federal authorities who searched for shared characteristics that defined *mexicanidad*, the lack of such distinctions thwarted easy categorical identification.

Those who supported broader definitions of citizenship argued that land distribution would bond campesinos of nebulous nationality to Mexico. One agrarian official wrote that land distribution could "develop patriotic sentiments and show that the campesinos could peacefully enjoy the land, thanks to the Revolution."[38] Land distribution would illustrate the "ideological and moral value of the Mexican Revolution, with its social reforms and practical improvements for everyday Mexicans." The author also believed that land reform ceremonies gave campesinos and agrarian officials the opportunity to show their pride and express their faith in the humanitarian principles of social justice as outlined by the revolution.[39] The memo's language is striking in its explicit agenda to create strong connections between the people of the Soconusco and the postrevolutionary Mexican government through economic change and cultural symbolism. Although no documents detail if agrarian reform ceremonies led campesinos to accept government rhetoric about the value of the Mexican Revolution, campesinos' intense loyalty toward Cárdenas's government illustrates some successes.

Narrower categorizations of *mexicanidad* often excluded members of particular indigenous groups that lived on both sides of the border. Mam and Tacanecans (a small indigenous group who settled on the Tacaná volcano) faced discrimination based on their indigenousness. During the early 1930s, Governor Grajales's policies toward native peoples in the Soconusco and Mariscal districts emphasized assimilation. The Mexican Mam had faced severe cultural repression under the Grajales regime, including prohibitions on speaking Mam and the burning of indigenous dress. The state government punished or deported those Indians who did not accept the governor's assimilation programs. Under Grajales, identifying Guatemalans as indigenous and Mexicans as mestizos became part of the state's negative definition of indigenous people as "foreigners." Because most Guatemalan immigrants belonged to particular ethnic groups, indigenous workers from the Sierra Madre regions who lacked a birth certificate or other official papers risked classification as Guatemalan.[40] Officially, the Cárdenas government supported pro-Indian policies and glorified Mexico's indigenous heritage. In Soconusco, however, *indigenismo* failed to gain much support because the Maya did not fit into the government's romanticized model of a "noble Indian." During the Cárdenas years, indigenous identity was seen as Guatemalan, not Mexican.

For many immigrants to Soconusco, links between indigenous identity and "foreignness" became another way for the government to control workers. In one small community, forty-five Mexican workers signed a letter objecting to their deportation to Guatemala. They were indigenous, and immigration authorities refused to believe they were Mexicans. While admitting that they lacked papers, the workers argued that their parents were "humble Indians" who in their ignorance did not always register their children during the Porfiriato, and even those who were supposedly registered had to struggle with "deficient" civil registries from that era.[41] The campesinos argued that the local *finquero* denounced them as foreigners because the community petitioned for an *ejido*. The landowner faced expropriation of part of his finca, which was the real reason for the deportations. These protests generally went unheeded by a government that also sought to incorporate indigenous cultures into a state-sanctioned cultural identity.

Exclusive definitions of nationality also depended on workers' behaviors— and their obedience to government officials. Guatemalans became "the other" against which the government defined a good Mexican worker. The Federal Labor Office in Tapachula sought to create "organizations [unions] for the defense of workers' rights ... taking care that all members should be accredited as Mexicans, given the palpable problem of the growing number of foreigners who live in the region." According to one government report, Guatemalan workers enjoyed better treatment and job assignments on the fincas because they hindered labor organizations and competed against Mexican campesinos.[42] Guatemalans subverted Mexican laborers by cultivating special treatment from the landowners.

Conversely, other government officials viewed Guatemalan workers as troublemakers who provoked problems on the fincas to the detriment of Mexican workers. One labor inspector claimed that the majority of the unionized workers on Finca España were Guatemalans who "dedicated themselves to causing difficulties." These Guatemalans complained about excessive work, even though the inspector claimed that they did not work even an eight-hour day. He implied that the Mexican workers (who did not belong to the union) worked harder than the Guatemalans did.[43] Both reports by the different government labor officials identify Guatemalans as the cause of labor problems, though for entirely different reasons. This illustrates how authorities used "Guatemalan" as a broad slur that served multiple purposes. Because national identity was so fluid at this time, the documents do not give any clear indication of who actually caused problems on the fincas. While wanting to favor Mexican nationals as beneficiaries of reform programs, labeling people as Guatemalan and Mexican allowed the government to exclude certain workers from participation in the postrevolutionary state.

Finally, dubious nationality for many workers gave the Cárdenas government an opportunity to shape some laborers into the government's ideal "Mexican" worker. Campesinos who lacked formal papers willingly conformed to official depictions of "good workers" in order to gain citizenship. The Cárdenas administration positively characterized laborers who complied with government dictates, while those who challenged the government received negative labels. In the *ejido* El Retiro, the agrarian engineer complained about stubborn *ejido* members who refused to accept a government land grant. The campesinos complained that the engineer assigned them inferior land, but the official claimed that villagers "were unwilling to understand the advantages" of their new situation as *ejiditarios*.[44] The disciplining action of the government did not necessarily have extensive power to eliminate other images of "good workers," but it did favor workers who accepted Cárdenas's political program.

In contrast to top-down processes of establishing citizenship through categorization, ordinary workers and peasants often defined citizenship based on horizontal associations. For many campesinos working in the Soconusco, the simple fact that they had labored in the region for several years qualified them for citizenship. They saw themselves as Mexican nationals because they developed relational ties through community, kinship, and work. These links to both people and places created a sense of belonging but conflicted with state-controlled characterizations of citizen. Claims to Mexican citizenship based on community and work relations weakened as economic and political pressures against laborers increased. Mexican campesinos (those who had obtained some form of government-sanctioned citizenship) had more legal rights and protections than those without such certification.

As pressures for land reform increased, community members began adopting official rhetoric that defined and excluded "Guatemalans." Mexican laborers rarely labeled Guatemalans as troublemakers, but they did protest about unfair competition for jobs. Even though unions and agrarian committees often included Guatemalan members in practice, union organizers continued to complain about Guatemalan campesinos who displaced Mexican workers.[45] Union members who worked for Alejandro Córdova protested that Córdova suspended Mexican workers because of economic downturns, replacing rank-and-file workers with Guatemalans. Instead of rehiring unionized workers as required by the collective contract, Córdova recruited Guatemalans and helped them enter Mexico illegally. Although unionized Mexican workers recognized Guatemalans' right to work "so that they could feed their families," they objected because Córdova violated his legal obligation to hire Mexicans first.[46] Workers protested against the planter, even though Guatemalan laborers got the jobs. The conflict on Córdova's finca highlights the increasing significance of nationality. Prior to the mid-1930s, planters commonly recruited laborers from both sides of the border. When the federal government implemented proworker policies, citizenship became a prerequisite that provided access to revolutionary benefits.

Planters, Agrarian Reform, and the Limits of Nationality

While rural laborers sought social, economic, and political rights as citizens, the national government could not necessarily protect campesinos from exploitation. Coffee growers claimed Mexican nationality, even though they often maintained cultural, social, and economic ties to Germany. Foreign-born *finqueros* constructed nationality both by meeting the state's desired characteristics and by creating relational networks that tied them to the planter community. For example, Tapachula's Chamber of Commerce included Mexican, Spanish, and German owners of both coffee and banana plantations in the Soconusco. As political events in Germany created tension for foreign-born members of the Chamber, the organization made a point of declaring that all of its members had their naturalization letters.[47] The linkages between foreign-born and Mexican coffee elites helped the former safeguard their economic and political interests. By aligning with Mexican landlords, the foreign-born coffee growers made it harder for the government and the peasants to claim that the planters represented foreign imperialistic interests that were contrary to the interests of the Mexican people.

Unofficial militias, or *guardias blancas*, contained campesino organizing efforts, illustrating limited state protection for impoverished rural citizens. Members of *guardias blancas* supported the landlords' efforts to prevent unionization and had free rein to attack "subversive" laborers. Work bosses extended their control over the agricultural laborers after the formal workday by becoming members of these militia groups.[48] By tolerating *guardias blancas*, agrarian officials effectively criminalized campesinos' unionizing efforts, even though legally, the Mexican constitution guaranteed workers the right to organize. Although the federal government formally opposed private militias, local acceptance of them obstructed peasant activism.

Planters also appealed either to the governor, to the regional military commander, or to the president directly to protect their property. Planters requested government support even though Cardenista policy allegedly protected campesino rights.[49] The effectiveness of landowners' petitions varied. Political alliances, economic conditions, and social conflicts influenced officials' choices about which citizens—elites or campesinos—deserved federal support. One landlord complained that local authorities did not act on his demand to remove invading campesinos from his finca. He appealed to Cárdenas, requesting federal army troops to clear the "troublemakers" from his land. When federal authorities took too long to respond, conservative Governor Grajales ordered the state militia to burn the campesinos' settlement on the finca.[50] In the end, landowners' ability to protect their interests by using local authorities or private militias against campesinos shows planters' power. It also illustrates the limits of nationality because the Mexican state did not equally protect the rights of rural workers against the elites. Even when campesinos and some government officials tried to implement labor and agrarian reform programs, alliances between planters and conservative authorities (both civil and military) gave growers access to force to discourage peasant claims.

Coffee growers willingly embraced citizenship rhetoric to undermine labor activism. By 1935, *finqueros* appropriated negative discourse about Guatemalans, effectively denouncing anyone who challenged planter authority as Guatemalan. Landlords identified workers who organized unions or petitioned for *ejidos* as Guatemalan and fired them.[51] Planters also delayed federal *ejido* grants to campesino communities by labeling prospective land recipients as Guatemalans, thus prompting lengthy government investigations to determine workers' nationality. For example, immigration officials deported men from the *ejido* Salvador Urbina, even though many could prove their Mexican citizenship. The campesinos argued that Finca San Vicente's owner arranged their deportation, preventing redistribution of finca land that agrarian officials granted to the *ejido*. The men's families were not deported, lending credibility to campesinos' claims that the men were Mexican and that local immigration authorities collaborated with the planters.[52] Another *finquero* adopted exaggerated antiforeign discourse when alleged Guatemalans invaded part of his finca. He argued that the campesinos targeted his land because "they know that I am Mexican and towards all of this country they have a savage racial hatred."[53] While his language was more extreme than most, he expressed the rising anti-Guatemalan sentiment implicitly sanctioned by the government. He also implied a link between the "racial" group of indigenous peoples and Guatemalan, as opposed to mestizo and Mexican.

Planters' anti-Guatemalan discourse coexisted with their continued recruitment of Guatemalan laborers for the fincas. Did this mean that nationality mattered little in the region? On the contrary, the fact that Mexican workers were able to petition for some rights from the federal government meant that Guatemalan laborers became even more attractive to growers because Mexican authorities provided few rights to foreigners. Landed elites cultivated strong paternalistic relationships with immigrant Guatemalans. In exchange for a compliant labor force, growers arranged for certificates of Mexican residency and even nationalized many workers.[54] Guatemalan workers often developed intense loyalty to the planters because of these actions. Enrique Braun, the owner of finca Santo Domingo, developed a close patron-client relationship with many Guatemalan workers on his finca. One former finca resident explained that during the early unionization campaign, workers divided over participation in the union. Many laborers felt that "Don Enrique" was a "very good man" and refused to join the organization. Guatemalan workers joined the union movement and claimed "Mexican" nationality only when it became clear that the government planned to expropriate the finca and distribute it among union members.[55] This ability to adopt externally defined characteristics of nationality became a key tool that campesinos used to challenge planter domination. However, the overall balance of power generally rested with *finqueros* because, ultimately, their rights as citizens trumped campesinos' rights as citizens.

1931–1941: Guatemalan Experiences of Nationalism

While Mexican campesinos received some recognition as citizens, in Guatemala, repressive authorities and planters minimized campesinos' rights to define Guatemalan nationality. Some Guatemalan officials inculcated nationality by teaching national characteristics to indigenous workers, particularly during the early years of President Jorge Ubico's regime. The central government expected villages to celebrate national festivals, including the anniversary of the Liberal Revolution of 1871. People gathered for official speeches, flag ceremonies, and singing the national anthem. Formal celebrations gave way to evening marimba concerts and dances.[56] These celebrations built on previous practices of national holidays. In 1921, the city of San Marcos described plans for celebrating the Liberal Revolution. In spite of concerns that the local roads might not be passable, the city planned public educational meetings, a ceremonial road opening, and a special lighting display.[57] Local celebrations sharply contrasted with daily practices of law enforcement that created a more punitive awareness of nationality.

Workers attended national celebrations, but communities lacked the sustained presence of federal reformers that reinforced positive images of the Mexican state. Audiences differed as well. In Soconusco, Cardenista officials often viewed campesinos as active participants in political theater, fostering perceptions of peasants as citizens. In San Marcos, Guatemala, local townspeople, military personnel, and some finca workers (those in overseer positions or higher) provided the audience—ordinary workers attended only occasionally. In fact, attendance at these celebrations was mandatory, even for off-duty soldiers. The military commander at Tacaná detained Sublieutenant Everardo Laparra López for not attending the local ceremony on President Ubico's birthday. Laparra López "escaped in his underwear" from his prison cell window. He fled to Mexico, filing a formal complaint against the commander. Authorities dismissed charges for missing the ceremony, but he was charged with escape and sentenced to a $Q50 fine. Forced celebrations and punishment undermined the nationalism by dictating unrealistic expectations for participation.

The hundred-year anniversary of leader Justo Rufino Barrios's birthday provoked a broader attempt to raise indigenous people's participation in national celebrations. Municipal presidents received small stipends from the federal government to offset the costs of a community commemoration. In the department of San Marcos, organizers of the anniversary celebration arranged a beauty contest among Mam villages. By juxtaposing the beauty pageant with the celebration of a national hero, regional officials hoped to link indigenous villages to national events. State authorities obligated all indigenous communities to participate in the pageant. Villagers had to "choose a girl from purely indigenous background, between 15–24 years old, pretty, and well-mannered. If the girl is ugly, the *alcaldes* will be fined." The rules continued: "The subcommittee [of the festival] must build houses, a Mam temple, a church, an ancient game with a dance room." This striking description links an imagined indigenous past to "modern" Guatemala—at a time where the dominant rhetoric favored improving "the indigenous race" through whitening, education, and structured labor. During the fiesta, the committee would choose the "most beautiful Indigena of the Sierra Madres." The girl (*muchacha* is continually used—not the more respectful *señorita*) would then spend the rest of the fiesta in the Mam temple. Committee members also planned a parade through the department capital of San Marcos. Ultimately, the festival would have a variety of other amusements, including performances of the "devil's trap," the dance of the conquest, followed by a community dance. Contestants' families received financial support to offset participation costs.[58] Blending indigenous activities with Justo Rufino Barrios's festival may be read as an attempt to acknowledge indigenous culture in Guatemala's history. By putting predominantly indigenous events on a major national holiday, the festival became a minimal attempt to incorporate the Mam into a broader national framework.

The festival's framework constituted only one part of its uniqueness. Local officials in San José Ojetenam chose sixteen-year-old Andrea Cifuentes, the daughter of a work boss on Finca Nueva Mundo, to represent the village. Her father initially agreed to Andrea's participation, but as the festival day grew near, he refused to allow her to attend. Instead, "his daughter fled to Mexico." In response, local police arrested Andrea's father and sentenced him to a $Q5 fine and five days of labor.[59] By punishing him, authorities asserted the Guatemalan government's power to control indigenous peoples. It also highlights resistance because the father refused to "display" his daughter to ladinos. Participating in national holidays became one way that workers in San Marcos experienced Guatemalan nationality. Officials briefly recognized indigenousness as Guatemalan, even though ladinos defined acceptable "Indian characteristics." Indigenous workers more commonly experienced Guatemalan nationality through coercive practices that defined indigenous citizens as laborers.

In spite of attempts to incorporate Mam campesinos into Guatemalan nationality, elites believed that indigenous peoples constituted a persistent threat to the nation. By 1935, campesinos experienced increasing repression because of the Ubico regime's concerns about indigenous rebellion. Local and regional officials patrolled the roads daily, looking for laborers without papers, smugglers, or any sign of social unrest. In San Marcos, police officers charged three men and a woman with hiding "bombs" because they "could try to commit some crime against social or political order." However, the judge ruled that villagers commonly used explosives of this sort in fiestas or for fishing. He commented that "the excessive zeal" of the agents did not prove that a crime existed.[60] The perception that workers were willing to commit crimes against the state fueled the decisions of the police and highlighted the race and class tensions that plagued Guatemala.

Local and regional Guatemalan officials also carefully watched events in Soconusco, Chiapas. They feared the radical influence of Cardenistas and interpreted local disturbances to Mexican influences, even if community problems caused unrest. For example, in 1937, the jefe politico of San Marcos made his annual inspection of the smaller villages in the department. When he arrived in Tacaná, roughly 800 Mam Indians had assembled in the main plaza. They complained that the local military commander unjustly harassed and imprisoned people, announcing that men had to join the cavalry but that he would exempt them for a small fee. The U.S. military attaché issued a report about the incident. "The Indians . . . claimed that the Vagrancy Law was being unjustly enforced and that Indians who had sufficient land under cultivation were being recruited into labor battalions by the local commander." The Indians became increasingly hostile when the commander attempted to dissolve the gathering and the jefe politico prevaricated. Ultimately, the official refused to "give appropriate consideration" to the Indians' complaints. Violence erupted on both sides. During the ensuing melee, Indians beat the military commander to death, but soldiers opened fire on the crowd. Twelve people were killed, and many more wounded. In the aftermath of the unrest, authorities arrested more than 200 Indians on charges of sedition. Several villagers fled to Mexico, yet local officials continued searching for them.

The U.S. military attaché reported that Guatemalan authorities feared that Mexican revolutionary ideals helped spark the unrest. In Tacaná, people worked coffee plantations in both Mexico and Guatemala. However, in a rather amazing conclusion, the attaché reported that the uprising "was not politically significant." The attaché blamed the local commander and the jefe politico of San Marcos for showing "a lack on knowledge of Indian psychology and a firm and proper handling of the situation."[61] The subtext of the attaché's argument concluded that had the officials acted forcefully from the beginning of the confrontation, the villagers would have submitted to authority. The attaché's conclusions point to his personal biases that overlooked worker activism. The document clearly points to strong connections between labor activism in Mexico and unrest in Guatemala. Ideas and strategies for rural organizing moved through migrant communities as workers returned from Soconusco. Planters and government officials alike worried about the spread of agrarian radicalism across the border. The Ubico government usually imprisoned Guatemalans deported by the Mexican government. However, in August 1934, orders from Guatemala City stipulated that "all individuals deported from Mexico [for being agrarian activists], must be immediately set free, and no one should obstruct the person's reintegration [into Mexico.]"[62] Agrarian radicalism in Mexico posed a significant threat to labor discipline on Guatemalan fincas, and Guatemalan officials quickly repressed expressions of worker unrest.[63] The spread of agrarian radicalism from Mexico to Guatemala underscores the impact of migration in sharing new ideologies. In the transnational social field of the Sierra Madres, practicing Mexican citizenship by exercising legal rights to organize workers and petition for land extended similar expectations of citizenship into Guatemalan indigenous communities.

Major unrest in villages caused rumors of political intrigue, but municipal reports suggest that keeping workers on fincas remained the primary challenge in San Marcos. *Finqueros* had trusted employees search for fugitive workers to force compliance with their labor contracts. One Guatemalan day laborer left work on Finca El Porvenir and crossed into Mexico. He worked for a month in Mexico before returning home. The landlord's overseer found the worker and alerted customs authorities because he brought back a pair of pants from his stay in Mexico. The laborer served twenty-three days in prison—twenty as his sentence for violating his contract and smuggling, and three days extra of public labor to cover the costs of food while he was in jail. In the documents, close monitoring of workers' labor obligations is much more common than village protests or uprisings. By controlling the daily lives of indigenous campesinos, *finqueros* and local authorities coerced Guatemalan laborers to work, reinforcing the idea that for indigenous Guatemalans, citizenship meant little more than mandatory labor obligations.

Court cases demonstrate rural Guatemalans' refusal to accept elite expectations of indigenous citizenship. Indigenous laborers continued smuggling, destroying or altering documents that recorded labor contracts, and overtly defying authority. For the state of San Marcos, the number of crimes against social order remained steady from 1934 to 1941 (between 10 and 15 cases per year), as did the number of charges for falsifying documents—altering or destroying *cédulas*—(between 7 and 10 cases per year). The number of smuggling cases increased slightly (between roughly 190 and 245 cases per year). Vagrancy and migration violations also grew marginally (from 6 in 1935 to 22 in 1941).[64] The persistence of "criminal behavior" suggests that the campesinos in San Marcos did not accept the legal codes about the informal economy. More important, the continuance of migration and vagrancy crimes highlights the illegitimacy of the labor system.

Conclusion

With the deteriorating economic situation in coffee (1938–1940), the benefits of the Mexican Revolution became increasingly limited because of a lack of resources. To adjust to the economic decline, Mexican officials intensified their attempts to exclude Guatemalans from reforms designed to benefit Mexicans. As agrarian petitions circulated through coffee fincas in the late 1930s and early 1940s, competition for land made rhetoric about the inclusion of Guatemalans scarce. In March 1939, the Cárdenas government instituted a major agrarian reform in Cacahoatán and Unión Juárez, two major coffee-producing municipalities. Officials divided more than 8,000 hectares among 1,636 campesinos. About half of the land was from Enrique Braun, a Mexican-German and supposedly one of the few planters who treated his workers well.[65] However, many campesinos denounced the agrarian reform. Echoing anti-Guatemalan rhetoric, some campesino organizations claimed "Mexicans" lost land to "Guatemalans," asserting that "foreigners" primarily benefited from land redistribution.[66] Tensions over economic resources strengthened the significance of state-dominated categorical identifications of nationality. The problems of an uncontrolled border meant the state lacked the ability to distribute resources to those it deemed acceptable.[67] Only those who officially proved their Mexican citizenship qualified for revolutionary benefits, and ordinary campesinos began adopting these classifications to improve their access to socioeconomic reforms.

As categorical identification of nationality strengthened, relational identification based on shared labor and living conditions weakened in some communities. In cohesive villages, concerns about nationality remained minimal. However, in communities divided by personal factionalism and limited resources, people used nationality as a tool to eliminate perceived economic competitors. Additionally, cultural attitudes toward indigenous groups influenced perceptions of who qualified for citizenship. Most people in Soconusco *ejidos* adopted mestizo cultural practices. They spoke Spanish and wore "modern" pants and skirts (as opposed to handmade indigenous clothing). Those who followed distinct cultural practices of religion, dress, and language, such as Mam Indians who became Jehovah's Witnesses or K'iche' speakers did not fit neatly into official definitions of Mexican citizens. They faced isolation or outright exclusion by Mexican authorities. By 1951, economist Moises T. de la Peña declared that the few indigenous people who remained in the Pacific zone (Soconusco) were Guatemalan immigrants.[68] The emphasis on categorical definitions of citizenship may also reflect limitations of available sources. Complaints about *ejido* grants or worker conflicts went to government officials, and to increase their effectiveness, campesinos adopted rhetoric used by authorities.

In Mexico, nationality incorporated both categorical and relational definitions of citizenship. Campesinos in Soconusco initially subverted official criteria for citizenship. Instead, inclusion into groups depended on relationships formed at work, in villages, and through networks of family and friends. In contrast, workers on the Guatemalan side of the border experienced nationality primarily through legal coercion and the power of the state. Following a trend that began in the late 1930s, "Mexican" campesinos in Soconusco increasingly have used categorical identification to distinguish themselves from "Guatemalans." This pattern has only strengthened over the past sixty years. Current dominant discourse in Soconusco describes Guatemalans as dirty, lazy, and a threat to Mexican laborers. This echoes rhetoric along the Mexican-U.S. border that labels Mexicans as dirty, lazy, and a threat to U.S. workers. Along the coffee-growing region of the Sierra Madre, campesinos adopted categorical definitions of nationality, which enabled government authorities to economically and politically control laborers. Yet laborers have continually challenged narrow definitions of nationality, frequently through horizontal community relationships in an attempt to create more inclusive meanings of citizenship that protect workers' rights.

NOTES

1. The author would like to thank John French, Leon Fink, and Juan Mora-Torres for their helpful comments and suggestions.
2. Crime: Contraband against Domingo López, José López, Simón Chávez, et al., December 14, 1935, Archivo General de Tribunales, San Marcos, Ramo Criminal, Juzgado de la 1a. Instancia, Indice Juicios (hereafter cited as AGCA/AGT-SM-RC), legajo 8F, expediente: 15.
3. Jesse Hoffnung-Garskof, *A Tale of Two Cities: Santo Domingo and New York after 1950* (Princeton, NJ: Princeton University Press, 2008), xv–xvii.
4. Rogers Brubaker and Frederick Cooper, "Beyond 'Identity,'" *Theory and Society* 29, no. 1 (February 2000): 14–17.
5. Alan Knight, "Cardensimo: Juggernaut or Jalopy," *Journal of Latin American Studies* 21, no. 1 (1994): 73–107; Gil Joseph et al., *Everyday Forms of State Formation: Revolution and the Negotiation of Rule in Modern Mexico* (Durham: Duke University Press, 1994).
6. Steven Lewis, *Ambivalent Revolution: Forging State and Nation in Chiapas, 1910–1945* (Albuquerque: University of New Mexico Press, 2005); Rosalva Aída Hernández Castillo, *Histories and Stories from Chiapas: Border Identities in Southern Mexico* (Austin: University of Texas Press, 2001).
7. G. K. Donald, Chargé d'Affaires, to U.S. Secretary of State, Guatemala, August 26, 1932, United States National Archives and Records Administration (hereafter cited as NARA) RG 59, 712.145/1.
8. *Memo: Registration of Guatemalan Citizens Resident in the United States of Mexico*, G. K. Donald, Chargé d'Affaires, to U.S. Secretary of State, Guatemala, August 26, 1932, NARA, RG 59, 712.145/1.
9. *Memo: Carrying on of Small Commerce along Frontier Regions*, G. K. Donald, Chargé d'Affaires, to U.S. Secretary of State, Guatemala, August 26, 1932, NARA RG 59, 712.145/1.
10. *Memo: Registration of Guatemalan Citizens Resident in the United States of Mexico*, G. K. Donald, Chargé d'Affaires, to U.S. Secretary of State, Guatemala, August 26, 1932, NARA, RG 59, 712.145/1.
11. G. K. Donald, Chargé d'Affaires, to U.S. Secretary of State, Guatemala, August 26, 1932, NARA, RG 59, 712.145/1.
12. "Guatemalan Invasion of Chiapas," *La Prensa*, August 4, 1932, forwarded by G. K. Donald, Chargé d'Affaires, to U.S. Secretary of State, Guatemala, August 26, 1932, NARA, RG 59, 712.145/1.
13. G. K. Donald, Chargé d'Affaires, to U.S. Secretary of State, Guatemala, August 26, 1932, NARA, RG 59, 712.145/1.

14. *Minutes of Meeting #3 between Mexico and Guatemala*, August 24, 1932, 4–5; G. K. Donald, Chargé d'Affaires, Guatemala, NARA, RG 59, 712.145/2.
15. Ibid.
16. "Summary of Meeting and Recommendations," August 26, 1932, 3, G. K. Donald, Chargé d'Affaires, Guatemala, NARA RG 59, 712.145/2.
17. *Antecedentes Históricos*, Sección Mexicana de la Comisión Internacional de Límites y Aguas México-Guatemala, Secretaría de Relaciones Exteriores, Mexico, available at http://www.sre.gob.mx/cilasur/; Moisés de la Peña, *Chiapas Económico*, vol. 2 (Tuxtla Gutiérrez, Chiapas: Gobierno del Estado, Departamento de Prensa y Turismo, 1951), 437; and Germán Martínez Velasco, *Plantaciones, trabajo guatemalteco y política migratoria en la Frontera Sur de México* (Tuxtla Gutiérrez: Gobierno del Estado de Chiapas, 1994), 31–34.
18. Jacobo Galván, interview with author, Ejido El Eden, Chiapas, Mexico, October 5, 1997; Juan Velásquez, interview with author, Ejido El Eden, Chiapas, Mexico, October 5, 1997; Felipe Robledo López, interview with author, Ejido Santo Domingo, Chiapas, Mexico, August 4, 1997.
19. David McCreery, *Rural Guatemala, 1760–1940* (Stanford: Stanford University Press, 1994), 286, 297.
20. Cindy Forster, *The Time of Freedom: Campesino Workers in Guatemala's October Revolution* (Pittsburgh: University of Pittsburgh Press, 2001), 29–31.
21. Crime: Contraband against Francisca López, 30 Julio 1932, AGT-SM-RC, Legajo 5D, expediente 7; second smuggling case against Manuel Lux, December 23, 1932, AGT-SM-RC, legajo 5D, expediente 14.
22. Crime: Contraband against Crisanto Hernández, December 10, 1935, AGCA/AGT-SM-RC, legajo 8F, expediente: s/n.
23. *Memo: Administration of Justice in Frontier Regions*, G. K. Donald, Chargé d'Affaires, to U.S. Secretary of State, Guatemala, August 26, 1932, NARA, RG 59, 712.145/1.
24. Crime: Violation of Migration Law against Manuel Pérez and Trancito García, November 16, 1935, AGCA/AGT-SM-RC, año 1935, Legajo 8K, expediente 13.
25. McCreery, *Rural Guatemala*, 202–3.
26. Forster, *The Time of Freedom*, 14–15; McCreery, *Rural Guatemala*, 300–307; Sarah Washbrook, "Enganche and Exports in Chiapas, Mexico: A Comparison of Plantation Labour in the Districts of Soconusco and Palenque, 1876–1911," *Journal of Latin American Studies* 39 (2007): 797–825.
27. McCreery, *Rural Guatemala*, 317–20.
28. Informe Administrativo, 31 Marzo 1934, for the towns of San Pablo, San Marcos, Malacatán, and Nuevo Progreso. AGCA/Archivo de la Secretaría de Gobernación y Justicia (hereafter cited as AGCA/ASGJ), Signatura B, Legajo 29949.
29. Friederike Baumann, "Terratenientes, campesinos y la expansión de la agricultura capitalista en Chiapas, 1896–1916," *Mesoamerica* 4 (1983); Steven Lewis, *Ambivalent Revolution*.

30. Crime: Illegal Detention against Fortino López, et al., April 10, 1935, AGCA/AGT-SM-RC, año 1935, Legajo 8C, expediente 10.
31. Crime: Vagrancy against Fulgencio Juárez, Francisco Tomás, et al., October 7, 1934, AGCA/AGT-SM-RC, año 1934, Legajo 7E, expediente 11; Washbrook, "Enganche and Exports in Chiapas, Mexico," 815–19.
32. Crime: Vagrancy against Florencio Gómez López, October 27, 1934, AGCA/AGT-SM-RC, año 1934, Legajo 7D, expediente 18.
33. Comité de Festejos to Jefe Politico of San Marcos, May 23, 1921, AGCA/ASGJ, Signatura B, Legajo 29567, Expedientes del Departamento de San Marcos, Correspondencia, unnumbered letter.
34. A. Almurga P., for Isabel Pérez and Marcelo López, to Juzgado Municipal de Paz, Tajamulco, July 27, 1934. AGCA/ASGJ, Signatura B, Legajo 29949, Expedientes San Marcos, Correspondencia.
35. Antonio García de León, *Resistencia y utopía: Memorial de agravios y crónica de revueltas y profecías acaecidas en la provincia de Chiapas durante los últimos quinientos años de su historia*, tomos I & II (México, D.F.: Ediciones Era, 1985), 194–200; Daniela Spenser, 'Economía y movimiento laboral en las fincas cafetaleras de Soconusco', in Daniela Spenser, et. al., (eds.) *Los empresarios alemanes, el tercer reich y la oposición de derecha a Cárdenas*, tomo I (México, D.F: CIESAS, 1988). 257–58; Alicia Hernández Chávez, *La mecánica Cardenista*, (Mexico, D.F.: Colegio de Mexico, 1979), 181–84.
36. María Eugenia Reyes Ramos, *El reparto de tierras y la política agraria en Chiapas, 1914–1988*, (Mexico, D.F.: UNAM), 59–61.
37. "Informe," Fernando G. Cortés, Partido Comunista Mexicana, Tapachula, June 7, 1938, AGN-LC, 404.1/343; Rosa Matúz de Rodríguez, interview with author, Tapachula, October 6, 1997; Jacobo Gálvez, interview with author, Ejido El Edén, August 12, 1997.
38. Memorandum, Chief of the Agrarian Department, to Manuel Ávila Camacho, Mexico, D.F., January 19, 1943, AGN-MAC 110.1/9.
39. Ibid.
40. Hernández Castillo, *Histories and Stories*, 18–41. Schoolteachers continued to stress assimilation through the early 1940s. Federal guidelines directed schoolteachers to encourage men to wear pants and women to wear skirts, instead of traditional clothing. "Plan General de Trabajo que desarrollará la Dirección de Educación Federal del Estado de Chiapas, durante el año escolar de 1935," AHSEP, Departamento de Escuelas Rurales, Dirección de Educación Federal, 236/10.
41. José Romero to Secretary of the Interior, Colonia Salvador Urbina, February 26, 1934, AGN-DGG, caja 5, 2.382(5)57.
42. "Memorandum," Federal Labor Office, #15 to Chief of the Labor Department, Tapachula, June 7, 1938, AGN-DAT, 218/11.
43. Francisco Aguilar M., to Federal Labor Inspector, Tapachula, March 25, 1938, AGN-DAT, 227/13.

44. Edmundo Nieto to President of the Comisión Agraria Mixta, Finca El Retiro, July 8, 1940, Tuxtla Gutiérrez, SEDA, Expediente: El Retiro, #1099.
45. Alejandro C. Vázquez, Sindicato de Trabajadores del Campo, Num. 20 to President Cárdenas, Finca Santo Domingo, July 25, 1936, AGN-DGG, caja 21A, 4; Angel Franco, Federación General de Trabajadores to President Cárdenas, Mexico, D.F., November 16, 1935, AGN-DGG, caja 42, 2.384.2(5)5699.
46. Francisco López to President Cárdenas, Tapachula, n/d, 1940, AGN-DGG, caja 12A, 11.
47. Juan Huthoff, Cámara Nacional de Comercio e Industria, "Circular #1," Tapachula, January 1941, AGN-DGG 2/331.9(5)36477.
48. Efraín Hernández to President Cárdenas, Colonia Lázaro Cárdenas, April 1, 1938, AGN-DGG caja 6, 2.382(5)16030, Tomo I; attacks on the houses Piedad Pagola to President Cárdenas, November 9, 1938, AGN-DGG caja 5, 2.382(5)16030, Tomo I.
49. H. J. Dike, Coapa Development Company to President Cárdenas, Finca Coapa, June 1, 1937, AGN-LC 404.1/7193.
50. Juan Pohlenz to President Cárdenas, Huixtla, April 24, 1934, AGN-DGG caja 5, 2.382(5)56.
51. Angelino Olivara, SUTICS Num. 20 to President Cárdenas, Finca Argentina, April 23, 1940, AGN-DGG, caja 12A, 54.
52. José Romero to Secretary of the Interior, Colonia Salvador Urbina, February 26, 1934, AGN-DGG, caja 5, 2.382(5)57.
53. Rafael Mota to President Cárdenas, Tapachula, March 28, 1938, AGN-DGG, caja 8, 43.
54. Spenser, "Economía y movimiento laboral," 269–72; Thomas Benjamin, *A Rich Land, A Poor People: Politics and Society in Modern Chiapas* (Albuquerque: University of New Mexico Press, 1989), 205.
55. Rosa Matúz de Rodríguez, interview with the author, Tapachula, Chiapas, October 6, 1997.
56. "Programa de los festejos para celebrar el LXVII aniversario de la revolución liberal del año 1871." Examples of these programs from San Rafael Pié de la Cuesta, Ayutla, Malacatán, June 30, 1934. AGCA/ASGJ, Signatura B, Legajo 29949, Correspondencia.
57. Comité de Festejos to Jefe Politico of San Marcos, May 23, 1921, AGCA/ASGJ, Signatura B, Legajo 29567, Expedientes del Departamento de San Marcos, Correspondencia, unnumbered letter.
58. Crime: Abuse of Authority, San José Ojetenam, AGCA/AGT-SM-RC, año 1935, Legajo 8F, expediente s/n.
59. Ibid.
60. Crime: Macario Cifuentes possessed bombs, AGCA/AGT-SM-RC, año 1935, Legajo 8C, expediente 9.
61. Walter H. McKinney, Chargé d'Affaires ad interim, to U.S. Secretary of State, April 14, 1937, NARA, RG 59, 814.00 Revolutions/91; and Report of Military

Attaché, Captain Jerome E. McGuire, USMC, March 18, 1937, NARA, RG 59, 814.00/90.
62. Jefe de Migración, Tapachula to Subsecretary of the Interior, August, 1934, as quoted in Martínez Velasco, *Plantaciones, trabajo guatemalteco y polírica migratoria*, 39–41; Forster, *The Time of Freedom*, 147.
63. Hoffnung-Garskof, *A Tale of Two Cities*, xv–xvii.
64. I calculated these numbers by counting the types of charges in the indices for Ramo Criminal, AGCA.
65. Francisco Zetina, Partido Comunista Mexicana, to Manuel Ávila Camacho, Tapachula, February 12, 1943, AGN-MAC 110.1/9. Braun's fincas received the brunt of the reform—more than half of the 8,000 hectares (4,957 ha.) came from Enrique Braun.
66. Liga de Comunidades Agrarias y Sindicatos Campesinos de Chiapas, *Resolución y antecedentes del problema agraria* (Tuxtla Gutiérrez, 1942), 13.
67. Ibid., 11–13, 16. "The borders are not even precisely defined, there are breaks in the border, and because of the exuberant vegetation, it is not possible to determine the dividing line between the two countries."
68. Hernández Castillo, *Histories and Stories*; de la Peña, *Chiapas Economico*, 290–92.

IV INTERNATIONAL FEMINISM AND REPRODUCTIVE LABOR

INTRODUCTION

Premilla Nadasen

Since the 1980s, scholarship on social reproduction and feminism has called into question some basic assumptions that have guided the field of labor history. Much of this literature has looked at women's paid and unpaid domestic labor—mothering, household maintenance, and care work—and the way this labor contributes to the perpetuation of capitalism. Historically, social reproduction has not been recognized as "real work" because of its racialized and gendered nature and because so much of it occurs in the home. Feminist scholars have persuasively argued that notions of work and labor need to be broadened to encompass both paid and unpaid social reproduction.

While reproductive labor might seem to fall within the ostensibly private realm of the home, in reality, it has been informed by—and informs—both economic transformations and state and international policy.[1] Indeed, the very notion of the home as an utterly "private" space is a product of the emergence of industrial capitalism in the nineteenth century. And since the beginning of the twentieth century, with the rise of the modern welfare state, government responsibility for aspects of social reproduction has increased with the implementation of policies such as social security for the elderly, the building of public hospitals, and compulsory education for children. Feminist scholars of the welfare state have examined how women's reproductive labor became the basis for women's inclusion in the welfare system.[2] In the United States, men benefited from the welfare state as full-time wage earners, but women were incorporated as dependents—as widows or as single mothers without a breadwinner in the family. State social policy, in most cases, reinforced the male breadwinner–female homemaker model and the gendered division of labor. Research on the welfare state has exposed the false binaries between public and private, state and family.

The work of social reproduction, or "care work," is also directly tied to capitalist production. Industrial capitalism spawned a consumer culture that changed the nature of social reproduction. Consumption for the purposes of household maintenance takes the form of everything from kitchen gadgets and cleaning appliances—such as potato peelers and washing machines—to canned goods and bar soap. While in some ways these products have eased the burden of social reproduction, they have also raised standards for parenting and cleanliness, redefining the responsibilities of women. So, mothers today spend less time churning butter and more time shuttling children to baseball practice.

The flip side of the consumer economy—and another example of the overlap between production and social reproduction—is how this labor is commodified and who is doing the work. Aspects of care work have a long history of commodification, whether this involved sending out clothing to be washed or hiring wet nurses. The commodification of care work forces us to examine the home as workplace and to consider the labor that takes place within it.[3] But, in addition, Pierrette Hondagneu-Sotelo has argued that the politics of social reproduction must take into account not only the paid and unpaid labor of women in the household but also the wages and working conditions of service-sector employees such as agricultural workers who produce prewashed packaged green salad. While immigrant workers constitute a large number of service workers, women of color are disproportionately represented in this labor sector. As Evelyn Nakano Glenn has argued, many women of color have moved "from servitude to service work." And they tend to be concentrated in the menial and manual tasks of social reproduction.[4] Women's service-sector work demonstrates that women are engaged in care work beyond the confines of their own homes, in hospitals, restaurants, nursing homes, and day care centers.

The general decline in manufacturing and increase in service-sector employment have moved women's labor from the margins to the center of labor organizing.[5] Over the past two decades, the growth of union membership has been located not in traditional manufacturing sectors, but in the service industries. Groups such as Service Employees International Union, UNITE-HERE, and neighborhood worker centers are establishing new patterns and methods of labor organization. They have integrated an analysis of race and gender, reached out to intermittent and part-time employees, and taken into account that many workers are undocumented and change employers frequently. As Eileen Boris and Jennifer Klein have demonstrated with their work on home health care aides, negotiating sometimes takes place with state agencies rather than one's immediate employer. In another example, the workers' centers of the 1990s modeled a kind of labor organizing centered in the community rather than the shop floor. In many cases, grassroots mobilization prompted innovative strategies for change.

Perhaps more than other occupational arenas, the work of social reproduction exposes the fault lines of race, class, and nation. As the chapters in this part demonstrate, these fault lines are starkly reflected in the debates about international feminism. Through their discussions of the role of labor feminists in International Labor Organization (ILO) deliberations about mandatory maternity leave and the competing views on domestic labor that characterized the International Women's Year (IWY) conference in Mexico City in 1975, Eileen Boris and Jocelyn Olcott contribute to scholarship on social reproduction and international feminism. These chapters illuminate the contestation about the meanings of maternity leave and how women's domestic labor can best be alleviated among feminists of differing class, race, and national backgrounds.

Like so many discussions of feminism today, the international gatherings—whether sponsored by the United Nations' Commission on the Status of Women or the International Labor Organization—reveal that there is no single definition of feminism or interpretation of social reproduction. There are, in fact, multiple voices and streams of feminist activity that may or may not find common ground. The phrase "international feminism" is sometimes reserved for early-twentieth-century gatherings of Western feminists—which Leila Rupp calls the international first wave—while the phrase "transnational feminism" refers to more recent grassroots organizing efforts by non-Western women.[6] But as Olcott and Boris demonstrate, gatherings that may fall under the rubric of "international feminism" grappled with the politics of race and class. Power shaped the terms upon which women came together in the international arena. Often dominated by Western feminists, the international gatherings raised the question of how to decenter the West in an international context.

The international feminist gatherings exposed the concerns and conflicting interests of women of different racial, class, linguistic, cultural, and national backgrounds. Fundamentally, they asked: Who defines women's interests? For First World feminists, legal equality, wage equity, and educational and professional opportunities were central issues. In contrast, non-Western women focused on development and economic empowerment. They could not separate women's equality from the struggle against colonialism, neocolonialism, and Western intervention. For these feminists, women's liberation involved challenging neocolonial control wielded by powerful international institutions such as the International Monetary Fund (IMF) and the World Bank, which they believed controlled their national governments. Forging a full-fledged international feminist alliance with an international feminist struggle, particularly one dominated by U.S. feminists, seemed to them to contravene their broader campaign for self-determination. This tension between rights and development framed much of the discussion in transnational feminist gatherings. But as Olcott demonstrates in her chapter, divisions and differences also informed interactions among women within national contexts. Race, class, and culture—as much as national origin—shaped women's understandings of feminism. Nevertheless, Latin American women, like their U.S. and Canadian counterparts, participated and engaged with other feminists from around the world. The outcome of these meetings was dissension, disagreement, and sometimes antagonism. Despite the differences, all these women were committed to pursuing an agenda for women's empowerment; as they affirmed at the 1995 Beijing Conference, women's rights are human rights.

Perhaps the strength of international feminism was not in establishing an elusive, abstract unity, but in fostering a dialogue about women's issues that centered on economic empowerment, reproduction, and gender. By asking whether it was possible to create a unified agenda for international feminism, women activists established feminism as a cultural construct and laid bare the contested views of the meaning of reproductive labor. By coming together around the issue of gender and reproduction, feminists demonstrated how the politics of gender transcended the nation-state and also how class, national identity, culture, and ethnicity profoundly complicated understandings of gender.

With the emergence of a neoliberal, globalized economy, the issues of feminism, reproductive labor, and transnationalism have become even more pressing. The move away from Keynesian economics, the dismantling of welfare states, a decline in well-paying manufacturing jobs with benefits and pensions, and the imposition of free-market policies on Third World countries through the mandates of the IMF and the World Bank have led to global shifts in the nature of women's reproductive labor along class lines. Kate Bezanson argues that social reproduction is the primary site of contestation in the neoliberal era.[7] Middle-class women with economic resources—in both more developed and less developed countries—are contributing more household income and have turned to the expanding service sector and to private household workers to fill the "care gap," as Arlie Hochschild calls it. Globally, there has been a greater reliance on poor women's productive and reproductive labor in the global marketplace, leading to what Rhacel Parrenas has called an international division of reproductive labor.

Poor women from less developed countries have taken wage employment at a much higher rate, often migrating great distances in search of such labor. While poor immigrant women have filled the growing demand for care and service workers among the middle class, their own social reproductive needs are often left unfulfilled. The "crisis" in child slavery and child labor, the booming transnational adoption market, and the increasing numbers of children in foster care all indicate how poor women are finding it harder to care for their own children.

The decline of the welfare state, which defined women as mothers; the increase in women's employment rate; and the expansion of the commodification of care work will undoubtedly redirect international feminism. While the tension between "rights" and "development" has long structured debates among international feminists, perhaps the recent economic trends will fuse these two concerns by establishing an agenda of "women's labor rights" that takes into account women's role in the workforce as well as the demands of social reproduction. Indeed, women workers who are organizing as domestic workers, informal workers, and service-sector workers are redefining not only feminism but also the landscape of the labor movement.

NOTES

1. Barbara Laslett and Johanna Brenner, "Gender and Social Reproduction: Historical Perspectives," *American Review of Sociology* 15 (1989): 381–404.
2. Mimi Abramovitz, *Regulating the Lives of Women: Social Welfare Policy from Colonial Times to the Present* (Boston: South End Press, 1988); Gwendolyn Mink, *The Wages of Motherhood: Inequality in the Welfare State, 1917–1942* (Ithaca, NY: Cornell University Press, 1996).
3. Eileen Boris and Cynthia Daniels, *Homework: Historical and Contemporary Perspectives on Paid Labor at Home* (Urbana: University of Illinois Press, 1989).
4. Mignon Duffy, "Reproducing Labor Inequalities: Challenges for Feminists Conceptualizing Care at the Intersections of Gender, Class, and Race," *Gender and Society* 19, no. 1 (2005): 66–82.
5. Dorothy Sue Cobble, *The Other Women's Movement: Workplace Justice and Social Rights in Modern America* (Princeton, NJ: Princeton University Press, 2004); Karen Sacks, *Caring by the Hour: Women, Work, and Organizing at Duke Medical Center* (Urbana: University of Illinois Press, 1987).
6. Ellen Carol Dubois, "Circling the Globe: International Feminism Reconsidered, 1920–1975," *Women's Studies International Forum* 32, no. 1 (2009): 1–3.
7. Kate Bezanson, ed., *Gender, the State and Social Reproduction: Household Insecurity in Neo-Liberal Times* (Toronto, ON: University of Toronto Press, 2006).

FURTHER READING

Abramovitz, Mimi. *Regulating the Lives of Women: Social Welfare Policy from Colonial Times to the Present*. Boston: South End Press, 1988.
Bakan, Abigail and Daiva Stasiulis. *Negotiating Citizenship: Migrant Women in Canada and the Global System*. Toronto: University of Toronto Press, 2005.
Bakan, Abigail and Daiva Stasiulis. *Not One of the Family: Foreign Domestic Workers in Canada*. Toronto: University of Toronto Press, 1997.
Baillargeon, Denyse, *Making Do: Women, Family, and Home in Montreal during the Great Depression*. Waterloo, ON: Wilfrid Laurier University Press, 1999.
Bezanson, Kate, ed. *Gender, the State and Social Reproduction: Household Insecurity in Neo-Liberal Times*. Toronto: University of Toronto Press, 2006.
Boris, Eileen, and Cynthia Daniels. *Homework: Historical and Contemporary Perspectives on Paid Labor at Home*. Urbana: University of Illinois Press, 1989.
Boris, Eileen, and Jennifer Klein. *Caring for America: How Home Health Workers Became the New Face of Labor*. New York: Oxford University Press, forthcoming.

Chaney, Elsa, and Mary Garcia Castro, eds. *Muchachas No More, Household Workers in Latin American and the Caribbean*. Philadelphia: Temple University Press, 1989.

Cobble, Dorothy Sue. *The Other Women's Movement: Workplace Justice and Social Rights in Modern America*. Princeton, NJ: Princeton University Press, 2004.

Dickinson, James, ed. *Family, Economy, and State: The Social Reproduction Process under Capitalism*. Toronto: Garamond, 1986.

Dubois, Ellen Carol. "Circling the Globe: International Feminism Reconsidered, 1920–1975." *Women's Studies International Forum* 32, no. 1 (2009): 1–3.

Duffy, Mignon. "Reproducing Labor Inequalities: Challenges for Feminists Conceptualizing Care at the Intersections of Gender, Class, and Race." *Gender and Society* 19, no. 1 (2005): 66–82.

Enloe, Cynthia. *Bananas, Beaches and Bases: Making Feminist Sense of International Politics*. Berkeley: University of California Press, 2001.

Epstein, Alexandra. "International Feminism and Empire-Building between the Wars: The Case of Viola Smith." *Women's History Review* 17, no. 5 (2008): 699–719.

Fine, Janice. *Worker Centers: Organizing Communities at the Edge of the Dream*. Ithaca, NY: Cornell University Press, 2006.

Francois, Marie Eileen. "The Products of Consumption: Housework in Latin American Political Economies and Cultures." *History Compass* 6, no. 1 (2008): 207–242.

French, John, and Daniel James. *The Gendered Worlds of Latin American Women Workers: From Household and Factory to the Union Hall and Ballot Box*. Durham, NC: Duke University Press, 1997.

Glenn, Evelyn Nakano. "From Servitude to Service Work: Historical Continuities in the Racial Division of Women's Work." *Signs* 18, no. 1 (1992): 1–43.

Gordon, Jennifer. *Suburban Sweatshops: The Fight for Immigrant Rights*. Cambridge: Harvard University Press, 2005.

Hochschild, Arlie Russell. *The Commercialization of Intimate Life: Notes from Home and Work*. Berkeley: University of California Press. 2003.

Hochschild, Arlie Russell, and Barbara Ehrenreich, eds. *Global Woman: Nannies, Maids and Sex Workers in the New Economy*. New York: Metropolitan Books, 2004.

Hondagneu-Sotelo, Pierrette. "International Division of Caring and Cleaning Work," in *Care Work: Gender, Class, and the Welfare State*, ed. Madonna Harrington Meyer. NY: Routledge, 2000: 49–162.

Hondagneu-Sotelo, Pierrette. *Domestica: Immigrant Workers Cleaning and Caring in the Shadows of Influence*. Berkeley: University of California Press, 2001.

Hutchison, Elizabeth Quay *Many Zitas: The Young Catholic Worker and Household Workers in Cold War Chile*. Labor 4, no. 4 (2009): 67–94.

Jelin, Elizabeth. *Family, Household and Gender Relations in Latin America*. London and New York: Kegan Paul International, in association with UNESCO, 1991.

Laslett, Barbara, and Johanna Brenner. "Gender and Social Reproduction: Historical Perspectives." *American Review of Sociology* 15 (1989): 381–404.

Luxton, Meg. *More Than a Labor of Love: Three Generations of Women's Work in the Home*. Toronto, ON: Women's Educational Press, 1980.

Luxton, Meg, and Harriet Rosenberg, eds. *Through the Kitchen Window: The Politics of Home and Family*. Toronto, ON: Garamond, 1986.

Milkman, Ruth. *L.A. Story: Immigrant Workers and the Future of the U.S. Labor Movement*. New York: Russell Sage, 2006.

Mink, Gwendolyn. *The Wages of Motherhood: Inequality in the Welfare State, 1917–1942*. Ithaca, NY: Cornell University Press, 1996.

Moya, Jose. "Domestic Service in Global Perspective: Gender, Migration, and Ethnic Niches." *Journal of Ethnic Migration Studies* 33, no. 4 (2007): 559–579.

Nadasen, Premilla. "Sista' Friends and Other Allies: Domestic Workers United and Coalition Politics" in *New Social Movements in the African Diaspora: Challenging Global Apartheid*, ed. Leith Mulllings. New York: Palgrave Macmillan, 2009: 285–298.

Nash, June C., and Helen Icken Safa, eds. *Sex and Class in Latin America: Women's Perspectives on Politics, Economics, and the Family in the Third World*. Brooklyn, NY: J. F. Bergin, 1980.

Nash, June C., and Helen Icken Safa, eds. *Women and Change in Latin America*. South Hadley, MA: Bergin and Garvey, 1986.

Olcott, Jocelyn. Revolutionary Women in Postrevolutionary Mexico. Durham, NC: Duke University Press, 2005.

Parrenas, Rhacel. *Servants of Globalization: Women, Migration and Domestic Work*. Palo Alto, CA: Stanford University Press, 2001.

Porter, Ann. *Gendered States: Women, Unemployment Insurance, and the Political Economy of the Welfare State in Canada, 1945–1977*. Toronto, ON: University of Toronto Press, 2003.

Repak, Terry A. *Waiting on Washington: Central American Workers in the Nation's Capital*. Philadelphia: Temple University Press, 1995.

Rupp, Leila. *Worlds of Women: The Making of an International Women's Movement*. Princeton, NJ: Princeton University Press, 1997.

Sacks, Karen. *Caring by the Hour: Women, Work, and Organizing at Duke Medical Center*. Urbana: University of Illinois Press, 1987.

Sangster, Joan. "Doing Two Jobs: The Wage-Earning Mother, 1945–1970," in *A Diversity of Women: Ontario, 1945–1980*, ed. Joy Parr. Toronto, ON: University of Toronto Press, 1995: 98–134.

Tinsman, Heidi. "The Indispensable Services of Sisters: Considering Domestic Service in the United States and Latin American Studies." *Journal of Women's History* 4, no. 1 (1992): 37–59.

11

"NO RIGHT TO LAYETTES OR NURSING TIME"

MATERNITY LEAVE AND THE QUESTION OF U.S. EXCEPTIONALISM

Eileen Boris

The Constitution provides no right to layettes or nursing time, observed William L. McGrath, employer representative to the U.S. delegation to the International Labor Organization (ILO).[1] Testifying before a Senate committee on treaty-making powers in 1953, McGrath mocked ILO deliberations over Convention 103, which mandated maternity leave for wage-earning women. He described an afternoon when "government, labor, and employer delegates, from nations all over the world, debated the question as to whether a woman nursing her baby, on time paid for by the employer, should do so in a single period of 1 hour per day, or 2 periods of one half hour each." To which Republican Senator Everett Dirksen of Illinois responded, "I do not suppose the baby was ever consulted about that?" McGrath replied: "And yet, you know the thing is not funny, the thing is just so tragic that you are just appalled by it all." The ILO Maternity Convention represented for this spokesman for the United States Chamber of Commerce not merely "socialistic" governments meddling with the family, as disgusting as he found that to be, but interfering with "volunteerism," insurance companies, and employer determination of benefits—practices that his organization was intent on maintaining.[2]

In the early postwar years, the U.S. Women's Bureau lamented how "visitors from other countries ask, time and again, why the United States . . . has no Federal law providing for a national system of maternity protection of its women workers."[3] McGrath's testimony highlighted the two intertwining myths central to this deficit: the privacy of the family and private enterprise. He lambasted European social insurance plans as "government takes over the function of the family," complaining that "the state provides against a multitude of contingencies for which, in a free society, the husband and the father as head of the family is supposed to provide."[4] He lamented the lack of distinction between the unwed and married under the convention's wording, "without benefit of marriage," preferring the solid "Anglo-Saxon" terms "legitimate and illegitimate."[5] The specter of sexuality run amok, symbolized by the unwed mother, haunted him. Like those who would fight against provision of social assistance to poor solo mothers, opponents of replacing the wages of pregnant workers acted as if such benefits would encourage out-of-wedlock pregnancy.[6]

But McGrath also viewed the ILO directives as interfering with collective bargaining, in which employers and unions negotiate worker benefits outside of state provisions. He countered the accusation that employers could not be trusted with maternity leave because they would discharge the pregnant woman by arguing that European employers "go along with the government" because "they can hire [women] for 25 to 35 percent less than they hire men."[7] In his mind, U.S. businessmen would not exploit mothers because they knew their proper place was not the factory or office, but in the home, and U.S. employers became the real protectors of babies through insurance purchased from private companies. Family wage ideology, in essence, reinforced a contributory contractualism that defined women as men's dependents and provided them lesser benefits even if they were the subscribers to workplace insurance.

That private provisions against sickness and disability would constitute the main provisions for most in the United States might have been foreseen but was not a foregone conclusion as World War II was ending. As an official of the Bureau of Manpower Utilization claimed, "The whole nation has broadened its concept of what facts are involved in obtaining efficiency of production." Wartime "health and welfare services," she predicted, "will continue."[8] New Deal social planners and labor feminists hoped that piecemeal federal programs would grow and even mothers on the job would be embraced in the bill of rights that certainly would emerge from Congress following President Roosevelt's call in January 1945 for greater economic security.[9] Before the solidification of the Cold War, during that euphoric moment in the mid-1940s when the United States appeared to stand for democracy and a higher standard of living, an expanded welfare state that covered all workers and their dependents seemed within the realm of political possibility.[10]

However, U.S. women would gain no right to layettes, nursing time, or cash income replacement for time away from their jobs. The failure to enact comprehensive family leave policies or even sign the revised ILO convention that Women's Bureau head Frieda Miller helped to formulate marks the "exceptionalism" that has distinguished the U.S. welfare state. No right to maternity leave thus appears as part of a larger story of truncated social citizenship, in which wage-earning women—caught in the vise of "female difference"—become the object of protective legislation rather than stand as rights-bearing subjects.[11]

During a period when a combination of political forces and ideological reluctance stymied extension of the 1935 Social Security Act, a private welfare state grew in the core sectors of the economy.[12] The weakness of the federal Women's and Children's Bureaus, the development of private-sector insurance under collective bargaining, the attack on government programs from Republican conservatives amid Cold War anticommunism, the recomposition of the female labor force with the growth of part-time work, the legacy of Jim Crow, and contradictory understandings of women's place all shaped the public-private system that lessened women's citizenship rights compared with men's and the rights of poor women and women of color compared with those women, mostly white, who gained entitlements from marriage to industrial workers—the primary beneficiaries of both public and private pensions and benefits.[13]

But to explain away these lacks as yet another example of a racially constructed residual or liberal welfare state is to substitute theoretical categorization for historical analysis.[14] Instead, this chapter complicates the notion of "American" exceptionalism by considering innovations that made the United States less an outcast than one of many states grappling with the pregnant worker during a period when social security systems were being developed throughout the world, including the eighteen nations, about a fifth of all ILO members, that ratified the original maternity convention during the two decades after its passage in 1919. Nearly half of these signatories were Latin American states.[15] Concerns for population increase, maternal and child health, and workforce demands motivated nations, though talk of "human rights" framed transnational discussions in which support for protective legislation and women's right to earn vied with each other.[16] Passing laws and signing global agreements signified concern with social issues, but actual implementation was another matter and could stymie rather than advance women's rights, especially when separate from comprehensive antidiscrimination and equal pay enforcement.

That women in the United States in the early post–World War II years remained subject to the vagaries of geographical and workplace locations was not so different from what women elsewhere experienced, especially if they lived outside major cities and worked in the domestic, service (i.e., retail and entertainment), or agricultural sectors. To put it another way, when compared with all but a handful of European programs, pregnant workers in the United States and elsewhere in the Americas labored under family wage regimes that privileged male breadwinning but required poorly paid work by certain groups of women, marked by class and often color or ethnicity. Pregnant workers in the Americas faced exposures to workplace hazards and pressures to leave employment or earn a living in casualized sectors (like family businesses, agriculture, industrial homework, and taking in washing and children) rather than in workplaces covered by union agreements or state laws. What historian Elizabeth Quay Hutchison concluded about Chile in the 1920s extends to other nations with maternity provisions during the first half of the twentieth century: "Despite legislators' intentions, early protective legislation contributed to economic and social pressures that made women's industrial labor more informal and precarious."[17] If we measure the norm by women's lives rather than constitutional or legislative decrees, then the United States was not so much of a laggard at mid-century; its exceptionalism in social policy was still under construction.

Looking at one global labor convention can illuminate social policy within the United States and its connection to transnational debates over wage-earning women. For more than a century, both international women's and transnational labor movements offered spaces to exchange ideas, provide support, and build solidarity. To be sure, these organizations reflected political and philosophical diversity, as well as the relative privilege of those from colonial and imperial nations. But rarely have historians discussed women and labor together as part of these transnational interactions. Women's historians have explored the making of global feminist networks, with a focus on women's rights in either the pre–World War I period or the late twentieth century.[18] Those who evaluate international meetings between 1920 and the Cold War tend to let conflicts between the National Women's Party (NWP) and its international network and labor feminists in and outside of the United States dominate assessments. Such analysis reaffirms the dichotomy between equal rights, tied to a gender-first ideology, and protective legislation, associated with a class-based defense of women industrial workers, reinscribing conflict in the United States onto the world stage. Gender analysis of the ILO repeats this pattern.[19] Stepping outside that discussion can illuminate how support of social security, maternity leave, and other "work and family" policies could advance women's rights and gender equality on the job and in the polity. A transnational approach reveals circuits of exchange between U.S. labor feminists and international policy making, complicating the standard story that champions an abstract equality over a characterized difference and elevates the NWP over the Women's Bureau network. It helps us see how U.S. labor feminists sought women's equality through supports targeted to wage-earning mothers, dissolving the dichotomy between equality and difference.[20]

Policy emerges not only from the particularities of the nation-state but also as part of transnational deliberations. In addressing the private, indeed intimate, issue of pregnancy in its public manifestation for employed women, U.S. policy makers were in dialogue with policies elsewhere, even if only as part of Cold War posturing. Labor feminists in the United States envisioned paid leave for pregnant workers and influenced revisions of Convention No. 3 through the participation of the Women's Bureau's Frieda Miller. Other policy makers, like maverick Senator William Langer (Republican of North Dakota), believed that the United States should keep up with the rest of the world. There existed homegrown as opposed to international precedents for government-sponsored maternity leave in the United States. Rhode Island's cash disability program, maternity benefits under the Railroad Retirement Act, and a failed attempt for civil service employees in Washington, D.C., represent roads not taken toward a more inclusive social insurance regime that would have covered pregnancy and recognized maternal wage earners as workers holding labor rights. How society organizes the work of reproduction highlights not only the racialized gender division of labor but also the construction of power and authority between state, market, and families. The United States nearly alone of industrial nations lacks paid leave. But by considering U.S. efforts in light of the ILO and Latin America practices, we see that in the immediate postwar years, this situation was not as apparent as policy distinctions appear in hindsight.[21]

International Conventions before World War II

With the AFL's Samuel Gompers chairing its organizing commission, the ILO emerged in 1919 from the end of World War I. Instituted to establish global labor standards, it operated through a tripartite structure: each nation sent government, employer, and labor representatives. It sought to eliminate inhumane working conditions, counter the economic injustice that many believed fueled political instability, and remove disincentives to reform by setting comparable practices worldwide. The United States joined the ILO only in 1934 but soon began to shape international labor conventions. For example, Social Security policy maker John Winant, former governor of New Hampshire, headed the organization on the eve of World War II; he worked closely with Frieda Miller.[22]

Women experts and labor leaders played a central role, revealing the workings of an early-twentieth-century feminism that simultaneously embraced inclusion and female difference. While the ILO instructed its director to "employ a certain number of women on his staff," a kind of sexual division of labor within reform circles led to appointing women experts especially "when any question regarding women's labor was to be considered." This directive appeared appropriate since women reformers had adopted legislated labor standards as a more viable strategy than collective bargaining for female wage earners crowded into few occupations.[23]

Before the initial 1919 meeting in Washington, D.C., labor feminists, who knew each other from prewar consultations, met to hammer out an agenda that would carry over into the official discussions.[24] The Commission on Employment of Women developed what became the Maternity Protection Convention, but not without debate.[25] To counter employer representatives who sought to undermine "radical" provisions by citing medical experts, British Women's Trade Union League founder Mary Macarthur underscored the class dimensions of maternity leave. "If it is undesirable that [women] should cease work it must be desirable that they should be employed, therefore we may expect to see leisure women and the wives of employers going to work six weeks before their confinement," she reasoned.[26]

Convention No. 3 was prescriptive—"not a single State was in a position to ratify it at once," the ILO Director recalled two decades later.[27] It covered commerce, where more women worked than industry; allowed for six weeks of leave before confinement; and mandated six weeks after delivery. It included job protection and cash benefits from either a public system or social insurance "sufficient for the full and healthy maintenance of herself and her child, as well as free attendance by a doctor or certified midwife." Upon return to employment, the wage-earning mother had the right to nurse "half an hour twice a day during her working hours."[28] Nations were to adopt enabling legislation or amend existing standards. The ILO would recommend protection for agricultural workers in 1921.[29]

These multiple provisions proved daunting for even ratifying countries. It took decades for most to include clerical and other workers in commerce. Between 1919 and 1952, the number of ratifiers grew only to thirty-five. While only nine of twenty-nine paid benefits to women compelled to leave employment in 1919, forty nations, including nonratifiers like Great Britain, had some sort of social insurance for maternity two decades later. By 1952, when the ILO addressed revisions, state practices still fell short of dictates.[30]

International labor standards remained aspirational rather than binding, with wide discrepancies. The Dominican Republic had a contributory scheme that required women to make fifteen contributions in the ten months prior to pregnancy, with husbands giving double the amount to insure spouses. In contrast, Uruguay, though a ratifier, lacked compulsory social insurance. Many states had inoperable laws, including Bolivia, Colombia, Costa Rica, Guatemala, Mexico, Panama, El Salvador, and Venezuela. Cuba, as well as Argentina, had "a special scheme of compulsory insurance for maternity benefits alone." Cuban workers contributed 25 percent of wages and employers 5 percent of payroll in 1944. The wives or common-law partners of male workers could obtain funds to meet delivery costs, while pregnant workers upon ceasing employment received a cash benefit for six weeks before and after delivery and also qualified for obstetrical aid. Along with Costa Rica, Guatemala, and Panama, ratifier Chile continued to place the burden of benefits on the employer. Chilean feminists denounced this arrangement for providing a disincentive to hire women. In 1952, however, they were able to obtain legislation that replaced employer subsidy with state subsidy of maternity leave. Legal challenges against wayward employers rarely resulted in the recovery of lost jobs.[31]

Most states replaced only part of the wage following a qualifying period for contributions into social insurance. In some, notably Denmark, France, and Great Britain, public funds kicked in. Medical care also diverged from ILO directives, though some national insurance schemes included it, and Britain provided care through the National Health Service. Latin American nations allowed for shorter but more frequent nursing breaks, and many also mandated provision of crèches for establishments with specified numbers of women workers. Mexico, another nonsigner, had included similar maternity provisions in its Constitution of 1917, but failed at enforcement. In general, huge gaps existed between standards and practices.[32]

Regional meetings further highlighted maternity as part of labor standards for women workers. Latin Americans looked to European and U.S. developments and participated at international meetings as part of an overall modernizing agenda. Chile, for one, drafted maternity legislation to match the 1919 convention; the Obligatory Insurance Law of 1924, passed as a military decree, extended to domestic servants and included medical expenses and eight weeks of leave.[33] At the Second Labor Conference of American States (Havana meeting), held for ILO members in 1939, delegates adopted a multifaceted program on women's work, including equal pay for equal work and extension of minimum wages to industrial homework—an aspect of protection presented by Mexico and a particular concern of U.S. delegates, who sought to curtail outwork. With mainland garment manufacturers taking advantage of homeworkers in Puerto Rico, U.S. labor feminists understood the regional—if not global—system of production that linked the states with the rest of the Americas.[34]

Maternity provisions adopted at the Havana meeting extended the 1919 convention through greater specification of employer duties and state responsibilities. They matched the positions of labor feminists from the Women's Bureau who dominated the U.S. delegation. But Cuban public health officials also pushed these provisions. Employers should not fire the pregnant woman on account of her condition, but should reassign her to appropriate work and offer her former, or an equivalent, position after confinement. Sickness should justify extending required leave, nursing time should not generate pay reductions, and the state or insurance should cover medical attention. The allowance provided during compulsory leave should be a standard rate rather than determined by a woman's previous contributions into social insurance and should extend into any period of disability as well. Significantly, the delegates resolved to levy taxes on "the total working force, male and female," "so as to avoid establishing a direct relation between the engagement of a woman worker and the payment of contributions for maternity benefit."[35]

The moral and religious economy of Catholic nations encouraged protection of even unborn children and their mothers.[36] Similar attitudes justified excluding unmarried women from guarantees. In the 1920s, Mexican factory owners defended themselves by claiming that compliance would "be immoral given that many of the women lead irregular lives or live catch as catch can in this sense." Such operatives, as Ann Farnsworth-Alvear discovered among those laboring in Colombian mills during the 1940s, "left because of a pregnancy." A woman may have "received 'the severance pay and bonus that she was entitled to because of her pregnancy and dismissal.'" Just as likely, she quit before her "dishonor" became known. Even if mothers were welcome in factories, the condition of pregnancy, especially for the single, brought discrimination rather than a job waiting on her return.[37]

That many maternity measures hindered women's employment highlights actual contestation within nations—between employers and unions, between feminists and health and welfare administrators, and among experts. In Brazil, for example, maternity legislation belonged to the modernizing, if paternalistic, labor standards promulgated by Getúlio Vargas in the early 1930s. Historian Barbara Weinstein heard from interviewees that "by the 1940s it became difficult for a woman of marriageable age to get a factory job since employers feared having to provide maternity leave and child care facilities." But employers ignored such laws because enforcement was nearly nonexistent.[38] Chilean feminists sought to protect children's health, historian Karin Rosemblatt argues, and thus looked for alternative means to achieve that end without discriminating against women.[39] Just as ILO delegates had responded to the death toll of World War I in promulgating Convention No. 3, maternity leave served as a symbolic indicator of the intent to preserve a future population, a eugenic representation but perhaps also emblematic of concern for the condition of poor mothers and their offspring.[40] Maternity policy belonged to the realm of labor regulation and social reproduction more than women's right to work—a major concern of U.S. labor feminists who participated in ILO deliberations.

Labor Feminists In and Outside of the State

Wartime employment of U.S. women put maternity leave on the collective bargaining agenda after 1943, but so did labor feminists within the government and unions.[41] These women varied in their strategies to advance women's equality at work, with some weary of protective legislation and others holding fast to such standards. Many held beliefs quite in keeping with international discussions, notably the 1939 Havana meeting, and they were well aware of provisions elsewhere. Frieda Miller was a U.S. delegate to the ILO in 1936 and a special assistant to the U.S. ambassador in London, a former director of the ILO, during the early war years.[42] She implicitly criticized her own nation in observing, "The Beveridge plan [in England] provides assistance to young children, and even in Cuba, men [as well as women] pay a tax that supports maternity benefits. Every child [does] have two parents."[43]

The war encouraged public responses, however inadequate or short-lived, to the needs of wage-earning mothers. Though mothers' labor force participation was hardly new, it captured national attention across the United States. In 1940, married women constituted 35 percent of the female labor force; by 1947, after reconversion from war industry, they were nearly half.[44] Day care centers, flexible hours, food services, equal pay, and maternity care became available to some war workers.[45] Wartime controls curtailed wages but advanced the growth of fringe benefits, foremost of which were pensions and health insurance.[46]

During the fighting, the Women's and Children's Bureaus recommended standards for industry in consultation with union, obstetrical, and public health experts. The Children's Bureau focused on child welfare and thus viewed women first as mothers, while the Women's Bureau was more concerned with women in the labor force and their rights as wage earners. Both still preferred that mothers not engage in employment, but the Women's Bureau defended women's right to earn by referring to her necessity to make ends meet.[47] After the war, Miller judged "income maintenance" as urgent as the need to promote the physical and emotional wellness of both mother and child, another goal of maternity leave.[48]

The large numbers of women in factories during wartime justified issuance of standards. In a joint 1942 report, both agencies emphasized maternal and child health. The Children's Bureau especially sought to convince employers that dismissal of pregnant women harmed, rather than protected, this health, especially since "the danger of miscarriage is greatest during the early months, and women who fear to lose their jobs will not tell of their condition." It recommended changing the job of the worker "to keep a pregnant woman a useful and efficient employee if she wishes to continue to work."[49] Protective goals led both agencies to call for health exams and prenatal care, rest periods, day shifts of eight hours and a forty-hour week, restrictions on type of work, and minimum prenatal and postpartum leave (six weeks before and two months after—longer than the 1919 standards). They assumed "that some would find it necessary to work and that provision for maternity care and leave should not jeopardize a woman's job or her seniority privileges." Thus they also supported "job protection for a reasonable period."[50]

In 1944, the War Labor Board "ordered" government contracts to contain a clause on maternity leave. This clause included up to a one-year leave, reemployment before hiring of other women, and undisturbed seniority rights.[51] Its "'Model' Pregnancy Policy," based on Children's Bureau guidelines, restricted work after the thirty-second week of pregnancy and six weeks after childbirth, with return approved by a woman's physician. Employees were to retain seniority, though no provision existed for paid leave.[52] The standing of the War Department undoubtedly generated the authority necessary for such a disciplinary and supervisory stance. But the model came too late, as the war was ending.

Labor feminists found justification for maternity policy in "social function" or "interest of society." Children became "citizens who carry on its civilization," which made birth a social asset. Maternity, then, was not "an illness," to be covered by new disability policies. But labor feminists wondered, "On what grounds would you ... pay? We aren't going to have any pregnant men. It is one of nature's discriminations. How do you rationalize it?" For Miller, maternity leave was like unemployment: It could "be borne as reasonably by industry or by the state as are the costs ... where the work just peters out for a period."[53] Katherine Lenroot of the Children's Bureau also presented maternity payments as a form of social insurance "spread over the whole society." A national program better served women than benefits gained through union contracts because universal requirements evened costs between employers, curtailing the disincentive to hire women. As the United States later would comment to the ILO, this principle resembled the "social acceptance of universal taxation" for school facilities.[54] Still some, like Julia O'Connor Parker of the Electrical Workers, feared that "special payment" would undermine the fight for "equal pay and equal treatment of women as citizens and workers rather than as women." Against maternalist notions of the mother-citizen, she stressed obtaining rights and equality.[55]

At war's end, labor feminists struggled for improved union contracts while trying to gain Miller's "basic, general social policy."[56] They sought "maintenance of seniority rights for this absence as for other absences," inclusion in benefit packages, and the choice of bargaining for standards in union agreements. Simultaneously, they fought for a "full social security program like Murray-Wagner-Dingell," which would include health coverage and supersede private agreements, and campaigned in the states for expanded criteria for unemployment compensation to cover "a woman who is pregnant but still able to work."[57]

With the failure to expand social security, unions sought their own sickness benefits, sometimes including pregnancy under group health insurance. Packinghouse and electrical workers gained a provision that maintained seniority rights for a year after a woman left for pregnancy and childbirth. The United Automobile Workers crafted a model maternity clause that provided leave of absence for up to a year, with retention and accumulation of seniority.[58] Still, Women's Bureau field representative May Bagwell concluded, "In most local unions no attention had been paid to this question. Some plants even discharged women when their pregnancy became known." Trade union women wanted more: Like Ruth Young of the left-wing United Electrical Workers at a Women's Bureau Conference, they asked, "Can we get some pay during that period?" Dolores Pinta of the Farm Equipment union concurred: Plants should pay "for their time off."[59]

Maternity clauses in union contracts revealed, Miller argued, "what kind of provisions ultimately should be developed as legislation." But unwilling to let collective bargaining take its own course, the bureau again pushed for model standards.[60] It sought to mobilize women to stand up for their rights by investigating the union contract, advising that they should "talk with union officers about getting a maternity clause if there is none; ask the bargaining committee to request the company to adopt a sound maternity policy; and be willing to accept responsibility and encourage other women workers to serve on committee and run for office so that women's problems could be presented by women."[61]

The details of existing provisions created an uneven landscape. By 1952, three-fourths of manufacturing firms and half of other enterprises maintained job security following maternity. Four-fifths of union contrasts contained leave of absence clauses, though only a sixth of unions, mostly in manufacturing, specified maternity leaves. Most teachers who worked in large cities (population over 100,000) had leave, but those in small cities did not—they often were on year-to-year contracts. Some school districts required teachers to take off as soon as they became aware of pregnancy, the majority before the sixth month. Because reinstatement could take place only at the beginning of the year or semester, the length of leave could extend to over a year. If no suitable position existed when a teacher was ready to return, she waited for an appropriate vacancy. Most leave was unpaid.[62]

Revising the ILO Convention

Labor feminists brought such positions into the international arena. After the war, the ILO sought to revise the maternity convention. The Women's Bureau supplied technical advice to the U.S. delegation and drafted its report. Under its prodding, the United States became one of only five nations commenting on the proposed revision. That two-thirds of wage-earning women were married, Miller argued, made "the modernization of Convention No. 3 . . . substantively one of considerable urgency."[63] This point reflected the Bureau's overall goal of protecting "women who carry the double burden of a paid job and motherhood."[64] Miller stressed the challenge of the "Iron Curtain countries," which "have recognized the importance of this question as far as building up a healthful and secure labor force," such as East Germany with its law "for the Protection of Mothers and Children and the Rights of Women" that included paid maternity leave. Here realpolitik entered the equation: "If the ILO now sidesteps this important matter," she advised, "this action may well be taken up as one more propaganda item against the ILO and against the U.S. as a leading policy maker in that organization."[65] Indeed, during ILO deliberations in June 1952, the Polish government delegate Mrs. Kalinowska mocked the gap between labor feminist aspirations and conditions in the United States, "that highly industrialised country which spends billions of dollars on armaments and yet possesses meager maternity protection in only four out of its 48 States and, as is well known, has even up to the present no social health insurance."[66]

Even though the United States rarely ratified ILO conventions, since they addressed "matters appropriate for action by the constituent states" and appeared too socialistic for Congress, it helped to formulate them. At a time when some domestic workers in the United States were gaining entrance into social security, the Women's Bureau asked to broaden maternity coverage worldwide "to all employed women, including domestic workers, farm workers, and employees of non-profit extended coverage in the revised organizations." Along with Guatemala, which sought protection of its predominantly agricultural workforce, the United States allied itself with worker representatives, who proposed expanding the convention beyond industry and commerce. Inclusion of home-based labor, however, generated resistance for being difficult to regulate and central to the organization of less "developed" economies. Thus the convention produced a text that allowed countries to temporarily ignore these extensions to allow, as Miller explained during the drafting process, "for adaptation to fit the circumstances in the different countries." The revision also provided greater flexibility in the amount of leave and widened the basis for such benefits to include either "compulsory insurance or public service . . . out of public funds." Here the U.S. proposal generously interpreted its own hybrid system by having those ineligible for social insurance to "be entitled to adequate benefits under social assistance."[67]

The United States also sought a stronger right to job security and greater safeguards for pregnant workers when on the job. Preferring compulsory insurance, Miller insisted that methods of financing "avoid discrimination against women workers," rejecting schemes that levied payroll taxes on employers alone or on the basis of number of women workers. To tax employers directly would curtail female employment and hinder "equal pay and equal opportunities for women who were employed."[68] This argument echoed sentiments embedded in the Equal Rights Amendment, a plank still rejected by the Women's Bureau for undermining women's labor laws. "Any tax that may be imposed," the United States commented, "should have general application, *without distinction as to sex*" (italics added)[69] Despite its embrace of protective labor legislation for women, the Bureau sought to promote women's equality at the workplace while taking into consideration those factors, like pregnancy, that could differentiate women from men. But unlike Cuba, where protests by male workers led to coverage for their wives under a compulsory contribution scheme, it continued to tie maternity leave to female employment.[70]

The revised ILO convention embraced the major U.S. suggestions, which paralleled comments of about a dozen other nations. While agreeing with World Health Organization standards for the length of leave and workplace conditions, the United States particularly emphasized "free choice" of physicians in keeping with its private medical system.[71] On the question of nursing facilities, it voted against the provision, having originally had "no suggestions" because "this aspect of maternity is not closely related to U.S. experience."[72] The final document contained the ideals of U.S. labor feminists, who would be unable to translate best practices into widespread social policy in the divided system (public-private, state-federal) of U.S. social provision.

Neglected Models: Rhode Island and the Railroad Retirement Board

While the Women's and Children's Bureaus pushed for industrial standards, two programs included maternity under unemployment disability insurance. Neither led to a more expansive insurance, and thus the circumstances of these exceptions are worth exploring. In 1942, Rhode Island passed a Cash Compensation Act as part of its unemployment insurance program that reimbursed those temporarily unable to labor. The act developed out of the struggle between employers and unions over the mounting funds in the state's unemployment insurance (UI) reserves. The cash sickness program resulted, financed by using one percent of the employee contribution. The act originally "defined sickness as inability 'to perform any services for wages.'" Pregnancy was not mentioned, but neither was it excluded. Unemployment compensation administrators decided to include pregnancy claims.[73]

Originally considered under the same terms as other conditions, maternity benefits became a major "drain" on the fund (as did benefits for retirees), and soon the legislature accepted their continuation in the cash sickness program through curtailing benefits. In 1946, the legislature reduced maternity benefits from the standard twenty-six weeks to fifteen, and then in 1950 to twelve consecutive weeks divided half before and half after birth—the 1919 ILO recommendation. Amendments also increased the minimum employment requirement, which became based on the four quarters prior to an individual leaving work. Pregnancy claims represented 40 percent of those filed by women in 1949 and 1950 and nearly a quarter of all claims for that period. They lasted longer than any others except for the most severe disabilities, with 42 percent terminated only by the time limit. Part of the controversy stemmed from a feeling that women who had no intention of returning to jobs took advantage of the fund.[74]

Why pregnant workers gained benefits remains unclear. The Women's Bureau in 1960 pointed to the sheer numbers of women, 40 percent of covered laborers in 1954. A center of light manufacturing, especially jewelry and textiles, Rhode Island continued throughout the 1950s to have one of the highest percentages of women workers.[75] Still, philosophical or political factors had to enter into the initial decision. Margaret F. Ackroyd, chief of the Division of Women and Children in the Rhode Island Department of Labor, was an active member of the network of labor law administrators in close communication with the Women's Bureau and may have influenced the decision to include maternity. Certainly, she fought against elimination of the benefits, asking the Bureau in May 1949 for additional information to support her efforts.[76] Other members of this labor law network pushed to duplicate Rhode Island's program. Only after the 1978 Pregnancy Discrimination Act mandated that pregnancy be treated the same as other conditions that led to temporary inability to perform on the job did New York, California, New Jersey, and other states that paid for disability finally join Rhode Island.[77]

The 1946 amendments to the Railroad Retirement Act provided the only cash benefits for pregnant workers under federal auspices. Judged central to the economy and burdened with a history of disruptive labor strife, the railroads came under federal regulation well before the New Deal. An appointed corporatist board—with representatives from government, labor, and employers—handled pensions and, during the war, considered "manpower" questions as well. Under the leadership of pension expert and planner Murray Latimer, the Railroad Retirement Board pushed for amendments that served both to bring railroad workers up to standards set in 1939 for Social Security, notably for widows (survivor's insurance) and to launch a more comprehensive social insurance program, compared by opponents, as well as its developers, to Britain's Beveridge plan. The board would protect "against the five major hazards of economic insecurity—old age, disability, death, unemployment, and sickness." Maternity leave was generous: eight weeks prior to delivery and about sixteen and half weeks afterward, more than six months, with daily benefits pegged to earnings. The power of the Railroad Brotherhoods and concern with industrial efficiency, as well as pressures to adjourn, explain passage.[78]

A recognized innovation was the inclusion of sickness, accident, and maternity benefits that opponents classified as health insurance "under the cloak of unemployment."[79] As a member of the New Jersey State Chamber of Commerce complained, "It is obvious that these benefits are not paid to compensate the worker for a wage loss, but rather represent for this country an excessive, untried and radical concept of social insurance which is not compatible with the American theory of government." Opponents never saw these benefits as legitimate and in the next Congress attempted to overturn them—without success.[80]

Maternity leave appeared "a minor part of the whole sickness-benefit program."[81] (Women composed no more than 5 or 6 percent of the workforce, and their numbers fell with the winding down of the war.) This inclusion represented administrative convenience as much as social conviction that such leave belonged in any comprehensive insurance program. The counsel to the Railway Labor Executives' Association insisted, "You cannot solve the problems which maternity illness produces by merely deciding not to include them." Trying to figure out whether a woman's illness came from pregnancy or some other cause even if she was pregnant "would require a great deal of administrative folderol, and, when you get all through with it, what have you accomplished?" he asked. "You have accomplished the exclusion from payment of something which by all reasonable human standards ought to be paid anyway."[82] Old ideas about women justified a progressive measure.

Opponents remained unconvinced that pregnant women were workers, but defenders of the measure noted during 1947 hearings that "the rights that that woman has can only be acquired by being a railroad employee in the same way that the pension rights that an individual gets after he retires, when he is no longer a railroad employee, can only be derived from his service as a railroad employee."[83] In other words, labor already performed earned pregnant women the right to worker benefits. Maternity stayed in. Like Rhode Island, a large percentage did not return to these jobs.[84]

Why Not Government Workers?

The incorporation of maternity leave under unemployment insurance languished at the national level, in part undermined by Social Security rules that unemployment funds could not be used for other purposes. Civil Service leave offered another venue for forging a model maternity policy. Early in 1948, Republican Senator William Langer introduced "maternity relief for government employees," a bill to provide sixty days of paid leave to married women with at least ten months of federal service. He requested information from Miller, who sent over materials from the ILO, including an evaluation of Convention No. 3 and a digest of legislation from Latin America, "because they are the only group of countries for which recent comprehensive information is available." His staff further investigated coverage of government employees in the Americas and elsewhere. Senator Langer looked at programs worldwide in formulating the resulting legislation.[85]

A Midwestern populist, isolationist, and anticommunist, Langer supported increased social security benefits, civil rights for African Americans, and federal workers' pay and dignity. He was a cosponsor of the Equal Rights Amendment. He felt strongly about the maternity proposal, shutting down Senate business one day when the legislators had blocked his bill. "Every other civilized country on the face of the earth pays its women employe[e]s in cases where it is necessary for them to have a leave of absence from their Federal jobs to give birth to their children," Langer declared, contending that "married women working for the Government are childless because they are not allowed time off with pay to have babies." Though reported favorably out of committee, the Senate never took up his measure, even after its reintroduction in the next Congress.[86]

Defenders of the proposal joined notions of rights with the old mothers and soldiers analogy that had well served promoters of mothers' pensions decades before. For Frieda Miller, the bill represented "an initial step toward material recognition of motherhood's contribution to the national welfare."[87] The staff director of the Civil Service Committee compared maternity leave to the National Selective Service Act.[88] Labor spokesmen, in contrast, emphasized antidiscrimination as a right. Denial of maternity leave interfered with women's "freedom to choose the kind of lives they wish, including the right to marriage and to have children," testified Walter J. Mason for the American Federation of Labor. "When they marry, as is their right, they should have the right to retain their jobs," he contended. "If this is a real right, they must have maternity leave with pay." Otherwise, women were "denied effective opportunity for marriage."[89] Such a notion of equality anticipated one strand of feminist argument in the 1980s, which claimed that lack of job protection for the pregnant deprived women, but not men, of the right to procreate.[90]

Mason believed that the federal government should offer model employment provisions. Langer's bill, Miller agreed, allowed "the Government an opportunity to take the lead toward accomplishment of the ultimate objective of maternity protection for all employed women by adopting such legislation for its own women workers." In pointing to the Civil Service Commission's recognition of "the principle of equal pay for equal work for women," she reformulated maternity leave as a worker right. Ever hopeful in 1948 that proposals for national health insurance would pass, Miller recognized that these provisions would cover only private firms, as she later noted about unsuccessful amendments to social security in 1949 that would have incorporated maternity under disability benefits.[91] Legislation for government employees still would be necessary.[92]

Langer's bill sank under the larger political and economic structures that blocked any expansion of health benefits. Whether out of concern over the cost of hiring temporary replacements or for partisan political reasons, despite the urging of the Women's and Children's Bureaus, the Bureau of the Budget advised the Civil Service Commission that Langer's proposal was "not in accord with the program of the President."[93] The presence of black women on the lowest levels of the civil service may have influenced opposition.

The question remains, Why did Langer introduce this bill? Part of the answer appears in his response to McGrath's testimony in 1953, when Langer presided over hearings to restrict the Executive's treaty-making powers. The North Dakotan lectured that "the greater conservatives in our Senate, men whom you esteem and members of your organization, voted in favor of maternity leave and said that our Government should pay for the care of the babies.... The point is that it is the care of the baby that is involved." He insisted: "You cannot name me a civilized country—and I include Japan and Germany—a single country aside from the United States, where the Federal Government does not give a leave of absence to women employees, married or unmarried, who are going to have a baby."[94] Nationalism and pronatalism mixed with a sense of women's rights in this vision of equity.

Exceptionalism Revisited

Historian Dorothy Sue Cobble rightly notes, "At the end of the 1950s, the United States had forged a path rejected by almost all other industrialized countries: it made no social provision for loss of income due to childbearing." If we limit comparison to Europe, as does Cobble following the disappointment of the labor feminists of that time, the United States appears as an exception better left behind than followed. States provided unemployment compensation for only "involuntary quits," which did not include pregnancy.[95] What did exist was a private system that was neither universal nor very generous. But despite better laws, other nations in the Americas resembled the United States in the practice of maternity leave and benefits during this period. Seen in transnational perspective, social policy in the United States looked a lot like the practice of nations far less industrialized.

Proposals for baby unemployment, social security for caregivers, and wage replacement for parental leave languished on the federal level even after passage of the 1993 Family and Medical Leave Act, which at least provides some job security to those in covered workplaces. The U.S. exception has become the global norm under rampant neoliberalism. In 2000, the ILO revised Convention 103, making it much more to William McGrath's liking. It currently provides greater flexibility for nations, tacking onto all provisions the idea that national laws would supersede the convention. It allowed member nations to exclude groups of workers after consultation with employer organizations and unions. At the same time, the revisions balance women's rights and female difference, protecting the health of mother and child, as well as income replacement and worker rights. The ILO Director General Juan Somavía called the new maternity convention, No. 183, "a perfect example of how gender equality is at the heart of decent work." In his mind, protection no longer interfered with equality.[96] Whether workers' rights will translate into women's rights still remains unresolved in the case of the pregnant worker. That social reproduction stands at the center of the organization of production, however, persists.

NOTES

1. I thank Jill Jensen and Ruth Fairbanks for sharing their work and insights, Julie Greene for comments, and a Faculty Research Grant from the UCSB Academic Senate and funding from the Hull Chair. Transcript attached to Memo to Edward B. Persons from Frieda Miller, "Suggestions for the agenda of the 35th Session of the International Labour Conference (1952)," November 10, 1950, 6-2-7-3 (2), Box 67, Office of Director, General Correspondence, 1948–63, Papers of the U.S. Women's Bureau, RG86, National Archives. On McGrath, Edward C. Lorenz, *Defining Global Justice: The History of U.S. International*

Labor Standards Policy (Notre Dame, IN: Notre Dame University Press, 2001), 173–76.

2. "Statement of W. L. McGrath, President, The Williamson Heater Co., Cincinnati, Ohio on Behalf of the Chamber of Commerce," *Treaties and Executive Agreements*, Hearings before a Subcommittee of the Committee on the Judiciary, United States Senate, 83rd Congress, 1st Session, on S.J. Res. 1 and S.J. Res. 43 (Washington, DC: Government Printing Office, 1953), 337–42, esp. 341.
3. "Maternity Protection of Employed Women," *Women's Bureau Bulletin* no. 240 (Washington, DC: Government Printing Office, 1952), 1.
4. "Statement of W. L. McGrath," 545–46.
5. Ibid., 539–40.
6. Gwendolyn Mink, *Wages of Motherhood: Inequality in the Welfare State* (Ithaca, NY: Cornell University Press, 1995).
7. "Statement of W. L. McGrath," 541–42, 545.
8. "Urges Expansion of Welfare Work," *New York Times*, November 4, 1944.
9. Roosevelt in "Extension of Remarks of Hon. Henry M. Jackson," *Appendix to the Congressional Record*, v. 92, pt. 11, 79th Congress, 2d session, 1946, A3708.
10. Eileen Boris, "Labor's Welfare State: Constructing Workers, Defining Citizens," in *Cambridge History of American Law*, vol. 3, ed. Michael Grossberg and Christopher Tomlins, (New York: Cambridge University Press, 2008) 319–58.
11. Alice Kessler-Harris, *In Pursuit of Equity: Women, Men, and the Quest for Economic Citizenship in 20th-Century America* (New York: Oxford University Press, 2001), 210–11.
12. Nelson Lichtenstein, "From Corporatism to Collective Bargaining: Organized Labor and the Eclipse of Social Democracy in the Postwar Era," in *The Rise and Fall of the New Deal Order, 1930–1980*, ed. Steve Fraser and Gary Gerstle, 122–52 (Princeton, NJ: Princeton University Press, 1989); Jennifer Klein, *For All These Rights: Business, Labor, and the Shaping of America's Public-Private Welfare State* (Princeton, NJ: Princeton University Press, 2003).
13. Boris, "Labor's Welfare State"; Evelyn Nakano Glenn, *Unequal Freedom: How Race and Gender Shaped American Citizenship and Labor* (Cambridge: Harvard University Press, 2002).
14. Julia S. O'Connor, Ann Shola Orloff, and Sheila Shaver, *States, Markets, Families: Gender, Liberalism, and Social Policy in Australia, Canada, Great Britain, and the United States* (New York: Cambridge University Press, 1999).
15. There were eighteen signatories, eight from the Americas: Chile (1925), Cuba (1928), Uruguay (1933), Colombia (1933), Argentina (1933), Nicaragua (1934), Brazil (1934), and Venezuela (1944). "Maternity Protection of Employed Women," 40.
16. Preparatory Asiatic Regional Conference of the ILO, "Labour Policy in General Including the Enforcement of Labour Measures," Report 2 (New Delhi, India: ILO, 1947), 184–91; Asunción Lavrín, *Women, Feminism and Social Change in Argentina, Chile and Uruguay, 1890–1940* (Lincoln: University of Nebraska Press, 1995).

17. Elizabeth Quay Hutchison, *Labors Appropriate to Their Sex: Gender, Labor, and Politics in Urban Chile, 1900–1930* (Durham, NC: Duke University Press, 2001), 200.
18. Bonnie S. Anderson, *Joyous Greetings: The First International Women's Movement, 1830–1860* (New York: Oxford University Press, 2000); Valentine M. Moghadam, *Globalizing Women: Transnational Feminist Networks* (Baltimore: Johns Hopkins University Press, 2005).
19. Sandra Whitworth, "Gender, International Relations and the Case of the ILO," *Review of International Studies* 20 (1994): 389–405; Carol Riegelman Lubin and Anne Winslow, *Social Justice for Women: The International Labor Organization and Women* (Durham, NC: Duke University Press, 1990),
20. Helen Laville, "A New Era in International Women's Rights? American Women's Associations and the Estblishment of the UN Commission on the Status of Women," *Journal of Women's History* 20 (Winter 2008): 34–56.
21. Lorenz, *Defining Global Justice*, 12–19; ILO, *Maternity Benefits in the Eighties: An ILO Global Survey (1964–84)* (Geneva: ILO, 1985); "The Americas," 11–15, shows the United States alone in the region lacks national social insurance–based maternity leave.
22. "ILO History," at http://www.ilo.org/public/english/about/history.htm; Jill Jensen, "From Geneva to the Americas: The International Labor Organization and Inter-American Social Security Standards, 1936-1948," *International Labor and Working Class History* No. 80 (forthcoming Fall, 2011).
23. Lubin and Winslow, *Social Justice for Women*, 25–32; Eileen Boris, *Home to Work: Motherhood and the Politics of Industrial Homework* (New York: Cambridge University Press, 1994).
24. Lubin and Winslow, *Social Justice for Women*, 25–32; Nitza Berkovitch, *From Motherhood to Citizenship: Women's Rights and International Organizations* (Baltimore: Johns Hopkins University Press, 1999), 86–91.
25. "Labor Conference Ends 30-Day Session," *New York Times*, November 30, 1919.
26. League of Nations, *International Labor Conference, First Annual Meeting* (Washington, DC: Government Printing Office, 1920), 173.
27. Quoted in Lubin and Winslow, *Social Justice for Women*, 30.
28. ILO, 35th Session, *Revision of the Maternity Protection Convention 1919 (No. 3)* (Geneva: ILO Office, 1952), 3; "Maternity Protection of Employed Women," 39.
29. Maryse Gaudier, "The Development of the Women's Question at the ILO, 1919–1994: 75 Years of Progress towards Equality," at http://www.ilo.org/gender/Events/lang--es/docName--WCMS_106521/index.htm.
30. *Revision of the Maternity Protection Convention 1919*, 4.
31. Ibid., 5–11; "Maternity Protection of Employed Women," 43–44; Social Security Administration, Bureau of Research and Statistics, Division of Coordination Studies, "Social Security Programs in Costa Rica et al," May 5, 1947, 1, 3, 5; Karin A. Rosemblatt, *Gendered Compromises: Political Cultures & the State in Chile, 1920–1950* (Chapel Hill: University of North Carolina Press, 2000), 81–82.

32. *Revision of the Maternity Protection Convention 1919*, 5–11; "Maternity Protection of Employed Women," 43–44; Susie S. Porter, *Working Women in Mexico City: Public Discourses and Material Conditions, 1879–1931* (Tucson: University of Arizona Press, 2003), 176–77, 183.
33. Hutchinson, *Labors Appropriate to Their Sex*, 205–6, 218, 221.
34. *Mexican Labor News*, November 16, 1939; Boris, *Home to Work*.
35. ILO, "Conditions Adopted by the Conference," *Official Bulletin*, 25 (April 1, 1944), 41–44.
36. Hutchinson, *Labors Appropriate to Their Sex*, 204.
37. Porter, *Working Women in Mexico City*, 183; Ann Farnsworth-Alvear, *Dulcinea In the Factory: Myths, Morals, Men, and Women in Colombia's Industrial Experiment, 1905–1960* (Durham: Duke University Press, 2000), 165–66.
38. John D. French, *Drowning in Laws: Labor Law and Brazilian Political Culture* (Chapel Hill: University of North Carolina Press, 2004); e-mail communication from Barbara Weinstein to E. Boris, July 21, 2008.
39. Rosemblatt, *Gendered Compromises*, 80–82.
40. *International Labor Conference, First Annual Meeting*, 173.
41. Dorothy Sue Cobble, *The Other Women's Movement: Workplace Justice and Social Rights in Modern America* (Princeton, NJ: Princeton University Press, 2004).
42. Lorenz, *Defining Global Justice*, 110–11, 124.
43. Quoted in Cobble, *The Other Women's Movement*, 128.
44. "Statement of Frieda S. Miller in Favor of S. 784 to Provide Maternity Leave to Federal Employees before the Civil Service Committee," February 18, 1948, in Miller Papers, A37, box 8, folder 168, Schlesinger Library.
45. Amy Kesselman, *Fleeting Opportunities* (Albany: State University of New York Press, 1990).
46. Klein, *For All These Rights*.
47. Sonya Michel, *Children's Interests/Mothers' Rights* (New Haven: Yale University Press, 1999).
48. "Statement of Frieda S. Miller in Favor of S. 784."
49. USDOL, Children's Bureau, *A Maternity Policy for Industry* (Washington, DC: Government Printing Office, 1944), 1–3.
50. *Standards for Maternity Care and Employment of Mothers in Industry*, 1942, Box 190, Division of Research, Women Workers in World War II, RG86, National Archives; Subcommittee of the Interdepartmental Committee on Children and Youth, *Planning Services for Children of Employed Mothers* (Washington, DC: U.S. Department of Labor, Women's Bureau, May 1953), 26; Allison L. Helper, *Women in Labor: Mothers, Medicine, and Occupational Health in the United States, 1890–1980* (Columbus: Ohio State University Press, 2000), 67–82.
51. "War Labor Board Policy on Women Workers," attachment to Louis Rocque from Lillian Hatcher, May 5, 1948, UAW Fair Practices Collection, Box 14, folder 10, Wayne State.

52. Bess Furman, "Maternity Aid Set for 500,000 Women," *New York Times*, July 27, 1944; Kriste Lindenmeyer, *"A Right to Childhood": The U.S. Children's Bureau and Child Welfare, 1912–46* (Urbana: University of Illinois Press, 1997).
53. Official Report of Proceedings before the Women's Bureau of the Department of Labor, "Conference of Women Representatives of Labor Unions on War and Post-War Adjustment of Women Workers," 103–5; unpublished typescript, April 19, 1945, Box 178, folder "Conferences 1945," Division of Research Records Re: Women Workers in WWII, 1940–1945, RG86, National Archives. *Revision of the Maternity Protection Convention.*
54. *Revision of the Maternity Protection Convention*, 34.
55. "Conference of Women Representatives of Labor Unions," 104–5.
56. Ibid., 106–7, 118.
57. Ibid., 106–7.
58. Ibid., 108–9, 100–103; UAW-CIO Women's Bureau, *Women Then and Now* (Detroit: UAW, 1954), 29.
59. "Maternity Leaves Urged for Workers," *New York Times*, May 1, 1945; Conference of Women Representatives of Labor Unions," 101, 103.
60. "Maternity Leaves Urged For Workers,"
61. "Protection in Maternity Urge Labor Bureau," *Minneapolis Labor Review*, May 10, 1945.
62. "Maternity Protection of Employed Women," 25–26, 29.
63. Memo to Edward B. Persons from Frieda Miller, November 10, 1950.
64. USDOL, "Observations of the United States Government with Respect to Revision of Convention No. 3 Concerning the Employment of Women before and after Childbirth," November 1950, 6-2-9-3, Box 67, Office of Director, General Correspondence, 1948–63, RG86, National Archives.
65. Memo to Mr. Edward B. Persons from Frieda Miller, November 10, 1950, 2.
66. International Labour Conference, *Record of Proceedings*, Thirty-fifth Session, Geneva, 1952 (Geneva: ILO, 1953), 343.
67. Memo to Edward B. Persons, from Frieda S. Miller, WB, October 30, 1952, 1, 6-2-9-3, Box 67, Office of Director, General Correspondence of the Women's Bureau, 1948–63, RG86, National Archives; "Observations of the United States Government with Respect to Revision of Convention No. 3," 4; International Labour Conference (ILC), "Revision of the Maternity Protection Convention 1919 (No. 3)," *Report VII* (Geneva: International Labour Office, 1952), 14; ILC, "Committee on Maternity Protection," June 1952, 3–4, 5, 13, ILC 35-510-17 Committee on Maternity Protection Reports (Signed), ILO Archives, Geneva; Mora comment, III/2, V/6; Miller comment, VII/2; Twelfth Sitting discussion, XII/6–9, XIII/1–4, in ILO, 35th Session, Committee on Maternity, June 1952, ILC 35-510-14, ILO Archives.
68. Memo to Edward B. Persons from Frieda S. Miller, October 30, 1952, 4–5.
69. ILC, "Revision of the Maternity Protection Convention 1919 (No. 3)," 34.

70. Comment of M. Budiner to Miss Fairchild, 27.9.52, Minute Sheet, 5, WN 5-62/5-3, ILO Archives.
71. *Revision of the Maternity Protection Convention 1919*, 12–40; *Maternity Protection* (Geneva: ILO, 1965), extract from the Report of the 35th (1965) Session of the Committee of Experts.
72. "Points the U.S. Government Recommends for Consideration by the Governing Body in Connection with Revision of Convention 3 (1919), "Employment of Women before and after Childbirth," March 11, 1948, 5, 6-2-9-3(3), Box 67, Office of Director, General Correspondence, 1948–63, RG86, National Archives. For opposition in 1952, see Memo to Persons from Miller, October 30, 1952, 1.
73. USDOL, Bureau of Employment Security, *Rhode Island Disability Insurance Program* (Washington, July 1954), 4–7; "Maternity Protection of Employed Women," 8–9.
74. "Maternity Protection of Employed Women," 8–9; "Recent Developments in Rhode Island Cash Sickness Benefits," *Monthly Labor Review* 63 (July 1946): 21–24.
75. "Maternity Benefit Provisions for Employed Women," 34; "Maternity Protection of Employed Women," 8.
76. Letter to Margaret L. Plunkett, Chief, Division on Women's Labor Law and Civil and Political Status, Women's Bureau from Margaret F. Ackroyd, May 31, 1949, 2-40-5-1, file: Rhode Island, maternity, Box 23, Office of Director, General Correspondence, 1918–1963, RG86, National Archives.
77. Lise Vogel, *Mothers on the Job: Maternity Policy in the U.S. Workplace* (New Brunswick, NJ: Rutgers University Press, 1993).
78. Jack M. Elkin, "The 1946 Amendments to the Railroad Retirement and Railroad Unemployment Insurance Acts," *Social Security Bulletin* 9 (December 1946): 23–33, 49–50.
79. "Statement of J. Dewey Dorsett," in *Railroad Unemployment Insurance Act*, Hearings before a Subcommittee of the Committee on Interstate and Foreign Commerce, House of Representatives, 80th Cong., 1st Sess. On H.R. 3150 (Washington, DC: Government Printing Office, 1947), 10. This bill would have repealed the unemployment benefits of the 1946 act before they even went into effect. It failed.
80. *Amendment to Railroad Unemployment Insurance Act*, Hearings before a Subcommittee of the Committee on Labor and Public Welfare, United States Senate, 80th Cong., 1st Sess. On S. 670 (Washington, DC: Government Printing Office, 1947), 57.
81. Testimony of Lester P. Schoene," *Railroad Retirement (Rebuttal Testimony)*, Hearings before the Committee on Interstate and Foreign Commerce, House of Representatives, 79th Cong., 1st sess. On H.R. 1362, part 3 (Washington, DC: Government Printing Office, 1945), 1112.
82. Testimony of Lester P. Schoene," *Railroad Retirement (Rebuttal Testimony)*, 1112–13.

83. *Railroad Unemployment Insurance Act*, Hearings, 80.
84. Daniel Carson, "First Year of Sickness Insurance for Railroad Workers," *Social Security Bulletin* 12 (February 1949): 16; *Maternity Protection of Employed Women*, 5–6; *Maternity Benefit Provisions for Employed Women*, 22–23; *Annual Reports of the Railroad Retirement Board*, National Archives, Great Lakes Branch.
85. Miller to Langer, December 10, 1947, December 22, 1947; Mary Cannon to Mary Irwin, January 20, 1948, Box 263, folder 1, Langer Papers, University of North Dakota Library.
86. "Maternity Relief for Government Employees," Remarks of Mr. Langer, *Congressional Record—Senate*, vol. 94, pt. 1, 80th Congress, 2nd Sess., 1948, 140810, reprinting testimony of Frieda Miller and Martha Eliot from the Women's and Children's Bureaus; "Langer to Reintroduce His Bill for 60-Day Maternity Leaves," *Evening Star* (Washington, DC), December 7, 1948.
87. Letter to Mr. Kenneth Meiklejohn, Solicitor's Office from Frieda S. Miller, attached to Letter to Honorable Frank Pace., Jr., Director, Bureau of the Budget, from Secretary of Labor, June 10, 1949, which repeats her language, Box 20, Office of Director, General Correspondence, 1948–53, 2-1-5-1, RG86, National Archives.
88. *Maternity Leave for Government Employees*, Hearings Before A Subcommittee of the Committee on Post Office and Civil Service, United States Senate, 80th Congress, 2nd Session on S. 784, February 17 and 18, 1948 (Washington, D.C.: Government Printing Office, 1948), 39.
89. Ibid., 36–37.
90. Vogel, *Mothers on the Job*, 78–88.
91. On proposed amendment to social security disability, see "Statement of Miss Frieda S. Miller . . . submitted to the Ways and Means Committee of the House of Representatives in support of certain amendments to the Social Security Act," H.R. 2893, Mr. Doughton, 81st Congress, April 15, 1949, in Miller Papers, A37, box 8, folder 168, Schlesinger Library.
92. "Statement of Frieda S. Miller," 3; letter to Meiklejohn.
93. See Secretary of Labor to Pace Jr., *Maternity Leave for Government Employees*, 31.
94. Statements of the Chairman, *Treaties and Executive Agreements*, Hearings, 541–42.
95. Cobble, *Other Women's Movement*, 130.
96. Somavía quoted in Chakravarthi Raghavan, "Radical Solutions Needed for Poverty and the Working Poor," Third World Network, 5 June 2000 at http://www.twnside.org.sg/title/radical.htm; "C183, Maternity Protection Convention, 2000," at http://www.ilo.org/ilolex/cgi-lex/convde.pl?C183.

12 THE BATTLE WITHIN THE HOME

DEVELOPMENT STRATEGIES AND THE COMMODIFICATION OF CARING LABORS AT THE 1975 INTERNATIONAL WOMEN'S YEAR CONFERENCE

Jocelyn Olcott

In 1963, Domitila Barrios de Chungara observed her first meeting of the Housewives Committee of the militant Siglo XX tin miners' union.[1] By her telling, her husband had thought she would attend one meeting and then "continue in the corner of my house."[2] She carried on with the Thursday afternoon meetings, where she and her *compañeras* would discuss union business and then spend time "embroidering or doing things we enjoyed" before going home. According to an account she offered seventeen years later, her husband, a committed union member, became irate. He stopped giving her money from his meager paychecks, started drinking, and, for the first time in their marriage, he beat her. He did not forbid her to attend the meetings, but when she asked him for money, he snarled that she should ask the union for a salary, since she spent so much time working for it. She stopped attending the meetings, and when a union leader asked her why, she explained her predicament. The unionist suggested she remind her husband "who cleans, who cooks, who attends to the little ones at home."

When she recommenced her union activities, her husband stopped speaking to her, so Barrios de Chungara went on strike. At her father's urging, she continued to cook, but she suspended all other domestic labors. When her husband complained, she retorted, "Since you say that I don't do anything, bring someone who can do things, who can clean, who can cook. And have her come right away because there's a mountain of diapers here." As the days went by, she reportedly tore up curtains and some of her husband's pants to use as diapers. The following month, she resumed her household labors again but kept track of all her hours and, at the end of the month, presented her husband with a bill for 240 pesos—three times his monthly wages. They finally resolved their differences, according to her narrative, when the Housewives Committee invited him to speak about the union movement, positioning him as an organizing authority. "That's how my husband understood me," she recalled, "and since then he participates with me in everything. That is the battle that I had to win within my home."

This parable, part of an informal talk Barrios de Chungara delivered to rural women's groups, neatly illustrated her lesson that men and women needed to work together to combat their class enemies rather than fighting against each other. She published her talk in a pamphlet adorned with cartoon-style drawings of Bolivian peasants facing off against Uncle Sam and dissolute Bolivian elites. She recounted that when she attended the 1975 UN-sponsored International Women's Year (IWY) conference, she observed two types of liberation. "One," she explained, "of those who think that women will be free when they are equal to men in all their vices. That is called 'feminism.' . . . That form of struggle is for moneyed women, who have everything and just want to imitate the vices of men."[3] The other form of liberation, she asserted, was "so that our opinion is respected inside and outside the home." This respect, she insisted, would be achieved through class struggle. "When we struggle men against women," she elaborated, "we are only pleasing the capitalists, who have created *machismo*, which dictates that men don't accept women's participation, thus dividing us so that we cannot struggle together, united. For this reason, the capitalists have also created feminism, that is, that women fight against men." To avoid any confusion about who were the "capitalists," this explanation was accompanied by a cartoon of Uncle Sam standing spread-eagle, pushing a group of men to one side and women to another (figure 12.1). Barrios de Chungara's pamphlet caricatures—both literally and figuratively—the ideological feuds between 1970s Marxists and feminists (figure 12.1). Arguments often degenerated into a chicken-or-the-egg debate over

FIGURE 12.1 Domitila Barrios de Chungara, *La mujer y la organización*. 1a ed. La Paz, Bolivia: UNITAS, CIDOP, CIPCA, 1980.

the tired question of whether women's emancipation must precede or follow economic justice—the feminist imaginary of class collaboration to wage a "battle of the sexes" versus the Marxist paradigm of revolution through class struggle—with fervent partisans in both camps.

However, Barrios de Chungara's pamphlet also highlights a critical and unresolved problem within both Marxism and feminism: how to liberate women from what Lenin dubbed "the barbarously unproductive, petty, nerve-wracking, stultifying and crushing drudgery" of domestic labor.[4] This "battle within the home"—the struggle for the recognition and alleviation of unpaid reproductive labor—became a central issue at the International Women's Year Conference, the site of Barrios de Chungara's alienation from feminism.[5] Preceded by two "encounter sessions"—one on women and development and another for journalists—the IWY events drew some 1,200 delegates to an intergovernmental conference, held at the northern end of Mexico City in the Ministry of Foreign Relations in Tlaltelolco Plaza, and another 6,000 participants to a parallel nongovernmental organization (NGO) tribune, which took place in the southern part of the city in the medical center of the Mexican Institute for Social Security. The Mexico City conference marked the first of the UN women's conferences—including 1980 in Copenhagen and 1985 in Nairobi and 1995 in Beijing. The Mexico City conference was among the very first of the UN conferences to include a parallel NGO tribune.

In most accounts of these conferences, written largely by scholars and activists who attended some or all of them, Barrios de Chungara stands as the authentic voice of the subaltern, and her bravery in standing up to speak truth to power at the UN tribune marks the turning point in international second-wave feminism toward a dialectical resolution of the conflict. As the historian Francesca Miller explains that by the Nairobi conference, "Women of diverse cultures and ethnicities and social and economic strata became aware of the urgency and immediacy of one another's concerns."[6] This sense of synthetic resolution, however, emerges from a focus on conflicts between participants in the industrialized and developing worlds and on issues in the public sphere. However, if we see the fault line as running not between the North and South, the Third and First worlds, or the industrialized and developing nations but rather between those who saw commodification as emancipatory and those who saw it as alienating, then the only resolution we see by the 1995 Beijing conference is a clear victory of the former camp. By examining the debates over reproductive labor—including the unpaid "caring" work of childcare, housekeeping, food provision, and the maintenance of critical community networks—this concern about commodification comes more sharply into focus. Current scholarship on transnational labor has given some consideration to uncommodified reproductive labor, particularly the phenomenon of "transnational motherhood."[7] Overwhelmingly, however, scholars have focused on commodified labor, including the transnational circulation of domestic laborers, hospital and nursing-home attendants, and sex workers.[8]

Policymakers and activists at the Mexico City events responded to geopolitical struggles, local political battles, and ideological convictions by seeking to naturalize strategic choices, making, for example, the socialization of childcare or wages for housework seem the "common sense" solutions to this knotty problem and a corollary question about whether participation in the labor market would liberate women from patriarchy. However, alongside this question sat the even thornier problem of what labor "counted" as such. Prevailing productivist emphases of modernization and development strategies stressed commodified labor—wage labor and production for markets—and either devalued or effaced the subsistence labor that occupied most women's energies.

The IWY events took place during the UN's Second Decade for Development, amid the heyday of the Women in Development (WID) program that, as development economist Naila Kabeer explains, centers on the "efficiency argument"—the "idea that women were productive agents whose potential had been underutilized under welfare-oriented approaches."[9] If development programs simply expanded to include women, the logic ran, women would become efficient contributors to development and would gain bargaining power at home.[10] Policy makers often marked women's progress by the extent to which they participated in the wage labor force and the so-called active life. Embedded in the liberal discourses of productivism at the 1975 IWY conference, then, are the seeds of a neoliberal project that by the 1990s called for the commodification of everything from air to water and the beginnings of the microfinance movement. To U.S. labor historians, developmentalist arguments are likely to recall Barbara Nelson's observations about the "two-channel welfare state," demonstrating how Workmen's Compensation programs came to be seen as an entitlement based on "socially legitimate, standardized decision criteria," while Mother's Aid programs were seen as charitable and discretionary.[11] The WID projects similarly sought to "shift attention from *welfare to equality* for women in the development process."[12]

In proclaiming 1975 as International Women's Year, the UN stated its goals as "the achievement of equality between the sexes, the integration of women into development and the enhancement of women's contribution to world peace."[13] The UN Commission on the Status of Women had initially proposed the themes of development and equality, and the General Assembly added the theme of peace during its 1972 session.[14] Still, the October 1974 report from the Economic and Social Council (ECOSOC), which oversaw the IWY activities, specified three agenda items for the intergovernmental conference as equality, development, and producing a World Plan of Action.[15] The theme (much less the goal) of "peace" seemed to have dropped out entirely; as one Mexican newspaper editorialized, "Development is the new name for peace."[16]

Both observers at the time and retrospective accounts have described the tensions between development and equality as reflecting geopolitical disputes, reiterating the Marxist-feminist debates over which objective must take priority over the other. Amid widespread decolonization movements, postcolonial nations—particularly the Group of 77 (G77) nonaligned countries—had come to dominate the UN's General Assembly, and they linked development with the implementation of a New International Economic Order (NIEO) that promoted more equitable trade relations and sovereign control over natural resources. The emphasis on equality, in this context, appeared as part of the U.S. State Department's broader opposition to these efforts. "These are the three main differences," reported New York City NOW member Elaine Livingstone from one of UN planning sessions, "the developing countries feel that women cannot gain equality until their countries are more developed economically, Mexico and a few other countries feel that a new economic order must come first, and the USSR feels that peace is the first priority. The United States and the United Kingdom stressed that women cannot wait until these large world problems are solved, that women's problems are not a reflection of society's problems, but part of them, therefore when women's status improves so will the economy and chances for peace."[17]

Debates over how to relieve women of the burden of uncommodified reproductive labors, however, raised a far more difficult problem than the tensions between Marxists and feminists or the many other fault lines that appeared during the conference. Some observers dismissed these concerns as the bourgeois feminist demands of "housewives," concurring with Barrios de Chungara's implication that these were the concerns of "moneyed women." Others offered an array of solutions, ranging from the socialization of reproductive labor to the restructuring of families. This chapter sketches the context for these debates and then considers the centrality of reproductive labor to these discussions and the conference's failure to address it. With a pronounced developmentalist ethos broadly shared across the political and ideological spectrum, efforts to resolve the reproductive-labor problem stalled amid widely held convictions that commodification offered the path to global development.

Despite the conspicuous challenges of addressing reproductive-labor issues, IWY organizers held out the promise that this historic conference offered an unprecedented opportunity to reshape household labor relations. The IWY, the UN's press release promised, "gives the international community a unique opportunity to promote genuine equality between men and women, not only in law but in everyday life."[18] Margaret Bruce, the head of the UN's Commission on the Status of Women, told a meeting of the American Association of University Women (AAUW) at the UN that "IWY, it is hoped, will result in a worldwide consciousness raising."[19] The interplay between the intergovernmental conference and the NGO tribune spotlighted concerns about how the feminist mantra that the "personal is political" would manifest in UN policy recommendations. With locales appropriate to their respective activities, the intergovernmental conference focused on geopolitical questions while the NGO tribune gave greater consideration to social issues, including quotidian matters such as household labor. To be sure, the official tribune agenda, written by the more established NGOs that enjoyed consultative status with the UN, such as the YWCA and International Planned Parenthood Federation, did not dwell on such matters, devoting more time to the safer, policy-oriented discussions of public health, population control, electoral politics, educational and labor rights, and economic development schemes. Still, the significant participation of smaller NGOs and individual activists meant that the NGO establishment could not retain control over tribune sessions, much less hallway palaver and dinnertime kvetching.

The one point of agreement—in both the conference and the tribune and across ideological, political, and cultural divides—was about the need to alleviate women's domestic labor burden. The draft World Plan of Action—the document used as a starting point at the intergovernmental conference and the subject of heated debate among tribune participants—insisted that a "reassessment of the functions and roles traditionally allotted to each sex within the family and the community at large is essential. The necessity of a change in the traditional role of men as well as women must be recognized. In order to allow for women's equal participation in all societal activities, men must accept shared responsibility for home and children."[20] In her inaugural address to the NGO tribune, Mexican First Lady María Esther Zuno de Echeverría, railed against the "false, mutilating dilemma" that forced women to choose between, on the one hand, having families and accepting a "miserable existence, overwhelmed by constant pregnancy, poverty, excessive workloads, and poor health" or, on the other, a life of intellectual and personal creativity.[21] Swedish Prime Minister Olof Palme stressed the importance of relieving women of domestic obligations, giving both men and women more balanced lives.[22] The Colombian Esmeralda Arboleda Cuevas, attending the conference as a UNESCO advisor, told a reporter that men should assist "even in washing the children's diapers; they must help with domestic matters."[23]

The demands of reproductive labor—the issue that, on its face, seemed most likely to unite this diverse gathering—proved to be as divisive as any other, however. Feminists from around the world hoped that their experiences as homemakers would provide the ground for unity and solidarity. Despite profound political and cultural differences and a conspicuous language gap, for example, Betty Friedan asserted that if she could simply sit next to one of the Chinese delegates at a reception, "some woman-to-woman things would get across."[24] Such assumptions, though, ignored stark differences in the conditions of women's reproductive labor. A Latin American woman responding to Friedan at the tribune explained, "In Latin America, the problem is not that the men are in power, but rather it is that the great imperialist powers cling to their privileges. For you, the most important problem is to liberate yourselves while preserving your quality of life; for the underdeveloped, we are liberating ourselves to be able to eat.... You ask for solidarity among all women; tell me, can a servant and her mistress unite?"[25] Like Barrios de Chungara's caricature of U.S. feminism, such challenges framed the conflict in terms of geopolitical and class conflicts. Placing the commodification of reproductive labor center stage, this participant joined a growing chorus lamenting that the emancipation of the mistress required the exploitation of the servant.

"Yes, It Would Be Good If He Helped Me a Little More": Strategies and Struggles

In addition to taking place during the UN's Second Decade for Development, the IWY conference followed major UN conferences on food and on population, both of which stressed the promise of improved technologies and population control. Amid this progressive and liberal ethos, the overwhelming tenor of the IWY conference portrayed women's domestic subordination as a drag on development. Licelot Marte de Barrios, the head of the Dominican delegation, argued that so long as women remained in a secondary position to men, they would "act as a brake on the country's evolution."[26] Historian Judith Zinsser, who attended the Copenhagen and Nairobi conferences, indicates that in Mexico City "ending the subordination of women was not a goal in itself" but rather served as a means of achieving development objectives.[27]

The first area of debate centered on how, in a developmentalist regime, to count women's unpaid household labor. Using metrics like gross domestic product (GDP) to gauge economic growth, analysts inevitably concluded that unpaid reproductive labor badly needed modernization. In the early 1970s, interventions by feminist social scientists had interrogated the impact of economic policies on women's unpaid labor, including the exclusion of that labor from data such as the GDP and other productivity measurements.[28] Viola Victorine Burnham, the wife of the Guyanese prime minister, insisted, "Women's labor in the home is not unproductive labor" but rather forms part of the female labor force.[29] Nonetheless, such assertions gained little traction within either the Marxist or liberal development strategies that prevailed at the IWY events.

Ignoring women's massive contributions to food production and other subsistence labor, IWY propaganda and planning documents stressed that women remained a squandered resource in development efforts and that rendering women more efficient and productive would advance Third World countries on the road toward economic security. Overwhelmingly, the modernization of gender roles in this conception depended on the *commodification* of women's labor. The New York–based organization UN We Believe sponsored a series of glossy ads promoting the conference, including one showing a man in profile with a woman shadowed in profile behind him under the headline "Half the brainpower of the world is out of service" (figure 12.2). The caption below explained, "Half the minds on *earth* belong to women. Who knows the penalties of holding back their development? Who knows what product of human thought will never

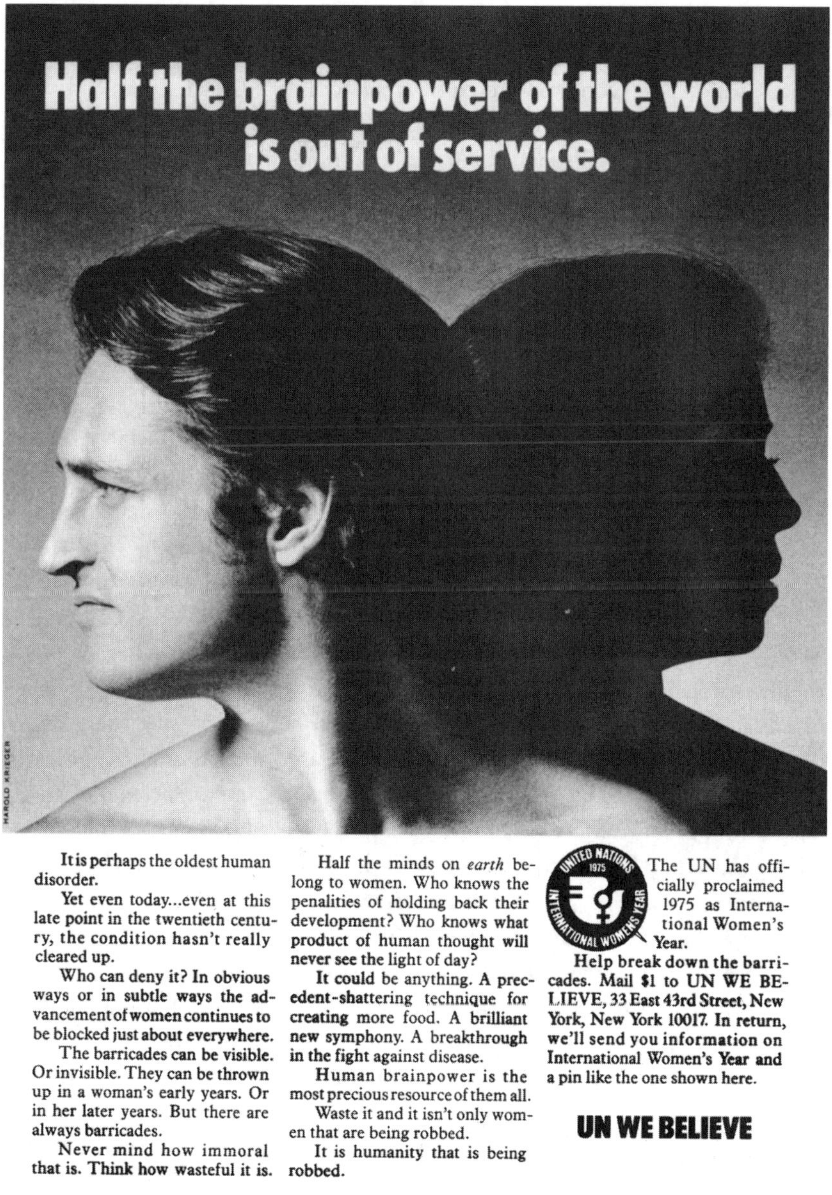

FIGURE 12.2   UN We Believe advertisement for International Women's Year. *Courtesy of UNA-USA*

see the light of day?"[30] NOW similarly sponsored a series of ads with the tag line "Woman Power. It's much too good to waste."[31] Eric Ojala, the director of social and economic policy for the UN's Food and Agriculture Organization, pointed to the "intolerable and colossal waste of human potential that women represent" and argued that the IWY should concentrate on integrating women into agricultural production and rural development.[32]

This insistence that the labor market would emancipate women pervaded IWY events as delegates cited labor force statistics to demonstrate both women's emancipation and economic and cultural modernity. First lady Jehan Sadat evidenced Egypt's modernization by indicating that women comprised 35 percent of its labor force.[33] Vilma Espín boasted that, as a triumph of the Cuban Revolution, women constituted 25 percent of the labor force and 44 percent of the workers in light industry.[34] Not to be bested, Patricia Hutar, leading the U.S. delegation, countered that women thrived under capitalism, comprising 45 percent of the U.S. labor force. Valentina Tereshkova, meanwhile, insisted that fully half of Soviet women contributed to economic activity, running businesses and accounting for 31 percent of legislators. "There are no obstacles in our country," she explained to one reporter. "There, everything is created and guaranteed so that woman can develop fully, just like a man. There are palpable testimonies."[35] The UN itself celebrated images of women in nontraditional jobs. The cover of one *IWY Bulletin*, published by the UN's Centre for Social Development and Humanitarian Affairs, featured a stylized photo of an all-women's road-construction crew in Lesotho (figure 12.3).[36] While the *Bulletin* offered no discussion of the photo or the program it represented, the text of the newsletter itself reinforced WID's productivist goals of shifting women from "welfare" programs to "productive" labor.

These formulations stressing the importance of the labor market and "productive" labor obscured the value of women's uncommodified labor and largely ignored the fact that the vast majority of women performed substantial and indispensable labor in food production and preparation, in some regions taking responsibility for nearly all food production.[37] The *New York Times* cited a Yale University study finding that in many cultures, women performed some of the most onerous tasks, such as carrying water, wood, and food.[38] The IWY tribune newspaper reported that the average Zairois woman worked in manioc fields four to eight hours a day, up to 312 days per year. On the journey from her field to the village—a trek that might cover a distance as far as ten kilometers—she would collect and carry thirty to forty kilograms of firewood.[39] Central American women expended similar labor tending livestock, grinding corn, and collecting water. A Kenyan respondent estimated that women produced 90 percent of the village food supply; a South Indian woman put the figure for her community at 75 percent. A group of *campesinas* attending a four-week agricultural training program in Tenango del Valle, Mexico, during the conference estimated that they spent an average of sixteen hours per day on reproductive labors.[40] A veteran employee of the UN Economic Commission for Africa estimated that women performed between 50 and 80 percent of the continent's agricultural production.[41] Development discourses that stressed "productive" (i.e., commodified) labor, however, ignored these efforts.

The tribune organizers recognized the effects of reproductive labor demands on women's opportunities, but they envisioned private solutions, such as the redistribution of household labor between men and women. By this logic, once

FIGURE 12.3 Lesotho women's work crew, from the cover of *IWY Bulletin*, no. 1 (July 1974). *UN Photo/anonymous*

women enjoyed equal income-earning opportunities with men, the comparative advantage of keeping women at home and sending men into the labor market would vanish, leading men and women to assume equal shares of unpaid domestic labor. Thus, they fought for wage parity and equality in educational and professional opportunities. However, as sociologist Monisha Das Gupta argues, second-wave feminists ignored the "gendered logic of capitalism" and the diversity of household arrangements, favoring the "commodification rather than socialization of the feminized work of cooking, cleaning, and caring."[42]

Other participants sidestepped the knotty question of who would perform reproductive labors by calling for their "socialization," even if often combined with a liberal emphasis on labor-market participation. Helvi Sipilä, the only woman in the UN secretariat and the secretary general of the IWY, stressed that the most important policy issue was the liberalization of divorce laws and the creation of child care centers "so that women can have as much time available to them for their individual development as men do."[43] The G77 delegations, pointing to women's double labor burden, issued a statement calling for, among other measures, the "accelerated transfer of the heaviest domestic labors to public services."[44] Across town, a coalition of Mexican communist and socialist organizations staged a counterconference calling for the complete socialization of domestic labor.[45]

The wages-for-housework campaign that had gained some traction in the United States and Europe did not have many advocates at the IWY meetings, perhaps because most socialist-feminists, the strategy's most vocal advocates, boycotted the conference as a liberal, bourgeois enterprise.[46] Although some socialist-feminists expressed concern that wages for housework would reinforce the sexual division of labor, others insisted that it would "get money into the hands of women" and challenged the notion that women would "join" the working class only by getting a "second job" in the paid labor force.[47] Despite the absence of partisans, the idea did get some airing in discussions. Françoise Giroud, the French minister for women's issues, advocated for government-paid mothers' wages, indicating that children provided women with a "powerful weapon" for their struggle. "Instead of fighting to obtain men's work," she explained, women "should try to conserve this control."[48] In a pamphlet published before the conference opened, a group of Mexican feminists explicitly challenged the Leninist formula to remove women from "domestic slavery" in order to draw them into "productive labor." "This 'Year,'" they argued, "should posit a just valuation of women's labor, as much in its domestic aspects as in the factory or the office." While strategies such as wage parity, socialization, and wages for housework sought to address the labor side of the household-labor problem, other approaches focused on the household side. Certainly, many feminists hoped that a reallocation of domestic labor would result naturally from wage parity, and advocates of "mothers' wages" predicted a strengthening of women's bargaining power within households.

The IWY tribune organizers, many of whom planned the IWY tribune while also organizing the NGO forum for the UN's 1974 World Population Conference in Bucharest, sought to alleviate women's domestic labor duties by promoting family planning and "responsible parenthood."[49] The Population Conference had sounded alarm bells about the "population bomb," emphasizing the threat not of per capita consumption of resources in industrialized centers but rather the gross numbers of people in poorer regions.[50] The public agencies in the United States had encouraged involuntary sterilizations of Mexican American, Puerto Rican, and black women, and Indira Gandhi's government in India had offered women and men incentives to accede to their own sterilization. The IWY tribune's emphasis on family planning, therefore, stemmed not only from the population panic among its liberal organizers but also from a recognition that advocating family planning would draw financial support for the tribune.[51] Radical women's organizations both within the United States and abroad lambasted this eugenicist approach, tagging family planning policies as genocidal rather than liberatory, sparking accusations against the "population control establishment" and charges of "indiscriminate birth control" in lieu of policies to mitigate starvation wages and the uneven distribution of resources.[52] One columnist in the Mexican daily *Excélsior* lamented the racist implications of the population bomb sloganeering, which discouraged women from having children that consume "food, goods and space that rightfully belong to others" and implied they posed an obstacle to women who wanted to "liberate themselves, to work and to study." Such logic, she elaborated, made children "enemies of their parents, of their siblings, and of society itself."[53]

The socialization and commodification strategies would reorganize this labor but generally retain the sexual division of labor. If women were to perform less reproductive labor, there were two possible outcomes: that less reproductive labor would be performed overall or that men would take on more of it. Per the draft World Plan of Action, however, most officials at the intergovernmental conference supported the redistribution of household labor. In his inaugural remarks, President Luis Echeverría stated that "there are no labors suitable to women or to men; there are tasks suitable to humankind."[54] Secretary General Sipilä insisted that education must include raising men's and women's awareness so that neither would shoulder the entire burden of domestic labors. "Men should stay home for a period of time," she explained, "attending the children and domestic labors so that there is an authentic equality between the two humans who make up the couple."[55] West German youth minister Katharine Focke similarly called for policies that encouraged men to share the burden of domestic labor, while Vilma Espín insisted that the recently implemented Cuban Law of Family Relations would accomplish the same ends.[56]

Seeking a more popular perspective on the questions of family structure and household labor, *Washington Post* reporter Marlise Simons canvassed participants in an IWY-related agricultural training program in Tenango del Valle, Mexico.[57] Naval de Sornoza, who cultivated rice on Ecuador's Pacific coast, barely made enough to buy food for her six children and pay rent on a two-room home. She made no mention of a husband or other adult members of her household. María Reynosa, who had come from the Ecuadorian highlands, informed the reporter, "My husband and I are completely equal. . . . We do the same work on the land and sleep in the same bed at night." At the end of their workday, however, Reynosa washed and cooked while her husband waited to be served. "If you call that discrimination," she conceded, "well, yes, it would be good if he helped me a little more." The report revealed skepticism about transforming gender ideologies from above. A Colombian man purportedly forbade his wife from attending the training program, insisting, "What do they need a year for if men are the boss and always will be?" Prudencia Kuri, who worked on an agricultural collective outside Lima, said that a new law in Peru guaranteed equal rights. "The last time we had a meeting of our commune we received an announcement. From now on the women had permission to speak up in the meetings, just like the men, it said."

Outside the intergovernmental conference, participants and observers indicated that such official proclamations would remain empty promises without a radical restructuring of families. The prominent Mexican sociologist Rodolfo Stavenhagen called for a "redefinition of the structure and role of the family in modern society," favoring the models of the Chinese commune and the Israeli kibbutz.[58] "In the process of economic development," Stavenhagen explained, "rural families tend to disintegrate and men's and women's roles are increasingly differentiated. The monetary economy, migrations, and proletarianized labor produce strong tensions within the traditional family institution that is bound to subsistence agriculture." While men adapted better to "productive labor," he elaborated, women "cannot adjust in the same way, owing to their family ties, imposed by biology and cultural tradition." Their labor, he continued, "is undervalued by a society that only attributes importance to activities in which the market intervenes."

At a tribune session on families, Dutch sociologist Ruut Veenhoven and Kenyan legal scholar Opinya Okoth-Ogendo both encouraged laws that would accommodate more diverse family formations that would distribute labor more equitably.[59] Okoth-Ogendo described families as an obstacle to social change, and Veenhoven celebrated the growing social emphasis on happiness over conformity. Pointing to various European experiments in communal living, as well as examples of diverse social formations, Veenhoven insisted, "family is not the salvation... the individual should have the ability and the capacity to choose and to depend on more extensive nuclei than the traditional family, since we cannot say that its structure is best."[60]

Meanwhile, rural and working-class women from developing countries, women like Domitila Barrios de Chungara or María Reynosa, advocated a strategy that dismayed many feminists: mandating a family wage for men that would allow women to avoid the double shift of performing both subsistence and wage labor. Barrios de Chungara elaborates her concern in her *testimonio*:

> One day I got the idea of making a chart. We put for example the price of washing clothes per dozen pieces, and we figured out how many dozen items we washed per month. Then the cook's wage, the babysitter's, the servant's. We figured out everything that we miners' wives do everyday. Adding it all up, the wage needed to pay us for what we do in the home... was much higher than what the men earned in the mine for a month. So,

that way we made our *compañeros* understand that we really work, and even more than they do in a certain sense. And that we even contribute more to the household with what we save. So, even though the state doesn't recognize what we do in the home, the country benefits from it, because we don't receive a single penny for this work. And as long as we continue in the present system, things will always be like this. That's why I think it's so important for us revolutionaries to win that first battle in the home.[61]

This position challenged the developmentalist divide between productive and reproductive labor and recognized—more than commodification or socialization strategies did—that reproductive labor constituted a full-time job that could not be adequately performed by a few underfunded public institutions or by the haphazard division of labor between men and women who also held paying jobs.[62] Many activists saw feminists' insistence on equality as blunting their most effective weapon: a politics structured around highly essentialized and biologized gender differences. The longtime Uruguayan activist Dr. Sofía de Demicheli warned women to proceed cautiously with their own liberation. "The woman who wants to compare herself to man in everything either speaks from rote or doesn't know what she says," she chided. "The result is so absurd that the man that she wants seems in all ways like a woman. Women in pants, men in skirts. Unisex. *Hijo de mi vida*, those are aberrations."[63]

This posture rested upon an insistent heteronormativity that reacted against both challenges to conventional family structures and the presence of lesbian activists at the IWY tribune. Barrios de Chungara, like many Latin American observers, particularly marked their alienation from discussions of women's sexuality at the IWY tribune. Pointing to interventions by "lesbians and prostitutes"—nearly always referenced in one breath as markers of Western feminist dissolution—Barrios performed her Marxist politics through a pronounced and vitriolic homophobia.[64] Daily editorials in the Mexican press lamented the presence of *marimachos* [dykes] and celebrated interventions by "true feminists" such as Arianna Stassinopoulos (now Huffington) extolling the virtues of motherhood.[65]

High-profile representatives echoed this emphasis on gender complementarity. Jehan Sadat told a press conference that Western feminism "does more harm than good, since we have to find balance within the family and in no way stage a revolution against men but rather work together."[66] Sri Lankan Prime Minister Sirimavo Bandaranaike insisted in her opening remarks to the conference, "We must not think of the man and the woman separately but rather of the couple."[67] Mexican First Lady María Esther Zuno de Echeverría similarly asserted, "Man and woman cannot be considered in isolation nor as signifying antagonism. They should fulfill themselves through integration and reciprocity. . . . Man and woman are not rivals; man and woman do not substitute for one another; man and woman signify unsurpassed complements; man and woman are the very essence of equality, development, and peace."[68]

208 · INTERNATIONAL FEMINISM AND REPRODUCTIVE LABOR

All of these positions rested more on aspirations than experiences. Even as they stressed the importance of placing more women in leadership positions, many feminists imagined a world where, ceteris paribus, women would enter the public realm of politics and professions as unmarked citizen subjects. With enough tweaking of policy—promoting juridical equality, wage parity, and meritocratic educational and professional opportunities—sex would be no more germane to status than handedness or eye color. Socialist women activists similarly envisioned a postrevolutionary social and political utopia in which sex was not salient.[69] And many Third World women aspired to a life of relative material security in which intact, heteronormative families depended on the family wage of a male head of household—precisely the system that activists like Friedan wanted to overthrow—so they could remain aloof from the increasingly market-oriented world economy. None of these conditions pertained, but they remained powerful imaginaries amid prevailing discourses of modernization and development, and IWY participants willingly suspended their disbelief long enough to make assertive claims for their respective positions.

The Devil in the Details: Punting on Policy Recommendations

On the last day of the IWY conference, the *Washington Post* ran an editorial cartoon showing a woman on her hands and knees scrubbing the meeting-hall floor, highlighting one of the events' most obvious failings (figure 12.4). Despite the widespread agreement that women's reproductive labor burdens preceded all

FIGURE 12.4 Cleaning up after IWY, from the *Washington Post*, July 2, 1975. *Mike Peters editorial cartoon (New) © 1975 King Features Syndicate*

other impediments to improving women's status, the final policy recommendations retained a focus on incorporating women into the labor market. Although the NGO tribune by design did not issue a formal statement of its positions, the intergovernmental conference issued two: the Declaration of Mexico, authored by G77 countries, which listed Zionism and apartheid as obstacles to women's emancipation, and the World Plan of Action, which removed this language to secure the support of Israel and the United States. Both documents contained vague references to the importance of lightening women's reproductive labor burdens to allow them greater intellectual development and social and political participation but foundered on the question of who would perform this labor. The World Plan of Action's original statement that "men must accept equal responsibility for home and children" had been replaced with a vaguer proposal encouraging "socially organized services . . . to lighten household chores."[70] The conference manifesto encouraged women to organize "self-help" activities and urged employers to have a "positive attitude" toward hiring women. Policy proposals centered on literacy and vocational training programs and expanded employment opportunities. The document did list, among the fourteen goals for 1980, the "recognition of the economic value of women's work in the home in domestic food production and marketing and voluntary opportunities not traditionally remunerated."[71] However, unlike the proposals to integrate women into labor markets, this objective did not correlate with specific recommendations in national and regional action plans. Prescriptions for "employment and related economic roles" focused on employment opportunity, wage parity, training in technical and management skills, support for cooperatives and microenterprises, abolition of protective legislation and discriminatory hiring practices, and promotion of "concerted efforts . . . to bring about a marked improvement in the position of women in employment."[72] The issue apparently had gained enough attention to merit acknowledgment but not enough to demand concrete policy prescriptions.

The debates over women's unpaid reproductive labors were overshadowed in the end by deliberations over Zionism and the NIEO. The objective of "women's emancipation" required a serious reckoning with he contradictions of uncommodified reproductive labor that sat precisely in the liminal space between culture and economics that international policy makers and activists found impossible to reach. Reproductive labor practices varied dramatically not only between industrialized and "developing" countries but also between rural and urban areas, between professionals and laborers, and among races and ethnicities. Rather than fostering the predicted unity among women, discussions about motherhood and reproductive labor set these differences in stark relief. Most IWY participants—especially in the intergovernmental conference—would not have performed their own reproductive labor but rather would have paid poorer and darker women, reinforcing the ideologies of race and caste that seemed antithetical to their commitments to combating racism and discrimination of all forms.[73] Amid the developmentalist emphasis on labor and productivity, such divides played a particularly pronounced role in identity formation. As women from wide-ranging political, cultural, and ideological walks performed their identities for the national and international media during the course of the conference and tribune, the possibilities for agreeing on this most intimate realm of labor and identity diminished rather than increased. In this sense, issues such as apartheid and disarmament—and even anti-Zionism—offered more promise for unifying an international women's movement than challenges closer to home.

NOTES

1. This chapter has benefited tremendously from critical feedback not only at the Newberry conference on Labor History across the Americas but also at the 2006 Latin American Labor History Conference at Duke University, the seminar on the United States and the Cold War at the New York University, and the Women and Work conference at the City University of New York Center for Worker Education. I am particularly grateful for the thoughtful suggestions of Eileen Boris, Susan Ferber, John French, Julie Greene, Liz Hutchison, Alice Kessler-Harris, Tom Klubock, Premilla Nadasen, Michael Nash, Tom Rogers, David Sartorius, Pete Sigal, Barbara Weinstein, and Marilyn Young.
2. Domitila Barrios de Chungara, *La mujer y la organización*, 1a ed. (La Paz, Bolivia: UNITAS, CIDOP, CIPCA, 1980), 17–23. All translations are my own unless stated otherwise.
3. Ibid., 8.
4. Vladimir Il'ich Lenin, *Collected Works*, 45 vols., vol. 29 (Moscow: Foreign Languages Publishing House, 1960), 429.
5. Reproductive labor can be conceptualized to include a wide range of activities, including biological reproduction (such as childbearing, surrogacy, wet-nursing), social reproduction (such as socialization, networking building, education), and maintaining forms of public respectability within communities. Sex work arguably falls somewhere in the interstices between these areas, but some 1970s feminists placed it within the purview of reproductive labor, pointing to lesbianism as a way to avoid the demands of sexual service.
6. Francesca Miller, *Latin American Women and the Search for Social Justice* (Hanover and London: University Press of New England, 1991), 201. For similar assessments, see Bina Agarwal, "From Mexico 1975 to Beijing 1995," *Indian Journal of Gender Studies* 3, no. 1 (1996): 88; Valentine M. Moghadam, *Globalizing Women: Transnational Feminist Networks* (Baltimore: Johns Hopkins University Press, 2005), 6.
7. See, for example, Pierrette Hondagneu-Sotelo and Ernestine Avila, "I'm Here, but I'm There: The Meanings of Latina Transnational Motherhood," *Gender & Society* 5, no. 11 (1997).

8. See, for example, Doreen J. Mattingly, "The Home and the World: Domestic Service and International Networks of Caring Labor," *Annals of the Association of American Geographers* 91, no. 2 (2001), Alice Kessler-Harris, "Gender and Work: Possibilities for a Global, Historical Overview," in *Women's History in Global Perspective*, ed. Bonnie G. Smith (Urbana and Chicago: University of Illinois Press and the American Historical Association, 2004), Barbara Ehrenreich and Arlie Russell Hochschild, *Global Woman: Nannies, Maids, and Sex Workers in the New Economy*, 1st ed. (New York: Metropolitan Books, 2002), Alice Kessler-Harris, "Reframing the History of Women's Wage Labor: Challenges of a Global Perspective," *Journal of Women's History* 15, no. 4 (2004), Katharyne Mitchell, Sallie A. Marston, and Cindi Katz, "Life's Work: An Introduction, Review and Critique," in *Life's Work: Geographies of Social Reproduction*, ed. Katharyne Mitchell, Sallie A. Marston, and Cindi Katz (Oxford: Blackwell Publishing, 2004), Lourdes Benería, *Gender, Development, and Globalization: Economics as if All People Mattered* (New York: Routledge, 2003).
9. Naila Kabeer, *Reversed Realities: Gender Hierarchies in Development Thought* (London: Verso, 1994), 8. The past fifteen years have witnessed a boom in feminist studies of development, including critical analyses of the WID and Gender and Development (GAD) approaches. For reviews of this literature, see Jane S. Jaquette and Gale Summerfield, *Women and Gender Equity in Development Theory and Practice: Institutions, Resources, and Mobilization* (Durham, N.C.: Duke University Press, 2006), Suzanne Bergeron, *Fragments of Development: Nation, Gender, and the Space of Modernity* (Ann Arbor: University of Michigan Press, 2004).
10. S. Charusheela, "Empowering Work? Bargaining Models Reconsidered," in *Toward a Feminist Philosophy of Economics*, ed. Drucilla K. Barker and Edith Kuiper (London: Routledge, 2003), 287–303.
11. Barbara J. Nelson, "The Origins of the Two-Channel Welfare State: Workmen's Compensation and Mother's Aid," in *Women, the State, and Welfare*, ed. Linda Gordon (Madison: University of Wisconsin, 1990), 136–37.
12. Kabeer, *Reversed Realities*, 6.
13. OPI/CESI Note IWY/December 19, 1974.
14. *Meeting in Mexico: The Story of the World Conference of the International Women's Year (Mexico City, June 19–July 2, 1975)* (New York: United Nations, 1975).
15. [Margaret K. Bruce], "Report of the Economic and Social Council," October 23, 1974, National Organization for Women, New York City Chapter (hereafter NOW-NYC) Records, box 23, folder 11.
16. *Excélsior*, June 19, 1975.
17. Elaine Livingstone to Arlie Scott et al., March 22, 1975, Betty Friedan Papers, Arthur and Elizabeth Schlesinger Library on the History of Women, Radcliffe Institute for Advanced Study, Accession No. 71-62; 77-M105; Carton 107, file 1248.
18. CESI Press Release, OPI/CESI Note IWY/December 19, 1974.

19. NARA, RG 220, (National Archives and Records Administration & Record Group) Records of the U.S. Center for International Women's Year; Subject Files, 1973–1975; A-AS; Box 1; folder AAUW.
20. World Conference of the International Women's Year Mexico City 1975, and United Nations Association. Al-Ber Costa Chapter, *Women in Action* (s.l.: Al-Ber Costa Chapter of the United Nations Association, 1976), 2.
21. *Excélsior*, June 20, 1975.
22. *El Universal*, June 24, 1975.
23. *Xilonen*, 23 June 1975, 6.
24. Betty Friedan, "Scary Doings in Mexico City," in *"It Changed My Life": Writings on the Women's Movement* (Cambridge: Harvard University Press, 1998), 454.
25. *El Universal*, June 21, 1975. *El Universal* underscored this disparity by juxtaposing this story with an article on rural malnutrition and two photographs of unidentified but well-heeled women in western dress eating outside the conference. One described the subject as "devouring" an ice cream.
26. *El Universal*, June 21, 1975.
27. Judith P. Zinsser, "From Mexico to Copenhagen to Nairobi: The United Nations Decade for Women, 1975–85," *Journal of World History* 13, no. 1 (2002): 147.
28. Sheila Rowbotham, *Woman's Consciousness, Man's World* (Harmondsworth, England: Penguin, 1973); Mariarosa Dalla Costa and Selma James, *The Power of Women and the Subversion of the Community*, 2nd ed. (Bristol, England: Falling Wall Press, 1973) Ester Boserup, *Woman's Role in Economic Development* (New York: St. Martin's Press, 1970).
29. *El Universal*, 17 June 1975.
30. NARA, RG 220, Records of the U.S. Center for International Women's Year; Subject Files, 1973–1975; A-AS, Box 1.
31. NOW-NYC Records, Tamiment 106, box 15, folder 10.
32. *El Universal*, June 21, 1975.
33. *El Universal*, June 18, 1975.
34. *El Universal*, June 17, 1975.
35. *El Universal*, June 19, 1975.
36. *IWY Bulletin*. For a study of developmentalist ideology in Lesotho, see James Ferguson, *The Anti-Politics Machine* (Cambridge: Cambridge University Press), 1990.
37. *Christian Science Monitor*, July 30, 1975.
38. *New York Times*, June 28, 1975.
39. *Xilonen*, June 30, 1975.
40. *Washington Post*, June 30, 1975.
41. *El Universal*, June 22, 1975.
42. Monisha Das Gupta, "Housework, Feminism, and Labor Activism: Lessons from Domestic Workers in New York," *Signs: Journal of Women in Culture and Society* 33, no. 3 (2008): 537.

43. *El Universal*, June 16, 1975.
44. *El Nacional*, June 30, 1975.
45. See Mexican secret-police reports from 27 and June 29, 1975, Archivo General de la Nación (AGN, Mexico City), Investigaciones Políticas y Sociales (IPS), Caja 1163-A, Vol. 1, Hojas 520–21, 532, 587–90.
46. The text most commonly read among feminist groups favoring wages for housework was Dalla Costa and James, *The Power of Women and the Subversion of the Community*.
47. Carol Lopate, "Letter to the Movement: Women and Pay for Housework," *Liberation* (May–June 1974): 8–11 [available in Tamiment 138, Leslie Cagan Papers, Box 5, Folder 3]; "Unpaid Labor," *Hera* (March 1975): 16, and "We Are All Workers—Part 2," *Hera* (July 1975): 28–29 [Tamiment 412, Boxed newspapers, Box 477]; "Why Wages for Housework International Is Not a Participant in the Socialist Feminist Conference" [Baxandall Papers, Box 1, Folder 40 in Tamiment Library].
48. *El Universal*, June 22, 1975.
49. "Responsible parenthood" was one of seven major focus areas of the International Council on Women at least by 1972 (See ICW to ECOSOC, July 1972; International Council of Women collection, Box 1, Folder 8, Sophia Smith Collection, Smith College, Northampton, Mass.).
50. Paul R. Ehrlich, *The Population Bomb* (New York: Ballantine, 1968); Matthew Connelly, *Fatal Misconception: The Struggle to Control World Population* (Cambridge: Harvard University Press, 2008), chapters 7 and 8; Laura Briggs, *Reproducing Empire: Race, Sex, Science, and U.S. Imperialism in Puerto Rico* (Berkeley: University of California Press, 2002).
51. International Planned Parenthood Federation was the most prominent NGO involved in organizing the tribune, influencing not only its agenda but also its press coverage. On promoting family planning to secure financial support for the tribune, see Rosalind Harris to Esther Hymer (both NGO tribune organizers), June 10, 1974, Sophia Smith Collection, International Women's Tribune Centre collection, Acc. #89S-27, Box 1; notes on ONGO letterhead, December 17, 1974, about using family-planning agenda to raise money from UNFPA and "population sources," Sophia Smith Collection, International Women's Tribune Centre collection, Acc. #89S-27, Box 3.
52. On "population control establishment," see Bonnie Mass, "The Politics of Population Control: Birth Control, Population Control, and Self-Help," address delivered to the Harvard Medical School Women's Conference on Health, March 1975, Bobbye Ortiz Papers, Box 17, Subject File Latin America 2/4, Duke University Rare Book, Manuscript, and Special Collections Library. On "indiscriminate birth control," see Domitila Barrios de Chungara and Moema Viezzer, *Let Me Speak! Testimony of Domitila, a Woman of the Bolivian Mines* (New York: Monthly Review Press, 1979), 199–200.
53. Magdalena de Bastien, "¿Liberación Femenina? Como siempre, slogans y manipuleo," *Excélsior*, 29 June 1975.

54. *El Universal*, June 20, 1975.
55. *Excélsior*, June 16, 1975.
56. On Focke, see *El Universal*, June 18, 1975; on Espín, see *El Univeral*, June 17, 1975.
57. *Washington Post*, June 30, 1975.
58. Rodolfo Stavenhagen, "Redefinir la función de la familia," *Excélsior*, June 17, 1975.
59. Described in secret-police report from June 27, 1975, AGN, IPS, Caja 1163-A, Vol 1, Hojas 539–41.
60. *Excélsior*, June 28, 1975.
61. Barrios de Chungara and Viezzer, *Let Me Speak!* 35.
62. Younger, unmarried Mexican women often embraced the developmentalist production-consumption divide. The women's sector of the Confederación de Jovenes Mexicanos, for example, argued: "When women leave off being an object of consumption and transform themselves into a subject of production, then they will be liberated" (*El Universal*, June 21, 1975).
63. *El Nacional*, June 26, 1975.
64. Jocelyn Olcott, "Cold War Politics and Cheap Cabaret: Performing Politics at the 1975 International Women's Year Conference" *Gender and History* 22:3 (November 2010), 733–754. Barrios de Chungara and Viezzer, *Let Me Speak!* 197–98.
65. See, for example, *Excélsior*, July 3, 1975; *Excélsior*, July 1, 1975; *El Universal*, June 23, 1975.
66. *El Universal*, June 24, 1975.
67. *El Universal*, June 21, 1975.
68. *Excélsior*, June 16, 1975. The final sentence references the IWY slogan.
69. In one of the more bizarre debates at the official conference, delegates to a subcommittee discussed whether to add sexism to the list of factors (which already included racism, imperialism, apartheid, and Zionism) that impeded women's emancipation. Representatives from Russia, Bulgaria, Bangladesh, and Somalia pointed to the word as a "nasty North American neologism," and the resolution failed by a vote of 26–20, with 10 abstentions (*Xilonen*, June 30, 1975).
70. World Conference, *Women in Action*, xiv; *Excélsior*, July 3, 1975.
71. *Meeting in Mexico*, 69.
72. Ibid., 79.
73. For discussions of these tensions, see Ana Lau, "El nuevo movimiento feminista mexicano a fines del milenio," in *Feminismo en México, ayer y hoy*, ed. Eli Bartra, Anna M. Fernández Poncela, and Ana Lau (Mexico: Universidad Autónoma Metropolitana, 2000), 15, Heidi Tinsman, "The Indispensable Services of Sisters: Considering Domestic Service in the United States and Latin American Studies," *Journal of Women's History* 4, no. 1 (1992), H. Pereira de Melo, "Feminists and Domestic Workers in Rio de Janiero," in *Muchachas No More: Household Workers in Latin America and the Caribbean*, ed. Elsa Chaney and Mary Garcia Castro (Philadelphia: Temple University Press, 1989).

V LABOR RECRUITMENT AND IMMIGRATION CONTROL

INTRODUCTION

Camille Guérin-Gonzales

The surge of interest in transnationalism, globalization, and internationalism marks a return, in many ways, to an earlier vibrant period of knowledge production—the 1920s and 1930s—when academics, activists, and artists envisioned North America as far more interconnected with other nations of the world than those who would write about and research and represent North American peoples and places in the subsequent era of the Cold War.[1] In the Cold War years, the shift away from what many had come to see as universalizing grand narratives reinvigorated exceptionalist ideas about the United States at the same time that it opened the door for greater attention to differences within the United States that threatened ideals of American exceptionalism.[2] The reifying of national identity that accompanied this turn made it difficult to recognize similarities of experience across borders and the ways in which the very concept of the United States is dependent upon policing borders that both separate and connect it to other nation-states. In the late twentieth century, however, a whole host of developments challenged such notions—the breakup of the Soviet Union and the rise of postcolonial nation-states, the push for global "free trade," and, in the United States, the efficacy of the anti–Vietnam War movement and ultimately the sagging fortunes of a labor movement predicated on national boundaries. As a result, scholars on the left increasingly came to see, once again, the global interconnectedness of human experience, in general, and of working people and the products they produce, in particular. This, in turn, has prompted renewed interest in labor migration and its control.

The following chapters offer important insights into the uneasy tension between exclusionary practices of nation building in the early years of the twentieth century and the continued reliance of the United States on the transnational migration of labor. The authors examine the process of state building without seeing that process or its ultimate geographical expression—fixed borders and sovereign states—as determining migration patterns or migrants' sense of belonging—far from it, in fact. They suggest new ways of thinking about the study of human migrations by using a transnational approach to examine the microlevel life projects of individual migrants and groups of migrants and, in the process, illustrate the entwined historicity and contingency of those movements to, from, and around North America. And they tackle three questions of particular interest to the study of workers, the nation-state, and transnationalism: How did internationalism shape the meanings of identity and citizenship? How did international migration challenge ideas of American exceptionalism? And how did migrant workers draw on their transnational experiences to gain control over their everyday lives?

Gunther Peck, in "Feminizing White Slavery in the United States: Marcus Braun and the Transnational Traffic in White Bodies, 1890–1910," looks at how a government-sponsored campaign to restrict the importation of contract workers in the early years of the twentieth century shape-shifted into a campaign to prevent the traffic in women "for immoral purposes." Driving the two campaigns was a discursive strategy that drew on a shared understanding of the horror of "white slavery." Peck skillfully traces the history of slavery as a keyword in American history to explore how white workers in the nineteenth century appropriated the term to define their enthrallment to an exploitative wage system they called "white slavery" and thus demonstrated that their bondage threatened the very foundations of the nation. He then examines the ways in which the meaning of "white slavery" changed by exploring how a federal bureaucrat entrusted with combating white slavery was able almost single-handedly to redefine the term to mean the enslavement of women for sex work.

Peck demonstrates how a middle-level bureaucrat, the Bureau of Immigration's chief undercover agent—and an immigrant himself—parlayed his ability to cross national borders into a position of authority as arbiter of national identity and belonging. He did this by occupying two positions in uneasy tension: He was an official champion of national sovereignty and a protector of borders from undesirables. Peck examines how the agent negotiated these two positions as part of a quest for personal power that would both solidify his identity as an American and authorize him to police national boundaries, the better to protect his transformation from an immigrant to a fully integrated citizen of the nation. This quest shaped the strategies the agent employed to police the national border and helps explain the ease with which he set aside his campaign against contract labor abuses and embraced one that targeted traffickers in women transported to the United States "for immoral purposes." Peck's story illuminates how the managerial revolution in the early twentieth century empowered a new class of bureaucrats to police national boundaries and thus to shape the nation. The transformation Peck describes, from a concern with contract labor to one over the traffic in women, thus exposes the complicated international negotiations that took place in these years over national identity and citizenship.

Michael Snodgrass is similarly concerned with negotiations over national identity and citizenship. His chapter, "Patronage and Progress: The Bracero Program from the Perspective of Mexico," takes up the story of contract labor as it again became a national concern in the second half of the twentieth century. The Bracero Program brought millions of Mexican workers to the United States temporarily and legally over a period of two decades, ending in the 1960s, and Snodgrass examines the program from a variety of Mexican perspectives—that of the federal government, that of intellectuals, that of labor leaders, and, most helpfully, that of returned braceros and their loved ones. At the heart of his chapter are residents of Jalisco with whom Snodgrass has conducted wide-ranging interviews. In the course of his analysis, Snodgrass draws out contrasts between the views of migrant men and those of the women who stayed behind, as well as between the perspectives of braceros from rural and urban Jalisco.

It may be surprising to some U.S. history scholars who are accustomed to rehearsing the hypocrisies and exploitation inherent in the Bracero Program to hear the positive benefits bracero families attribute to their transborder experience, and this sense of surprise can only help us complicate our understanding of the program. Snodgrass's work thus contributes to a rich literature by scholars who have long incorporated analysis of migration experiences from the perspective of *el otro lado*.[3] Younger scholars, like Kelly Lytle Hernández, are also doing pathbreaking work in this regard.[4] Snodgrass also prompts us to engage questions of memory and meaning-making—to consider the structures of feeling and the transformations, both discursive and political economic, that inform contemporary Jalisco residents' recollections of bracero experiences from a half-century ago.

Lara Putnam's analysis of 1920s immigration restriction in Central America, the Caribbean, and the United States serves as another example of transnational historical insight. In "Unspoken Exclusions: Race, Nation, and Empire in the Immigration Restrictions of the 1920s in North America and the Greater Caribbean," Putnam explains how the 1924 Johnson-Reed Act in the United States and its opaque but effective process of implementation vis-à-vis the British Caribbean both participated in and spurred a transnational ban on black immigration throughout the region. That ban, in turn, fostered anticolonial projects in the British Caribbean.

Putnam begins by surveying the Caribbean migrations that helped to establish extensive black populations in the late nineteenth and early twentieth centuries in places as disparate as Panama, Costa Rica, Venezuela, Honduras, Cuba, and New York City. Having put those peoples in the places where 1920s immigration restriction would find them, she then examines the early confusion that reigned over the status of Afro-Caribbeans—were they residents of the

Western Hemisphere, which was excluded from the quotas established by the Johnson-Reed Act, or were they British colonials, and thus subject to the quotas?

When all was said and done, Putnam shows, the Johnson-Reed Act ended up functioning as "a total ban on black immigration," even as it covered its exclusionary tracks. This story in and of itself makes a crucial historiographical contribution. But she also examines the widespread adoption of restrictive immigration policies throughout Latin America and the Caribbean in this same period. And she documents in evocative detail the effects of such policies on Afro-Caribbean individuals and explains how those effects engendered anticolonial responses. Putnam's essay complements Deborah Thomas's study of nationalism and globalization in Jamaica and helps us understand the myriad innovative ways people have translated national policies to gain more power over their everyday lives.[5]

Together, Gunther Peck, Michael Snodgrass, and Lara Putnam illustrate in vivid, practical detail how transnational studies deepen our understanding of migration to, from, and within North America and the Caribbean. In doing so, these chapters and their larger analytical agenda will inform many a labor and working-class history, indebting us for their historical insights into when, where, and how working people move and about the meanings they give those movements.

NOTES

1. Two excellent overviews of this knowledge production are Robin D. G. Kelley, "'But a Local Phase of a World Problem': Black History's Global Vision," in "The Nation and Beyond, Transnational Perspectives on United States History," special issue, *Journal of American History* 86, no. 3 (December 1999): 1045–77; and Michael Forman, *Nationalism and the International Labor Movement: The Idea of the Nation in Socialist and Anarchist Theory* (University Park: Pennsylvania State University Press, 1998).
2. For an elaboration of this argument, see David Thelen, "The Nation and Beyond: Transnational Perspectives on United States History," in "The Nation and Beyond, Transnational Perspectives on United States History," special issue, *Journal of American History* 86, no. 3 (December 1999): 965–75; and Michael Denning, *Culture in the Age of Three Worlds* (London: Verso, 2004).
3. E.g., Gunther Peck, *Reinventing Free Labor: Padrones and Immigrant Workers in the North American West, 1880–1930* (New York: Cambridge University Press, 2000); David Gutierrez, *Walls and Mirrors: Mexican Americans, Mexican Immigrants, and the Politics of Ethnicity* (Berkeley: University of California Press, 1995); Lawrence A. Cardoso, *Mexican Emigration to the United States, 1897–1941* (Tucson: University of Arizona Press, 1980); Camille Guérin-Gonzales, *Mexican Workers and American Dreams: Immigration, Repatriation, and*

California Farm Labor, 1900–1939 (New Brunswick, NJ: Rutgers University Press, 1994); George Sánchez, *Becoming Mexican American: Ethnicity, Culture, and Identity in Chicano Los Angeles, 1900–1945* (New York: Oxford University Press, 1993); Francisco E. Balderrama and Raymond Rodriguez, *Decade of Betrayal: Mexican Repatriation in the 1930s* (Albuquerque: University of New Mexico Press, 2006); and Harry E. Cross and James Sandos, *Across the Border: Rural Development in Mexico and Recent Migration to the United States* (Berkeley: Institute of Governmental Studies, University of California, 1981).

4. Kelly Lytle Hernández, "The Crimes and Consequences of Illegal Immigration: A Cross-Border Examination of Operation Wetback, 1943–1954," *Western Historical Quarterly* (Winter 2006): 421–44, and *Migra: A History of the U.S. Border Patrol* (Berkeley: University of California Press, 2010).

5. Deborah Thomas, *Modern Blackness: Nationalism, Globalization, and the Politics of Culture in Jamaica* (Durham, NC: Duke University Press, 2004).

FURTHER READING

Bashi, Vilna. "Globalized Anti-Blackness: Transnationalizing Western Immigration Law, Policy, and Practice." *Ethnic and Racial Studies* 27, no. 4 (2004): 584–606.

Boehm, Deborah. "'Now I Am a Man and a Woman!': Gendered Moves and Migrations in a Transnational Mexican Community." *Latin American Perspectives* 35, no. 1 (2008): 16–30.

Choy, Catherine Cenita. *Empire of Care: Nursing and Migration in Filipino American History*. Durham, NC: Duke University Press, 2003.

Cohen, Deborah. "From Peasant to Worker: Migration, Masculinity, and the Making of Mexican Workers in the U.S." *International Labor and Working-Class History* 69, no. 1 (2006): 81–103.

Fink, Leon. *The Maya of Morgantown: Work and Community in the New South*. Chapel Hill: University of North Carolina Press, 2003.

Frank, Dana. *Bananeras: Women Transforming the Banana Unions of Latin America*. Boston: South End Press, 2005.

Guérin-Gonzales, Camille, and Carl Strikwerda, eds. *The Politics of Immigrant Workers: Essays on Labor Activism and Migration in the World Economy since 1830*. New York: Holmes and Meier, 1998.

Gutiérrez, David, and Pierrette Hondagneu-Sotelo, eds. *Nation and Migration: Past and Future*. Special Issue of the *American Quarterly*. Baltimore: Johns Hopkins University Press, 2009.

Harzig, Christiane. "Domestics of the World (Unite?): Labor Migration Systems and Personal Trajectories of Household Workers in Historical and Global Perspective." *Journal of American Ethnic History* 25, nos. 2–3 (2006): 48–73.

Herod, Andrew. *Labor Geographies: Workers and the Landscapes of Capitalism*. New York: Guilford, 2001.

Hoerder, Dirk. *Cultures in Contact: World Migrations in the Second Millennium.* Durham, NC: Duke University Press, 2002.

McKeown, Adam. *Chinese Migrant Networks and Cultural Change: Peru, Chicago, and Hawaii, 1900–1936.* Chicago: University of Chicago Press, 2001.

Ngai, Mai. *Impossible Subjects: Illegal Aliens and the Making of Modern America.* Princeton, NJ: Princeton University Press, 2004.

Peck, Gunther. *Reinventing Free Labor: Padrones and Immigrant Workers in the North American West, 1880–1930.* New York: Cambridge University Press, 2000.

Rodríguez, Marc, ed. *Repositioning North American Migration History: New Directions in Modern Contintental Migration, Citizenship, and Community.* Rochester, NY: University of Rochester Press, 2004.

Weber, Devra. *Dark Sweat, White Gold: California Farm Workers, Cotton, and the New Deal.* Berkeley: University of California Press, 1994.

13 FEMINIZING WHITE SLAVERY IN THE UNITED STATES

MARCUS BRAUN AND THE TRANSNATIONAL TRAFFIC IN WHITE BODIES, 1890–1910

Gunther Peck

In the waning days of William Jefferson Clinton's presidency, the U.S. Congress passed a remarkable law, the Trafficking Victims Protection Act of 2000 (TVPA).[1] Far more than an ironic coda to the sex scandal of Clinton's second term or the Republican Party's self-destructive sexual purity campaigns, the Trafficking Act put the U.S. federal government squarely against a burgeoning form of international commerce: the buying and selling of men, women, and children "by force, fraud, or coercion," for unfree labor around the globe. According to the text of the 2000 act, "at least 700,000 persons annually, primarily women and children, are trafficked within or across international borders," and some 50,000 of these victims "are trafficked into the United States each year." While traffickers "primarily target women and girls, who are disproportionately affected by poverty," the "transnational crime" of trafficking in persons was not limited to the sex industry but also included the "forced labor" of migrants around the globe, most of them unable to exercise the right to quit because of legal, cultural, and geographic isolation. Whether sex workers, child laborers, or illegal migrant workers, all trafficked workers shared similar experiences: They were transported by traffickers across international boundaries, they assumed their jobs "by force, fraud, or coercion," and they were, according to the framers of the 2000 law, "a contemporary manifestation of slavery."[2]

Using the language of slavery to describe a cluster of unfree labor relationships represented no accidental or careless choice of words on the part of the law's framers and supporters. To the contrary, it reflected a growing popular and political consensus that slavery, once banished from North American soil by the Civil War and the Thirteenth

Amendment, had returned in startling and sickening fashion. This consensus was reflected in the broad bipartisan support the Trafficking Act enjoyed during its passage and subsequent reauthorization under the Bush administration in 2003, one of the rare legislative campaigns in which Senators Sam Brownback of Kansas and Paul Wellstone of Minnesota enthusiastically cooperated during a decade of sharpening partisan discord in Washington.[3]

But while a sense of history seems intrinsic to these contemporary abolitionist efforts, the current mobilizations evince little awareness of the diverse forms of human trafficking that had inspired previous generations to action or of the historical changes in discourse and policy that parallel contemporary developments. Indeed, between 2000 and 2003, when the TVPA was reauthorized under the Bush administration, a significant shift occurred in how U.S. State Department officials interpreted and sought to enforce the antitrafficking legislation. While female victims were prominent in congressional hearings and testimonies right from the beginning of the 2000 law's passage, by 2003 legislators and policy makers primarily featured trafficking stories of sexual violation and rape. Implementation of the TVPA likewise shifted by 2003, from a general concern with stopping human trafficking to a more targeted global campaign against legalizing prostitution.[4]

In the first decade of the twentieth century, a similar transition occurred in the discourse about human trafficking and slavery. At the end of the nineteenth century, a diverse group of middle-class reformers, Populist farmers, and working-class men and women used the language of trafficking and "white slavery" to summarize a host of working-class complaints involving wage earners and farmers in virtually every quarter of the nation. Boston labor reformer Louis Albert Banks, for example, described female seamstresses and "the worthy poor" in Boston as "white slaves" needing emancipation in 1892, while Irish miner John Fitzpatrick of Pennsylvania described both his unionized compatriots and newer imports from Italy and Hungary as "white slaves of monopolies" throughout the late 1880s and 1890s. Populist leader James Weaver claimed in 1890 that there were "over fifty millions of white slaves" among the nation's farmers and wage earners, all of them slaves at the hands of "America's moneyed aristocracy.[5] In 1910, by contrast, white slaves referred primarily to immigrant prostitutes and a growing number of American-born women who had allegedly been seduced and coerced into a life of sexual slavery in one of the nation's many urban brothels. The white slave trafficker was not a monopolist or a capitalist, according to middle-class moral reformer Edward Bell in 1910, but a pimp, usually a foreign-born immigrant from Eastern Europe.[6]

While enormous differences separate the Progressive Era from the past decade, the parallels between campaigns against white slavery and those against human trafficking do invite comparative questions: Why have stories about sexual traffic and sexual violence so effectively—and consistently it would seem—displaced stories about working-class labor? How should we analyze the feminization of human trafficking discourse, both in the present and in its past iterations? What lessons might the feminization of white slavery during the Progressive Era hold for contemporary abolitionists and policy makers seeking to redress the tragedies associated with trafficked migrants today?

To answer these questions, we need first to ponder the historical plasticity of antislavery language as well as the controversies generated by efforts to deem certain forms of trafficked labor as "slavery." Throughout the eighteenth century, for example, the traffic in indentured servants to North America, much of it founded on "force, fraud, and coercion," stimulated some servants to claim they had become enslaved in North America. While the majority of indentures did not claim enslavement, references to them as white slaves had become fairly commonplace by the 1790s. The language of white slavery likewise helped stimulate a much broader political movement against the traffic in children and orphans sold to work in Britain's cotton mills in the 1820s, while in the United States the language of white slavery fueled working-class critiques against the buying and selling of all human labor for wages in the 1830s and 1840s. Such efforts generated considerable political attention and controversy among working-class actors in both Britain and the United States. Indeed, many indentures and factory workers resolutely resisted the designation of slave as much as they resisted the coercion that fueled such comparisons to the "peculiar institution" of chattel slavery. Lowell mill girls going out on strike in 1836, for example, marched together chanting "O, I will not be a slave, I can not be a slave, O, I will not be a slave," even though many of their supporters (and a few detractors) described them as white slaves. In 1848, abolitionist Frederick Douglass expressed considerable skepticism about using the term "white slavery" to describe the coercions that wage workers were experiencing in Northern factories, canals, and railroads, challenging an assembled gathering of abolitionists and working-class white slaves to switch places with his black brothers and sisters currently toiling in Virginia. None responded to Douglass's call. Similar critiques of white slavery discourse emerged in the Progressive Era, more often than not from radicals like Emma Goldman, who described campaigns against white slavery as a politics for "baby people," a middle-class and paternalistic distraction from the real politics of working-class insurgency.[7]

Douglass's and Goldman's skepticism was and is useful, highlighting an important starting point for any analysis of human trafficking as a form of slavery. Though some trafficked migrants have embraced the label of slave, most historically have not, and most scholars of indentured servitude, child labor, and forced prostitution go to some pains to describe their coercions as *not* being a form of slavery, regardless of whether the language of white slavery became prominent.[8] Conflating the experience of indentured servants with African slaves not only obscures the very real legal and political differences that emerged between them in the late seventeenth and early eighteenth centuries, for example, but also risks minimizing the horrors of African slavery and validating the claims of contemporary white supremacists.[9] The varied coercions that British child laborers and immigrant prostitutes in North America experienced in the nineteenth and early twentieth centuries were likewise not commensurate with what millions of Africans experienced in plantation slavery in the New World, a *legal* system that made all descendants slaves by birth and that used race to mark the condition of their enslaved status. Put another way, no trafficked migrant called a slave, however fungible, mistreated, or exploited, has ever been enslaved or had their progeny enslaved, *because* of their race or their whiteness. White slaves were enslaved not because of their skin color, but in spite of it.

But while skepticism of the language of white slavery is warranted, it does not follow that we should necessarily understand its extension to trafficked migrants as a mere metaphor only, a hyperbolic perception of white victimhood. Rather than asking whether white slavery or the slavery of human trafficking has been "real," I instead begin with the assumption that the diverse forms of human trafficking represented as slavery have indeed been coercive and unfree. If we are to properly historicize human trafficking and the ideas of racial slavery that have conditioned our perceptions of it, we need first to understand the origins and nature of that coercion. Unlike plantation slavery, where control of a slave's labor hinged on restricting her or his mobility, the coercions of human trafficking have been generated by a migrant's mobility. For the trafficked migrant, coercion begins not with one's legal status as a slave, but by the varied ways a migrant's transnational movement and political status en route become commodified and controlled by middlemen: padrones, coyotes, labor agents, corrupt border officials, consular officers, and merchants. The ways that these international middlemen—these "entrepreneurs of space," as I described padrones in my first book—commodified migrants' passages have varied by context and locale, but they converge in transforming what many consider to be a hallmark of freedom—the capacity to move or to quit—into cornerstones of coercive power.[10] For trafficked migrants, the right to quit has been rendered meaningless not by legal sanction, but by geographic, cultural, and political circumstance. What does the right to quit mean if you are sixty miles from the nearest shelter and have no means of transportation? Does it matter that you voluntarily signed a work contract in your home village if you arrive in a strange locale and discover you've no path of return except through the same middleman who sent you there in the first place?

To understand how mobility becomes coercive, how migrants have become trafficked in the past and the present, we need to pay attention not only to the costs of movement but also to the traffickers themselves, the middlemen who have used both proximity and distance from state powers to gain chokeholds over particular migrations, controlling the flow of specific bodies across political and cultural boundaries. Most middlemen have gained power without legal or state sanction, working on the geopolitical margins of a nation's or an empire's capacity to regulate traffic, whether for goods or people. Understanding the history of human trafficking, then, necessitates not only seeing the changing physical geography of human migrations but also examining the changing claims and capacities that sovereign states have made to control mobile subjects who move across or outside territorial borders. Indeed, efforts by states to police traffic, whether of goods or people, have long been foundational to how modern states have conceptualized their sovereignty and their power as national communities. Because most forms of human trafficking have historically flourished on the frontiers of imperial and national sovereignty, investigating the history of human trafficking requires studying the relationships between traffickers and the border authorities who sought, with mixed results, to police them.[11] Those relationships have been filled with heroic languages of intervention and ironic reversals for both border authorities and reformers, revealing symbiotic connections as well as conflicts between traffickers and state reformers and actors.

In this chapter, I examine the work of one such border authority, Marcus Braun, the U.S. Bureau of Immigration's chief undercover detective between 1900 and 1910, who investigated human trafficking throughout Europe and North America. Marcus Braun's discoveries were important in shaping both the work of the U.S. Bureau of Immigration and the public's shifting perceptions of precisely who was a victim of human trafficking in the first decade of the twentieth century. His discoveries did not single-handedly transform how Americans saw and understood the traffic in white bodies, but an examination of his career sheds important light on how and why white slaves became feminized over the course of the decade. "Feminization," I argue, was bound up with the intrinsic challenge of seeing "slavery" within the business of human traffic. For white slavery abolitionists, whether border officials, temperance reformers, feminists, labor organizers, or elite business leaders, the challenge of distinguishing white slaves from white citizens created both conceptual hurdles and political opportunities. For immigration bureaucrats, efforts to stamp out the white slave traffic led to policy failure, policy revision, and bureaucratic expansion simultaneously. On the one hand, Braun discovered that it was far easier to condemn sexual violence and to see prostitution as a sign of white slavery than it was to condemn the complex ways capitalism was making all human labor, and especially international migrants, disposable. Such feminization briefly empowered subaltern bureaucrats like Braun, who for a time became the chief government investigator of the new traffic in female white slaves. But Braun's discoveries ironically blurred the very boundaries between heroic border authorities and villainous human traffickers that he labored to construct as an undercover investigator. Just so did border agents like Braun fall from grace, and America's nascent immigration bureaucracy learn to thrive and expand on its policy failures. Put another way, while

Braun's investigations failed to clarify who was and who was not a white slave, his transnational detective work nonetheless legitimated the nationalistic and even heroic purpose of the U.S. Immigration Bureau and its many immigration agents.

Who was Marcus Braun and why did he become an antislavery crusader against human trafficking? Born in Hungary, Braun emigrated to the United States in 1892 and, like many of his Jewish, Yiddish-speaking compatriots, he joined the expanding ranks of America's immigrant working class. Braun did not long remain a mechanic, however, but threw himself into language training and became a journalist for Hungarian-language and then English-language newspapers in New York City. By 1899, Braun had not only learned English but founded a new political organization: the Hungarian Republican Club of New York City, which endorsed rising political star Theodore Roosevelt. Braun's political activities paid off handsomely when the new president pressed for Braun's appointment as a "special investigator" to the U.S. Bureau of Immigration in 1903.[12]

As an undercover U.S. immigration agent, Braun's principal task in the spring of 1903 was to use his language expertise in Europe to investigate the origins of contract labor, a practice whereby employers imported immigrant workers under contract directly to jobs in North America, typically using them as strikebreakers and paying them cheap wages. For the previous thirty years, labor reformers and immigration officials alike had sought to stop the practice and to enforce legislation that outlawed it. In 1885, the Knights of Labor and their allies across the country had successfully persuaded Congress to pass the Foran Act, which forbade the importation of workers into the nation under contract. These contracts and the poor immigrants who accepted them were, according to labor leaders and activists like John Fitzpatrick, an example of how white slavery was injuring the freedom of once-independent American producers. Braun's task as an immigration inspector was to find the origins of this white slavery in Europe's labor markets and to stamp it out, a task that Terence Powderly, former Knights of Labor leader and U.S. commissioner-general of immigration throughout the 1890s, heartily endorsed.[13] As a one-time member of America's immigrant working class, then, Braun's work as an agent of the U.S. Bureau of Immigration was quite extraordinary. Though a Republican, he was by background and temperament subaltern, committed, like Powderly, to improving the conditions of workers in North America by policing the "unscrupulous immigrants" who violated America's borders.

In his 1903 report, Braun amply documented the coercions that emigrants experienced at the hands of steamship agents and emigration authorities throughout Europe. In trying to discover how labor market traffic coerced emigrants, Braun "travelled about 25,000 miles by railroad and about 600 miles by special conveyances, visiting . . . the following European ports: Hamburg, Bremen, Stettin, Fiume, Trieste, Odessa, Naples, Genoa, Marsielles, St. Nazaire, Havre, Antwerp, Rotterdam, Southampton, London, and Liverpool." At nearly every turn, Braun encountered the work of Europe's most powerful steamship agent, Frank Missler of Bremen, who controlled annually the passages of more than 200,000 emigrants on the Holland-America, Red Star, and North German Lloyd lines. Missler employed hundreds of subagents in Hungary, Austria, Bulgaria, Serbia, and Greece, many of them clerks, teachers, and even local priests, who scoured villages, according to Braun, armed with circulars advertising specific jobs in North America and guaranteeing entry into the United States should they pay their commissions. Missler's subagents also worked with local moneylenders who not only sold tickets to emigrants at double their actual cost but also lent them passage money at extremely high interest rates, often compelling emigrants to take out mortgages on their family lands over time. Perhaps most troubling to Braun, Missler's men trained emigrants to evade the Foran Act, coaching them on how to answer the questions of U.S. border officials without revealing the existence of the work and passage contracts that had brought them from European village to North American factory.[14]

In locating specific individuals responsible for the flow of contract laborers to North America, Braun greatly pleased his superiors in the U.S. Bureau of Immigration. Unlike immigration inspector A. S. Anderson, who complained in 1903 that "there is a great deal of confusion over the status of [U.S. immigration] laws" in Europe, Braun never criticized the inconsistencies of the Foran Act or U.S. immigration policies, which simultaneously demanded that immigrants state that they had no job awaiting them and that they would not become a public charge.[15] Instead, Braun sought and found European causes for coercion in the American labor market: White slavery originated not in U.S. factory conditions or in its own contradictory immigration policies, but in the abuses of men like Frank Missler, whose "unscrupulous and greedy activity" had created an "unnatural emigration of paupers and assisted emigrants."[16] Braun's interpretation of Missler not only comported well with the moral and nationalistic sensibilities of his superiors in the Bureau of Immigration but also vindicated their bureaucratic authority. Indeed, he called for an expansion of the bureau's political work in 1903. After traveling from Europe to Vera Cruz, Mexico, in September to investigate one of Missler's "backdoors" into the United States. Braun concluded that "the inspection force at the Border of Mexico and the United States . . . [should] be increased considerably, and that such force should be mounted so as to form a sort of flying column, thus enabling them to . . . prevent the coming in of these inadmissible aliens."

While outspoken for an immigration agent, Braun was hardly unusual in being nationalistic. Braun's Jewishness and fluency in Yiddish, Hungarian, French, and German were, however, creating striking tensions between his role as a subaltern cultural interpreter, traveling the circuits of transnational labor exchange, and his rhetoric as a proud American citizen. While Braun located the origins and immoral character of contract labor coercion almost entirely within

Europe, for example, he also relied on foreign governments for much of his information and fully cooperated with local police and state officials in Europe. Indeed, Hungarian officials were initially intrigued by Braun's investigations into Frank Missler and together with Braun arrested several of Missler's steamship subagents in Hungary.[17] Here Braun acted as an enforcer of Hungarian laws as well as U.S. Bureau of Immigration directives. Braun's Jewish heritage proved a trickier subject, however, as he evinced little sympathy in his official reports for Jewish emigrants. One of the first emigration cases that Braun pursued in Europe was that of "a Polish Jew by the name of Osias Freund who was rejected by the physician at Ratibor" and had boarded a ship for America anyhow. Braun sought to have Freund deported from New York. After witnessing the aftermath of a pogrom against Jewish residents in Kishineff, Russia, in June 1903, Braun coldly remarked that "the late race riots and massacres are liable to bring about quite an exodus of a very undesirable class of aliens." Unlike some immigrant elites, Braun deemed his new American identity incompatible with any outward embrace of Jewishness, at least in 1903. To the contrary, the coin of his new American citizenship was contingent on suppressing such links and even amplifying certain prejudices against immigrants—that new immigrants were teeming with contract laborers and, as Braun put it in his published report, "paupers, criminals, exconvicts, prostitutes, and diseased" men and women.[18] And yet it was precisely Braun's links to these "undesirable" emigrants, as he put it, that explained why he was working for the U.S. Immigration Bureau in the first place. He was hired not so much for his fluency in the rhetoric of American nationalism—though that certainly helped—as for his fluency in German, Hungarian, French, and Yiddish. Braun's nationalism and internationalism, while in conflict with each other in his reports, were also inextricably linked, two sides of one coin.

Braun's success as an U.S. immigration agent, then, was symbiotically linked to the same traffic he investigated. He gained power not like Frank Missler, by taxing the mobility of emigrants' geographic passages to and from North America. Rather Braun acquired bureaucratic influence by shaping the transnational exchange of ideas about traffic that circulated between nations and cultures. As long as Braun could mediate the distance between American and Yiddish culture and language, between images of labor market villainy and the actual patterns of coercion created by transnational migration, between desirable and undesirable immigration, Braun's power as a cultural broker and a U.S. immigration agent enhanced one another. But as Braun soon discovered in 1905, many of the tropes he used to describe labor market coercion and national virtue, including the language of antislavery, were exceptionally unstable, particularly in the hands of bureaucratic competitors.

Braun's new assignment in the spring of 1905 began peacefully enough when he returned to Europe to "investigate . . . the alleged activity of charitable associations, both Hebrew and others, in sending undesirable aliens to the United

States," as well as "to inquire into the matter of importing contract labor to the United States to work on the railroads, in the mines, and upon large public works in various parts of the country."[19] When Braun returned to his native Hungary, he discovered an expansion of coerced migration not under the tutelage of the "unscrupulous" agent Frank Missler, but under the thumb of an expansive government-run employment agency. Rather than passing laws that would further criminalize the activities of men like Missler, Hungarian officials had passed in 1904 a new emigration law that gave the "central ticket office" of the state-owned Cunard Steamship Line monopolistic control over the vast commerce of migration that was transforming the Hungarian countryside. Instead of Missler's subagents, hundreds of civil service workers traveled throughout Hungary's peasant populations "with a drum from street to street," spreading fabulous tales of wealth in the United States and selling fares through the "Central Ticket Office." Any citizen applying for a passport, moreover, was immediately visited by a ticket office representative, while "every railroad conductor," according to Braun, "was under the instruction to maintain a careful watch that no person should get beyond the Hungarian border without first securing tickets from the 'monopoly.'" The parasitic "blood-suckers" and "usurers" that Hungarian emigrants now condemned—and which Braun quoted in his reports—were not Missler and his men, but civil service workers for Hungary's own state-run monopoly. Braun's "heroic" allies in the Hungarian state had become villains, white slavers rather than emancipators of the coerced and enslaved Hungarian peasant-emigrant.[20]

Had Braun more time to contemplate these ironic narrative reversals, he might have been better prepared for the scandal that subsequently erupted around him and his European investigations. As the critical nature of Braun's investigations circulated back to Austrian authorities, they began spying on Braun and plotted a well-coordinated campaign of their own to discredit him and his findings. On May 9, 1905, Braun returned to his hotel in Budapest and "caught detective Galmar," an employee of the Hungarian Ministry of the Interior, "tampering with my mail box" and opening his official correspondence from U.S. Commissioner-General of Immigration Frank Sargent. Braun responded to Galmar by promising to "knock him down" and to "denounce publicly this outrageous procedure." But Hungarian officials preempted Braun by announcing through official press bureaus over ensuing days that "Marcus Braun . . . was exposed today to be a swindler" and had been "bribed by the North Atlantic Steamship Trust, for the purpose of compromising the Cunard Line." In subsequent press attacks, Braun was described paradoxically as both a "Hungarian Jew" and "an obnoxious foreigner," whose meddlings in his former homeland of Hungary had tarnished the nation's sovereignty and honor. The Vienna *Deutscher Volksblatt* compared Braun to the worst steamship agents and white slavers on the European continent: "We wish him Bon Voyage, may he in the circle of

Missler... think about how he can make the powers at Washington believe, that via Fiume only criminals like himself, while via Hamburg and Bremen, only angels emigrate."[21]

Known as the Marcus Braun Affair, the scandal not only strained U.S.-Austro-Hungarian relations, leading Theodore Roosevelt to publicly consider sending U.S. battleships to the Adriatic Sea, but turned upside down neat distinctions between desirable and undesirable immigrants, heroic immigration authorities and unscrupulous foreign agents. Braun, the Americanized Jewish anti-Semite, had become, in the twinkling of an eye, a familiar anti-Semitic stereotype himself, a swindling criminal who, like Missler, profited directly from the traffic in human migrations. The scandal afforded Hungarian authorities a chance not only to rebuke Braun's challenge to their monopolistic control over emigration but also to critique U.S. immigration policy and the allegedly arbitrary behavior of U.S. border authorities in deporting thousands of Hungarian emigrants as contract laborers over the previous months. Such deportations were only one aspect of the coercive power that Braun and border inspectors wielded in both Hungary and the United States. Inspecting emigrant bodies for signs of trachoma and other diseases, carefully questioning emigrants in "special boards of inquiry" at every American port, detaining and deporting immigrants who answered questions incorrectly or who showed signs of moral, political, or economic weakness—these new powers not only exemplified the growing power of "modern" border bureaucracies but also mirrored the work of labor market entrepreneurs who also read workers' bodies and probed their responses to questions in determining their worth as migrants. The very exchangeability of moral roles in the Marcus Braun affair highlighted the coercive power that transnational migration invested in state and private actors on both sides of the Atlantic Ocean.[22]

For Braun, the scandal not only compromised his ability to continue his undercover investigations into Jewish emigration societies and contract labor migrations but also weakened his power as a cultural broker within the Bureau of Immigration and the Hungarian ethnic community in New York. Particularly vexing to Braun were press reports in both Hungarian and American newspapers that questioned his integrity and motives.[23] "I can hardly get to any place without having representatives of the press after me," Braun confessed to Commissioner Sargent in one missive, adding that "the awful strain I had to undergo in connection with this affair has worked havoc with my nervous system."[24] Not only did the *New York Times* print articles critical of his actions in Austria but also his portrayal of Hungarian emigrants infuriated many of his ethnic compatriots. "The Hungarians of New York have been exercised over the reports published in the American newspapers, on authority of Marcus Braun, regarding the character of Hungarian emigrants," began one article, a situation that Braun sought to assuage at a meeting with 150 Hungarians at the Café Boulevard in New York in the summer of 1905. "Marcus Braun made it known that the accusations in the

English newspapers against the Hungarians should not be considered to be anything but newspaper 'ducks'. . . . His reports sent to the Government did not contain the accusations which were published." Yet even while Braun backpedaled his criticisms of the character of Hungarian emigrants, he sharpened his nativist attacks against undesirable emigrants over the ensuing months, condemning "paupers, criminals, and others equally undesirable" and the efforts by foreign governments to keep alive "the patriotic spirit for the fatherland in the minds of these colonies" of immigrants. Braun's strenuous efforts to be an American patriot, an honorable Hungarian ethnic, and eventually a defender of Jewish people not only fomented striking tensions in his public statements but also highlighted challenges intrinsic to his role as a cultural broker and translator within the Immigration Bureau.[25] As an undercover investigator, Braun believed—or hoped—he could fix and define the specific contours of white slavery and the many differences between free and coercive migration that the discourse mapped onto the bodies of new immigrants. As the subject of newspaper stories and object of editorial commentary, however, Braun quickly discovered just how difficult it was to control the traffic in images about white slavery and his own race and national virtue, despite his credentials as a white slavery abolitionist.

The strain of the Marcus Braun affair not only "worked havoc with his nervous system" but also led to his forced resignation from the Bureau of Immigration in August 1905. Braun responded to his ouster by seeking to restore his reputation as an immigration authority and a devoted American nationalist. In 1906, he published *Immigration Abuses: Glimpses of Hungary and Hungarians*, a recounting of his adventures and entanglements as an immigration agent between 1903 and 1905. The book primarily reiterated Braun's assertions against the Austro-Hungarian government and his claims of being an honest and virtuous American patriot. One of Braun's most interesting claims was that "autocratic" Austro-Hungarian authorities had attempted to entrap and discredit him by planting a letter on him proving that he was a white slaver, "an exporter of young women for immoral purposes." Braun had mentioned the existence of that plan in a letter to Commissioner Sargent in 1905, but the plot occupied a much larger place in his published recounting, an episode that highlighted to Braun the treachery and corruption of Hungarian authorities. Perhaps most intriguing, Braun omitted in *Immigration Abuses* that he had learned of the Hungarian government's plot against him by "employing another detective of the Royal Hungarian State Police for my own purposes," as he stated to Sargent in 1905. Such details clouded the moral distinction that Braun sought to project between a corrupt and decadent European regime, where both prostitution and graft flourished, and the virtuous American polity that he proudly represented as an immigration agent.[26]

Braun's intervention into the publishing world was a modest success at best, as *Immigration Abuses* never became a best seller. But it did accomplish one important purpose: restoring Braun's reputation as a heroic antislavery investigator to the one person who possessed the power to make a difference, President Theodore Roosevelt, who after meeting with Braun and reading portions of his book, had him reinstated within the Bureau of Immigration in November 1906.[27] Yet Braun's reinstatement raised as many questions as it answered about his future as an undercover investigator. How would he revive the balancing act of embodying American national virtues on the one hand and exploiting his international language skills on the other? Having been tagged an "obnoxious foreigner" by the Hungarian state, how would he henceforth perform his undercover investigative work in Europe, and who would take him seriously, besides President Roosevelt, in the United States? Given his unhappy experience with the metaphor of white slavery in 1905, in which Hungarian authorities framed him as a white slaver, would Braun eschew or embrace a new assignment as a white slave investigator?[28]

Further complicating Braun's challenge was the ongoing redefinition of white slavery from wage earning to prostitution within the United States by 1906. Led by British purity reformer William Coote, who traveled to New York that year to found the National Vigilance Association, a group devoted to the "safe-guarding of unprotected girls and women and the suppression of the white slave traffic," white slaves were increasingly seen and imagined as white prostitutes in need of heroic rescue.[29] The conflation of prostitutes with white slaves had long been developing in Great Britain, where in 1885 William Stead's sensational exposé of a mother's sale of her fourteen-year-old daughter into the hands of a "white slave trader" had appalled and fascinated the British nation. In the United States, by contrast, white slavery still connoted primarily working-class and populist stirrings between 1900 and 1907, as a brief perusal of white slavery publications from those years suggests.[30] A comparison of the feminization of white slavery abolitionism in Britain and the United States suggests that the strength of labor abolitionism in the United States, an organizing tradition that articulated a critique of wages as a form of slavery throughout the nineteenth century, partially explains the late moment of white slavery's feminization in the United States.[31] Even as the strength of labor abolitionism was ebbing in the U.S. labor movement by 1900, Terence Powderly's antislavery rhetoric and influence over immigration policy remained strong, committing the U.S. Bureau to aggressive efforts toward stopping contract labor and working-class renditions of "white slavery." For American Federation of Labor President Samuel Gompers, by contrast, wage work was a necessary foundation of working-class experience and organizing. Fighting "white slavery" by enforcing the Foran Act held less appeal than stopping courts from using the injunction against unions.[32]

These shifts in political economy and culture would become dramatically apparent when Marcus Braun accepted a new undercover assignment in the summer of 1908 to make a "thorough investigation of the White Slave Traffic in its relation to the Immigration Laws and the violations thereof," a "white slave traffic" that was immigrant prostitutes rather than contract laborers. Braun took his new definitional mandate from European treaties that sought to abolish the traffic in white slaves, or prostitutes, beginning in 1902, which the United States finally signed under President Roosevelt's leadership on June 15, 1908. Henceforth, white slaves were to be seen—and investigated—as prostitutes rather than contract laborers. The Foran Act was not exactly a dead letter, but no longer would it inspire the language or energy of an antislavery crusade within the U.S. Immigration Bureau.

Braun's new assignment contained both risks and opportunities. He might redeem his national reputation as a heroic fighter against slavery, or he might inflame racist hostilities against Jewish immigrants. Moreover, the meanings of white slavery seemed more unstable than ever in 1908, as the conflation of white slaves with prostitutes was still fairly new to Braun and was not universally shared by activists on the left or by Braun's peers in the bureau. By the time Braun finished his white slavery investigations in the summer of 1909, however, white slavery had become a moral panic virtually synonymous with prostitution. Henceforth, even labor radicals like Joe Hill presumed the white slave to be a prostitute. While the feminization of white slavery in the United States seemed long overdue when compared with Europe and Britain, the process itself was not inevitable, as national differences in political economy and culture clearly mattered and help explain the different timing of white slavery's transformations. Equally important, the work of individual actors, whether Terence Powderly's efforts to stop contract labor as U.S. immigration commissioner, Theodore Roosevelt's championing of international treaties against international prostitution in 1908, or Marcus Braun's subsequent investigations in 1908 and 1909, each made incremental changes in the larger process of feminization. Marcus Braun's significance lies not so much in any single-handed transformation of white slavery discourse, but in the ironic and revealing ways he sought to influence popular discourse as a border bureaucrat and his novel efforts to make white slaves visible, whether contract laborers in 1903 and 1905 or prostitutes in 1908 and 1909.[33]

Unlike his previous assignments, Braun's research detail in the summer and fall of 1908 was confined to the United States and to the immigrant prostitutes who had been allegedly imported by white slavers. The domestic context of Braun's work—the fact that this problem was in America's backyard—alone may have accounted for the sensational impact of his discoveries. But equally important and revealing were the rhetorical devices Braun used in writing his final report. "Matter of fact man though that I am," Braun began, "never yet did I feel so thoroughly aroused, I might say inspired with the importance of the work entrusted to me." By confessing the sincerity and purity of his motives, Braun sought to remove himself from any potential affiliation with the "human flesh merchants" he subsequently described in his report. For Braun, this meant sundering any perceived tie to his Jewish ancestry. "I felt called upon to help eradicate a crime," Braun continued in his prologue, "a condition of affairs which is a crying shame upon our much boasted 20th century Christian civilization." Sounding every bit like a Christian purity reformer, Braun then dropped the bombshell of his findings: "There are more than 50,000 foreign born prostitutes in the United States . . . and there are about 10,000 procurers and pimps, 'Human flesh merchants' plying their ghoulish trade, and I am very conservative with my estimate." By placing quotes around his own language, Braun oddly noted his indebtedness to a larger community of Christian reformers, even while simultaneously peppering his narrative with claims of veracity and objectivity. "The White Slave Traffic . . . is to the Department no longer a surmise or a suspicion, no longer a matter of hearsay," Braun claimed, "but a matter of fact. . . . We have the names of the leading spirits engaged in it, we know the methods employed and we know the existence of an international band of scoundrels engaged in it." Even more provocative, Braun claimed to have discovered literal marketplaces in which white bodies were bought and sold. "We know of the existence of a kind of 'exchange' or a 'clearing' house through which these dealings in rotten, corrupt human flesh are made."[34]

Braun used these sensational "discoveries," many of them indebted to moral reformers' rhetoric and narrative conventions within penny press exposés, to make a series of bold policy recommendations. First, he called for the creation of an entirely new department within the Bureau of Immigration, "a separate squad of officers to handle the white slave cases . . . composed of at least sixty picked Immigrant Inspectors, judiciously divided into districts, under one responsible Head." Second, Braun sought to greatly expand the legal authority and advantages of the bureau, recommending that "blank warrants should be placed at the disposal of Officers who may be detailed to perform the duties of investigating and eradicating the traffic in white women." In addition, Braun called for the suspension of any citizenship rights to immigrant prostitutes and to any men "married" to them. "If my recommendations are adopted," Braun concluded, "I am sure that ere one year will be gone by, we will have stopped the importation of women for the purposes of prostitution."[35]

Although Braun's recommendations did not lead to any immediate changes within the Bureau of Immigration, they did eerily prefigure the formation of the Federal Bureau of Investigation in 1911, whose main task, among others, was to investigate white slavery cases across the nation. Braun's more immediate impact, however, was on the public's perception of white slavery. His report, though unpublished, soon found its way into public circulation after the National Vigilance Committee requested and received a copy of it in October 1908. Within a year, several leading vice crusaders cited Braun's work as authoritative proof of the existence of white slavery, despite the remarkably slim evidence that Braun actually marshaled. Braun's rhetoric not only comported well with the Christian sensibilities of moral reformers but also successfully combined the authority of a policy maker with the narrative skill of a muckraking journalist: "conservative" disclaimers about one's findings, a delay in presenting one's evidence to build a sense of suspense and horror, a confessional mode of delivery, and titillating and sexualized references to the human body and to images of groping hands throughout the report. "We can put our fingers on the ulcerous spot," Braun claimed at one point when speaking of the location of white slave auctions, while in another he lamented, "I fear the girl Lucienne has slipped through our fingers." Braun's description of pimps was likewise erotic and corporeal. "They work in unison and hand in hand, as if they were members of some secret society bound to each other indissolubly."[36]

Braun's was hardly the first or the last white slavery investigation that inadvertently blurred the boundary between vice reformer and vice trafficker, between white slave abolitionist and white slaver. In 1885, British journalist William Stead wound up in prison for allegedly having purchased his heroine's virginity in order to write his story. Likewise, white slave crusader H. W. Lytle blurred the boundary, perhaps intentionally, between moral reform and pornography in his celebrated *From Dance Hall to White Slavery*, publishing separate editions in 1912, one with a "respectable" woman and the other with a nude woman on the cover, radically different images of white slavery bracketing the same text. Lytle seems to have been conscious of the ironies of his crusading role, including photographs of himself holding a gun with the words *truth*, *love*, and *nitroglycerine* written on the gun's barrel.[37]

Braun's report, however, was not written to titillate or to sell copies within a literary marketplace, however indebted its narrative strategy and conventions about sexuality may have been to men like Stead and Lytle. Braun's goals as an immigration agent were simultaneously more practical—to galvanize opposition to prostitution—and more elusive: to maintain bureaucratic power as a trafficker in the ideologies of traffic. Braun's report, in addition to making sensational claims, was filled with anxieties about its content, suggesting the depth of his struggle to redeem and secure cultural authority within the bureau. "Never since my connection with the Bureau of Immigration," Braun wrote in his report, "did I make my final report with such trepidation as I do now." Indeed, Braun acknowledged his failure to make "a thorough investigation of the white slave traffic," blaming his lack of evidence on the difficulties of documenting sexual commerce and the practice of "tipping off," whereby a pimp "causes an exodus" from a brothel and thus "annihilates and destroys the careful work done by preliminary examinations and official inquiries." Braun used the rhetoric of moral social reform—describing pimps as "merchants of human flesh"—in part to persuade his superiors of the merits of his investigations and recommendations. But even here, Braun's anxieties infused his comments to the commissioner-general. "Though, Sir, I might cause your blood to boil with horror and indignation," wrote Braun at the beginning of his report, "I must tell you we do not know what terrific dimensions this awful nefarious practice has assumed." But would Sargent's blood boil from rage at the injustices of white slavery? Or at Braun's failure to determine the precise contours of sexual traffic in his investigation?[38]

One suspects that Braun's anxieties were at least partially connected to his use of the language of white slavery itself, one that he fully realized was charged with anti-Semitic potential. Braun attempted to justify his new use of white slavery rhetoric by comparing prostitution to the older forms of coercion recently known as white slavery—contract labor. To Braun, the comparison left little doubt as to which social relation was more coercive: "What is the clandestine importation of . . . a gang of men under contract to perform certain labor . . . in comparison to the importation of Daughters of Eve, the sex of Mother, Wife, Daughter, Sister for the purpose of prostitution? Why to me, it seems absolutely insignificant." Working-class complaints about coercive contracts paled in comparison to the depredations of "human flesh merchants," according to Braun. Yet this had not always been the case, particularly in Braun's own investigative work in 1903. For Braun, white slavery's transformation from contract labor to prostitution reflected the greater narrative and moral power of prostitution as a public issue, as well as the fact that he now served as a direct result of President Roosevelt's intervention within the Bureau of Immigration.[39] Indeed, his power as an undercover agent depended on his ability to make visible the immigrant prostitutes thought to be white slaves and to make their traffickers accountable.

The feminization of white slavery discourse in the United States, then, had many causes and many participants, but it did not result from anything intrinsic to the market for commercial sex, despite Braun's assertions to the contrary. The market for sex was not inherently more coercive than the labor market. Nor had the comparative number of immigrants being trafficked for sex work as opposed to factory labor increased dramatically over the previous decade. Rather, the feminization of white slavery discourse grew out of changes within a traffic in ideas about labor market traffic and new opportunities that the language of antislavery provided Progressive Era bureaucrats seeking to justify their work and make it heroic. Braun's success in articulating persuasive narratives about white slavery reflected a knot of competing cultural, political, and personal interests. For Braun, the transformation of white slavery from contract labor to prostitute had less to do with the actual nature of sexual or labor market commerce than with a shifting set of opportunities for assimilating himself as an Americanized Jewish professional and securing the favor of powerful American leaders. Working as a crusader against contract labor in Europe in 1905 had earned him the anti-Semitic epithet of being an "obnoxious foreigner." Working as a crusader against prostitution in the United States in 1908, by contrast, enabled him to burnish his patriotic credentials, even if it meant briefly passing as a Christian. Indeed, in the summer of 1909, Braun seemed to be at the top of his game, heralded by Protestant reformers and immigration bureaucrats alike as a heroic defender of American freedoms and national virtues.

The growing white slavery panic was not good to most Jewish professionals and businessmen, however. Even among Jewish intellectuals, success as a Jewish person in the United States bore the taint of being a pimp or white slaver. In Jewish author Reginald Kauffman's popular white slavery novel, *The House of Bondage*, published in 1909, the villain is, like Braun, a successful Hungarian Jew described in the following manner: "The hair on his head was black and curly.... His lips were thick when he did not smile and thin when he did, with teeth very white; and his gray glance had a penetrating calculation that made the girl instinctively draw her coat together and button it." Kauffman depicted his Jewish slave trader not as entirely primitive or black, but rather as a complex mixture, a kind of gray in-between person with both thick and thin lips, civilized and bestial habits. The danger he represented was not only of market "calculation" run amok, but of cultural "mongrelization" and racial miscegenation, a fear reflected in the literal form of the villain's name, Max Crossman. How ironic, then, that both villain and victim in white slavery discourse could be from the same ethnic group: "white" Jewish women being exploited by "mongrelized" Jewish slave traders. For Marcus Braun, the whiteness of white slavery abolitionism was not only elusive but also a double-edged sword, as likely to cut the hands that embraced it as to empower.[40]

The instability of Braun's power as a cultural broker within the Bureau of Immigration was soon manifest in the spring and summer of 1909, when in the wake of his popular success in the United States, Braun was sent to Europe to research the continental origins of the white slavery traffic. Braun's mission soon foundered, as it had on his last trip to Europe, on the resistance various governments presented. Meeting with French Interior Minister M. Hennequin, Braun found him "to be very well posted on the subject of the white-slave traffic ... but he seemed to object to my being here on a mission which he thinks properly belongs to the Prefecture de Police of Paris.... If the government of the United States wants to investigate the traffic in white women, we should ask the French government to investigate it for us." In Britain and Belgium, authorities expressed less resistance to Braun's investigations but offered their cooperation only if "an English or a Belgian girl ... is lured to the United States."[41]

Braun took these setbacks in stride, but the rebuke he received from the new U.S. Commissioner-General of Immigration Daniel Keefe, left him confined and demoralized. After asking for an assistant and seeking permission to travel to Spain and Switzerland, where Braun had discovered some promising leads, Keefe wrote a sharply critical letter to Braun denying his travel requests, rebuking him for using "six superfluous words" in a recent cablegram, and demanding that he write weekly reports and "finish entirely with your work in one city before proceeding to another." Braun protested that he would "never be able to do my work thoroughly" if he had to finish his work in one city at a time, "for the nature of... the subject is such that the threads run from one city to another." The traffic in women, however voluntary or coerced, was indeed transnational as Braun realized, one that required his own mobility across national boundaries. Keefe refused Braun's requests, however, and like his European counterparts, approached the white slavery problem in resolutely national rather than transnational terms.[42]

Although England, France, Germany, Spain, and several other European countries had pledged their international cooperation in signing a white slavery treaty in 1902, the issue increasingly fueled nationalist resentments and anger by 1909. As prostitutes, white slaves functioned as symbols of a racially pure nationhood that had been defiled by the immoral acts of foreign-born pimps, more often than not a Jewish man. The resistance to Braun by European officials in 1909 did not seem primarily motivated by anti-Semitism, but the memory of the "Marcus Braun affair" and the slander he endured hung around Braun's neck throughout the summer of 1909. Indeed, Keefe refused Braun permission to return to Hungary, fearing a new international incident and a revival of the anti-Semitic images that had damaged Braun's and the Bureau of Immigration's credibility. As Braun sarcastically claimed, "There seems to be a fear on the part of someone in our government service, that my mere entry in the Austro-Hungarian Monarchy would immediately cause a great war between the United States and the aforesaid country."[43]

Increasingly hemmed in by nationalist and anti-Semitic anxieties among both European and American border bureaucrats, Braun continued his investigative work in France and Germany, focusing on the one group of white slaves for whom authorities would provide him information: Jewish prostitutes. Braun cooperated with a "high police official of the German government," one Hans von Tresckow, who discovered a booming traffic in Jewish girls on the Austrian-German frontiers. "These girls, children of poor Jewish families in Galicia and Russian Poland are lured away under the most contemptible tricks and taken via Bremen, which lately has become a distributing point, to Triest, and there embarked for South America."[44] Braun's interest in these Jewish "white slaves," as he described them, raises a number of intriguing questions about his motives under trying circumstances. Was Braun again creating distance between himself and "undesirable" Jewish immigrants? Or was he seeking to aid the lowest of his "race," thereby improving the status of all Jews as whites? Perhaps the confinement of Braun's research to Jewish immigrants by both American and European authorities had provoked Braun to embrace Jewish rather than American nationalism. His report on Jewish prostitutes going to South America certainly moved beyond the national criteria laid down to him by Commissioner Keefe.

Regardless of whether Braun had begun to harbor Zionist sympathies, nationalist energies harnessed by the white slavery panic soon overtook him, weakening his ability to broker the many linguistic and cultural boundaries between the United States and Europe. Soon after Braun sent his report on Jewish white slavery in South America to Washington, the *Boston Transcript* published a story stating that several European governments "aid and abet in shipping immoral women to the U.S.," a deliberate and astonishing violation of their white slave agreements. Most damaging to Braun, the newspaper listed him as its principal source. The sensational exposé, so characteristic of the growing traffic in white slavery storytelling, exemplified how little control Braun had over the traffic in ideas that had helped bring him to prominence. Braun furiously denied the claim to his German hosts, especially German commissioner Tresckow, and reprimanded Commissioner Keefe, asking him "not to give out any information to the press which might seriously impair the success of my mission." Whether Keefe had deliberately sandbagged Braun is unclear, but the damage had been done to Braun's reputation as a sympathetic and culturally fluent foreign national. Henceforth, he received no cooperation from German officials, and French officials lodged a formal complaint with the U.S. ambassador and threatened to deny him entry into the nation.[45]

Conclusion

In one of his last letters to Commissioner Keefe before retiring from the Bureau of Immigration in 1909, Braun attempted to understand why he was unable to procure good evidence about white slavery and why he was thus losing power as an immigration inspector. "In cases of trafficking in prostitutes . . . I found difficulties to obtain official information . . . because the conception of what constitutes a 'white slave' is quite different in Europe than it is in the United States." Braun explained that the expansive definition of white slavery in America, which lumped mistresses and prostitutes into one category, was quite objectionable to authorities in Europe, many of whom described American immigration laws as "simply outrageous." Yet in blaming his difficulties on cultural differences between Europe and America, Braun also obscured their role in his rise to authority within the Bureau of Immigration. Moreover, Braun minimized the profound impact that European notions of white slavery had on white slavery in the United States. Indeed, one of the key reasons that white slavery had become feminized in the United States were the commitments that European nations had made to eliminate the "traffic in white women" in 1902, a political mobilization that inspired U.S. immigration authorities to send Braun to American cities and Europe in search of white slaves and white slavers. The success of Braun's transnational investigative work had long depended on cooperating with local police officials in Europe, even if Braun condemned them later in his reports.[46] Likewise, his return to prominence as an investigator in 1908 was directly linked to a traffic in ideas and images about white slavery that flourished between Europe and North

America, a traffic that was generated, at least partially, by the very same cultural differences he condemned in his final missive as an immigration inspector.

Yet national differences in the meaning of white slavery between Great Britain and the United States do not by themselves explain how or why feminization occurred in the United States. Peculiarities in national culture—the nineteenth-century strength of labor abolitionism in the United States, for example—certainly predisposed the United States to experience a dramatic shift in white slavery's meanings in the early twentieth century, but the disinvestment of North American workers in antislavery ideology did not cause the feminization of white slavery. There are at least two reasons this explanation is inadequate. First, working-class renditions of white slavery had not, in fact, disappeared by 1910 but continued to animate critiques of wage work as a form of slavery on both the left and increasingly the right over the course of the twentieth century.[47] The survival and even proliferation of working-class critiques of traffic suggest they have played an ongoing role in the feminization of trafficking discourse, providing a sense of moral energy, however flawed, to middle-class efforts to imagine and justify "rescuing" poor women from prostitution at home and abroad. The complex class relationships between working-class actors and middle-class reformers are only partially comprehended by a focus on national culture and its apparently exceptional characteristics in the United States.

Second, focusing on national differences tends to reify national cultures into essential qualities, ignoring how permeable national cultures are, as well as how the "transatlantic crossings" of people, things, and ideas changed them in the United States over time.[48] White slavery's feminization developed as a historical process by which immigrant middlemen like Braun bridged and linked national and international understandings of race, freedom, and rescue, often with surprising and contradictory results. One of the greatest ironies of the transatlantic crossings that shaped white slavery's feminization, however, was that Braun, the cosmopolitan, became the key advocate for the domestication of white slavery, calling for the elimination of the word *alien* in the prosecution of the 1907 immigration law in his 1908 report. Wrote Braun, "If we could not have that word 'alien' in the present law, we could prosecute every Procurer who happens to be an American Citizen." Here Braun's recommendation dovetailed neatly with the agendas of urban and domestic reformers seeking to build the power of the progressive state in policing a host of vice problems. Braun's call was heeded not only in the creation of new urban laws across the country against prostitution and procurers but also in the language of the Mann Act, which nationalized the problem of sexual traffic by criminalizing the movement of "prostitutes" across both state and national borders in 1910. Just so did immigrants serve as canary birds for social reform.[49]

The nationalization of white slavery and its feminization not only went hand in hand, then, but also were both crafted by internationally minded middlemen like Marcus Braun, seeking to solve fundamental problems of visibility within white slavery abolitionism. Braun's efforts to clarify the boundaries of white slavery and his own heroic role by expanding the purview of white slavery crusades from immigrants to citizens created a number of unforeseen developments. With the government's prosecution of Jack Johnson as a white slaver in 1911, the problem of white slavery traffic seemed to lose all connections to its transnational origins. Increasingly, African American men rather than Jewish or Italian pimps were prosecuted as white slavers, men whose black skin made clear in the minds of American bureaucrats, north and south, distinctions between consensual and coercive market relations. Although Marcus Braun's reaction to Johnson's prosecution is unknown, the Mann Act's policing of African American sexuality provided Braun a new opportunity for bolstering his American identity. As it had in the antebellum era, white slavery in the United States once again became a way of privileging white victimhood over black. As Ernest Bell put it in 1910, the war on the white slave trade had become a struggle "against the blackest slavery that has ever stained the human race." Marcus Braun, the Jewish immigration agent who would be white, no doubt heartily agreed.[50]

NOTES

1. I would like to thank the following individuals for their generative insights and criticisms on drafts of this article: Jeremy Adelman, Edward Balleisen, Wini Breines, Faulkner Fox, John French, Gary Gerstle, Julie Greene, William Jordan, Kevin Kruse, Gerda Lerner, Nancy McClean, Frank Mort, Daniel Rodgers, Christine Stansell, and Sean Wilentz.
2. U.S. Congress, Victims of Trafficking and Violence Protection Act of 2000, October 28, 2000, Public Law 106–386, 114 Stat. 1466, Sec. 102, a & b, Purposes and Findings.
3. Anthony M. DeStefano, *The War on Human Trafficking: U.S. Policy Assessed* (New Brunswick: Rutgers University Press, 2007), 33–34.
4. The shift in emphasis from human trafficking to sex trafficking is partially explained by differences between Democrats and Republicans; see DeStefano, *The War on Human Trafficking*, 35–38, 102–3.
5. Louis Albert Banks, *White Slaves: or the Oppression of the Worthy Poor* (Boston: Lee and Shepard Publishers, 1893); John Fitzpatrick, *The White Slaves of Monopolies* (Harrisburg, PA: Lane Hart, 1884); Brian Donovan, *White Slave Crusades: Race, Gender, and Anti-Vice Activism, 1887–1917* (Urbana, IL: University of Illinois Press, 2006); David Roediger, *The Wages of Whiteness: Race and the Making of an American Working Class* (London: Verso Press, 1992), 32ff.
6. Ernest A. Bell, *Fighting the Traffic in Young Girls or the War on the White Slave Trade* (Chicago, 1910); David J. Langum, *Crossing over the Line: Legislating Morality and the Mann Act* (Chicago: The University of Chicago Press, 1994), 15–47.

7. Harriet Robinson, *Loom and Spindle: Or, Life among the Early Mill Girls* (New York: Thomas Y. Crowell & Company, 1898), 145; Frederick Douglass, *Liberator*, April 28, 1848; Emma Goldman, "The Traffic in Women" (1911), in *Red Emma Speaks*, ed. Alis Kate Schulman (New York: Schocken Books, 1983), 178.
8. Edmund Morgan, *American Freedom, American Slavery: The Ordeal of Colonial Virginia* (New York: Norton, 1975), 123; Jill Lepore, *The Name of War: King Phillip's War and the Origins of American Identity* (New York: A. A. Knopf, 1998), 135. Other historians have recently ignored historical differences between servants and slaves. See, for example, Don Jordan and Michael Welsh, *White Cargo: The Forgotten History of Britain's White Slaves in America* (Edinburgh: Mainstream Publishers, 2007).
9. David Duke, *My Awakening: A Path to Racial Understanding* (Covington, LA: Free Speech Press, 1998).
10. Gunther Peck, *Reinventing Free Labor: Padrones and Immigrant Workers in the North American West, 1885–1930* (Cambridge: Cambridge University Press, 2000).
11. Jacqueline Berman, "The Left, the Right, and the Prostitute: The Making of U.S. Antitrafficking in Persons Policy," *Tulane Journal of International and Comparative Law* 14 (2006): 269–93; Laura Agustin, "The Disappearing of a Migration Category: Migrants Who Sell Sex," *Journal of Ethnic and Migration Studies* 32, no. 1 (January 2006): 29–47; and Elizabeth Bernstein, "The Sexual Politics of the 'New Abolitionism,'" *differences: A Journal of Feminist Cultural Studies* 18, no. 3 (2007).
12. Marcus Braun to Frank Sargent, June 13, 1905, London, pp. 1–14, File # 52011/B, Box 87, folder 1, Records of the U.S. Bureau of Immigration, Immigration Subject Correspondence, RG 85, U.S. National Archives, Washington, D.C.
13. Robert J. Steinfeld, *Coercion, Contract, and Free Labor in the Nineteenth Century* (Cambridge: Cambridge University Press, 2001), 29–38.
14. Marcus Braun, "Report of Special Immigrant Inspector Marcus Braun," August 24, 1903, New York, pp. 86–87, File 52320/47, Folder One, Box 97, RG 85.
15. A. S. Anderson to F. H. Larned, Acting Commissioner-General, Washington, D.C., June 4, 1903 in File 52320/47, Folder one, box 97, RG 85.
16. Marcus Braun, "Report of Special Immigrant Inspector Marcus Braun," August 24, 1903, New York, p. 95, File 52320/47, Folder One, Box 97, RG 85.
17. Marcus Braun to Commissioner General of Immigration, June 3, 1903, Granica, Russian Border, p. 1, File # 52320/47, folder one, Box 97, RG 85.
18. Report of Special Immigrant Inspector Marcus Braun, August 24, 1903, New York, NY, p. 95, File # 52320/47, folder 1, Box 97, RG 85.
19. F. P. Sargent to Marcus Braun, Ellis Island, New York Harbor, March 27, 1905, File 52011/A, Box 78, RG 85.
20. Braun to Sargent, June 3, 1905, File 52011/B, box 78, folder 1, RG 85; Braun to Sargent, June 13, 1905, p. 13, ibid.

21. Braun to Bellamy Storer, United States Ambassador, May 9, 1905, File 52011/A, Box 78, RG 85; Braun to Sargent, May 22, 1905, ibid.; Vienna *Deutscher Volksblatt*, June 1, 1905, cited in Braun to Sargent, June 13, 1905, File 52011/B, Box 78, folder 1, RG 85.
22. Braun to Frank Sargent, June 13, 1905, pp. 1–3, File # 52011/B, folder 1, Box 78, RG 85.
23. See, for example, "The Return of the Native," *New York Times*, May 24, 1905; and "In Mockery of Marcus," *New York Times*, August 15, 1905.
24. Braun to Sargent, June 13, 1905, London, England, Folder # 52011/B, folder 1, Box 78, RG 85; Mrs. Marcus Braun to F. H. Larned, July 17, 1905, File # 52011/B, folder 2, Box 78, RG 85.
25. "Braun to the Hungarians," *New York Times*, July 1, 1905; "Aliens Enrich Europe with Money Made Here," *New York Times*, January 18, 1906.
26. Marcus Braun, *Immigration Abuses: Glimpses of Hungary and Hungarians* (New York: The Pearson Advertising Company, 1906).
27. Braun to Sargent, June 13, 1905, London, England, Folder # 52011/B, folder 1, Box 78, RG 85; Mrs. Marcus Braun to F. H. Larned, July 17, 1905, File # 52011/B, folder 2, Box 78, RG 85.
28. Report of Special Immigrant Inspector Marcus Braun, August 24, 1903, New York, p. 91, 93, File 52320/47, folder 1, Box 97, RG 85; On slavery among Greek "boys," see the deposition of William Mentis to U.S. Immigration Inspector Andre Seraphic, April 18, 1903, Philadelphia, "Greek Boys" file, Contract labor Violations, Port of Philadelphia, RG 85, National Archives, Philadelphia Branch.
29. Edward Janney to the Commissioner of Immigration, October 20, 1908, File 52484/1-B, Box 110, Immigration Subject Correspondence, Rg 85.
30. W. T. Duncan, *The Story of a White Slave* (Emporia, KS: 1906); J. E. Robuck, *Archie McDonald of South Carolina: A Victim of Circumstantial Evidence under the Pressure of Negro Slavery Abolition Prejudice. Fifty years—1850 to 1900—a "White Slave"* (Birmingham, AL: Leslie Printing and Publishing Co, 1909); Charles Sheldon French, *The Worship of the Golden Calf. A Story of Wage-Slavery in Massachusetts* (Dalton, MA: C. Sheldon French, 1908); *The White Slavery: A Study of the Present Trade Union System* (Akron, OH: The Werner Company, 1909).
31. Roediger, *The Wages of Whiteness*, 80–87.
32. Julie Greene, *Pure and Simple Politics: The American Federation of Labor and Political Activism, 1886–1917* (Cambrdige: Cambridge University Press, 1998).
33. Frank Larned, Acting Commissioner General of Immigration to Marcus Braun, July 2, 1908, Washington, D.C., File # 51777/197, RG 85.
34. Marcus Braun to Frank Larned, September 29, 1908, New York, NY, pp. 2–4, File # 52484/1A, Box 110, RG 85.
35. Braun to Larned, September 29, 1908, pp. 29–30, File # 52484/1-A, Box 110, RG 85.

36. Braun to Larned, September 29, 1908, New York, NY, pp. 4–6, File 52484/1-A, Box 110, RG 85; Edward Janney to the Commissioner of Immigration, October 20, 1908, New York, NY, 52484/1-B, Box 110, RG 85.
37. W. H. Lytle, *From Dance Hall to White Slavery: The World's Greatest Tragedy* (Chicago: Charles C. Thompson Co, 1912); and W. H. Lytle, *Tragedies of the White Slave* (Chicago: Padell Book and Magazine Co, 1912).
38. Braun to Larned, September 29, 1908, New York, NY, pp. 1, 2, 6, File # 52484/1A, Box 110, RG 85.
39. Ibid., p. 2.
40. Reginald Wright Kauffman, *The House of Bondage* (New York: Grosset and Dunlap Publishers, 1911), 19; "Jews and the White Slave Trade," *Literary Digest*, December 4, 1909, 993–94; Edward Bristow, *Prostitution and Prejudice* (New York: Schocken Books, 1983); Matthew Frye Jacobson, *Whiteness of a Different Color: European Immigrants and the Alchemy of Race* (Cambridge, MA: Harvard University Press, 1998).
41. Marcus Braun to Commissioner General, Paris, April 23, 1909, pp. 1–2, File 52484/1D, Box 110, RG 85; Braun to Commissioner General, Paris, April 22, 1909, File 52484/1D, Box 110, RG 85.
42. Daniel Keefe to Marcus Braun, April 23, 1909, Washington, D.C., File 52484/1D, Box 110, RG 85; Braun to Commissioner General, May 61, 1909, Berlin, pp. 1–2, File 52484/1D, Box 110, RG 85.
43. Braun to Commissioner General, June 18, 1909, Berlin, p. 3, File # 52484/1-D, Box 110, RG 85.
44. Ibid., p. 2.
45. Braun to Commissioner General, July 26, 1909, Berlin, pp. 1–3, File # 52484/1-E, Box 110, RG 85.
46. Braun to Commissioner General, July 26, 1909, Berlin, p. 2, File # 52484/1-E, Box 110, RG 85; Braun to Commissioner General, September 16, 1909, New York, p. 2, File # 52484/1-F, Box 110, RG 85.
47. Indeed, claims about a historic traffic in "white slaves" are an essential weapon in the arsenal of contemporary white supremacist David Duke, who dedicates a chapter of his best-selling book, *My Awakening to the History of Working-Class "White Slavery,"* to the topic.
48. Daniel Rodgers, *Atlantic Crossings: Social Politics in a Progressive Age* (Cambridge, MA: Belknap Press of Harvard University Press, 1998).
49. Braun to Larned, September 29, 1908, New York, p. 26, File # 52484/1-A, Box 110, RG 85.
50. Geoffrey Ward, *Unforgivable Blackness: The Rise and Fall of Jack Johnson* (New York: A.A. Knopf, 2004).

14

PATRONAGE AND PROGRESS

THE BRACERO PROGRAM FROM THE PERSPECTIVE OF MEXICO

Michael Snodgrass

During the 1980s, record migration levels and intensified policy debates stimulated an outpouring of scholarship on Mexican immigration to the United States.[1] Since then, social scientists and journalists on both sides of the border have examined emigration's multifaceted effects on contemporary Mexico. Historians of Mexico have yet to follow their lead. While award-winning histories about those immigrants' experience *within* the United States abound, scholars continue to neglect the historical impact of emigration and return migration on Mexico itself.[2] Indeed, historians of migration devote more attention to the immigrants who settled in late-nineteenth- and twentieth-century Mexico than to the emigrants who departed in ever greater streams. As a result, leading textbook surveys devote cursory attention to the issue, reducing emigration to an effect of rural poverty rather than a process of great complexity, magnitude, and consequence in its own right.[3] Contemporaries knew otherwise. From the 1920s onward, emigration regularly dominated headlines and policy debates, while Mexican films and folk ballads taught lessons about the promises and pitfalls of life in the United States, the almost singular destination of Mexico's emigrants.[4] By the early twenty-first century, Mexico became the world's leading emigrant-sending nation. Consistent with both historical and contemporary precedents, this evolution into an emigrant nation owed a good deal to state policy.[5]

This chapter examines the most consequential of these federal government initiatives: the Bracero Program, a migratory labor agreement that Mexico first negotiated with the United States during World War II. The Bracero Program began as a bilateral response to fears of labor scarcity and food shortages, as native-born U.S. farmworkers abandoned the fields for military service or industrial jobs. While some wartime migrants labored on railway maintenance crews, the majority were contractually restricted to harvesting crops. These braceros, as seasonal labor migrants became known, were hailed by Mexico's government and by host communities for their heroic contribution to the economic mobilization. However, what began as a temporary "guest worker" policy proved so successful—from the perspective of growers, both governments, and the migrants themselves—that it lasted until 1964. Indeed, more braceros arrived each year in the 1950s than during the war years combined, and the Bracero Program became the largest U.S. experiment to date with the importation of foreign contract labor.[6]

In the United States, early-twenty-first-century debates about "immigration reform" and talk of another large-scale guest worker program have renewed attention to the neglected history of the braceros. Cautionary tales about the program's negative effects abound. Building on the observations of contemporary critics, historians of agricultural labor highlight the Bracero Program's detrimental consequences for U.S. farmworkers. Real wages stagnated and, in some cases, fell. Living and working conditions barely improved, despite greater government oversight. The nascent unionization of the 1930s was stymied, too, as the agricultural labor force became more transitory, dispersed, seasonal, and deportable. The setbacks experienced by farm labor contrast markedly with the organizational and socioeconomic gains made by industrial workers during these decades of postwar American prosperity.[7] The staggering poverty discovered in farmworker communities by the early 1960s thus lent credence to charges that the Bracero Program was little more than a system of "imported colonialism," as one AFL-CIO official called it. The migrant farmworkers so celebrated for their wartime contribution to American agriculture came to be seen as "The Slaves We Rent." Today the Bracero Program is frequently demonized on the Internet as a system of "legalized slavery," an expression borrowed from Lee G. William, a U.S. Department of Labor officer who supervised bracero employment.[8] These critical views of the Bracero Program parallel those heard in Mexico, then and today.

A labor policy that prompted a largely regional debate in the United States evoked a national outcry in the braceros' homeland. The Bracero Program became the most controversial policy implemented by the state in the 1940s and 1950s. For many, the state's proemigration policy was an affront to national dignity. How, the critics demanded, could the government encourage hardworking young men to abandon the homeland and go north to be exploited by gringo farmers on lands that were once Mexican? Moreover, they claimed, aspiring braceros were bribed by venal officials, shipped north in cattle cars, and then sent back with little to show for their labor except some new boots and meager savings. Today, due to lawsuits by former braceros, Mexicans also know that corrupt bureaucrats in Mexico City made off with the compulsory savings deducted from braceros' pay.⁹ Meanwhile, for the government's opponents, the "bracero problem" exposed flaws in the state's domestic policy. For the critics, emigration was symptomatic of a failed revolution.

Scholars of U.S. labor, immigration, and Chicano history have researched diverse facets of the Bracero Program, from its diplomatic origins and legal implications to its economic, cultural, and demographic effects on the American West.¹⁰ This chapter examines the Bracero Program from the Mexican perspective, analyzing less the program's critics than its influential supporters, be they renowned scholars and statesmen or leaders of Mexico's once powerful union movement. It first analyzes migration policy up to and during the Bracero Program. I explore why the federal government perceived and promoted migration to the United States as a means of achieving human and material progress at home. Meanwhile, migration permits became sources of political patronage allocated by the ruling Institutional Revolutionary Party to working-class beneficiaries in central-western states like Jalisco, in Mexico's emigrant-sending heartland. We hear why the strongest defenders of the program remain its alleged victims: the former braceros themselves. In their recollections, the hardships confronted and sacrifices made barely tarnish the benefits that seasonal migration offered: good pay, frequently decent treatment, and the opportunity to improve their families' lives upon return.¹¹ Seen from the perspective of Jalisco, we understand how a guest worker program that undermined conditions for farmworkers in the United States produced beneficial returns for Mexican communities, where the Bracero Program nurtured and sanctioned a culture of migration that persists to this day.

Citizens on a Mission

Throughout its twenty-two-year history, the Bracero Program remained a product of both U.S. domestic policy and foreign relations. A powerful American agricultural lobby first pressured a divided U.S. Congress to consider the program. Claims of labor shortages by southwestern growers—and favorable responses from policy makers—were hardly novel. What made this accord unprecedented were its scale and the decision by the U.S. government to assume the role of labor contractor itself. Once approved, it fell on a reluctant State Department to negotiate the bilateral agreement with its Mexican counterparts. Some American diplomats initially feared that any discrimination against migrants would undermine the Good Neighbor Policy and wartime cooperation. But U.S. immigration officials had learned in the early twentieth century that migrants returned home with "a distinct affection for the United States." The U.S. ambassador arrived at the same upbeat conclusion about the braceros: "The knowledge they are receiving of our customs, habits and ways of living will bring a greater appreciation of our culture and our problems, which should add to a better understanding of our country. The effects of these programs will long outlive the war conditions that make them necessary."[12] By the 1950s, as anti-Americanism swept much of Latin America, social scientists discovered that braceros indeed developed positive views of the United States. The migration accord was therefore defended during the Cold War as an effective antidote to communism.[13]

The Mexican government proved less reluctant about the proposal. Officials from the labor and foreign affairs ministries astutely negotiated a migratory accord with all the advantages that their wartime bargaining power then offered. They were determined that migrants would no longer suffer the racist abuses and coerced deportations their predecessors had known in the 1920s and early 1930s. Officials justified the program as a legal means of regulating migration and safeguarding emigrants from the dangers posed by human traffickers and illegal immigration, which escalated in the early 1940s. "It would be great if a country never faced the periodic need to permit its *campesinos*' departure," wrote Mexican Secretary of Foreign Relations Jaime Torres Bodet. "But it would be foolish not to guarantee adequate working—and living—conditions while they carry out their tasks."[14] As a temporary guest worker program that offered contractual guarantees on wages, working conditions, living standards, and return transportation—regulations that would be enforced by Mexican labor inspectors within the United States—the Bracero Program marked a radical departure from past labor migrations. These protective clauses and the mechanisms to enforce them explain why Americans sympathetic to migrant workers initially endorsed the policy and why the program's greatest beneficiaries, the growers, remained its most shameful critics.[15] No one foresaw the extent to which the program's expansion in the 1950s would undermine the capacity to enforce bracero rights in rural America.

For Mexico, therefore, the potential benefits were several. The bilateral accord promised fair treatment and a safe return. The ostensible exclusion of skilled workers and *ejidatarios* (land grant recipients) would avert domestic labor and food shortages. Mexican officials also insisted on a punitive clause permitting its consuls to blacklist regions whose growers or merchants discriminated against migrant workers. By 1951, they had sanctioned the states of Texas and Idaho and dozens of counties in the Mississippi Delta for unchecked cases of discrimination and contract violations.[16] Finally, both Mexican authorities and U.S. diplomats enveloped the program in the rhetoric of wartime solidarity. While Mexico's industrial workers waged their "battle for production" in the mines and mills, the braceros headed north to contribute further to the Allied cause. According to one progovernment newspaper, the nation was not "simply an exporter of human labor resources." Rather, the Bracero Program made Mexico "a valuable ally of the democracies in the fight against the totalitarian powers." Therefore, "these workers must be considered not as immigrants but as Mexican citizens on a mission."[17] Perhaps most important, as seasonal migrants they were destined to come home. Policy makers therefore highlighted the potential benefits of return migration to justify a program that far outlasted the struggle against totalitarianism.

Seen from the perspective of Mexico City, the Bracero Program marked the culmination of a forty-year debate on the "problem" of emigration. Since the 1920s, the issue had posed a real dilemma for postrevolutionary governments. After all, in the years that preceded the 1910 revolution, the old regime's critics blamed the policies of Porfirio Diaz for the "depopulation of Mexico." "By the thousands our compatriots have had to cross the homeland's border," the Partido Liberal Mexicano charged, "fleeing plunder and tyranny. This evil must be solved and it will, by the government that offers expatriates the means to return to their birthplace." In 1906, these revolutionary activists demanded land reform and state-subsidized repatriation to get the emigrants back home and working on their own farms.[18] Their proposal became official policy in the early 1930s. But by then, the devastating effects of revolution and civil war in Mexico—and active recruitment by U.S. employers—caused emigration to reach unprecedented levels.[19]

The 1920s therefore witnessed the first meaningful debates among Mexican intellectuals and statesmen on the issue of emigration. Many cited the negative consequences on Mexico's postrevolutionary economic reconstruction: the fear of labor shortages, the loss of ambitious and hardworking youth, pressures to raise wages, and so forth. In the northern industrial capital of Monterrey, for example, local employers grew alarmed when U.S. labor contractors recruited skilled Mexican workers from the steel mill and railway shops in the early 1920s.[20] In response, the state posted propaganda in northbound trains warning aspiring braceros of the dangers posed by deceitful contractors and undocumented migration. The press in major sending regions cooperated, with hardship stories about economic exploitation and racial discrimination. Consular officials often authored the reports, and some returned home to write scathing critiques meant to counter an emerging theory that migrants benefited from their sojourn to the modern, industrial north.[21]

At the same time, more influential statesmen and scholars offered upbeat arguments in support of emigration. One 1922 report circulated by an anonymous consular official compared Mexican migrants with the more established Italian community. He argued that with proper guidance from the state, Mexicans would enter industry, learn new skills, organize themselves abroad, and remit their earnings through immigrant savings banks. Indeed, not unlike some modern development specialists, Italian statesmen regarded emigrant remittances as a means to achieve a national balance of payments and to promote regional economic growth.[22] The comparative perspective became common among proemigrant statesmen such as Jaime Torres Bodet, the diplomat who helped negotiate the original Bracero Program. From his perspective, seasonal migrations to the United States were as beneficial to Mexico as the northern flight of Spanish and Italian workers into postwar Western Europe.[23] Meanwhile, policy makers highlighted the effects of return migration to defend the Bracero Program from its domestic critics.

Here is where the intellectual and political influence of the famed Mexican anthropologist Manuel Gamio becomes apparent. In 1926 and 1927, Gamio undertook a survey of Mexican immigrants in the United States. The relevance of the study—one of the first sponsored by the Social Science Research Council—rested on Gamio's twin focus: on the migrants' ongoing connections to their homeland and the subsequent effects of their return. His flawed methodology—just seventy-six subjects, many from middle-class backgrounds—skewed the results. But what mattered was his conclusion: that the experience was beneficial for both Mexico and its migrants, despite the hardships and abuses they suffered. In fact, Gamio's study found evidence that emigration achieved the very ends sought by postrevolutionary policy makers at home. The "bitter humiliations" of racism, for example, strengthened one's national identity. "It is a notable fact," he reported, that migrants "learn immediately what their *patria* means, and they always think of it and speak of it with love." Gamio collected evidence of remittances, discovered the migrants' western Mexican origins, and observed them returning with better clothes, tools, and farm implements. Emigration also promoted state projects to educate and uplift the rural masses. Migrants improved their diets, hygiene, and housing standards. They developed "discipline and steady habits of work," "learned to handle machinery," and realized a degree of social mobility.[24] Most important, they would bring these new aspirations and behavioral traits home and work to achieve a better life upon return. Gamio's own migration policy proposals foreshadowed the very demands that Mexican officials brought to the table when they negotiated the Bracero Program. By the 1940s, Gamio not only advised migration policy makers. His research set the terms by which the state defended its controversial policy.[25]

No Mexican wartime (and then postwar) policy received greater media attention—and more sustained criticism—than the Bracero Program. Domestic opposition was "so unfavorable and widespread," one U.S. diplomat wrote, "that a real tribute must be paid to the Mexican Government for its adherence to the program in the face of such public criticism."[26] Critics came from across the political spectrum. Nationalists and leftists decried a system that sent ambitious men to perform demeaning tasks as yet another form of neocolonial exploitation by gringo capitalists, one that deepened Mexico's economic dependency on the United States. Church officials feared emigration's effects on families back home and accurately warned of the braceros' exposure to both Protestant missionaries and an immoral atmosphere of drinking, gambling, and prostitution at the labor camps. No aspect of the program aroused stronger condemnation in the Mexican press than that which the State Department had feared: the racist mistreatment of the braceros in the United States. The issue, one American official noted, "is enough to make all Mexicans see red and it is practically the only subject on which Mexicans of all classes and all political persuasions seem to agree. It has been used by both leftist and rightist newspapers to attack the US."[27] Muckraking press exposés dramatized the discriminatory abuses faced by braceros abroad and the inability of Mexican or U.S. officials to fully enforce contractual guarantees on wages, housing, food provision, and so on. Many blamed the injustice as much on recalcitrant growers as on the complacency of Mexican consulates. Among such critics was the politically powerful Confederation of Mexican Workers (CTM), whose leaders pressured the state to better enforce bracero rights after their investigators learned of a corrupt consul who discouraged a union drive among railroad braceros.[28] Publicly, however, the CTM fully endorsed a program that delivered significant benefits to many Mexican workers.

Mexico's federal government responded by lauding its emigration policy as a progressive precedent. Editorials in the state-owned press correctly emphasized that this "collective contract for agricultural laborers" extended legal protections to farm labor for the first time in U.S. history. The Bracero Program therefore promised the "liberation" of native-born workers as well. (Officials in the U.S. Labor Department confided to Mexico's Denver consul that it bolstered their efforts to pressure American agribusiness to improve labor conditions.) Most important, the government insisted, this postrevolutionary generation of migrants were not the hapless victims or docile peasants that critics assumed: "The Mexican worker, now accustomed to being treated as a human being within his own country, and to demanding the rights guaranteed by advanced labor laws, will never subject himself to those old forms of work that were more like slavery than free labor."[29] This proved true. Bracero recruits knew their rights before departing—or learned them up north—and protested their abrogation. Mexico's Foreign Relations Ministry archives hold hundreds of files documenting bracero protests and successful efforts to redress their grievances. Consular officials recovered lost wages, fined employers, and blacklisted entire counties for violating the accord. Effective enforcement declined as the program's growth in the 1950s outgrew the consular offices' reach. But braceros continued to resist what they perceived as contractual violations through formal claims, with wildcat stoppages, or by skipping out to return home or seek better jobs elsewhere.[30] Meanwhile, despite the shortcomings, demand for bracero contracts always outpaced the supply.

From its inception, one American historian recalled, "The tremendous news [of the Bracero Program] caused something like a gold rush."[31] Each year thereafter, the federal government received hundreds of letters and telegrams—from desperate farmers, small-town mayors, or union locals—pleading for migration permits for themselves, their communities, or their rank-and-file members. Its appeal proved strongest in the traditional sending states of west-central Mexico, where the revolutionary government's policies of agrarian reform and anticlericalism had violently divided communities one generation earlier. By the 1950s, the region's mining towns, communal farms, and blue-collar neighborhoods were sending thousands of braceros north each year. They went with the official blessing of both the state and its allies in the union movement, which endorsed emigration in the very terms set by Gamio two decades earlier. "Thousands of men who left here impoverished, badly dressed, [and] poorly fed will return... in possession of a fair sum of money [and] a greater appreciation of work," the CTM's official paper believed. "These Mexicans have seen the world now, and will not be too willing to return to their former life, to villages without electricity, without drinking water, without libraries, but well provided with taverns and priests." Having served in el Norte as "citizens on a mission," these agents of change were coming home "to serve as a fighting brigade in the struggle for Mexico's economic awakening."[32]

Back Home in Jalisco

The western state of Jalisco is the birthplace of such quintessential Mexican traditions as mariachi music, tequila, and rodeo cowboys (*charros*). It also known in Mexico as a producer of emigrants. During the Bracero Program, Jalisco and the neighboring states of Guanajuato, Michoacán, and Zacatecas sent about 45 percent of the legal migrants north.[33] That was because the federal government allocated these traditional sending states a disproportionate share of bracero permits. Exactly why these states received large bracero quotas remains unstated in the archival sources. The policy appears to reflect a mix of historical continuity, popular demand, and socioeconomic and demographic calculations. First, here is where a culture of Mexican migration first took root in the early twentieth century. In the 1920s, Paul Taylor found that nearly 70 percent of the Mexican immigrants surveyed in Chicago and northwest Indiana hailed from this region, far from the sparsely populated northern border. (The finding so intrigued Taylor that he ventured to Jalisco to research a pioneering study on the sending community of Arandas.)[34] Then, when the federal government first announced bracero contracting in 1943, tens of thousands of men from these states traveled to Mexico City and overwhelmed the recruitment center. By 1946, authorities relocated the processing centers to Irapuato (Guanajuato) and Guadalajara (Jalisco), before U.S. pressure led to their establishment in northern railway hubs like Monterrey. Finally, among the thousands who petitioned Mexican presidents for bracero *permisos* are a disproportionate number from these states. By the late 1940s, municipal officials in depressed mining villages and drought-stricken farm towns were seconding their constituents' requests.[35]

Early in the program's development, state officials also developed a formula to calculate quotas based on local agricultural needs and labor supplies. The complex model accounted for commodities produced, hectares planted, land tenancy patterns, and population density. Yet no figures accompanied the formula, so it remains unclear whether such calculations resulted in the disproportionate quotas. In their studies of rural development, Sandos and Cross offer the best historical analysis of the economic and labor market conditions that created a vast pool of potential emigrants in the region. After 1910, three decades of revolutionary violence and agrarian reform caused a decline in full-time hacienda employment and a shift to subsistence farming. But postrevolutionary governments failed to deliver sufficient credit, irrigation, or extension services to land grant communities (*ejidos*) or small farmers. Rather than address local agrarian grievances, the state's green revolution bypassed this sending region to promote highly capitalized commercial agriculture in northern Mexico. Thus after a lull in the 1930s, pressures to migrate resumed, especially among the sons of small landholders during a period of mounting population growth. The Bracero Program thus offered one way out of this development dilemma. Meanwhile, this region where Catholic rebels (Cristeros) fought the federal army in the 1920s became the geographic heartland of another antigovernment movement, the Sinarquistas, by the early 1940s. "By quickly moving discontented young men out of the region and into the US," Sandos and Cross argue, "the Mexican government began to diffuse the Sinarquista movement at its base."[36]

Most observers assumed, as Manuel Gamio had argued decades earlier, that "emigration acts as a real safety-valve for men out of work." Keeping "would-be immigrants" home, Gamio suggested, would foster high unemployment and then "social struggle . . . disorder and conflict."[37] The safety valve thesis dates back to early-twentieth-century studies of westward migration and European immigration to the United States. In Mexico's case, contemporary social scientists—their perspectives shaped by Cold War fears of Latin American revolution—concurred that migration alleviated the social stresses left unresolved by state development policies. "Politically and socially," one landmark study noted, "the exodus of discontented, hungry campesinos served as a safety valve throughout the bracero program's history."[38] Did state officials utilize the Bracero Program to maintain rural peace through emigration? Government infiltrators considered the neofascist Sinarquistas to be a militant, well-organized movement with a large and highly disciplined base among the "humble classes" of western Mexico.[39] But no evidence links their departure to an explicit state policy of targeted migrations. When asked, old-timers in Jalisco scoff at the suggestion that state officials utilized bracero quotas toward such political ends. Sinarquismo, they note, had disappeared once large-scale contracting began in the early 1950s. Meanwhile, states like Jalisco received a disproportionate share of bracero quotas into the 1960s while Guerrero and Morelos were allotted a pittance, despite the postwar reemergence of agrarian radicalism in that region closer to Mexico City. Those states got military repression rather than bracero quotas.[40]

It is worth noting that the government allocated few bracero quotas to the Los Altos (Highlands) region of Jalisco—a stronghold of both the Cristero rebellion and the Sinarquista movement.[41] Those it received went to cronies of local political bosses. So many young *alteño* migrants did as their fathers and grandfathers had done and headed north on their own, *de alambre*, as they referred to their illegal migration "across the wire" at Arizona or California. It was easy then. When he headed north for the first time in 1955, the first English expression that Gerardo López learned was "go ahead," the words a Border Patrol agent spoke while encouraging his entry. By the 1950s, former migrants recall, the *alteños* could tap into migratory networks dating to the 1920s that led men from Valle de Guadalupe to Santa Monica, or those from the nearby village of Mezcala to San Francisco. Those contracted as braceros often abandoned fieldwork to head to these cities. They attribute their undocumented migrations not to desperation but to their own resistance to the Bracero Program. In their minds, a bracero contract offered only hard labor in the fields, imposed contractual limits on their mobility, and, they believed, discounted the cost of the food and housing provided by employers. So they maintained their independence and shunned the costs and long wait that acquiring bracero contracts entailed.[42]

To the extent that the Bracero Program served political ends, it did so *not* by offering prized bracero contracts to potential dissidents but by rewarding friends and members of the ruling Institutional Revolutionary Party (PRI) as it built its nationwide political machine. In Jalisco, the Bracero Program offered a means for municipal officials to enrich themselves and maintain a base of support in a region that historically harbored strong antigovernment sentiments. The bracero contract—a fairly well-paid if short-term stint in the United States—served as one form of patronage that an erstwhile PRI boss could deliver to his constituents or their sons, be they from a merchant family or a nearby farm. Cronyism and self-enrichment became endemic among a new generation of *ejido* leaders, union bosses, and low-level government functionaries in postrevolutionary Mexico. The Bracero Program simply offered small-town mayors or their underlings the chance to sell permits, reward their allies, and supplement their salaries. Indeed, a black market in contracts flourished, despite press exposés of corruption and the occasional investigation by Mexico's Interior Ministry into such scandals.[43] Aspiring braceros accepted paying the bribe as one of the many costs of migration.

The Bracero Program functioned differently in the Valles region of Jalisco. Here the PRI utilized it not to enrich corrupt functionaries but to reward the working-class members of the "revolutionary family," as the ruling party referred to its coalition with organized workers and peasants. In the region to the south and west of Guadalajara is where Jalisco's semiarid high plains give way to well-watered forests and lush fields planted with corn, peanuts, and, most famously, sugarcane. The workers and peasants of this semitropical zone benefited more from that state's postrevolutionary land and labor reforms than any others in Jalisco. In the mid-1930s, agrarian activists won their struggle for lands once owned by the region's wealthiest planters. By 1941, the sugar mill workers succeeded in their own battle for union recognition. The mill workers secured significant benefits over the next decade: eight-hour days, better wages, company housing, and better schools for their kids.[44] Their union locals dominated municipal politics over the coming decades. During the Bracero Program, the state allocated more contracts per capita to the region's sugar workers and communal farmers than to any other part of Jalisco. Their case demonstrates that the government used the migratory agreement to reward the ostensibly loyal (male) beneficiaries of its land and labor reforms.

That favoritism became evident in 1945. Men from Jalisco were still prohibited by the state government—which feared harmful labor shortages—from being contracted as braceros (although thousands ventured individually to Mexico City and achieved that very goal). So at the behest of union leaders in the Ameca Valley, the federal Labor Department secured the governor's approval to contract 2,000 sugar workers. Their departure caused no harm to the local economy because the prime bracero contracting months of May through October coincided with the sugar industry's *tiempo muerto*, the down season between harvests. Whatever one's rank in the occupational hierarchy, nearly all workers migrated, for earnings in the fields of California surpassed even the relatively high rates offered by the mill. So it was that the sugar workers of towns like Ameca and Tala became braceros, and privileged ones at that. For several years in the late 1940s, the union boss Filemón Avalos convinced migration authorities to process his men right in Ameca's town square. That privilege did not last long. But in contrast to so many braceros from Jalisco, the mill workers never paid a mayor or union boss for a contract. And their union hired buses to transport them to the contracting center in Sonora, alleviating another financial burden that most hard-pressed braceros (and their families) shouldered themselves. So while contemporary social scientists—and the state's critics—asserted the safety-valve thesis frequently during the 1950s and 1960s, it seems that, in fact, the program sought to achieve distinct political ends: rewarding the state's allies in the labor movement. As a result, a culture of migration took root in this region of Jalisco where no prior tradition existed.

The Bracero Program marked a watershed in Jalisco's emigration history. It consolidated the dependence of dozens of rural communities (and several Guadalajara neighborhoods) on seasonal migration and channeled their labor disproportionately into commercial agriculture. It therefore altered the nascent emigration patterns of the 1920s by steering the state's migrants away from Midwestern cities and industry and into the fields of California and Texas.

Finally, it dramatically increased the sheer number of migrants departing. Take undocumented departures into account—they met or exceeded bracero permits issued—and during the 1950s at least 30 percent of working-age males from Jalisco labored in the United States each year.[45] But what were return migration's immediate and long-term effects on the braceros, their families, and the communities that sent them north? We know that, over the past 100 years, their *migradolares* have financed land acquisition and home construction and made possible the purchase of tractors, trucks, and consumer goods otherwise unavailable to Mexico's rural poor. Unlike the 1920s, Jorge Durand notes, migrants who returned from bracero contracts found Jalisco to be more stable, prosperous, and therefore suitable for investment.[46] But how many returnees managed to invest in productive enterprises? Moreover, policy makers envisioned that emigration would produce a cultural transformation of the countryside, not just produce capital for small-scale investments. Did it?

In subsequent years, social scientists who studied sending communities in western Mexico found evidence to both confirm and counter Manuel Gamio's forecast. Nathan Whetton's pioneering ethnography asserted that migrants acquired new "habits of diet and dress and new ideas concerning agriculture." But, he went on, "some are restless and reluctant to settle down again in the same isolated villages from which they migrated, and some of those are moving into Mexico City."[47] Twenty years later, when bracero migrations had become a lifestyle in rural Michoacán villages, Belshaw found limited effects on the rural economy. As one bracero commented, "I found that I can live better and I learned something about cultivation, but I found that I can do nothing because there they have resources and here one has nothing." Belshaw concurred that the braceros learned few agricultural skills that applied to their smallholding agrarian lifestyles. But villagers did become "new men." "They acquired a new dignity and self respect, sloughed off their fatalism, and began to realize it was in their power to change things." Those who benefited most consistently in economic terms were local merchants. The braceros who parlayed their stints abroad into new careers at home did so as carpenters, cargo haulers, or barbers, investing their savings into the tools of new trades. But what most impressed ethnographers who studied rural Mexican villages were the migrants' new attitudes, which ranged from greater self-reliance to less deference toward "the political leader or the rural patron," as studies of return migrants in early-twentieth-century Italy also find.[48]

Visit any town square in small-town Jalisco today, and one is certain to encounter veteran braceros willing to share their experiences with a mix of reluctance, authority, pride, and nostalgia. When queried, the former migrants who collaborated in this study initially shrugged off the possibility that their emigration produced the positive results promised by state policy makers.[49] Some recall leaving home with no great *ilusiones* (goals) other than to find work or seek adventure. The bracero contracts offered an escape from Mexican village life and promised better wages for steady work, all of which appealed to the landless sharecroppers' or farmers' sons who dominated Jalisco's male population. "We did not improve ourselves at all," Javier Salazar recalled of himself and his fellow Amecans. "We didn't advance at all . . . that was just a dream." Aurora Medina's father first left her family of eighteen children when she was ten years old. Laid off from the sugar mill, he earned his first bracero contract as compensation from Mexican labor officials. He returned sporadically over the next ten years and rarely with anything more than used clothes for his kids. As for savings, Aurora surmised with a tone of embarrassment, "Well, either he didn't save much or who knows what." When interviewed, former braceros' wives and widows are typically first to admit that a husband's vices abroad often determined a family's ability to benefit. Guadalupe Gonzalez's husband, for example, took a liking to cards and left his earnings at the gambling tables that flourished in bracero labor camps. Women back home, meanwhile, fed their kids by cleaning homes, vending food, and (when possible) moving back to their parents' house. "All that time he was struggling up there," Maria Rodriguez recalled, "we were struggling down here as well."[50]

While many seemed reluctant at first, the former braceros interviewed for this project admit, often at the insistence of their wives, that they indeed harbored clear objectives upon departing for El Norte. Landless laborers and sharecroppers dreamed of buying a parcel of land. Some realized their dreams. But most left with more modest goals and built on their accomplishments as the Bracero Program proceeded. As Mexican presidents boasted in their state-of-the-nation reports, the braceros collectively earned considerable sums. (By the mid-1950s, total remittances were Mexico's third greatest source of foreign exchange after mining and tourism.)[51] They dedicated those savings toward countless ends. Migrants returned with gifts for themselves and their wives: radios, sewing machines, boots, hats, perfume, and cloth. What remained got them through the next few months. Many paid off debts and set money aside for next year's journey. Labor migrations allowed some of Jalisco's rural poor to avoid debt altogether, a universal but often unattainable dream of agrarian peoples everywhere. It is easy to underestimate how profound a change seemingly meager savings could offer. As a former bracero pointed out, there was no industry and only poorly paid farm labor available in Guanajuato by the 1950s. The region around San Francisco del Rincón, near the Jalisco border, had seen its hat-weaving industry decline in the preceding decade. Therefore, "everyone around here benefited greatly from the braceros." This was a moment, Viviana Gómez recalled, when "hunger disappeared from this place."[52]

Braceros from places like San Francisco or the neighboring Los Altos region of Jalisco were frequently second- and third-generation migrants, and they capitalized on the lessons of their forefathers. Lupe Romo recalled that of his twelve classmates back in the hamlet of Valle de Guadalupe, nine ended up studying

English with him at the same night school in Santa Monica. Many would stay on in Los Angeles to labor in the building trades or in landscaping. They saved and purchased property back home—as well as in formerly working-class neighborhoods in Santa Monica and San Francisco—and finally retired to comfortable lives in Tepatitlán, the now-prosperous county seat. Romo attributed this exceptional story of success to his village's history of emigration, one that the region's braceros were uniquely qualified to capitalize upon. They were expected to not just return with savings, but to achieve mobility as a result of the migrations. Many learned to stay on or skipped out of contracts, moving to urban California and saving considerable sums. Eustacio Franco recollects that he saved an average of $1,800 annually in the 1950s, working in the fields or in construction. During ten years of bracero and undocumented labor, the one-time sharecropper saved for family maintenance, then invested in dairy cows, and eventually purchased his own small ranch. Several braceros from Tepatitlán earned fame and helped stimulate further migrations when they returned, bought land, and planted the area's first peach and apple orchards.[53] Emigration became and remains such an ingrained and lived feature of *alteño* identity that today the region's booming agribusiness and textile industries depend on immigrants from Central America.

Those who departed the Valles region, on the other hand, left with distinct goals. The sugar workers of Ameca typically applied their earnings toward urban real estate, purchasing lots or renovating their homes. Those who migrated from the region's many *ejidos* harbored other goals. Bicycles became ubiquitous, many residents recall, for they offered a quick and modern means to get out to the nearby fields. (Mexican farmers typically lived on the outskirts of town.) Few realized Gamio's vision of peasants investing in tractors. Why would they, when most farmed no more than ten to twenty acres? But farmers replaced their old donkeys with a pair of horses and, when they saved more, retired the horses for costlier but "smarter, more peaceful and durable" teams of oxen. They could then purchase larger and more effective steel plows.[54] Other *ejidatarios* invested their savings just as state agriculture officials expected: purchasing hybrid seeds or the newly available fertilizers. Javier Salazar added that his earnings allowed him to modernize his agricultural practices without recourse to the government's agricultural credit bank, which he recalled for its high interest rates. Material change thus came to the countryside in gradual and piecemeal fashion. However, it resulted in greater agricultural productivity and in easier working lives on the small farms and *ejidos* of Ameca. Here, then, we find that the Bracero Program was less a reflection of a failed agrarian reform policy than a means by which it might succeed.[55]

From its inception, its proponents marketed the Bracero Program to a critical public as a means to uplift the rural masses. Gamio, after all, devoted more of his influential research to the cultural consequences of emigration than to the issue of remittances. Ideally, braceros were expected to work, observe, learn, and return to apply their newfound knowledge. Many understood that the goal was to improve life at home. "The idea was to progress," Jesus Amezquita recalled, "to buy a little parcel of land, some cows, and to make oneself a capitalist." This, he noted, was not a simple task, and many invested their savings in land to only lose it, for they lacked "administration skills."[56] When asked what they learned, most former braceros first chuckle at the notion. They recall laboring in strawberry fields or on lettuce farms, acquiring knowledge that meant little for those without land, sufficient water, or regional markets. But upon further reflection (or additional queries), most former braceros recognize that their migrations did produce new knowledge and cultural change back home. Few braceros earned enough to invest in tractors, but they gained experience in handling and repairing them and capitalized on that as the region's large landowners began investing in farm machinery in the later 1950s. "Emigration elevated the culture of this region," Francisco Romo says confidently and proudly of his hometown, Tepatitlán. "We brought great ideas back from there," Javier Salazar remembered. The *ejidatario* not only returned home with some financial resources. He learned to appreciate the new hybrid seeds and how to sow them to maximize and conserve costly fertilizers. Others returned to plant new crops, like the onions and potatoes they harvested in Michigan, less to market them than to improve their own diets.[57]

Change came to the braceros' homes and communities as well as their lands. When asked, Javier Salazar noted that he learned from observation as he ventured into the farm towns of California's Central Valley or befriended Mexican American families who invited him into their homes. He noted their clean and paved floors, their neat dress and appearances. He saw that they insisted on sending their children to school. Not all braceros ventured north with the same sense of adventure and curiosity. But those who did learned and brought the lessons home. Nearly all braceros from Ameca, for example, returned to invest their earnings in home purchases or improvements. "That is what cultura is," claimed Francisco Gonzalez, "having a bathroom, a real roof, and a tile floor." Emigration "was a huge learning experience and it brought profound change." Ameca, he concluded "escaped from its stagnation" as a result of the braceros.[58] In nearby Tala, former mill worker Manolo Zavala observed that, after migrating north, "We began to open our eyes a little more." Subsistence farming, cane cutting and sugar mill labor were no longer sufficient to achieve the new expectations generated by the bracero experience. "We all wanted concrete houses after we saw how they lived up there. . . . And now it was possible thanks to money from [the United States]." Sugar mill workers like Zavala saw considerable improvements in their lives with unionization in the early 1940s. Over the next two decades, the union pressured the mill to build a vast Colonia Obrera of worker housing, a modern school, and a community recreation center. But not all locals enjoyed the privilege of mill work. Thus winning bracero contracts helped the mill's vast contingent of seasonal contract workers or the region's cane-farming *ejidatarios* to aspire to the same opportunities as the well-paid union mill workers.

Former braceros attribute these cultural changes to their emigrations and experiences. But their hometowns were subjected to various external influences that may, had the Bracero Program ended with the war, have arrived regardless. Over the course of the 1950s, once isolated districts in the Los Altos and Valles regions of Jalisco saw the arrival of paved highways from Guadalajara, electricity to the county seats, more secondary schools, radio, and even the mobile cinemas that the U.S. Consulate sent out to teach the locals about modern agriculture, hygiene, and housing.[59] So the winds of change came from many directions. But the braceros' experience abroad certainly left them more open to new ideas and outlooks than they otherwise might have been. "It was a massive success (*un exitazo*)," Juan José Zepeda believes, "because we really became civilized." Offering a metaphorical conclusion, he then added, "We left as a bunch of illiterate hicks and came back wearing eyeglasses and with pens in our shirt pockets."[60]

The Bracero Program brought great change to the sending communities of Jalisco and its neighboring states. The effects were like those experienced in the emigrant-sending regions of southern Europe, where the state sanctioned the emigration and return migration of native sons well into the twentieth century.[61] The Bracero Program did not, perhaps, result in the changes that Manuel Gamio and like-minded policy makers promised. After all, Gamio focused his investigation on settlers in urban America, emigrants like Francisco González's father. He left Jalisco in the 1920s to work in the railway yards and then a restaurant in downtown Chicago. Thirty years later, he left his wife in charge of the family's store and headed north again as a bracero. In eighteen months, he saved enough to build a new home. But he drew a clear and unfavorable distinction between 1920s Chicago and postwar Arizona. "Up there [in Illinois]," his father told González, "we lived like people; we were clean and wore suits . . . not like some animals out in the cotton fields." The Bracero Program renewed migratory flows, but it altered the experience by consolidating a link between farmwork and Mexican emigration. Of course, thousands of emigrants resisted their relegation to field labor and skipped their contracts in search of urban employment. However, most accepted the contractual terms established by the binational accord in return for the steady work, wages, or adventure that the bracero program promised and frequently delivered. Moreover, most braceros returned home with positive recollections that contrast markedly with the Bracero Program's depiction as a form of "legalized slavery," a view as common in the 1960s as on the Internet today. This, of course, reflects a tendency among oral history interviewees to recall the past with a sense of nostalgia. But from their perspective, seasonal labor in the fields of El Norte permitted them to maintain their families, make their lands more productive, and open their eyes to a world beyond their hardscrabble villages and neighborhoods. The benefits they gained from that experience, and the lessons it taught to their children, helped to institutionalize the culture of migration for which western Mexico is so renowned today.

Conclusion

The Bracero Program ended where it began, in the halls of the U.S. Congress. The bill to terminate it unilaterally—Mexico had no say in the matter—passed by a mere seventeen votes, despite a groundswell of concern for the plight of migrant workers. No sooner did it end than César Chávez and the United Farm Workers launched the first successful effort to organize field laborers in postwar U.S. history. Meanwhile, the last braceros returned to Mexico when the 1964 harvest concluded. More than twenty years had passed since thousands of eager young men departed the Mexico City train station as "citizens on a mission." A generation later, migrants returned to a nation living through a "Mexican miracle" of sustained economic growth and political stability. During the Bracero Program's twenty-two-year run, their homeland evolved into a model of Third World development, an industrializing nation of modern cities that soon hosted the 1968 Summer Olympic Games. By then, urban Mexico exerted a greater pull on rural migrants than the fields of El Norte. But Mexico's unprecedented rate of population growth—one of the world's highest—alarmed policy makers who otherwise took pride in the state's capacity to develop jobs at home. In 1965, Mexico initiated the Border Industrialization Program, a new binational agreement that gave birth to the sprawling assembly plants near the U.S.-Mexican border known as maquiladoras. But they developed slowly, and, contrary to their planners' vision, they preferred to hire young women rather than the men who once migrated. So when Mexico's miracle of growth ended abruptly in 1982, communities whose ties to the migrant trail dated to the Bracero Program headed north from Mexico once again. The former guest workers now invited themselves. But their renewed exodus built on a migratory culture that twenty-two years of bilateral, state-sanctioned emigration had institutionalized in Mexico's traditional sending states.

NOTES

1. Research funding for this project came from a Fulbright Faculty Research Fellowship (2007) from the U.S. Department of Education and a Research Support Funds Grant (2006) from the Office of Research and Sponsored Programs at Indiana University Purdue University–Indianapolis. This chapter benefited from the provocative questions offered by colleagues at the Newberry Conference on Labor History across the Americas and the inspiration and editorial advice of Julie Greene. Gracias a todos.

2. An important exception is the sociologist David Fitzgerald's *A Nation of Emigrants: How Mexico Manages Its Migration* (Berkeley: University of California Press, 2009).
3. Examples include Theresa Alfaro-Velcamp, *So Far From Allah, So Close to Mexico: Middle Eastern Immigrants in Modern Mexico* (Austin: University of Texas Press, 2007); Michael Meyer, William Sherman and Susan Deeds, *The Course of Mexican History*, 8th ed. (New York: Oxford University Press, 2007). One exception is Moisés González Navarro, *Extranjeros en Mexico y los mexicanos en el extranjero, 1821–1970* (Mexico City: El Colegio de México, 1993).
4. Claire Fox, *The Fence and the River: Culture and Politics at the US-Mexico Border* (Minneapolis: University of Minnesota Press, 1999); Maria Herrera-Sobek, *Northward Bound: The Mexican Immigrant Experience in Ballad and Song* (Bloomington: University of Indiana Press, 1996).
5. Mark I. Choate, *Emigrant Nation: The Making of Italy Abroad* (Cambridge, MA: Harvard University Press, 2008); Nana Oishi, *Women in Motion: Globalization, State Policies and Migration in Asia* (Stanford, CA: Stanford University Press, 2005).
6. The U.S. government issued nearly 5 million contracts to bracero migrants, with annual averages peaking at more than 400,000 in the mid-1950s. At least as many undocumented migrants, unable or unwilling to secure bracero permits, ventured north during the same period. Michael Snodgrass, "The Bracero Program, 1942–1964," in *Beyond la Frontera: The History of Mexican-U.S. Migration*, ed. Mark Overmyer-Velásquez (New York: Oxford University Press, 2011), chapter 4.
7. For example, farm wages in California fell from 64.7 percent of national manufacturing wages (1948) to 46.6 percent (1959). President's Commission on Migratory Labor, *Migratory Labor in American Agriculture* (Washington, DC: Government Printing Office, 1950), 56–62; Ernesto Galarza, *Merchants of Labor: The Mexican Bracero Story, an Account of the Managed Migration of Mexican Farm Workers in California, 1942–1960* (Charlotte, NC: McNally and Loftin, 1964).
8. Truman Moore, *The Slaves We Rent* (New York: Random House, 1965); union official quoted in Mae Ngai, *Impossible Subjects: Illegal Aliens and the Making of Modern America* (Princeton, NJ: Princeton University Press, 2004), 13; Williams cited in J. F. Otero, "Immigration Policy: Drifting toward Disaster," *AFL-CIO American Federationist* 88 (February 1981).
9. Ricardo Sandoval, "Braceros Want an Old Promise Met," *Dallas Morning News*, January 27, 2002; Susan Ferriss, "Braceros Line Up for Wages Withheld during WWII," *Sacramento Bee*, October 27, 2008.
10. Kitty Calavita, *Inside the Sending State: The Bracero Program, Immigration, and the INS* (New York: Routledge, 1992); Stephen Pitti, *The Devil in Silicon Valley: Northern California, Race, and Mexican Americans* (Princeton, NJ: Princeton University Press, 2003).
11. Deborah Cohen, "From Peasant to Worker: Migration, Masculinity, and the Making of Mexican Workers in the US," *International Labor and Working-Class History* 69 (2006): 81–103.

12. G. S. Messersmith, U.S. Embassy Mexico City, to Washington, August 11, 1943, in Records of the Foreign Service Posts of the Department of State, Record Group 84, 850.4, United States National Archives and Records Administration (hereafter NARA: RG 84); Mark Wyman, *Round-Trip to America: The Immigrants Return to Europe, 1880–1930* (Ithaca, NY: Cornell University Press, 1993), 6.
13. Michael Belshaw, *A Village Economy: Land and People of Huecorio* (New York: Columbia University Press, 1967), 132–33.
14. Jaime Torres Bodet, *La victoria sin alas . . . Memorias* (Mexico: Porrúa, 1970), 508–9.
15. Carey McWilliams, *North From Mexico: The Spanish-Speaking People of the United States* (Philadelphia: J.B. Kippincott, 1949), 266–70.
16. Ernesto Gamboa, *Mexican Labor and World War II: Braceros in the Pacific Northwest* (Austin: University of Texas Press, 1990); Memphis Consul Cano de Castillo, 1951 correspondence, Trabajadores Migratorios, box 6/31 in Archivo Histórico "Genaro Estrada" de la Secretaría de Relaciones Exteriores de México (hereafter Archivo SRE).
17. Messersmith, Mexico City, July 16, 1942, NARA: RG 84, 850.4, box 352; *El Nacional*, Mexico City, February 4, 1943 (quoted).
18. Mercedes Carreras de Velasco, *Los Mexicanos que devolvió la crisis, 1929–32* (Mexico: Secretaría de Relaciones Exteriores, 1974), 44–45.
19. Mark Reisler, *By the Sweat of Their Brow: Mexican Immigrant Labor in the US, 1900–40* (Westport, CT: Greenwood, 1976).
20. Michael Snodgrass, *Deference and Defiance in Monterrey: Workers, Paternalism, and Revolution in Mexico, 1890–1950* (New York: Cambridge University Press, 2003), 47–50.
21. Alfonso Fábila, *El problema de la emigracion de obreros y campesinos mexicanos* (Mexico: Talleres Gráficas, 1928); Enrique Santibáñez, *Ensayo acerca de la inmigración mexicana en los Estados Unidos* (San Antonio, TX: Clegg, 1930).
22. Consular report in Archivo General de la Nación (Mexico City): Ramo Obregón-Calles, 711-M-30, which cites Prime Minister Luzzatti on emigration's positive effects on Italy's development.
23. Torres Bodet, *La victoria sin alas*, 510.
24. Manuel Gamio, *Mexican Immigration to the United States: A Study of Human Migration and Adjustment* (Chicago: University of Chicago Press, 1930), 128, 156–57, 178–84.
25. Arthur Schmidt, "Manuel Gamio in the United States," in *Strange Pilgrimages: Exile, Travel, and National Identity in Latin America, 1800–1990s*, ed. Ingrid Fey and Karen Racine (Wilmington, DE: Scholarly Resources, 2000), 171–73.
26. Messersmith, Mexico City Embassy, May 18, 1944, NARA: RG 84, 850.4, box 488.
27. Guy Ray, Mexico City Embassy, October 6, 1943, NARA: RG 84, 840.1, box 330.

28. Enrique Lozano to (CTM leader) Fidel Velasquez, October 3, 1944, and Gamio to President Avila Camacho, 1944, reprinted in *Boletín del Archivo General de la Nación*, Mexico 4, no. 14 (October–December 1980).
29. *El Nacional*, May 18, 1944; Denver Consul Martínez to Mexican Embassy, September 20, 1943 in Archivo SRE, 1458-2.
30. See Archivo SRE: Trabajadores Migratorios files for written protests and consular records of farmers and growers associations charged with violations. Bracero resistance in Gamboa, *Mexican Labor and World War II*; and Cohen, "From Peasant to Worker," 92–98.
31. Leslie Byrd Simpson, *Many Mexicos*, 4th ed. rev. (Berkeley: University of California Press, 1966), 347.
32. *El Popular* (Mexico City), October 21, 1944.
33. The northern states of Durango and Chihuahua sent 20 percent more. Thus six states with a quarter of Mexico's population sent two of every three braceros north. From figures in James Sandos and Harry Cross, "National Development and International Labour Migration: Mexico 1940–65," *Journal of Contemporary History* 18, no. 1 (1983).
34. Paul Taylor, *Mexican Labor in the United States*, vol. 2 (reprint; New York: Arno, 1970), 48–50; Taylor, *A Spanish-Mexican Peasant Community: Arandas in Jalisco, Mexico* (Berkeley: University of California Press, 1933).
35. Messersmith, Mexico City, August 11, 1943, NARA: RG 84, 850.4, box 352; Eaton, Durango Consulate to Washington, January 31, 1945 NARA: RG 84, Durango General Records, 1936–46, Box 72; Presidente Municipal Guanajuato to Governor, July 19, 1944, in Archivo General del Estado de Guanajuato: Gobierno box 1.19.83.
36. Sandos and Cross, "National Development and International Labour Migration," 55.
37. Gamio, *Mexican Immigration*, 178–84.
38. Richard Craig, *The Bracero Program: Interest Groups and Foreign Policy* (Austin: University of Texas Press, 1971), 60.
39. Gobernación intelligence reports on Sinarquista activism in Jalisco and Guanajuato in AGN, Dirección General de Investigaciones Políticas y Sociales, boxes 771–73.
40. Interviews with Juan Jose Zepeda Santos and Andrés Dueñas Rodríguez, Ameca, Jalisco, May 15, 2007.
41. Following based on interviews with Rodrigo Barba Villegas and Juan Jauregui Jiménez, Valle de Guadalupe, Jalisco, May 24, 2007; Jose Vásquez García, Arandas, Jalisco, May 31, 2007; Ruben Oñate García, Arandas, Jalisco, June 1, 2007; Gerardo López Gómez, Tepatitlán, Jalisco, April 9, 2007.
42. See Snodgrass, "The Bracero Program, 1942–1964," for the hardships migrants endured during the bracero recruitment process in Mexico. Interviews with Guadalupe Romo, Tepatitlán, Jalisco, April 9, 2007; Manuel y Rogelio Rodríguez Pulido, San José de Gracia, Michoacán, June 26, 2008.

43. Jose Lázaro Salinas, *La emigración de Braceros: visión objetiva de un problema mexicano* (Mexico: Cuauhtemoc, 1955); Unión de Braceros to Presidente Municipal of Guadalajara, August 17, 1952, Archivo Municipal de Guadalajara, 1-02-14.
44. Based on interviews with former braceros and mill workers from Ameca, Tala, and Villa Corona, Jalisco.
45. Based on figures in Gloria Vargas y Campos, *El problema del bracero mexicano* (Mexico: Universidad Nacional Autonoma de México, 1964), 82–85; Dirección General de Estadística, *Anuaria Estadístico de los Estados Unidos Mexicanos, 1968–1969* (Mexico: Sec. Industria y Comercio, 1971), 31.
46. Jorge Durand, Emilio Parrado, and Douglas Massey, "Migradollars and Development: A Reconsideration of the Mexican Case," *International Migration Review* 30, no. 2 (1996): 423–44.
47. Nathan L. Whetten, *Rural Mexico* (Chicago: University of Chicago Press, 1948).
48. Belshaw, *A Village Economy*, 130–31; Richard Hancock, *The Role of the Bracero in the Economic and Cultural Dynamics of Mexico* (Stanford, CA: Hispanic American Society), 1958, 122–23; Wyman, *Round-Trip to America*, 160–72.
49. The following paragraphs rely upon forty interviews conducted by the author in 2007 and 2008 in western Mexico. I use them here as empirical evidence and to illuminate the experiences, values, and traditions that shaped individual memories and collective identities in this emigrant-sending region. The frank and ultimately positive recollections that former migrants express are consistent with evidence from bracero oral histories collected elsewhere. The most far-reaching is the Bracero History Archive (http://braceroarchive.org), an online collection of more than 500 interviews collected by the University of Texas–El Paso's Institute of Oral History in conjunction with the Smithsonian's National Museum of American History.
50. Interviews with Javier Salazar Areola, Ameca, Jalisco, May 14, 2007; Aurora Medina Sanchez, Ameca, May 15, 2007; Guadalupe González Gomez y Domingo González Mesa (not related), Ameca, May 16, 2007; and Maria Rodríguez Bautista, Ameca, May 16, 2007.
51. Ngai, *Impossible Subjects*, 143.
52. Interviews with Pedro Domínguez Arrellano and Viviana Gómez Vásquez, San Francisco del Rincón, Guanajuato, June 13, 2007.
53. Interviews with Jesús López Gómez and Guadalupe (Lupe) Romo, April 9, 2007; and Eustacio Casillas Franco and Francisco Romero, March 28, 2007, all in Tepatitlán, Jalisco.
54. Interview with Dominguez Arrellano.
55. Interviews with Salazar Areola and Jose Manuel (Manolo) Zavala Salazar, Tala, Jalisco, June 28, 2007.
56. Interview with Jesus Amezquita Ulloa, Lagos de Moreno, Jalisco, June 12, 2007.

57. Interviews with Romero and Viviana Gómez Vásquez and Benjamin Rosas López, San Francisco del Rincón, Guanajuato, June 13, 2007.
58. Interviews with Salazar and Francisco Javier Gónzalez Núñez, Ameca, May 16, 2007.
59. U.S. Consulate program in Archivo Municipal de Arandas (Jalisco), Dec. 1951, box 2.
60. Interview with Juan Jose Zepeda Santos, Ameca, Jalisco, May 15, 2007.
61. Dino Cinel, *The National Integration of Italian Return Migrants, 1870–1929* (New York: Cambridge University Press, 1991); Wyman, *Round-Trip to America*; Portuguese case in Caroline Brettell, *Anthropology and Migration: Essays on Transnationalism, Ethnicity, and Identity* (Walnut Creek, CA: AltaMira, 2003).

15

UNSPOKEN EXCLUSIONS

RACE, NATION, AND EMPIRE IN THE IMMIGRATION RESTRICTIONS OF THE 1920S IN NORTH AMERICA AND THE GREATER CARIBBEAN

Lara Putnam

The 1924 Johnson-Reed Act is studied as a milepost of nativist populism and racist Anglo-Saxonism within U.S. history. But the United States was not alone in legislating new race-based restrictions on entry, citizenship, and employment in the interwar years. To the contrary, states around the world moved in this era to adopt new, linked technologies to control borders, identify persons, and limit employment and mobility on the basis of national belonging. These were the years in which consuls, passports, visas, and work permits took on their modern forms. The industrialized North Atlantic—both its sending societies in Europe and receiving societies in North America—was first to adopt the mechanisms and ideologies of identification and exclusion. But by the turn of the twentieth century, the other American receiving societies—the agro-export economies in South and Central America—were moving rapidly in the same direction. After several generations in which Asian and Middle Eastern migrants bore the brunt of restrictive legislation and overt state racism here, the 1920s saw those of African ancestry systematically excluded as well for the first time. It was the several hundred thousand British Caribbean men, women, and children living outside their islands of origin who would pay the price.

This chapter examines the formal immigration restrictions enacted in Central America, the Caribbean, and the United States in the 1920s and uses newspaper sources from around the region to reconstruct the actual implementation of the new legal structures. The impact of the Johnson-Reed Act on Afro-Caribbean immigration is unmarked or misrepresented within even recent and comprehensive scholarly analyses of U.S. immigration history: an understandable outcome of the ambiguities and slippages through which U.S. restrictionist legislation was made to work. By careful interpretation of terms like *country*, *nation*, and *self-governing*, the institutional actors charged with enforcing the Johnson-Reed Act—which contained no explicit restrictions on the entry or citizenship of Afro-descended peoples—made it function as a total ban on black immigration. Ironically, in this case it was the homeland of Jim Crow segregation that masked its program of antiblack exclusion, while in the Spanish-speaking circum-Caribbean republics, lands where lines of color and ancestry were far more fluid and rarely given governmental sanction, black immigration was openly and officially outlawed on the explicit basis of race. Meanwhile, within the British Empire, the fact of the Crown's acquiescence as those British subjects of African and Asian ancestry—and no others—were stripped of their right of entry by nation after nation undercut the pretense of race-blind imperial equity that had so long sustained Britannia's rule. Thus this moment of pan-American state racism, expulsion, and return migration was a crucial stage in the growth of racialized anticolonialism in the British Caribbean.

Circum-Caribbean Migration in the Late Nineteenth and Early Twentieth Centuries

In the first generation after the abolition of slavery in the British Caribbean in 1834, separate migratory circuits developed in the Eastern and Western Caribbean. Scores of thousands of freed people and their descendants from Barbados and other Windward Islands sailed south to Trinidad, and sometimes on to Venezuela or even farther to Brazil, establishing themselves as smallholders growing provisions for the region's busy ports or finding work in burgeoning export sectors like cocoa farming in Trinidad or gold panning along the Orinoco River. In the Western Caribbean, Jamaicans similarly used their newly won freedom to seek opportunities far from home, on railroad projects in Colombia, Costa Rica, or Honduras or growing new export crops—most prominently, bananas—along the Caribbean littoral of Central America. Attempts to build a canal across the isthmus of Panama, first by French concessionaires in the 1880s and then under the aegis of the U.S. government after Panama's assisted secession from Colombia in 1903, both drew on this nascent regional labor market and in turn intensified shipping, communication, and kin ties to draw ever greater numbers of British West Indians into the transnational migratory sphere.

The completion of the Panama Canal in 1914 left tens of thousands of laborers without work and curtailed opportunities for the saloon keepers, laundresses, and peddlers who had flocked to the isthmus to meet canal laborers' needs. As war in Europe sent international sugar prices sky-high, migrant streams shifted northward to the cane fields of the Greater Antilles.[1] In 1913, the United

Fruit Company recruited a thousand-odd British West Indians from their Costa Rican banana plantations to provide manpower for the expansion of sugar holdings newly acquired by the company in eastern Cuba.[2] The sugar plantations of the Dominican Republic drew Eastern Caribbean migrants in a parallel and contemporaneous process. While a 1913 Cuban presidential decree sought specifically "white European workmen" demobilized in Panama, offering "a bonus of $5 for each immigrant of the desired class brought," Cuban sugar growers eagerly employed the Afro-Caribbean laborers already on the move around the region.[3] In 1916, 1,288 of the 7,133 Jamaicans arriving in Cuba reported that their last place of residence had not been their country of birth; in 1917, 2,141 out of 7,889 arriving Jamaicans said the same.[4]

All told, at least a hundred thousand British Caribbeans and twice that number of Haitians would reach Cuba from the 1910s to the 1930s, and these totals may omit sizable numbers of temporary migrants who escaped official registry: A 1924 report estimated that 65,000 "Jamaican negroes" came to Cuba annually.[5] The cane fields of Oriente and Baraguá had replaced Panama and Colón as the prime destinations of the Western Caribbean migratory system. Years later, Miss Sitty recalled the rural Jamaica of her childhood years: "Plenty bwoy, ... people always lef and say them going to Cuba. Was only Cuba was the going ... and you only hear when they come, they talk the twang."[6] While some stayed in Cuba long enough or traveled often enough to pick up Spanish phrases—to "talk the twang" upon return—for others, Cuba was a brief way station. Brother S. spent two years in Cuba before taking work on a "fruiter" in 1920, a banana steamer traveling between Port Antonio and New York City: "And from what I got from that job, I was able to buy half an acre of land over where I am living there now."[7]

Brother S. was not alone in reaching New York harbor from the Caribbean in these years, and many chose to stay longer than he did. Even as migration from the British islands to the Spanish-speaking rimlands was expanding at the start of the twentieth century, West Indian elites noticed a smaller but growing movement to New York City as well. Often, these were scions of the islands' colored middle classes or the children of rural black proprietors whose success with export crops had enabled them to educate their children beyond the absorption capacity of the islands' middling ranks (where "decent employ" still went preferentially to those of the lightest skin and most established pedigrees). A Kingston *Daily Gleaner* editorial in 1905 lamented both the outflow of able-bodied laborers to Panama, Costa Rica, and Mexico and the emigration "of another sort," the "drift of our more intelligent and energetic young men to the United States."[8] As completion of the Panama Canal in 1914 simultaneously dried up employment opportunities in the Western Caribbean and multiplied the movement of ships, sailors, and savvy between the isthmus and the U.S. eastern seaboard, the numbers of British West Indians trying their luck in the metropolis to the north climbed. Numbering some 3,500 annually from 1903 to 1913, Afro-Caribbean arrivals to the United States averaged 5,000 per year over the following decade and reached more than 10,000 in the single year of 1924. By then, the nation was home to nearly 100,000 foreign-born blacks, the majority of them from the British Caribbean and almost all the rest Spanish-speakers and French-speakers from the same region. Roughly half of all black immigrants resided in and around New York City. Florida's coastal cities, linked to the Greater Antilles for generations through migrations temporary and permanent, boasted large Caribbean communities as well, and smaller numbers clustered in Boston and other New England ports.[9]

Though across the British Caribbean (as elsewhere in this heyday of transoceanic migration) men outnumbered women among those departing, still there were scores of thousands of women among those reaching Costa Rica, Panama, and Cuba from Western Caribbean islands and Trinidad, Guiana, Venezuela, and the Dominican Republic from the Eastern. Some women traveled with male partners or to join them; others journeyed with or to female kin and companions. Some women left children behind in the care of relatives or placed in service, while others brought infants, toddlers, or youths along with them.[10] Those boarding a Kingston-bound steamer in a Honduran port in a 1926 short story by Barbadian-born, Panama-raised Eric Walrond included "a woman and an amazing brood of children" ("one pulled, screaming, at her skirt, one was astride a hip, another, an unclothed one, tugged enthusiastically at a full, ripened breast") and "a tar-black Jamaica sister, in a gown of some noisy West Indian silk, her face entirely removed by the shadowy girth of a leghorn hat ... the edge of her skirt in one hand, after the manner of the ladies at Wimbledon, in the other a fluttering macaw."[11]

Migration and the related circulation of goods and earnings had become integrated into working-class Caribbean lives. Outside observers marveled at the "most extraordinary collection of personal property and 'household goods'" that accompanied "deck passengers" from Kingston to Panama, "as friends on shore handed over the side, and those on board received and stowed away, pathetic little bundles containing all that some poor creature possessed, imposing tin boxes and portmanteaux, pillows, beds, chairs, cooking vessels, garments, fruit, flowers, sugar-cane, an endless stream flowing over the side of the vessel"—all of which, somehow, by the time the steamer headed out to sea would be "neatly arranged and in order.... Chairs, beds, boxes ... all placed so that their owners could sit and rest and eat by day and sleep, or rest, by night."[12] Departures "to foreign" had become routinized and were routine parts of interpersonal ruptures. Aunt Dore was born in rural Jamaica in 1888 and interviewed in 1975. When she was young, she reported, if a man and woman fought, like as not one would "go a foreign." "Plenty a man you heard gone a sea and dem never come back, dem tek up dem clothes and dem gawn lef' the woman.... Or the woman would a shame. Shame.

She would a shame when the the scandal come up and she run whe gawn anoder place, you never hear gun fire of her."[13]

The evolving geography of migratory ties was inscribed in notices published in the region's newspapers, disavowing responsibility for disappeared spouses' future debts or seeking news of kin long gone from home: "MISSING: Nina V. Dove, age about 26, coloured, short and stout, worked as a domestic servant. When last heard from in June 1929 was in Havana. Please communicate with Salvation Army Headquarters, Kingston, Ja. Mother in Kingston anxious for news." And another: "Pollock, Mathilda (Mrs.). Coloured, native of Jamaica. Left Jamaica February 1912 for Cristobal, Canal Zone. Last heard from in 1915. Anyone knowing of her whereabouts, please communicate with Captain Moffett, The Salvation Army, Headquarters, Kingston, Jamaica."[14] Some 10,000 copies of the evangelical Christian magazine where these notices were placed were sold each month on street corners in ports from eastern Guatemala to the Leeward Islands: Wherever Miss Dove and Mrs. Pollock had traveled within the Greater Caribbean migratory sphere, there was some chance they would be found. Thus the customs and institutions created over two generations of intraregional migration wove emerging destinations into the fabric of Caribbean life. Religious and fraternal groups new and old spanned the migratory sphere. Barbadian friendly societies took in thousands of pounds in deposits from Panama each year; Afro-Caribbean migrants initiated Salvation Army corps in Costa Rica, Honduras, Cuba, and the Dominican Republic; the Montserrat Progressive Society, Grenada Mutual Association, Sons and Daughters of Barbados, and countless similar groups held weekly meetings in Harlem, Colón, and points in between.[15]

Imperial ties likewise bound migrants together, while also tying them into an even larger imagined community. One of the first public endeavors of the young Marcus Garvey, then a timekeeper on a United Fruit banana plantation in Costa Rica, was the organization of a "Coronation Committee" to celebrate the ascension of George V in 1911. One arch commentator in the Limon *Times* found it "very strange" that "Mr. Garvey ... who has only lived in the faith of the existence of a royal personage" should be taking the initiative in lieu of "others who claim a prior right to do," such as "His Brittanic Majesty's Vice Consul, other Scotchmen, Englishmen, and even Canadians who have been privileged to enjoy the true feelings of loyalty, in that, they have been reared in the immediate vicinity of royalty and its surroundings."[16] A racial hierarchy of imperial belonging—in which (white) Canadians somehow originated closer to "the immediate vicinity of royalty" than black Jamaicans like Garvey—apparently seemed self-evident to this author. But Garvey's contemporaries evinced remarkable confidence regarding their full status as "His Britannic majesty's subjects," as one group wrote from Chiriqui Prison in Panama in 1919, "oppressed Britishers" who "as Britishers ... refuse to yield to any ... unlawful and inhuman treatment ... because we know we belong to the great British Empire."[17] Actions backed up such formulaic phrases:

in matters of empire, British West Indians had skin in the game. During the Great War, the banana port of Bocas del Toro, Panama, not only generated hundreds of volunteers for the British West Indies Regiment but also through public subscription paid their passage to Kingston to join up. Australia-born Winifred James organized a bazaar in Bocas in 1916 that raised more than a hundred pounds sterling for the British Red Cross, a sum "rather wonderful," given that "in such times as these many of the negroes do not average more than ten or twelve shillings a week."[18] To James's shock, the white wives of United Fruit Company employees had refused to attend "if the negroes are to be allowed to come. Are they crazy? Why, nine-tenths of the population are negroes and so are all the British subjects with the exception of a dozen white people.... The negroes were my own people and I couldn't turn them down if I wanted to: they were fighting with us, they were eager to help with their money."[19] Hers was the racially inclusive Britannia invoked three years later by those "oppressed Britishers" of diverse island origin who from the depths of Chiriqui Prison sought justice from "the Great British Empire of which we shall always be pleased and proud to form a part."[20]

Grassroots imperial pride coexisted with newer and potentially contradictory supranational claims. Trinidadian Henry Sylvester William founded the Pan-African Association in London in 1901, a harbinger of the "race-consciousness" that—as banner, as bar—would come to define the century.[21] A decade later, Marcus Garvey, traveling the well-worn circuit from Central America to Jamaica and on to Harlem, founded the Universal Negro Improvement Association (U.N.I.A.) to develop and disseminate this vision. But for all Garvey's polemical prominence, the U.N.I.A.'s growth was more symptom than cause of the era's racially defined black internationalism.[22] Jamaican-born Socialist and Harlem intellectual W. A. Domingo called the "world-wide reaction of the darker races to their common as well as local grievances ... one of the most significant facts of recent development" and attributed it largely to migratory trends. Harlem alone was home to 35,000 black immigrants, whose disparate island origins yet shared current plight created nested and overlapping loyalties. "Here they have their first contact with each other, with large numbers of American Negroes, and with the American brand of race prejudice.... Unlike others of the foreign-born, black immigrants find it impossible to segregate themselves into colonies; too dark of complexion to pose as Cubans or some other Negroid but alien-tongued foreigners, they are inevitably swallowed up in black Harlem.... Forming a racial majority in their own countries and not being accustomed to discrimination expressly felt as racial, they rebel against the 'color line' as they find it in America"[23] The Jamaican-born father of poet June Jordan reached Harlem in this era after years in Panama. "He was a 'race man,' an admirer of Marcus Garvey, an enthusiast for theories about African origins of the human species, a zealous volunteer boxing instructor at the Harlem YMCA, devotedly literate in the available Negro poetry and political writings—and also, he would angrily insist that he was not 'black,' not a 'Negro.' Looking at him, you'd have to say that my father was extremely handsome, possibly white, and at least 50 percent Chinese."[24] Such complexities of self-identification, external labeling, and political allegiance were hardly anomalous in the transnational migratory sphere that had shaped his youth and that he, and thousands like him, had reshaped with their subsequent travels. But the spaces open to men like Granville Ivanhoe Jordan were about to be drastically curtailed.

Migration Restriction in the Interwar United States

Until the 1920s, British Caribbeans faced no categorical limitation on migration to the United States; after 1925, they faced a de facto ban in the Colossus of the North and a slew of de jure bans all around the Greater Caribbean. Yet despite the significance of this shift—both in its immediate material impact and as a symbol of the shifting politics of race and nation in the twentieth-century Americas—scholars have been either silent or confused about what happened and how.[25] This is not happenstance, nor a sign of faulty research. Rather, it replicates the widespread confusion at the time about how the new U.S. legislation would affect black British subjects in the Americas. This confusion, too, was not happenstance but a direct consequence of the way legislation was crafted and implemented: in particular, the way in which it enacted but did not enunciate race.

To the intellectuals demanding legislation, race was the most fundamental division between human groups. Yet to their eternal frustration, the reality of human fluidity confounded efforts to operationalize the fervent fiction of race. The lack of fixed markers through which individuals could systematically be identified as belonging to one and only one race meant that U.S. legislation aiming for racial selectivity was framed in terms of "national origins," to be determined by documentation of birthplace and political filiation, with language and religion playing a supporting role for certain groups. Mae Ngai has noted that although most discussion of the 1924 Johnson-Reed Act focuses on the distinctions it drew between more and less desirable European "stocks," more fundamentally the legislation and its implementation drew a bright line between European and non-European aspirants. The national origins quota system confirmed the whiteness of Europeans and Euro-Americans even as it reified supposed cultural differences among them; in contrast, it assigned non-Europeans indelible "ethnic and racial identities that were one and the same."[26] Europeans were to be counted, compared, and controlled by the federal government; non-Europeans were banned categorically (in the case of Asians) or left to the ad hoc judgment of border guards (in the case of Latin Americans).

This was the era in which race-based Asian exclusion was enunciated most openly and emphatically. Case law in the 1920s (in particular, *Ozawa* in 1922 and *Thind* in 1923) broadened the cachement of "Asiatics" excluded from citizenship by law, adding Japanese and South Asians to the Chinese whose exclusion under that heading had been established a half-century earlier. No members of "races ineligible for citizenship" were allowed entry to the United States as immigrants. Thus the legislation and case law of the 1920s marked the end of the gentleman's agreement through which the U.S. and Japanese governments had worked to limit Japanese emigration to the United States without the perceived humiliation of naming the Japanese as racial undesirables alongside the excluded Chinese.[27] However, there was no ban on the acquisition of citizenship by men and women of "Negro" race. On the contrary, within living memory in the United States, Afro-descended freed people had been incorporated into citizenship en masse. The Jim Crow procedures that turned African Americans' full citizenship in theory into second-class citizenship in practice were enacted locally and extralegally. To revisit the eligibility for citizenship of members of the "Negro race" would require contentious debate that would shine a bright light on antidemocratic practices that withstood challenge precisely because they were regional rather than national, ingrained by terror rather than proclaimed by law. Thus restrictionists in the 1920s did not attempt to institute race-based exclusion for those of African ancestry parallel to that which disqualified Asians.

In sum, by relying on the terms "national origins" and "eligibility for citizenship" as the mechanisms for what were intended to be racial preferences and exclusions, authors of restrictive legislation in the 1920s created neither a mandate nor a mechanism for the exclusion of black immigrants. In the United States, then, black exclusion was instituted de facto rather than de jure, through practices that ensured absence rather than statutes that proclaimed inadmissibility. Ambiguity and confusion were in this sense integral rather than incidental.

Congress's first adoption of a quota and numerical cap system in 1921 radically reduced immigration from many European countries. But immigrants from the countries of the Western Hemisphere were exempt from the quota system. Western agro-business interests had prevailed upon Congress to leave open their access to Mexican migrant workers, in part by insisting Mexicans were "birds of passage" disinclined to remain on northern soil any longer than their labor was needed. The new legislation consolidated mechanisms to ensure this lack of permanence. Those crossing the border could be banned on the basis of failure to pass literacy tests, on the grounds that they came in the prohibited condition of contract laborers, or because they were "Likely Public Charges." Absent categorical exclusion, Mexican workers could be allowed entry—or subsequently expelled—at the discretion of border agents responsive to the needs of local elites.[28] The same held true for Cuban workers arriving in Florida or French Canadians in northern New England.

The implementation of the 1921 law treated immigrants from European colonies and dominions in the Americas like those from American republics:

Jamaicans and Barbadians stood in the same condition as Canadians, Mexicans, and Cubans. It is no coincidence that, as we have seen, the years after 1921 saw migration to the United States from the British Caribbean reach its greatest heights. However, the 1924 Johnson-Reed Act, which from the point of view of European, Asian, and Mexican immigrants represented a continuation or intensification of the 1921 restrictions but not a categorical transformation, from the point of view of Afro-Caribbeans marked a total and radical rupture. Inhabitants of Britain's "non-self-governing" colonies in the Western Hemisphere now were to receive visas under the (enlarged) British quota. Aristide Zolberg's summary of what the 1924 legislation meant for the British Caribbean offers an utterly reasonable interpretation of the law as written: "Blacks living under colonial rule were eligible within the quotas of their respective imperial powers, and presumably at their discretion. Given the large British allocation and the relatively low demand for visas from the British Isles, this provided opportunities for blacks from the English-speaking Caribbean."[29] This is not, however, the way things worked.

The Johnson-Reed Act was signed into law on May 26, 1924, but the new quota system (requiring the creation of schedules of nationalities and determination of the portion of the 1890 U.S. population represented by each "stock") was not slated for implementation until 1927 and was ultimately postponed until 1929. The impact on the British Caribbean, however, was felt almost immediately. "Emigration of Jamaicans To U.S. Stopped," read the banner headline in the Kingston *Daily Gleaner* on June 14, 1924. News and rumors flew across the family networks that linked circum-Caribbean destinations. On July 7, the New York–based African American *World* reported rising consternation: "West Indian Negroes living in New York are excited over announcement that emigration from Jamaica to the United States has been stopped, at least temporarily, and that the American Consul at Kingston has been instructed by Washington that only passports of Americans desiring to come north are to be vised." Applicants had been told that the law taking effect July 1, 1924, had blocked the extension in Jamaica of visas for the United States. Alarms sounded: "Taking from the insular possessions the unrestricted privileges of the British self-governing dominions will check Negro immigration from the West Indies. In recent years 10,000 or more West Indian Negroes have been coming to New York annually. It is estimated that they make up one-third of the 200,000 Negro population in Harlem." The New York paper then quoted recent—and utterly erroneous—reporting from the Kingston *Gleaner* about how the number of visas to be issued in Jamaica would be determined: "From what can be gathered, only 2 percent of the population of Jamaicans, resident of the United States in 1890, will be allowed to enter the United States in any one year." This procedure would have meant treating Jamaica as equivalent to a European nation, a total contravention of the taxonomy of race and culture underlying the 1924 legislation, which, as we have seen, highlighted national and cultural distinctions among the "white races" but treated "colored races" as having, essentially, no meaningful country of origin. Finally, drawing a connection between race-based black exclusion and race-based black nationalism that would echo repeatedly around the Caribbean in the coming years, the *World* quoted Marcus Garvey as saying that the new U.S. policy made emigration to Liberia even "more logical than before."[30]

As July drew to a close, U.S. consular officials remained as confused as the Gleaner editors as to how the availability of visas for Jamaican or other British Caribbean emigrants was to be determined. On July 30, the *Gleaner* reported that at least sixty Jamaicans were visiting the U.S. consulate daily to discover if they would be allowed to sail for the United States as planned, while the local American consuls were doing their best to get instructions but as yet could provide no answers. "The steamship companies, too, are working in the same direction: they will not take people from Jamaica only to find that they have to bring them back." The editors expected that the "ambiguities with regard to passports, landing, residence for a time in the States" would be cleared up in a matter of days. Repeating previous misinformation, the *Gleaner* proclaimed: "We know, of course, that Jamaica is to be allowed, like other British countries, to send to the States two percent per annum of the people who emigrated from this island to the States in 1890, but the number of Jamaicans who went to America in that year has not yet been ascertained: at any rate, the American Consulate here has not yet been informed what it is." There were further points of confusion. It was said that "bona fide" visitors, those planning to stay less than six months, supposedly would not need any papers at all, perhaps not even passports. "That would be a great convenience, but is that really the regulation? In other words, does this rule mean what it says?" Meanwhile, "the steamship companies have shown no disposition to book passengers without official documents." The authors reported similar confusion over whether the quota arrangement would apply to "people from Cuba, Hayti, Canada, Mexico and some other countries"—early interpretations had suggested they would be free to travel as before, but now rumors flew of Canadians barred at the border.[31]

The confusion over details of migratory restriction in *Gleaner* coverage was paired with a remarkably clear-sighted and panoramic understanding of the political, economic, and ideological processes that had converged to recast U.S. policy. The United States had long considered itself "the land of the free, . . . the asylum of oppressed nationalities," but "quickly this attitude gave place to one almost of panic" as citizens imagined that "from the war-ravaged countries of Europe great hordes were preparing to emigrate to the cities of America. This must be prevented; and the moment it was accepted that some restriction of immigration was necessary the conviction grew until it became an obsession." Recognizing links between demographic and economic protectionism in the emerging nativist platform, the *Gleaner* suggested that the United States would soon legislate "not only almost impassable tariff walls, but absolutely impassable immigration walls." This redefinition of national interest could not be understood without reference to shifting ideologies of race. "For a new theory has begun to be promulgated. It is preached that the highest human type is the Nordic type, the fair-haired and blue-eyed people of North Europe, and the aim of those in America who have been captivated by this doctrine is to keep America for the Nordic type. How this is to be done, after all types have for decades been admitted freely into the States, is not mentioned. How it is to be done in a country with a large Negro population passes all understanding."[32]

August 1924 found reports of some 200,000 would-be migrants—40,000 of them British Caribbeans—stranded in Havana, their attempted transit to the United States either barred by the new quota system or derailed by the need to seek a visa through the consular office in their polity of origin.[33] Letters to the editor of the *Gleaner* insisted that the "Motive for Placing West Indians on Quota Basis" could be nothing other than race. Writing from New York City, PROLETARIAT observed that in the 1921 law, the only distinction drawn was between Old World immigrants, admitted under an annual quota capped at 3 percent of 1910 population of that group, and New World migrants who were "free to enter, provided they met the requirements of health, literacy, etc., that are imposed upon all immigrants. No distinction was made between colonies that were self-governing and those that were not." Under the new law, in contrast, all immigrants "from colonies with a preponderant population of African descent are placed on a quota basis, and in view of the fact that there were so few of these people in the United States in 1890, their quota will practically result in their permanent exclusion." (Note again the belief that British colonies would be treated as nations for the purpose of quota determination.) The criteria of "self-governance" was a flimsy cloak for racist intent. "The Law makes no distinction between Cuba, practically an American protectorate, Haiti, San Domingo, Peru, Nicaragua, Costa Rica (vassal states) and Mexico, Brazil and Argentina." The use of the term *self-governing*, unique to the British Empire, "proves clearly the object sought": "the exclusion of West Indians, who are mostly of African descent." After all, PROLETARIAT observed, if it were numbers that mattered, the 117,000 immigrants entering the United States from Canada in 1923 would be of greater concern than the 13,000 West Indian arrivals.[34]

PROLETARIAT's letter is further notable for its heartfelt conviction— proven dead wrong by subsequent events—that support for British West Indians would be forthcoming from two sources: U.S. African Americans and the British Crown. "This matter has been brought to the attention of American coloured people who count for something and it is believed that in this year of political uncertainty the Republican Party who is responsible for excluding the few coloured people who came to the country, will be made to pay dearly for its treachery." Expecting solidarity from African Americans along lines of color, the author also expected support from the Foreign Office along lines of imperial fidelity. Surely the British government would intervene on behalf of those British subjects whose mobility had been truncated, just as they would if white Britishers had received the same affront. "Realising that it will be difficult to have the discriminating feature of the Act removed immediately, Jamaicans and other West Indians should urge their government to negotiate with the British Government and Washington to have definite quotas allotted. Little Malta has succeeded in securing its own quota of ten persons annually, and I have no doubt that Jamaica can have its proper share of the British Empire quota, which could be computed on the basis of the proportion of Jamaicans leaving for the United States ten years before the Great War."[35] Nothing of the sort would happen, and as we shall see, the issue of the lack of British official protests when discriminatory legislation affected subjects of color abroad would gain ever more salience as race-based restrictionism spread across the Greater Caribbean over the following decade.

Within a few short months, it had become clear that the new U.S. laws, which nowhere mentioned, much less outlawed, immigration by those of African ancestry, intended to keep black aliens out of the United States and would be entirely successful. "Writer says U.S. Limitation Act has Achieved Object of Its Framers: Quota Arrangement: Declares Fact Stands Out the Desire is to Keep Out African Descendants," proclaimed the *Gleaner* in November 1924.[36] From more than 12,000 in 1923, black immigration dropped to less than 800 in 1924.[37] The deliberations and decision making behind this radical shift remain opaque. At the logistical level, though, the reduction was accomplished through stringent limits on the number of visas allotted to U.S. consulates in the Caribbean, and immediate authority over the allocation of visas among British territories resided with the U.S. quota control officer in London.[38] Reliance on U.S. consuls in migrants' land of origin to screen individual aspirants was key to what Zolberg has identified as the "remote control" migratory regime instituted by the 1920s regulations; in this case, the consuls' gatekeeper function went further, visa allocation creating de facto categorical restrictions not enunciated on the national origins schedules. Sources reported from Barbados in August 1924, "The American Consul has received a cable from the Visa Control Office of Great Britain which allots 10 non-preference quota visa numbers to this colony, of which 10 percent are to be issued each month, or one visa per month."[39] The figure was so small compared with established demand that its absurdity required no comment.

Yet many insisted on believing that the distribution of visas within the British Empire was at the discretion of British officials. In 1926, a petition from the Governor's Council of the Cayman Islands to the Colonial Office described the hardship the ban on U.S. entry had caused Cayman Islanders, whose economy had long been inextricable from that of south Florida. The petitioners suggested the U.S. government place the Caymans "for the purposes of immigration in the category with the Latin American Republics and the Greater Antilles" or that the

Foreign Office give the Caymans a special quota of their own, as "it is presumed that the Imperial government has the allotment to various dominions and colonies of the total number on the British Quota." Alongside this passage an anonymous Colonial Office functionary inscribed the emphatic marginalia: "No."[40] Private citizens likewise believed that British officials in Kingston or London controlled the allocation of visas for the United States. Scores of letters are preserved in the Jamaica National Archives from petitioners seeking to emigrate to the United States or reunite with family there. Still unsure in 1929 as to how such determinations were made, one colonial official called up the consulate and added a written note to the file of fruitless inquiries: "The Consul of the U.S.A. informs me (by telephone) that the quota for Jamaica is 140 per annum and that he has a waiting list of over 3,000."[41] In Barbados in 1927, labor leaders asserted that the whole of the British West Indies received only 200 emigrant visas a year, of which only five were allocated to Barbados.[42]

Under the 1924 regulations, the legal wives and legitimate children (under age eighteen) of U.S. citizens were allowed to emigrate to the United States as nonquota immigrants. Yet in Jamaica and elsewhere, only members of the established middle class used marriage sanctioned by church and state to cement conjugal partnerships. Illegitimate births routinely accounted for two-thirds of all children born on the islands. In other words, for the vast majority of British Caribbeans, the 1924 restrictions not only banned new departures for the United States but also cut off the circulation of family members and maintenance of transnational kinship networks that had been so central to the spread and prosperity of the circum-Caribbean migratory sphere. Typical was Catherine Shaw, who wrote to colonial officials in Kingston from Atlantic City, New Jersey, in 1931 begging that her eleven-year-old niece from Montego Bay be permitted "to come and live with me as my own daughter. I am able to take good care of her. I am a widow of 32, a Christian and do a good deal of church work. But at home it is quite lonesome, and my brother has thirteen (13) children and will give me Lucille."[43]

A devout and childless widow, a brother with too many mouths to feed—this was precisely the kind of circumstances that prompted fluid and frequent "child-borrowing" on the island, and until the 1920s, children had shifted across imperial or national borders with equivalent ease (although, as with intraisland child-borrowing, with varying degrees of pain and love).[44] But U.S. law, while urging quota control officers to make "the unit of consideration be the family and not the individual," recognized only the legitimate child, wife, or husband of a U.S. citizen as "family members" who could bypass the quota limits on annual entry by nationality.[45] Consensual partners of U.S. citizens, or the spouses or children of noncitizen immigrants, would have to join the thousands of others queuing for a turn that would never come. Such was the case of Eric McKay, about whom Enoch Hylton wrote in 1929, "His mother and Uncle lives in the

U.S.A. for many years and has left him under my protection. Now he has grown a lad of 15 years they are wanting him to school in America, his Uncle is a Dr. in Georgia U.S.A. and is responsible for him, I notify the American Consol about the matter, and after several papers had been passed, they turn him down. I can't understand McKay has no body as a relative in Jamaica save me as his Guardian."[46] Hylton's "can't understand" marks the disjunct between a vernacular logic of transnational family ties and a legal logic of territorial exclusivity never before brought to bear against Caribbean subjects. As legislatures across the region embraced antiblack exclusion, even the prosperous middle classes found themselves facing barriers of race and national origin that no amount of church decency or devotion to schooling could breach.

Spanish American Republics and the Emerging International Restrictionist Regime

Had the restrictionists who lobbied for the Johnson-Reed Act had their way, the limits on inter-American migration would have been both more extensive and more explicit. In the wake of the legislation's passage, Senator Johnson's Committee on Immigration and Naturalization (to which Eugenics Record Office head Charles Davenport and his deputy Harry Laughlin were regular advisors) solicited a report from Princeton economist Robert Foerster on "The Racial Problems involved in Immigration from Latin America and the West Indies to the United States." Had the United States just cut off its nose to spite its face? "The provisions drastically limiting the immigration of oriental people prevent the immigration into the United States of Chinese, Japanese, and some other peoples possibly desiring to enter this country after residence in the other American countries, but no law has been enacted imposing any similar restriction upon the immigration of races which constitute the dominant stocks in the Latin American countries."[47] With the arrival of Europeans now restricted, U.S. demand for unskilled workers would inevitably stimulate migration by "the mestizo," "on the whole more willing and able to work than the pure-blooded Indian," and by "pure-blooded negroes of West Indian birth," who had already proved themselves "willing to migrate for employment."[48] Any short-term economic benefit paled in comparison with the long-term cost. "Only when the racial effects of immigration are considered is it seen that effects of an economic or political character may go forward without end. . . . There are evident differences between the traits of a hundred thousand Swedish immigrants and a hundred thousand negro or Mexican immigrants; when these immigrants have themselves passed away there will still be manifest differences between the children of the Swedes and the children of the Negroes or Mexicans."[49]

The compromise between U.S. nativists and agribusiness interests that left the southwest border a back door within immigration policy thus carried second-order consequences for British Caribbeans as well. If it was not to be politically possible to restrict immigration into the United States from Latin America and the (formally) independent republics of the circum-Caribbean, at least one might attempt to ensure that the "racial stock" of those populations did not get even worse. Restrictionists pursued this goal through efforts both public and covert to find, strengthen, and guide institutional allies abroad. For instance, Charles Davenport worked closely with Dr. Domingo Ramos—leading Cuban health authority and elected member of the International Commission on Eugenics—as Ramos organized the First Pan-American Conference of Eugenics and Homiculture in Havana in 1927.[50] The first item on the agenda was "Immigration in relation to physical, mental and moral conditions of population"; Davenport's own lectures to the assembled dignitaries covered "Immigration and Race Crossing" and "Race Crossing, with Picture Plates." Latin American delegates recognized that maintaining their status as partners rather than objects of the U.S. restrictionist project required at least lip service to protecting their nations' "racial stocks" from further "undesirable elements." For Ramos, it was a "necessity that all of we Nations of America reach a single defined conclusion, and apply the measure equally, given that, fortunately, up until now there is no migration problem among the nations of the Americas, since Panama and the United States, who have made restrictive immigration laws, in those laws do not refer to the other countries of America."[51] Other elements of Ramos's proposed Eugenics Code proved irremediably controversial, but racist xenophobia seemed to be the one project on which all could agree. The draft finally adopted pledged, "The nations of America will issue and apply laws of immigration with intention to bar the entry into their territory of individuals from races whose association with the natives may be considered biologically undesirable."[52]

An international conference on emigration and immigration policy in Havana months later ended in frustration when other nations refused to adopt the ambitious and expensive monitoring system U.S. organizers had advocated.[53] However, this was not the end of U.S. restrictionists' efforts to guide Latin American populations in a eugenic direction through immigration control. Harry Laughlin, whose testimony had shaped U.S. national origins legislation earlier in the decade, advised the Cuban government even as Davenport's efforts to encourage hemisphere-wide regulation faltered. Yet by 1930, Laughlin's role in "aiding" the Cubans, as he put it, "in drafting their new immigration law on a eugenical basis," was seen even by his own superiors as a delicate matter at best. In response to a communiqué from above warning him away from any appearance of racialist "propaganda," Laughlin disavowed activist intent. "I understand from your letter quite clearly the policy of the Institution in this matter and I shall take special pains to conform with it." He would only "let the Cuban Government have access to any objective studies which we have made in the field of human migration in relation to future composition of the family-stocks of any country."[54] Like Foerster and Davenport before him, Laughlin insisted that eugenic science merely provided dispassionate demographic truth. "Through all the studies we have made on immigration we have appreciated all the while that the subject was full of dynamite and consequently, in keeping with the policy of the Institution, [crossed out text] even when advising with the House Committee on Immigration and Naturalization in Washington or with the Psychopathic Laboratory of the Municipal Court of Chicago, there was never any urging that the individual or a family or a state do a certain thing."[55]

Although Laughlin's foreign advocacy work had been reined in, the Eugenics Record Office's interest on immigration policy on the other American republics continued apace. In the early 1930s, and in collaboration with the Organization of American States, Laughlin began work on an exhaustive survey of the immigration-control laws and structures then in place in each independent nation in the Western Hemisphere. The legislative panorama the resultant 1936 report captured testified to the wide currency this view had garnered within Latin America. New restrictive immigration laws had been put in place by almost every national state in the Americas in the fifteen years before he wrote. In every case, immigration laws now mandated, on paper at least, both selection on the basis of individual fitness (denying entry to those with physical or mental deficiencies; those "dangerous for the public peace," anarchists in particular; and those indigent or "likely to become a public charge") and the categorical exclusion of races or nationalities deemed inherently *nocivos*, that is, damaging or threatening. While the precise wording and timing of legislation varied from country to country, the groups excluded tended to be the same, as did the order in which they had been added to the list of the categorically forbidden: Chinese or "those of yellow race"; Gypsies; Arabs, Syrians, or Turks; Blacks or Africans; and, in the most recent innovation, as yet not widespread, Jews.[56]

What had driven such a broadly shared trend? While U.S. actors' lobbying and scientific alliances certainly favored eugenicist rhetoric and restrictive laws, their actual promulgation in the Spanish-speaking republics of the greater Caribbean, at least, reflected a particular domestic political and economic conjuncture as well. By the 1920s, declining terms of trade had undercut export profits and as a result loosened traditional agro-export oligarchies' grip on state institutions. New voices were vying for and sometimes claiming political power: middle-class populists, leaders of organized labor, in each case promoting an expanded definition of state obligations to *el pueblo* (the people) and *la nación* (the nation). Along with this expanded state role, here as elsewhere, came a new concern to demarcate the boundaries of eligibility for such public goods.[57] The dynamic set the stage for xenophobia. When times turned hard, employers recalcitrant, or crowds too demanding, scapegoating "aliens" for stealing jobs and spreading vice proved as irresistible to politicians here as it did in Boston, East London, and Berlin.

Up to the 1920s, no circum-Caribbean republic had explicitly banned black immigration on the basis of race. By 1942, almost all of them did. A cascade of restrictive laws installed prohibitive fees, restricted employment, and then banned black entry outright in each of the receiving societies of the British Caribbean migratory sphere: Honduras (1923, 1926, 1929, 1934), El Salvador (1925), Mexico (1926), Panama (1926, 1928, 1941), Venezuela (1929, 1937), Nicaragua (1930), Guatemala (1931, 1936), the Dominican Republic (1932, 1933), and Costa Rica (1942).[58] The only major circum-Caribbean receiving society that did not explicitly enshrine antiblack racist criteria in immigration law in this period was Cuba. There, a 1933 presidential decree ordered the "forcible repatriation" of all unemployed foreigners; several months later, the Law of Nationalization of Labor mandated that 50 percent of all occupations be filled by natives. Although the language was race-blind, implementation was not. It was black immigrants, rather than the twice-as-numerous Spanish immigrants, who were expelled.[59]

Even in the preceding era of nominally open borders, immigrants had met physical and financial abuse at the hands of receiving-society officials and employers. Of course, native working folk faced abuses from these two groups as well, so that in turn-of-the-century Central America, say, the vulnerability of English-speaking migrants born in another polity and that of Spanish-speaking migrants born in another province were not systematically different. The emerging restrictionist regime did not erase internal conflict and corruption from the system, and these characteristics could, as before, sometimes work in migrants' favor.[60] But the new laws' international spread limited migrants' options for exit, weakened their bargaining position vis-à-vis employers, and moved the bar for what kinds of mistreatment by local officials would be disavowed by national governments. Thus even where arbitrarily enforced—sometimes especially then—racially restrictive laws shifted the baseline balance of power to the detriment of targeted migrants. Accounts of Panama's new immigration laws in 1926 worried that United Fruit's Bocas del Toro operations depended on workers continuously crossing the Costa Rica–Panama border as they cultivated fields and crewed banana trains: A reporter had it on "high and reliable authority" that the company's division manager had cabled Boston to advise "the cessation of operations so soon as the measure is put into effect in its present form."[61] Somehow, magically, corporate operations continued apace. But two years later in Bocas, Jamaican passengers were being pulled off trains at the border on a local magistrate's insistence that "the Immigration Law is in full force"—yet allowed to understand that it "would only be carried out during pay-day season." The editors of the local *Central America Express* called for "prompt action ... to prevent the fleecing of British West Indians in this manner," yet there is no evidence that any action occurred.[62]

Laws mandating categorical exclusion undercut any claims by sojourners to civil protections or due process. In 1938 and 1939, Venezuelan guards seized longtime Grenadian and Trinidadian residents from their homes, motored them out to sea, and pushed them overboard at gunpoint to swim the half-mile to Trinidad's southern shore.[63] As in this case, the seaborne routes that had served to expand migrants' horizons, options, and earnings now became nodes of vulnerability as well. One Jamaican and three Honduran youths stowed away on a New York–bound steamer from Puerto Cortés, Honduras: "In accordance with American law, the stowaways were handed over to the Immigration Authorities, who re-shipped them on the same steamer on her leaving New York on the return voyage to Cuba and Central America." Angered by William Jones's refusal to work for his keep on the way home, the captain—who had handcuffed the stowaways on arrival in Havana harbor "to prevent their flight from the ship, as the latter would be subject to a fine of £100 for each that escaped"—locked Jones in an unventilated steel-walled space adjacent to the boiler room and "Allowed [him] to Meet Death by The Slow and Painful Method of Roasting Alive."[64] As the sensationalist coverage suggests, the case was hardly typical. Yet it reflected a new regulatory order that fused specific legalities with systematic illegalities, an order in which nominal remote control of borders created new risks specific to immigrants and no longer shared by native workers, however grim their Depression-era plight.

Empire Laid Bare: Restrictive Legislation and the Destabilization of British Rule

The fracturing of the Greater Caribbean migratory sphere through a combination of international pressures, national politics, and global economic crisis threatened British colonial rule in multiple ways at once. At a material level, the loss of migration outlets dried up earnings and remittances when they were needed most, even as new waves of returnees made scarce island jobs even scarcer. Meanwhile, returnees brought more than their hands and hunger: They also introduced new social visions, like the Africa-focused religious revivals (Ras Tafarianism most famously) that flowered in West Kingston. More fundamentally, the conjuncture cast the fault lines in the facade of imperial unity into high relief. In the emerging international order, one role of sovereign states was to defend the interests of their nationals abroad: to project state power as a bulwark against migrants' disempowerment and to treat official disrespect for immigrants' racial nature as an insult to the nations from which they came. China and Japan (whose migrants to the Americas had been the earliest targets of racial scapegoating) had taken the lead in affirming this equation: hence, for instance, the 1907 Gentlemen's Agreement that restricted Japanese arrivals without publicly insulting the race or the nation. But while British West Indians tried to insist that insults to them were insults to the British Empire more broadly, the colonial government declined to treat it so. Some foreign service officers did decry Spanish American governments' "flagrant disregard of British, if coloured, interest."[65] Yet, even this formulation—by an unusually committed advocate—made explicit the presumption that color qualified claims of imperial belonging. Again and again, the sequelae of restrictive legislation exposed British ambivalence over its possession of colored subjects and those subjects' possession of British rights.

The lines of print and oral communication that wove together the circum-Caribbean migratory sphere gave British Caribbeans a panoptic view of the crisis and its racial patterning. "The privations caused by non-employment especially among the coloured people is not felt in Costa Rica alone, in Cuba there is awful suffering," read a typical update in the Port Limon papers in 1930. The international scope of antiblack nationalism was clear. "Whatever work there is to be got in that island is given to the natives preferably; pretty much as is the custom here hence the lack and stringency among the Jamaicans there, is very serious. A couple of weeks ago 34 of these who were found to be suffering from Starvation had to be repatriated."[66] Similar hardship gripped British West Indian communities in Panama, the Dominican Republic, Venezuela, and beyond, in each case due to the combination of regional economic straits and the intentional actions of local political leaders, who increasingly reserved employment for nationals, raised fees on foreign residents, demanded forced labor of those who could not pay the new fees, and threatened (and sometimes carried out) mass deportations.

One Clayton Lloyd Alexander Jeffers, native of St. Kitts and resident in San Pedro de Macoris, Dominican Republic, spelled out the historical depth and current breadth of the crisis in a petition to the King of England in 1933: "Owing to the grim circumstances, caused by the ever increasing population of our respective countries, and the lack of labour to maintain us—we were forced to seek our daily bread in these Latin American Countries. . . . We thy subjects; descendants of our ill-fated and enslaved ancestors whom the Good and Honourable Deceased Queen Victoria herself, signed the documents of slavery 'abolition,' . . . now find ourselves not as free-born British subjects—but actual slaves for these American sugar plantations here in these Spanish Republics." Jeffers's appeal to monarchical concern for "the British vast and Grand Empire, over which the sun never sets," echoed the rhetoric of the Chiriqui prisoners fourteen years before. But his was a story of loyalty betrayed, by the "dark, sinister and underhand dealings practiced by the so-called British Counsellors here upon we Your Majesty's black subjects." "Ill-treated, sometimes shot down like dogs," "the unfortunate ones of my race" now found themselves rejected even by those lands previously eager to exploit them. "We have become a stumbling block to their inhabitants, an awful shame to ourselves, and a terrible disgrace to the illustrious banner of Old England beneath whose brilliant colours we so oft have resort for protection and have sadly been disappointed."[67]

A confidential 1931 report from Josiah Crosby, British Minister in Panama, analyzed with acuity the systemwide crisis confronting British West Indian sojourners, while also revealing much about those "so-called British Counsellors" who failed to offer men like Jeffers the imperial protection they sought. Crosby evinced far more sympathy for the circum-Caribbean governments' desire to "defend" themselves against the "threat" of "Africanization" than he did for the Afro-Caribbean men and women affected. "The West Indian is coming to be regarded in the countries adjacent to the Caribbean Sea as a racial and economic menace, as something to be feared and excluded. And it must in fairness be admitted that there is justification for such an attitude in the interests of the original population, to which the negro—racially difficult of assimilation—shows himself to be superior alike in his capacity for labour and his power of multiplication."[68] Crosby described the rising intensity of antiblack agitation by Panamanian politicians and then noted similarities elsewhere. Dispatches "from His Majesty's Minister in Guatemala . . . report[ed] that the government of that country has followed the example of Panama in framing legislation prohibiting the immigration of persons of the negro and yellow races." Venezuela and Costa Rica were doing likewise, "whilst in the United States, of course, the entry of all aliens, including negroes, is drastically restricted. In other words, the ordinary outlets hitherto available for the surplus populations of the British West Indian islands are being closed."[69] What would happen to those migrants who chose or were forced to return to their (or their parents') island of origin? What would happen to the straitened island economies forced to absorb them?

The Colonial Office worried in response: "Any Barbadian who returned to that colony at the present time would only increase the difficulties that exist there as the result of overpopulation and might tend to upset the equanimity with which the present period of depression is being met by the masses of that island. Any large number of discontents returning from Panama or the Central American Republics to Barbados might give cause for anxiety and might even result in the occurrences of riotous outbreaks."[70] The description was prescient. By the mid-1930s, some 2.5 million people resided in the British Caribbean colonies from British Honduras in the west to the Windwards in the east. Prices were high, wages low, and reliable employment a distant memory. After a decade of closed doors and plummeting remittances, of repatriations both voluntary and forced, port city shantytowns swelled with embittered returnees and desperate rural jobseekers alike. There were hunger marches and railway strikes in Belize in 1934 and 1935, sugar plantation strikes in Guyana in 1934, 1938, and 1939, marches of the unemployed in Port-of-Spain and an oilfields strike in Trinidad in 1934 and 1937, tax protests in St. Vincent in 1935, riots sparked by political deportations in Bridgetown in 1937, and strikes by sugar workers that spread to a state of emergency in Jamaica in 1938. News of these "labour rebellions" catapulted the Caribbean islands to the forefront of British public debate over the continuance and character of colonial rule.[71]

A parallel debate was already underway within British Caribbean communities, and those located far from home were marking closely the disparities of imperial concern that the Crown's tepid response to antiblack immigration restriction had revealed. An editorial in the Limon, Costa Rica, *Searchlight* in May 1930 asked why Queen Victoria's Day was no longer celebrated with the fervor of previous decades: "Formerly it was the greatest pride of any British subject to be able to claim fellowship under the British flag. Boastingly you could hear on every side 'I am a British subject' on equal magnanimity that the Romans used the proud phrase 'Romanus sum ego' when Rome was in her glory."[72] It was the lived experience of second-class subjecthood, argued the editors, that had undermined the illusions of the African-descended West Indians who had previously been the most loyal of His Majesty's subjects:

> The coloured man . . . is indeed, as was said by one of our most popular coloured men in this country some twenty years ago "a British object," an object of derision in the eyes of even less cultured peoples; he is legislated against by nearly every country, and yet such legislation is not protested against by the British Consular Offices. Formerly a British Passport demanded from the inhabitants of every Country that the proud holder be allowed to travel *free without let or hindrance and be afforded every assistance in his travels*, under Security of the dominant British Flag, but now he dare not go to certain countries, even though he was instrumental in making that country with his Brawn, his Brain, and his Blood, as he did Panama.[73]

If the British crown allowed racial distinctions to vitiate imperial protections for colonial subjects abroad, it could not cry foul when the people of the colonies embraced racial solidarity as a challenge to imperial legitimacy. "Is it any wonder then that Empire day goes by undignified, unnoticed? Is it any wonder that the Indian, the Egyptians, and negroes would like to shake off British dominance and see their own destinies? For after all what is it worth to be a British subgest [sic] in foreign parts especially to the Negro, the Chinese, or Hindu? Nothing but indignities by depreciation & discrimination against in trade, in labour, in Social equality." Second-class subjecthood, made visible by the new regime of race-based restrictionism, would not be endured: "Discontent will be rampant and the indifference to the indignities of such observances will continue to grow until 'Albion' changes her tactics to these what she calls inferior races which in reality are only inferior in 'opportunities' or finds herself stripped of her belongings."[74]

What changes a century had wrought! The abolition of slavery in the British Caribbean and the subsequent expansion of the U.S. informal empire had together set the stage for the creation of a migratory sphere that cut across territorial boundaries of republics and empires. Now those republics and that unacknowledged empire were enforcing a new logic of territorial belonging that once again radically restricted the freedoms of the African-descended people in the region, who felt themselves, as Clayton Lloyd Alexander Jeffers had warned the king, ever less "free-born British subjects" but rather "slaves for these American . . . plantations here in these Spanish Republics." Having given their brawn, their brains, and their blood to bring modern progress to the Greater Caribbean, black migrants were now told that their bodies and their blood had no place in modern progressive nations. In letters to the editor, petitions, and public meetings, the targets of exclusionary policies denounced the hypocrisy and demanded the justice Britannia claimed to embody. Would the empire stand by "these industrious subjects of King George" who labored "all over the western Hemisphere colonizing every body's country, with no place of their own to colonize, only to be told so soon as he has made it hygienically fit for habitation 'Get out of here! you are no longer needed get back from whence you came.'"[75]

Again, the link was explicit between the imperial abdication of responsibility for protecting the rights of subjects of color abroad and the increasingly loud demands for political rights at home. It was "on account of all these insults and indignities why we find Captain Cipriani of Trinidad in his discourses in London before the Labour Conferences, striking out in no uncertain tones for "Self Government" in the Colonies; while Dr Harold Moodie"—upstanding leader of London's West Indian intelligentsia—"points out the seriousness of the Government's inattention to 'my people' as he terms them by its Racial Prejudice. . . . If Britain thinks that because she has and is dominating a quarter of this earth's surface she is destined to go on doing so forever; she had better be at once undeceived."[76]

Conclusion

Less than two decades before this editorial was penned on the occasion on Empire Day, a young Marcus Garvey had been pounding the pavement in this selfsame Port Limon, raising subscriptions and planning parades to celebrate Coronation Day. Decolonization in the British Caribbean somehow went from inconceivable to irreversible over the course of the two decades that bracketed the Second World War. That editorial and dozens like it suggest that the British acquiescence to migratory restrictions—first in the United States, then across the Americas—that categorically excluded some of its subjects while welcoming others played a fundamental role in undermining the fiction of race-blind imperial belonging. British rule in the Caribbean had endured for three centuries by the time these articles were published, yet its dissolution was only twenty-five years away. Albion would indeed find herself "stripped of her belongings" by the initiative of Caribbean men and women—some prominent, others anonymous— who had come of age in the years when mass migration, and then massive migration restriction, recast individual destinies and remade collective identities in and around the Caribbean.

An integral part of that story was the role of the United States in pioneering the creation of a new international restrictive regime. The constellation of constraints ushered in by the 1924 Johnson-Reed Act didn't proclaim antiblack exclusion, yet the discriminatory impact was clear for all to see. Meanwhile, the combination of visa requirements and remote-control regulation of mobility not only truncated families and reduced opportunities around the region but also created new patterns of illegality and vulnerability specific to "alien" workers that are all too familiar to us today.

NOTES

1. Julie Greene, *The Canal Builders: Making America's Empire at the Panama Canal* (New York: Penguin, 2009), chapter 9.
2. The *Canal Record* [Panama Canal Zone], October 28, 1914; Alejandro de la Fuente, *A Nation for All: Race, Inequality, and Politics in Twentieth-Century Cuba* (Chapel Hill: University of North Carolina Press, 2001), 102.
3. "Cuba Wants European Laborers," *Canal Record*, December 10, 1913. Cf. Jorge L. Giovannetti, "Colonial Labor and Imperial Designs: Regional, Hemispheric, and Atlantic Frontiers of Caribbean Migrant Workers, 1917–1948" (paper presented at the seminar "Workers, the Nation-State, and Beyond: The Newberry Conference on Labor History across the Americas," Chicago, September 18–20, 2008).
4. Cuba, Secretaría de Hacienda, Sección de Estadística, *Informe y movimiento de pasajeros* (Havana, 1916 and 1917).
5. "West Indian Labor May Be Lost to Cuba," *New York Times*, August 16, 1924.
6. "Life in Jamaica in the Early Twentieth Century; A Presentation of Ninety Oral Accounts" (unpublished transcripts housed at Institute of Social and Economic Research, University of the West Indies, Mona, Kingston, Jamaica), Volume St. James, 62StjFC, Flamstead, "Ded lef pickney, lef to the mercy of God," 23. Ellipses in original.
7. "Life in Jamaica," Volume Portland, 35Pmb Grange Hill, "Formerly of the Band of Mercy," 16.
8. Editorial, "Problem of the Immediate Future," Kingston *Daily Gleaner*, August 29, 1905.
9. Winston James, *Holding Aloft the Banner of Ethiopia: Caribbean Radicalism in Early Twentieth-Century America* (New York: Verso, 1998), 356–57; Irma

Watkins-Owens, *Blood Relations: Caribbean Immigrants and the Harlem Community, 1900–1930* (Bloomington: Indiana University Press, 1996).

10. Lara Putnam, "'Children of the Dispersion': Circum-Caribbean Migration and the Varieties of Race Consciousness in the Early Twentieth Century," in Jazz Age Caribbean Crucible: Migration, State Racism, Popular Culture, and Black Internationalism," unpublished manuscript.
11. Eric Walrond, "The Yellow One," in *Tropic Death* (New York: Boni and Liveright, 1926), 66.
12. Herbert Bury, *A Bishop among the Bananas* (Milwaukee, WI: Young Churchman, 1911), 110.
13. "Life in Jamaica," Volume St. Catherine, Respondent 49StcFb Orangefield, Aunt Dore. Interviewed March 1975, p. 18. In the last sentences, "Nuh" works to stress the self-evident nature of the statement: thus, "Isn't it obvious that she must be beat. Isn't it obvious that he must beat her."
14. "Missing," *West Indies War Cry*, November 1929. Archived at Salvation Army Territorial Headquarters, Kingston, Jamaica.
15. Bonham Richardson, *Panama Money in Barbados, 1900–20* (Knoxville: University of Tennessee Press, 1985), 207, passim; Watkins-Owens, *Blood Relations*, 68–74.
16. "A Good Suggestion," Letter to the Editor, [Limon] *Times*, April 19, 1911. Biblioteca Nacional de Costa Rica, microfilm Periódicos de Limón.
17. Petition to C. C. Mallet, British Minister, Panama, from Reginald Brown, Chiriqui Prison, January 16, 1919, in National Archives of the United Kingdom [henceforth, PRO] FO 288/200: Foreign Office: Consulate, Panama: General Correspondence (December 31, 1918–July 31, 1919); cf. Giovannetti, "Colonial Labor and Imperial Designs."
18. Winifred James, *Out of the Shadows* (London: Chapman and Hall, 1924), 65, 66, 74.
19. Ibid., 65, 66.
20. Petition to Mallet from Brown, January 16, 1919.
21. Owen Charles Mathurin, *Henry Sylvester Williams and the Origins of the Pan-African Movement, 1869–1911* (Westport, CT.: Greenwood, 1976).
22. James, *Holding Aloft the Banner*.
23. W. A. Domingo, "The Tropics in New York," *Survey Graphic*: Harlem, Mecca of the New Negro 6, no. 6 (March 1925), 648; see http://books.google.co.ve/books?id=eTfx4WoHwQIC.
24. June Jordan, *Soldier: A Poet's Childhood* (New York: Basic Civitas, 2000), 5.
25. Higham, *Strangers in the Land: Patterns of American Nativism, 1860–1925* (New Brunswick, NJ: Rutgers University Press, 2002); Roger Daniels, *Guarding the Golden Door: American Immigration Policy and Immigrants since 1882* (New York: Hill and Wang, 2004), 49–78; Mae Ngai, *Impossible Subjects: Illegal Immigrants and the Making of Modern America* (Princeton, NJ: Princeton University Press, 2004); Watkins-Owens, *Blood Relations*.

26. Mae Ngai, "The Architecture of Race in American Immigration Law: A Re-Examination of the Immigration Act of 1924," *Journal of American History* 89 (1999): 70; Ngai, *Impossible Subjects*, 27, passim.
27. Ibid., 37–50; Aristide Zolberg, *A Nation by Design: Immigration Policy in the Fashioning of America* (New York and Cambridge: Russell Sage Foundation and Harvard University Press, 2006), 262.
28. Francisco Balderrama and Raymond Rodriguez, *Decade of Betrayal: Mexican Repatriation in the 1930s* (Albuquerque: University of New Mexico Press, 1995).
29. Zolberg, *A Nation by Design*, 262; cf. 479, n. 19.
30. "Jamaica Negro Influx Is Checked: Exodus from That and Other West Indian Isles Halted by Alien Law," *World* [New York, NAACP], July 7, 1924.
31. "Some Confusion," Kingston *Daily Gleaner*, July 30, 1924.
32. Ibid.
33. "Today's News: Foreign," Kingston *Daily Gleaner*, August 11, 1924.
34. "American Ban on Emigration: Motive for Placing West Indians on Quota Basis," Letter to the editor from "PROLETARIAT," New York City, August 6, 1924, in Kingston *Daily Gleaner*, August 18, 1924.
35. Ibid.
36. "The Immigration Restriction in U.S.: Writer Says U.S. Limitation Act Has Achieved Object of Its Framers," Kingston *Daily Gleaner*, November 24, 1924. Reprints article by W. A. Domingo from [New York] *Amsterdam News* of October 15.
37. Ibid.; James, *Holding Aloft the Banner*, 355.
38. See, for instance, letter from British Embassy in Washington, D.C., to Sir Austen Chamberlain, Colonial Office, December 15, 1927; copy contained in Jamaica National Archive, 1B/5/77/133. Cf. "Jamaica Falls in U.K. Quota, Says Washington Report," Kingston *Daily Gleaner*, August 2, 1924.
39. "Barbados Quota," Kingston *Daily Gleaner*, August 27, 1924.
40. PRO, CO 318/384: West Indies: General, 1926. Caymans United States Immigration Regulations.
41. Jamaica National Archive, 1B/5/77/24: Emigration to USA (Individual Enquiries).
42. Richardson, *Panama Money in Barbados*, 237.
43. Jamaican National Archive, 1B/5/77/24: Emigration to USA (Individual Enquiries): Letter from Catherine Shaw, July 31, 1929.
44. On Jamaican "schoolgirls" in Limon, see Lara Putnam, "Work, Sex, and Power in a Central American Export Economy at the Turn of the Twentieth Century," in *Gender, Sexuality, and Power in Latin America*, ed. Katherine Bliss and William French, 133–62. (Lanham, MD: Rowman & Littlefield, 2006).
45. United States Department of State, *Admission of Aliens into the United States: Notes to Section 361 Consular Regulations. Revised to July 1, 1932* (Washington, DC: Government Printing Office, 1932), 83.

46. Jamaica National Archive, 1B/5/77/24: Emigration to USA (Individual Enquiries): Letter from Enoch Hylton, November 14, 1929.
47. Robert F. Foerster, "The Racial Problems Involved in Immigration from Latin America and the West Indies to the United States," in *Hearings of the Committee on Immigration and Naturalization, House of Representatives, March 3, 1925* (Washington, DC: Government Printing Office, 1925), 304.
48. Ibid., 333.
49. Ibid., 334–35.
50. Actas de la Primera Conferencia Panamericana de Eugenesia y Homicultura de las Repúblicas Americanas, celebrada en la Habana, Cuba, desde el 21 hasta el 23 de diciembre de 1927 (Habana, 1928). See Nancy Leys Stepan, *"The Hour of Eugenics": Race, Gender, and Nation in Latin America* (Ithaca, NY: Cornell University Press, 1991), 174–77; Lara Putnam, "Eventually Alien: The Multigenerational Saga of British Western Indians in Central America, 1870–1940," in *Blacks and Blackness in Central America: Between Race and Place*, ed. Lowell Gudmundson and Justin Wolfe (Durham, NC: Duke University Press, 2010).
51. Actas, 70–71.
52. Actas, 323.
53. United States Congress, "Second International Emigration and Immigration Conference, March 27, 1928. Committed to the Committee of the Whole House on the state of the Union and ordered to be printed. Mr. Burton, from the Committee on Foreign Affairs, submitted the following supplementary report to accompany H.R. 10167."
54. "H. Laughlin draft of letter to Carnegie Institution of Washington President J. C. Merriam, defending his lobbying for immigration restriction in Cuba." Digital image consulted at http://www.eugenicsarchive.org/html/eugenics/index2.html?tag=1110.
55. Ibid.
56. Harry Laughlin, "The Codification and Analysis of the Immigration-Control Law of Each of the Several Countries of Pan America, as expressed by Their National Constitutions, Statute Laws, International Treaties, and Administrative Regulations, as of January 1, 1936" (mimeo, Eugenics Record Office, Carnegie Institution of Washington, October 1936).
57. John Torpey, *The Invention of the Passport: Surveillance, Citizenship and the State* (Cambridge: Cambridge University Press, 2000); Andres Wimmer and Nina Glick Schiller, "Methodological Nationalism and Beyond: Nation-State Building, Migration, and the Social Sciences," *Global Networks* 2, no. 4 (2002): 301–34.
58. Elizabeth M. Thomas-Hope, "The Establishment of a Migration Tradition: British West Indian Movements to the Hispanic Caribbean in the Century after Emancipation," *International Migration* 24 (1986): 559–71; Bonham Richardson, "Caribbean Migrations, 1838–1985," in *The Modern Caribbean*, ed. Franklin Knight and Colin Palmer (Chapel Hill: University of North Carolina Press, 1989); Lauro Capdevila, "Una discriminacion organizada: las leyes de

inmigracion dominicanas y la cuestion haitiana en el siglo," *Tebeto: Anuario del Archivo Histórico Insular de Fuerteventura* no. 5, Special Issue: *En torno a las Antillas hispánicas* (2004): 438–54.
59. de la Fuente, *A Nation for All*, 104–5, 194–98.
60. Putnam, "Eventually Alien"; Putnam, "Work, Sex, and Power."
61. "Panamanian Law Hits the United Fruit Company," Kingston *Daily Gleaner*, December 9, 1926.
62. "Jamaicans in Bocas del Toro," Kingston *Daily Gleaner*, February 9, 1928.
63. PRO, CO 318/436/15: Treatment of British West Indians in Venezuela: Compensation Claims.
64. "Jamaican Youth's Horrible Death on Board German Ship," Kingston *Daily Gleaner*, July 2, 1926.
65. Letter from Ernest Gye, British Legation, Caracas, to Foreign Office, September 5, 1938. PRO, CO 318/436/15: Treatment of British West Indians in Venezuela: Compensation Claims.
66. "The Sufferings in Cuba," Limon *Searchlight*, June 7, 1930: Biblioteca Nacional de Costa Rica, microfilm Periódicos de Limón.
67. Copy of petition from C. Jeffers to King, January 20, 1933. PRO, CO 318/408/3: Immigration of British West Indians to Central and South America, 1932.
68. Dispatch from Sir J. Crosby, H.M. Minister at Panama, September 21, 1931. PRO, CO 318/404/13: Immigration of British West Indians into Central and South America.
69. Ibid.
70. Minute, Frank Stockdale. Ibid.
71. Richard Hart, "Labour Rebellions of the 1930s in the British Caribbean Region Colonies," *SHS Occasional Paper Series* no. 15 (Caribbean Labour Solidarity and the Socialist History Society, 2002).
72. "24th MAY," Limon *Searchlight*, May 31, 1930. Emphases in original.
73. Ibid.
74. Ibid.
75. "What Steps Will Britain Take," Limon *Searchlight*, October 4, 1930.
76. Ibid. Moodie, a Jamaican-born physician who led efforts against discriminatory practices in Britain, would found the League of Coloured Peoples the following year.

VI TRANSNATIONAL LABOR POLITICS

INTRODUCTION

Bryan D. Palmer

Does the working class have a country?[1] It is an old, and extremely complicated, question. Empirically, the query can easily be answered in the affirmative, as there is demonstrable evidence that workers have only rarely mobilized in truly internationalist ways. "Cross-border solidarity may seem logical, but in practice it is not," writes Marcel van der Linden.[2] And yet it is equally the case that the broad structural processes of class formation in the modern world have always been a profoundly *internationalist* undertaking. The primitive accumulation that both Karl Marx and Rosa Luxemburg saw as fundamental to the realization of global capitalism's extensive reach often preceded the founding of nation-states and has always traversed and transcended their borders. It brought together free and unfree labor, congealing the dissimilar components of the differentiated strata of the producers through strategies of dispossession, colonization, conquest, recruitment, and migration.[3]

Indeed, very early in the making of the global proletariat, transnational currents of resentment, resistance, and rebellion raised multiple voices of discontent within the "many-headed hydra" that Peter Linebaugh and Marcus Rediker have identified as the bourgeois-led Age of Revolution's unkempt underside.[4] Haiti's slave revolt of 1791 was the "motley crowd's" equivalent of the French Revolution.[5] The Irish diaspora *and* the often genocidal displacement of Amerindian populations in both the southern and northern hemispheres were just as surely consequences of empire's relentless and routinely destabilizing destructions.

All of this may seem to inhabit the world of the prepolitical. To be sure, prior to the creation of the world's first workers' state in the Soviet Union in 1917, the articulation of a transnational politics of labor was seldom voiced in the unambiguous language of class. "Proletarian internationalism" is thus a decidedly twentieth-century project, at least at the level of proclaimed objective. It can perhaps be best understood as the visible tip of a historical iceberg of raucous resistance, long obscured in the agitated seas that were the chaotic channel of class formation on a world scale.

From the core of the Industrial Revolution's transformative impact in the early nineteenth century emanated indications of labor's transnational politics. Often this took the form of resistance to colonization's unmistakable capacity to deny rights in the peripheral political economies of empire that the oppressed and exploited in the metropolitan center had come to appreciate as entitlements not to be trifled with. Thus in 1837, with the distant colonies of Canada on the verge of rebellion, London's Chartists issued a circular headed "Democracy or Despotism" and rallied 2,000 strong "to vindicate the political rights of their fellow-men in Canada."[6] Indeed, working-class radicals staunchly defended bourgeois-democratic rights over the course of the nineteenth century, perhaps nowhere more clearly than in the International Working Men's Association or First International's staunch support of the Polish Insurrection of 1863.[7] The very imagery of the workers' movement was also transnational, grounded in generally "western" stereotypes that were racialized and gendered.[8] There were, however, openings in the symbolic edifice of labor's iconography that challenged such Eurocentric tendencies.

May Day, for example, came to be an internationally celebrated workers' festival honouring Chicago's Haymarket struggle of 1886, which involved mobilizing for the eight-hour day, protesting police violence, street confrontations that included the explosion of a bomb, and the execution of anarcho-communist workingmen by the state. Marches, commemorative gatherings and dinners, mass strikes, and a regular outpouring of publications reprinting the famous trail speeches of the martyrs created a transnational politics of memory and mobilization that reached beyond Europe and the United States into the global south. Celebrated for the first time in Mexico in 1913, May Day was inaugurated with anarchist-inspired strikes for the eight-hour day, protests against the country's military rulers, and memorials to the martyrs of 1887. As late as the 1980s, miners' homes in remote enclaves of Bolivia might sport embroidered cloth window hangings reading, yet again, "Long Live the Martyrs of Chicago."[9]

The transnational politics of labor remains, like the question of whether workers have a country, a complex, indeed disturbingly difficult, subject. The intellectual challenge here includes the need to ground any study of the transnational in a sophisticated understanding of both the national and the local, the difficulty of mastering the sources and languages necessary if this is to be achieved, and reckoning with the historical realities that have regularly thwarted workers' efforts to cross the borders that have in so many ways limited them. The two chapters that follow provide insights into how labor's transnational political initiatives unfolded and how we might expand our own interpretive boundaries in pursuing such topics.

Shelton Stromquist offers a forceful reminder that the transnational coexists comfortably with the local. He recounts a subterranean history of working-class socialists struggling to remake urban environments. Such mobilizations connected activists in the English-speaking world in the 1890–1914 years and, as Stromquist shows, link past struggles to the contemporary politics of labor reform in the global south. Much of the forceful transnational authority of Fabianism in Australia, Canada, the United States, and the United Kingdom rested on the socialist effort to reclaim the city. The local was translated to a wider global audience as speaking tours brought Sidney and Beatrice Webb, Ben Tillett, Tom Mann, E. R. Hartley, and others "out of darkest England" and into the light of New World cities, from Broken Hill, New South Wales, to Brooklyn, New York. Old-fashioned American machine politics, in locales such as Cleveland, Detroit, and Toledo, mirrored the fin-de-siècle municipal socialism of Independent Labour Party [ILP] politicos in places like Engels's archetypal proletarian city, Manchester. Much of this agitation, now viewed with hindsight, seems prophetic of the struggles for reform characteristic of Latin American countries such as Brazil and Venezuela in the opening decade of the twenty-first century: "The Socialist acknowledges the right of the unemployed to have the opportunity to work given to him—and the unemployed woman too," wrote an ILP MP, F. W. Jowett, in 1907. "If a Socialist majority had the responsibility of governing a city, they would take steps at once to . . . meet their obligations to the unemployed. . . . They would, acting under the best expert advice available, select some considerable piece of land, either already in the possession of the city, or that could be acquired by purchase, which, being either laid idle or used wastefully, needed human labour . . . and as the land was reclaimed for its most useful purpose they would provide for its permanent occupation and continued use."[10] We are reminded of E. P. Thompson's statement in the preface of *The Making of the English Working Class*: "Causes which were lost in England might, in Asia or Africa, yet be won."[11]

The notion that *any* nation's working class could be made as a homogeneous entity is, with the exception of the most insular and particular examples such as Iceland, untenable. In recognizing the significance of migration to global class formation, we necessarily confront a process of the blending of peoples and politics. Working-class struggles invariably congealed a potent mix of emotions and principles, unfolding at the interface of diverse cultures. Labor upheavals in the United States in 1916–1922, for instance, were paced by internationalist attachments to revolution and Soviet-inspired experiments in workers' control, as immigrant workers embraced nationalist independence movements in their homelands and the entitlements of unionized collective bargaining rights in their adopted country. When a former student of John R. Commons and a leading voice in the labor relations and social work fields of progressive America, John A. Fitch, looked at one of the major class conflicts of this tumultuous era, he saw "a strike for wages carried on in a revolutionary atmosphere."[12] His words could well have been emblazoned on the banner of 1919.

John H. Flores explores how Mexican migrants to Chicago's working-class districts forged a sense of themselves in their new blue-collar surroundings. As Mexicans streamed into the Windy City's steel mills, packinghouses, railway yards, and pluralistic proletarian neighborhoods, they brought with them the radical liberalism of a reform nationalism associated with the Mexican Revolution of 1910–1920. Chicago's labor movement embraced internationalism and anti-imperialism as important mobilizing forces. Flores highlights how what Benedict Anderson has called "print capitalism" facilitated this process of cross-fertilization, drawing attention to the important role of Mexican nationalist publications in providing a foundation on which the coercive assimilation of the host society could be effectively resisted.[13] He shows how the migrant Mexican milieu of Chicago in the interwar years nurtured cross-class alliances of intellectuals and journalists, workers and small entrepreneurs, all of whom pioneered voluntary associations, "community" festivals, and educational initiatives. Constructing a multiracial Mexican nationalist identity, this activist contingent merged with communist and socialist forces in the 1930s as popular-frontist impulses, international events like the Spanish Civil War, labor mobilizations, and settlement house programs stimulated a radical transnational politics. The result was a moment of possibility in which the promise of revolutionary Mexican nationalists actually linked political arms with several multiethnic Chicago labor organizations, including the International Worker's League, the Illinois Labor Alliance, the Steel Workers Organizing Committee, and the Packinghouse Workers Organizing Committee.

The alliance of liberal-radical Mexican nationalists and United States communist, socialist, and labor organizations, seemingly in the offing in the late 1930s, could not, however, weather the storm of opposition that came from Mexican forces embracing an entirely different politic. The right was also capable of mounting a transnational politics; it, too, had its intellectual, journalistic, and print voices. Ultimately, Chicago's Mexican "community" fractured, and the project of bringing together workers and revolutionary nationalists foundered on the shoals of a religiously orchestrated, anticommunist politics of assimilation. An experiment in transnational labor politics had seemingly come to an end, echoed in the lament of a migrant worker in the Jazz Age pop tune, "El Enganchado," or "The Hooked One":

> Many Mexicans don't care to speak
> The language their mothers taught them
> And go about saying they are Spanish
> And denying their country's flag...
> My kids speak perfect English

And have no use for Spanish,
They call me "fadder" and don't work
And are crazy about the Charleston.

"I am tired of all this nonsense" was the last chorus of this sad soliloquy.[14]

We can close with the case of Quebec in the 1960s and early 1970s. The French-speaking province of Canada provides an illuminating example of how a radical nationalist upsurge can draw on and extend transnational labor politics. In Quebec, the cause of nation and independence was articulated in class ways and drew sustenance from internationalism and the politics of anticolonialism that was a powerful force over the course of the 1960s.

For the Québécois, the "nonsense" of being a conquered people was two centuries old as the 1960s erupted. In less than a decade, the ancien régime became passé. To be sure, the disintegration had been in the making for some time, and certainly began as early as 1949, when a bitter strike in the asbestos-producing communities of the Eastern Townships signaled that the holds of the Catholic Church (which had for decades organized much of the province's workforce into "confessional" unions), the authoritarian provincial state, and the English-speaking capital were weakening. By the early 1960s, a so-called Quiet Revolution led to a state-orchestrated modernization that reconfigured Quebec. A massive infrastructure of education, health, and welfare was supplemented by development megaprojects of economic nationalization, in which the creation of Hydro-Quebec by future advocate of independence, René Lévesque, was widely perceived as a crown jewel in the renegotiation of federal-provincial relations. Soon the hounds of dissent were unleashed. A new generation of francophone youth and intellectuals fed the resentments of their long-standing oppression with a steady diet of anticolonialist, anti-imperialist tracts, dining out on comparisons of themselves with Castro's and Guevara's bearded revolutionaries, Algerian freedom fighters, Black Power advocates in the United States, Vietnam's National Liberation Front, and Uruguayan Tupamaros.

It was in this concentrated period of radicalization, reaching from 1963 to 1968, that the Front de Libération du Québec (FLQ) was born and that one of its leading militants, Pierre Vallières, penned the decade's most influential Canadian New Left manifesto, *White Niggers of America* (1968). Vallières and the FLQ were the underground of a rising tide of revolutionary Québécois politics that fused questions of national oppression and class exploitation in ways that found comparable expression in an increasingly secular and militant workers' movement. Trade union conventions urged labor to embrace a Second Front beyond the workplace, extending its power into a generalized struggle for social justice. From Montreal's Central Trade Council, the fiery radicalism of Michel Chartrand championed an eclectic mix of radical causes, including francophone language rights, defense of imprisoned FLQ "terrorists," opposition to the war in

Vietnam, tenants' and consumers' rights, housing reform, and, of course, a seemingly endless eruption of often violent and provocative strikes. As the unions linked arms with clandestine advocates of revolutionary violence, marched in festive May Day parades where "The Internationale" was the anthem of choice, and found that their members were as interested in reading *The Autobiography of Malcolm X* or Frantz Fanon's *The Wretched of the Earth* as they were in listening to the federalist message of Ottawa, a new politics of possibility dawned. Quebec suddenly gave rise to a proliferation of revolutionary organizations, radical publications, and spirited mobilizations. Worker militants joined with student rebels, community activists, and a wide swath of *indépendantistes*. University occupations, anti-imperialist conferences, FLQ bombings, strike violence that ended in deaths, and escalating levels of municipal and provincial state repression signaled that Quebec was on the break point.[15]

Precipitating the province into a crisis were the 1970 FLQ kidnappings of two representatives of constituted authority and the subsequent murder of one of those seized, Quebec Minister of Labour Pierre Laporte. With the passage of the War Measures Act, indiscriminate arrests of hundreds of radicals, and the presence of Canadian armed forces in Ottawa, Montreal, and Quebec City, the stage was set for a retreat from the politics of direct action. The labor movement remained the single most powerful component in Quebec's "community of resistance," and the one sector that retained most vigorously its capacity to challenge entrenched interests. In 1971 and 1972, general strikes and common front manifestos drew directly on the transnational politics of 1960s youth and labor radicalizations, transforming Quebec into a symbol of rising syndicalist aspiration throughout North and South America in the early 1970s. Workers demanding their rights as trade unionists experienced the militancy of class struggle as intimately related to the demand that they should indeed have a country, something that had been denied them for centuries. This served as an inspiration in a transnational politics of class struggle that crossed borders and transcended the nation-state.

NOTES

1. For an outline that addresses the issues raised by the question, see Eric J. Hobsbawm, "What Is the Workers' Country?" in Hobsbawm, *Workers: Worlds of Labor* (New York: Pantheon, 1984), 49–65.
2. Marcel van der Linden, *Workers of the World: Essays toward a Global Labor History* (Leiden: Brill, 2008), 263–64.
3. Karl Marx, *Capital: A Critical Analysis of Capitalist Production*, vol. 1 (New York: International, 1967), 713–74; Rosa Luxemburg, *The Accumulation of Capital* (New York: Monthly Review, 1968), 388–418.

4. Peter Linebaugh and Marcus Rediker, *The Many-Headed Hydra: Sailors, Slaves, Commoners, and the Hidden History of the Revolutionary Atlantic* (Boston: Beacon, 2000).
5. C. L. R. James, *The Black Jacobins: Toussaint L'Ouverture and the San Domingo Revolution* (New York: Dial, 1938).
6. Stanley Ryerson, *Unequal Union: Confederation and the Roots of Conflict in the Canadas, 1815–1873* (Toronto: Progress, 1968), 64.
7. See *The General Council of the First International, 1864–1865: The London Conference, 1865, Minutes* (Moscow: Foreign Languages Publishing, 1964).
8. Eric J. Hobsbawm, "Man and Woman: Images on the Left," in Hobsbawm, *Uncommon People: Resistance, Rebellion, and Jazz* (London: Weidenfeld & Nicolson, 1998), 94–112; Sally Alexander, Anna Davin, and Eve Hostettler, "Labouring Women: A Reply to Eric Hobsbawm," *History Workshop Journal* 8 (Autumn 1979): 174–82.
9. James Green, *Death in the Haymarket: A Story of Chicago, the First Labor Movement, and the Bombing That Divided Gilded Age America* (New York: Pantheon, 2006), 284–320; Green, "The Globalization of a Memory: The Enduring Remembrance of the Haymarket Martyrs around the World," *Labor: Studies in Working-Class History of the Americas* 2 (Winter 2005): 11–23.
10. F. W. Jowett, *The Socialist and the City* (London: George Allen, 1907), 84–85.
11. E. P. Thompson, *The Making of the English Working Class* (New York: Vintage, 1963), 13.
12. John A. Fitch, "Lawrence: A Strike for Wages or Bolshevism?" *Survey* 42 (April 5, 1919): 45.
13. Benedict Anderson, *Imagined Communities: Reflections on the Origins and Spread of Nationalism* (London: Verso, 1983).
14. Paul Taylor, *Mexican Labor in the United States: Chicago and the Calumet Region* (Berkeley: University of California Press, 1932), vi–vii, quoted in Herbert G. Gutman, *Work, Culture & Society in Industrializing America* (New York: Vintage, 1977), 8–9.
15. For a recent overview of all of these developments, see Bryan D. Palmer, *Canada's 1960s: The Ironies of Identity in a Rebellious Era* (Toronto: University of Toronto Press, 2009), 311–65. Note, as well, Sean Mills, *The Empire Within: Postcolonial Thought and Political Activism in Sixties Montreal* (Montreal & Kingston: McGill-Queen's University Press, 2010).

FURTHER READING

Eley, Geoff. *Forging Democracy: The History of the Left in Europe, 1850–1900*. New York: Oxford University Press, 2002.
Gabaccia, Donna and Franca Iacovetta, eds. *Transnational Lives: Italian Workers of the World*. Toronto: University of Toronto Press, 2002.

Gutman, Herbert G. "Work, Culture, and Society in Industrializing America, 1815–1919." *American Historical Review* 78 (June 1973): 531–88.

Hobsbawm, Eric. *Workers: Worlds of Labor*. New York: Pantheon, 1984.

Hoerder, Dirk, ed. *"Struggle a Hard Battle": Essays on Working-Class Immigrants*. DeKalb: Northern Illinois University Press, 1986.

Hoerder, Dirk. *Cultures in Contact: World Migrations and the Second Millennium*. Durham, NC: Duke University Press, 2002.

Keck, Margaret. *The Workers' Party and Democratization in Brazil*. New Haven: Yale University Press, 1992.

Kirk, Neville. *Labour and Society in Britain and the USA*, vol. 1: *Capitalism, Custom and Protest, 1780–1850* and vol. 2: *Challenge and Accommodation, 1850–1939*. Aldershot, England: Scolar, 1994.

Linebaugh, Peter, and Marcus Rediker. *The Many-Headed Hydra: Sailors, Slaves, Commoners, and the Hidden History of the Revolutionary Atlantic*. Boston: Beacon, 2000.

Montgomery, David. "Immigrants, Industrial Unions, and Social Reconstruction in the United States, 1916–1923." *Labour/Le Travail* 13 (1984): 101–14.

Morgan, Kevin, Gidon Cohen, and Andrew Flinn, eds. *Agents of the Revolution: New Biographical Approaches to the History of International Communism in the Age of Lenin and Stalin*. Bern: Peter Lang, 2005.

Silverman, Victor. *Imagining Internationalism in American and British Labor*. Urbana: University of Illinois Press, 1999.

Vallières, Pierre. *White Niggers of America*. Toronto: McClelland and Stewart, 1971.

van der Linden, Marcel. *Workers of the World: Essays toward a Global Labor History*. Leiden: Brill, 2009.

van der Linden, Marcel, and F. L. van Holthoon, eds. *Internationalism and the Labor Movement, 1830–1940*. Leiden: Brill, 1988.

16 CLAIMING POLITICAL SPACE

WORKERS, MUNICIPAL SOCIALISM, AND THE RECONSTRUCTION OF LOCAL DEMOCRACY IN TRANSNATIONAL PERSPECTIVE

Shelton Stromquist

E. R. Hartley, a master butcher by trade and member of the Independent Labour Party, was a contentious presence in the Bradford (England) City Council after his election in 1895. By his own account and those of others, he shattered the clubby decorum that ruled the chambers whether liberals or conservatives dominated. He challenged the routine election of committee chairs, balked at salary increases for city engineers when employees who collected night soil had been denied raises, and gave a fellow councilor "such a basting [as] he will never forget and probably never forgive" over a proposal that unsanitary conditions in poor neighborhoods should simply be subject to "natural evolution." On one occasion, faced with constant interruptions and heckling from conservatives on the council "who had evidently been in the club room" and who challenged the facts in his comments on the water supply for poor neighborhoods, an exasperated Hartley turned on them and declared, "If you'd get less whiskey, you'd soon know a good deal more." He noted in his diary, "There was a silence one c'd feel."[1]

As one of a small minority of labor men on the Bradford Council, Hartley's campaign for "municipal socialism" seemed a perpetual, all-consuming, and at times quixotic battle. He and his colleagues might gather to recharge their spirits with an inspiring lecture on a Sunday afternoon at the Labour Church and a visit to a local saloon, where they sat "at the tea table" and in good humor exchanged war stories of the latest fights in council, but they battled on, savoring small procedural and occasional substantive victories.[2] As the Bradford *Labour Echo* reported, the Labour councilors in one session lost lopsided votes over providing land for subsistence farming by the "outdoor poor," closer inspection of the leasing of municipal lands to private interests, and the construction of a new art gallery. The editor reflected on these results and dominance of a council majority representing propertied interests.

> It would be easy to hold our local Councillors—or those who form the majority—up to ridicule on account of their attitude towards the matters mentioned. But we must remember that the Council is what the people make it. Our work lies with the Electors. When we have done our work with the electors, different men will be sent to the Council Chamber, and with the advent of another order of municipal representation will come more enlarged and enlightened views of the possibilities of municipal government.[3]

Hartley and his comrades in Bradford were hardly alone or as inconsequential as they may at times have appeared. I argue in this chapter that popular struggles for the control of cities played a crucial role in the development of a new species of local working-class politics. Driven by deteriorating conditions of urban life, economic insecurity, and intensifying labor conflict, workers across the industrializing world of the late nineteenth century experimented with new forms of political mobilization and forged a sense of common purpose that transcended locality and nation-state. Their struggles contended, on the one hand, with propertied elites' traditional defense of their interests in cities and, on the other, with liberal reformers, whose preference lay generally in technocratic and organizational reforms that displaced a direct role by workers in city politics and in many ways undermined popular participation. My focus is on one particularly fertile period—1890 to 1920—when, across the industrializing world, workers and their allies crafted a new urban politics that posed fundamental challenges to elite control and reformers' designs for the city. But this period hardly exhausts the record of such struggles. In the late eighteenth and early nineteenth century, plebeian crowds and working-class movements had asserted their grievances in ways that precipitated a wave of political reforms designed to contain that insurgent movement, most notably in England.[4]

Cities and Nation-States

But why the city? And why municipal politics? Much of the historiography of labor and socialist political development in the nineteenth and twentieth centuries has effectively bypassed the city as a political space, emphasizing the emergence of nationally competitive and parliamentary-oriented labor and socialist parties and consigning the realm of municipal politics to the margins, as a peripheral and secondary aspect of the story of labor's political mobilization.[5]

And political theorists, too, as Canadian political scientist Warren Magnusson has demonstrated, have since the eighteenth century made state sovereignty the focus of analysis and neglected the local (and municipal). In fact, according to Magnusson, the challenge of representative government as it emerged in the eighteenth century was to manage and sustain the "gap between the rulers and the ruled" in ways that would "ensure responsible government rather than mob rule." As new, and in many ways limited, forms of representative democratic government evolved, the city and its government took on a specific, if subordinate role. In his view,

> The municipality is designed to provide an enclosure for popular politics, and so to render that politics safe for the state, the market, and the other forms of government to which we are subject. The state in turn encompasses these enclosures and formally centres politics upon itself. It creates its own vortex, which pulls the media, the movements, the parties, the pressure groups, and the political scientists toward it.[6]

The decentering and enclosure of the city and its politics has been, then, a matter of both practical politics and political theory (and a supporting historiography).

From their earliest appearance as trading entrepôts and spontaneous sites of new political space in the medieval world and before, cities posed something of a problem for emergent royal, imperial, and ultimately democratic nation-states. As engines of economic enterprise and congealing property, they had tangible value. But as autonomous sites of civic identity and political activity, they perpetually threatened and even destabilized the emerging nation-state order of things. Hence in the eighteenth and nineteenth centuries, most decisively in Britain and its satellite states and imperial domains, parliaments undertook the reform of city governance in ways that promised to contain and subordinate the governing authority of cities, while securing such government as they had for property-owning elites, especially the new class of manufacturers, whose interests it was deemed necessary to protect.[7] With interesting variation, the pattern in other European countries and European settler states bore great similarity to the English experience.[8]

Cities saw their functions differentiated from states in two respects. First, paramount responsibility for the protection of property came to be identified with the state, beyond the reach of local control, which was increasingly deemed unreliable and potentially dangerous to the rights of private property. Second, cities became literally political and administrative creatures of the state.

Among the factors narrowing cities' right of self-government was a growing fear of the threat to property that popular sovereignty might pose. By the end of the nineteenth century in the United States, the self-governing power of cities had been so severely restricted as to virtually preclude measures that might effectively regulate the powers of private corporations without the express sanction of state legislatures, in whom ultimate authority rested.[9] Local struggles for "home rule" and popular political movements seeking to expand cities' domain of democratic self-government faced significant restrictions imposed by courts and legislatures. Progressive reformers in both England and the United States harbored ambiguous sentiments toward the democratization of municipal politics. The influential nineteenth-century American legal theorist Judge John Dillon defended "the need to protect private property from attack and indicated his reservations about the kind of democracy then practiced in the cities." Dillon, like many in the progressive reform community, advocated government by the "best men," striking a careful balance between protecting government from excessive control by private corporations and protecting private corporations from unwarranted interference by government, especially local government.[10]

In England, this ambivalence toward popular democratic rule in cities was embodied in the writings of none other than Fabian socialists Sidney and Beatrice Webb. Their influence radiated far beyond the shores of Britain. In 1898, they toured Australia, New Zealand, and the United States, with a particular eye on the status of local government. The Webbs and their Fabian socialist allies were hardly disinterested observers. Over the course of the 1890s, they had been intimately involved in the expanding reform agenda of the London County Council through a progressive political coalition.[11] And on their return to England, they would soon embark on a prodigious and devastatingly critical study of the history of local government in the United Kingdom.[12]

Remarkable, among other things, is how little attuned the Webbs were to the democratic, working-class political insurgency stirring in the cities they toured.[13] They took no account and presumably had no interest in the new Labor government about to take power in the legendary silver mining town, Broken Hill, New South Wales, where just a year before, Ben Tillett, leader of the dockworkers in London, had dedicated the local Trades Hall. Nor in Melbourne, Sydney, or Brisbane do they appear to have consulted or even rubbed shoulders with municipal labor activists battling in the electoral trenches against established propertied elites whose claimed right to govern in the best interests of all people was under challenge, though they did offer unflattering observations about the Labor Party parliamentarians and their socialist "poor relations."[14]

Sidney Webb's involvement in London education in the 1890s through his chairmanship of the Technical Education Board under the London County Council (LCC) and his founding of the London School of Economics provided the ideal venues for pursuit of his meritocratic conception of municipal change. The Webbs' vision of centralized municipal services, the consolidation of municipal bodies, and, indeed, the imposition of national standards and regulation, while comporting with the views of his Progressive Party allies on the LCC, flew in the face of both Conservative opponents and emerging ILP and Labour Party views.[15] According to historian Alan McBriar, Labour Party activists in London, among them Ramsey MacDonald, "who had come to dislike Webb, had found new virtues in the 'primary democracy' of ad hoc local authorities."[16] Among other things, such divisions reflect divergence within the ranks of labor and socialist activists over how best to pursue power and what vision of the municipality such a pursuit implied.

Sidney Webb's conception of the work and method of improving society distinguished him sharply from the likes of William Morris and the strain of utopian socialism Morris upheld, yet also from Labour Party activists who themselves split over the primacy and place of municipal political activism. As Webb wrote before joining the Progressives in pursuit of a seat on the London County Council in 1890, "Prophets nowadays do not found a partial community which adopts the whole faith; they cause rather the partial adoption of their own faith by the whole community."[17]

No formulation better distinguishes the separate strands of municipal reform, one of which required the empowerment of a new working class prepared to engage in municipal trench warfare with the political agents of propertied elites and another (the Webbs and their Progressive allies) which embraced a vision that foresaw the rise to power and influence of educated and socially conscious middle-class professionals, a process the Webbs called "permeation." Such divisions appear in the emerging political movements of labor across the industrializing world in the 1890s and early twentieth century.

Local Democracy in Practice: Program, Politics, and Internationalism

The most striking feature of labor and socialist politics at the municipal level in the late nineteenth and early twentieth centuries is the remarkable uniformity of its *programmatic* vision. Labor, socialist, and feminist activists across the industrializing world crafted programs that promised immediate relief and popular, democratic control of the local urban worlds inhabited disproportionately by workers. Women, although generally denied suffrage, nonetheless played pivotal roles as social investigators, propagandists for reform, theoreticians, and outspoken advocates for broader suffrage. Where the franchise permitted women's participation in local and school board elections, they seized the opportunity not only to vote but also to run for office.[18]

Utopian strains of this localist vision crop up repeatedly in different contexts in the late nineteenth century.[19] Echoing the words of French anarcho-socialist, Paul Brousse, Canadian political scientist Warren Magnusson suggests that early municipal socialists believed that "localism . . . prefigured the socialist society" and took advantage of the "geographically uneven development of capitalist society" to create models to which other workers might aspire. This vision implied the shift from a local capitalist marketplace to a collectivist world of consumption, mediated by the local state. In such cities, workers

> could live in public housing, ride public transit, rely on public utilities for water, power, lighting and telecommunications, send their children to public schools, get health care at public hospitals and clinics, go to the public swimming baths, recreation centres, parks and theatres, eat at public restaurants, and depend on public pensions and other benefits for people with inadequate incomes.

Local authorities would directly employ citizens on public works, and workers' organizations would "participate in planning and developing their own community."[20] In London, Progressives who gained control of the London County Council in 1889 articulated a similar vision. As English historian Pat Thane has noted, "Fundamental issues of human survival—death and sickness rates, levels of income, the quality of living space—became politicized as never before." The LCC sponsored "house-building, purified water supplies, work creation, a commitment to . . . 'fair wages and conditions'" in all city contracts, and improved conditions of employment for "the growing army of municipal employees."[21] Many leading German social democrats regarded suspiciously the emergence of a distinct wing of their movement committed to political action at the municipal level. Indeed, "Gemeinde-Sozialismus" became embroiled in the controversies surrounding Eduard Bernstein's advocacy of revisionism. Nonetheless, some voices in the SPD envisioned a more transformative, locality-based socialism and crafted municipal programs that reflected those goals. As a Hamburg delegate told the 1902 Party Congress, he hoped

> that cities in substantial numbers will contribute to the transformation of social relationships and create a wholly new social organism, and that democratic self-determination of cities can serve as a means to create a new social order.[22]

Similar programmatic outcroppings appeared everywhere across the industrial world of the turn of the century.

On closer examination, the programmatic similarities seemed to spring from strikingly parallel if not precisely simultaneous developments. A new laborist politics came into being out of the mass strikes and industrial turmoil spawned by the great worldwide depression of the 1890s. But each of these municipal movements was hobbled to some degree by a restrictive municipal voting franchise that enabled local elites to maintain power in the face of an increasingly politicized working class. The relationship of each of these movements to reform-oriented interests in their respective "liberal" parties both hindered and enabled their development. In situations where labor could not achieve majority presence on city councils, small numbers of elected labor or socialist councilors often created temporary, pragmatic alliances with liberal reformers to accomplish surprising results. In each case, the years immediately preceding the outbreak of the Great War saw increasing municipal socialist electoral strength and success, interrupted but not wholly stifled by the war itself. Democratizing electoral franchise reform followed in the wake of the war, creating a new political environment that saw rising levels of municipal success for labor and socialist parties.

The Industrial Revolution, then, made cities sites of profound social and economic change. By 1890—much earlier in some places—the magnetic pull of urban labor markets and insecure conditions of employment had intensified problems of congestion; epidemic disease; squalid housing; inadequate urban transit; unreliable supplies of water, milk, and essential foodstuffs; and chronic unemployment. If onerous working conditions precipitated new forms of labor organization, the conditions of daily living also produced new forms of urban politics.

But similar circumstances alone did not dictate these outcomes. This programmatic parallelism and similar patterns of municipal political mobilization and activism were no mere accident. They were fed directly by the agency of working-class political actors themselves and a locally grounded internationalism that seemed a "natural" by-product of the global capitalist transformation.

Recent scholarship documenting the transatlantic and transglobal flow of social reform ideas and programs in the late nineteenth and early twentieth centuries reminds us how interconnected these histories were. Nowhere was this flow more evident than in the realm of urban reform.[23] The cross-fertilization of political ideas and the transnational experience of political organizers were impressive. Edward Bellamy's *Looking Backward* became a ubiquitous text, sold throughout the western world in cheap agitational editions to finance organizing campaigns. Henry George's single-tax idea swept through Australia, New Zealand, Britain, and Sweden, shaping the thinking of working-class activists and middle-class reformers. The Knights of Labor and, somewhat later, the Industrial Workers of the World (IWW) exerted a powerful influence in Australia and New Zealand, as they did in parts of Europe and Latin America.[24] At key points in this period, Americans like Milwaukee social democrat Walter Thomas Mills or New Zealand revolutionary activist Patrick Hickey moved easily between the milieus of their respective countries. Hickey led the Blackball miners' strike in 1908 and the "Red Feds" after several years of organizing for the Western Federation of Miners in Colorado, and he subsequently ran for and held municipal office in New Zealand and Australia. Sidney and Beatrice Webb visited the United States, Australia, and New Zealand just before the turn of the century, preceded Down Under by the legendary British docker Ben Tillett and followed soon thereafter by Labour Party activists Tom Mann and E. R. Hartley. The traffic moved the other way as well. A young Christchurch organizer, "Jimmy" Thorn, went off for four years to organize for the Independent Labour Party in Britain; Australian railway union leader Claude Thompson had circulated widely in the industrial union and labor party circles of Europe and America, acquiring along the way honorary memberships in the American Labor Union and the Western Federation of Miners; evolutionary socialist Eduard Bernstein spent a decade exiled in London, imbibing the experience of independent labor activists and imparting his own evolving ideas to sympathizers in London. Axel Danielsson in Malmö, Sweden, participated in the Scandinavian Workers Congresses of the early 1890s and meetings of the Second International, bringing that internationalism to the Swedish readers of his newspaper, *Arbetet*.[25] What made such circulation feasible was that these political itinerants and their ideas entered worlds that were undergoing remarkably similar social and political changes; they spoke a common *political* language, read each others' tracts, and believed they faced common problems. With an eagle eye, the labor press in each country observed developments in the others; delegates to international socialist gatherings brought back colorful reports of the successes comrades had achieved elsewhere.[26] Common threads defined these local struggles across national boundaries.

As if emerging from political darkness, groups of working-class activists broke the spell of municipal governance propertied elites had fostered. They entered into a realm that promised freedom and the opportunity to address fundamental conditions in their day-to-day lives. They challenged the decorum and markers of social status that had reigned in the defense of property and the interests of rate-payers. With the illusion of "consensus" shattered, the fissures of class permitted new conceptions of workers' rights and a redefined understanding of democratic community to emerge, buoyed by an invigorated politics that made new claims for the use and control of public space, the rights of city workers, and the basic need for clean water, sanitation, electricity, and affordable public transit. A few cases illustrate the nature of these struggles to democratize the city.

Christchurch, New Zealand: "Which Side Are You On?"

As the dust settled in Christchurch, New Zealand, after a hard-fought municipal election in early May 1913, local Labor activists surveyed the results with some satisfaction. They had elected five of their members—referred to in the liberal press as "Social Democrats"—and garnered nearly 6,000 votes, 40 percent of those cast. Though still a minority on the council, they clearly felt empowered by the victory.[27] And in the election's aftermath, the staid tenor of council deliberations took a dramatic turn.

The election of the council's standing committees, usually a routine and uncontested matter following city elections, "caused a lengthy and at times warm discussion," according to one press report, "in which party feeling now and then ran high."[28] An unspoken tradition of nonpartisanship, at least in name, had been the norm in council deliberations. The governing class regarded parties as an inappropriate and unwelcome intrusion in municipal affairs. When Labor member James McCombs accused the "Citizens' Association" of taking more than its share of committee positions, Mayor Holland lashed back, "There is no Citizens' Association here. . . . I want to say here that there are no parties in the Council." Another Labor councilor asserted that "there was no use disputing the fact that party had become a clear-cut issue," and he was prepared to stay all night if necessary to settle the matter. The partisan tone of the floor debate brought the boisterous public gallery into play and a threat from the mayor to clear the hall if decorum were not promptly restored. Finally, Jim McCullough, newly elected Labor member and brother of local Labor notable J. A. McCullough, pointed out that some councilors could be seen consulting typewritten slips of paper with preselected names for different committees. It appeared that after all "things were cut and dried." McCullough raised the temperature of the debate a few more degrees. "If the other party wanted to fight they would get it on the floor of the Council. The Social Democrats were not there to be snuffed out and if they could not get justice one way they would fight it out on the floor of the Council." Before the councilors resorted to fisticuffs, cooler heads prevailed, a compromise was reached, and the councilors agreed to increase the membership of each committee to six, each having at least two Labor members.[29]

The election of 1913 was no anomaly in the universe of early-twentieth-century municipal politics. And in Christchurch, candidates had run for council seats with explicit labor backing before 1913. In 1907, for instance, Jimmy Thorn, the unquenchable local labor activist, reported a plan afoot to contest the municipal election with support of a dozen local unions. He wrote to a colleague in Dunedin that he had "kicked up a shindig" in a city council meeting by speaking of "the mediocrities of which it was composed" and claiming that it lay "in the hands of greedy rack rent landlords and money grubbing employers."[30] Thorn belittled his Liberal-Labour colleagues who professed to see "nothing wrong," and he also chided those Social Democrats who "would have us waste our strength with shadows." To the contrary, as he prepared a stump speech to his fellow socialists about "Socialism and Municipal Politics," he proclaimed, "I've got a catalogue of woes to talk about. That Labour man that has no grievances is a Liberal."[31] Although the campaign yielded no victories in that election cycle, it set the stage for future campaigns.

Between election campaigns, the interests of labor remained focused on the municipal arena, with periodic petitions and interventions in council affairs. In the fall of 1908, the Trades and Labour Council protested the city's raising fees to exorbitant levels for the city baths, and the Independent Political Labour League (IPLL) sent a delegation to council, asking it to institute a municipally owned market for fresh and inexpensive vegetables and fish. "His Worship the Mayor" referred the matter to committee, where, apparently, it disappeared.[32] In 1909, the annual preelection ritual of stripping innumerable lodgers, home-residing sons, and other unqualified municipal voters from the rolls produced a large number of challenges to reinstate would-be voters for the impending referendum on the Saturday half-holiday for shop workers. Months before, labor supporters T. E. Taylor and J. McCombs had addressed the council on that very issue in support of the clerks and office workers, many of whom were disfranchised.[33]

The politicization of council business continued apace in 1910 with petitions and deputations from the Trades and Labour Council and other labor sympathizers over the pay and hours for city laborers and drivers. Seeking first to exclude such deputations and ignore the petitions, the council gradually found itself divided over the extent to which interested citizens ("New Zealand Labour Party, South Christchurch Branch") and trade unions should be heard during council meetings. Unaccustomedly polarized in a series of votes at successive meetings in March through June, the council by close margins chose to exclude deputations of interested parties and turned down the wages and hours recommendations of its own Works Committee. Clearly, the business of governing the city had become more contested.

By the election of 1911, a new political environment seemed in place. A number of the petitioners from the previous year now entered the contest directly as candidates for council, and T. E. Taylor, highly respected MP from Christchurch and vocal advocate for labor's interest, stood for mayor. On petition, the council permitted more generous enrollment of electors, and either as a matter of policy or deference, the town clerk disqualified fewer of them. Indeed, the election results proved impressive. T. E. Taylor was resoundingly elected mayor, his allegiances to labor clear but his formal association somewhat less so. The Canterbury Trades and Labour Council subsequently congratulated the new "Labour Councilors" and the "Municipal Representation Committee" that had worked so diligently on their behalf.[34]

The ascension of T. E. Taylor as mayor promised a new day. His predecessor acknowledged an unprecedented "swing in the pendulum of municipal politics." Accepting the office, Taylor noted that "the attempts of Labour to secure representation on the Council had aroused interest in municipal affairs." While acknowledging that "the Labour Party" had not achieved its full objectives, he noted that now "there was a little leaven in the Council that might ultimately leaven the whole lump." He proceeded to enumerate the issues he hoped to pursue: street improvements, especially in poor neighborhoods; higher wages for city employees; a better water supply, public markets, and milk supply; and this without raising local rates.[35]

No sooner had Taylor and his Labor colleagues assumed their positions in the Christchurch Council chambers than they began to challenge both the procedure and substance of city council business. In a series of tie votes broken by the mayor, council granted permission to a whole variety of organizations seeking to hold public meetings in the central Cathedral Square, a public space previously denied for such purposes. The successful petitioners ranged from the Salvation Army and the Sydenham Gospel Mission to the Industrial Workers of the World, the New Zealand Socialist Party, and the Christchurch Prohibition League. The mayor also submitted a lengthy report on his proposal for major street reconstruction throughout the city, including working-class neighborhoods, and proposed to hold mass meetings to build support for his proposals. (Dust and muck were perpetual problems in poorer neighborhoods, where macadam roads were unknown.) On other matters, the mayor and the minority of Labor councilors had more difficulty mustering a majority in the closely divided council. The wages of city employees continued to be such an issue, where they were stymied.[36]

Mayor T. E. Taylor's sudden death just three months after his election dealt the new administration a devastating blow. An outpouring of grief from all segments of the community proved truly unprecedented. In a moving testimonial, Hiram Hunter, labor councilor and head of the Tramway Drivers' Union, spoke to the unfinished agenda Taylor had left—the empowerment of city health inspectors, "the elimination of slums" and the establishment of a city-owned fish market and municipal quarry. "There was not a plank in the Labour platform that Mr. Taylor overlooked." By the spring of 1913, the forces of labor again mobilized through a Municipal Labour Representation Committee (LRC), sought to reclaim and enlarge the territory they had won with Taylor's election in 1911, and then lost abruptly when conservative businessman Henry Holland succeeded him as mayor.[37] An election broadside on behalf of candidates "known as the Social-Democratic candidates or Labour 'ticket'" claimed the support of a coalition that included the North Canterbury Labour Representation Committee, the Socialist Party, Fabian Society, Unity Committee, Trades and Labour Council, and the Women's Institute, all united "for the purpose of securing adequate representation of the wage-earners of Christchurch." They belittled the notion that "businessmen" were somehow more capable than practical workingmen of efficiently running city affairs. The administration that succeeded Taylor had squandered the opportunity to acquire the gas monopoly, to increase public access to electricity in workers' homes, to arrest the spread of disease by controlling the milk supply, and to limit the profiteering of middlemen by instituting a public market.[38]

Although the LRC did not achieve the Labor control of city council it sought, the elected Labor councilors brought a new level of popular interest to municipal affairs and a new recognition of the underlying polarities that might govern such affairs in the future. As sitting Labor councilor Hiram Hunter wrote before the election, "It is no use to try and evade the fact that there are two parties in municipal as well as general politics. . . . Which side are you on? There is no middle course. Either you are of the exploiting class, or you are being exploited."[39]

While the election of a "Labour mayor" in 1911 was without precedent in New Zealand, the municipal victory in Christchurch and the politicization of municipal affairs that underlay it follows a pattern that can be discerned in many municipalities in Australia and New Zealand in the prewar years.[40] In fact, "Jimmy" Thorn, who played such a crucial role in igniting working-class municipal activism in Christchurch, moved to England for several years to work as an organizer for the Independent Labour Party (ILP) and Robert Blatchford's Clarion Van.[41] Although the precise timing and specific history varies from one municipality to another, similar patterns can be observed in Broken Hill, Brisbane, Redfern (Sydney), Richmond, Footscray, Fitzroy, and Essendon (Melbourne), Australia. City affairs began to tilt under the influence of the political gravity labor brought to local politics. Sometimes the progress was more symbolic than real or so incremental as to be barely discernible, but in other cases, a minority labor interest in council drew to its ranks sympathetic liberal councilors and on occasion could constitute an effective, if ephemeral, majority.[42] Labor's presence made a difference, if only by being able to shine the bright light of public attention into municipal affairs that had previously been shrouded from public view by an illusory consensus and the arcane clubbiness of elite governance.

Broken Hill, New South Wales, Australia: A Model of Municipal Labor Governance

When Ben Tillett, Britain's legendary leader of the dockworkers, visited Broken Hill, NSW, in September 1897 to dedicate the new Trades Hall, he took the opportunity to remind local workers about the importance of municipal politics. He thought "the municipal problem was coequal in seriousness to the Parliamentary problem" and believed it quite unacceptable "that so advanced a set as the workers of Broken Hill had only two representatives in the council." The following year, they elected two more, and two more in each of the succeeding several years, but the *Barrier Truth* asserted that it was less Tillett than the persistent and dedicated organizing and campaigning of local workers that produced this result.[43]

Whatever the combination of factors, the most stunning municipal victories of the 1890s in Australia came in this silver-mining town deep in the outback of New South Wales. A bitter strike defeat in 1892 had set the stage for new political assertiveness by labor at the municipal level. What differentiated Broken Hill was the dramatic success of that initiative and the sustained record of achievement after 1900 of labor's first municipal government in all of Australia.[44] Jabez Wright, a local undertaker with trade union roots, was first elected to the Broken Hill City Council on a labor platform in 1896 and almost immediately, even as a single councilman, made his presence felt. Joined the next year by another labor man, they in turn witnessed the addition of two more labor councilmen in 1898. By 1899, the additional labor seats won produced a council chamber evenly divided between labor and the mining company "independents."[45] The stage was set for labor's dramatic victory in 1900.[46]

In reporting the stunning victory, *The Tocsin* (Melbourne) noted, "The defeat of the miners . . . at Broken Hill, some few years ago, was really a blessing in disguise." The miners had thereafter devoted themselves to politics with some success at both the municipal and state parliamentary levels. Specifically, they seized "the immense possibilities there are for securing reforms in the local council." With a majority of eight ("two miners, a teamster, an ore-dresser, a cabinet maker, a labourer, an undertaker, and the secretary of the Miners' Association") in a council of twelve, they could move with some freedom to implement their agenda, the first step of which was to elect as mayor the person the mining companies referred to as "that meddlesome old agitator," Jabez Wright. They might actually be forced, according to contemporary chronicler George Dale, to "disgorge to the community the actual amount of rates annually" that they owed the city.[47] After six months of local labor government, the *Tocsin* enumerated its first fruits.

> With the advent of the Labour majority, the contractor disappeared, and all the work required by the council is now done direct by its own employes on the day labour system. The council has its own workshops, builds its own drays, and effects all necessary repairs, etc., in connection with its property. The trades union wage for labourers at Broken Hill is 7s. 6d per day; the council's minimum wage for labourers is 8s.4d. per day . . . and the trades union wage and the eight hours principle are rigidly observed for all kinds of mechanics in the employ of the Council.[48]

The excitement generated by the new municipal regime was palpable, despite the fact that the mining companies immediately challenged in court the new rates imposed on them. The new council had plans afoot for a new public bath, a municipal slaughterhouse, and a publicly owned sanitary water system. Broken Hill's Labor government stood as a beacon in Australasia, "the only institution of its kind . . . where representatives of Labour number two-thirds of its [council] members." And Labor would remain in control of the municipality for the next generation and beyond. George Dale reported that in 1918 the city was electing its seventeenth Labor mayor.[49] Its accomplishments, entirely consistent with Labor's municipal goals elsewhere, provided a noteworthy balance sheet that included: "the erection of the baths, the introduction of the sealed pan system [street paving], the regular removal of all garbage, the establishment of the abattoirs, street lighting, the improvement of the parks," and the creation of a free public library, "including perhaps more sociological works than any similar lending library in the Commonwealth."[50] The physical fabric of the city changed in dramatic ways—the baths (with an indoor swimming pool 90 by 30 feet and Turkish baths) stood "a stone's throw" from Trades Hall, a new public library, a rebuilt technical college, the newspaper offices of the Labor paper, the *Barrier Truth*, and the Social Democratic Club, where workers socialized and heard lectures. In 1904, the club expanded to include a bar and reading and meeting rooms. The editor of the *Truth*, R. S. Ross, addressed the temperance critics of the bar in socialist terms: "I was willing that there should be collective ownership in beer and that beer should be dispensed for cooperative benefit and not for private profit." Membership in the club subsequently boomed.[51]

The *Barrier Truth* faithfully reported each week the hand-to-hand combat on the floor of the Broken Hill municipal council but carried as well a prominent weekly column titled "Municipal Socialism" in which the exploits of comrades in municipalities around the globe were reported.[52] The columns conveyed the sense of a common war waged on innumerable municipal fronts: "The fact that other eyes are on us must never be forgotten. A weakness in any one regiment, or even company, is a corresponding weakness in the whole army of labor, while the effects of a victory anywhere must be felt everywhere."[53] Another such front was Manchester, England, the cradle of the Industrial Revolution.

Manchester, England: The Politics of Public Space

Fred Brocklehurst may have seemed an unlikely candidate for jail in the summer of 1896. From being a one-time piecer in a silk mill at the age of ten and subsequently a printer's devil on the *Manchester Courier*, he had found his way to Queen's College, Cambridge, in 1890 and, after earning a degree, became secretary for the Labour Church in Manchester. By the mid-1890s, he was an active member of the Independent Labour Party.[54] The party was already having a measurable impact in local elections across the North. In Manchester, two members had been elected to the city council in 1894, and two more, including Brocklehurst, would follow in 1897. By the latter year, Bradford ILPers joined Manchester with four seats in their council, and Keighley, Stockton, Leicester, Wolverhampton, and a number of other towns across the United Kingdom had elected two. School boards and Boards of Guardians were likewise being infiltrated by Independent Laborites.[55]

But Brocklehurst's "criminal" notoriety in 1896 came as a result of a principled stand on behalf of labor's right to freedom of speech and the use of public space for agitational purposes. The battle that year revolved around a challenge to the ILP's unauthorized use of a natural amphitheater in a secluded public park, Boggart Hole Clough, for public meetings. As early as 1893, Manchester City Council had debated and rejected a petition from "an outside body" to use Alexandria Park for a Sunday celebration of May Day. In that debate, Alderman John Harwood had argued "that the parks were intended for the use chiefly of children and ladies and those who were in need of quiet recreation and he hoped that they would never be allowed to be used for public meetings of any kind."[56]

In 1896, conflict erupted again, this time on a grander scale, over the use of Boggart Hole Clough, where the local Fabian Society had held public gatherings as far back as 1892.[57] But in May 1896, the Parks Committee under its chairman, George Needham, decided to force the discontinuance of such meetings conducted by "a certain party." City authorities issued summonses against leaders of the ILP who had appeared at the most recent gathering. In the face of fines and threats of imprisonment, party activists pushed ahead with a new series of meetings in June for which additional summonses were issued. Fred Brocklehurst reported lightheartedly in the *Clarion* the "offenses" for which the accused were cited.

> Harker... was prosecuted for writing a note and passing it to the speaker; Brierley for holding an umbrella over his head when it rained; Smalley for helping a park attendant in keeping order; Vowers for "nothing in particular"; Tweedale and Moss for standing quietly for ten minutes at the edge of the crowd; Hempsall for smoking a cigar within six yards of the speaker; Mrs. Pankhurst for lending her umbrella for the purposes of the collection; and Hall "for the unpardonable crime of opening his mouth."[58]

Brocklehurst and Hall eventually served a month under brutal conditions in the Strangeways Gaol. Others received varying fines, though the prosecuting authorities, including the grandson of William Cobbett, declined to press charges against the prominent women involved, including Emmeline Pankhurst and her daughters, Cristabel and Sylvia. Before the dust settled, Boggart Hole Clough attracted to its now weekly meetings such Labour notables as Keir Hardie, Tom Mann, Ben Tillett, J. Bruce Glasier, and Pete Curran, with crowds ranging from 10,000 to 50,000.[59]

The issue continued to percolate through the summer's council proceedings with a report on how other municipalities regulated public spaces and a series of contentious votes in the council over the conditions under which activities in the parks were to be allowed. The ILP weighed in with the view that "the parks of this City are the common property of all the citizens," asserting the right to hold meetings in parks and asking that no new bylaw be adopted without a direct vote of the citizens. A petition of 1,670 citizens calling such meetings "an intolerable nuisance" asked the mayor to "support the Parks Committee in their arduous duty of upholding the honour, dignity, and independence of the Council."[60] A counterpetition, signed by 2,644 memorialists, called on the mayor to convene a public meeting in the evening "to the end that it may be attended by citizens whose avocations prevent them from attending a meeting held in the day time" to affirm the right to hold meetings in open spaces. In the end, a substantial council majority overrode the sentiments of the ILP councilors and their liberal allies by instituting regulations that denied the right of persons to "sing, preach, lecture, or take part in any meeting for political, religious, or other purposes, or take part in any public show, performance, or demonstration in the park." Over labor's opposition, a caveat provided an avenue for grants of special permission on a case-by-case basis, though the ILP councilors did secure the deletion of an obnoxious addendum permitting the exclusion of any person "not dressed in decent clothes."[61] While passage of the bylaw appeared to be a defeat for the ILP and its allies, attempts by Chairman Needham to block ILP meetings in the coming year proved unsuccessful. And even more tellingly, in the November 1897 election, Councilor Needham lost his seat in Harpurhey Ward, near Boggart Hole Clough, to none other than Frederick Brocklehurst. With the entry of two additional ILPers to the Manchester City Council and in the changed political climate after the Boggart Hole Clough controversy, the terrain of municipal affairs became an even more contentious battleground for labor.[62]

Brocklehurst joined fellow ILPers on the Manchester Council: recently elected William Maben, a joiner, and continuing councilors, J. E. Sutton, a former miner and checkweighman, and Jesse Butler, a union secretary.[63] Although still a small minority, the labor councilors set about immediately making their presence felt. Brocklehurst and Maben entered into the proceedings energetically, and speaking with notable "effect" to the full council, Brocklehurst "never failed to gain the respectful attention of his fellow members." In so doing, he "disregarded the unwritten 'rule' that new members should be silent for at least twelve months."[64]

Building on the efforts of Sutton and Butler to force consideration of the eight-hour day for city street employees, the construction of new city-owned housing for workers displaced by slum clearance, and the ongoing efforts to use public space for political gatherings, the new labor quartet assembled a majority to protect the right to music in the parks on Sundays, pushed forward a plan to curtail tramway franchises so as to enable municipalization in the near future, forced repeated scrutiny by council of wages and working conditions of city employees, and blocked efforts to give "rate-paying companies" a vote in municipal and parliamentary elections.[65] Although defeated in their attempts to institute a local single tax of all unoccupied properties held by private interests, abolish the office of alderman, and adopt a trade union "standard" of wages and hours for all contractors with the city, the labor group injected a whole new set of issues into the business of governing the city and in the process challenged established, long-standing "rules" regulating the decorum and procedures of the body. Brocklehurst was also elected the same year to the school board and agitated for the abolition of school fees in the primary grades, for higher salaries for assistant teachers, and for curtailing subsidies for "voluntary" religious schools. Brocklehurst demanded that the schools "give the children of the poor an equal chance educationally with the children of the rich."[66]

The impact of municipal labor representation should not be underestimated in Manchester or other industrial cities such as Bradford, Halifax, Rochdale, Keighley, and Huddersfield, as well as Liverpool and Leeds, where similar inroads were made.[67] Brocklehurst's quieter but no less effective ILP colleague on the council, William Maben, mounted effective agitation around the demand for new sanitary municipal housing, against "smoke nuisance" and other poisonous contaminations of poor neighborhoods, and for better wages for city laborers, but he succumbed to bronchitis in his second term at age fifty-one.[68] His funeral was well attended by city officials, including the lord mayor and a deputation from the council, along with activist colleagues from the SDF and ILP. But as the labor journal *Justice* reported, "More touching was the presence of some two to three hundred poor people, who had come some four to five miles on this bitterly cold day to testify their love and respect for, as one of them said, 'One who was a poor man like ourselves, and who worked for the like of us.'"[69]

Detroit, Cleveland, and Toledo: Pragmatic Politics in a Municipal Reform Triangle

Peter Witt had some acquaintance with the rough-and-tumble of class politics and labor strife in Cleveland. As an iron molder, he had struck and been blacklisted; he and his labor associates had campaigned vigorously for populist local candidates; and he developed his own lantern-slide presentation, "Cleveland before St. Peter," indicting the monopoly rule of local elites, which he presented all over the city to gatherings of trade unionists and reformers. When the Democrats recruited single-taxer Tom Johnson to run for mayor in 1901, Witt joined the campaign and, following the election, was appointed to run Johnson's "tax school." Eventually as city clerk in the second Johnson administration, he masterminded a single-tax-inspired redesign of the local tax system.[70] Johnson's enfant terrible inspired his boss with his no-holds-barred attacks on privilege. At a memorable city council session in which the private street car monopoly rejected out of hand the city's terms for gradual municipalization, Johnson recalled,

> Witt not only denounced the policy and methods of the railway company, charging that in the past it had bribed councilmen, corrupted legislators,

used dishonest judges, and for months had the City Hall watched by a private detective, but one by one he called the men present by name and shaking his finger at them declared the responsibility of each for the particular things of which he held that man to be guilty.[71]

Tammany boss George Washington Plunkitt memorably referred to municipal reform politicians as "morning glories [that] looked lovely in the mornin' and withered up in a short time, while the regular machines went on flourishin' forever, like fine old oaks."[72] Although Plunkitt may have underestimated the staying power and class character of much municipal reform, he did capture something of the evanescent and pragmatic reforms that swept through American cities in the period 1890 to 1920 and beyond. What such movements lacked in formal party organization that extended from one city to the next, they nevertheless embodied in a programmatic consistency that united these "social justice" reformers, whether they were affiliated with Democratic, Republican, Nonpartisan, Socialist, Labor, or Public Ownership parties. This new municipal political gospel may not have been identical in Hazen Pingree's Detroit, Samuel Jones's Toledo, Tom Johnson's Cleveland, Victor Berger's Milwaukee, Eugene Schmitz's San Francisco, Edward Dunne's Chicago, or countless other reform and socialist regimes in smaller industrial cities, but in certain respects, they reflected similar impulses and political outcomes.[73] It is appropriate to speak of them programmatically in the same breath with Christchurch, NZ, Broken Hill, NSW, Manchester, England and hundreds of other cities around the globe.

In an international context, the United States does not immediately come to mind as the birthplace of a new and vigorous labor and socialist political movement, in part because of the long shadow cast by Werner Sombart and his historiographical heirs.[74] But it is also a byproduct of the failure of historians to take seriously the realm of municipal politics. I would argue that in the United States the vigor of "municipal socialism," broadly defined, compared favorably with its counterparts in much of the industrializing world through World War I. Why local labor and socialist activists faced more serious barriers to building a *nationally competitive* social democratic party in this period is a different question, requiring a different explanation.[75]

One of the most compelling arenas in which to examine the emergence of this new urban politics is a triangle of cities on the Great Lakes whose political transformation was relatively concurrent and that embodied the promise and limitations of those politics in the American context. Detroit, Toledo, and Cleveland each elected a maverick politician as mayor, whose conscience but also political antennae had been stimulated by the labor upheavals of the late nineteenth century. All were or had been industrialists, but all had imbibed the reform currents circulating widely in labor and working-class circles—Henry George's single tax (Tom Johnson was a convert and disciple), municipal ownership of utilities (all three supported it), Christian socialism (Jones, in particular, moved in those circles), and urban populism (which had made some mark in all three cities). In building or attracting local reform constituencies, they turned away from their conventional party ties (Republican for Pingree and Jones and Democratic for Johnson) and toward a cross-party coalition of reformers, workers, and even socialists. Although each served multiple terms as mayor, each also reshaped local politics in ways that lasted well beyond their own mayoral service. Pingree moved on to the governorship but left an institutional legacy of reform in Detroit that would last for decades. Jones ran for governor as a nonpartisan but was succeeded in the mayoralty by his protégé, Brand Whitlock. And although Tom Johnson died within a year of leaving office in 1909, his political legacy continued in the hands of the cadre of operatives he had brought into his administration, not the least of whom were Peter Witt, Newton D. Baker, and Frederic Howe.[76]

Each of these reform administrations came up against the state-imposed limitations on municipal home rule unequivocally reinforced by the Supreme Court in *Hunter v. City of Pittsburgh*, 1907. Frustrated in their ability to secure the right to thoroughly municipalize streetcar service, Pingree, Jones, and Johnson each pursued higher office and sought to pressure state legislatures to revise the terms under which cities were chartered and managed their own affairs. Each was ultimately unsuccessful, despite igniting a broader movement for municipal charter reform.[77]

What is most striking about each of these cases is the consistency in their programs for reform and the extent to which such reform programs overlapped those of municipal socialists in a host of other cities. Within the limits of the authority they could muster, they municipalized some city services, notably water, electricity, and street maintenance. They built public baths in poor neighborhoods; created parks and recreation spaces that were open to working-class residents' use; instituted new forms of municipal welfare and employment relief; addressed the problems of poor housing, impure air, and inadequate sanitation; reformed law enforcement and city jails in ways that ensured greater fairness; set in motion public inspection of markets and perishable foods like milk, fish, and meat; and took steps to regulate and acquire streetcar lines for operation as public utilities. City workers came to be paid, by and large, standard union wages for a reasonable workday. In all these respect, cities in this reform triangle moved in directions similar to, or even in advance of, their labor and socialist municipal reform colleagues in cities across the industrializing world of the early twentieth century.[78]

Conclusion

The cases discussed here suggest ways in which workers and their political allies built from below a new democratic politics in the city, despite a restrictive municipal franchise, judicial impediments to genuine self-government, and a stifling or outright repressive elite political culture. They cast their struggles in an international context, even as they challenged the drift of their own political movements toward a national parliamentary orientation. In the politics of the city, workers saw an arena where their most basic day-to-day needs could be addressed and where the defensive bulwarks put up by propertied interests seemed most entrenched and most determinedly resistant to genuine democratization. Workers in Christchurch, New Zealand, tore away the mask of nonpartisanship that local elites had used to cover the reality of class rule in the municipality and challenged the decorum, procedures, and substance of what local government had been. In Broken Hill, New South Wales, Australian silver miners and their working-class allies achieved a stunning victory in the municipal contest of 1900 and proceeded over years of unbroken Labor government to demonstrate concretely what difference self-government could make in the daily lives of workers, once the control of powerful mining interests was broken. In Manchester, England, as in so many municipalities around the globe, victories came incrementally, the result of political hand-to-hand combat in the trenches of the city council, the school board, and the "Guardians of the Poor." The fight for labor's right to use public parks, like Boggart Hole Clough, for political rallies and other working-class cultural events may have ended with only partial victory, but it set the stage for new rounds of local struggle that changed the political terrain in ways that promised more substantial future victories. A reform triangle of cities in the Progressive-era United States (Detroit, Toledo, and Cleveland) revealed a new kind of pragmatic urban working-class politics that proved capable of adapting a common municipal reform program to the specific partisan political environment of different U.S. cities, with impressive results. These (and many other) cases of municipal labor and socialist politics at the turn-of-the-century reveal a remarkable degree of programmatic and strategic consistency transnationally, nourished by the common insecurities of urban industrial life and the shared experience of political activists determined to build a locally-grounded, grassroots democratic movement of global proportions that would address them.

NOTES

1. E. R. Hartley Diary, vol. 1, January 9, 1900; February 13, 1900; Minutes of the Bradford City Council, February 11, 1896; see also Molly Jackson, "Edward R. Hartley, a Monograph Compiled by his Grand-Daughter," West Yorkshire Archives Service, Bradford Public Library.
2. The *Labour Echo* (Bradford), October 5, 1895.
3. Ibid., February 22, 1896.
4. See E. P. Thompson's essays, "The Moral Economy of the English Crowd in the Eighteenth Century," *Past and Present* 50 (1971): 76–136, and *The Making of the English Working Class* (New York: Pantheon, 1964); Georges Rude, *The Crowd in*

History: A Study of Popular Disturbances in France and England, 1730–1848 (New York: Wiley, 1964); Eric J. Hobsbawm, *Labouring Men: Studies in the History of Labour* (London: Weidenfeld and Nicholson, 1964).
5. This national historiographical emphasis is ubiquitous in the labor histories of those nation-states encompassed by this project. See, for example, Duncan Tanner, *Political Change and the Labour Party, 1900–1918* (Cambridge: Cambridge University Press, 1990); Bede Nairn, *Civilising Capitalism: The Beginnings of the Australian Labor Party* (Melbourne: Melbourne University Press, 1989); Geoff Eley, *Forging Democracy: The History of the Left in Europe, 1850–1900* (New York: Oxford University Press, 2002); Marcel van der Linden, "The National Integration of European Working Classes, 1871-1914: Exploring Causal Configurations," in idem., *Transnational Labour History: Explorations* (Aldershot: Ashgate, 2003).
6. Warren Magnusson, *The Search for Political Space: Globalization, Social Movements, and the Urban Political Experience* (Toronto, ON: University of Toronto Press, 1996), 8, 10.
7. Bryan Keith-Lucas, *English Local Government in the Nineteenth and Twentieth Centuries* (London: Historical Association, 1977); Derek Fraser, *Power and Authority in the Victorian City* (New York: St. Martin's Press, 1979).
8. Albert Shaw, *Municipal Government in Continental Europe* (New York: Century, 1895); E. P. Hennock, *Fit and Proper Persons: Ideal and Reality in Nineteenth-Century Urban Government* (London: Edward Arnold, 1973), 299–307; G. W. A. Bush, *Decently and in Order: The Government of the City of Auckland, 1840–1971* (Auckland, New Zealand: Collins, 1970); Sven Beckert, *The Monied Metropolis: New York City and the Consolidation of the American Bourgeoisie, 1850–1896* (New York: Cambridge University Press, 2003); David Harvey, *Paris: Capital of Modernity* (New York: Routledge, 2003).
9. See later discussion of the "municipal reform triangle" (Detroit, Toledo, Cleveland) and the fight for home rule.
10. Gerald E. Frug, *City Making: Building Communities without Building Walls* (Princeton, NJ: Princeton University Press, 1999), 45–46 (quotation on 45).
11. A. M. McBriar, *Fabian Socialism and English Politics, 1884–1918* (Cambridge: Cambridge University Press, 1966); Paul Thompson, *Socialists, Liberals and Labour: The Struggle for London, 1885–1914* (London: Routledge, 1967); and Susan D. Pennyback, *A Vision for London, 1889–1914: Labour, Everyday Life and the LCC Experiment* (London: Routledge, 1995).
12. Sidney and Beatrice Webb, *English Local Government from the Revolution to the Municipal Corporations Act*, 11 vols., 1906–1927 (Reprinted: Hamden, CT: Archon, 1963).
13. Eric Hobsbawm, "The Fabians Reconsidered," in Hobsbawm, *Labouring Men* (New York: Anchor, 1967), 295–320; also Royden Harrison, *The Life and Times of Sidney and Beatrice Webb, 1858–1905: The Formative Years* (London: Macmillan, 2000).

14. Beatrice Potter Webb, *The Webb's Australian Diary, 1898* (Melbourne: Pitman and Sons, 1965), 41, 73; *Visit to New Zealand in 1898: Beatrice Webb's Diary with Entries by Sidney Webb* (Wellington, New Zealand: Price Milburn, 1959). See also Bruce Scates, *A New Australia: Citizenship, Radicalism and the First Republic* (Cambridge: Cambridge University Press, 1997), 12–13; Race Mathews, *Australia's First Fabians: Middle-Class Radicals, Labour Activists and the Early Labour Movement* (Cambridge: Cambridge University Press, 1993).
15. Alan McBriar, "Sidney Webb and the LCC," in *The Webbs and their Work*, ed. Margaret Cole (London: F. Muller, 1949), 89–92.
16. Ibid., 90.
17. Sidney Webb, *Socialism in England*, 1890, 7, quoted in Harrison, *The Life and Times of Sidney and Beatrice Webb*, 209.
18. See Melanie Nolan, "Gender and the Politics of Keeping Left: Wellington Labour Women and Their Community, 1912–1949," in *Communities of Women: Historical Perspectives*, ed. Barbara Brookes and Dorothy Page (Dunedin, New Zealand: Otago University Press, 2002); Particia Hollis, *Ladies Elect: Women in English Local Government, 1865–1914* (Oxford: Clarendon Press, 1987).
19. On the influence of utopian socialist, William Lane, in Australia, see D. J. Murphy, "Queensland," in *Labor in Politics: The State Labor Parties in Australia, 1880–1920*, ed. D. J. Murphy (Brisbane, Australia: Queensland University Press, 1975), 132–33, 136–37, 150–51; Verity Burgmann, *'In Our Time': Socialism and the Rise of Labor, 1885–1905* (Sydney, Australia: George Allen and Unwin, 1985), 19–34; and for the continuing influence of the Paris Commune, *The Paris Commune of 1871: The View from the Left*, Eugene Schulkind, ed. (London: Jonathan Cape, 1972).
20. Warren Magnusson, *The Search for Political Space*, 167, 164–65.
21. Pat Thane, "Labour and Local Politics: Radicalism, Democracy and Social Reform, 1880–1914," in *Currents of Radicalism: Popular Radicalism, Organized Labour and Party Politics in Britain, 1850–1914*, ed. Eugenio F. Biagini and Alastair J. Reid (Cambridge: Cambridge University Press, 1991), 246.
22. *Protokoll über die Verhandlungen des Parteitages der Sozialdemokratischen Partei Deutschlands*, München, 14 bis September 20, 1902 (Berlin: Vorwärts, 1902), 220.
23. Shelton Stromquist, "'Thinking Globally, Acting Locally': Municipal Labor and Socialist Activism in Comparative Perspective, 1890–1920, *Labour History Review* 74, no. 3 (2009): 233–56. For a different but related realm, see Daniel Rodgers, *Atlantic Crossings: Social Politics in a Progressive Age* (Cambridge, MA: Harvard University Press, 1998).
24. Marcel van der Linden, *Revolutionary Syndicalism: An International Perspective* (Aldershot, England: Scolar, 1990),
25. See for example, E.R. Hartley's Australian Diaries, E.R. Hartley Papers, West Yorkshire Archives Service, Bradford; Fred J. Hokin, "Twenty Years of Hustling in Nineteen Countries—Claude Thompson, a character sketch," flyer, Box 7, Voltaire Molesworth Papers, Mitchell State Library, New South Wales.

26. See reports in publications as diverse as Robert Blatchford's *Clarion*, the German SPD's, *Kommunale Praxis*, Axel Danielsson's *Arbetet*, and Victor Berger's *Social Democratic Herald* (Milwaukee).
27. For an account of the results of the 1913 municipal election in Christchurch, see Jim McAloon, "Working-Class Politics in Christchurch, 1905–14" (master's thesis, University of Canterbury, 1986), 221.
28. Christchurch, N.Z., City Council Minutes, May 12, 1913, Christchurch City Archives.
29. Canterbury Trades and Labour Council, Minutes, Christchurch, May 22, 1913 MacMillan-Brown Archives, Canterbury University.
30. J. Thorn to J. T. Paul, January 23, 1907, J. T. Paul Papers, Hocken Library, Dunedin.
31. Ibid.
32. Canterbury Trades and Labour Council, Minutes, March 21, 1908; Christchurch City Council Minutes, April 27, 1908.
33. Christchurch City Council Minutes, December 21, 1908; March 27, 1909; and April 5, 1909.
34. Ibid., March 20 and April 3, 1911; Canterbury Trades and Labour Council Minutes, Christchurch, April 29, 1911.
35. Christchurch City Council Minutes, May 3, 1911.
36. Ibid., May 15, June 26, and July 10, 1911.
37. T.E. Taylor Papers, 1 v., newspaper cuttings, Canterbury Museum, Christchurch. J. A. McCullough to "Tom," April 28, 1913, Outward Correspondence; J. A. McCullough Diaries, vol. 4, 5, May 15, 1913; see also, Melanie Nolan, *War and Class: the Diaries of Jack McCullough* (Wellington, New Zealand: Dunmore Publishing, 2009).
38. "Labour Representation," by Hiram Hunter, and "Parting of the Ways," in election broadside, "The Social Democratic Press. A Journal Devoted to Municipal Progress," Christchurch, April 25, 1913, E. J. Howard Papers, Local Body Election Scrapbook, Hocken Library, Dunedin.
39. Hiram Hunter, "Labour Representation."
40. See municipal programs of the PLL in NSW, Labour-in-Politics annual meetings in Queensland, and the IPLL and NZLP in New Zealand.
41. James Thorn to J. T. Paul, 3/10/10, J. T. Paul Papers, Hocken Library, Dunedin, New Zealand.
42. J. A. McCullough discusses the efforts to bring labor-leaning candidates more closely into the "Labour Party" fold in a series of letters to Ramsey MacDonald, September 7, 1910; to T. E. Taylor, November 7, 1910; and to George Davis, November 7, 1910, in J. A. McCullough Papers, Outward Correspondence, Canterbury Museum, Christchurch.
43. The *Barrier Truth*, March 16, 1900, 2, quoted the local newspaper, the *Bulletin*, attributing the municipal victory of 1900 as due at least in part to Ben Tillett. See also, Brian Kennedy, *Silver, Sin, and Sixpenny Ale: A Social History of*

Broken Hill, 1883–1921 (Melbourne: Melbourne University Press, 1978), 84.

44. George Dale, *The Industrial History of Broken Hill* (Melbourne, Australia: Fraser and Jenkinson, 1918); Brian Kennedy, *Silver, Sin, and Sixpenny Ale*; and Bradon Ellem and John Shields, "Making the 'Gibralter of Unionism': Union Organising and Peak Union Agency in Broken Hill, 1886–1930," *Labour History* 83 (2002): 65–87.
45. "Mayors and Councillors of Broken Hill," compiled by Janette Mackenzie (looseleaf notebook, 2001); "Nominee List for the Broken Hill Council Elections, 1888–2004 (with occupations), compiled by Brian Tonkin, 2004, Broken Hill Library.
46. Broken Hill City Council minutes, February 27–April 9, 1896; *Barrier Truth*, February 18, 1899.
47. *Tocsin*, July 26, 1900; Barrier *Truth*, February 17 and 24, 1900.
48. *Tocsin*, July 26, 1900.
49. Dale, *The Industrial History of Broken Hill*, 260–61.
50. Ibid., 260.
51. Kennedy, *Silver, Sin and Sixpenny Ale*, 93.
52. See, for instance, *Barrier Truth*, January 21, March 11, and December 30, 1899; January 13 and 27, 1900.
53. *Barrier Truth*, February 18, 1899.
54. Naomi Reid, "Brocklehurst, Frederick (1866–1926)," *Dictionary of Labour Biography*, vol. 6, ed. John Saville, Joyce Bellamy (London: Palgrave Macmillan, 1982), 39–42; and "Mr. Councillor Frederick Brocklehurst, B.A.," *Manchester Faces and Places*, v. 16 (Manchester: Woodhead, 1905), 209–14.
55. "Directory of I.L.P. Members on Public Bodies," *Minutes of the Fifth Annual Conference of the I.L.P.*, London, April 19–20, 1897, 33–39; see also David Howell, *British Workers and the Independent Labour Party, 1888–1906* (Manchester, England: Manchester University Press, 1983), 337, 463.
56. *Manchester Times*, May 5, 1893. Comparable conflicts over the use of public space are found in many cities.
57. Naomi Reid, "Boggart Hole Clough and Free Speech," *Dictionary of Labour Biography*, vol. 6, 42–43; also Parks and Cemeteries Committee, Minutes, City of Manchester, v. 16, July 3, 1896, 152–3.
58. *Clarion*, June 20, 1896, quoted in Reid, "Boggart Hole Clough and Free Speech," 43.
59. Naomi Reid, "Boggart Hole Clough and Free Speech," 44–45.
60. Minutes, Council of the City of Manchester, July 28, 1896, 754–57.
61. Ibid., 757, 760.
62. Naomi Reid, "Boggart Hole Clough and Free Speech," 45; also *Northern Echo* (Darlington), November 9, 1897.
63. Tom Regan (Alderman), compiler, "The Labour Group: A Chronological & Alphabetical Record of the Labour Group on the Manchester City Council,

1894–1966" (1967), Local Studies and Archives, Manchester Public Library.
64. "Mr. Councillor Frederick Brocklehurst, B.A.," *Manchester Faces and Places*, 213.
65. Manchester City Council Minutes, vol. 1894–95, May 22, 1895, 719; October 2, 1895, 1384; vol. 1895–96, July 28, 1896, 741–73; September 9, 1896, 1384; vol. 1896–97, January 6, 1897, 243–44; April 7, 1897; vol. 1897–98, vol. 2, August 3, 1898, 1665; October 5, 1898, 1918–20; vol. 1898–99, February 1, 1899; February 15, 1899, 350, 353–54; April 26, 1899, 515–16; June 21, 1899, 771–73; vol. 1899–1900, November 9, 1899, 17–18; December 16, 1899, 141–42; May 2, 1900, 492–93; vol. 1900–1901, April 3, 1901.
66. *Manchester Courier and Lancashire General Advertiser*, November 4, 1897; Manchester School Board, Minutes, v. 52, March 21, 1898, 257–8, v. 53, May 23, 1898, v. 54, November 28, 1898, 393–4, v. 55, December 19, 1898, 130, 135.
67. Other case studies that highlight labor's municipal efforts include Keith Laybourn and David James, eds., *"The Rising Sun of Socialism": The Independent Labour Party in the Textile District of the West Riding of Yorkshire between 1890 and 1914* (Bradford, England: West Yorkshire Archives Service, 1991); Sam Davies, *Liverpool Labour: Social and Political Influences on the Development of the Labour Party in Liverpool, 1900–30* (Keele, England: Keele University Press, 1996); Leon Fink, "The Forward March of Labour Started: Building a Politicized Class Culture in West Ham, 1898–1900," in *Protest and Survival: The Historical Experience: Essays for E. P. Thompson*, ed. John Rule and Robert Malcolmson, 279–321 (London: Merlin Press, 1993).
68. Naomi Reid, "Maben, William (1849–1901)," *Dictionary of Labour Biography*, vol. 6, 179–81.
69. *Justice*, January 12, 1901, quoted in Naomi Reid, "Maben, William (1849–1901)," 80–81.
70. Shelton Stromquist, "The Crucible of Class: Cleveland Politics and the Origins of Municipal Reform in the Progressive Era," *Journal of Urban History* 23, no. 2 (1997): 192–220; Peter Witt, *Cleveland before St. Peter, a Handful of Hot Stuff* (Cleveland, OH: C. Lezius, 1899); Louis F. Post, "Notes for a biography of Peter Witt," Peter Witt Papers, Western Reserve Historical Society, Cleveland, OH.
71. Tom Johnson, *My Story* (1911; reprint, New York: AMS, 1970), 258.
72. William Riordan, *Plunkitt of Tammany Hall* (1905; reprint, New York: E. P. Dutton, 1962), 17.
73. See Shelton Stromquist, *Reinventing "the People": The Progressive Movement, the Class Problem, and the Origins of Modern Liberalism* (Urbana-Champaign: University of Illinois Press, 2006), 76–82, on Cleveland, Milwaukee, and Hearst's New York campaign.
74. Werner Sombart, *Why Is There No Socialism in the United States?* Translation of *Warum gibt es in den Vereinigten Staaten keinen Sozialismus?* (1906; translated and reprinted, New York: Macmillan, 1976); Robin Archer, *Why Is There No Labor Party in the United States?* (Princeton, NJ: Princeton University Press,

2007); Eric Foner, "Why Is There No Socialism in the United States?" *History Workshop* 17, no. 1 (1984): 57–80.

75. My own perspective on this question focuses attention on constitutional and political-structural factors, as well as the related power of property-owning and employing classes to break the back of sustainable mass trade union organizing before the 1930s.

76. Melvin Holli, *Reform in Detroit: Hazen S. Pingree and Urban Politics* (New York: Oxford University Press, 1969), 169; also Hoyt L. Warner, *Progressivism in Ohio, 1897–1917* (Columbus: Ohio State University Press for the Ohio Historical Society, 1964).

77. Robert E. Bionaz, "Streetcar City: Popular Politics and the Shaping of Urban Progressivism in Cleveland, 1880–1910" (doctoral dissertation, University of Iowa, 2002); Melvin Holli, *Reform in Detroit*, 188–95; and Tom Johnson, *My Story*, 198–205.

78. Socialist municipal administrations in literally hundreds of U.S. cities followed essentially congruent paths to those discussed here. See Richard W. Judd, *Socialist Cities: Municipal Politics and the Grass Roots of American Socialism* (Albany: State University of New York Press, 1989), 69–94, especially 73–74; Donald Critchlow, *Socialism in the Heartland: The Midwestern Experience, 1900–1925* (Notre Dame, IN: University of Notre Dame Press, 1986).

17 A MIGRATING REVOLUTION

MEXICAN POLITICAL ORGANIZERS AND
THEIR REJECTION OF AMERICAN
ASSIMILATION, 1920–1940

John H. Flores

This chapter examines immigrant political culture, the phenomenon of transnational social movements, and the formation of binational identities through a study of a Midwestern Mexican immigrant community during the early to mid-twentieth century. It reveals the relationship between international and local politics by reconstructing the history of a segment of the Mexican population of Chicago, which I term the "revolutionary generation." These political activists, whose ranks included men and women, white-collar workers, blue-collar laborers, and rural folk, formed liberal, conservative, and radical associations in Chicago. As diverse and divisive as these immigrants were, I group them together as a political generation because their collective ideology was shaped by their experience and understanding of the Mexican Revolution (1910–1920). After migrating to Chicago, they began adapting their particular understanding of revolutionary politics to the city with the aim of shaping the identities and influencing the political outlooks of Mexicans residing within the United States. While the various revolutionary factions eventually made their way to Chicago, this chapter focuses on the liberal and radical wings of this political generation and compares them as they evolved outside the borders of the Mexican nation-state.[1]

During the early 1920s, Mexican liberals migrated to Chicago. They possessed some formal education and subscribed to a reformist ideology that emerged in Mexico during the revolution. Once in Chicago, liberals carried out a program of middle-class uplift that celebrated Mexican biracial identity and history, while emphasizing ethnic solidarity and the importance of an education. Mexican liberals believed that education could empower migrants and facilitate their upward mobility while allowing them to retain their Mexican citizenship and allegiance to Mexico. Ultimately, the combined forces of the Great Depression and the arrival of the conservative (or traditionalist) faction of the revolutionary generation jointly contributed to the decline of the Mexican liberal movement of Chicago.

By the mid-1930s, the rise of fascism in Europe, the international Communist Party's shift toward a Popular Front strategy, and most important, the ascendancy of President Lazaro Cardenas in Mexico (1934–1940) inspired a few lingering liberals and a growing number of blue-collar workers to embrace radical Cardenista politics, which once again oriented Mexican Chicago toward Mexico. Like the liberals before them, Mexican radicals underscored the importance of education but linked their educational endeavors to a leftist political project that stressed antifascism, anti-imperialism, international labor solidarity, and the economic value in participating in the Chicago labor movement. Although liberals and radicals subscribed to different political visions, they shared an intense commitment to the Mexican state, which was made possible by the heterogeneity of revolutionary politics and the revolving-door style of Mexican governmental rule in the period before the entrenchment of the Institutional Revolutionary Party. Moreover, liberals and radicals knew that Mexico did not recognize dual citizenship. Consequently, between 1920 and 1940, they carried out distinct political projects in Chicago but collectively encouraged migrants to reject U.S. citizenship and political assimilation.

On January 12, 1925, a liberal journalist named Julian Xavier Mondragon, a businessman named F. Patron Miranda, and five other Mexicans gathered together in a small office at 20 East Jackson Street. On this day, the office was "filled with great stir and activity" as they all worked feverishly "taking clippings" from "great stacks of '*El Universal Ilustrado*'" and other imported Mexican newspapers. Working together, Mondragon and his cohort were planning the unveiling of *Mexico*, the first Spanish-language newspaper in Chicago that would represent the specific interests of Mexican sojourners. At this point in time, Chicago's Spanish-language press typically fell into three categories: religious newsprints published by a handful of Protestant churches, apolitical papers printed by high school Spanish-language departments, and newspapers written by self-identified "Hispanic Americans" that reflected a "Pan-American" ideology that called for the unification of Latin Americans.[2] Mondragon and Miranda were active in Pan-American circles, but they were first and foremost Mexican nationalists who wanted to publish a paper devoted to Mexican-oriented topics. Before immigrating to the United States, Mondragon had written for *El Universal Ilustrado* in Mexico City, and after arriving in Chicago, he secured employment at the *Tribune*. Miranda, meanwhile, appears to have invested in a tailoring business and was now turning toward a career in advertising. Mondragon and Miranda believed that Chicago was ripe for a Mexican-centric paper. The city's Mexican population was growing, and a class of educated migrants had arrived who wished to create a liberal intellectual culture in Chicago.³

During the 1920s, Chicago industries' desire for immigrant labor contributed to a substantial increase in new immigrants. Between 1900 and 1930, the city's Mexican population soared from about 200 persons to more than 20,000. These migrants were among the million or more Mexicans who were uprooted by the revolution and immigrated to the United States between 1900 and 1930. Although most Mexicans gravitated toward Texas and other Southwestern states, between the start of World War I and the mid-1920s, Midwestern labor agencies began to recruit Mexican laborers to fill agricultural and industrial job openings created by World War I production demands and later by the restrictive Immigration Acts of 1921 and 1924. Railroad companies in Chicago began to hire significant numbers of Mexicans in 1916. By 1928, sixteen Chicago labor agencies had recruited some 18,000 Mexican laborers. Labor agencies often enlisted Mexicans to work in Midwestern agriculture, but after arriving in Chicago, many migrants went to work for industrial and manufacturing companies who provided immediate jobs and higher wages. By the late 1920s, Mexicans represented about 40 percent of the maintenance-of-way railroad workforce of the city, 12 percent of steel and metal employees, 5 percent of the meatpacking labor force, and about 15 percent of all cement, rug manufacturing, and fruit-packing laborers.⁴

After securing employment, migrants began to rent property throughout Chicago. As a whole, Mexicans were not bound by any employer, neighborhood, or parish. In fact, their dispersion led them into residential contact with African Americans, white ethnics, and other Mexicans whose regional origins and educational attainment varied considerably. By the mid-1930s, about 50 to 60 percent of the Mexican population of Chicago, some 10,000 to 15,000 migrants, lived in three neighborhoods: the West Side, South Chicago, and the Back of the Yards. The other 40 to 50 percent of Mexican Chicago resided throughout the rest of the city. Around 38 percent of Mexicans emigrated from northern Mexico, and another 60 percent arrived from west-central Mexico. The west-central population included migrants from small towns and an estimated 6 to 7 percent from Mexico City. Living and working side by side, Mexicans from diverse regional and educational backgrounds exposed each other to their particular region's political tradition. In the Chicago context, urban and learned migrants from Mexico City, such as Julian Xavier Mondragon, often befriended and educated those around them. While there appear to have been fewer Mexican women than men in Chicago during the 1920s, Mexican women became vital leaders within Chicago's Mexican liberal movement, which began in Mexico during the revolution.⁵

The Mexican Revolution was driven by military generals and the ideological beliefs of liberal intellectuals. In response to President Porfirio Diaz's thirty-year dictatorship (the Porfiriato), a growing faction of liberal scholars began demanding social reforms. As well-educated individuals who believed in the power of ideas, Mexican liberals emphasized public education as the key that could reshape society. Through newspapers and monographs, liberals condemned the Porfiriato and championed parliamentary democracy, freedom of speech, freedom of the press, and an understanding of freedom of worship that was directly tied to their notion of education. Although the sentiment varied, most liberals were anticlerical and believed that Mexico's meager educational system was restrained by an antiquated structure controlled by the Catholic Church. By secularizing Mexican society, liberals believed they could create a more learned, democratic, and prosperous Mexico. Consequently, liberals advocated the expansion of a state-supported, secular education system that would uplift the general population while spreading the gospel of liberalism.

This liberal-reformist movement blossomed after Diaz relinquished power and fled to Europe in 1911. Diaz's self-exile emboldened liberals, who quickly began to experiment with public education projects. After Diaz abdicated, a young Jose Vasconcelos and other liberal academics created the *Ateneo de la Juventud*. *Ateneo* intellectuals advocated the philosophies of Immanuel Kant, Arthur Schopenhauer, and Henri Bergson, whom they drew on to critique the positivist philosophy of the Diaz administration. In 1912, Vasconcelos helped form the People's University, which took the ideas of the *Ateneo* to the masses through cost-free education courses and public lectures delivered near labor shops in urban areas. After obtaining the presidency in 1920, Alvaro Obregon appointed Vasconcelos to be secretary of education. Between 1920 and 1924, Vasconcelos advanced the liberal-reformist agenda by creating more than a thousand rural schools, building nearly 2,000 public libraries, and printing and distributing thousands of textbooks that advanced a liberal interpretation of the Mexican Revolution.[6]

The revolution unleashed a reformist movement that filtered down to all segments of Mexican society, including Mexico's massive number of emigrants. The case of Tomas Echeverria illustrates this point. While living in Mexico, Echeverria worked as a mason. He had been a devout Catholic and at one point even aspired to the priesthood. During the revolution, he began to read about liberalism and soon became skeptical of organized religion. Although he possessed what a contemporary described as a "grammar school" education, Echeverria read Nietzsche and Schopenhauer, who was then hailed by the Mexican liberal intelligentsia. Grappling with the "agony of having all of his past ideas torn and shaken," Echeverria found purpose in the philosophy of the American pragmatist William James. After migrating to Chicago, Echeverria started collecting monographs and formed a personal library of more than a hundred texts. Speaking about Protestants in Chicago who had tried to court him, Echeverria said:

I have never been especially attracted by the Protestant Church. Its teaching does not agree with what I learned in physiology and natural science. I would like to find some group which was thoroughly modern to which I could belong, some philosophy of life which I could follow, something which would unify my thinking.

Indeed, worldly Mexican migrants such as Echeverria who had received an unorthodox education during the revolutionary era were having trouble finding a place for themselves in the modern American city of Chicago. After exploring the "liberal American Churches in Hyde Park," Echeverria came to the conclusion that his background as a Mexican and his work as a laborer set him apart from the Hyde Park congregations, which he identified as consisting of "business and professional people."[7] Echeverria was by no means an anomaly. During the 1920s, Mexican professionals and laborers who had migrated to the city shared Echeverria's sense of estrangement. As these migrants came into contact with each other, they addressed their alienation by transplanting a Mexican liberal culture to Chicago through the creation of Spanish-language newspapers and Mexican associations.

On January 18, 1925, Mondragon, Miranda, and their colleagues inaugurated *Mexico: The Paper of the Homeland*. They were able to do so by drawing on Miranda's finances and contacts as a businessman, Mondragon's skills as a journalist, and the relationships they had cultivated among a growing body of liberal organizations. For about a year and a half, Mondragon managed *Mexico* while Miranda worked as an editor. Although the paper changed hands between 1926 and 1930, Mondragon remained active in the Mexican community. Through *Mexico*, Mondragon and Miranda set a historical precedent. They had created a paper aimed primarily at the Mexican population of Chicago. Under Mondragon's leadership, *Mexico* endorsed Mexican liberal associations, encouraged migrants to seek out English- and Spanish-language instruction, connected migrants to the Mexican Consulate, and discouraged Mexicans from becoming U.S. citizens.[8]

During the early 1920s, Mexican liberals began forming organizations by utilizing the institutional resources of the Chicago settlement houses. By the late 1920s, the existing evidence suggests that migrants who arrived in Chicago with more capital created associations that were independent of the settlements. In South Chicago, for instance, liberals did not establish all of their organizations through the generally influential Byrd Memorial Community Center. In this neighborhood, formally educated Mexicans arrived with capital and united with blue-collar migrants who secured well-paid and stable employment in local steel mills. This coalition possessed the finances and stability to create Mexican-controlled autonomous associations. The three most active groups in South Chicago were Lux en Umbra, a Masonic lodge; the Mexican Blue Cross, a social welfare group led by Mexican women; and the Society of Independent Mexican Laborers, a blue-collar mutual aid organization. Each subscribed to a liberal ideology that differed along an axis of elitism to reformism. While all three groups were endorsed by *Mexico*, their constituencies and activities suggest that blue-collar laborers and reform-minded liberals shifted the liberal community away from an elitist agenda and toward a more inclusive plan that emphasized social reform.[9]

In South Chicago, Mexican Masons initially sought to create a patriotic but exclusive intellectual coalition. However, the needs of the largely blue-collar Mexican population of the city sparked debates between liberal elitists and reformers who subscribed to a more inclusive vision of community. In October 1928, a group of migrants in South Chicago contacted the Valley of Mexico Lodge of Mexico City and founded a Masonic lodge named Lux in Umbra No. 50 as a division of the Rito Nacional Mexicano. Under the direction of Venerable Master Luis Alvarez Castillo, Lux began recruiting "honorable" Mexicans who worked as professionals or owned small businesses. Seeking legitimacy and community prestige, Lux courted the Mexican Consul, General Carlos Palacios Roji, who soon supported the lodge's initiatives. Drawing on their own finances, Masons held exclusive events on their private property, which included several restaurants, such as La Gardenia in South Chicago and the South American on the West Side, owned by Brother Luis Flores. By November 1929, Lux constructed a temple, where it held joint events with U.S. Masonic lodges. *Mexico*, meanwhile, publicized its festivities as examples of glorious tributes to Mexican patriotism.[10]

In January 1929, Lux created a winter solstice celebration that endorsed postrevolutionary Mexican nationalism, an ideology advocated by liberals in Mexico who sought to unify a politically and ethnically heterogeneous population by celebrating Mexico's multiracial and culturally liberal heritage. During the solstice ceremony, Brother Roman H. Fortoso recited a poem by the journalist Amado Ruiz de Nervo, which paid tribute to President Benito Juarez, or the "Indian of Guelatao," as the Chicago liberal press called him. "Sir," read Fortoso, "let me tell you about the glory of your race, the glory of the bronze men, whose Indian clubs have been cut on so many helmets and shields, Oh the courage . . . Oh Eagle Knights!" Brother Fortoso selected Nervo's poem because it paid tribute to President Juarez, the culturally liberal Zapotec indigene who secured the Mexican presidency in 1858 and drove the French invading nation-state out of Mexico. President Juarez had become the icon of Mexican liberalism during the 1920s. He, like so many Mexicans, was "bronze"-skinned, yet through education, he rose in prominence, obtained the presidency, successfully defeated a European power, and then directed Mexican society down a liberal path of secularization and education. Liberals in Chicago, like liberals in Mexico, rejected the racially essentialist denigration of the Mexican indigene and chose to underscore the adaptability of liberal ideology. Rather than emphasize a vision of whiteness, Fortoso's reading of Nervo reminded Mexicans in Chicago of their brownness, which liberals conflated with a reading of Mexican indigenous history that framed indigenes as poets, intellectuals, and creators of civilizations. "My name was Netzahualcoyotl and I was the [Poet] King of Texcoco," bellowed Fortoso, "within the mist of paganism ... [I] built a pyramid, and on it, always during the brilliance of the first star and to the son of Huehuetl, I raised my chant." Lux celebrated a proud but selective vision of Mexican history.[11]

As Brother Fortoso and other Masons gathered to recite nationalist poetry, migrants who read about Lux's festivities began submitting letters to *Mexico* critiquing liberal associations that "led to nothing." Educated Mexican women responded to these criticisms by forming the first liberal-reform organization in Chicago, the Mexican Blue Cross. The Blue Cross began in Texas as a social welfare organization that provided migrants with health and child care assistance. *Mexico* and other Spanish-language newspapers picked up on the activities of the Texan Blue Cross and began praising their work. These articles ran in conjunction with letters that critiqued elitist liberal organizations. In response, Milla Dominguez, a professional singer from Mexico City who was married to the vice consul of Chicago, joined a coalition of Mexican women and inaugurated the West Side Blue Cross in 1929. Although Dominguez claimed to privilege domesticity over public activism, in practice, she devoted much of her time to fund-raising and networking on behalf of the Blue Cross. As a former entertainer, Dominguez initially served as the Blue Cross's director of festivities. By 1931, she was elected to the presidency of the South Chicago Blue Cross Executive Board. Early on, Dominguez drew on her middle-class contacts and broadened the Blue Cross's social network by partnering with several Mexican doctors, such as S. G. Meixueiro, Eliud Garcia Trevino, and Oscar G. Carrera, who was a vocal advocate of working-class migrants. In April 1930, a subbrigade of the Blue Cross was created in South Chicago. There, Dominguez, several Mexican doctors, and other West Side Blue Crossers elected an entire board of Mexican women to lead this subbrigade. These women developed an outstanding reputation in South Chicago. While some men, such as Dr. Carrera, assisted the Blue Cross, the organization was led by Mexican women who devoted themselves to migrants who had little access to social welfare services.[12]

Despite its egalitarian intentions and middle-class backing, the Blue Cross lacked the finances to carry out large-scale activities. Instead, Blue Crossers and other women's associations, such as the Sociedad Femenil Mexicana, collected clothing for poor families, bought Christmas presents for orphans, visited the elderly in hospitals, started a support network for widows, and through their connections to Mexican doctors, created an educational network that addressed intimate matters, such as women's "sexual hygiene" practices. To raise revenue for these activities, Blue Crossers turned to the ideology of Mexican nationalism, a decision that was inspired by blue-collar workers. Beginning in April 1930, *Mexico* received letters signed by Mexican laborers who stressed that "true patriot[s]" and "real [Mexican] citizen[s]" would support the Blue Cross and "our countrymen who are dispossessed." Mexican workers ultimately recommended that the Blue Cross create nationalist fund-raisers, which would build community support by commemorating "the struggle and deeds of our Mexican heroes."[13]

At this point in time, liberal associations had held exclusive nationalist affairs that were typically closed to the public. Few liberal organizations had yet to create inclusive nationalist events that sought to court broad-scale community participation. Based on the recommendations of Mexican workers, the Blue Cross decided to build community support by blending revenue-raising with nationalism. On May 5, 1930, the Blue Cross held two Cinco de Mayo festivals that "commemorate[d] the anniversary of the glorious Puebla expedition" that defeated French colonial troops. As a result of their organizational contacts and their emphasis on Mexican nationalism, more than four hundred Mexicans attended the Blue Cross festival at Ashland Auditorium while another four hundred migrants participated in a parallel event at Community Hall. Throwing his support behind these nationalist celebrations, Chicago's Mexican Consul, Rafael Aveleyra, appeared at both events. On the West Side, Dr. Trevino delivered a speech "prais[ing the Mexican] General Ignacio Zaragoza, and other heroes" who fought against French domination, while Consul Aveleyra delivered a personal lecture on Mexican history. *Mexico* gleefully bolstered the nationalist overtones of the celebrations, citing that migrants had "turned out in mass to do homage to the memory of our heroes, and to show the interest which we still have in the far away land of the Mother country."[14]

Blue-collar migrants were moved by the Blue Cross's dedication to the broader community and soon began forming coalitions with white-collar liberals. During the early 1930s, blue-collar groups, such as the Independent Mexican Laborers and Campamento Emilio Carranza of the Woodmen of the World, were invited to participate in Blue Cross activities. After attending the Blue Cross's Cinco de Mayo celebration in 1930, Jose R. Vega, the president of the Independent Laborers, wrote a passionate letter to *Mexico* in admiration of the women of the Blue Cross: "These women have made themselves the idols of men. Each one of the members of this benevolent institution will encounter a supporting hand and heart, eager to help them glorify the dignity of the Mexican woman through their cultural and social work. I wish to stress the fact that the women of this worthy organization have the backing of the Mexican workers." Mexican women were incredibly active in Chicago during the 1920s, and Mexican workers who participated in the liberal-reform movement recognized and appreciated their labor. By September 1931, the Independent Laborers and Campamento Carranza joined Consul Rafael Aveleyra, Dr. Eliud Garcia Trevino, and several reform groups in a citywide campaign against alcoholism.[15]

As liberals worked with blue-collar migrants, some organizers began to focus solely on the issue of education. From the liberal's perspective, a poor education placed migrants at an economic disadvantage in Chicago and contributed to their sense of alienation, which might lead to U.S. naturalization. Jesus Mora, a frequent contributor to *Mexico*, argued that migrants were unaware of "the wonderful traditions of our [Mexican] race." Their poor formal education, Mora insisted, led migrants to "feel ashamed of their origin[s] and deny their country either by changing their citizenship or by making up their mind not to come back [to Mexico]." Mora and other liberals believed that education and patriotism went hand in hand. One of *Mexico*'s first prints lashed out against "[Mexicans] Who Deny Their Country." This editorial declared that "the true Mexican" was the "dark skin[ned]" and "herculean" "workman [who sent] a check to his mother, to his wife or to his children," who "proclaim[ed] his nationality once and a thousand times . . . saying very proudly to everyone THAT HE WAS BORN IN MEXICO, that that is his country and that he would give everything for his country, including his life." Unlike the "true Mexican," the "renegade" denied his nationality "no matter how dark-skinned he [was]" and would even try "passing themselves off as Spanish." Indeed, as Mexican liberals consistently rebuffed U.S. assimilation, they concurrently rejected an American ideology of whiteness and opted to embrace a more inclusive Mexican nationalism and its emphasis on the biraciality of the Mexican people.[16]

Over time, Mora and *Mexico*'s publishers had come to argue that Mexicans considered adopting U.S. citizenship and even passing as Spaniards because of U.S. racial and national chauvinism. By Mora's reasoning, U.S. racism did not discourage Mexicans from taking out citizenship papers. On the contrary, racism contributed to migrants' sense of alienation and encouraged them to consider U.S. assimilation through naturalization. "[T]he sons of 'Uncle Sam'" express an "air of superiority . . . toward the Mexicans," asserted Mora. "They believe that we are still uncivilized beings," they "reproach us for our illiteracy," and "because their color is white, they classify us as 'colored people.'" Due to migrants' poor education and their predominantly nonwhite skin color, contended Mora, Mexicans were looked down upon, which led some to deny their national origins. Mondragon believed that migrants' low national self-esteem was a consequence of the period before "[Francisco I.] Madero's [Mexican] Revolution," when Mexicans "were kept in the most profound ignorance and no opportunities for education were given [to] them." Mondragon agreed with Mora; without education, Mexicans would remain unpatriotic and unable to intellectually defend themselves against U.S. racial and national elitism. Mondragon and Mora therefore never fixated on the limits of essentialist notions of race. Instead, they advocated that education could be used as a vehicle to gain material advances and personal self-respect within Chicago.[17]

Between the mid-1920s and the mid-1930s, Mexican liberals encouraged migrants to take advantage of educational opportunities in Chicago, particularly English- and Spanish-language instruction. Well aware of the market advantages to learning the English language, white-collar and blue-collar Mexicans enrolled in English courses Chicago officials created to help assimilate the city's foreign-born population. Between 1926 and 1927, more than 637 Mexicans enrolled in the Chicago Board of Education's night school English-language courses, and another 845 registered between 1927 and 1928. Settlement house workers jubilantly claimed that Mexicans were one of the few immigrant groups whose participation nearly matched their population size within Chicago. In 1920, Mexicans represented about 2 percent of the Chicago population, and they constituted 1.8 percent of the 47,718 immigrants who enrolled in the board's classes. Settlement house workers and city officials cited these figures as proof that Mexicans wanted to assimilate. Following in the footsteps of the board, Hull House established an English course specifically for Mexicans in 1927 and enrolled more than 100 migrants. Mexican women attended English-language classes at Hull House and represented about a third of the students attending an English class at Henry Booth House. While social workers and city officials viewed migrants' aspiration to learn the English language as an indicator of their desire to become U.S. citizens, migrants consistently refused to relinquish their Mexican citizenship. A report by the Immigrants' Protective League suggested that only two Mexicans opted to naturalize in the Chicago region in 1926, a mere five in 1927, and a total of fifteen in 1928 when the Mexican population of the city stood as high as perhaps 20,000 persons.[18]

Mexico and other Spanish-language papers encouraged Mexicans to learn the English language, but they also urged migrants to reject U.S. citizenship and to safeguard the Spanish language. In Mondragon's words, the Spanish language needed to be sustained for the sake of "our helpless [Mexican] children who ... speak the English language much better than their own beautiful Spanish." Believing that Mexican children would lose touch with Mexico if they lost the Spanish language, Mondragon advocated creating educational courses in the Spanish "mother tongue" for Mexican children and adults. Consequently, beneath the radar of the Board of Education and the settlements, Mondragon and other liberals carried out their own educational projects, which included English-language lessons with an additional emphasis on sustaining and improving migrants' Spanish-language skills. In 1924, Mondragon and a colleague started a language course at a local Young Men's Christian Association. In Brighton Park, a Mr. Rodriguez used an empty storefront as a classroom to assist Mexican adults with their English competency while teaching Mexican children the Spanish language. On the Near North Side, a Mr. Herrera used his residence as a classroom and taught a language course to a group of about eight migrants on a weekly basis. On Ashland Avenue, A. Talamentes, a former teacher in Mexico, taught a language class out of his apartment. Throughout Mexican Chicago, liberals carried out an educational program intended to preserve the Spanish language and to build relationships with the broader Mexican population of the United States, which included Mexican protestants.[19]

In Chicago, Mexican liberals began working with Protestants because of local, national, and, most important, foreign developments. Locally, during the mid-1920s, several Protestant denominations in Chicago had started to court what they perceived to be a growing Mexican population. Mondragon and other liberals took advantage of the educational resources that Baptist, Presbyterian, and Methodist churches offered migrants as they attempted to convert them. Mexican liberals in Mexico and in Chicago were critical of the Catholic Church and therefore expressed few qualms about working with Protestants. Nationally, in the 1930s, liberals in Chicago initiated a dialogue with their counterparts in the Southwest, many of whom were Mexican Protestants. In May 1930, *Mexico* published "The Swallows of Becker" by Alberto Rembao, a Methodist minister and liberal intellectual who had developed a scholarly reputation in the Southwest. Rembao had recently started to question the liberal conviction that migrants would eventually return to Mexico. In Mexico, Rembao had worked as an educator in the state of Jalisco. After immigrating to the United States, he found employment as a journalist for *La Prensa* in San Antonio, the largest Mexican-controlled newspaper in the United States. He later wrote for *La Opinion* in Los Angeles and then in 1930 began publishing *La Nueva Democracia* in New York City. As a migrant who had worked in several U.S. cities as a journalist, an educator, and a Methodist minister, Chicago's Spanish-language press treated Rembao as an authority figure on contemporary immigration issues. In his editorial for *Mexico*, Rembao began by declaring that he was "speak[ing] as a Mexican of Mexicans, with the pride of my blood, race, and citizenship." He explained that migrants were once like "swallows" or birds-of-passage who sought to escape revolutionary turmoil by sojourning to the United States. While it was "painful to say the truth," Rembao now reasoned that migrants were never going to return to Mexico because they had found work in the United States, they had established large families on this side of the border, and their children were losing the Spanish-language "mother tongue" and were internalizing American cultural values. "The American public schools," bemoaned Rembao, "bombard us at night through our own children who preach to us the doctrines which are taught to them during the day."[20]

Mondragon and other liberals came to terms with Rembao's argument as they personally witnessed the growth of the city's population of Mexican children. During the 1920s, many Mexicans arrived in Chicago without children. As late as 1930, out of a study of 3,616 Mexican households, 1,602 were childless. As the population of Mexican children grew, however, Mondragon came to the conclusion that Mexican children would serve as the pendulums that would swing the community toward or away from Mexico. Building on previous arguments that linked discrimination to migrants' self-esteem, Mondragon held that Mexican children were the victims of the alienating "racial discrimination" that encouraged Mexicans to deny their nationality. Claiming that Mexican children often had to cope with discrimination "in private," Mondragon argued that a Mexican community center could provide a place of refuge for children so that they could escape the "outrages suffered by many of our people." A center could further function as a school building to teach the Spanish language to whole families. Pleading to the Mexican community through *Mexico*, Mondragon implored his readers to support the construction of a center that would allow the community to "occupy a place of honor amongst other foreign colonies in this modern 'Babylon' called Chicago." In the end, Mondragon managed to establish the center through his relationship with Protestant reformers, specifically by working with a Methodist minister of Puerto Rican and Irish descent named Guillermo Baquero O'Neill. At the center, Mondragon started a Spanish-language class for children and adults, he created a Spanish-language library, and he began contacting Mexican artists and intellectuals in Mexico and academics at the University of Chicago and Northwestern University, all in an effort to strengthen the Mexican liberal community.[21]

Although the liberal movement was experiencing a period of growth, international developments would soon derail Mondragon and the liberals' plans to direct the political orientation of Mexican Chicago. Between 1926 and 1929, liberal and Catholic conflicts in Mexico exploded into the bloody Cristero Rebellion, which pushed antiliberal and proclerical Mexican conservatives, or traditionalists, out of Mexico and into the United States. Traditionalists wanted to improve Mexican society, but they were unwilling to abandon the Catholic Church and the Catholic ethic that was said to be a defining characteristic of the Mexican people. In Chicago, traditionalists joined Catholic churches, such as Our Lady of Guadalupe in South Chicago and St. Francis of Assisi on the West Side. On the West Side, traditionalist associations, such as the Mexican Nationalist Union, critiqued liberals for praising anticlerical government officials in Mexico, and they challenged their right to serve as representatives of the Mexican community in Chicago. Then, between 1929 and 1937, the Great Depression devastated Mexican Chicago. More than a third of the Mexican population lost jobs, and while liberals pleaded with migrants "to patronize the stores of our people," the weight of the recession proved too great, and numerous Mexican-owned businesses went bankrupt, reducing the financial and institutional support that upheld the liberal community. Finally, as the Depression became more severe, city, state, and federal authorities began pressuring Mexican nationals to repatriate. Mexican liberals were ambivalent about repatriation. On the one hand, they condemned deporting Mexicans against their will, particularly when the process involved coercion and violence; on the other hand, liberals did not consider themselves "Americans." They worked with Mexican Consul Rafael Aveleyra to assist migrants who wanted to return to Mexico, and they even critiqued the Mexican government for bureaucratically impeding return migration. During the Depression, hundreds of Mexicans worked with the Mexican Consulate of Chicago to return to Mexico as effortlessly as possible. Within this context, Mondragon and other liberals who remained in Chicago witnessed the decline of their movement. As they began to lose their influence in Chicago, they initiated a countercampaign against the traditionalists to save what was left of their community.[22]

Joining the *Liberal* in 1933, Mondragon went on the offensive. When traditionalists leafleted Chicago in favor of the Cristero guerrillas who rebelled against the Mexican government in 1926, the *Liberal* asked them to "go to school... so that they may be able to define the words: Citizenship, Revolution, [and] Right[s] of Man. Because in their utmost inconsistent sheet they exposed their ignorance and clearly show [they are] coward[s and] traitors." Liberals believed that the traditionalists' poor writing, seditious critique of the Mexican government, and devotion to the Catholic Church were all part of a counterrevolution. Through the *Liberal*, Mondragon defended the revolution and the legacy of liberal leaders, such as the "most meritorious statesman of the Americas Licensed Don Benito Juarez," the "Great Indian who knew how to manage one by one the administrators of the [Catholic] convents and other similar centers where the most impudent immorality of the epoch was in force." For Mondragon and other liberals, Juarez's Laws of Reform benefited Mexico by reducing the power of the Catholic Church, widening the division between church and state, and thereby "teach[ing] us [Mexicans] to respect God as God, and Man as a Man." Mondragon was by all accounts a die-hard liberal.[23]

By the 1930s, the Mexican Martyrs, a traditionalist organization operating out of St. Francis, began distributing the *Mexican Ideal* to combat the *Liberal*. The *Liberal* now started referring to the traditionalists as "Associations of Stupid Persons" who wanted to return to the "35 year[s] of [Porfirio] Diaz" when Mexicans were kept "ignoran[t]," "illiterate," and with "no schools." The migrants who wrote for the *Liberal* explained, however, that they were not anti-Catholic; they were patriotic Mexican liberals who as children "kept the picture of Our Lady of Guadalupe together with that of Benito Juarez" over "the head of [their] bed[s]." Yet, this synthesis of liberalism and Catholicism was of little concern to traditionalists. From their perspective, the liberal movement of Mexico and of Chicago possessed an anticlerical, and perhaps elitist, dimension that was at odds with their understanding of Mexican identity and culture. As the Depression wore on, liberals lost their small-business support while the traditionalists, working out of Catholic churches, continued to organize against liberal organizations. Consequently, between 1930 and 1937, the bankruptcy of Mexican small businesses, the repatriation of liberal leaders, and the rise of the traditionalists together contributed to the decline of the Mexican liberal movement of Chicago.[24]

By the late 1930s, a few liberals and an increasing number of blue-collar workers began to regroup within the Mexican Popular Front (Front), a transnational organization tied to CPMEXICO (Partido Comunista Mexicano, CPMEXICO). The Front first emerged in Mexico City as a consequence of pro-labor governmental policies and CPMEXICO's shift toward a Popular Front strategy. The Depression prodded Mexico's postrevolutionary government to carry out a number of broad-scale social reforms. Under President Lazaro Cardenas (1934–1940), the government distributed millions of acres of land to rural folk, passed labor legislation that reinvigorated a national unionization movement, and facilitated the growth of massive worker organizations, such as the Confederation of Mexican Workers, whose membership included hundreds of Marxian militants. Through this corporatist project, the Cardenas administration, like the liberal politicians before them, sought to cultivate a national identity out of the heterogeneous Mexican population, and they, too, believed that education could unify, uplift, and direct the Mexican people. Cardenas, therefore, expanded the power and scope of the Secretariat of Public Education. In his effort to manage the increasingly militant and Marxian state-sanctioned worker organizations, the Cardenas administration endorsed teaching "socialist education." Although the concept of socialist education varied, exponents typically blended the liberal citizenship-rights ideas enshrined in the Mexican Constitution of 1917 with the discourse of Marxism, often encouraging Mexicans to participate in collective but civic action. As Mexican politicians continued to endorse, define, and grapple with the application of socialist education, international conditions led CPMEXICO to shift toward a Popular Front orientation.[25]

In response to the growing threat of European fascism and the directives of the Soviet Comintern's Seventh Congress, in August 1935 CPMEXICO formed the Organizing Committee of the Anti-Imperialist Popular Front (Front) in Mexico City. Over the next six months, the Front aligned itself with labor, agricultural, student, and women's groups to form a broad coalition that could defend Mexico's "independence" from European fascists and Mexicans who sided with U.S. "imperialist capitalism." Assessing the role of the United States in global affairs, the Front drew a distinction between the United States as a nation-state and the United States as an exporter of "imperialist capitalism," which they implied emanated from the financial sector of the U.S. economy. By the Front's logic, to combat fascists and traitorous Mexicans aligned with foreigners, the Front needed to support loyal Mexican businessmen, government officials, and the Cardenas administration, which they identified as patriotic and sympathetic to labor. Moreover, the Front celebrated Cardenas's commitment to socialist education, which Front activists defined "as a progressive system of education" that would be "totally and effectively free education" and would advance the "the anti-imperialist consciousness of the [Mexican] youth."[26]

During the 1920s, the Mexican liberal movement had immigrated to the United States; by the mid-1930s, Mexican radicals were making their way north. In January 1936, Mexicans in Cleveland, Ohio, established a chapter of the Front under the guidance of a delegation from Mexico City. A few weeks later, Nicholas M. Hernandez formed section one of the Chicago Front at the University of Chicago settlement in the Back of the Yards. Not long after, Fidencio Moreno started section three at Hull House on the West Side. In South Chicago, A. Escamilla launched a section at the Byrd Memorial Community Center. Unemployed during the Depression, impoverished Mexicans were once again establishing associations through the Chicago settlement houses. By February 1936, Hernandez joined forces with Henrique Venegas and Jesus Flores, both formally educated individuals. Venegas owned a pool hall and a cigar shop in South Chicago and a restaurant on the West Side. Flores, an immigrant from Mexico City, appears to have obtained a high-level education in Mexico, but his family's origins and his politics were rooted in the working class. By 1937, Mexicans had established five sections of the Front, which were located throughout Chicago.[27]

Unlike the liberals who preceded them, Hernandez, Venegas, and Flores sought to create a radical organization that would primarily court and serve blue-collar workers. In an effort to enlist Mexican laborers while providing them with an opportunity to voice their concerns, Hernandez and his comrades held a massive recruitment meeting at Bowen Hall at Hull House. In South Chicago, A. Escamilla had won over Juan Uribe, who edited the *Struggle*, a Spanish-language paper established before the Depression. Through their use of the *Struggle*, the Front filled Bowen Hall to capacity, forcing some fifty migrants to remain standing during the assembly. While the majority of the attendees were male, Mexican women were also present. Both "professionals" and "laborers" attended the recruitment fair, but "the latter [laborers] outnumbered the former [professionals] by a ratio of at least twenty to one."[28]

During the meeting, blue-collar workers bemoaned the Depression and what they described as a culture crisis. Speakers took turns lamenting that they had left their "cultural advantages" in Mexico and had been unable to "transplant" their way of life to the United States. Hernandez, Venegas, and Flores offered to address the attendees' disaffection through a plan that meshed with the Front's commitment to a "cost free Socialist Education" and the "[elevation of the anti-imperialist consciousness of the] youth." Cheered by the attendees, Front organizers proclaimed they would call upon the Cardenas administration to finance the construction of Spanish-language schools in Chicago aimed at Mexican youth. They reasoned that Mexican adults and children deserved access to Spanish-language libraries and educational courses, and they declared that they would start a scholarship program for "talented young students who may return to Mexico" to be trained in the "arts and professions" so they could become "leaders of their own people both here and in Mexico." Front organizers, reminiscent of liberal activists, understood that the future of Mexican Chicago rested in the hands of youth. Moreover, while they sought to train Mexicans to serve as binational leaders, like the liberals before them, Mexican radicals were extremely nationalistic and, therefore, discouraged migrants from relinquishing their Mexican citizenship.[29]

In the context of the tumultuous 1930s, Mexican political activists had come to believe they were participants in a global struggle against imperialism and fascism, which, if left unchecked, could threaten Mexico's sovereignty. Mexican radicals therefore embraced education as the means by which to transmit their brand of left-wing Mexican culture to Mexicans living in the United States. Unlike the liberals, the Front did not advocate education for the purpose of upward mobility. For the Front, education was the vehicle that would "transplant" a Mexican-origin radical culture to Chicago, a cultural movement that advocated working-class empowerment through education, championed the "patriotic" Cardenas administration, and sought to radicalize migrants by encouraging them to participate in international and local political and labor activities.

A week after the Hull House conference, Section One came together to elect their governing body of officers. Committed to uneducated blue-collar workers, Front organizers applied a developmental pedagogy to their organization. During the election, Venegas was chosen as general secretary; Hernandez, secretary of propaganda; Flores, secretary of education; and a migrant named Jose Pedraza was asked to serve as the secretary of interior. Although Venegas, Hernandez, and Flores possessed strong language skills, many new recruits did not. In the past, liberal associations advocated working with blue-collar groups, but the Front sought to compel laborers to serve as community leaders. Subscribing to a radical ideology that stressed working people's empowerment through education, the Front refused to use formal education as a litmus test for leadership. The case of Jose Pedraza best illustrates this point. During a meeting in March, Pedraza said he planned to resign from his post because of his poor language skills. In broken Spanish, Pedraza explained: "When I see you one at a time, when I see you all together I lose my tongue. Now if it was a matter of ploughing [sic] a field that would suit me better. You can't get bananas from an orange... from apple trees.... Neither can you get fine words from a man who has not gone to school." Moved by his sincerity, Front officers applauded Pedraza and rejected his resignation. Decided by popular vote, the Front appointed a formally educated migrant to aid Pedraza as his "auxiliary secretary" so that Pedraza could continue at his post.[30]

Pedraza's insecurities set off an internal debate within the Front concerning the relationship between education, leadership, and the future of Mexican

Chicago, which profoundly affected Flores, reaffirming the magnitude of the Front's educational mission. Flores reasoned that Front organizers needed to educate blue-collar migrants, but they had to link their educational activities to a "history of their own people," which would prepare them to participate in political and labor activities in Mexico. Flores and other Front activists had come to believe that many Mexicans might be returning to Mexico after all, given the severity of the Depression and the U.S. government's initiative to repatriate and deport Mexicans living in the United States. To strengthen the ties between Chicago and Mexico, Flores reached out to the Secretariat of Public Education (SEP) in Mexico City. Through contacts at the SEP, Flores began receiving batches of Spanish-language textbooks and mimeographed materials. With this collection, he started a cost-free Spanish-language library that included texts on politics, economics, and the labor movement in Mexico. Although Flores would eventually self-repatriate, during his tenure as a Front officer, Section One started a Spanish-language library, Spanish-language courses for children and adults, a public debate team, and a lecture series that drew in international guest speakers, all in an effort to bridge the divide between Mexican Chicago and Mexico under Cardenas.[31]

Under Flores's guidance, the Front started a Spanish-language class for children. Possessing almost no finances and dealing with working-class people with families, Flores had to develop an innovative educational program. In the end, he was able to create the children's course by drawing on the educational skills of Mexican women, utilizing the settlement's cost-free facilities, and adhering to a family-convenient class schedule. While Front organizers met for their weekly meeting in the living room of the University of Chicago settlement, Mexican children gathered in the game room to be taught by a Mrs. Garcia and her assistant, both of whom were associated with the Front. The success of the children's class led the five sections to begin a citywide fund-raising campaign to create a summer school project that would include courses in the Spanish language, Mexican history, and geography.[32]

By March 1936, the Front was enrolling Mexican children in its Spanish-language course, but the Spanish class for adults had yet to come to fruition. Although the Front could draw on its own members to teach basic Spanish skills, they wanted a professional to teach adults. Initially turning to the Mexican Consulate for assistance, they encountered immediate opposition from Consul Eugenio Pesqueira. Mexican consuls had a significant degree of autonomy in Chicago and chose to assist, hinder, or ignore Mexican migrants based on personal preferences that were influenced by Mexico's political climate. While Consul Aveleyra had endorsed Chicago's liberal associations, Consul Pesqueira detested the radical Front, and he repeatedly sidestepped their invitations to meetings, events, and cooperative proposals and even publicly rejected its self-proclaimed connection to the Cardenas government, stating the Front "had nothing to do with the Mexican government" and was by and large a "selfish group." In May 1936, Pesqueira returned to Mexico and was replaced by Consul Antonio Schmidt and Vice-Consul Manuel Aguilar, who wholeheartedly embraced the Front and a liberal association that was still active in Chicago. With the changing of the guard, Section One gained the support of a consular worker named Dr. Ramon Alcazar who had obtained a high-level education in the state of Guadalajara, Mexico. After he was approached by the Front, Dr. Alcazar agreed to teach a cost-free course that would include Spanish-language instruction in addition to topics in Mexican history, civics, and geography.[33]

Front activists had labored for months to start their Spanish-language courses, and they were doing so for a radical political purpose. Beginning in March 1936, the Front sponsored a lecture series that included CPMEXICO partisans. In April, the Front invited Angelica Arenal to the University of Chicago settlement. At the time, Arenal worked as a journalist for *El National* in Mexico City but was living in New York City with her husband, David Alfaro Siqueiros, the renowned muralist and CPMEXICO activist. Arenal had just participated in the leftist International Conference for Writers in New York and was about to fly to Spain to write a series of articles on the Spanish Civil War. Speaking to the Chicago Front, Arenal delivered a "zealous" speech about the "the plans being unfolded by El Frente Popular in Mexico in favor of the Mexican workers." She provided Mexicans in Chicago with a firsthand account of "the progress made in education in Mexico" and concluded by offering Mexican workers in Chicago a "fraternal salutation" from their kin, the "workers of Mexico." In solidarity, the Chicago Front pulled together a monetary collection, which they entrusted to Arenal to deliver to the Mexico City Front. As a radical journalist and CPMEXICO fellow traveler, Arenal's presence in Chicago spoke to the Front's determination to import radical Mexican-origin politics to the city, while keeping Mexicans in touch with the political currents of the homeland.[34]

Between April 1936 and March 1937, things began to move quickly, as the Front made contact with numerous leftist associations in Chicago. Just as liberals were willing to work in Pan-American circles during the 1920s, Mexican radicals were inclined to join radical organizations, but they did so as committed Mexican citizens. The Chicago multiracial and multiethnic milieu led Mexican radicals to work with leftists of various national backgrounds. In June 1936, the Chicago Front invited a labor organizer from Cuba to the settlement. There, he delivered a lecture about U.S. companies' "exploitation" of Cuban workers, which was "enthusiastically received" by the Front. In August, the five sections began to hold meetings to discuss the Spanish Civil War, during which they emphasized the "economic liberation of the Spanish speaking peoples" and specifically the "working classes in Spain." Following these meetings, Nicolas Hernandez, the Front's secretary of propaganda, delivered a speech titled "Significance of the Frente Popular throughout the Whole World!" in which he tied the fate of the

Spanish Civil War to the future of the Mexican working class. Hernandez argued that the "monied classes have been constantly oppressing the laboring class and for that reason the latter has been uniting throughout the world." If the Republicans were to lose the civil war, Hernandez reasoned, their loss might embolden the Mexican "capitalist class" to initiate a civil war against Mexico's "working class." Front organizers now moved to mobilize Mexicans on behalf of the Spanish Loyalists living in Chicago. The Mexican Front soon met with the Spanish Popular Front and worked with them to facilitate the arrival of Spanish delegates, author Isabel de Palencia, the theologian Reverend Luis Sarasola, and Marcelino Domingo of the Republican Left Party, coming to the Midwest to raise funds for the Republican cause.[35]

While working with Spanish radicals, the Mexican Front began connecting Mexican blue-collar workers in Chicago with the labor movement in Mexico. In May 1936, Flores's brother went on strike in Mexico City. Through his brother's correspondence, Flores began generating discussions with migrants about strike techniques in Mexico. At the end of the month, the five sections invited the Confederation of Mexican Workers (Confederacion de Trabajadores de Mexico, CTM) to Chicago. At the time, CTM was the largest confederation of unions in Mexico and was working closely with the Cardenas administration. At Union Hall on the West Side, the Front received CTM delegates Dr. Manuel Villasenor, Eduardo Inez, and Dr. Rafael Carrillo, who collectively spoke about the significance of CTM in contemporary Mexican politics. Believing that the settlements would disapprove of its increasingly radical activities, Section One called a secret meeting on the rooftop of the University of Chicago settlement. There, representatives of all five sections discussed the "effects of the capitalist system in Mexico and the U.S.," and a few Mexicans began to blame the "system" for the impoverishment of the Mexican worker in both countries.[36]

A few weeks after the covert meeting, the Front's multiethnic world continued to widen when it decided to assist several labor groups, including the International Worker's League (League), the Illinois Workers Alliance (Alliance), the Packinghouse Workers Organizing Committee (PWOC), and what appears to have been the Steel Workers Organizing Committee. In August of 1936, Section One invited the League's Joseph Roth to the University of Chicago settlement. There, Roth argued that the U.S. government was using the procedure of deportation as a strike-breaking weapon against immigrant noncitizen laborers. A University of Chicago settlement worker who overheard Roth's talk documented "his ideas [as] destructive rather than constructive." Section One then joined the Illinois Workers Alliance of Cook County, which claimed to stand for the "Economical, Social, Political, and Educational Advancement of the Workers." By 1937, Mexicans were working in Alliance Locals 32 and 36, which were collectively lobbying the Illinois state legislature on behalf of Works Progress Administration employees. Returning from an Alliance convention near Grant

Park, Front delegates claimed that many "W.P.A. groups" had spent their time discussing "the oppression on the working class from the part of the capitalistic group." By 1937, Front activists began meeting with PWOC and steelworker unionists. As PWOC organized the Back of the Yards, Front members assisted them by holding prounion meetings in Spanish. During one campaign, several PWOC organizers worried that Mexicans would resist unionization, given that several Catholic churches had taken a critical position on the PWOC. The PWOC organizers remembered Front activists telling them, "Don't worry about the Mexicans, we'll get you the signed [union] cards." The following day, PWOC received multiple cards signed and initialed "FPM" or Frente Popular Mexicano. As Front militants immersed themselves in the Chicago unionization movement, white unionists started pressuring Front members to become U.S. citizens. Time and again, Front organizers refused. In fact, Front activists chastised Mexican workers who even considered it, calling them "gringo renegades," the term Mexican liberals used to disparage Mexicans who deliberated about U.S. naturalization. Throughout their term in Chicago, Front activists reaffirmed migrants' commitment to Mexico. As late as 1940, less than 10 percent of the Mexican population of Chicago had taken out U.S. citizenship papers.[37]

As the Front gained a reputation within Mexican Chicago as a radical Cardenista association, once again, Mexicans who subscribed to competing visions of Mexican identity and culture went on the offensive. At St. Francis on the West Side, the Mexican Martyrs who had campaigned against the liberals now turned their attention to the Front. Through the *Ideal Mexican*, the Martyrs warned migrants about reading leftist literature. They supported the "nationalists" in the Spanish Civil War, claiming they would "liberate" Spaniards from "Bolshevik degradation," and they argued that "Communism was crucifying [Christ in] Mexico" under Cardenas or the "Chicharronero" ("the one who fries pork"), as the traditionalist press called him. At the University of Chicago settlement, Jose Rosales began maneuvering officials against Section One. At Hull House, Hortensia de la Mora started challenging Section Three. For de la Mora, migrants were "simple" and "uneducated." Consequently, an "intellectual" radical association, such as the Front, was "perhaps a bit dangerous because of this!"[38] Rosales had participated in the 1920s liberal movement, but after joining the settlement as a social worker in the 1930s, he began disagreeing with the Front's ultraleftism and started to work behind the scenes to undermine their activities.[39]

Unaware of the forces moving against them, the Front carried on with its radical agenda. In January 1937, Section One invited a Mexican national named Natalio Vazquez Pallares to the University of Chicago settlement. Pallares was a law student at the University of Guadalajara, where Dr. Alcazar had received his education, and was serving as the general secretary of the student branch of the Front in Mexico. During his second lecture, "Socialist Education in Mexico,"

Pallares argued that the U.S. educational system was "controlled by capitalism" and structured to train U.S. students in technical fields so that the "Rockfellers [sic], and the Morgans could better exploit [their] high technical knowledge." Unlike the U.S. educational system, under Cardenas, Mexican education taught students to contribute to the welfare of all Mexicans. Pallares concluded by reaffirming that Mexico's educational system was "socialist" because it taught Mexican children that "since the laboring masses are the real producers, they should receive a larger share of the wealth produced within the country."[40]

Emboldened by Pallares, the Front now sought to strengthen its ties to the Chicago groups that claimed to represent the interests of "the laboring masses ... the real producers." In late January, Section One received an invitation to join the American League against War and Fascism, a CPUSA affiliate that recruited a wide range of activists. After learning of the league's invitation, Jose Rosales and an unnamed settlement house administrator expelled the Front from the University of Chicago settlement. Throughout Chicago, Mexican traditionalists and settlement house officials, who opposed radical extremists, worked together to drive the Front from its liberal base. As this occurred, a new wave of Mexican political actors arose to positions of leadership. These activists, Mexicans who considered themselves "Mexican American," questioned the Front's political orientation toward Mexico and ultimately argued that Mexicans should become U.S. citizens, while maintaining a cultural tie to Mexico. By the late 1940s, Mexican American associations, such as the Mexican Civic Committee, led the Mexican community of Chicago down a new path and left the liberals and radicals behind them.[41]

This chapter suggests that the Midwestern Mexican political experience is best understood in relation to the ebbs and flows of Mexico's political currents. During World War I, industries in Chicago recruited thousands of Mexican immigrant laborers, many of whom were profoundly affected by the Mexican Revolution. This revolutionary generation, as I call them, arrived in Chicago and formed political associations that oriented migrants toward Mexico. Immigrant political activists were invested in their country's future because they believed that their vision of Mexico was possible in the unpredictable period before the entrenchment of the Institutional Revolutionary Party. In the 1920s, self-taught and formally educated liberals, often from Mexico City, arrived in Chicago and carried out a social service and educational campaign that sought to facilitate migrants' upward mobility while encouraging them to adopt a liberal identity. Given that the Mexican government did not recognize dual citizenship until 1998, patriotic liberals wanted to win migrants to their agenda while discouraging them from U.S. naturalization. As liberals rejected American assimilation, while adopting revolutionary "cosmic race" nationalism, they concurrently rejected the American ideology of whiteness. Distancing themselves from Catholic parishes, anticlerical liberals drew on Mexican small businesses for support. In the context of the Great Depression, Mexican small businesses went bankrupt, significantly contributing to the decline of their movement.

In the context of the Great Depression, Mexico's political currents flowed to the left, leading to the rise of the populist presidency of Lazaro Cardenas (1934–1940). Inspired by Cardenas, a few liberals and numerous blue-collar laborers in Chicago reached out to the Front, a radical organization formed in Mexico City by CPMEXICO and Cardenista partisans. Adapting the Front's politics to Chicago, Mexican radicals initiated a socialist education project that connected migrants to unionization and politically radical movements in Mexico. Chicago's ethnically and racially diverse environment led Mexican leftists to form coalitions with radical Cubans, Spaniards, and white Americans, some of whom were members of the CPUSA and the CIO. The Mexicans who were drawn to the CIO's Packinghouse Workers Organizing Committee were not New Deal Democrats but proud Mexican citizens motivated by the radical turn in Mexican-origin politics. Some American unionists encouraged migrants to become U.S. citizens, but like the liberals before them, Mexican radicals were extremely nationalistic and ultimately unwilling to relinquish their Mexican citizenship. Mexican liberals and radicals had a cultural impact on Mexicans' decision to assimilate. As late as 1940, less than 10 percent of Chicago's Mexican population had naturalized. While migrants were choosing not to become Americans, their children were following a different path. As liberals and radicals fearfully understood, U.S.-born Mexican children were legally American citizens, received an English-language education, and were immersed in American culture. By the mid-1940s, these Mexican Americans became politically active in Chicago and eventually succeeded in decoupling Mexican citizenship from Mexican culture, thereby engendering a politically viable binational "Mexican American" identity.

NOTES

1. I would like to thank Leon Fink, Eric Arnesen, Susan Levine, Juan Mora Torres, Perry Duis, Shelton Stromquist, Jose Angel Hernandez, Jaime Pensado, John Rosen, Sam Mitrani, Joseph Lipari, Agustina Lizcano, Martha Flores, and Erin Mulloy for commenting on various versions of this chapter. Throughout it, I use the terms *Mexican* and *migrant* to refer to people of Mexican origin. Regarding the term *migrant*, based on census and Catholic parish records, Francisco Rosales estimated that only 3 percent of Mexican Chicago in 1930 had been born in the United States; see Rosales, "Mexican Immigration to the Urban Midwest during the 1920s" (doctoral dissertation, Indiana University, 1978), 106.
2. Journal, 73, 79–80, Robert Redfield Papers, Box 59, Subseries 12, Special Collections, Regenstein Library, University of Chicago.

3. Image of Mondragon in *La Noticia Mundial*, September 16, 1927; *El Heraldo de las Americas*, November 15, 1924, translated by author; Journal, 1–2, 73, Redfield Papers, Box 59, Subseries 12.
4. U.S. Bureau of the Census, *Fourteenth Census of the United States 1920*, vol. 3, *Composition and Characteristics of the Population by States* (Washington, DC: Government Printing Office, 1922); U.S. Bureau of the Census, *Fifteenth Census of the United States: 1930, Population*, vol. 3, part 1 (Washington, DC: Government Printing Office, 1930).
5. Louise Ano Nuevo Kerr, "The Chicano Experience in Chicago: 1920–1970" (doctoral dissertation, University of Illinois at Chicago, 1976), 23.
6. Michael C. Meyer, William L. Sherman, and Susan M. Deeds, *The Course of Mexican History*, 7th ed. (Oxford: Oxford University Press, 2003), 463–68, 539–42, 4704; Charles A. Hale, *Emilio Rabasa and the Survival of Porfirian Liberalism: The Man, His Career, and His Ideas, 1856–1930* (Stanford, CA: Stanford University Press, 2008).
7. Except, 1928–31, CFLPS, Box 53; Robert C. Jones and Louis R. Wilson, *The Mexican in Chicago* (Chicago: Comity Commission of the Chicago Church Federation, 1931), 23.
8. *Mexico*, January 18, 1925, trans. Author; Journal, 73, Redfield Papers, Box 59, Subseries 12; *Correo Mexicano*, November 18, 1926, trans. Author, Paul S. Taylor Papers (PSTP), Carton 11, Folder 54, Bancroft Library, University of California, Berkeley.
9. Journal, 64, Redfield Papers, Box 59, Subseries 12; Scrap Book of Robert C. Jones, 1927; *Mexico*, February 25, 1930; *El Nacional*, March 4, 1931, CFLPS, Box 52; *Mexico*, October 13, 1928, CFLPS, Box 53.
10. Image of Benito Juarez in *La Noticia Mundial*, September 16, 1927; Field Notes, Societies, 123, PSTP, Carton 11, Folder 64; *Mexico*, November 3, 1928; November 24, 1928; January 5, 1929; February 20, 1929; June 29, 1929; November 9, 1929, CFLPS, Box 53.
11. Amado Nervo, *Anthologia Poetica E Ideario De Amado Nervo: Editores Mexicanos Unidos, Poesia* (Mexico City: Editores Mexicanos Unidos, 1999), selection trans. Author; *El Nacional*, July 15, 1933, CFLPS, Box 52; *Mexico*, January 5, 1929, CFLPS, Box 53; Gabriela F. Arredondo, "Navigating Ethno-Racial Currents: Mexicans in Chicago, 1919–1939," *Journal of Urban History* 30, no. 4 (2004): 399–427.
12. *Mexico*, January 18, 1925, trans. Author; *La Noticia Mundial*, August 21, 1927, trans. Author; *Mexico*, June 2, 1928; November 12, 1929; April 12, 1930; April 29, 1930; May 6, 1930; May 15, 1930; *El Nacional*, June 20, 1931; Scrap Book of Robert C. Jones, 1927, CFLPS, Box 52; Scrap Book of Robert C. Jones, 1927, CFLPS, Box 53; Robert C. Jones's Field Notes, 1928, interview with Dr. Francisca Luna, PSTP, Carton 11, Folder 49; Las Sociedades Contestan a la Cruz Azul Mexicana, PSTP, Carton 11, Folder 68; Integracion de la Junta Patriotica de Aquel Lugar, Chicago, Fondo 2006–20, Archivo de Relaciones Exteriores (SRE), DF, Mexico.

13. *Mexico*, November 11, 1928; November 28, 1928; December 5, 1928; December 15, 1928; December 29, 1928; March 15, 1930; April 5, 1930; April 12, 1930; May 1, 1930; *El Nacional*, December 17, 1930, CFLPS, Box 52.
14. *Mexico*, April 24, 1930; May 6, 1930; May 8, 1930; May 20, 1930, CFLPS, Box 52.
15. *Mexico*, May 8, 1930; *El Nacional*, May 2, 1931; May 9, 1931; September 19, 1931, CFLPS, Box 52.
16. *Mexico*, November 3, 1928, CFLPS, Box 52; *Mexico*, January 1925, trans. Redfield, Redfield Papers, Box 59, Subseries 12.
17. *Mexico*, November 10, 1928; December 19, 1928, CFLPS, Box 52.
18. Anita Jones, "Conditions Surrounding Mexicans in Chicago," (masters thesis, University of Chicago, 1928), 100–103; *Mexico*, June 2, 1928; December 15, 1928; *El Nacional*, December 23, 1933, CFLPS, Box 52; Adena Miller Rich, "The Administrative Organization and Extent of Naturalization in the Chicago District," June 1928, 51, Immigrants' Protective League (IPL), Box 1, Folder 3, Special Collections, University of Illinois at Chicago; "Aliens Naturalized in the Chicago District, 1922–28," IPL, Box 1, Folder 1.
19. *Mexico*, December 15, 1928, CFLPS, Box 52; Journal, 1–2, 18, 42–57, 101, Redfield Papers, Box 59, Subseries 12.
20. *Mexico*, May 20, 1930, CFLPS, Box 52; Alberto Rembao, *Outlook in Mexico*, Outlook pamphlets on Latin America (New York: Friendship Press, 1942); *Lecciones de filosofía de la religion* (Matanzas: Publicaciones del Seminario Evangelico de Teologia, 1958); *The Growing Church and Its Changing Environment in Latin America: From Missions to Mission in Latin America: Study Conference of the Committee on Cooperation in Latin America* (New York: The Committee, 1958).
21. Kerr, "The Chicano Experience," 33; *Mexico*, December 5, 1928; *El Nacional*, July 18, 1931; March 12, 1932, CFLPS, Box 52; *El Nacional*, October 24, 1931; May 7, 1932; June 4, 1932; November 19, 1932; *El Mexicano*, May 2, 1934, CFLPS, Box 53; *Chicago Daily Tribune*, December 14, 1923; December 15, 1923; December 12, 1923; December 24, 1923; January 14, 1924; July 10, 1930; June 6, 1932; April 9, 1939; Dr. Luna Interview, 1928, 17, PSTP, Carton 11, Folder 49.
22. Kerr, "The Chicano Experience," 70; *Mexico*, January 23, 1929; March 29, 1930; *El Nacional*, May 14, 1932; May 28, 1932; *El Liberal*, August 12, 1933; Interview with Mr. Antonio L. Schmidt by Hernandez, May, 19, 1937, CFLPS, Box 52; *El Nacional*, August 13, 1932; *La Defensa*, January 18, 1936, CFLPS, Box 53; Field Notes, Societies, 123, PSTP, Carton 11, Folder 50.
23. *El Liberal*, May 13, 1933; June 17, 1933, CFLPS, Box 52.
24. *El Liberal*, June 17, 1993; July 22, 1933; September 16, 1933;6-17-33, 7-22-33; *Sunday Times*, May 26, 1935, CFLPS, Box 52; *El Ideal Mexicano*, September 6, 1936, CFLPS, Box 53.
25. Ruth Berins Collier and David Collier, *Shaping the Political Arena: Critical Junctures, the Labor Movement, and Regime Dynamics in Latin America* (Notre

Dame, IN: University of Notre Dame Press, 2002); Mary Kay Vaughan, *Cultural Politics in Revolution: Teachers, Peasants, and Schools in Mexico, 1930–1940* (Tucson: University of Arizona Press, 1997).

26. Primer Congreso Nacional del Frente Popular Antimperialista (PCNFPA), 27 y 28 De Febrero de 1936; Letter from Benjamin Erosa Peniche to Luis I. Rodriguez, undated; Letter from Lic. Esteban Garcia de Alba to Gobernador Constl. Del Estado, February 11, 1936, Lazaro Cardenas del Rio (LCR), 433/121, Archivo General de la Nacion (AGN), Distrito Federal, Mexico.

27. *Mexico*, January 24, 1925; January 31, 1925; February 7, trans. Author; *Mexico*, January 23, 1929; *La Defensa*, February 8, 1936, CFLPS, Box 52; *El Nacional*, August 13, 1932, CFLPS, Box 53; Letter from Dr. C. S. Shuman to Adena Miller Rich (December 4, 1935), Lista De Clubs Y Sociedades Mexicanas (April 1937), Rich Papers, Box 1, Folder 11; Secretario de Propaganda, Gran Junta Popular Flyer in Anderson, Book No. 310, The Sunday Afternoon Discussion Group (SADG), May 20, 1936, University of Chicago Settlement House Collection (UCSH), box 25, folder Mexican Work (MW), Chicago History Museum.

28. Anderson, Book No. 310, SADG, "Meeting at Hull House," February 2, 1936, UCSH, box 25, folder MW.

29. PCNFPA, 8, LCR, 433/121, AGN; Anderson, Book No. 310, SADG, "Meeting at Hull House," February 2, 1936, UCSH, box 25, folder MW.

30. Anderson, Book No. 310, SADG, February 9, 1936; February 16, 1936; March 1, 1936, in UCSH, box 25, folder MW.

31. Mexican Adult Grays (May 5, 1936), Mexican Adult Group Report (Dorothy Anderson Report for June 1936), Anderson, Book No. 310, SADG, February 9, 1936; February 17, 1936; March 2, 1936; April 26, 1936; June 29, 1936, UCSH, box 25, folder MW.

32. Anderson, Book No. 310, SADG, February 23, 1936; June 14, 1936; June 24, 1936, UCSH, box 25, folder MW.

33. *La Alianza*, May 1936, July 1936; *La Defensa*, October 31, 1936, CFLPS, Box 52; *La Defensa*, May 30, 1936, CFLPS, Box 52 & 53; "Mrs. De la Mora requests," Mexican Group, March 3, 1936, Rich Papers, Box 1, Folder 11; Anderson, Book No. 310, SADG, February 2, 1936; February 17, 1936; February 21, 1936; March 8, 1936; March 21, 1936; April 19, 1936; April 26, 1936; July 1, 1936; August 12, 1936, UCSH, box 25, folder MW.

34. *La Defensa*, April 11, 1936, CFLPS, Box 52; Mrs. Rich, March 31, 1936, Rich Papers, Box 1, Folder 11; ASAMBLEA GENERAL, Angelica Arenal and Consuelo Garcia Moran, Domingo 5 de Abril, flyer, Anderson, Book No. 310, SADG, March 21, 1936; April 5, 1936, UCSH, box 25, folder MW; Angelica Arenal, *Paginas Sueltas con Siqueiros* (Mexico City: Editorial Grijalbo, 1979), 111.

35. "In Support of Spanish Democracy" flyer; Anderson, Book No. 310, SADG, June 3, 1936; August 26, 1936; Meeting of the Frente Popular (MFP), November 1, 1936; November 22, 1936, all in UCSH, box 25, folder MW.

36. *La Defensa*, May 30, 1936, CFLPS, Box 52; Anderson, Book No. 310, SADG, May 20, 1936; August 5, 1936, UCSH, box 25, folder MW.
37. "The Unemployed and W.P.A. Workers Must Organize" flyer; MFP, October 25, 1936; Anderson, Book No. 310, SADG, May 20, 1936, all in UCSH, box 25, folder MW; Herbert March, interviewed by Elizabeth Ballanoff, transcript, Roosevelt University, November 16, 1977; Arredondo, "Navigating Ethno-Racial Currents," 418, 427, n. 158; Record Group 21, U.S. District Court, Northern District of Illinois, Chicago, Naturalization Order Books, 1921-1986, April 1, 1921 (List 1) to January 2, 1940 (List 3617), National Archives and Records Administration, Great Lakes Region, Chicago, Illinois.
38. Mexican Group, March 3, 1936, "Mrs. De la Mora requests that," Rich Papers, Box 1, Folder 11.
39. *El Ideal Mexicano*, November 8, 1936; January 3, 1937, CFLPS, Box 52; *El Ideal Mexicano*, October 25, 1936, CFLPS, Box 53; MFP, October 25, 1936, UCSH, box 25, folder MW; Mexican Group, March 3, 1936, "Mrs. De la Mora requests that," Rich Papers, Box 1, Folder 11.
40. MFP, January 10, 1937; January 24, 1937, UCSH, box 25, folder MW.
41. MFP, January 31, 1937; Report, Meeting of the Study group meeting on Wed. evenings, May 7, 1937, both in UCSH, box 25, folder MW.

VII LABOR INTERNATIONALISM

INTRODUCTION

Nelson Lichtenstein

The rights of workers and of citizens coincide most efficaciously when trade unions, collective bargaining procedures, labor standards, and welfare regulations are contained within and bounded by sovereign states that exercise their power in a robust, intrusive, and self-contained fashion. These were the kind of "thick" states that were most prevalent, for good or evil, during the middle years of the twentieth century. We know a lot about the retrogressive side of such regimes, the Stalinist, fascist, or autocratic dictatorships that deprived citizenship of any real meaning and destroyed the capacity of the working class for self-organization.

But "thin" states have their own dangers for the working class and for the maintenance of a vibrant sense of citizenship. As a locus for working-class demands, protections, and civic participation, the modern state may well be undergoing a dramatic thinning process as transnational corporations become increasingly detached from and subversive of the traditional exercise of state regulatory power.[1] Indeed, the rise of a system of global supply chains, with their multilayered set of factories, vendors, and transport links, has created a world system in which legal ownership of the forces of production has been divorced from operational control. The global economy has been transformed during the past several decades, from one in which large manufacturers were dominant to one in which transnational retailers and other service-sector enterprises prevail. This shift has generated a system in which accountability for labor conditions is legally diffused and knowledge of the actual producers is far from transparent. The globally dispersed and opaque system of production that exists today means that if workers fight for their rights in one factory, the manufacturer might well shift its production to a "friendlier" one—often in another country. Production is readily moved around the globe—even from China, which has reportedly lost manufacturing to other Asian countries (such as Vietnam) as a result of rising wages and the implementation of a new contract labor law.[2]

Thus does this global system devalue, constrain, and thin the nation-state, whose capacity to regulate and structure labor and employment standards becomes increasingly attenuated. Needless to say, this thinning of state capacity is not what Karl Marx had in mind when he predicted the withering away of the state. Marx wrote during an era when states and the ideology that sustained them were still fragile, when empires were barely militarized, and when the tools of economic and social regulation were just being forged. The idea that workers of the world might unite was therefore not merely ideology but had a material basis predicated on the mobility of labor, the weakness of state regulation, and the underdevelopment of the nineteenth-century nation-state. But the thinning of state capacity in the twenty-first century returns us to a world quite familiar to Marx and his comrades, when political boundaries and economic regimes did not necessarily coincide and when the labor movement stood in search of a mechanism by which standards, rights, and political voice might be exercised in a world economy that was both highly integrated and poorly regulated.

The contemporary thinning of the state and simultaneous thickening of the transnational supply chains has had an impact on the way scholars and activists conceive of the modern labor question and its remedies, making some of the ideas and movements that came to the fore in the nineteenth century relevant once again. The definition, measurement, and advocacy of human rights now constitutes a pervasive way in which we define the extent to which individuals hold and exercise citizenship. The idea had its origins first in the nineteenth-century fight against slavery in the Caribbean, the American South, and the Belgian Congo and then in the twentieth-century effort to protect ethnically identifiable groups from persecution at the hands of hypernationalist states in Europe, the Middle East, and elsewhere. The Universal Declaration of Human Rights, originally formulated in 1948, stands as a monument embodying a Euro-American conception of such human rights, including strong provisions, eclipsed during the Cold War, insisting on labor's capacity for self-organization.[3]

Likewise, the century before the onset of World War I was one of a global labor migration; studies of immigration, refugee policy, and guest workers now often address the meaning of citizenship and its relevance to workplace relations. This is obviously true in terms of contemporary immigration debates, but as Mae Ngai, Gary Gerstle, Leon Fink, and Cindy Hahamovitch demonstrate, the relationship between American conceptions of citizenship and exclusion have had a dramatic impact on the expectations of those immigrant workers and the way employers accommodate or resist that mentality.[4] Meanwhile, the United States is not the only country grappling with such issues. In Europe, the Middle East, and within China itself, the relationship between a layered conception of citizenship and the rights of labor has generated conflict and contention.

It is in this context that legal scholars in the United States have also taken a renewed interest in the Thirteenth Amendment, which banished "involuntary servitude" in all those lands subject to U.S. constitutional writ. Because the main body of American jurisprudence limited the scope of the emancipation amendment to the abolition of chattel slavery alone, most students of free labor thought the Thirteenth amendment had little relevance to American work life, even in the South. But as James Pope and Risa Goluboff have recently demonstrated, the amendment had an important post-Reconstruction afterlife, first as a warrant the labor movement used to negate Lockner-era limitations on the right to strike and organize and then in the 1940s as a weapon that even some federal litigators deployed to undermine debt peonage and racial discrimination on the farms and in the factories that employed both black laborers and white.[5]

The Thirteenth Amendment and its British Empire counterparts were the product of the agitation and mobilization instigated by antislavery societies, which we might label the very first nongovernmental organizations (NGOs). Those NGO-like antebellum organizations created the template for a kind of citizen advocacy, which, as Jeffrey R. Kerr-Ritchie so aptly demonstrates, did not shy away from acts of militant civil disobedience and near-insurrectionary collective lawbreaking. When states are weak or internally fractured, such institutions fill the vacuum. Thus today, scores of NGOs make it their business to expose human rights violations and push forward a social, economic, and legal framework to which sovereign states must accommodate themselves.

This dynamic is at work within the labor movement of the United States as well. As American unions seek a new source of legitimacy, they have become enthusiastic converts to the new—or renewed—discourse equating labor rights and human rights. The AFL-CIO has underwritten an NGO, American Rights at Work, which has sought reform of American labor law; likewise, the union federation now celebrates December 11 as International Human Rights Day with almost as much verve as the traditional Labor Day in September. Human Rights Watch and other NGOs also have turned their attention to the American work regime, publishing a series of reports and investigations that seek to measure U.S. workplace practices by the standard established in the Universal Declaration of Human Rights and the conventions that govern freedom of association and speech adopted by the International Labor Organization (ILO).[6]

The renewed interest historians and global studies scholars have taken in the ILO also reflects a search for an effective mechanism by which the rights and standards of global labor might be protected in an era when the nation-state seems increasingly ineffectual. The ILO itself was founded during the turmoil following World War I. Although clearly designed as a mild social democratic alternative to Bolshevism, the ILO also arose out of the prewar effort to legalize, codify, and ameliorate international relations by means of conventions and formal treaties governing commerce, war, and labor standards.[7] In its early years, the ILO depended on strong states to frame and enforce its writ, a condition that all too often subordinated the organization to the racial and geostrategic interests of the major powers.[8]

But nineteenth-century states were still notably thin. In his stimulating study of slave states, fugitive slaves, and the abolitionist impulse, Kerr-Ritchie describes a world in which the boundaries between slave and free are plastic and capable of radical reconfiguration. Like the newly emergent capitalist economies and deregulated labor markets of Eastern Europe and East Asia in our own time, the slave labor regime was geographically unstable during the first seven decades of the nineteenth century. By surveying the entire Caribbean and the North American continent, Kerr-Ritchie demonstrates that those who sought to flee from slavery or protest its existence needed to keep an up-to-date atlas handy. Was Texas slave or free? Until 1829, slavery enjoyed legal protection, lost it when Mexico liberated itself from Spain, and became lawful once again when Texas won independence, only to face abolition at the end of the Civil War. But free labor for African Americans lasted little more than a decade, after which something very close to enslavement descended on East Texas when white elites made use of peonage laws and racial terror.

Likewise, in other parts of the United States, as well as in Canada and the Caribbean, the boundaries between slavery and freedom were in flux, not the least because of the agency of the enslaved men and women who turned themselves into refugees and fugitives, a quasi-citizen-like status that denaturalized the existence of the slave border and brought into question the very legitimacy of the states and nations that maintained such a geolegal distinction. Any resemblance to contemporary debates over the status of illegal aliens, the rights of undocumented workers, and the activities of the U.S. Immigration and Customs Enforcement agency may well be merited. As in antebellum America, a conflict that conflates the nature of citizenship and the status of labor has thinned a state's capacity to regulate its borders, if only because of popular resistance and employer opportunism. The Mexican-U.S. border represents one site of such a contestation, but so, too, do the European Union–Eastern Europe boundary and the internal provincial segmentations that once made the divide between rural and urban China an economic and social frontier not dissimilar from that of an international boundary.

Indeed, historians have often expected that nations, states, and labor markets should be coterminous, but as Jacob Remes points out in his chapter on Toronto printers, that was not the case in the nineteenth century. The era from 1914 to about 1989 now seems something of an anomalous moment in world labor history, when national boundaries and labor markets did approximate each other more than in eras before or since. Thus in the 1860s and 1870s, Toronto printers forged their consciousness and their politics in a world in which they belonged simultaneously to a North American working class, to a British imperial nation, and to a Canadian polity. That the Toronto printers did not in fact live within a stable and unified nation provides compelling evidence for Remes that "the modern ideological supremacy of the nation is contingent and historically specific." These printers were living in an exceedingly thin state, thereby making the study of transnational, subnational, or nonnational communities essential to explain the character of working-class life in Toronto and elsewhere.

With an entirely open border between the United States and Canada, the proletarian internationalism of the Toronto printers had both an economic reality and a sound ideological footing. "Tramping" between one print shop and the next—between Toronto and Chicago, for example—was legal, legitimate, and frequent. Strike support had a tangible benefit because a lost work stoppage, even in a distant city, brought in its train a flood of desperate printers seeking new jobs at whatever pay the market might bear—hence the naturalness of the *International* Typographical Union.

But in a move that would foretell the thickening of the state and the rise of a late-nineteenth–early-twentieth-century form of imperialist nationalism, the Toronto printers became increasingly conscious of themselves as subjects of the British Empire and citizens of the Canadian nation-state. They did so not only because of the racial affinities upon which the English-speaking parts of these entities were based but also because a demand against the state had a good chance of actually generating some payoff if that polity were powerful, bounded, and needing popular legitimacy. Thus the future of working-class nationalism during the next century lay not with the transnational empires—although the British made a pretty good attempt at it—but with the nation-state, even if, as in Canada, it was internally divided by language, culture, and religion and overshadowed by its southern neighbor. In Canada as elsewhere, tariffs and immigration controls conspired to finally make the market and the polity one and the same.

Leon Fink's interrogation of ILO efforts to raise labor standards on the high seas demonstrates why the promise of international cooperation proved so difficult during the twentieth century and why it remains equally elusive today. For generations, the maritime industry has been quintessentially global, seemingly detached from regulation by any single nation-state because owners, operators, shippers, charterers, and insurers, not to mention the officers and crew, are all of different nationalities. Indeed, it became standard practice for most ships to register under flags of convenience in states like Panama and Liberia that require few taxes and have no relationship to the citizenship of the owners or operators. These are thin states indeed, mere slivers of insubstantial regulation who offer no resistance to the global pressures that have depressed wages and working conditions in the trade.

Thus, as Fink remarks, any history of the ILO seafaring conventions has a remarkably present-day feel, even if those discussions took place eighty years ago, when maritime powers like Britain and the United States played a more active role. At that time, construction of an ILO maritime labor standard was shot through with racial and national self-interest; indeed, the effort by the British, ship owners as well as seamen, to actually create a uniform standard was crippled from the start by the maintenance of a set of hours and wages for Indian seamen far below that of Northern Europeans.

But the main problem for the ILO and for its effort to establish a single labor standard for all seamen was not exclusively racism or the maintenance of a seaborne colonial relationship. Even more important was the effort by most of the developed nations to protect and preserve a merchant marine, which seemed a geostrategic imperative for many mid-twentieth-century states. Ships built in the United States and manned by U.S. sailors benefited from a massive governmental subsidy. This had the effect of dividing the world maritime workforce into a nationally protected aristocracy, well protected by subsidies, government regulations, and strong trade unions, and a vast seagoing proletariat largely subject to the economic vicissitudes and physical dangers generated by a world of global commerce in which states are thin, legal responsibility elusive, and competition fierce.

NOTES

1. Gay W. Seidman, *Beyond the Boycott: Labor Rights. Human Rights, and Transnational Activism* (New York: Russell Sage, 2007), 23–27, where she discusses the thinning of the modern regulatory state.
2. Nelson Lichtenstein, *The Retail Revolution: How Wal-Mart Created a Brave New World of Business* (New York: Henry Holt, 2009), 1–9, 35–52. Excellent essays covering workers, entrepreneurs, and states in a single industry are found in Gary Gereffi, David Spender, and Jennifer Bair, eds., *Free Trade and Uneven Development: The North American Apparel Industry after NAFTA* (Philadephia: Temple University Press, 2002).
3. Mary Ann Glendon, *A World Made New: Eleanor Roosevelt and the Universal Declaration of Human Rights* (New York: Random House, 2001), 193–241, passim. And see John D. French and Kristin Wintersteen, "Crafting an International Legal Regime for Worker Rights: Assessing the Literature since the 1999 Seattle WTO Protests," *International Labor and Working-Class History* no. 75 (Spring 2009): 145–68.
4. Mae Ngai, *Impossible Subjects: Illegal Aliens and the Making of Modern America* (Princeton, NJ: Princeton University Press, 2005); Gary Gerstle, *American Crucible: Race and Nation in the Twentieth Century* (Princeton, NJ: Princeton University Press, 2002); Leon Fink, *The Maya of Morganton: Work and Community in the Nuevo New South* (Chapel Hill: University of North Carolina Press, 2003); Cindy Hahamovitch, *The Perfect Immigrant: Jamaican Guestworkers in the Land of Jim Crow* (Chapel Hill: University of North Carolina Press, forthcoming).

5. James Gray Pope, "The Thirteenth Amendment versus the Commerce Clause: Labor and the Shaping of American Constitutional Law, 1921–1957," *Columbia Law Review* 102, no. 1 (January 2002): 1–122; Risa Goluboff, *The Lost Promise of Civil Rights* (Cambridge: Harvard University Press, 2007), 111–40; 238–52.
6. See, for example, two outstanding reports published by Human Rights Watch, *Unfair Advantage: Workers' Freedom of Association in the United States under International Human Rights Standards* (2000) and *Discounting Rights: Wal-Mart's Violation of US Workers' Right to Freedom of Association* (2007).
7. Elizabeth Borgwardt, *A New Deal for the World: America's Vision for Human Rights* (Cambridge: Harvard University Press, 2005), 61–70.

FURTHER READING

Anderson, Benedict. *Imagined Communities: Reflections on the Origin and Spread of Nationalism.* London: Verso, 1991.

Glenn, Evelyn Nakano. *Unequal Freedom: How Race and Gender Shaped American Citizenship and Labor.* Cambridge: Harvard University Press, 2002.

Gordon, Linda. "Transnational Labor Citizenship." *Southern California Law Review* 80 (March 2007): 503–87.

Hahn, Steven. *A Nation under Our Feet: Black Political Struggles in the Rural South from Slavery to the Great Migration.* Cambridge: Harvard University Press, 2003.

Harvey, David. *A Brief History of Neoliberalism.* New York: Oxford University Press, 2005.

Lichtenstein, Nelson. *The Retail Revolution: How Wal-Mart Created a Brave New World of Business.* New York: Henry Holt, 2009.

MacGillivray, Alex. *A Brief History of Globalization.* London: Constable & Robinson, 2006.

Ngai, Mae. *Impossible Subjects: Illegal Aliens and the Making of Modern America.* Princeton, NJ: Princeton University Press, 2005.

Seidman, Gay. *Beyond the Boycott: Labor Rights, Human Rights, and Transnational Activism.* New York: Russell Sage, 2007.

Tabili, Laura. *"We Ask for British Justice": Workers and Racial Difference in Late Imperial Britain.* Ithaca, NY: Cornell University Press, 1994.

18 FUGITIVE SLAVES ACROSS NORTH AMERICA

Jeffrey R. Kerr-Ritchie

There is little doubt that the creation of national borders on the continent of North America has encouraged numerous cross-border movements for freedom over the years.[1] Repression in the United States has led Americans to move both south and north. After U.S. authorities forced the Church of Jesus Christ of Latter-day Saints to ban polygamy, some Mormon farmers left Utah and settled in the Galeana district of Chihuahua, Mexico, during the early twentieth century. Jack Johnson, the first black heavyweight boxing champion of the world, fled to Canada from Chicago before embarking for Europe to beat several trumped-up charges of illegally transporting white women for the purposes of prostitution in 1913. His real "crimes" were being the black boxing champion and publicly flouting the color line through numerous interracial relationships with white women. In the 1960s Vietnam War, U.S. fugitives from the draft crossed into Canada to avoid participating in an increasingly unpopular and deadly military conflict. On the other hand, the United States has frequently provided sanctuary for oppressed peoples on the continent. In 1893, a local uprising in Santo Tomas, Chihuahua, to unseat Mexican dictator Porfirio Diaz was crushed by government troops. The surviving insurgents crossed into the United States to regroup and mobilize new supporters before they returned to northern Mexico to continue their rebellion. The same year Johnson left the United States, Mexican revolutionary leader Pancho Villa escaped from jail and relocated to El Paso, Texas. In our own time, poor people from Central America and Mexico constantly cross into the United States without papers and work without documentation in pursuit of an economic freedom denied them at home.[2]

This chapter provides a historical examination of these pathways to freedom with a focus on cross-border fugitive slave activities in continental North America during the nineteenth century. The argument is made in four parts. We begin with examples of fugitive slaves crossing borders in search of individual liberation. During the nineteenth century, territorial conflict abounded between the British, Spanish, Americans, and Mexicans. This territorial conflict provided a gateway to freedom for thousands of fugitives who gravitated toward free areas beyond the borders of the American republic, including Spanish Florida, independent Mexico, and British Canada. This important demographic undercurrent deserves greater attention than it has received thus far. The second section examines diplomatic responses to these escapees, especially the signing of international treaties to prevent fugitive escape. The role of fugitives in provoking these agreements has not been sufficiently understood, and the conventional treatment of these treaties within national frameworks ignores their crucial continental context. The third part focuses on the contributions of fugitive slaves to antislavery mobilization across borders. These organizing efforts in different nations and territories took place because such efforts were either illegal or difficult to accomplish within the existing confines of the nation-state. The fourth section examines the creation of fugitive settlements across borders, especially in Florida, central Canada, and Mexico. These black communities served as beacons of freedom to fugitives and were among the first postemancipation settlements on the North American continent. The major contextual point of this cross-national analysis is that territorial conflict provided a gateway to freedom for fugitives. The major objective of this chapter is to provide a cross-national examination of fugitive movements, laws, and communities in support of transnational history.

I

During the seventeenth and eighteenth centuries, imperial tensions between the British and the Spanish facilitated fugitive flight southward from the British mainland colonies of South Carolina and Georgia to Spanish Florida. In 1688 and 1689, for example, colonial officials noted that fugitives had sought refuge in the Spanish colony.[3] In 1728, planter Thomas Elliott and others requested government assistance because they had "fourteen Slaves Runaway to St. Augustine." That same year, the colonial governor of South Carolina complained to the London colonial office that the Spanish were "receivieing [sic] and harbouring all our Runaway Negroes."[4] The extent of this flight, together with the usefulness of fugitives as laborers, translators, and settlers, encouraged the Spanish to establish a fugitive settlement near Saint Augustine called Gracia Real de Santa Teresa de Mose in 1739. Although the English established the colony of Georgia as a buffer during the early 1730s, this simply transferred the fugitive "problem" to the southern border of the new colony. The fugitive "problem" disappeared with the British annexation of Florida in 1763, when fugitives were no longer able to seek Spanish asylum, until Florida was returned to Spain at the end of the American Revolutionary War in 1783.[5]

The establishment of a slaveholding American republic did not lessen colonial tensions and guaranteed the continuation of fugitive flight. During the War of 1812, international conflict between the United States, Britain, and Spain facilitated the southward escape of slaves. Fugitives continued to flee the plantations and farms of the southeastern seaboard, with mixed results. Some obtained and retained their freedom by mixing with the Seminole Indians and fought in two major wars (First and Second Seminole Wars). Others were either returned to U.S. slavery or reenslaved by American Indians. The area was annexed by the United States in 1819 and eventually made safe for slaveholding with the establishment of Florida as the twenty-seventh state in the Union in 1845.[6]

Territorial tensions between the United States and Mexico also encouraged fugitive flight. This former Spanish colony won its independence in 1821 and within a decade terminated slavery, an institution with roots stretching back to the seventeenth century. According to the decree signed by President Vicente Guerrero in the federal palace on September 15, 1829, "Slavery is forever abolished in the republic," all former slaves "are free," and former "proprietors of slaves shall be indemnified" once funds were available. The decree was passed to commemorate independence, enhance "public tranquility," and to restore natural rights to all.[7] This law, however, actually freed few slaves except in Texas, which at the time was filling up with slaveholders and slaves, and led to the secession of Texas. The windy title of American abolitionist Benjamin Lundy's 1836 pamphlet made the point: *The war in Texas; a review of the facts and circumstances, showing that this contest is the result of a long premeditated crusade against the government set on foot by slaveholders, land speculators, etc., with the view of re-establishing, extending and perpetuating the system of slavery and the slave trade in the Republic of Mexico.*[8] Nearly two decades later, former U.S. slave in Canada Samuel Ringgold Ward explained that the U.S. "war with Mexico was conceived and brought forth, on purpose to lengthen the cords and strengthen the stakes of slavery."[9] More recently, Rosalie Schwartz put it this way: "The whole issue of the abolition of Negro servitude might well have been moot in Mexico, had it not been for the nation's contiguity with an expansive, slave-owning society on her northern border and the historical circumstances which brought conflict to the frontier area."[10]

Although Mexico's abolition law liberated only about 10,000 people, it was to have an impact on slaves in the slaveholding American South.[11] Fugitives from expanding southwestern slavery crossed the Rio Grande in search of freedom. During the brief life of the Texas republic between 1836 and 1845, the enslaved population increased in the area largely through the slave trade and bringing new slaves into the region. At the same time, fugitive slaves embarked for the free soil of Mexico. Texas president Sam Houston, for example, lost two domestic slaves who sheltered in Matamoros, just across the Rio Grande from Brownsville. U.S. military personnel marching to the Rio Grande in 1845 reported: "Three slaves of officers have run away. Of course every inducement is offered by the enemy." This explanation downplays fugitive agency in seeking freedom during opportune wartime conditions. By the 1850s, there were large numbers of fugitives living in Mexico. According to the *Austin State Times*, hundreds of thousands of fugitives inhabited Mexico in 1854. This figure was probably an exaggeration and might have been motivated by a desire for greater security for slave-owners' property and perhaps even further annexation by the federal government. John Ford estimates about 3,000 fugitive slaves from Texas were living in Mexico in the 1850s; Rosalie Schwartz suggests there were "several thousand" fugitives in Mexico during the 1850s."[12]

In *A Journey through Texas*, published in 1857, New England journalist Frederick Law Olmsted devoted several pages to borderland fugitives. One fugitive he interviewed told a fascinating story:

> He very civilly informed me, in answer to inquiries, that he was born in Virginia, and had been bought South by a trader and sold to a gentleman who had brought him to Texas, from whom he had run away four or five years ago. He would like right well to see old Virginia again, that he would—if he could be free. He was a mechanic, and could earn a dollar very easily, by his trade, every day. He could speak Spanish fluently, and had traveled extensively in Mexico, sometimes on his own business, and sometimes as a servant or muleteer. Once he had been beyond Durango, or nearly to the Pacific; and, northward, to Chihuahua, and he professed to be competent, as a guide, to any part of Northern Mexico. He had joined the Catholic True Church, he said, and he was very well satisfied with the country.

Olmsted went on to report: "Runaways were *constantly* arriving here; two had got over, as I had previously been informed, the night before. He could not guess how many came in a year, but he could count forty, that he had known of, in the last three months." These cross-border fugitives were not always successful. Olmsted "supposed a good many got lost and starved to death, or were killed on the way, between the settlements and the river." Although many of them brought money and a little property, some lived in profligate ways, ending up "very poor and miserable." Others learned the language, were "industrious," and lived "very comfortably." "The Mexican government," Olmsted continued, "was very just to them, they could always have their rights as fully protected as if they were Mexicans born." Some of these fugitives made good social marriages. Indeed, despite the poverty of many fugitives, their improved social condition was familiar enough to become a local witticism: "It is repeated as a standing joke—I suppose I have heard it fifty times in the Texas taverns, and always to the great amusement of the company—that a nigger in Mexico is just as good as a white man, and if you don't treat him civilly he will have you hauled up and fined by an alcade [magistrate]."[13]

Two decades after the U.S. war with Mexico, wartime conditions again facilitated fugitive slaves crossing North America. Former Texas slave Jacob Branch, at age eighty-six, recalled wartime cross-border fugitive flight:

> After war starts lots of slaves runned off to git to de Yankees. All dem in dis part heads for de Rio Grande river. De Mexicans rig up flat-boats out in de middle de river, tied to stakes with rope. When de culled people gits to de rope dey can pull deyself 'cross de rest de way on dem boats. De white folks rid[e] de 'Merican side dat river all de time, but plenty slaves git through, anyway.[14]

This is an interesting piece of evidence for several reasons. Most scholars have recorded fugitive flight to Union-occupied positions in the South rather than across the border to Mexico. Also, it seems that Mexicans assisted the fugitives in their escape. Furthermore, regular white patrols did not deter slaves from escaping across the river. Finally, it must have been an unforgettable scene for Mr. Branch to recall it in such detail nearly eight decades later.

Fugitives also crossed northward into the British imperial domain. After the implementation of legal abolition in the British colonies in 1834, fugitives from American slavery increasingly sought refuge northward in British Canada, especially present-day Ontario. Historian Robin Winks estimates there were 12,000 fugitive slaves living in British Canada by 1840.[15] But the real exodus occurred during the 1850s. As a result of the passage of the Fugitive Slave Act in 1850 in the United States (discussed later), many fugitive slaves and free blacks left the northern states for the comparative safety of Canada. It has been estimated that about 3,000 fugitives relocated in the months immediately following ratification of the law. Fugitives Anthony Hollingsworth, Daniel Lockhart, Fred Wilkins, and Jerry McHenry, all of whom had been rescued from American slave catchers, relocated to Canada. Those who aided and abetted their escape, like Samuel Ward and John Lisle, also moved to Canada to avoid federal prosecution. In his *Autobiography of a Fugitive Negro*, published in London in 1855, Ward explained that he and his family decided to move to Canada because of the lack of prospects in the United States and the possibility of incarceration for assisting in the escape of fugitive Jerry McHenry from Syracuse, New York, in contravention of the Fugitive Slave Act: "I had already become hopeless of doing more in my native country; I had already determined to go to Canada. Now, however, matters became *urgent*."[16] Furthermore, numerous fugitives worked their way via the Underground Railroad through the midwestern states of Ohio, Illinois, and Michigan into southern Ontario. This region bordering on the Detroit River and Lake St. Clair contained the counties of Essex and Kent. Many towns in the area—Windsor, Sandwich, and Amherstburg—saw a large increase in their black populace. Scholars estimate between 40,000 and 60,000 people of African descent were living in Canada by 1860, with some historians claiming a populace of more than 100,000. Most of these people resided in Canada West, and most arrived during the 1850s.[17]

It is clear that most fugitive slaves in North America did not leave the colonial or independent polity. Whether they traveled near or far, slave runaways carved out niches of freedom within the territorial confines of the colonial society or nation-state within which they were legally enslaved. For example, most scholars agree that fugitive slaves escaped southern U.S. slavery for either local, regional, or northern destinations during the antebellum era.[18] Their search for freedom occurred within a national framework, albeit one in which borders between slavery and freedom were constantly shifting.

At the same time, however, a significant number of fugitive slaves crossed national borders in search of permanent freedom. They did this at various times and in a variety of ways. The key contextual point was that territorial conflict between rival powers and states provided a *gateway* to freedom for fugitives, and that fugitives did not balk at the chance to repeatedly exploit these tensions. This slave self-emancipation occurred within the context of expanding and contracting American slavery, the emergence of British colonial abolition in Canada, and imperial rivalries between the Americans, British, Spanish, and Mexicans. The primary inducement was less official state policies than the prospect of permanent freedom during a time of shifting national and free-unfree borders. The transformative role of fugitive slaves, and how this took on continental significance, goes unappreciated if the focus remains only upon movements within national boundaries.

II

As a result of fugitive flight across the North American continent, treaties were drawn up between nations and colonial powers to prevent fugitive escapes, as well as to return those fugitives who had already escaped from slavery. These treaties between the United States and Mexico and British Canada between the 1820s and 1840s met with limited success. (At the same time, fugitive laws within the United States pointed to shifting borders between slave and free territories that were also important.) As a consequence of this limited success, territories adjacent to slaveholding lands were annexed to secure borders. Although these territorial grabs proved successful, and new lands were added to the slaveholding American South, the borders continued to prove porous as fugitive slaves simply went beyond them.

In the aftermath of the establishment of the independent republic of Mexico in 1821, many new emigrants settled in the state of Coahuila y Texas. These included slaveholders and their slaves. One consequence was the frequent flight of fugitives to Mexico. Benjamin Milam, an early frontier settler, complained to Joel Robert Poinsett, the first U.S. minister to Mexico: "I have been in the frontiers of Texas for some time and have observed that the Stait of Louisiana have lost a grait maney slaives that have taken refuge in this Republick of Mexico."[19] Between 1825 and 1832, a series of diplomatic initiatives between the two North American republics began. The major purpose was to establish relations of amity, commerce, and navigation between the two nations, but no less important was the need to arrange for the return of fugitive slaves from Mexico to U.S. territory. Despite vigorous treaty negotiations, strong consideration of two separate articles concerning fugitive slave return, and powerful U.S. pressure to get the treaty and these articles ratified, the Mexican Chamber of Deputies repeatedly rejected the fugitive slave clause. Their opposition was partially motivated by natural rights law, together with the practical understanding of the usefulness of the labor of free men in an underpopulated region. Both nations ratified the treaty on April 5, 1832, but without the fugitive slave clause.[20]

After the passage of British colonial abolition in 1834, fugitives from American slavery increasingly sought refuge northward in Canada, especially present-day Ontario. Their status prompted American slaveholder requests for extradition. Recognizing the irrelevance of American fugitive law in Canada, U.S. slaveholders tried to use an 1833 British-Canadian extradition act for returning escaped criminals as a means of repatriating fugitive slaves. Three cases involving fugitive escapees from Kentucky—and American requests for their extradition between 1833 and 1837—tested Anglo-American relations. Thorton Blackburn and Lucie Blackburn were arrested in Detroit, Michigan, under the 1793 U.S. Fugitive Slave Act but were rescued by their supporters and crossed into British Canada, where they settled in eastern Toronto. Solomon Mosely stole himself and his master's horse and was arrested and ordered returned, but a group of antislavery supporters helped him to escape to Canada. Jesse Happy also stole himself and a horse to aid his escape. These fugitives' thefts were considered instrumental to personal escape by the colonial authorities. As Sir Francis Bond Head, lieutenant governor of Upper Canada, put it in a letter to Lord Glenelg, the British colonial secretary in London:

> It may be argued that a slave escaping from bondage on his master's horse is a vicious struggle between two parties of which the slave owner is not

only the aggressor, but the blackest criminal of the two—it is the case of the dealer in human flesh versus the stealer of horse flesh.

This pattern of fugitive escapes, U.S. extradition requests, and British denials continued until the Nelson Hackett case in 1842. Hackett, a self-emancipated slave from Arkansas, stole a horse, coat, saddle, and gold watch, as well as himself. Since some of these items were not considered indispensable to his escape, the governor-general ordered Hackett's return for criminal intent, according to the 1833 extradition treaty. This was the first time a fugitive had been returned from Canada. The combination of abolitionist furor and the legal ambiguities of the Hackett case resulted in the passage of the Webster-Ashburton Treaty in 1842. The new law eased border disputes between the United States and British Canada, and although some abolitionists feared it would create new slave catchers, it appears that no fugitive was extradited from Canada under the 1842 treaty.[21]

These fugitive cases between 1833 and 1842 highlight three important points concerning the relationship between imperial abolition and American slavery. First, American fugitives deemed British soil safer after the legal abolition of colonial slavery in 1834. Although they were to subsequently encounter racism and exclusion in British Canada, fugitives were originally motivated by their belief in greater liberties under the British flag. As historians William and Jane Pease put it: "If the tales of a Canadian paradise were in part misleading, perhaps it was just as well, for they guided the Negro to a land where the law both promised and gave what in the United States was denied him."[22] Second, British denials of American extradition can best be understood within the broader context of an unfolding imperial commitment toward abolition and paternal governance. The position of fugitive slaves in British Canada had already been determined by a series of important legal decisions: Chief Justice Mansfield's decision against slave ownership in England in 1772, Upper Canada's Lieutenant Governor Simcoe's ruling against slave importation in 1793, the abolition of the British transoceanic slave trade in 1808, and the final termination of British colonial slavery in 1838. By this last date, slavery had become illegal throughout the empire, any former slave was instantly free on British soil, and the British Empire was de facto a paternal institution.[23] Third, black and white mobs of antislavery activists often proved more important in freeing fugitives than either British legal decisions fueled by colonial paternalism or Anglo-American diplomacy. The Blackburn family and Solomon Mosely were freed through armed struggle. This collective stance represented a continental means of self-defense and liberation, a cross-national form of resistance otherwise lost in local, regional, and national analyses.[24]

In the aftermath of the victorious American war with Mexico in the late 1840s, southern slaveholders demanded federal support for returning runaway slaves. The continental expansion of the American empire brought with it the spread of slavery and demands for federal protection of personal property, especially fugitive slaves. Authored by Virginia senator and slaveholder James M. Mason, the Fugitive Slave Act was debated, passed, and finally signed by President Millard Fillmore on September 18, 1850. It empowered federal marshals to support southern slaveholders' efforts to "pursue and reclaim" fugitive slaves "from service and labor" through either a warrant or legal seizure "without due process." It essentially beefed up the pursuit, capture, and return of fugitive slaves by buttressing state rights with federal legislation. It further betokened a legal assault on the pursuit of freedom by slaves, a massive new threat to fugitives living in free states, and the potential for kidnapping those people of African descent who were born free.[25]

Fugitive battles became central to the political mobilization against American slavery from the early 1850s onward. Major conflicts broke out between federal agents, slaveholders, and armed posses versus fugitives and self-defense mobs. Historian Thomas Campbell calculates 156 fugitive slave cases involving 300 slaves during the 1850s. Scholars James and Lois Horton estimate more than 80 well-publicized fugitive slave rescues and attempted rescues. Armed vigilance groups engaged in the self-defense of fugitives often carried out these actions. In September 1851, the attempt to capture fugitive slaves in Christiana, Pennsylvania, by slaveholder Edward Gorsuch and a posse was successfully repulsed by dozens of black men and women armed with guns, corn cutters, scythe blades, staves, clubs, and stones. These self-defense acts were reminiscent of earlier border skirmishes in support of fugitives from Kentucky.[26]

Newspaper reports of these fugitive battles contributed to this political mobilization. These fugitive *causes célèbres* were extensively reported in black and abolitionist newspapers. The press industry had taken off during the 1830s because of technological improvements, cheaper print, and educational advances. By 1850, it has been estimated that two-thirds of black adults in six northern U.S. cities had rudimentary reading skills. Many must have shared the news with those who could not read. By the early 1850s, these readers had learned of a series of spectacular fugitive cases. This press coverage undoubtedly served to fire abolitionist and antislavery imaginations. Every fugitive struggle placed the issue of slavery directly into the hearts and minds of literally thousands of people in North America. Reports of these incidents propagated continental struggles over slavery. The Boston *Liberator* reported on fugitive escapees from southern U.S. slavery to British Canada and elsewhere. Many readers first learned of Fredrick Wilkins's rescue from Boston as the "Shadrach" case in the *Voice of the Fugitive*, printed from Sandwich, Canada West. In an article headlined "Colored Population Wide Awake," this fugitive abolitionist newspaper informed readers that "six and even seven hundred colored citizens, many of whom are fugitives, are here, and are determined to stand by one another, and live or die together."[27]

At the same time, slaveholders in Texas (admitted to the Union as the twenty-eighth state in 1845) sought federal support for the protection of their property and the return of fugitive slaves. The same year as the Fugitive Slave Act was passed, the state legislature approached the U.S. Congress requesting an agreement with Mexico that "all criminals, robbers, persons held in bondage, or fugitives from justice" should be returned. This legal language says a great deal about the way these politicians understood justice and property rights; it stands in marked contrast to the perspective of fugitives, whose search for freedom was against injustice and what they would have considered the criminal act of enslavement. Texas's politicians failed, and Mexico continued to refuse to return fugitive slaves from its territory. Similar efforts at extradition in 1857 also proved fruitless.[28] In short, fugitive slaves who escaped to either the British colony of Canada or the republic of Mexico were more likely to remain permanently free than those fugitive slaves who sought freedom within U.S. territorial confines, especially after the federal expansion of slavery in 1850.

III

The expansion of American slavery brought with it a corresponding expansion of antislavery mobilization. This involved the transnational movement of slaves, fugitives, free blacks, activists, abolitionists, and intellectuals during the middle decades of the nineteenth century. Their travels took them across North America and the North Atlantic. They raised monies, wrote autobiographies, joined abolition groups, started newspapers, and created new organizations—all with the primary objective of overthrowing American slavery.[29]

It is important at the outset to acknowledge abolitionist and antislavery activities within the nation-state.[30] Historians have devoted a great deal of ink to these activities, including the Underground Railroad, the antislavery movement, and the politicization of opposition toward southern slave power. One powerful example was the emergence of personal liberty laws by northern and western states as a means of challenging federal intrusion in the pursuit of fugitives during the 1840s and 1850s. At the same time, we cannot ignore the unprecedented power of the federal government in clamping down on these activities. Fugitive Anthony Burns and thousands of his abolitionist supporters could not prevent the combined might of U.S. military personnel, the Massachusetts militia, and the Boston police from returning Burns to slavery in Virginia in June 1854.[31] Famous altercations like these proved that antislavery activities were difficult in northern states, becoming harder after 1850, and more likely to be successful beyond U.S. borders.

One of the most important consequences of the fugitive exodus to Canada West was the continental expansion of antislavery mobilization. Six months after the passage of the Fugitive Slave Act in 1850, the Anti-Slavery Society of Canada was formed at City Hall, Toronto, Ontario, the first major antislavery organization in British Canada. Its auxiliary, the Toronto Ladies' Association for the Relief of Destitute Colored Fugitives, was formed in April 1851. Over the next two years, the Anti-Slavery Society of Canada established regional branches in Kingston, Hamilton, London, and St. Catherines. This successful expansion was partially due to the uncompromising organizing efforts of Maryland fugitive Samuel Ringgold Ward, who had relocated to Canada. Moreover, this period saw the pioneering establishment of an antislavery press in Canada. The *Toronto Globe*, established in 1844, increasingly attacked American slavery under the editorial direction of Scottish emigrant George Brown. In March 1854, the *Provincial Freeman* began regular publication under the nominal editorship of Ward. This soon passed to Mary Ann Shadd, free-born in Wilmington, Delaware, who moved to Windsor, Ontario, in 1851, where she opened a school for black children. It was through the pages of these newspapers that readers first learned about West Indian Emancipation Day celebrations, annual meetings every first day in August drawing large numbers of people of African descent with the dual aims of commemorating British colonial abolition in the past and mobilizing for the future abolition of American slavery.[32]

This mobilization was also very pronounced in the region of western Ontario, where many fugitives ended up relocating. Between January 1851 and February 1852, these fugitives played a central role in the establishment of an antislavery newspaper, a major black convention, and a new organization. One of the key individuals involved in these developments was American fugitive Henry Bibb.

Bibb was born in Shelby County, Kentucky, in May 1815, to enslaved mother Mildred Jackson and slaveholder James Bibb. As a youth, he was separated from his mother and endured several harsh periods as a hired slave. Of this period, he later wrote: "I was a wretched slave, compelled to work under the lash without wages and often without clothes enough to hide my nakedness." In 1834, he married Malinda, an enslaved woman, and they had one child, Mary Francis. After several unsuccessful escape attempts and forced returns to Kentucky between 1837 and 1841, Bibb made his final successful bid for freedom and settled in Detroit, Michigan. He searched for his family for the next three years, but stopped after finding out they had been sold and that Malinda had become the mistress of her new owner. Bibb threw himself into antislavery work and became quite prominent. In 1848, he married Mary Miles, a free black woman and teacher working in the Boston abolitionist movement. The following year, he published *Narrative of Life and Adventures of Henry Bibb, an American Slave*. After the passage of the Fugitive Slave Act, the Bibbs crossed into British Canada and settled in Sandwich.[33]

It was from this small town in western Ontario that the Bibbs established the *Voice of the Fugitive*, beginning publication on January 1, 1851. This bimonthly newspaper called for the abolition of American slavery, temperance, educational reform, agricultural development, and emigration to Canada. It published numerous articles on American fugitive cases, abolitionist meetings in the United States and Canada West, and postemancipation conditions in the Caribbean. It also advertised and reported annual commemorations of British West Indies emancipation, along with articles on temperance and moral reform, together with advertisements for small businesses, including confectioners, boarding houses, clothiers, and barbers. Within one year, the *Voice of the Fugitive* claimed more than a thousand paid subscribers. Many Canadian readers first learned about major fugitive cases, like the Shadrach rescue in Boston and the fugitive rescue at Christiana, Pennsylvania, from the pages of this newspaper. The same newspaper played an important role in informing readers in the United States about the formation of antislavery organizations, the establishment and welfare of black communal settlements, and Anglo-Canadian politics. Moreover, the *Voice of the Fugitive* listed selling agents throughout Canada West, as well as in Michigan, Massachusetts, New Jersey, New York, New Hampshire, Ohio, and Pennsylvania. Martin Delaney was the Pittsburgh correspondent; James T. Holly was the agent for Burlington, Vermont. Its reach even extended to the United Kingdom: African-American visitors Henry Highland Garnet and James W. C. Pennington corresponded from London.[34]

It was through the pages of the *Voice of the Fugitive* that Henry Bibb called for a North America Convention of Colored People to convene in Toronto during the second week of September 1851. To hold such a meeting in the United States, he observed, "would greatly endanger the liberty of thousands of self-emancipated persons." In contrast, Canada "bids defiance to all fugitive slave laws," and Toronto was a great commercial metropolis and central meeting place. Although the major objects would be brought before the convention, several correspondents informed Bibb what these might be, and he subsequently published them:

1. The immediate and everlasting emancipation of our race from slavery, and a manifestation of gratitude to the government of Great Britain, which has so nobly protected us in the enjoyment of liberty, whenever and wherever, we have stepped on her soil.
2. To abandon menial employments, as far as it may be practicable, and become owners and tillers of the soil.
3. To consider the vast interests of moral, mental and physical improvement.
4. To inculcate the idea of every man becoming the owner of his homestead.
5. The vital importance of our people becoming agriculturalists as a means of making themselves independent.
6. To recommend the emigration of free people of color, from the United States, for the settlement of Canada land.
7. To take proper steps for sustaining such presses only as will faithfully vindicate the rights of our people.

8. To bear testimony against the American colonization to Africa, as being prejudicial against color and pro-slavery.
9. To pledge ourselves to the defence of that government only that protects us in the enjoyment of liberty.[35]

This agenda deserves quotation in full because its emphasis on free soil, social uplift, independent land ownership, emigration, a fair press, antiprejudice, and self-defense represents the fugitive slaves' manifesto in an age of manifestos.

Over three days at the convention, the delegates discussed numerous resolutions in "spirited debate," including the unchristian nature of American slavery; the moral improvement of temperance, education, and wealth accumulation; and cultivation of the soil. Earlier calls for immigration to Canada West were repeated. It was resolved "that the convention recommend to the colored people of the U.S. of America, to emigrate to the Canadas instead of going to Africa or the West India Islands, that they, by so doing, may be better able to assist their brethren who are daily flying from American slavery."[36]

In the aftermath of the meeting of the North America Convention of Colored People, three of the delegates—Henry Bibb, John Fisher, and James Tinsley—issued "An Address to the Colored Inhabitants of North America," which was published in the October 21, 1851, edition of the *Voice of the Fugitive*. As one might expect from a representative address, many of the convention's themes and resolutions were repeated, including outrage at the Fugitive Slave Act, calls for moral improvement, and emigration to Canada. But there was also a more militant tone to this address, anchored in the politics of fugitive self-emancipation. After outlining the unique oppression of "colored inhabitants," the hypocrisy of American republican slavery, and the nominal freedom of free coloreds in the United States, the address turned to its main theme of stressing that abolition was in the hands of the people of color in North America. While grateful to "the true-hearted abolitionists, who have stood by us in the darkest hours of adversity," the manifesto stressed that it is we who should be "standing in the front ranks of the battle, until our kinsmen, according to the flesh are disenthralled." The history of the oppressed demonstrates that they have succeeded in liberating themselves only through their own exertions. In the words of the English poet George Byron: "Hereditary bondsmen! know ye not, Who would be free, themselves must strike the first blow?" The best way to accomplish this was through slave rebellion: "Three millions and a half of men, armed with the righteous cause of freedom, and the God of Justice on their side, against two hundred and fifty thousand tyrants [southern slaveholders], could sweep them like chaff before the wind." Moreover, fugitives would undermine the system of American slavery. "We believe it to be an indispensable duty," read the address, "that every 'hereditary bondsman' owes to himself, first to run away from slavery, and to carry off with him whatever may be necessary to effect his escape." This last sentence drew from a long history of slave self-emancipation, stretching from the Kentucky cases in the late 1830s through to two of the address writers—Bibb and Tinsley—who were fugitives from U.S. slavery.[37]

IV

Along with antislavery organization and mobilization, fugitives crossed borders to create fugitive settlements, including black communities in Spanish Florida, British Florida, British Canada, the Republic of Mexico, and elsewhere. These settlements met with mixed success. Furthermore, they often served as footballs in an ideological game between defenders of slavery, who argued that such settlements proved that emancipation did not work, and abolitionists, who disseminated the opposite view that they demonstrated the unequivocal success of ex-slave freedom.[38] Amid the polemics, however, let us not forget why fugitives crossed borders, what they hoped to accomplish, and the role such settlements played in provoking territorial expansion.[39]

As noted previously, the creation of the United States did not prevent fugitives from continuing to escape. This led to the creation of fugitive settlements in Spanish Florida. By 1812, black settlements among the Seminole Indians consisting of "several hundred fug[i]tive slaves from the Carolinas & Georgia" were reported by irate southern slaveholders. A U.S. surveyor described separate villages with well-constructed houses and carefully cultivated fields and large herds of livestock.[40] In late 1814, the British military built a fort called British Post at Prospect Bluff, near Pensacola, which included some hundred fugitives who had enlisted in the army in exchange for future freedom. In the following year, an estimated 1,000 fugitives settled in the fort's environs, protected by a garrison of about 300 fugitives and some Choctaw and Seminole warriors led by a black leader called Garcon. This black fort was to become a "beacon light" for slaves, who flocked to its promise of freedom and guaranteed protection.[41]

It also served as a constant threat to the security of southern slave owners along the borders. The U.S. authorities were eventually persuaded to attack and destroy the fort, blowing up 270 of its inhabitants and capturing 64 prisoners. As a consequence, the fugitives fled eastward, where they built villages down the seacoast to Tampa Bay. Here, they lived and drilled in preparation for the impending invasion by the Americans. When it came, a thousand Seminole Indian and fugitive slave warriors proved no match for General Andrew Jackson's 3,300 troops, including American Indians opposed to the Seminoles. By the summer of 1818, the black and Indian settlements had been destroyed, their former residents killed, captured, or exiled. In February 1819, the Adams-Onis Treaty was signed between the United States and Spain. It ceded all of Florida for $5 million, dropped the U.S. claim to territory north of the 42nd parallel in the Pacific

Northwest, and ceded the U.S. claim to Texas. The treaty established the continental boundary between the United States and Spanish territories to the Pacific Ocean. More important, a territory that had provided a refuge for fugitives, virtually without interruption since the late seventeenth century, was now made safe for the expansion and protection of slaveholding interests. Historian Kenneth Porter has made the important point: "The original impulse behind these invasions was general American expansionism, inspired by the same frontier land-hunger as was also directed in the same general period against Canada; but another objective, which became increasingly important and eventually developed into a primary purpose, was to safeguard the slave system in adjacent states by breaking up the runaway Negro settlements in Florida."[42] He could have added Mexico.

Fugitives from the United States also settled north of the border in southern Ontario, British Canada. In 1830 and 1842, fugitives settled at Wilberforce and Dawn. Although these fugitive settlements were plagued by poor land, lack of alternative employment opportunities, and leadership problems, they did at least provide the basis for the creation of free black institutions—families, churches, schools—as well as asylum and relief from U.S. slavery, with its slaveholders, slave catchers, federal officials, and system of slave laws.[43]

Probably the most renowned fugitive settlement was Elgin. Named after British Canada's governor, it was incorporated on August 10, 1850, as the "King's Settlement" at Buxton, Ontario. Benjamin Drew's 1856 collection of fugitive slave narratives in Canada, *A Northside View of Slavery*, estimates its population numbered nearly 800 adults, many of them fugitive slaves who had originally resided in the northern United States before relocating to Canada. According to the director's fourth annual report of 1853:

> 130 families have settled on the lands of the association, and improved farms in the neighborhood: these families contain 520 persons in all. 500 acres are cleared and under fence; 135 cut down and partially cleared. Of the cleared land, 236 acres are in corn; 60 acres in wheat; 29 in oats, and 90 in other crops: making in all 415 acres under cultivation. The number of cattle in the settlement is 128. There are 15 horses, 30 sheep, and 250 hogs. The temperance principle is strictly acted on through the whole settlement,—no intoxicating drinks being either manufactured or sold. The Sabbath is generally observed; and most of the settlers attend some place of worship. The number of children at the day school is 112; at the Sabbath school, 80. They were all improving, both in secular and scriptural knowledge: a number of the more advanced pupils were studying Latin, with a view to future usefulness.

Isaac Riley's personal story humanizes this bare statistical report. Although he recalled a benevolent form of slavery in Missouri, he still decided to escape "with my wife and child to Canada." "Among the French near Windsor [Canada]," he continued:

> I got small wages—2s. or 1s. 6d. a day, [at] York: and morning and night up to my knees in water,—still I preferred this to abundance in slavery. I crossed over and got work and better pay in Michigan. They would have liked to have me remain, and offered to build a house for me. But I did not feel free in Michigan, and did not remain. I went to St. Catharines, and got fifty cents a day. By and by, I heard of Mr. King's settlement,—I came here, and have got along well. My children can get good learning here.

Dr. Samuel R. Howe, who represented the Freedmen's Inquiry Commission, agreed that this "settlement is a perfect success."[44]

Another settlement was the Refugee's Home Society (RHS). This organization was rooted in changes along the Detroit-Windsor frontier. The rapid influx of fugitives had resulted in the meeting of a local black convention at Sandwich, southern Ontario, in 1846. Its major objective was to form a new black settlement to aid fugitives through the provision of land, homes, and education. Over the next few years, the Sandwich Mission obtained about 1,200 acres, which was to be divided into 10-acre lots and resold to black settlers, with 25 acres reserved for a school and a church. Although little came of this plan, the Sandwich group became the basis for the Fugitives Union Society, a black moral improvement association located in Windsor. In May 1851, a new group of white abolitionists in Detroit were moved to form an organization whose primary object was to "extend to them [fugitives] the helping hand in their struggle to establish homes among strangers, whose laws protect them from the grasp of the American slave-hunters." The resulting body merged with the Sandwich group to form the RHS in January 1852. Its leaders included white abolitionists E. P. Benham and Horace Halleck in Detroit, American Missionary Association worker David Hotchkiss in Amherstburg, American fugitive and black settlement leader Josiah Henson, and Henry and Mary Bibb in Windsor. The RHS plan was to buy "50,000 acres of farming land, in Canada, on which to settle refugees from slavery." By 1855, it had purchased 2,000 acres and provided homes for 150 fugitives. Three years later, the RHS acquired another 290 acres along the Puce River east of Windsor, thus expanding the existing black community.[45]

There were also settlements of people of African descent south of the Rio Grande. On October 13, 1857, U.S. Consul Franklin Chase, based in Tampico, Mexico, wrote to U.S. Assistant Secretary of State John Appleton about one of these settlements:

> A decree was issued at the city of Mexico on the July 2, 1857, granting the formation of a new colony in the state of Vera Cruz and District of

Tampico called "Eureka." This concession is made to a person by the name of Luis N. Fouche, a colored native of the State of Florida, who has obligated himself to furnish his colony with one hundred families of the same race. They are to be considered as Citizens of the Mexican Republic but exempted from the payment of all taxes other than municipal, and also from the performance of military service, except in the case of foreign invasion, when they are to come under all obligations of other Mexican Citizens.

It is unclear why this decree was issued, beyond the Mexican government's desire to populate regions with productive emigrants, as well as potential fighters against U.S. incursions. (One can imagine these black emigrants would have been as eager to repulse slaveholder attacks as their cousins in Canada.) Consul Chase continued: "Several families have already arrived here, and preliminary preparations are in progress for the final establishment of the new Colony, but from the information I have obtained from them, I feel convinced that their new enterprise will not be attended with success."[46] The fugitive poverty described earlier by Frederick Olmsted supports Consul Chase's feeling, although it does not appear to have stopped black cross-border emigration. In 1857, forty people of African descent left New Orleans for Vera Cruz and formed another settlement at Tlacotalpan. Other black settlements were reported at Nacimiento, Coahuila, and elsewhere in Mexico. Although conditions were often hard, wages low, and the language and culture initially alien, many fugitives embraced their new lives of freedom. Much like their fugitive cousins in British Canada, these emigrants were attracted by an alternative set of freedoms, as well as official protection offered by cross-border movement and settlements that were guaranteed by the existing government.[47]

It should be clear by now that national borders played an important role in fugitive flight, as well as the establishment of fugitive settlements. Crossing borders was more likely to result in permanent freedom, as well as the opportunity to begin a new life away from the travail of slavery. At the same time, there were borders within national borders that facilitated fugitive movement. We have already seen this with the shifting of borders between slave and free states in the antebellum United States. The Great Dismal Swamp, situated along the North Carolina–Virginia border, is 1.3 million acres of quagmire, bog, and inhospitable terrain. It was once peopled by a motley crew of poor whites from the two states, American Indians especially of the Tuscarora nation, and fugitive slaves. There were concentric rings of external and internal residents, many of whom spent their entire lives within the confines of the swamp. There were also maroon communities deep in the interior regions, who, according to Edmund Jackson of *The Liberty Bell* in 1852, constituted a "singular community of blacks, who have won their freedom and established themselves securely in the midst of the largest slaveholding State of the South . . . [and] from this extensive swamp, they are seldom, if now at all, reclaimed."[48] Refuges like the Great Dismal Swamp suggest that long-term self-emancipation was even possible within national borders.

V

This cross-border treatment of fugitives, laws, and settlements is noteworthy for several reasons. First, those fugitives who crossed borders were much more likely to remain permanently free because the long arm of the slaveholding state could not reach them. This was not always the case. A citizen from Washington County, Texas, reportedly crossed into Mexico with a posse and captured and returned a fugitive.[49] On the other hand, the lesson of the failure to extradite fugitives from British Canada and the Mexican Republic to the United States during the 1830s and 1840s sent a clear message to fugitives; it was also no doubt the reason for so many crossings after the passage of the 1850 law, as well as during the Civil War. Second, cross-border fugitives were a major loss of capital investment for slaveholders because it was so difficult to obtain their return. Samuel Ward explained that each fugitive from the American South in the mid-1850s "carried off in his own person from 400 to 2,000 dollars."[50] If 1,000 fugitives left annually, slaveholders would have lost between $400,000 and $2 million. This explains the wide array of political activities by southern slaveholders and their supporters—extradition treaties, national slave laws, territorial annexation—to try to retrieve their lost property. Third, there were important cross-national dimensions to some domestic laws that get overlooked if we focus only on legal acts within national frameworks. The emigration of free blacks and fugitives from the northern United States to Canada as a consequence of the 1850 law is only the most obvious example. Another was the 1829 abolition of slavery in Mexico. Despite its noble sentiments, it was primarily motivated by Mexican politicians' desire to dissuade the development of slavery along the new nation's borderlands.

Moreover, annexation was also driven by the need to stamp out potential refuges for fugitive slaves. This simple point, made nearly seventy years ago by Kenneth Porter in the pages of *The Journal of Negro History*, was probably also true regarding carving the state of Texas out of northern Mexico. If we are familiar with the notion of the southwest territories being made available for American slaveholders, we should also become more acquainted with the notion that these new territories provided beacons of liberty to enslaved people. In addition, fugitive settlements not only inspired numerous enslaved people but also, as the first postemancipation communities in North America, challenged the argument of slavery's defenders that slaves could not exist without slavery and would perish if free. The continental struggles of fugitives suggests otherwise. Most important, fugitive cross-national movements suggest that the nation-state, with its laws, boundaries, and territorial integrity, could be indispensable to the successful realization of long-term freedoms. Fugitives *knew* the significance of national borders, even if some contemporary scholars dismiss the relevance of the nineteenth-century nation-state in the lives of ordinary men and women.[51] Finally, these fugitive movements, linked with those described at the opening of this chapter, belong to a long tradition of continental pathways to freedom beyond our conventional understanding of national struggles for rights and freedoms.

NOTES

1. Thanks to Emily E. LaBarbera Twarog for shepherding this project, to Shelton Stromquist and Elizabeth Lindquist for editorial improvements, to the participants at the 2008 Newberry Conference session, and to my research assistant, John Tilghman, for tracking down some archival sources. Shukran to the editors of this book, especially John French, for providing me with an opportunity to expand this chapter beyond its original Anglo-American framework. This chapter is dedicated to the pioneering cross-national scholarly insights of Fred Landon, Kenneth Porter, and Rosalie Schwartz.
2. Friedrich Katz, *The Life & Times of Pancho Villa* (Stanford, CA: Stanford University Press, 1998) 26, 90, 193; Arthur Ashe, *A Hard Road to Glory: The History of the Afro-American Athlete, 1619–1918* (New York: Amistad, 1988), 39.
3. Rosalie Schwartz, *Across the Rio To Freedom: U.S. Negroes in Mexico* (El Paso: Texas Western Press, 1975), 3.
4. Peter H. Wood, *Black Majority: Negroes in Colonial South Carolina from 1670 through the Stono Rebellion* (New York: W. W. Norton, 1975), 304–5.
5. Schwartz, *Across the Rio*, 3–4; Kenneth Wiggins Porter, "Negroes and the Seminole War, 1817–1818," *The Journal of Negro History* 36, no. 3 (July 1951): 250–1. The bias of much of the historical literature can be seen in the designation of fugitive slaves as a "problem." For fugitive slaves, the problem was finding freedom in colonial and national systems of slavery.
6. Schwartz, *Across the Rio*, 6; Fergus M. Bordewich, *Bound for Canaan: The Epic Story of the Underground Railroad, America's First Civil Rights Movement* (New York: Amistad, 2006), 111–12; Porter, "Negroes and the Seminole War," 278.
7. Junius Rodriguez, ed., *Encyclopedia of Emancipation and Abolition in the Transatlantic World*, vol. 3 (New York: Sharpe Reference, 2007), 689.
8. Eugene C. Barker, "The Influence of Slavery in the Colonization of Texas," *Mississippi Valley Historical Review* 11, no. 1 (June 1924), 3. Barker's article makes the opposite argument: that slavery's expansion and the protection of existing slavery played no part in Texas's revolution.
9. Samuel Ringgold Ward, *Autobiography of a Fugitive Negro* (1855; reprint, New York: Arno, 1968), 114.
10. Schwartz, *Across the Rio*, 8.

11. Robin Blackburn, "Haiti, Slavery, and the Age of Democratic Revolution," *William and Mary Quarterly* 63, no. 4 (2006): 10. This was about the same number of slaves freed in New York State two years earlier on July 4, 1827.
12. Schwartz, *Across the Rio*, 26–27, 31, 33, 60, n. 114; *Rip Ford's Texas*, ed. by Stephen B. Oates (Austin: University of Texas Press, 1963), 196.
13. Frederick Law Olmsted, *A Journey through Texas* (1857; reprint, Lincoln: University of Nebraska Press, 2004), 323–25. Italics in the original.
14. Jacob Branch, *The American Slave: A Composite Autobiography*, vol. 4 in *Texas Narratives*, part 1, ed. George P. Rawick (Westport, CT: Greenwood, 1972), 141.
15. Robin W. Winks, *The Blacks in Canada: A History* (New Haven, CT: Yale University Press, 1971), 168–77.
16. Ward, *Autobiography*, 126–27. Italics in the original.
17. J. R. Kerr-Ritchie, *Rites of August First: Emancipation Day in the Black Atlantic World* (Baton Rouge: Louisiana State University Press, 2007), 144.
18. Steven Hahn, *A Nation under Our Feet: Black Political Struggles in the Rural South from Slavery to the Great Migration* (Cambridge, MA: Belknap, 2003), 57.
19. Schwartz, *Across the Rio*, 8-9. Spelling in the original.
20. Ibid., 9–18.
21. Kerr-Ritchie, *Rites of August First*, 124–25; Karolyn Smardz Frost, *I've Got a Home in Glory Land: A Lost Tale of the Underground Railroad* (Toronto, ON: Thomas Allen, 2007).
22. Kerr-Ritchie, *Rites of August First*, 125–26; Jane H. Pease and William H. Pease, *Black Utopia: Negro Communal Experiments in America* (Madison: State Historical Society of Wisconsin, 1963), 46. Jason H. Silverman's *Unwelcome Guests: Canada West's Response to American Fugitive Slaves, 1800–1865* (Greenwood, CT: Associated Faculty, 1985) provides the most persuasive case for racism toward fugitives in Canada.
23. The major exception was British India, where slave abolition was delayed until 1842 because the colony fell under the jurisdiction of the East India Company, not the British Parliament.
24. Silverman, *Unwelcome Guests*, 37; Winks, *Blacks in Canada*, 169–70; Ward, *Autobiography*, 123.
25. Junius P. Rodriguez, ed., *Slavery in the United States: A Social, Political, and Historical Encyclopedia*, vol. 2 (Santa Barbara, CA: ABC-CLIO, 2007), 636–39; Kerr-Ritchie, *Rites of August First*, 169.
26. Kerr-Ritchie, *Rites of August First*, 170–71.
27. Ibid.
28. Schwartz, *Across the Rio*, 32, 50–51.
29. For fugitives' transatlantic antislavery mobilization, see Kerr-Ritchie, *Rites of August First*.
30. A point raised by Jim Barrett and Nelson Lichtenstein at this chapter's original presentation at the Newberry Conference.

31. James Brewer Stewart, *Holy Warriors: The Abolitionists and American Slavery* (New York: Hill and Wang, 1976), 157–58.
32. Kerr-Ritchie, *Rites of August First*, 135–36, 139–40.
33. Henry Bibb, *Narrative of the Life and Adventures of Henry Bibb: An American Slave, Written by Himself* (1849); reproduced online: http://docsouth.unc.edu/neh/bibb/menu.html; Kerr-Ritchie, *Rites of August First*, 146.
34. *Voice of the Fugitive*, January–December, July 30, 1851; Kerr-Ritchie, *Rites of August First*, 147.
35. *Voice of the Fugitive*, July 30, 1851; Kerr-Ritchie, *Rites of August First*, 148–49.
36. Kerr-Ritchie, *Rites of August First*, 151.
37. *Voice of the Fugitive*, October 22, 1851; Kerr-Ritchie, *Rites of August First*, 152–53.
38. Kerr-Ritchie, *Rites of August First*, 230–32.
39. See p. 367.
40. Porter, "Negroes and the Seminole War," 253.
41. Ibid., 260–61.
42. Ibid., 263–75 (quote on 254); Alan Brinkley, *The Unfinished Nation: A Concise History of the American People*, vol. 1: *To 1877* (New York: McGraw Hill, 1993), 213–15. Kenneth Wiggins Porter, *The Negro on the American Frontier* (New York: Arno, 1971). For Porter's professional life, see August Meier and Elliott Rudwick, *Black History and the Historical Profession 1915–1980* (Urbana: University of Illinois Press, 1986), 106.
43. Kerr-Ritchie, *Rites of August First*, 159–60; Harvey Amani Whitfield, *Blacks on the Border: The Black Refugees in British North America, 1815–1860* (Burlington: University of Vermont Press, 2006), 45.
44. Benjamin Drew, *A North-Side View of Slavery* (Boston: J. P. Jewett, 1856), 291–308; reproduced online: http://docsouth.unc.edu/neh/drew/drew.html; Samuel R. Howe, *Refugees from Slavery in Canada West* (1864), 70–71, in Fred Landon, "The Buxton Settlement in Canada," *The Journal of Negro History* 3, no. 4 (October 1918): 366. Landon taught at the University of Western Ontario from where he pioneered studies of borderland slavery, abolition, and politics, much of which was published in *The Journal of Negro History* during the 1920s.
45. Kerr-Ritchie, *Rites of August First*, 153.
46. Franklin Chase to John Appleton, October 13, 1857, U.S. Dept. of State, Dispatches from the U.S. Consuls in Tampico, 1824–1906, Dispatch Number 27, Microcopy Number T241, Record Group 59, National Archives.
47. Schwartz, *Across the Rio*, 40–44.
48. Brent Morris, "'Running Servants and All Others': The Diverse an[d] Elusive Maroons of the Great Dismal Swamp," in *Voices from within the Veil: African Americans and the Experience of Democracy*, ed. William H. Alexander et al. (Newcastle, UK: Cambridge Scholars, 2008), 85–112, quote on page 85.
49. Schwartz, *Across the Rio*, 32–33.
50. Ward, *Autobiography*, 104.
51. For an alternative view, see chapter 5, Dirk Hoerder's contribution in this book.

19 MOVABLE TYPE

TORONTO'S TRANSNATIONAL PRINTERS, 1866–1872

Jacob Remes

When the Toronto Typographical Union met in June 1866, two resolutions were moved and carried.[1] James Hynes moved "that those members of this Union now under arms for the defence of the country be exempt from dues." Hynes referred to printers called up as militiamen to repel an attack on Canada by the Fenian Brotherhood, a U.S.-based Irish republican organization. Earlier that month, eight hundred Fenians had invaded Canada from U.S. soil in the hope that they could force Britain to grant Irish independence.[2] Later, William Winter moved that the union's month-old charter from the Indianapolis-based National Typographical Union "be suitably framed."[3] The charter effectively subordinated the TTU to the NTU, and Winter's motion celebrated the TTU's joining an American labor organization.

It was an accident of timing that the Fenians chose to attack British North America from the United States the same month that Toronto's organized printers voted to join the U.S.-based NTU. At first glance, Hynes's and Winter's motions seem contradictory—the first honoring patriots who defended Canada from an American invasion, the second celebrating membership in an American union. But the motions appear contradictory only in contemporary conceptualizations of nationality and citizenship, by which we expect that nations, states, and labor markets should be coterminous. In the mid-nineteenth century, Toronto's skilled workers had no such expectations. Rather, they belonged to three different yet overlapping communities that were neither functionally nor ideologically contradictory. Toronto's printers belonged simultaneously to a North American working class, a British imperial nation, and a Canadian polity. The TTU's concurrent adoption of the two motions suggests that the relevance of these different communities differed with the audience and the context. Toronto's printers mobilized each of these identities at different moments and in different contexts, depending on whom they wanted to influence.

This chapter examines a group of skilled, male workers in a specific locality: 461 unionized printers in Toronto. While its focus is local, it examines how these individuals acted as transnational subjects. Historians have of late decentered the nation as a category of historical analysis. By showing the ways in which nation has been a historically unstable concept, scholars have challenged our contemporary notions of nationality and citizenship.[4] Legal scholars similarly draw on the experiences of contemporary migrants to consider what citizenship might look like decoupled from the normative nation-state.[5] This chapter furthers that literature by showing that Toronto printers participated in imagined communities of different sorts, and that they drew on these complementary communities when they were relevant to different parts of their lives. That Toronto printers did not live within a stable and unified nation provides compelling evidence that the modern ideological supremacy of nation is contingent and historically specific. Their experience suggests that transnational, subnational, or nonnational communities and categories of analysis might better serve historical scholarship. Tracing the transnational lives and ideologies of Toronto printers facilitates a better understanding of their relationship to their international union, to their political representatives, and to the broader British Empire.

Historians have recently addressed migration and transnationality in what they term United States–Canada borderlands. Building on an older historiography of diplomacy and population movements, these historians paradoxically center a political boundary and decenter the nation-state. They show how local people created communities that spanned the political boundary, and they highlight groups like runaway slaves and aboriginal peoples who depended on it. The most successful histories show how these border-crossing populations contested the putative boundary even while both states tried to impose their lines and regulations on them. Toronto printers did not live in a liminal space between a stable "United States" and a stable "Canada." Rather, they were located simultaneously and firmly within a Canadian political community and a North American working-class community. They were also positioned firmly within the British Empire, a community that the borderlands historians have thus far neither explained nor engaged. Borderlands scholars are most perceptive when they explain the creation of a culturally meaningful border as a historically contingent process, but their intrinsic focus on the border suggests the limitation of their transnational frame.[6]

Other scholars have reevaluated traditional narratives of the changing relationship between Canada and Great Britain in the late nineteenth century. Drawing from Carl Berger's germinal work, they point out that Confederation did not mark a turning away from Britain, but rather was part of a long process in which Canadians found new ways of expressing British nationalism and a coexisting Canadian patriotism.[7] As Phillip Buckner argues, the growth of a Canadian identity and community concurred with the growth of a sense of Britishness among the same people.[8] He and others trace the constitutional and political evolution of Canada's imperial connection, note how schools and newspapers inculcated and reflected imperial ideology, and demonstrate that middle-class Canadians often looked toward Britain for cultural cues rather than to the United States.[9] Berger, an intellectual historian, suggested that the ideology of imperial unity "found no favor with the working classes," and later scholars have continued to focus on middle-class and elite imperialism, nationalism, and patriotism.[10] In offering a social historical examination of the way skilled workers in Canada understood their relationship with Greater Britain, this chapter expands that scholarship to emphasize the working class and highlights the complex relationship with the United States.

The June 1866 meeting of the TTU illuminates Toronto printers' simultaneous location in three overlapping, transnational communities. The printers at that meeting acted within a well-defined community of North American printers.[11] These printers traveled across the United States and Canada throughout their careers. They joined a U.S.-based institution like the NTU, and the NTU welcomed them, precisely because printers in the United States and Canada worked in a single, unified labor market. Yet they also recognized differences between themselves and those in "the republic to the south." Many of them had personal ties to a British imperial nation. Of the ten men at the June 1866 meeting, between two and five were born in the British Isles.[12] Even those born in Canada recognized affective ties to "the mother country," with which they shared a language, a queen, and an ethnicity. The printers emphasized their Britishness in later years, when they appealed to their rights as English workmen and cheered Queen Victoria.

Finally, the Toronto printers belonged to a political community in Canada. This Canadian community emerged when the printers made claims on the new Canadian state, as they did at election time or when they sought to influence the law. Just as the TTU joined the National Typographical Union, it also worked with the local coopers' union to form the Toronto Trades Assembly, through which it hoped to have influence over local employers and politicians.[13]

Toronto's printers spoke to their different communities at different times for different purposes. This is not to say that the printers were variously more "North American" or more "British" or that they felt more "North American" at a union meeting and more "Canadian" at a political one. They left no records of their feelings, so we cannot know whether these identities battled for supremacy in the printers' souls, only how they deployed references to them in their rhetoric and symbolic actions. Nor does our public evidence reveal where printers considered their home. What the printers' behavior and words reflect are the ways they made claims on different types of people based on shared memberships in different communities. Thus, as North American workers, they made claims on their employers (for higher wages and shorter hours) and their fellow printers (to respect their union's authority); as British subjects, they made claims on the larger public (to support their right to organize and strike); and as Canadians, they made claims on their elected officials and the state (to change specific laws). These were not, to use one metaphor, different hats the printers put on or took off as they needed, or to use another, chits that they put away in a drawer when they were not using them. They wore all the hats at once and held all three chits in their hands.[14] Their group memberships overlapped, and printers accessed them as they found them relevant.

These three communities came into stark relief in 1872. On March 25, Toronto's printers struck to demand a nine-hour workday, so beginning a major battle with the employing master printers. George Brown, the publisher of the *Globe* and leader of the Reform Party, demanded that local authorities arrest the strike committee for seditious conspiracy. The case was dismissed, however, after the Dominion government, led by Conservative Prime Minister Sir John A. Macdonald, passed the Trade Unions Act, modeled on the British Trades Union Act, which had been enacted a year before.[15] The Macdonald legislation made unions and strikes unambiguously legal and had the predictable political effect: Toronto's organized working class rallied around him and his party's candidates during the hard-fought parliamentary election that summer. Although the strike depleted the TTU's treasury and membership rolls, it won shorter hours and established the TTU as a force within local industry and the labor movement.[16] The strike and the rhetoric around the passage of the Trade Unions Act illuminate the relationship that the printers had with Britishness and Canadianness and the ways in which they appealed to Britain and Canada at different times. Also debated in 1872 was the unpopular Treaty of Washington, in which U.S. and British diplomats resolved a number of disputes concerning Canada. In the election, the treaty served as a proxy for Canadians debating what their relationship should be both with Britain and with the United States.[17] Such debate exposed the ways Canadian workers imagined themselves to be part of the British Empire and thus different from their southern neighbor.

A North American Working Class: Toronto's Printers and the United States

The continental community of workers to which Toronto printers belonged can be most simply described as a unified labor market. The tramping printer is well known in Anglo-American labor historiography, as printers in Europe and North America frequently left one city in search of better employment elsewhere.[18] The

TTU minute books record 461 men who attended membership meetings between January 1866 and February 1872, yet the official membership list for February 1872 included only 270 members, of whom 19 were traveling. Even allowing for the one recorded death and a handful of hypothetical, unrecorded retirements, this means that roughly 200 men circulated through but did not settle in Toronto during this period.[19] Frequent travel meant that conditions in one city directly affected those of another. Thus North American printers built institutions that would support local organizations and regulate travel. Moreover, sojourns not only created an impetus for institution building but also built a sense of community. Printers arriving in Toronto brought news of how other local unions operated and of what demands they made on their employers. Such movement created affective ties among workers in different locales.

The chart shows the cities Toronto printers traveled to and from during this period. The data suggest several things about tramping patterns. First, move-

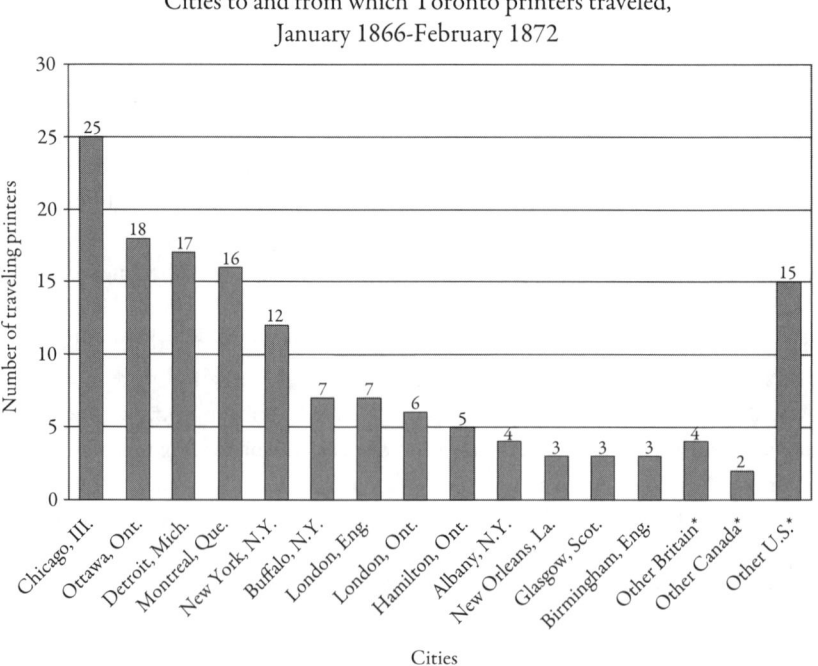

FIGURE 19.1 In the minutes of their meetings TTU secretaries recorded the city from which a newcomer presented a traveling card, and occasionally indicated where a Toronto printer went when he left the city. This graph shows the frequencies with which each city appeared in the minutes taken between January 1866 and February 1872. Most of the time, the secretary only recorded cities in which there was a union organized, and rarely did the secretary record the cities to which printers departed. The chart includes all cities mentioned in the minutes, regardless of whether printers were coming or going.
*Other: Cities with one or two appearances in the minutes.
Source: Toronto Typographical Union minutes

ment among cities was decidedly transnational. A majority of exchanges were with American cities. Second, some cities were favored: The four most popular cities account for slightly more than half (52 percent) of the known exchanges. Third, these cities were not determined by their proximity to Toronto or their relative size. Chicago, for instance, is farther from Toronto than any North American city on the list apart from New Orleans, but it is the city most represented. Buffalo had ten fewer exchanges than Detroit, although it is about 140 miles closer and had more than half again the latter's population.[20] It is apparent that tramping printers chose cities based on affective or institutional ties, not simply ease of access. In other words, sojourning not only built a transnational community of printers in different cities but also depended on that community.

The union served a valuable purpose in such a transient industry because it regulated movement between cities. A printer from a unionized city had to have been a member there if he wanted to join the union in his new city; men even sometimes joined the Toronto union immediately before departing from the city. Conversely, it meant that a printer who refused to join the union in one city could not expect a welcome in another union city. The NTU umbrella organization routinized the sharing of information; the Toronto union regularly received circulars from other locals with the names of "rats" who had violated union rules and should be denied employment among union printers. It established networks for sharing specific intelligence. When a man appeared in Detroit claiming to have been a member of the Toronto union, the Detroit secretary could write to his counterpart to investigate. A continental union not only regulated the movement of individual printers but also helped to manage the flow of printers as a group. A poor state of trade in one city could easily spread to the next if unemployed printers all flocked to their neighbors. Toronto printers had an incentive to support strikes even in far-off American cities because if New Yorkers lost their jobs, they might arrive in Toronto, depressing wages there. Supporting other unions' struggles also meant, of course, that Toronto printers could expect similar help in times of need. Printers throughout North America worked to build continent-wide institutions that helped them regulate the labor market to their advantage.

The movement of North American printers, and the politics of that transience, rested largely on their status as skilled workers, on the mobility and freedom guaranteed them by their whiteness, and on the professional privilege their union defended at the expense of women and younger men. Membership in a transnational union gave transient printers power because it meant that if they could not find a job, or if they became fed up with wages, conditions, or their ability to organize, they could easily move elsewhere. For unskilled or nonunion workers, such travel could put them at risk of coming under the power of labor agents or padrones; members of a transnational craft union could instead rely on their brother members. Thus travel and distance increased, rather than decreased, the freedom of their labor.[21] This freedom of movement—and the other freedoms that went with it—also depended on the printer's gender. Women were deliberately excluded from membership in the union, and they were easily excluded from the fraternity of sojourners, too. An unaccompanied woman would have found intercity travel more dangerous than a man, she was more likely to be encumbered with children, and she would not find the welcome of brother printers in her new city.[22] Moreover, Canadian labor historians have increasingly emphasized the role of race in the formation of white, working-class culture.[23] Though Toronto's unions do not appear to have feared nonwhite competition for jobs, they did join in anti-Chinese politics.[24] By protecting the privileges of the skilled male worker, providing fellowship in a new city, and creating social networks through which information flowed, the presence of a continental union helped to blunt the otherwise considerable difficulties of travel across large distances.

In the mid-nineteenth century, North America was a single labor market for skilled artisans. The same benefits that banding together brought Baltimore and New Orleans printers flowed from an alliance between Toronto and Chicago, because travel between the latter two cities was, if anything, easier than travel between the former pair. The difficulty of crossing the border was negligible. Inspection of travelers for the purpose of regulating immigration did not begin at the U.S.-Canada border until the 1920s, with the intensification of American immigration restrictions. No one even recorded the names of migrants until 1906.[25] When William Dean Howells, then a fledgling newspaper correspondent, traveled up the St. Lawrence Valley in 1860, he wrote of the exoticness of "British" Toronto, telling of differences in clothing and accent. But his parenthetical mention of his crossing the border suggests the ease with which printers could do it: "I strolled up from the wharf to the Rossin House, (the custom-house officer having politely passed my trunks and small valise and portfolio without examination,) and at the hotel perceived for the first time that I was no longer in my beloved native land." Indeed, the border crossing was so easy and insignificant that Howells was perhaps the only travel writer of the period to even describe the process.[26]

It should therefore not be surprising that the National Typographical Union began early to expand into British North America.[27] In 1860, when the New Orleans local sought advice from the NTU on how to deal with sojourners from Toronto, the NTU studied the issue and eventually invited the Toronto Typographical Society to take out a charter.[28] The invitation reached Toronto in December 1864, the same time the union in Saint John, New Brunswick, joined the NTU.[29] Why it took five years to go from a proposal to inviting these unions to join is not clear, although the disarray the Civil War created for the NTU and the need to amend the union's constitution to expand into Canada seem logical explanations. The Toronto union delayed its response until April 1865, when, after some debate, a committee was appointed to study the matter. The following month, the Toronto Typographical Society chose to become the Toronto Typographical Union, the NTU's ninety-first affiliate.[30]

While membership in the national union—which soon changed its name to the International Typographical Union of North America to reflect its transnational membership—is the most concrete evidence of the Toronto printers' association with the United States, it is by no means the most important. Membership in the NTU only institutionalized ties that had existed for years. Even before formal membership in the national union, Toronto's printers had been deeply embedded in a growing North American working-class culture, beyond frequent cross-border travel. As early as 1836, the Toronto union had struck, demanding that employers match the wages paid in New York.[31] The Toronto union had policed the labor market in cooperation with its American counterparts. In September 1860, for instance, the secretary of the Buffalo union wrote that James S. Martin was a "rat," so Toronto printers refused to work alongside him until he "made ample reparations" to the Buffalo union.[32] Toronto printers also had affective ties to printers in the United States, forged by their own travels. In 1861, for instance, DeVere Hunt read to the meeting a letter from U. J. Tracie, then in New Orleans. While it is unclear which city Tracie considered home, he traveled frequently between New Orleans and Toronto, and it is likely that Hunt went to Louisiana based on his friend's experience there. Similarly, the month after Tracie's letter, A. Black, another man who had worked in Toronto, wrote a letter from California, warning that there were too many printers there for too few jobs.[33] Appropriately for a printers' union, newspapers reinforced community. The TTU began in 1862 to subscribe to the *Printer*, a New York publication. The suggestion came from DeVere Hunt, showing again that the most frequent travelers showed the most interest in building a transnational community.[34] Sojourners like Hunt built through their travels and other connections the affective and social communities that they and other printers created locally through shared work, battles over job control, and sociability.[35]

All this occurred before the Toronto union joined the NTU, an affiliation that reinforced and strengthened the common community that already existed. In the five years following affiliation, Toronto printers came increasingly in contact with their colleagues to the south. The corresponding secretary received more frequent notices from other unions, announcing their current roster of members or denouncing "rats." Toronto's printers participated in a vigorous debate in 1867 over a proposed new constitution for the ITU, exchanging letters with other subordinate unions and even appointing a special committee to canvass the members and ask their opinion.[36] More significant, perhaps, the TTU donated generously to strike and relief funds in New York, Buffalo, Brooklyn, Erie, and Chicago.[37] Of those five American cities, three—New York, Buffalo, and Chicago—frequently exchanged members with Toronto.

The printers' newspaper, the *Ontario Workman*, reflected and reproduced a community of North American workers. Readers learned which American cities promised employment and which would be bad choices. Columns of American news were heavy with stories of industrial disputes in the United States and reports of boom conditions in certain cities; similarly, columns of labor news frequently included American notices. The "Labor Notes" column of the April 25, 1872, edition, for instance, carried news that "good painters and bricklayers are in demand in Detroit," that the master builders in New York were considering adopting the short hour system, that Brooklyn workers had held a mass meeting to demand the eight-hour day, and that a cigar makers' strike in Leavenworth, Kansas, had ended. The news from North America was frequently practical. For example, the newspaper carried an announcement of a new shingle factory opening in Waterloo, Ontario, and a notice that the Pennsylvania Railroad Company in Altoona employed 2,550 men, in both cases suggesting where men in Toronto could go in search of work, just as columns of strike news warned them where not to go.[38]

Not all of the U.S. coverage was purely practical, however. As with most small, weekly newspapers of the period, the *Ontario Workman* was primarily filler. A typical eight-page issue contained only three pages of news, and of those, the copy was often recycled from other sources and barely counted as news. Page two contained a serialized story, and page three was filled with short stories, either explicitly fictional or effectively so. Similarly, the sixth page was usually not news; it often carried a column called "Chips and Sawdust," which consisted of one-line jokes and anecdotes. Pages seven and eight were often filled with advertisements or more anecdotes and curiosities. Most of the time, the filler was American, identifiable because the stories took place in an American city, because they made reference to American politics, or because they were credited to an American publication. The *Ontario Workman*'s printing of American filler, while probably not intended to bind together a North American working class, had that effect: Workers in Canada and the United States read the same things.

Toronto printers drew on this North American workers' culture in their actions related to labor issues. When in 1872 Toronto workers began agitating for the nine-hour day, they held a mass meeting chaired by the TTU's J. S. Williams. The featured speaker was a Mr. Trevallick, a representative from the National Labor League of the United States.[39] In matters relating to the continental labor market, the Canadianness of Toronto and its printers seemed barely to matter; instead, the TTU emphasized similarities with the United States. Repeatedly, the TTU rejected outright or ignored proposals from the Montreal union to create a Canadian block within the ITU. In 1867, it refused to send a common "delegate from Canada" to the international convention.[40] Two years later, the Montreal union suggested that they work together to try to organize unions in other cities in Canada; the question was referred to a committee that never reported back, and the proposal died of neglect.[41] The TTU also rejected an offer to hold the annual convention of the international in Toronto; Montreal accepted two years later.[42] While Montreal was attempting to create a Canadian community of printers, Toronto continued to learn from American cities. In 1868, for instance, the union once again followed the lead of several American cities—identified as such in the annual report—in revamping the working card system.[43] Other Ontario unions seemed to follow the lead of Toronto in imagining a continental community of printers. The London (Ontario) Typographical Union even went so far as to hold a dinner honoring Benjamin Franklin's birthday.[44]

The only indication of special relations among Canadian unions is that the Toronto union consistently gave much more generously to the strike funds of their compatriot unions, even imposing special levies on members to support strikes in Montreal and Ottawa.[45] This may have reflected the fact that there was more exchange of workers among Canadian cities than most other cities—recall that the American unions that received aid also frequently sent workers to Toronto—but it may also have been an indication that Toronto's printers felt a greater allegiance to their counterparts in Canadian cities than in American cities. There is nothing to suggest, however, that when the Montreal and Ottawa unions wrote requesting aid, they called on their Toronto brethren in terms of a shared Canadian identity.

A British Imperial Nation: Toronto's Printers and England

While Toronto's unionized printers saw themselves within a North American labor market and imagined themselves part of a North American community of workers, they also paid fealty to Britain and recognized strong affective ties to what they called "the mother country." They particularly used the language of British nationalism when they demanded justice or otherwise made calls to a community larger than or different from the working class. Thus they summoned the British nation while engaged in their dangerous battle with George Brown over the right to unionize and strike. Before the 1872 strike, there had been almost no suggestion that British nationality mattered. In January 1870, for instance, the union requested that its corresponding secretary "open Communication with some of the Typographical Unions of Great Britain," but the nature or purpose of that communication was left unstated, and the secretary never reported back on its result.[46] But during the 1872 strike, the printers had to appeal to a broader public in order to appeal for rights, so they called on a common, cross-class sense of Britishness.[47]

The printers struck in March 1872 for a shorter working day, but after twenty-four of their leaders were arrested for conspiracy, the issue became the right to strike and thus the very right to effective unions. Printers framed the question as one of liberty and rights due all citizens, rather than as simply a matter that concerned the working class. Thus they crafted appeals to the nation at large and demanded the rights due them as British subjects. To do this, they emphasized their allegiance to England and the Queen and downplayed their affiliation with American workers. When demanding a nine-hour day, for instance, they described their movement as English in origin and distinct from the short hour movement in the United States.

When printers and their advocates appealed to others through references to England, the Queen, and their allegiance to the mother country, they participated in what I call British imperial nationalism. Although writers and speakers referred to *England* as the mother country and pronounced it the wellspring of Canadian culture, they also celebrated Canada as the epitome of the *British* ideal of English, Irish, and Scots living together in harmony. Despite the emphasis on England, a united Britishness was imagined as the imperial ideal. Like all nationalisms, it sought to describe and create an imagined community of a large number of people of diverse classes and to ascribe them a political culture.[48] Different speakers enunciated their views of the nation differently, but they shared certain elements. First, there were frequent, even ritualistic, references to Queen Victoria and her family. Second, there was a sense of community with people in Britain. Third, there was the insistence that all British subjects, regardless of where they were located within the empire, had the right to English liberty. Because English liberty was something that was imagined to bind together all subjects, regardless of class, Toronto printers made appeals to British nationalism when they spoke to people of different classes.

A common aspect of global British imperial nationalism was the invention of the Queen as a potent imperial symbol.[49] The Toronto printers' fight for the nine-hour day occasioned many public demonstrations, and the election of 1872 gathered workers for many public meetings. Each of these ended with three cheers for the Queen, a ritual reminder that all those present were bound together in fealty to her. When Toronto workers gathered to thank John A. Macdonald for his support during the strike and to present a memento to Lady Macdonald, the couple took their seats to the strains of "God Save the Queen."[50] At times, references to the royal family seem ritualistic. At a rally in April to support the printers, James Beaty, a Tory member of Parliament and the publisher of the only newspaper to acquiesce to the printers' demand for shorter hours, began his speech with patriotic thanks for "the recovery of the Prince of Wales. He knew," wrote the *Ontario Workman*, "the sympathy that had been felt through the country and the British Dominion by every Christian, not only for the Prince but for his widowed mother during the illness of the Prince."[51] Prince Edward had indeed been gravely ill with typhus, but that had been five months previous; the newspapers had reported his recovery since January. In April, the news was of his healthy holiday trip to Rome.[52]

There were other invocations of the monarchy. The *Ontario Workman* printed a lengthy report of a speech by British Conservative opposition leader Benjamin Disraeli on the financial benefits of the monarchy. Disraeli noted that the cost to taxpayers of the American Congress and each state legislature was double "the charges to the people of England . . . for the entire expense of maintaining the Royal family, and managing their State affairs." The article was longer than most the paper printed, but such ritual invocations of the monarchy reminded readers that trade unionists were not republicans intent on turning Canada into the United States.[53] The London *Times* never reported Disraeli's speech, suggesting that Canadians saw greater need to reject republicanism than did metropolitan Britons.[54]

Ideologies like nationalism are never stable. We should then read the *Ontario Workman* both as evidence for an extant nationalism and as a mechanism by which nationalism was replicated. Just as the newspaper both helped to create and reflected a North American working class through news coverage of American events, it helped build British imperial nationalism by printing many cheery or inspirational stories about events in England and elsewhere in the empire. While it did print labor news from Britain, it was usually in a column of other "foreign news," mixed in with reports from the continent and elsewhere. These reports reflected a British nationalism that cut across class lines, though they also espoused a nationalist ideology that was itself not classless. Printers and their allies worked to construct a nationalism that, while binding them to other classes, was especially relevant to skilled workers.[55] Even this distinctly working-class nationalism, however, served to bind people across class.

While a multiclass, national community was helpful to workers during confrontations with employers, the 1873 visit of Joseph Arch, the leader of the English National Agricultural Labourers' Union, showed that it could pose dangers. Toronto's labor leaders—among whom were many printers—found it difficult to make common cause with Arch when he came to Ontario to investigate Canada as a possible destination for resettlement of his members. Indeed, Arch found more in common with the printers' nemesis, George Brown, than with his class allies. Because Toronto's working-class ties were with the United States and its ties to Britain were relatively unclassed, there was little ideology to bind Arch to the interests of Toronto's printers. The emigration scheme that Arch had come to investigate was inherently imperial, and the British imperial nationalism on which it was based did not recognize class division or solidarity. Toronto's labor leaders were unable to use class allegiance to convince Arch to repudiate Brown; Brown conversely looked past his hostility to unions to embrace Arch. Just as working-class activists could appeal to a cross-class national identity to garner support from middle-class observers, employers could erode class solidarity with a similar appeal.[56]

Although the British nation was an imagined community, many of the readers of the *Ontario Workman* did not have to imagine Britain in one sense: They had been born there. Of the 130 TTU members in February 1872 who had been counted by the census the previous April, 59 percent had been born in the British Isles. In Toronto as a whole, only 44 percent of the population was British-born. Census takers also asked about national origin—in modern parlance, ethnicity— which meant that even those who had been born in North America had to identify a European country to which they felt some allegiance. Of the 130 union printers enumerated, 38 percent (49) identified themselves as English, 43 percent (56) as Irish,[57] 16 percent (21) as Scottish, two as French, and one each as Dutch and German. These proportions are roughly the same as in the general Toronto population.[58] Their act of identifying themselves as British to the census taker both reflected and constructed the imagined community of the British Empire.[59] Speakers at public meetings often used their personal immigration stories to insist that Toronto workers shared the rights enjoyed by workers in England. At a meeting of 4,000 workers to express indignation over the arrest of the strike committee, Richard Nye, the English-born secretary of the Cabinet Makers' Union, proclaimed that he "was from the shores of Old Albion" and demanded "liberty and justice to which they, as British subjects owing allegiance to Her Majesty the Queen and the good old Union Jack, were rightly entitled to."[60] Britain, then, was not only the mother country in rhetoric but also literally a familial homeland. But just as children seek to differentiate themselves from their parents while continuing to assert their close ties, so did Toronto's printers and those who sought to win their political support. A poem written especially for the *Ontario Workman*'s inaugural issue described the relationship this way: "Canadian hearts, let us be loyal, / and remain 'neath England's wing / Till she can no longer guard us— / Then to Canada e'er cling."[61] Yet printers still emphasized their loyalty to and commonality with metropolitan Britain.

This seeming confusion was particularly evident during political debate surrounding the Treaty of Washington. Concluded in 1871, the treaty resolved disputes between the United States and Britain that stemmed from the Civil War and from trade and fishing rights, a number of which directly concerned Canada. Among the key questions was how Britain would compensate the United States for the losses incurred during the Civil War from the *Alabama*, a Confederate warship built in Liverpool. Although John A. Macdonald was among the British negotiators, he accepted under pressure compromises that proved unpopular in Canada. In particular, the United States refused to pay reparations to Canada for the Fenian incursions, claiming that it was not responsible for the actions of renegades. Although Britain eventually calmed Canada with $2.5 million in loan guarantees, the treaty suggested to Canadian voters that their militiamen who died fighting off Fenians were worth less than the property damage that U.S. merchant ships had suffered from the *Alabama*. Because of this controversy, discussion of the treaty was emblematic of the complex relationship between Canada and Britain. The *Ontario Workman* approvingly reprinted a speech by the British opposition politician Earl Russell demanding that someone—the United States or Great Britain—make Canada whole for its losses, implicitly suggesting that the treaty was not good enough because Canada was not well treated by it. Russell noted that the Americans were paid for the *Alabama*, from which no lives were lost. "It was not so, unhappily in the case of Canada," he noted.[62] (Russell had been the foreign secretary who allowed the *Alabama* to sail, so he was not disinterested in the matter.) Yet whatever the Canadian working-class objections to the treaty, the editors of the *Ontario Workman*, at least, were prepared to support it because of its connection to the Crown and Macdonald's government, and they urged their readers to treat the election as a referendum: "If the people are in favour of ratifying the Treaty, they maintain the Government. If on the contrary, they are in favour of pursuing a policy antagonistic to that of the Imperial Government, then they will endorse the Opposition."[63] When it looked briefly as if the American Senate would refuse to ratify the treaty, the newspaper blamed it on "popular Anglophobia," suggesting again that the treaty was closely aligned to Britain in the Canadian imagination.[64]

Because nationalism can function to unify people of disparate classes and experiences, Toronto's printers most frequently made appeals to the British nation when they were looking beyond their class for help and support. This was most noticeable in the discussions surrounding Macdonald's Trade Unions Act, passed in Parliament on June 14, 1872. The primary argument for the act was that Canadian labor law should be equivalent to that in Britain, so that, in the words of the *Ontario Workman*, "operatives from the Mother Country would have the same freedom of action, and the same right to combine for the accomplishment of lawful objects, as they had in England."[65] Printers and their allies made specific calls to Britishness before Macdonald introduced the new legislation, for instance, at two large rallies in downtown Toronto. "Englishmen are all tarred with the same brush—very fond of liberty and freedom," proclaimed Richard Nye. The arrest of the printers' strike committee was "un-English and unjust oppression."[66] The same week, Macdonald announced his intention to bring Canadian law into line with that of "home."[67] The next week, a meeting in St. Catharines, about ten miles from the U.S. border, brought together supporters of the nine-hour movement throughout Ontario, and they all made appeals to Britain to support their demands for shorter hours and the right to strike. James Ryan, the chair of the Hamilton Nine Hour League, proclaimed Benjamin Disraeli's support for the short hour movement. Torontonian William Doughtie assured his audience that "in the British Isles where Trades' Unions have the full protection of the law," workers remained loyal to the state. Doughtie warned that without protection in Canada, the best workers would go to the United States. "He wished," wrote the *Ontario Workman*, "God-speed to the industrial pursuits of that country, but as a

British subject he would prefer to see those men treated in a manner that would induce them to stay in Canada."[68] Doughtie, Ryan, and the others spoke literally to fellow workers, but they needed no convincing. The rhetoric appeared directed at a middle-class public whose primary shared community with the workers was the British imperial nation.

It was not just printers and their allies who appealed to nationalism; politicians seeking their votes did the same, for they, too, were reaching across class to workers. (As we will see later, working-class politicians speaking to working-class audiences did not need to make reference to a unifying British nation.) This tactic seemed to work best for the Tories, whom Toronto workers were more likely to support anyway. When Reform candidates employed it, they demonstrated how working-class nationalism was contested. Toronto Centre was among the hardest fought ridings in the 1872 election, with considerable dishonesty and vast sums spent on both sides. Reform leader George Brown described the fight as "the keenest & bitterest I ever knew," and Conservatives, too, agreed that the election was dirty. (In the end, Reformer Robert Wilkes defeated Frank Shanly, but by only 28 of 2,404 votes cast.)[69] So despite organized labor's hostility to Brown and his "Grits," Wilkes scheduled a meeting to campaign among workingmen, where he would give a talk titled "Capital and Labor." But when things got out of hand, appeals to British nationalism were in vain. Wilkes began his speech trying to prove his sympathy with workers and their right to organize and strike. But when he described the previous repression of unions in England, Tory workers in the audience heckled him, demanding that he stop talking about England. "Tell us something about Toronto," a voice called out. "Tell us about Canada!" "Mr. Wilkes thought that most of them were interested in and had sprung from the 'old root,'" a decidedly unsympathetic *Ontario Workman* paraphrased. "Although some raised the cry of independence, he would say England for ever." Although the audience cheered this declaration, Wilkes could only continue his talk "amid considerable uproar," and by the end of the meeting, the Conservatives had taken over the stage and passed a resolution denouncing Wilkes as under the control of Brown, "the well known avowed enemy of the workingmen of Canada." By the time the event ended with three cheers each for the Queen, Shanly, and Macdonald, Wilkes had slunk off and was nowhere to be found. The working-class audience had rejected a transparent attempt to appeal to their British nationalism, and in fact, one of their speakers reclaimed that rhetoric. Alluding to his own immigration from Scotland, labor leader Andrew Scott declared to cheers, "If the employers of this country had imitated those of the old country, there would have been a better feeling existing between them at the present time."[70] Scott's comment suggested a way that Canadian workers saw their country as partially distinct from Britain, and it hinted at the way they existed not only within a British imperial nation but also within a Canadian polity.

A Canadian Polity: Toronto's Printers and the Dominion

If Toronto printers imagined their class to be continental and their nationality to be imperial, what did it mean to be Canadian? The printers appealed to Canadianness generally when dealing directly with politicians or when making a claim on the state, rather than on their employers or their national community. Before the 1872 strike, for instance, reference to Canada was slight, and, as we have seen, the TTU generally rebuffed Montreal's efforts to take more action based on a shared Canadian identity. The two exceptions, both in April 1869, prove the rule: They were instances in which printers made demands on the state. First, the TTU signed a Montreal petition regarding copyright law reform.[71] Two weeks later, it joined a special meeting of the bookbinders' union to protest a proposed repeal of a tariff on imported books.[72] Otherwise, matters relating to Canada qua Canada seemed not to interest the TTU until the election of 1872. Then, printers relied on Canadian appeals to demand favors from politicians beyond what they could win through appeals to Britishness.

Just as Toronto's printers were not troubled by any apparent contradiction between their North American class community and their British imperial nation, so, too, did neither of those categories conflict with their ability to be fully Canadian. To them, as to other Canadians, expansion in the West, building the transcontinental Canadian Pacific Railway, or fostering Canadian industry were simultaneously both domestic, Canadian concerns and imperial, British matters.[73] As we have seen, Canadian workers spoke of Britain and Britishness when they wanted to appeal to all members of the British imperial family, regardless of class. When they spoke specifically of politics or demanded action from the Dominion government, they spoke of Canada. In the pages of the *Ontario Workman* and in other instances where historians can hear a working-class voice, we see a clear example of what historian Douglas Cole categorized as nationalism toward the British imperial nation and patriotism toward the Canadian polity.[74]

In meetings of workers and in the newspaper they cooperatively published, workers mentioned the Dominion and its interests when they wanted a policy different from that in Britain. For example, workers wanted tariffs to protect them from cheaper American imports, but such a policy contravened the British imperial policy of free trade. So tariff advocates contrasted Canada with Britain to show how protectionism was appropriate for the former, even when it had been rejected in the latter. Henry Witton was a Tory candidate in Hamilton and himself a worker. At a campaign meeting, he defended Macdonald's platform, arguing that the Dominion needed a distinctly Canadian trade policy. "When England adopted Free Trade, she was a century in advance of other nations, but Canada was a young country, and the difference was obvious. Articles that Canada did not produce should come in free of duty," Witton said in the *Ontario*

Workman's paraphrase. His speech ended "with a review of the glorious prospects of the Dominion and an appeal to the electors to vote on the side of good and patriotic government."[75] Here Witton, as a working-class politician, emphasized a Canadian community in urging a policy to be enacted in Ottawa and constructed a patriotism that referred specifically to the Canadian state.

Organized labor made a similar argument about the Criminal Law Amendment Act, which Macdonald had introduced at the same time he legalized strikes with the Trade Unions Act. It, too, was copied from English law, but workers on both sides of the Atlantic found it objectionable.[76] When the *Ontario Workman* argued against the law, it used both British and Canadian rhetoric. Before Parliament passed the act, the newspaper noted that even in England trade unions were working to have it repealed—a reminder of a shared British identity—and then called specifically on Canadian unions to "bring all their influence to bear against" the bill.[77] When a Reform politician sought to criticize Macdonald before a working-class audience, he denounced the labor laws Macdonald introduced, saying that they "may suit the working man of aristocratic England, but it was totally unsuited to those of democratic Canada."[78]

The *Ontario Workman* and working-class speakers also used language about Canada when seeking a contrast with the United States, especially when the two countries were perceived as being in competition, as for immigrants. In these cases, the newspaper was usually demanding action from Parliament—in other words, making a demand on the state. In the United States, the paper claimed, the eight-hour movement was more successful, the franchise was universal, "every inducement is offered to immigrants," and "employers cannot insult workmen with impunity." If Canada did not compete, "we shall sink to the condition of a mere appendage to the States' contract, because we have not the courage to expand,—become a province when we ought to become a nation."[79] The president of the Hamilton Nine Hours League also used the rhetoric of Canadian competition with the United States: "If the capitalists and manufacturers in the United States can grant their men their moderate request what is to hinder our employers in Canada from doing the same?"[80]

One indication of the way Toronto printers used the idea of Canada to request favors from the state is that those requests frequently came from regional labor organizations. Until the Toronto Trades Assembly was organized in April 1871, the TTU had cooperated with other local unions on matters of Canadian legislation in ad hoc alliances. After the printers helped found the TTA, such activities were usually directed through it. At the TTA's very first regular meeting, the assembled delegates discussed the Homestead Act.[81] When Toronto workers wanted to thank the prime minister for the Trade Unions Act, the invitation came not from the TTU, but from John Hewitt, the corresponding secretary of the Toronto Trades Assembly. The event itself, as we have seen, was dominated by British nationalist music and rhetoric, but when Hewitt wrote, he thanked

Macdonald for his "timely efforts in interests of the operatives of *this Dominion*."[82] Throughout the seven-year life of the Trades Assembly, one of its major purposes was to lobby the Dominion government for legislation on a variety of topics, including immigration and prison labor.[83] Localism and patriotism were apparently closely tied.

By far the most common time the *Ontario Workman* mentioned Canada was in discussing electoral politics. This should not be surprising; during a Dominion election, anyone discussing politics necessarily speaks of the Dominion. But what is particularly noteworthy is that while middle-class politicians like Macdonald and Wilkes appealed to working-class crowds with references to Britain, Henry Witton, the working-class Tory candidate, spoke of Canada. At a Hamilton campaign meeting to support Witton and another candidate, Macdonald was described as "a patriot," and Witton called himself the "happiest man in Canada."[84] The *Ontario Workman* trumpeted his nomination in decidedly Canadianist terms: "This is the first occasion in the history of our country in which a *bona fide* workingman has been brought before the electors," it crowed; "our country" here meant Canada, not Britain.[85] That Witton would soon show himself to be controlled by Macdonald and quickly trade his "rough coat" for "evening clothes," in the memorable phrasing of the governor general's wife, Lady Dufferin, was, of course, unknowable; in the meantime, he was elected as a workingman by other workingmen, and he had been able to speak to his constituents specifically of Canada.[86]

Discussions of Canada in partisan politics—along with debates over tariffs and immigration—heralded the start of a new era of nationalist rhetoric. Hints of a Canadian nationalism, related to but distinct from British imperial nationalism, were evident in 1872. With the exception of two naval garrisons, British troops withdrew from North America, leaving Canada to protect itself and creating an opportunity for martial nation building.[87] The militia held a training encampment at Niagara the summer of 1872, which both relied on and reproduced Canadian nationalism.[88] On the same page as a report on the short hour movement in Scotland and several brief, humorous stories from the United States, the *Ontario Workman* ran a Hamilton man's ode to the nine-hour movement: "Arouse ye men of Canada, ye sons of freedom rise," it began, urging that "the world forget the Shamrock, the Thistle and the Rose."[89] This vision of Canada extended beyond simply being a polity or a state, but it also acknowledged an imperial nationalism of which Canada was the epitome. In this growing vision, Canada remained a part of the British World—indeed, was a better version of Britain—but also began to develop its own territorial nationalism.[90]

It is in the Canadianist rhetoric of 1872 that we can begin to see a growing congruence between nation, labor market, and state. This increasing alignment of the three was itself an international phenomenon: At the same moment that Canadians were electing their second parliament, the *Ontario Workman* reported the collapse of the First International.[91] Without too much exaggeration, one may see the end of the First International as the beginning of a period of state and nation formation throughout the world. The United States introduced a padrone statute in 1874 and the anti-Chinese Page Law in 1875, the first federal immigration restrictions. They served to emphasize the central state's authority over boundary making and decisions about who could be a part of the nation.[92] Canada introduced the Dominion Lands Act in 1872 to encourage settlement in the West as a bulwark against American encroachment on Canadian sovereignty and then followed with the establishment of the North West Mounted Police in 1873 to further project central Canadian power on the West.[93] In 1879, the Macdonald government—returned to government after five years in opposition—introduced a National Policy protective tariff to support Canadian manufacturing.[94]

The 1870s were the beginning of a lengthy era of unprecedented challenges to the nature of the bourgeois state. States like the United States and Canada responded by firming up their boundaries and building a sense of nationalism to tie together their citizens. Thus the multiple communities to which Toronto's printers belonged in the late 1860s and early 1870s became devalued. This was a long process, culminating in the acceptance of nationalism as the legitimating political ideology in the post-Versailles world, the permanent adoption of passport regimes, and the adoption, in the United States and Canada, of drastically exclusive immigration laws.[95] The success of this statist, nationalist project throughout the world has obscured the particular circumstances of its birth and blinded us to the ways people interacted before the nation-state's success.[96] The several communities in which Toronto's printers lived and acted demonstrate a way in which skilled workers could make claims on different types of people at different times.

NOTES

1. Sarah Deutsch, Dorothy Fujita-Rony, Paula Hastings, Bryan Palmer, Gunther Peck, Joan Sangster, John Herd Thompson, and Susan Thorne read various versions of this chapter and offered valuable comments, suggestions, and questions. I extend thanks to them all. Of course, all errors of fact or interpretation are solely my own.
2. Hereward Senior, *The Last Invasion of Canada: The Fenian Raids, 1866–1870* (Toronto, ON: Dundurn Press in collaboration with the Canadian War Museum, Canadian Museum of Civilization, 1991).
3. Minutes for June 13, 1866, Toronto Typographical Union Minute Books, series A, reel 1a, Toronto Typographical Union No. 91 Papers, Fonds 1272, Archives of Ontario. Hereafter TTU Minutes.

4. Antoinette Burton, "Who Needs the Nation? Interrogating 'British' History," *Journal of Historical Sociology* 10 (September 1997): 227–48; Donna Gabaccia, "Is Everywhere Nowhere? Nomads, Nations, and the Immigrant Paradigm of United States History," *Journal of American History* 86 (December 1999): 1115–34.
5. Jennifer Gordon, "Transnational Labor Citizenship," *Southern California Law Review* 80 (March 2007): 503–87; Linda Bosniak, "Citizenship Denationalized," *Indiana Journal of Global Legal Studies* 7 (2007): 447–509.
6. J. J. Bukowiczyk et al., *Permeable Border: The Great Lakes Basin as Transnational Region, 1650–1990* (Pittsburgh, PA: University of Pittsburgh Press, 2005); Sheila McManus, *The Line Which Separates: Race, Gender, and the Making of the Alberta-Montana Borderlands* (Lincoln: University of Nebraska Press, 2005).
7. Carl Berger, *The Sense of Power: Studies in the Ideas of Canadian Imperialism, 1867–1914* (Toronto, ON: University of Toronto Press, 1970). I use here the vocabulary suggested by Douglas Cole, "The Problem of 'Nationalism' and 'Imperialism' in British Settlement Colonies," *Journal of British Studies* 10 (May 1971): 160–82.
8. Phillip Buckner, "The Creation of the Dominion of Canada, 1860–1901," in *Canada and the British Empire*, ed. Phillip Buckner (Oxford: Oxford University Press, 2008), 67, 83–84.
9. Buckner, "Creation," 79–80; John Herd Thompson "Canada and the 'Third British Empire', 1901–1939," in *Canada and the British Empire*, ed. Phillip Buckner (Oxford: Oxford University Press, 2008), 87–106; James Sturgis, "Learning About Oneself: The Making of Canadian Nationalism, 1867–1914," in *Kith and Kin: Canada, Britain and the United States from the Revolution to the Cold War*, ed. Colin Clifford Eldridge, (Cardiff: University of Wales Press, 1997), 104–108.
10. Berger, *Sense of Power*, 5.
11. "North American" here means Canada and the United States; Mexico's inclusion (or not) in this community and labor market is beyond the scope of this chapter.
12. Of the ten, the 1871 census lists five as born in Ontario and two as Irish-born Protestants. Three are unlisted, a further indication of their mobility. Bruce S. Elliott, general ed., *Index to the 1871 Census of Ontario*, vol. 24, Toronto (Toronto: Ontario Genealogical Society, 1992), now helpfully digitized and available at http://www.collectionscanada.gc.ca/databases/1871-ontario/index-e.html.
13. TTU Minutes, March 4, 1871.
14. Rebecca Scott, "Public Rights and Private Commerce: A Nineteenth-Century Atlantic Creole Itinerary," *Current Anthropology* 48 (April 2007): 237–56.
15. The records of the conspiracy case are in File 7074, "J. S. McMillan et al.," Criminal Assize Indictments, Box 193, Series 392, RG 22, Archives of Ontario (hereafter Criminal Assize File). On the closing of the case, see Edward Blake's

notes to himself, December 18, 1886, Envelope 3, Box 17, Series B-3-e, Fonds 2, Blake Family Papers, Archives of Ontario.

16. Sally Zerker, "George Brown and the Printers Union," *Journal of Canadian Studies* 10 (1975): 87–88; George S. Kealey, *Toronto Workers Respond to Industrial Capitalism 1867–1892* (Toronto, ON: University of Toronto Press, 1980), 124–53.

17. John Herd Thompson and Stephen J. Randall, *Canada and the United States: Ambivalent Allies*, 2nd ed. (Athens: University of Georgia Press, 1997), 39–41.

18. E. J. Hobsbawm, "The Tramping Artisan," *Economic History Review*, n.s. 3 (1951): 299–320; Sally F. Zerker, *The Rise and Fall of the Toronto Typographical Union 1832–1972: A Case Study of Foreign Domination* (Toronto, ON: University of Toronto Press, 1982), 53–65.

19. The total number from 1866 to 1872 was compiled from the monthly reports of new members in the TTU minutes. The February 1872 membership list is in Criminal Assize file.

20. *Ninth Census of the United States, 1870*, vol. 1, table III, 176, 209.

21. Gunther Peck, *Reinventing Free Labor: Padrones and Immigrant Workers in the North American West, 1880–1930* (Cambridge: Cambridge University Press, 2000).

22. On the concerted exclusion of women from the Toronto union in a slightly later period, see Christina Burr, "'That Coming Curse – The Incompetent Compositress': Class and Gender Relations in the Toronto Typographical Union During the Late Nineteenth Century," *Canadian Historical Review* 74 (1993): 344–366. On gender and the printing trades generally, see Ava Barron, "An 'Other' Side of Gender Antagonism at Work: Men, Boys, and the Remasculinization of Printers' Work, 1830–1920," in *Work Engendered: Toward a New History of American Labor*, ed. Ava Baron (Ithaca, NY: Cornell University Press, 1991), 1–46. For a broader discussion of the way craft unions used gender, see Ileen A. Devault, *United Apart: Gender and the Rise of Craft Unionism* (Ithaca, NY: Cornell University Press, 2004).

23. Christina Burr, *Spreading the Light: Work and Labour Reform in Late Nineteenth-Century Toronto* (Toronto, ON: University of Toronto Press, 1999); David Goutor, *Guarding the Gates: The Canadian Labour Movement and Immigration, 1872–1934* (Vancouver: University of British Columbia Press, 2007); Adele Perry, *On the Edge of Empire: Gender, Race, and the Making of British Columbia, 1849–1871* (Toronto, ON: University of Toronto Press, 2001).

24. For example, see *Ontario Workman*, June 27, 1872; July 4, 1872.

25. Starting in 1894, Canadian railways were supposed to ensure the legal status of Canadians crossing the border. See Mai Ngai, *Impossible Subjects: Illegal Aliens and the Making of Modern America* (Princeton, NJ: Princeton University Press, 2004), 64–67; Bruno Ramirez with Yves Otis, *Crossing the 49th Parallel: Migration from Canada to the USA, 1900–1930* (Ithaca, NY: Cornell University Press, 2001), 36–49.

26. Robert Prince, ed., "The Road to Boston: 1860 Travel Correspondence of William Dean Howells," *Ohio History* 80 (Spring 1971): 118.
27. On very early printers' unions, see, Mark Lause, *Some Degree of Power: From Hired Hand to Union Craftsman in the Preindustrial American Printing Trades, 1778–1815* (Fayetteville: University of Arkansas Press, 1991).
28. George A. Tracy, *History of the Typographical Union* (Indianapolis: The International Typographical Union, 1913), 190–93, 199, 206, 212–13. The printer who confused the New Orleans union seems to have been U. J. Tracie, who wrote a letter back to Toronto regarding "the strictness of the New Orleans Union" in 1861. TTU Minutes, April 2, 1861.
29. Eugene Forsey, *Trade Unions in Canada, 1812–1902* (Toronto, ON: University of Toronto Press, 1982), 47.
30. TTU Minutes, April 11, 1866; May 9, 1866.
31. F. H. Armstrong, "Reformer as Capitalist: William Lyon Mackenzie and the Printers' Strike of 1836," *Ontario History* 59 (1967): 191, 192–93.
32. TTU Minutes, September 7, 1860.
33. TTU Minutes, April 2, 1861; May 6, 1861.
34. TTU Minutes, July 1, 1862; November 14, 1866.
35. Gregory S. Kealey, "Work Control, the Labour Process, and Nineteenth-Century Canadian Printers," in *Workers and Canadian History* (Montreal, QC: McGill-Queen's University Press, 1995), 209–237; Wayne Roberts, "The Last Artisans: Toronto Printers, 1896–1914," in *Essays in Canadian Working Class History*, ed. Gregory S. Kealey and Peter Warrian (Toronto, ON: McClelland and Stewart, 1976), 125–142.
36. TTU Minutes, August 10, 1867; September 11, 1867; October 9, 1867; November 13, 1867; December 11, 1867; January 12, 1868.
37. TTU Minutes, November 13, 1867; March 12, 1868; September 8, 1869; October 14, 1871.
38. *Ontario Workman*, August 1, 1872; July 25, 1872.
39. J.M.S. Careless, *Brown of the Globe*, 2 vols., (Toronto, ON: Macmillan, 1959–1963), 2:288.
40. TTU Minutes, March 20, 1867.
41. TTU Minutes, September 8, 1869. The fact that such a project was not mentioned in the 1869 annual report suggests strongly that nothing happened. TTU Minutes, January 12, 1870.
42. TTU Minutes, July 1870. The ITU convention was held in Montreal in 1873. Tracy, *Typographical Union*, 267.
43. TTU Minutes, January 13, 1869.
44. TTU Minutes, February 9, 1870. On Canadian printers' reverence for Franklin, see Kealey, *Toronto Workers*, 85.
45. TTU Minutes, April 23, 1869 ($150 to the Montreal union), February 9, 1870 ($75 to the Ottawa union).
46. TTU Minutes, January 12, 1870.

47. For examples of this pattern elsewhere in the British Empire, see Paul A. Pickering "A Wider Field in a New Country: Chartism in Colonial Australia," in *Elections: Full, Free and Fair*, ed. Marian Sawer (Annandale, New South Wales: Federation Press, 2001), 28–44; Laura Tabili, *We Ask for British Justice: Workers and Racial Difference in Late Imperial Britain* (Ithaca, NY: Cornell University Press, 1994).
48. Benedict Anderson, *Imagined Communities: Reflections on the Origin and Spread of Nationalism*, rev. ed. (London: Verso, 1991).
49. David Cannadine, "The Context, Performance and Meaning of Ritual: The British Monarchy and the 'Invention of Tradition,' c. 1820–1977," in *The Invention of Tradition*, ed. Eric Hobsbawm and Terence Ranger (Cambridge: Cambridge University Press, 1983), 101–64.
50. *Ontario Workman*, July 18, 1872, 4.
51. *Ontario Workman*, April 18, 1872, 1.
52. The *Times*, November 22, 1871; November 29, 1871; December 1, 1871; January 19, 1872; March 30, 1872; April 9, 1872.
53. *Ontario Workman*, June 13, 1872, 6.
54. A search for key words from the *Ontario Workman* article on the speech yielded no articles in the *Times Digital Archive*.
55. Burr, *Spreading*, 8–16.
56. David Goutor, "'Stand by the Union, Mr. Arch': The Toronto Labour Establishment and the Emigration Mission of Britain's National Agricultural Labourer's Union," *Labour/Le Travail* 55 (Spring 2005): 9–35.
57. It is important to note that "Irish," in the Canadian usage, has a different valance than in the American usage. To wit, only sixteen of these fifty-six men of Irish ancestry said they were Catholic. On the different meanings of "Irish," see Donald H. Akenson, *Small Differences: Irish Catholics and Irish Protestants, 1815–1922, an International Perspective* (Kingston, ON: McGill-Queen's University Press, 1988).
58. A "Semi-Annual Circular" of the TTU, listing February 1872 members, is in the Criminal Assize file. The place of birth and national origins of the printers come from the 1871 census manuscript and Elliot, *Index to the 1871 Census*.
59. Anderson, *Imagined Communities*, 164–70. On the Canadian census in particular, see Bruce Curtis, *The Politics of Population: State Formation, Statistics, and the Census of Canada, 1840–1875* (Toronto, ON: University of Toronto Press, 2001).
60. *Ontario Workman*, April 25, 1872, 1.
61. *Ontario Workman*, April 18, 1872, 2.
62. *Ontario Workman*, June 27, 1872, 5.
63. *Ontario Workman*, May 23, 1872, 4.
64. *Ontario Workman*, May 30, 1872, 4.
65. *Ontario Workman*, May 9, 1872, 4.
66. *Ontario Workman*, April 25, 1872, 1.

67. *Ontario Workman*, April 25, 1872, 4.
68. *Ontario Workman*, May 2, 1872, 1.
69. Donald Swainson, "Robert Wilkes," in *The Dictionary of Canadian Biography*, available at http://www.biographi.ca/009004-119.01-e.php?&id_nbr=5318.
70. *Ontario Workman*, August 8, 1872, 1.
71. TTU Minutes, April 14, 1869; May 12, 1869.
72. TTU Minutes, April 28, 1869.
73. Buckner, "Creation," 73–74.
74. Cole, "Problem."
75. *Ontario Workman*, August 8, 1872, 5. On Witton as a workingman, see *Ontario Workman*, June 25, 1872, 4.
76. The act meant that despite the general legalization of trade unions, their actions were still regulated under conspiracy statutes. Gaston V. Rimlinger, "Labor and the Government: A Comparative Historical Perspective," *Journal of Economic History* 37 (March 1977): 215; Paul Craven, "Workers' Conspiracies in Toronto, 1854–72," *Labour/Le Travail* 14 (1984): 69–70.
77. *Ontario Workman*, May 23, 1872, 4.
78. *Ontario Workman*, August 1, 1872, 5.
79. *Ontario Workman*, May 30, 1872, 4.
80. *Ontario Workman*, June 13, 1872, 4. This article was reprinted from the *Hamilton Spectator*, which at the time favored the nine-hour movement.
81. Forsey, *Trade Unions*, 92.
82. D. G. Creighton, *John A. Macdonald: The Old Chieftain* (Toronto, ON: Macmillan, 1955), 134. Emphasis added.
83. Forsey, *Trade Unions*, 95.
84. *Ontario Workman*, July 25, 1872, 5.
85. *Ontario Workman*, July 25, 1872, 4.
86. Bryan D. Palmer, *A Culture in Conflict: Skilled Workers and Industrial Capitalism in Hamilton, Ontario, 1860–1914* (Montreal, QC: McGill-Queen's University Press, 1979), 148.
87. Thompson and Randall, *Ambivalent Allies*, 41.
88. *Ontario Workman*, June 13, 1872, 4; June 20, 1872, 4.
89. *Ontario Workman*, May 23, 1872, 6. The next issue identified the poet as Thomas Davis.
90. On Canada as a "better Britain," see Buckner, "Creation," 74. On the development of "Canadian territorial nationalism," see Sturgis, "Learning about Oneself."
91. *Ontario Workman*, May 16, 1872, 8; August 8, 1872, 5.
92. Peck, *Reinventing*, 84–85; George Anthony Peffer, *If They Don't Bring Their Women Here: Chinese Female Immigration Before Exclusion* (Urbana: University of Illinois Press, 1999).
93. Cecelia Danysk, *Hired Hands: Labour and the Development of Prairie Agriculture, 1880–1930* (Toronto, ON: McClelland and Stewart, 1995), 17; Buckner,

"Creation," 74–75. McManus, *Line Which Separates*, also points to the mid-1870s as a moment of state building in the west.

94. Robert Craig Brown, *Canada's National Policy, 1883–1900: A Study in Canadian-American Relations* (Princeton, NJ: Princeton University Press, 1964); Kealey, *Toronto Workers*, 154–71; Kevin Henley, "The International Roots of Economic Nationalist Ideology in Canada, 1846–1885," *Journal of Canadian Studies* 24 (Winter 1989–1990): 107–21.
95. See Ngai, *Impossible Subjects*, 9–10.
96. On the adoption of nationalism by late-nineteenth-century states, see Anderson, *Imagined Communities*, 46–49.

20 GLOBAL SEA OR NATIONAL BACKWATER?

THE INTERNATIONAL LABOR ORGANIZATION AND THE QUIXOTIC QUEST FOR MARITIME STANDARDS, 1919–1945

Leon Fink

As the very artery of international commerce, merchant shipping offers an ideal setting for examining the changing regulatory regimes applied by both individual states and ultimately an organized world community to workers across the nineteenth and twentieth centuries.[1] With the rise of powerful nation-states joined by a global marketplace in the nineteenth century, recruitment and regulation of a seafaring labor force emerged as both a high priority and a vexing problem for western powers like the United States and Great Britain. In the post–World War I era to which this chapter directs our attention, a combination of the deskilling impact of steam and diesel power, the hypercompetition among shipping powers, and a worldwide reach for cheap labor threatened wage and living standards established by a previous generation of collective bargaining and political accommodation. No occupational sector thus looked with greater hope to the establishment of the International Labor Organization (ILO) in 1919 as a mechanism for restoring a semblance of order and humane treatment in the labor market. Given the diversity of the international seafaring labor force, however, regulation—whether global or national in inspiration—inevitably reflected the racial, ethnic, and imperial designs of the regulators themselves. When ethnic as well as deep political and economic differences prevented global regulations from taking hold, national actors, by the mid-1930s, took matters into their own hands. Despite its many failures, however, by 1948, the ILO and especially the ILO maritime division beckoned as one of the few broadly international bodies to survive, with both its machinery and aspirations intact, the wreckage of economic depression, another world war, and the large-scale collapse of democracy.

The world treated the early-twentieth-century seafarer as a more modern if decidedly less heroic functionary than his eighteenth- or nineteenth-century counterpart. The change began with the shipping vessels themselves. Though sailing ships continued to carry a substantial portion of the world's trade up to the world war (though even these often carried steam engines as auxiliary means of propulsion), the twentieth-century configuration would be one of iron (and later steel) hulls and steam (and later diesel) engines. The transformation also inevitably complicated an older comradeship below deck. Employers increased the percentage of unskilled workers: Not only were the crew now divided between deckhands, firemen (or stokers), and (especially on passenger liners) stewards but also the distinctions in pay and status between officers and engineers on the upper end and able-bodied seamen and firemen or stewards on the lower end grew ever starker.[2] By 1913, the president of the American Steamship Association utterly dismissed union attempts to maintain a three-year service requirement for "able-bodied" quotas and status:

> The work performed by the deck hands aboard a modern steamer, with short masts, little rigging, and almost no sails, is of the most ordinary kind of unskilled labor that can be imagined, consisting for the most part of washing decks, scrubbing paint, and polishing brasswork, the center of gravity, so to speak, having shifted from the deck to the engine department, where the really technical part of a steamer's work is now performed.... To insist that it requires three years' experience to acquire adequate facility is "absurd"—three months at most would be amply sufficient.[3]

Not surprisingly, the public image of the seaman suffered as well. Once a literary symbol of human freedom and noble character fighting off threats from various antagonists, the modern-day jumble of unskilled laborers recruited from across the world for an arduous, seagoing life provided a less ennobling fictional tableau. The dean of the new realist sea writers was Joseph Conrad, who, as a young Polish emigré, had worked on eighteen (mostly British) ships until his "retirement" in the mid-1890s.[4] In what would become a common trope, Conrad juxtaposed an idyllic, manly, preindustrial age of sail to the conflictual, degraded, and utterly regimented routine of the steamship. Highlighted by his depiction of the quarreling officers and crew's disgraceful abandonment of beleaguered passengers on the wrecked tramp steamer *Patna* in his best known novel, *Lord Jim*, Conrad effectively disparaged the loss of virtue and character in a regimented world of industrial marine labor.[5]

The theme equally resonated with Eugene O'Neill, who, first inspired by a Conrad novel, shipped out at age twenty-one on one of the disappearing square-riggers and then included the sea in nineteen of his forty-four plays as "an integral part of the action."⁶ Driscoll, the hard-living protagonist of O'Neill's early S.S. *Glencairn* series, thus disparages his steamship workmates who have asked him for a song: "Ye've heard the names av chanties but divil a note av the tune or a loine av the words do ye know. There's hardly a rale deep-water sailor lift on the seas, more's the pity."⁷ In starker terms still, the Irish stoker Paddy speaking to his American buddy, Yank, in *The Hairy Ape* (1921) contrasts the days of "clippers wid tall masts touching the sky—fine strong men in them" with that of "bloody engines pounding and throbbing and shaking . . . choking our lungs wid coal dust . . . caged in by steel from a sight of the sky like bloody apes in the Zoo!" Marginalized both on ship and off by respectable society, Yank's combustible anger lands him in prison, from where he can identify vicariously with working-class political rebels. Listening from his cell to a denunciation by a U.S. senator of the Industrial Workers of the World as "the Industrial Wreckers of the World," Yank erupts, "Wreckers, dat's de right dope! Dat belongs! Me for dem!"⁸

Another gripping illustration of the downward passage of sailors from exotics to drudges occurs in *The Death Ship* (1926 German edition, 1934 first English edition), a novel by the biographically mysterious writer, B. Traven, best known for *The Treasure of the Sierra Madre* (1935). Likely (but not transparently) a German-born national who then moved to the United States and Mexico, the pseudonymous Traven evokes a maritime world of bureaucratic coercion and lifeless toil as witnessed by protagonist Gerald Gales, an American merchant sailor stranded in Europe without proper papers. With sardonic humor, Traven sketches the struggles of the lower depths of a floating international proletariat amidst rising nationalist barriers. Continually deported and effectively locked out of "civilized" society for want of demonstrable citizenship, Gales thus finds a berth only on the "death ship" *Yorikke*, filled with other workers in the same situation: "There have never been so many [death ships] as since the war for liberty and democracy that gave the world passports and immigration restrictions, and that manufactured men without nationalities and without papers by the ten thousand."⁹ Literally cast adrift, Gales's shipmates evolve a communicative strategy common to a British-dominated shipping world: "Every sailor of any nationality knows some thirty English words, which he pronounces in such a way that after half an hour you may get a rough idea of what he wishes to say."¹⁰

Jamaican-born Claude McKay, like his Harlem Renaissance compatriot Langston Hughes, experienced the racial diversity of the sea firsthand.¹¹ Bound for a meeting of the Communist Congress in Moscow in 1922, McKay first worked his way over from New York to London as a stoker on a merchant ship.¹² Both of his two early novels, *Home to Harlem* (1928) and *Banjo* (1929), make reference to the friction of race and work from the author's experience at sea and portside in New York, London, and Marseilles. In the first novel, the main character's freighter "stank between sea and sky: The white sailors who washed the ship would not wash the stokers' water-closet, because they despised the

Arabs. And the Arabs themselves made no effort to keep the place clean, although it adjoined their sleeping berth."[13] In the second novel, the southern black vagabond Banjo, hanging out with Afro-Caribbeans in Marseilles, in the end rejects a life at sea given the hostility that "colored seamen" find there. In particular, he becomes aware of British policy (abetted by the national seamen's union) to drive colored seamen out of England. "Colored seamen," Banjo observes, "who had lived their lives in the great careless tradition, and had lost their papers in low-down places to touts, hold-up men, and passport fabricators, and were unable or too ignorant to show exact proof of their birthplace, were furnished with the new 'Nationality Doubtful' papers."[14] As McKay, like B. Traven, recognized, state policy in the post–World War I world had come down hard on the wayward, and especially racially marked, seaman.

Industrialized work routines, miserable pay and conditions, a polyglot labor force breeding tensions and the threat of radical upheaval—these were main themes of sea writers across the early twentieth century. They were also the themes that ILO reformers, seeking to bring justice as well as stability to the world's shipping lanes, confronted during the organization's first decades of work. Conceived by liberals and social democrats amid post–World War I expectations (apocalyptic or millennial, depending on the observer) of mass strikes and armed uprisings, the ILO might best be considered a reformers' redoubt from revolution. That the air was already coming out of the original Bolshevik balloon as early as 1920 when the ILO got down to business immediately weakened the odds that it could pull off the grand social compromise it sought. Moreover, the ensuing years of rising nationalist tensions dwarfed the very "class conflict" international labor standards were meant to allay. As a result, momentum slowed and resources dwindled for projects of international cooperation on almost every front, and at the political level, one might fairly label the interwar ILO, like its mother ship, the League of Nations, "an almost total failure."[15] That said, the discussions within the organization on policy prescriptions for what latter-day commentators would call the "global economy" have a remarkably present-day feel. The ILO might thus well be seen as *the* pioneer attempt to deal with the effects of globalization on working people.

The United States played a fitful role in the ILO's development. Just as President Woodrow Wilson laid the foundations for the League and then watched helplessly as his country failed to join, so AFL President Samuel Gompers served as a moving spirit for the ILO, only to face the same rebuff from the U.S. Congress. During the Paris Peace Conference, Gompers, indeed, presided over the Commission on International Labour Legislation that drafted the constitution for the ILO. Yet, it surely pained the AFL leader, along with other eager American labor internationalists, to be forced to the sidelines during the inaugural International Labor Conference held October 1919 in Washington D.C.[16] Like the League of Nations, the ILO soldiered on in the absence of the world's newest superpower, although, in the case of the ILO, sustained interest from key labor, business, and civic groups led to a reversal of policy and belated U.S. entry in the organization in 1934.[17]

Though organically tied to the League of Nations—and subsequently the United Nations—organizational structure—the ILO embraced a unique representational and juridical process.[18] Adopting the British War Cabinet's formula for incorporating both business and trade union representatives in its counsels, the ILO embraced "tripartism," with each national delegation composed of government (two votes), employers (one vote) and workers (one vote) members.[19] From its inception, the ILO sought to establish minimal international standards—or "conventions"—for the treatment of workers that would, in turn, be accepted and incorporated into the national laws of affiliated governments.[20] The first ILO director, Albert Thomas, French socialist politician and wartime minister of munitions, approached the organization (which he affectionately called "*la maison*") with great expectations. As his English-language deputy eulogized, "Like Columbus, [Thomas] saw a world beyond the horizon of his fellows, and he laid his plans and settled his methods on other assumptions than theirs."[21]

Nowhere, moreover, were the aims and principles of the ILO more quickly on display than within the maritime field. The wartime collaborative efforts of Havelock Wilson's National Sailors' and Firemen's Union with the employers' Shipping Federation spilled over into larger efforts of standard setting within the umbrella of the ILO and its effective sponsorship of a series of seamen's conferences. Despite considerably smaller numbers than other occupational groups like railway workers or dockers, seamen commanded more immediate international attention, including the adoption of thirteen conventions during the interwar period alone.

Those seeking to draft what they called an "International Seamen's Code" at the 1920 Genoa conference—the first targeted industrial conference in the life of the infant ILO—justified their work with reference to both seamen and shipping interests. First, unlike most other workers, seamen were a polyglot, multilingual lot, regularly working "in several countries," as well as "on the world's highway, far removed from the usual reach of public authorities." As such, as an "international community," conference organizers asserted, they would be best served by a "uniform law." Second, anticipating the postwar return of cutthroat commercial competition between merchant fleets, the would-be legislators pointed to the difficulties in adopting "any new [single-nation-based] legislation because of its possible reaction to the advantage of the merchant fleet of a competing country. If, for instance, one State attempts by legislation to secure the improvement of seamen's living accommodations, it may find itself at a disadvantage vis a vis another State which fails or refuses to make a similar change in its laws."[22]

However compelling the larger logic, when it came to international standards, the devil was in the details. In the maritime field, a cardinal illustration of the difficulties of agreement lay in the basic principle of a limitation of working hours. Though "eight hours" had been adopted as a principle as early as the Versailles Treaty, attempts to apply it to maritime work had been tabled at the initial 1919 Washington Labor Conference and left to the first special maritime conference in Genoa, Italy, in 1920 to adjudicate. The thirty countries assembled there, however, quickly confronted a fact that would regularly frustrate the search for common standards for the next century: There was no single but rather several maritime labor markets, depending on both the physical and racial geography of commerce. South Asian seafarers, to take but one prominent example, had been paid a third to a fifth of the British (or European) wage since the mid-nineteenth century.[23] In response, how could the world body legislate a global norm?

Reporting from a special subcommittee meeting, governmental delegate Charles Hipwood, from the British Board of Trade, first voiced the problem to the assembled delegates in Genoa. Though all British parties agreed that "the present hours of Lascars [the Indian seamen who signed on to special 'Asiatic' articles for remuneration far below the standards of British seamen] should be reduced," he averred, "further than that we found it very difficult to go." On top of a draft convention Article 1 adopting the universalistic "principles of the 8 hr day and 48 hr week applied to every seamen employed on board a vessel of whatever nature, public or private" and "without distinction of nationality or race," Hipwood therefore proposed a special "Lascar" article allowing for a lower standard, to be subsequently negotiated among government, shipping, and Indian seamen representatives.[24]

As reports from the proceedings made clear, openly imperial powers like Belgium and France, as well as the shipping colossus, Great Britain, which clothed its South Asian empire in quasi-autonomous legal forms, could not square their interests with a simple, global "eight-hour" labor standard. Rather, they sought to allow for racially and/or geographically derived corollaries to the main trunk of an international principle. As Belgian government spokesman and director of the Royal Observatory, Georges Lecointe, explained of the African seamen employed by French boats on the Red Sea and Belgian black boatmen in the Congo, "They have not the same ability to work as the white men of course, and so, if a uniform régime were applied to them, the Belgian shipowners could no longer engage these people and . . . they would be deprived of their work." Until "native" skill levels reached those of their western contemporaries, therefore, Lecointe proposed to divide crew members into distinct ethnic groups with appropriate work hours assigned to each group.[25]

Among international labor legislators, however, it was not just "imperialists" who invoked the race card. Just as antebellum free-soilers sought to keep blacks, slave or free, from settling in their own northern states, so several ILO worker delegations feared—and sought to curtail—economic competition from a cheaper, "colored" labor force. The Australian government delegate, Robert

Storrie Guthrie, a former seaman and trade union leader, was perhaps most explicit in rejecting a separate "Lascar" article within the regulation of hours. Proud of his own country's "white" labor policies ("in Australia [we have] no black labour carrying one pound of cargo or one passenger along the 12,000 miles of our coastline"), he warned that Indian crews must be "confined to the Indian trade" or else "this Conference will have failed." By accepting a reduced standard for Indians, warned Guthrie, the ILO would inadvertently sanction the dreaded "Khalassi watch"—"it means men, with supervisors over them who use a whip, yes, a whip for the purpose of getting them awake when something has got to be done." In short, argued Guthrie, there could be but one seamen's code: "The war has been won, and in the conditions of the settlement of that war was this, that there should be a standardization throughout the world. Whether they were black or white did not matter to ourselves." To be sure, Guthrie's universalistic logic was echoed by some delegates who categorically denied any racialist intent. Italian seamen's leader Giuseppe Giulietti thus urged Indian seamen to trust to the power of the international workers' movement rather than national employer or governmental interests to lift them up. "The seamen of every nation belong to the same class," thundered Giulietti, "and we are fighting and working in order to unite all the seamen of the world. Do not forget the great war! Do not forget that at the present time, in Paris and other great cities, representatives of African people and of Indian people are organizing big societies in order to get complete freedom for the people they represent."[26]

The Indians, for their part, saw the hoary hand of protectionism behind every assertion of universal standards. Government spokesman Captain D. F. Vines of the Royal Indian Marines pleaded for respect for the Indians' place in international waters within a calibrated ILO standard of hours regulations to make up for their own lack of strong unions. Responding to the arguments of the union delegates, Vines reminded them that during the war Indian seamen had carried food and merchandise to Britain, France, and Italy: "You did not want to push them out then. Are you now going to try and push them aside?" Labor delegate A. M. Mazarello, representing passenger liner stewards determined not to limit their tip income, endorsed Vines's support for a Lascar article that "will permit India to follow the international movement without going too quickly, and will provide at the same time a protection for Indian sailors."[27] With each side sticking to its own "principled" position, maritime shorter hours legislation (which required a two-thirds majority to become an ILO convention) failed by a single vote in 1920. A breakthrough on this issue would wait another seventeen years.[28]

Even as substantive reform lagged, the tone of international discussion noticeably changed during the interwar years in one important respect. The protective, if condescending, discourse on the part of European governments toward the workers in their imperial possessions diminished and was replaced by the beginnings of self-representation from the developing world itself. In particular, new voices of anger and frustration were registering from the representatives of Asian seamen, who experienced conditions far worse than those of their western brethren and who no longer put any faith in separate "Asian" articles. In 1929, Indian ILO workers' delegate Muhammed Daud, a Calcutta lawyer who gave up his practice during the noncooperation movement to become president of the Indian Seamen's Union, described a desperate situation where 250,000 seamen were competing for 50,000 jobs and expressed "disappointment regarding the benefits for which we had hoped from this Organization." Despite repeated calls since the Versailles Treaty for "better wages, better regulation of hours of work, better treatment from the shipowners, and better treatment when in port," he saw little evidence of progress. "If the different Governments continue to act in this way," Daud warned, "there is the danger workers in the East will begin to turn their attention to the programme of Moscow."[29] Joining Daud in demanding a special study of Asian sea labor, Chau Chit Wu, adviser to the Chinese Workers' Delegation, claimed that 160,000 of his countrymen were employed by foreign shipowners in highly unfavorable conditions. Typically, he reported, they received two to three pounds per month, compared with the non-Asiatic rate of nine or ten pounds per month; similarly, hours restrictions (along with overtime pay) and workplace accident compensation were regularly relaxed for Chinese seamen. Indeed, they had twice conducted prolonged strikes from Hong Kong since 1922 against the "general contempt" and "inequality of treatment" shown them. Together, Wu and Daud urged support for state employment bureaus, as well as protection for the "freedom of association" in the conduct of trade unionism. In addition to securing an "Asiatic enquiry" in 1929, the rising new nationalist voices militated against separate Asian articles to any agreement. As late as the preparatory meeting for the 1936 International Labour Conference, British-based shippers were reportedly still proposing the old policy. But the Indian worker delegation (led by the Bengali coal trimmer Aftab Ali), now joined by shipowner representatives of Indian-owned firms looking to make their own compact with native labor, prevailed on the Indian High Commissioner Faroz Khan Noon (an heir to a wealthy Punjabi landowning family whose own nationalist aspirations—he would later serve as prime minister of Pakistan—probably inclined him to sympathy with fellow Muslim seafarers) to refrain from reviving what they viewed as an outdated and insulting formula.[30]

After years of deadlocked conferences and dashed hopes, ILO maritime reform was again propelled by the twin stormclouds of worldwide depression and Communist insurgency (this time within the international labor movement). The breakthrough for global standards on hours and manning provisions came at a special maritime conference in Geneva in 1936.[31] The government delegate from France and chairman of the conference preparatory committee, André Haarbleicher, director of the French Merchant Marine and officer of the Legion of Honor who would later die at Auschwitz, opened discussion with a warning that "there is considerable risk of social disturbance if this Convention is rejected."³² British trade union leader and Labour Party stalwart Ernest Bevin, who served as adviser to the worker delegation from the British Empire, pressed the point. Bevin condemned rising trade barriers and increasing restrictions on emigration that he likened to medieval acts limiting peasants from leaving their villages. "World organization," he suggested, "must take the place even of empires if we are going to solve modern economic and other difficult problems." Start with the "regulation of hours of labour on terms of equality," he counseled the trading powers of the globe; then we can further "narrow the field of competition" by eliminating selective government subsidies, quotas, and varying currency standards. Ensuring the seamen's welfare, said Bevin, was thus "but a step towards something bigger and better": "Anyone who votes against this Convention today is voting for the continuation of the miserable world chaos which we find around us, whereas a vote in favour of the Convention will be one contribution, however small, to the removal of that chaos."³³

Even as the Depression's heightening impact hardened resistance to higher standards among many employers—the British, Dutch, and Norwegians, for example, persisted with the twelve-hour day—two new factors had come into play on behalf of international standards. First, in many countries, "the wider extension of subsidies [to national shipping industries] gave seamen an opportunity to appeal to their governments to grant subsidies only where reasonable labor standards were in force."³⁴ Perhaps more significant still was the inaugural (and very active) presence of a U.S. delegation within the international organization itself. With a suspension of the rules and a special joint resolution that Massachusetts Republican Congressman George H. Tinkham labeled "one of the most contemptible intrigues ever attempted in the parliamentary history of this country," President Roosevelt had secured U.S. participation in the ILO in June 1934.³⁵ In keeping with the regulatory spirit of the early New Deal, ILO entry was directly linked to the domestic standards-setting machinery of the National Industrial Recovery Act and Agricultural Adjustment Act. "We can proceed faster and farther in this direction of standards," advised Rep. Samuel Davis McReynolds (D-TN), "if standards are also being raised in most of the other countries of the world."³⁶ Conflating domestic with international developments, California Representative Charles J. Colden called the ILO the "foundation stone upon which enlightened souls of every nation are attempting to build a new deal."³⁷

Indeed, for some of its U.S. enthusiasts, the ILO beckoned not only for its potential international benefits but also at least briefly as a savior of sorts of President Roosevelt's domestic reform agenda. After the Supreme Court's Schechter decision of May 1935 struck down both the NIRA and the AAA—thus leaving the president's economic program in shambles—use of the ILO convention process (like the more famous court-packing plan) offered a theoretical way around a constitutional bottleneck.³⁸ As U.S. Commissioner of Labor Statistics

Isador Lubin told Secretary of Labor Frances Perkins in May 1936, "We should establish the precedent of submitting [ILO] conventions to the Senate so that in the event we wish to test out the treaty-making power as a vehicle for securing social legislation a definite precedent will have been established."[39] The strategem took immediate effect in a June 1936 presidential message to Congress urging consideration of five ILO draft conventions, including "reduction of hours of work to 40 a week"—this a full year and a half before the president's domestic Fair Labor Standards Act, embodying the same principle, was enacted by Congress.[40]

However grandiose their expectations for the world body in general, the Americans clearly arrived at the ILO's 1936 maritime conference with enthusiasm. The U.S. delegation was led, across 1935 and 1936, by government delegate Robert W. Bruere, erstwhile editor of the Progressive reform ramrod, *The Survey*, and NRA adminstrator. He was accompanied by an employer representative from the U.S. flag carrier Moore & McCormack Co. and a labor delegate from the near-moribund International Seamen's Union, creating one of the few tripartite delegations united by strong reform and regulatory predilections. The rationale for unanimity was not far-fetched. Like France and Russia, the United States already enforced the eight-hour day and three-watch system, as opposed to the traditional two-watch system of four hours on and four off that added up, for most of the world's sailors, to a twelve-hour day. As Harvard economist Carl J. Ratzlaff had argued in 1932, "American employers and laborers [will be] directly [and positively] affected by the 'leveling' up work of an international economic organization such as the ILO."[41] Now second only to Great Britain as a maritime power, the U.S. presence decidedly advanced the chances for maritime reforms inside that world body.[42]

Pressure for regulatory economic action was generally intense by mid-1936. To fend off plunging price and production schedules, labor and governmental delegates at the Twentieth Session of the International Labor Conference in Geneva pushed for hours limits in multiple industries. Yet despite an energetic push for standards, particularly the forty-hour week, the textiles convention, the symbolic center for international industrial agreement (let alone similar measures for the construction, iron, and coal industries), failed to reach the needed two-thirds threshold for passage.[43] Indeed, of all the "landed" industries, only the peculiar arenas of the glass bottle industry (a classic repository of child labor) and public works (which, by definition, lacked private sector opponents) secured hours conventions.[44]

Finally, in the fourth such attempt since 1920 and amid what American delegate Bruere called "miserable world chaos," the Hours of Work and Manning Convention sailed through the 1936 conference. Though applying only to "international" voyages, exempting catering and clerical employees, and allowing exceptions according to "national regulations" or "collective [bargaining] agreements," the three-watch, eight-hour day-at-sea, and six-day-week-in-port system was thus enshrined as an international norm and slated to "come into force" as soon as it had been ratified by at least five of the major maritime countries.[45] Still, U.S. Labor Commissioner (and Columbia University economic historian) Carter Goodrich marveled that "in this most international of industries," the advocates of regulation had "won a signal and unexpectedly complete victory."[46]

Yet, even the passage of a convention exposed a degree of cynicism, as well as the practical limits associated with ILO diplomacy. The assenting majority, for example, included many votes from countries effectively unaffected by the outcome. Even as the Mexican government happily subscribed to the "fundamental principles of social doctrine," it allowed that the subject had "no immediate repercussions" on the national economy. China similarly offered eager support for the "eight-hour day," even though "we have no such [internationally trading] ships in our country." While supporting the measure, the Soviet Union found it almost equally inconsequential. "In our country," proudly proclaimed the government delegate, a Mr. Markus, "the abolition of private ownership of the means of production, the nationalisation of shipping, the liquidation of the capitalist class and the absence of private shipowners have put an end to the exploitation of seamen. Soviet seamen are working for themselves, for their own society, and consequently they work shorter hours than those of any other country in the world."[47]

Opponents of regulation, to be sure, did not find the convention terribly constricting. The government delegate for India, for example, though not casting a negative vote, made clear that the draft convention, representing too much of a departure from contemporary practices, would never be adopted by his country. Likewise, the Dutch, who claimed to have lost nearly 20 percent of their shipping due to others' industry subsidies and protectionist trade policy, would not countenance further intrusions on their marketplace maneuverability by paying overtime rates. "I am not in the easy position," rued C. J. P. Zaalberg, director of the Dutch National Society for the Protection of Shipping Interests, "of those . . . who say to themselves 'We have no merchant marine, but we want everybody in the world to have a happy life, and so we shall vote for this convention.'"[48] After all the argument and all the waiting, the 1936 Hours and Manning Convention never came into force: Ten years after its passage, only three nations (Australia, the United States, and Belgium) had ratified its terms.[49]

At best, a good gauge of international sentiment—and a model debating forum for competing visions of industrial regulation that might in turn be appropriated in collective bargaining agreements—the ILO consistently proved a source of unrequited love for even its most active suitors.[50] The British had long been cautious regarding the ILO's reach. The Americans as well, who had belatedly but all the more eagerly turned to the ILO to raise worldwide standards to a level in at least some minimal correspondence with its own, soon adopted other strategies. Indeed, witnessing the timing of events developing across congressional, parliamentary, and ILO clocks, it appears that government officials and their labor allies, even as they "played the international field," had simultaneously been hatching plans to "marry the girl next door" in the form of national shipping subsidies and seamen's protective legislation.

Protection, indeed, was the name of the international game by the mid-1930s. With the economy spiraling downward, the shipping nations sought to hold onto their share of the world market by various forms of subsidy. Great Britain had notably abandoned its signature free trade posture—adopting heavy duties and then later devaluing the pound and jettisoning the gold standard—in the post–World War I years. By 1935, Britain had also followed Japan, Italy, Germany, the Netherlands, and France in establishing operating subsidies for its tramp steamers in the British Shipping (Assistance) Act.[51] Having built itself overnight, or at least between 1917 and 1922, into the world's second largest merchant fleet, the United States was equally determined not to fall behind. By the 1930s, having redirected most of its government-built fleet into private hands, anxieties rose that the Americans once again were drifting into maritime impotence.[52] The coincidence of the *Morro Castle* (September 1934) and *Mohawk* (January 1935) passenger ship disasters—the first by fire, the second by seeming crew incompetence—further raised public anxieties.[53]

The result was the Merchant Marine Act of 1936. Modeled on regulatory rates and hours legislation adopted for the railroad and trucking industries in the Emergency Railroad Transportation Act (1933) and Motor Carrier Act (1935) and extending and amending preferences previously offered in a series of ocean-mail subsidy acts in the 1920s, the Merchant Marine Act simultaneously curried favor with the marine unions and the U.S. shipping and shipbuilding industries.[54] By justification, it harked back to Adam Smith's original exemption of a national shipping industry from free trade principles on grounds of national defense and economic security. One of the bill's key proponents, Representative S. O. Bland, thus pointed to a litany of historical embarrassments due to the nation's chronically inadequate seagoing capacity. In addition to the scare of 1914, when the United States found itself suddenly "cut off from the markets of Great Britain, France, Italy, Germany, and other nations of Europe with few exceptions," Bland thus invoked "the spirit of the martyred war President, William McKinley, who knew the humiliation which we suffered in the Spanish-American War, when we had not American ships or seamen sufficient for the war, when we had to search the ports of Europe for transports and colliers . . . when we had to enlist landsmen and foreign seamen to man our fighting vessels, and when returns show that fully one third of our naval crews were foreigners." President Franklin Roosevelt echoed Bland's logic in his 1935 legislative message to Congress, urging new legislation to "square this traditional ideal [of an American merchant marine] with effective performance."[55]

Faced with a competitively adverse sea, American policy makers in 1936 thus acted decisively (however impractically) to establish a U.S.-owned and manned oceanic fleet. Invoking the La Follette Act of 1915 as "one of the most humanitarian ever enacted by the Congress," New Dealer Sen. Royal Copeland (NY) determined to realize its ambitions for American seamen in a new form. "If there is one place," declaimed Copeland, "if there is one institution under the American flag which should be under the domination and control of loyal, patriotic Americans, it is a vessel upon the high seas."[56]

Appealing across class, regional, and partisan boundaries with this security argument, legislators sweetened a massive subsidy program for U.S. shipbuilders and shipowners (a newly created U.S. Maritime Commission would essentially fund the difference between the prevailing construction and operating price abroad and that at home) with an employment and welfare program for U.S. seamen.[57] The latter measures (divided between the act itself and amendments to the La Follette Act of 1915) authorized the new commission to prescribe minimum manning and wage scales for all U.S. oceangoing ships and required that within two years 90 percent of crews on subsidized ships—and 75 percent on all U.S.-flagged ships—"be citizens of the United States, native-born, or completely naturalized"—stipulations to be advanced by establishment of a government-sponsored Merchant Marine Academy for training seamen and officers and to be relaxed only under an emergency finding by the secretary of commerce.[58]

Unfortunately, any move to protect a single nation's seamen was likely to contain a nastier side as well. As in Britain's early lascar restrictions or in the English-language provisions of the U.S. La Follette Act, a racist, anti-immigrant, and specifically anti-Asian animus infected Anglo-American maritime labor reform in the Depression Era.[59] The British mold was first set in the Coloured Alien Seamen Order of 1925. This Order in Council from the British Home Office responded to the overlapping interests of employers, the Board of Trade, and the conservative National Union of Seamen in attempting to block "coloured" seamen from claiming full citizenship status on the imperial mainland. At first designed to distinguish alien (and especially Arab) passengers—marked for deportation—from bona fide seamen, the prosecution and very definition of *alien* proved elastic. Racial difference itself suddenly appeared to signal outsider status, forcing all "blacks" (including Indians) to register with the police in complicated documentation checks and threatening "widespread harassment of Black residents of British ports," until both panic and application of the order was dampened by countervailing pressures from the Colonial Office.[60]

Just as the Coloured Alien Seamen Order made things difficult for nonwhite maritime workers *on land*, so the labor clauses of the 1935 tramp shipping subsidy bill discriminated against them at sea. In accepting industry subsidies, Labour MPs had insisted on a full reversal of open-hiring practices and demanded a British-only employment policy on British ships. As with the earlier order, however, precisely defining "British nationals" within an extensive and complex imperial order proved a difficult and contentious process. Initially, many veteran Indian seamen lost their jobs, as employers scurried to comply with the new rules. Quickly, a labor shortage and internal conflicts within the seamen's union led to an agreement to treat British "protected persons" (from the war-acquired territories of Southern Arabia and East Africa) and "all classes of British subjects" (89) alike. Still, some, like the Goan seamen used to traveling on lascar articles but technically Portuguese subjects, were left out. Moreover, when the subsidy scheme was renewed in 1939, shipowners risked losing the subsidy if they employed Indian seamen outside "customary" routes; in addition, Indian-crewed ships received a lower subsidy since wage increases affecting British seamen since 1935 had not applied to them.[61]

The U.S. move to subsidized shipping carried a similarly racialized taint when it came to manpower definitions. Within a general clampdown on 1930s immigration (including the "voluntary" return to their homeland of nearly a million Mexicans), immigration restrictionists reintroduced legislation that had been routinely backed for years by the American Federation of Labor under the rubric of the Alien Seamen's Act of 1933.[62] The rationale for the bill lay in a perceived loophole—in fact, a component of the "right to quit"—of the 1915 act itself, under which all sailors had enjoyed the right to depart their ships in any American port for up to sixty days before signing on to another voyage under the best terms they could find. On the grounds that an appreciable number of seamen (and "bogus seamen")—estimates of total "deserter seamen" from all countries varied wildly from 50,000 to 500,000—otherwise excluded by law from entering the country, were manipulating this sea passage to join the U.S. labor force, the bill proposed severe new restrictions. Every arriving alien seaman would be "examined in quarantine" to determine his eligibility to disembark the ship. No vessel that included crewmembers racially excluded from applying for U.S. citizenship would be granted entry into a port. Finally, no vessel could depart a U.S. port with a smaller crew than it had entered with. Identifying Asiatic aliens as people whose "willingness to work for low wages and under any conditions make it impossible for the American workmen to compete with them," Texas Congressman Martin Dies (better known for his later service as the first chairman of the House Un-American Activities Committee) believed restriction would "not only help labor but promote law enforcement." "Many of these aliens," he explained, "become racketeers and criminals."[63] Probably due to the intense diplomatic pressure from U.S. allies, Senate leadership failed to match the ardor of the House, allowing the alien seamen initiative to lapse once again in 1933.[64]

Of course, the citizen-only clause that accompanied the 1936 shipping subsidy legislation offered another path toward restriction. Indeed, in addition to its strong native preference, by limiting even the potential 10 percent of noncitizens within a crew to those making a "valid declaration of interest to become a citizen," the bill neatly disqualified from service all Asians, who were already barred from citizenship.[65] The degree to which cultural prejudice trumped even the most naked economic self-interest in such matters was nowhere more blatant than in one curious turn amid the 1936 congressional debates. Just as the final *t* was being crossed in the Senate version of the "personnel" section of the new legislation, concern was expressed about the total ban on Asians in the stewards department on passenger liners. Speaking up for several West Coast shipping lines, Sen. Frederick Steiwer (R, Oregon) urged a special exemption of up to 20 percent "only in the steward's department" for "aliens ineligible for citizenship." Such a measure, Steiwer urged his colleagues, was necessary to accommodate passenger liners on the trans-Pacific run who regularly employed "some Asiatics": "The reason for the necessity of doing so is that many of the passengers on some of the runs are themselves Asiatics, and the ship operators find that it is impossible to employ a good class of American citizen to serve the Asiatic passengers."[66] For fear of losing rich passengers' accounts, the restrictionists were thus asked to give way slightly and allow a minimal presence of an accursed "coolie" class on American-flag ships. Despite an initial show of support, the Senate ultimately buried the proposal.[67]

Even the most poignant absurdity within the citizenship clause of the 1936 act could not deflect the law's restrictionist impulse. As it happened, an estimated 3,000 Filipino seamen had entered the U.S. merchant marine—especially as stewards—following the Spanish-American War and since established permanent residency with their wives and families. Now, as Resident Commissioner Quintin Paredes appealed to Congress, they were in a "serious predicament." Owing allegiance to the United States and subject under the Philippines Constitution to a call to arms in defense of the American flag, which still had complete sovereignty over their country, they nevertheless fit neither the "native born" nor "completely naturalized" options available under the 1936 act as resident "nationals," nor, except in special circumstances, could they apply for American citizenship. If now restricted to the quota for aliens under the new legislation, the 3,000 Filipino seamen would drop to at most 750. Again, the appeal fell on deaf ears.[68]

In 1947, *New Yorker* writer and labor historian (*Labor's Untold Story*, 1955) Richard O. Boyer offered a colorful reminiscence of his wartime experience on a troop transport ship and the heroic struggles of the left-wing National Maritime Union.[69] A central theme of Boyer's story was the realization, aboard ship, of the classic melting pot of American identity.

> Union leaders were proud of the fact, moreover, that there was little racial discrimination aboard the *Marquette*—although they said they had to fight to keep this so, since new officers and new crewmen appeared on each trip. They said that some of the best men in the crew were Negroes and that on the ship's muster roll were Egyptians, Chinese, Swedes, Persians, Englishmen, Liberians, Welshmen, Hondurans, Frenchmen,

Italians, Russians, Irishmen, Serbs, Mexicans, Croats, Ecuadorians, Puerto Ricans, South Africans, Spaniards, Icelanders and Filipinos, all of them naturalized Americans.[70]

Tales of interracial and interethnic solidarity are a mainstay of the survival narratives of the trade union movement around the world, including its British and American component parts. And there was probably no occupational group with more experience of international and cross-cultural contacts than merchant seamen. Indeed, it was that very experience that had set Anglo-American seamen's organizations as early as the turn of the twentieth century on a path to define a set of common, livable standards for all the world's seamen. That quest continued through a vigorous pursuit of ILO seamen's conventions. Yet, even those of a most democratic disposition in the west faced a difficult dilemma. Should they engage a worldwide market of people and products and try to impose humane standards there, just as they had done across a century of struggle in their home country? Or should they withdraw behind selective national standards to cushion the competitive market pressures?

At least for the two greatest shipping powers of the interwar world, the global sea of competitive shipping and motley maritime crews proved a more threatening than inviting proposition. As the initial decades of ILO experience suggested, there existed no obvious instrument by which minimal worldwide codes of skill, safety, and conditions of labor could be imposed. Both Great Britain and the United States, in a period of social democratic currents stirred by strong labor movements, opted to insulate their maritime labor forces, as well as their shipping industries, from outside competition. The economic impact of such measures, which will not concern us here, only accelerated the long-run decline of both shipping powers on the world stage. The social consequences were more immediate. As a result of the protectionist legislation, the "world" found aboard both British- and U.S.-flagged ships increasingly mirrored that found at home. The kicker in Boyer's paean to NMU pluralism was the final, almost invisible phrase—"all of them naturalized Americans." "Diversity" in the post–World War I Atlantic world would determinedly be limited to "naturalized" citizens. No matter the slogans or projected ideals, as B. Traven had recognized early on, this was not the stuff of which international solidarity could easily be fashioned.

For all its travails, internationalism on the high seas did not, perhaps could not, go away. It can only be briefly noted here that even as the Atlantic superpowers turned away from the rest of the maritime laboring world, that world did not stand still. In particular, both the Chinese and the Indian seafaring populations—the accursed objects of much western restrictive activity—already by World War II had gained important new leverage. In both cases, wartime service in the Allied cause, together with rising nationalist sentiment at home accentuated by resentment of imperial and/or racist disdain from western "superiors," triggered a rising assertiveness. Amid the collective fight against Japan, mass desertions by Chinese seamen in U.S. ports effectively forced an attenuation of long-functioning exclusion laws. In the case of the Indians, a succession of wartime strikes, together with pressing labor shortages, produced a dramatic jump in wages and benefits. Yet, as Gopalan Balachandran has argued, it was "only... in the context of the self-consciously modern project of the new nation-state—that Indian seamen finally shed their badge as 'coolies' to emerge as workers."[71] An important step on that path was the 1948 complaint to the ILO by A. K. Serang, son of founding Indian seamen's leader Mohamed Serang, about the corrupt hiring practices associated with the shipping company–recruitment boss control of the labor market. The First Asian Maritime Conference, held in 1953 in Ceylon, proved a turning point. Shortly thereafter, government-run seamen's employment offices were established in Bombay and Calcutta, as well as in Pakistan, Singapore, and Hong Kong.[72] The story, to be sure, carries a broader point. If western trade unionists often found international organizations like the ILO to be toothless tigers, their counterparts in developing nations often looked to them as both political and economic lifelines.[73] Moreover, in the post–World War II era, particularly with mounting concerns about conditions on ships attached to flags of convenience, both ILO standards like the global minimum wage and the mobilization of Third World seafarers would assume a new public prominence.

NOTES

1. I particularly thank Harold Lewis, Jeremy Seekings, Denver Brunsman, Nelson Lichtenstein, and Susan Levine for their suggestions and criticisms of earlier drafts of this chapter. Gopalan Balachandran and Ravi Ahuja helped me immeasurably in making sense of the Indian evidence. Finally, Thomas Dorrance provided valuable assistance in the course of my research.
2. Eric W. Sager, *Seafaring Labour: The Merchant Marine of Atlantic Canada, 1920–1914* (Montreal: McGill-Queen's University Press, 1989), 245–49.
3. H. H. Raymond testimony in Cong. Rec. 63rd Cong., 1st sess. Senate, 1913, 50, pt. 6: 5697.
4. Jurgen Kramer, "Conrad's Crews Revisited," in *Fictions of the Sea: Critical Perspectives on the Ocean in British Literature and Culture*, ed. Bernhard Klein (Burlington, VT: Ashgate, 2002), 157.
5. John Peck, *Maritime Fiction: Sailors and the Sea in British and American Novels, 1719–1917* (London: Palgrave, 2001), 170–73; Lillian Nayder, "Sailing Ships and Steamers, Angels and Whores: History and Gender in Conrad's Maritime Fiction," in *Iron Men, Wooden Women: Gender and Seafaring in the Atlantic World, 1700–1920*, ed. Margaret S. Creighton and Lisa Norling (Baltimore: Johns Hopkins University Press, 1996), 189–90. Cf. Hester Blum, *The View from*

the Masthead: Maritime Imagination and Antebellum American Sea Narratives (Chapel Hill: University of North Carolina Press, 2008), 112.

6. Arthur Gelb and Barbara Gelb, *O'Neill* (New York: Harper and Brothers, 1962), 157.
7. Eugene O'Neill, *Early Plays* (New York: Penguin, 2001), quotation from *The Moon of the Caribbees* [1917], 6.
8. Eugene O'Neill, *The Hairy Ape*, in *Three Great Plays* (Mineola, NY: Dover, 2005), 104, 129.
9. B. Traven, *The Death Ship: The Story of an American Sailor* (Brooklyn, NY: Lawrence Hill, 1991), 216. "Death" or "coffin" ships, said to be dispatched to be sunk for their insurance value by unscrupulous owners, were a prime target of the investigations of British reformer Samuel Plimsoll in the 1870s and 1880s.
10. Ibid., 237.
11. On Hughes's experience, see *The Big Sea: An Autobiography* (New York: Hill and Wang, 1940), and Elizabeth Schultz, "African-American Literature," in *America and the Sea: A Literary History*, ed. Haskell Springer (Athens: University of Georgia Press, 1995), 244–46.
12. Wayne F. Cooper, *Claude McKay: Rebel Sojourner in the Harlem Renaissance* (Baton Rouge: Louisiana State University Press, 1987), 171.
13. Claude McKay, *Home to Harlem* (New York: Harper & Brothers, 1928), 1.
14. Claude McKay, *Banjo* (New York: Harper & Brothers, 1929), 312; Schultz, "African-American Literature," 244.
15. Eric Hobsbawm, *Age of Extremes: The Short Twentieth Century, 1914–1991* (London: Michael Joseph, 1994), quotation on 34, and see more generally his treatment of the "Bolshevik biennium" (1917–1919) and its collapse, 54–84.
16. Harold B. Butler, "The Washington Conference" in James T. Shotwell, *The Origins of the International Labor Organization* (New York: Columbia University Press, 1934), I, 305–30; as Elizabeth McKillen notes, in embracing the ILO as an "advisory" rather than "compulsory" body, Gompers himself maintained his essential voluntarist principles even as he continued a World War I–era shift from "rigid antistatism" toward a "centrist alliance with [President] Wilson." "Betrayal or Realization of a Dream: The Transnational Labor Movement and the Birth of the International Labor Organization in 1919," Paper presented at Newberry Conference on Labor across the Americas, September 19–20, 2008, Newberry Library, Chicago.
17. Edward C. Lorenz, *Defining Global Justice: The History of U.S. International Labor Standards Policy* (Notre Dame, IN: University of Notre Dame Press, 2001), 75–103.
18. Though League members automatically became chartered members of the ILO, an opening was also left for non-League members to the join the ILO.
19. Edward J. Phelan, "British Preparations," in Shotwell, *Origins*, I, 105–26.
20. International Labour Organization, *The Rules of the Game: A Brief Introduction to International Labour Standards* (Geneva: ILO, 2005), 12–16.

21. Tribute by Francis Blancard in *Albert Thomas, 1878–1978* (Geneva: ILO Office, 1978), 5; E. J. Phelan, *Yes and Albert Thomas* (1936; reprint, New York: Columbia University Press, 1949), 58.
22. International Seamen's Code proposal, International Seamen's Conference, Genoa, Italy, June 1920, as reprinted in San Francisco, *Seamen's Journal*, September 29, 1920.
23. Ravi Ahuja, "Mobility and Containment: The Voyages of South Asian Seamen, c. 1900–1960", *International Review of Social History* 51 (2006), Suppl. no. 112.
24. "Hours of Labour and Their Effect on Manning and Accommodation," League of Nations, International Labour Office, Seamen's Conference, Genoa, July 9, 1920, 416.
25. Ibid., 417.
26. http://www.adb.online.anu.edu.au/biogs/A090139b.htm?hilite=Guthrie; "Hours of Labour," 421.
27. "Hours of Labour," 423–24; Gopalan Balachandran suggests that Mazarello (and thus the decisive maritime hours vote) may have fallen victim to the influence of P&O and government interests who supplied his interpreter. See "Conflicts in the International Maritime Labour Market: British and Indian Seamen, Employers, and the State, 1890–1939," *Indian Economic & Social History Review* 39 (2002): 94–95.
28. Arthur Marsh and Victoria Ryan, *The Seamen* (Oxford: Malthouse, 1989), 108–10; F. J. A. Broeze, "The Muscles of Empire: Indian Seamen and the Raj," *Indian Economic and Social History Review* 18 (1981): 52–55. Two less controversial conventions banning child labor under fourteen and restricting shipside recruitment bosses and brokers were approved in Genoa. Otherwise, prior to 1936, the only maritime measures to reach the two-thirds threshold required the signing of articles of agreement for all seagoing vessels (1926) and the repatriation of foreign seamen to their home country (1926); see http://www.ilo.org/ilolex/english/convdisp1.htm
29. Record of Proceedings, International Labor Conference, Geneva, 12th sitting, October 24, 1929, 157.
30. Ibid., 171–74, 176; Report of the Director, International Labor Conference, 14th Session, Geneva 1930, 244; Record of Proceedings, International Labour Conference, 21st and 22nd sessions, Geneva 1936, 126–27; Broeze, "The Muscles of Empire," 56, 61; Aftab Ali subsequently became a prominent trade union leader and politician in East Pakistan. Ravi Ahuja, "Mobility and Containment: The Voyages of South Asian Seamen, c. 1900–1960," in Rana Partap Behal and Marcel van der Linden, eds., "Coolies, Capital, and Colonialism: Studies in Indian Labour History," *International Review of Social History Supplements* (2006), 139.
31. Reawakening fears of worldwide revolution and social breakdown, the stock market crash and economic depression of the 1930s paradoxically lifted the global profile of the ILO as a potential agent in dealing with the employment

crisis. See Daniel Patrick Moynihan, "The United States and the International Labor Organization, 1889–1934" (doctoral dissertation, Fletcher School of Law and Diplomacy, 1960), 469.
32. Record of Proceedings, International Labour Conference, 21st and 22nd sessions, Geneva, 1936, 117.
33. Ibid., 133.
34. William Gorham Rice and W. Ellison Chalmers, "Improvement of Labor Conditions on Ships by International Action," *MLR* 42 (May 1936): 1181–1203, quotation on 1191.
35. Moynihan, "The United States," xi; Cong. Rec., 74th Cong, 1st sess., 1935, 78, pt. 2: 1683.
36. Cong. Rec., 73d Cong., 2d sess., 1934, 78, pt. 11:12580.
37. Cong Rec., 74th Cong., 1st sess., 1935, 79, pt. 3: 2583.
38. New Deal advocates certainly had reason to fear for the future of national labor and welfare legislation. Not until March 1937 did the Supreme Court (in the famous "stitch in time saves nine" case) reverse itself and uphold a state minimum wage law. Within weeks, it likewise upheld the National Labor Relations Act and the Social Security Act, thus both averting a constitutional crisis and rendering unnecessary such radically alternative paths as the ILO for domestic social legislation. Robert McElvaine, *The Great Depression: America, 1929–1941* (New York: Three Rivers, 1993), 286; Lorenz, *Defining Global Justice*, 108.
39. Lubin, as quoted in Lorenz, *Defining Global Justice*, 109.
40. Cong. Rec., 74th Cong., 2d sess., 1936, 80, pt. 9: 9999.
41. C. J. Ratzlaff, "The International Labor Organization of the League of Nations: Its Significance to the United States," *American Economic Review* 22 (September 1932), 450–51.
42. Rice and Chalmers, "Improvement of Labor Conditions," 1195.
43. On the 1936 world textile conference, see Lorenz, *Defining Global Justice*, 113–19.
44. W. Ellison Chalmers, "International Labor Organization: Results of International Labor Conference, June 1936," *MLR* (1936): 323.
45. http://www.ilo.org/ilolex/english/convdisp1.htm
46. Cater Goodrich, "International Labor Relations: Maritime Labor Treaties of 1936," *MLR* 44 (1937): 349, 354. A British collective bargaining agreement the previous summer adopting the rudiments of the three-watch system reportedly paved the way for the needed supermajority of delegate votes.
47. Record of Proceedings, International Labour Conference, 21st and 22nd sessions, Geneva 1936, 120, 127, 129. The Soviet delegate, a Mr. Markus, pointedly did not mention the suppression of the Kronstadt sailors' uprising in March 1921.
48. Ibid., 129, 121–22.
49. International Labour Conference, Report III (Part 2), "Lists of Ratifications by Convention and by Country," 91st Session, 2003.
50. Marsh and Ryan, *The Seamen*, 154–55.

51. Ronald Hope, *A New History of British* Shipping (London: John Murray, 1990), 365–66.
52. Roland, Bolster, and Keyssar, *The Way of the Ship*, 273, 325. The World War I–era oversupply of ships, combined with the Depression-era trade slump, drastically affected U.S. shipbuilding. See Jeffrey J. Safford, "The U.S. Merchant Marine in Foreign Trade, 1800–1939," in *Business History of Shipping: Strategy and Structure* (Tokyo, Japan: University of Tokyo Press, 1985), 111.
53. Joseph P. Goldberg, *The Maritime Story: A Study in Labor-Management Relations* (Cambridge: Harvard University Press, 1958), 182.
54. Ellis Hawley, *The New Deal and the Problem of Monopoly* (New York: Fordham University Press, 1995), 233–34.
55. Cong. Rec., 73rd Cong., 2d sess., 1934, 78, pt. 1: 665; Cong. Rec., 74th Cong., 1st sess., 1935, 79, pt. 3: 2859.
56. Cong. Rec., 74th Cong., 2d sess., 80; Furuseth's epithet and frequent presence at debates was invoked by Dem. Rep. William P. Connery (Mass.) on March 5, 1934, Cong. Rec., 73d Cong., 2d sess., 78, pt. 4: 3739.
57. The measures, tied together in debate, were passed as the ship-subsidy Merchant Marine Act of 1936 and as an amendment to the Seamen's Act of 1915. On the subsidy meassures, see Ralph L. Dewey, "The Merchant Marine Act of 1936," *American Economic Review* 27 (June 1937): 240–52; Roland, Bolster, and Keyssar, *The Way of the Ship*, 294–99.
58. Cong Rec., 74th Cong., 1st sess., 1936, 79, pt. 9: 10194; Cong. Rec., 74th Cong., 2d sess., 1936, 80, pt. 7: 7259; Joint Conf. Report 3041 (June 18, 1936), 1–8, quotation, 6. Reference to the late-shifting of the "personnel" sections of the 1936 legislation is made within the House debates: Cong. Rec., 74th Cong., 1936, 2d sess., 80, pt. 10571–72; Merchant Marine Act of 1936, Public Law No. 835, 74th Cong., sec. 301 (a) and (b).
59. On the exclusionist tint of the LaFollette Act, see see Jerold S. Auerbach, "Progressives at Sea: The LaFollette Act of 1915," *Labor History* 2 (Fall 1961): 344–60.
60. Laura Tabili, *"We Ask for British Justice": Workers and Racial Difference in Late Imperial Britain* (Ithaca, NY: Cornell University Press, 1994), 113–34, quotation, 121. For an account of the intimidating effect of such legislation, see McKay, *Banjo*. On the political gamesmanship (and limited real effect) behind the order, see Tony Lane, "The Political Imperatives of Bureaucracy and Empire: The Case of the Coloured Alien Seamen Order, 1925," *Immigrants and Minorities* 13 (1994): 104–29.
61. G. Balachandran, "Conflicts in the International Maritime Labour Market: British and Indian Seamen, Employers, and the State, 1890–1939," *Indian Economic & Social History Review* 39 (2002): 71–100, quotation 89.
62. Aristide R. Zolberg, *A Nation by Design: Immigration Policy in the Fashioning of America* (Cambridge: Harvard University Press, 2006), 267–70.
63. Cong. Rec., 73rd Cong., 2d sess., 1934, 78, pt. 4: 3735–41, quotation 3738.

64. Ibid., 3737; on international pressures, see "Representations by Foreign Governments Regarding Congressional Bills for the Deportation of Certain Alien Seamen," U.S. Dept. of State, Foreign Relations of the United States, diplomatic papers, 1932, General, Vol. 1 (1932), http://digicoll.library.wisc.edu/cgi-bin/FRUS/FRUS-idx?type=article&id=FRUS.FRUS1932v01&did=FRUS.FRUS1932V01.I0018&q1=alien%20seamen
65. Merchant Marine Act of 1936, Public Law No. 835, 74th Cong., sec. 301 (c).
66. Cong. Rec., 74th Cong., 2d sess., 1936, 80, pt. 9: 9916.
67. Cong. Rec., 74th Cong., 2d sess., 1936, 80, pt. 10: 10068–69.
68. House Committee on Merchant Marine and Fisheries, Hearings on H.R. 8532, 75th Cong., 2d and 3d sess., 1937–38, 710–12. It is likely that the Filipino mariner issue effectively disappeared into the exigencies of wartime mobilization. Special acts, for example, invited Filipinos into the U.S. Army, the Coast Guard, and Coast Guard Reserve in 1941 and 1942. Otherwise, the anomalous status of Filipinos in U.S. law vanished with independence in 1946. U.S. Cong., Permitting Filippinos to Become Members of Coast Guard Auxiliary and Coast Guard Reserve. S. Rp. 1636, 77th Cong., 2nd sess., 1942, Serial 10659.
69. The NMU had arisen amid the failed 1936–1937 strike as a revolt of rank-and-file militants versus a sclerotic and corrupt ISU leadership. On the complicated and often bitter maritime interunion battles of the 1930s, see Goldberg, *The Maritime Story*, 130–62; Bruce Nelson, *Workers on the Waterfront: Seamen, Longshoremen, and Unionism in the 1930s* (Urbana: University of Illinois Press, 1988), 223–49.
70. Richard O. Boyer, *The Dark Ship* (Boston: Little, Brown, 1947), 23.
71. Jonathan Hyslop, "Steamship Empire: Asian, African and British Sailors in the Merchant Marine, c. 1880–1945," *Journal of Asian and African Studies* 44, no. 1 (2009): 63–64; Gopalan Balachandran, "Producing Coolies, (Un)making Workers: A (Post-)Colonial Parable for the Contemporary Present," Paper presented to "Workers, the Nation-State and Beyond: The Newberry Conference on Labor across the Americas," Chicago, September 18–20, 2008.
72. Telephone interview with Abdulgani Serang (grandson of A. K. Serang and currently general secretary of the National Union of Seafarers of India, NUSI), March 3, 2009; "The ILO and Seafarers," *ITF Journal* 29 (Autumn 1969): 59.
73. See, e.g., Broeze, "The Muscles of Empire," 43–67; and Jeremy Seekings, "The ILO and Welfare Reform in South Africa, Latin America and the Caribbean, 1925–50," Paper presented at the conference "The Past and Present of the International Labour Organisation," International Institute of Social History, Ghent, Belgium, October 4–6, 2007 (copy courtesy of the author).

CONTRIBUTORS

Steven J. Bachelor is professor of history at Fairfield University. The author of a number of articles on postrevolutionary Mexico, he is completing a book manuscript titled *Miracle to Maquila: The Big Three Automakers in Mexico*.

Eileen Boris, Hull Professor and chair of the Department of Feminist Studies at the University of California, Santa Barbara, specializes in women's labors in the home and other workplaces and on gender, race, work, and the welfare state. Her latest books are, with Jennifer Klein, *Caring for America: Home Health Workers in the Shadow of the Welfare State* . (forthcoming from Oxford University Press) and, edited with Rhacel Salazar Parreñas, *Intimate Labors: Cultures, Technologies, and the Politics of Care* (Stanford University Press, 2010).

Aviva Chomsky is professor of history and coordinator of Latin American, Latino, and Caribbean Studies at Salem State University in Massachusetts. Her books include *A History of the Cuban Revolution* (Wiley-Blackwell, 2011), *Linked Labor Histories: New England, Colombia, and the Making of a Global Working Class* (Duke University Press, 2008), *They Take Our Jobs! And 20 Other Myths about Immigration* (Beacon Press, 2007), and *West Indian Workers and the United Fruit Company in Costa Rica, 1870–1940* (Louisiana State University Press, 1996), as well as several anthologies and translations. Her current projects include a history of international solidarity in the Americas.

Leon Fink is distinguished professor of history at the University of Illinois at Chicago and editor of *Labor: Studies in Working-Class History of the Americas*. He is currently completing a study of the regulation of global seafarers.

John H. Flores is assistant professor of history at Case Western Reserve University. He is currently working on a book manuscript titled *On the Wings of the Revolution: Transnational Politics and the Making of Mexican American Identities*, which examines Mexican-origin political and labor movements in metropolitan Chicago during the early to mid-twentieth century.

John D. French is a professor of history and African and African-American Studies at Duke University whose specialties include labor and politics in Brazil and the rise of alt-global politics. His books include *The Brazilian Workers' ABC: Class Conflict and Alliances in Modern São Paulo* (University of North Carolina Press, 1992), *Drowning in Laws: Labor Law and Brazilian Political Culture* (University of North Carolina Press, 2004), and the coedited *The Gendered Worlds of Latin American Women Workers* (Duke University Press, 1997). He is currently finishing a manuscript titled *Lula's Politics of Cunning: From Trade Unionism to the Presidency in Brazil.*

Julie Greene is associate professor at the University of Maryland at College Park, where she specializes in U.S. labor and working-class history. Her research and teaching interests span immigration and political history, the history of empire, and transnational approaches to the history of the Americas. Greene is the author of *The Canal Builders: Making America's Empire at the Panama Canal* (Penguin, 2009) and *Pure and Simple Politics: The American Federation of Labor and Political Activism, 1881–1917* (Cambridge University Press, 1998) and coeditor, with Eric Arnesen and Bruce Laurie, of *Labor Histories: Class, Politics, and the Diversity of the Working-Class Experience* (University of Illinois Press, 1998).

Camille Guérin-Gonzales is professor of history at the University of Wisconsin–Madison. She is completing a book-length study, *Mapping Working-Class Struggles in Appalachia, South Wales, and the American Southwest, 1890–1947* (forthcoming from University of Illinois Press), and is the author of *Mexican Workers and American Dreams: Immigration, Repatriation, and California Farm Labor, 1900–1939* (Rutgers University Press, 1994). A *manita* from northern New Mexico, her scholarship and teaching are dedicated to an understanding of difference and power in all their complexity and to the pursuit of social justice that flows out of that understanding.

Dirk Hoerder teaches North American social history, history of global migrations, and borderland issues at Arizona State University. His areas of interest are labor migration in the Atlantic economies, worldwide migration systems, and sociology of migrant acculturation. He was professor at Universität Bremen 1977–2008 and has also taught at York University, Duke University, Université de Paris VII, and the University of Toronto. His publications include *Cultures in Contact: World Migrations in the Second Millennium* (Duke University Press, 2002), which received the Social Science History Association's Sharlin Prize, and the coedited *The Historical Practice of Diversity: Transcultural Interactions from the Early Modern Mediterranean to the Postcolonial World* (Berghahn Books, 2003).

Jeffrey R. Kerr-Ritchie is associate professor of history at Howard University. He has authored *Freedpeople in the Tobacco South: Virginia, 1860 to 1900*

(University of North Carolina Press, 1999), *Rites of August First: Emancipation Day in the Black Atlantic World* (Louisiana State University Press, 2007), and an electronic anthology, *African American Social Movements* (ProQuest, 2005). His contribution to this volume draws from his current project "The Great Emancipators: How Slaves Destroyed Slavery in the Americas."

Neville Kirk is professor emeritus of labor and social history at Manchester Metropolitan University. He has published extensively in the fields of modern British and comparative and transnational British, U.S., and Australian labor history. He is currently writing a book titled *Labour and the Politics of Empire: Australia and Britain from 1900 to the Present Day* (Manchester University Press, 2010). He is also coeditor, with Don MacRaild and Melanie Nolan, of two forthcoming issues of *Labour History Review* on transnational labor history.

Alex Lichtenstein is associate professor of history at Florida International University. He is the author of *Twice the Work of Free Labor: The Political Economy of Convict Labor in the New South* (Verso, 1996) and "Making Apartheid Work: African Trade Unions and the 1953 Native Labour (Settlement of Disputes) Act in South Africa," *Journal of African History* 46 (July 2005). He is working on a cross-national study of race and labor in the United States and South Africa.

Nelson Lichtenstein is MacArthur Foundation Chair in History as well as Director of the Center for the Study of Work, Labor, and Democracy at the University of California, Santa Barbara. He is the author, most recently, of *The Retail Revolution: How Wal-Mart Created a Brave New World of Business* (Metropolitan Books, 2009) and editor of *American Capitalism: Social Thought and Political Economy in the Twentieth Century* (University of Pennsylvania Press, 2006).

Premilla Nadasen is associate professor of history at Queens College, City University of New York. Born in South Africa and raised in the United States, she is an activist and a writer who has given numerous public talks about race, gender, and social policy. She is author of *Welfare Warriors: The Welfare Rights Movement in the United States* (Routledge Press, 2005), winner of the John Hope Franklin Prize, and is currently writing a book on domestic worker organizing.

Catherine Nolan-Ferrell is associate professor of history at the University of Texas at San Antonio. Her book, *Negotiating Nationality: Transnational Workers, Citizenship, and Revolution in Southern Chiapas, Mexico, 1880–1950* is forthcoming from the University of Arizona Press.

Jocelyn Olcott, associate professor of history at Duke University, is the author of *Revolutionary Women in Postrevolutionary Mexico* (Duke University Press, 2005) and coeditor with Gabriela Cano and Mary Kay Vaughan of *Sex in Revolution: Gender, Politics, and Power in Modern Mexico* (Duke University Press, 2006; in translation with Fondo de Cultura Económica, 2009). Her essays have appeared in the *Journal of Women's History*, *International Labor and Working-Class History*, and *Latin American Perspectives*, as well as numerous anthologies.

Colleen O'Neill is associate professor of history at Utah State University and coeditor of the *Western Historical Quarterly*. She is the author of *Working the Navajo Way: Labor and Culture in the Twentieth Century* (University Press of Kansas, 2005) and coeditor with Brian Hosmer of *Native Pathways: American Indian Culture and Economic Development in the Twentieth Century* (University Press of Colorado, 2004). Her next book is a broad synthesis of American Indian labor history titled *Labor and Sovereignty: The Transformation of Wage Work in Indian Country*.

Bryan D. Palmer is the Canada Research Chair, Canadian Studies, Trent University, and the editor of *Labour/Le Travail*. His most recent books are *James P. Cannon and the Origins of the American Revolutionary Left* (University of Illinois Press, 2007), *Labouring Canada: Class, Gender, and Race in Canadian Working-Class History*, edited with Joan Sangster (Oxford University Press, 2008), and *Canada's 1960s: The Ironies of Identity in a Rebellious Era* (University of Toronto Press, 2009).

Andrew Parnaby is associate professor of history at Cape Breton University. He is the author of *Citizen Docker: Making a New Deal on the Vancouver Waterfront* (University of Toronto Press, 2008) and, with Andrew Neufeld, *The IWA in Canada: The Life and Times of an Industrial Union* (New Star Books, 2000).

Gunther Peck is associate professor of public policy and history at Duke University. He is the author of *Reinventing Free Labor: Padrones and Immigrant Workers in the North American West, 1880–1930* (Cambridge University Press, 2000) and numerous journal articles. His current book project is titled *Trafficking in Race: The Rise and Fall of White Slavery, 1700–2000*, which explores the history of human trafficking and the ideologies of freedom, slavery, and race that immigrants, their advocates, and border bureaucrats have used to describe and summarize the problem.

Lara Putnam, associate professor of history at the University of Pittsburgh, specializes in the study of gender, kinship, migration, and race. She is the author of

The Company They Kept: Migrants and the Politics of Gender in Caribbean Costa Rica, 1870–1960 (University of North Carolina Press, 2002) and is currently at work on two book-length manuscripts: the first, a history of the role of migrants' experiences in shaping political and cultural movements in the twentieth-century circum-Caribbean, and a second on the evolution of social policy and academic perceptions of the Afro-Caribbean family.

Jacob Remes received his PhD in history from Duke University in 2010 and is now Andrew W. Mellon/American Council of Learned Societies Recent Doctoral Recipients Fellow at the Centre for Interdisciplinary Studies in Society and Culture at Concordia University. He is currently revising his manuscript, "City of Comrades: Urban Disasters and the Formation of the North American Progressive State."

Joan Sangster teaches at Trent University, Peterborough, Canada, where she specializes in women's and working-class history. She has published books and articles dealing with the history of the Left; women, work, and the labor movement; the criminalization of women and girls; and Aboriginal women. Her forthcoming book with University of Toronto Press is *Transforming Labour: Women and Work in the Post–World War II Period*.

Vic Satzewich is professor of sociology at McMaster University in Hamilton, Ontario. He is past president of the Canadian Sociological Association. His books include *The Ukrainian Diaspora* (Routledge, 2002), *Racism and the Incorporation of Foreign Labour: Farm Labour Migration to Canada since 1945* (Routledge, 1991), and, with Nick Liodakis, *"Race" and Ethnicity in Canada* (Oxford University Press, 2007). He is currently working on a project on discretion within the immigrant selection system in Canada and another project on the Save the Children Fund and its response to famine in Russia and Ukraine in 1921–1923.

Michael Snodgrass is associate professor of Latin American history and international studies at Indiana University–Purdue University, Indianapolis. He is author of *Deference and Defiance in Monterrey: Workers, Paternalism, and Revolution in Mexico, 1890–1950* (Cambridge University Press, 2003). His articles have appeared in *Latin American Research Review*, *Labor: Working-Class History of the Americas*, and *International Labor and Working-Class History*. He is writing a history of emigration and return migration in Mexico from the 1890s to the 1970s.

Shelton Stromquist is professor of history at the University of Iowa. His research has focused on issues of class, politics, and labor conflict, with recent attention to the Progressive Era and the Cold War. His books include, *Reinventing "the People": The Progressive Movement, the Class Problem and the Origins of Modern Liberalism* (2006). His current book-length project is titled *Social Democracy in the City: Class Politics and Municipal Reform in Comparative Perspective, 1890–1920*. He is currently working on a comparative study of municipal labor and socialist politics from 1890 to the end of World War I.

Peter Way is professor of history and department head at the University of Windsor in Canada. He is the author of *Common Labor: Workers and the Digging of North American Canals, 1780–1860* (Cambridge University Press, 1993), as well as many articles in a variety of academic journals and edited collections. He is currently working on a book-length project titled *Artisans of War: Common Soldiers and the Making of Britain's American Empire in the Seven Years' War*.

INDEX

aboriginal labor, transnational history, 111–12
Ackroyd, Margaret F., 183
Act for the Instruction and Permanent Settlement of the Indians, 114
Adams-Onis Treaty, 376–77
Africa, UN Economic Commission for, 202
Africans
  enslavement and trans-shipment, 61
  forced labor, 24
  human cargo, 49
  United States immigration laws, 278
  working people, 23
Afro-Caribbeans
  1924 Johnson-Reed Act, 267–68
  migrations, 217–18
Age of Revolution, 295
agrarian reform, 150–52, 156–57
Agricultural Adjustment Act, 417
agriculture
  government policy, 129n.22
  indigenous peoples, 114
  small-scale and Squamish families, 120–21
Ahuja, Ravi, 50
Alabama warship, losses, 396–97
Albemarle, Lord, 60
Alemán, Miguel, 81, 86–87
Alianza de Tragajadores de Ford, 85–86
Almaguer, Tomas, 42
al Sadat, Jehan, 202, 207
American Association of University Women (AAUW), 198
"American Century," Luce, 81, 98n.3

American Dream, working-class patriotism, 28
American exceptionalism
  complication, 173, 187
  threatened ideals, 215
  welfare state, 172
American Federation of Labor and Congress of Industrial Organizations (AFL-CIO)
  American standard of living, 28
  Bracero Program, 246
  training for union organization, 90
American League against War and Fascism, CPUSA, 349
American Revolution, Mi'kmaq autonomy, 125
American Rights at Work, labor law reform, 357
American Steamship Association, union attempts, 410
"American Way," making Mexico's, 89–90
Americas
  forced labor migration, 24
  one theater of Seven Years' War, 75–76
Amezquita, Jesus, progress, 259
Amherst, Jeffery, slave labor, 60
Anderson, A. S., immigration, 227
Antara Polanco, Mexico City, 97
Anti-Imperialist Popular Front, CPMEXICO, 342
anti-Semitism, European resistance to Braun, 238–39
Anti-Slavery Society of Canada, formation, 372–73

anti-Vietnam War movement, efficacy, 215
Appleton, John, 378–79
apprentices, labor type, 71, 73
Arbetet, Bernstein, 310
Arch, Joseph, English National Agricultural Labourers' Union, 395
Arenal, Angelica, radical Mexican politics, 346
Argentina, maternity standards, 176
army
  building forts and garrisons, 75
  mundane labor, 74–75
  transition to capitalism, 62–63
Articles of War, Mutiny Act, 58
artisans, war, 69–74
Asian immigrants, restrictions, 267, 273–74, 280
Asian seamen, 415–16, 425
assimilation
  Grajales's policies, 148
  schoolteachers stressing, 160n.40
Atlantic world, states as conglomerate, 34–35
Austin State Times, fugitive slaves, 366
Australia
  labor history, 22n.6
  labor movement, 19
  maritime labor, 414–15
Australian Labor Party, trade union, 19–20
Austro-Hungarian government, Braun's assertions, 231
Autobiography of a Fugitive Negro, Ward, 367
automobile industry
  Automotive Integration Decree, 90–91
  Mexico and U.S., 83–84
  unionism in Mexico, 92–97
  United Auto Workers (UAW), 92
  violence and repression in Mexico, 96–97

Automobile Manufacturers Association, Mann, 91
Automotive Integration Decree
  assembly to full-scale manufacturing, 91–92
automakers, 90–91
Aveleyra, Rafael, 336, 341

Bachelor, Steven J., 52, 81–98, 431
Balachandran, Gopalan, 425, 427n.27
Bandaranaike, Sirimavo, 207
Banjo, McKay, 411–12
Banks, Louis Albert, 222
Barbados, 1924 Johnson-Reed Act, 275
Barrier Truth, Broken Hill's labor government, 314, 316
Barrios, Ernesto, 143
Barrios de Chungara, Domitila
  cartoon, 195*f*
  demands of housewives, 198
  Housewives Committee of the Siglo XX, 194
  pamphlet, 195
  reproductive labor, 207
  union activities, 194–95
  women's sexuality, 207
Basch, Linda, 39, 42
Battle of the Overpass, Reuther, 92
Battle of Wandiwash, British victory, 76
Baugh, Daniel, Britain's "blue-water" policy, 66
Beaty, James, 394
Beijing Conference (1995), women's rights, 166, 196
Belgium, 237, 414
Bell, Edward, white slavery, 222
Bellamy, Edward, *Looking Backward*, 309
Belshaw, Michael, bracero migrations, 256
Bender, Thomas, 24
Benedict, Dan, 92
Benham, E. P., 378
Benito Juarez, Don, 341

Berger, Carl, 385–86
Berger, Victor, 320
Bergquist, Charles, 24–25
Bergson, Henri, 332
Bernstein, Eduard, 308, 310
Between the Devil and the Deep Blue Sea, Rediker, 51
Beveridge plan, Britain, 184
Bevin, Ernest, 417
Bezanson, Kate, 166
Bibb, Henry
  fugitive settlement, 378
  Voice of the Fugitive, 373–76
Bibb, Mary, 373, 378
Blac, Christina Szanton, *Nations Unbound*, 39
Blackburn, Lucie, 369, 370
Blackburn, Thorton, 369, 370
black immigration, Jim Crow procedures, 268, 274
The Black Jacobins, James, 23
black populations, Caribbean migrations, 217–18
Bland, S. O., 420
blue-collar workers
  Blue Cross's dedication to community, 336
  education, 337–39
  radicals connecting, in Chicago, 347
  socialist education, 343–44
Blue Cross. *See* Mexican Blue Cross
Boggart Hole Clough, controversy, 317, 318, 322
Bolivia, maternity standards, 176
Bolivian peasants, cartoon, 195
bondage, martial labor, 76–77
Border Industrialization Program, 261
Boris, Eileen
  biography, 431
  home health care, 164
  maternity leave, 171–87
  social reproduction, 165
  U.S. exceptionalism, 172–73, 187
Boston Transcript, white slavery, 239
Bourinot, John, 116
Bourne, Randolph, 33–34
Boyer, Richard O., 423–24
Bracero Program
  change to communities, 259–61
  contracts to migrants, 262n.6
  debates about emigration, 249–50
  emigration policy, 251–52
  favoritism, 254–55
  influence of Gamio, 250
  interviewing former braceros, 257–58
  media attention, 250–51
  Mexican citizens on mission, 248–49
  Mexican workers to U.S., 217
  migratory labor agreement, 245–47
  mission, 247–52
  potential benefits, 248–49
  proponents, 258–59
  quotas for Jalisco, 253–55
  resistance, 251, 264n.30
  response of Mexican government, 248, 251
  western state of Jalisco, 252–61
Braddock, General, 59, 66
Bradford Council, Hartley, 303–4
Branch, Jacob, 367
Braun, Enrique, 152, 156, 162n.65
Braun, Marcus
  charitable associations, 228–29
  coerced migration in Hungary, 229
  demoralization by Keefe, 237–38, 239
  European research of white slave traffic, 237
  feminization of white slavery, 240
  human trafficking, 225–27
  immigrant prostitutes, 232–35
  Immigration Abuses: Glimpses of Hungary and Hungarians, 231–32
  interpretation of Missler, 227
  Jewish white slavery report, 239

Braun, Marcus (*Continued*)
  nationalism, 227–28
  redefinition of white slavery, 232
  report on prostitution, 235–37
  reports on Hungarian emigrants, 230–31
  reputation, 232, 238–39
  scandal, 229–31, 238
  U.S. Bureau of Immigration, 225, 227, 228
Brazil, enslaved Africans, 24
Bread and Roses strike (1912), 27
Breech, Ernest R.
  Ford Motor Company, 81
  "New World," 83
  University Club address, 84, 85
  visit to Mexico, 81–82
Brewer, John, 64–65
Britain
  "blue-water" policy, 66
  child laborers, 224
  East Indian trade, 76
  indentures and factory workers, 223
  white slave traffic investigation, 237
British Army
  empire building, 74–77
  Seven Years' War, 57–77
  slaves serving in, 78n.15
  strength of, in America, 67
British Board of Trade, 414
British-Canadian extradition act, fugitive slaves, 369
British Caribbean
  antiblack nationalism, 285
  black immigration, 283
  circulation of goods, 270–71
  impact of Johnson-Reed Act, 275–80
  imperial protections, 286–88
  legislation destabilizing British rule, 284–88
  limited migration to U.S., 273
  men vs. women, 270
  migratory circuits, 268–73
  personal property, 270–71
  petitioning King of England, 285–86, 288
British Columbia
  aboriginal laboring classes, 111
  Canadian federation, 122
  Mi'kmaq, 110–11, 124–25
  Squamish Indians, 117–19
  Squamish longshoremen, 110–11, 125
British Empire, 277, 278–79
British imperial nationalism, Toronto printers, 393–98
British India, slave abolition, 382n.22
British military, 59, 63–66
British Post at Prospect Bluff, fugitives in army, 376
British Red Cross, James raising funds, 272
British Shipping (Assistance) Act, 420
British soldiers, "scum of earth," 68–69
British West Indians, 283, 286–87
British West Indies Regiment, Great War, 272
British Women's Trade Union League, maternity leave, 175
British world, labor movement, 19
Brocklehurst, Fred, 316–19
Broken Hill, New South Wales, 306, 314–16
Brousse, Paul, 307
Brown, George, 373, 387, 393, 395, 398
Brownback, Sam, Trafficking Act, 222
Brownlie, Robin Jarvis, 111
Brubaker, Rogers, 44–45, 137
Bruce, Margaret, 198
Bruere, Robert W., *The Survey*, 418
Buckner, Phillip, 386
Bureau of Immigration, national borders, 216–17
Bureau of Manpower Utilization, sickness and disability, 172
Burnham, Viola Victorine, 200
Burns, Anthony, 372
Bush, George W., Trafficking Act, 222

Butler, Jesse, 318
"Buy American!" nationalism, 28
Byron, George, 375

Cabinet Makers' Union, 396
Calles, Plutarco, "New Law of
    Migration," 138–41
Calles government, Ford workers, 86
Cameron, Ardis, 27
Campbell, Thomas, 371
campesinos
    crossing the border, 143
    definitions, 138
    permitting departure, 248
    vagrancy, 145
Canada
    census, 403n.12
    Croatians, 41–42
    displaced to, after WW II, 40
    farm workers from Mexico, 40
    First Nations, 103–4
    French-speaking Quebec, 299
    fugitive settlements, 376–78
    fugitive slaves from U.S., 367–68
    indigenous history, 127n.5
    1924 Johnson-Reed Act, 275
    labor movement, 19
    military history, 59
    position of fugitive slaves in British,
        370
    relationship with Great Britain,
        385–86
    Toronto printers, 358–59, 399–402
    U.S-Canada relations, 42–43
    U.S. treaties for fugitives, 368–72
    War Measures Act, 300
Canadian New Left manifesto, *White
    Niggers of America*, 299
Canadian railways, 390, 399, 404n.25
Canterbury Trades and Labour Council,
    312
Cape Breton Island, Nova Scotia
    cod fishery, 114

indigenous peoples, 117
Mi'kmaq peoples, 112–13
Mi'kmaw peoples, 109–10, 125
population, 128n.14
Capital, Karl Marx, 61
capitalism
    army in transition to, 62–63
    collaborative, 84
    forces other than, 8
    global, 7
    industrial, 69
    supernational processes, 18
    U.S. education, 349
    world systems theory, 10n.20
Capitalism and Slavery, Williams, 23
Capital Moves, Cowie, 26
Cárdenas, Lazaro, 330, 342–44
Cárdenas presidency
    agrarian reform, 156–57
    Ford workers and mobilizations, 86
    federal reforms, 138
    Mexican Revolution, 146–50
    nationalization and mobilizations, 83
care work, social reproduction, 163, 164
Caribbean migrants
    black populations, 217–18, 283
    circulation of goods, 270–71
    communication, 271
    enslaved Africans, 24
    imperial ties binding, 271–73
    migratory circuits in Eastern and
        Western, 268–73
    slaves after emancipation, 25
    Spanish-speaking republics, 282
Caribbean women, Panama Canal, 14
Carrera, Oscar G., 335
Carter, Sarah, 41
Cash Compensation Act, Rhode Island,
    183–84, 185
Castillo, Sánchez del, 100n.48
Catholic Church, 299, 340–41
Cayman Islands, visa distribution,
    278–79

Centre for Social Development and Humanitarian Affairs, United Nations, 202
Champion, Henry Hyde, 19
Champs-Elysées, Paris, 97
Change to Win, American standard of living, 28
Chapel Island reserve, creation, 113
charrazo, Mexican labor history, 87–88
charrismo, union control, 89
Chartists, London's, 296
Chartrand, Michel, 299
Chase, Franklin, 378–79
Chávez, César, 261
Chelsea Hospital Out-Pension Books, 69
Chicago
  Dunne, 320
  education for migrants, 337–39
  Front's activists in, 342–49
  industries desiring immigrant labor, 331
  language classes, 338–39, 340
  May Day honoring Haymarket struggle, 296
  Mexican American identity, 350
  Mexican immigrant population, 331
  Mexican liberals forming organizations, 333–34
  Mexican migrants to, 298, 329–30
  Mexican nationalism, 334–36
  Mexican small businesses, 349–50
  population of Mexican children, 339–40
  radical Mexican politics, 342–49
Chicago Board of Education, Mexicans, 338
children
  Britain, 224
  Chicago's population of Mexican, 339–40
  Children's Bureau, 173, 179, 186
Chile, maternity, 173–74, 176, 177
China
  global political economy, 9
  racial scapegoating, 284
  restricting immigration from, 267, 273–74, 280
Chinese indentures, 49
Chinese Workers' Delegation, advisor Wu, 416
Chomsky, Aviva, 23–28, 431
Christchurch, New Zealand, 310–14
Christian Base Communities, 26
Christmas, Bernd, 126
Chrysler
  benefits to Mexican automakers, 89
  Mexico City factory, 97
  organization at Toluca plant, 93–94
  shootings, 94–95
Church of Jesus Christ of Latter-Day Saints, fugitives, 363
cities, municipal politics, 304–7
Citizens' Associations, accusations, 311
citizenship
  categorization, 150
  eligibility for, 274
  "good workers" to gain Mexican, 149–50
  Guatemalan-Mexican border, 137–38
  labor and borders, 358
  mandatory labor for Guatemalans, 156
  Mexican, 147–48
  nationality, 157–58
  rights for migrants, 40
  shipping legislation, 422–23
  United States and immigrants, 279–80
  working class, 355
Civil Register, Guatemala, 147
Civil Service Commission, equal pay, 186
Civil War, 67, 221
Clarion, Brocklehurst, 317
Cleveland, municipal reform, 319–21, 322
Clinton, William J., 221–22

Clive, Robert, 76
Córdova, Alejandro, 150
Coast Salish groups, potlatch, 119–20
Cobbett, William, 317
Cobble, Dorothy Sue, 187
coercions
  child labor, 224
  immigrant prostitutes, 224
  mobility, 224–25
  steamship agents, 226–27
  white slavery, 223–24
coffee growers
  economy, 143–44
  Mexican nationality, 150–52
Colden, Charles J., 417
Cold War
  alliance with U.S., 28
  American exceptionalism, 215
Cole, Douglas, 399
collective bargaining
  Alianza de Trabajadores de Ford, 85–86
  International Labor Organization (ILO), 172
  maritime labor, 419–20
colonialism
  conjoining of militarism and, 66
  English labor pattern, 71
  Native workers, 105–106
  shaping Europe, 23–24
Colonialism in Question, Cooper, 5
Coloured Alien Seamen Order (1925), 421–22
commercial fishing, indigenous people, 114–15
Commission on Employment of Women, Maternity Protection Convention, 175
Commission on the Status of Women, United Nations, 197, 198
Committee on Immigration and Naturalization, Johnson, 280
Commons, John R., 297

communication
  Caribbean migrants, 271
  immigrants, 43–44
  racial patterning crisis, 285
Communist influence, Mexican unionism, 92
Communist insurgency, maritime reform, 416–17
Communist Party, Popular Front, 330
Confederación de Trabajadores de México (CTM). *See* Confederation of Mexican Workers
Confederation of Mexican Workers
  bracero rights, 251, 252
  Chicago, 347
  corruption, 94
  labor confederation, 87–88
  militants, 342
Conrad, Joseph, 410
contract labor. *See also* white slavery
  Bracero Program, 246
  from, to prostitution, 233–37
  importation, 216–17
Cooper, Frederick, 3–6, 5, 137
Coote, William, 232
Copeland, Royal, 421
Coronation Committee, 271
Costa Rica
  black immigration, 283
  border with Panama, 283
  George V and Coronation Committee, 271
  maternity standards, 176
  U.S.-owned plantations, 28
Cowie, Jefferson, *Capital Moves*, 26
CPMEXICO (Partido Comunista Mexicano), 342, 346, 350
CPUSA, American League against War and Fascism, 349
Criminal Law Amendment Act, 400
Croatians, Canada, 41–42
Crosby, Josiah, 286
Cross, Harry, 253, 264n.33

Cuba
    immigration law, 281–82, 283
    1924 Johnson-Reed Act, 275
    maternity standards, 176, 178, 182
    Second Labor Conference of American States, 177
    sugar plantations, 269
    U.S.-owned plantations, 28
Cuban Revolution, 92, 200
Cunard Steamship Line, 229
Curran, Pete, 317
Czechoslovakia, formation of state, 41

Daily Gleaner, emigration of Jamaicans, 269, 275, 276–78
Dale, George, 315
Danielsson, Axel, 310
Das Gupta, Monisha, 203
Daud, Muhammed, 416
Davenport, Charles, 280, 282
Dawn, fugitive settlement, 377
Dawson, George, 118
The Death Ship, Traven, 411, 426n.9
Decade for Women, United Nations, 212
Declaration of Mexico, 209
de Demicheli, Sofia, 207
de la Peña, Moises T., 157
Denmark, social insurance, 176
depression. *See also* Great Depression
    maritime reform, 416–17
    revolution and breakdown, 427n.31
desertions, Seven Years' War, 57–58
de Sornoza, Naval, Ecuador, 205
Detroit
    converting to war production, 86
    Mexican autoworkers, 85–86
    municipal reform triangle, 319–21, 322
Detroit-Windsor, Refugee's Home Society (RHS), 378
Díaz, Hugo, 94
Diaz, Porfirio
    depopulation of Mexico, 249
    Ford negotiating with, 98 n.6
    social reforms, 331–32
    uprising, 363
Dies, Martin, 422
Dillingham Commission, migrants in U.S., 36
Dillon, Judge John, 306
Dirksen, Everett, 171
Dirlik, Arif, 8
Disraeli, Benjamin, 395, 397
domestic labor
    family structure, 205–6
    responsible parenthood, 204–5, 213n.49
    socialization, 204
    wages-for-housework campaign, 204
    women, 163
    women's burden, 198–99
Domingo, W. A., 272
Dominguez, Milla, 335
Dominican Republic
    black immigration, 283
    Haitians to, 25, 29n.10
    pregnant workers, 176
    sugar plantations, 269
Dominion, Toronto printers and, 399–402
Dominion Lands Act (1872), 402
"door-step" economy, phrase, 121, 134n.72
Doughtie, William, 397–98
Douglass, Frederick, 223
Drew, Benjamin, *A Northside View of Slavery*, 377
dual loyalty, immigrants, 44–45
Duffy, Michael, 63
Duke, David, 244n.47
Dunne, Edward, 320
Durand, Jorge, 256
Dutch National Society for the Protection of Shipping Interests, 419

Earl of Albemarle, slaves and Havana, 60
East Germany, Protection of Mothers and Children and the Rights of Women, 181

East India Company, British interests, 76
Echeverría, Luís, 95–96, 205
Echeverria, Tomas, Mexican migrant, 332–33
Economic and Social Council (ECOSOC), 197
Economic Commission for Africa, United Nations, 202
economy
  coffee growers, 143–44
  imperial frame, 38n.7
  migration, 37
education
  blue-collar migrants, 337–39
  Mexican radicals, 344
  reforms in Mexico, 332
  socialist, of blue-collar workers, 343–44
Elgin, fugitive settlement, 377
Elliott, Thomas, 364
El Salvador, 176, 283
Eltis, David, 25
El Universal Ilustrado, Mexican-centric paper, 330, 331, 333
emancipation
  slaves after, in Caribbean, 25
  women's labor, 200, 214n.69
Emergency Railroad Transportation Act (1933), 420
emigration
  Bracero Program, 249–50, 255–56
  Mexican government, 251
  steamship agents and coerced, 226–27
Empire Day, 288
England
  free and unfree labor, 70–71
  Manchester's politics, 316–19
  Seven Years' War, 57–77
  Toronto printers and, 393–98
English National Agricultural Labourers' Union, 395

Equal Rights Amendment, women's labor, 182, 185
Escamilla, A., 343
Escuelas Henry Ford initiative, 90
Eskasonie, Indians, 117
Espín, Vilma, 202
eugenicist approach, domestic labor, 205
Eugenics Code, Ramos, 281
Eugenics Record Office, 280, 282
Eureka, settlement in Mexico, 379
Europe
  Braun investigation, 237, 239–40
  colonialism shaping, 23–24
  resistance to Braun, 238–39
  steamships and coerced emigrants, 226–27
European Union, reluctance to ratify, 45n.11

Fabianism, transnational authority, 297
Fabian Society, 313, 317
Fair Labor Standards Act, domestic reform, 418
Family and Medical Leave Act (1993), passage, 187
family planning, domestic labor, 204–5
family structure, household labor, 205–6
Fanon, Frantz, *The Wretched of the Earth*, 300
Farm Equipment union, women, 180
farm workers
  Canada from Mexico, 40
  migrant, and Bracero Program, 246–47
Farnsworth-Alvear, Ann, 177–78
Federal Bureau of Investigation, formation, 234
Federal Labor Office, Tapachula, Mexico, 149
feminism. *See also* labor feminists
  alienation from, 196, 210n.5
  global feminist networks, 174

feminism (*Continued*)
    international, 163–67
    labor feminists in U.S., 174–75
    race, class, and culture shaping, 165–66
    struggle for moneyed women, 195
    struggle with Marxists, 195–96, 197
feminization, slavery, 225, 236–37, 240–41
Fenian Brotherhood, attack on Canada, 384
Fifth Avenue, New York, 97
Finca Clarita, Guatemala, 145
Finca Santo Domingo, 136, 152
Fink, Leon
    biography, 431
    immigration debates, 356
    labor standards, 359–60
    maritime standards, 409–25
finqueros
    exploiting campesinos, 147
    foreign-born, and nationality, 150–51
    labor contracts, 156
    labor laws, 145
    land owners, 143–44
Firestone, forced labor in Liberia, 53
First Nations, 103–4, 106
First Pan-American Conference of Eugenics and Homiculture, Ramos, 281
First World, industrialization, 28
First World feminists, 165
fiscal-military state, military revolution, 63–66
Fisher, Andrew, 19
Fisher, John, 375
fishing
    indigenous people, 114–15
    Mi'kmaq peoples, 115–16, 125, 129–30n.29, 130n.34
    Squamish in British Columbia, 122
Fitch, John A., 297–98
Fitzpatrick, John, 222, 226

Flores, Jesus, 343, 344–45
Flores, John H., 298, 329–50, 431
Florida, fugitive settlements, 364–65, 376
Focke, Katherine, 205
Foerster, Robert, 280, 282
Folbre, Nancy, 30n.16
Foner, Nancy, 33
Food and Agriculture Organization, United Nations, 201
Foran Act, 226, 227, 232, 233
Ford, Henry, 53, 98n.6
Ford, Henry, II, 81
Ford de México
    Breech's visit, 85
    charrazo episode, 87–88
    demonstration and violence, 95
    founding, 85
    Ruedas, 85
    strike petition, 86–87
Ford Motor Company
    Breech's visit to Mexico, 81–82
    Escuelas Henry Ford initiative, 90
    Mexican autoworkers, 52–53
    Mexico City's La Villa factory, 82, 84–89
Forster, Cindy, 142
Fortoso, Roman H., 334–35
Fouche, Luis N., 379
Foxen, Patricia, 25
France
    Jewish prostitutes, 238
    shipping, 414
    social insurance, 176
    white slave traffic investigation, 237
Franco, Eustacio, 258
free labor, general pattern, 25
Freeman, Carla, 4, 6
French, John D., 3–9, 18, 431–32
French Canadian, ethnic identity and socialism, 27
French Revolution, 295

Freund, Osias, 228
Freyder, John Baptist, 57
Friedan, Betty, 199
From Dance Hall to White Slavery, Lytle, 235
Front de Libération de Québec (FLQ), 299–300
Fugitive Slave Act (1793), 369
Fugitive Slave Act (1850), 367, 371, 372
fugitive slaves
  across North America, 363–81
  antislavery mobilization, 372–76
  creation of fugitive settlements, 376–80
  cross-border treatment, 380–81
  crossing borders for liberation, 364–68
  emigration, 380
  treaties and agreements, 368–72
Fugitives Union Society, Windsor, 378
fur trade
  aboriginal people, 111
  Cape Breton to Halifax, 115
  Mi'kmaq, 112, 125
  Squamish, 112

Gabaccia, Donna, 43
Galmar, Braun scandal, 229
Galván, Jacobo, 141
Gamio, Manuel, 250, 252, 253, 258, 260
Gandhi, Indira, 205
Garnet, Henry Highland, 374
Garvey, Marcus, 271, 272, 276, 288
"Gemeide-Sozialismus," 308
General Motors (GM)
  benefits to Mexican automakers, 89–90
  contract negotiations, 93
  Mexico City factory, 91–92, 97
  organization at Toluca plant, 93–94
  strike movement in Mexico, 95
George, Henry, 309, 320
George V, Coronation Committee, 271

Georgia, slaves, 364
Germany, Jewish prostitutes, 238
Gerstle, Gary, 27, 356
Giroud, Françoise, 204
Giulietti, Giuseppe, 415
Glasier, J. Bruce, 317
Glenn, Evelyn Nakano, 164
global economy, primitive accumulation, 295
  manufacturing, 355
global history
  fall of Soviet Union, 4
  project, 6
  public policy, 3
  role of nation-state, 27
globalization
  capital, 15
  exploitable labor force, 31n.17
  merchant capital, 58
  scholarly conceptualizations, 3–4
  traders and producers, 35
  transnationalism, 7
  word, 3, 6
globalizzazione, term, 9n.2
global labor, feminist networks, 174
glocal, term, 6
glocalization, term, 6
Gloucester textile trades, bread riots, 69
Gómez, Viviana, 257
Gómez López, Florencio, 145
Godínez, Bernardo, 146
Goldman, Emma, 223
Goluboff, Risa, 357
Gompers, Samuel, 12–13, 19, 175, 232, 412
Gonzalez, Ellice, 123–24
Gonzalez, Francisco, 259, 260
Gonzalez, Guadalupe, 257
González, Simeona, 145
Goodrich, Carter, 419
Gorsuch, Edward, 371
Gracia Real de Santa Teresa de Mose, 364
Grajales, Victórico, 147, 148

Great Britain
  Beveridge plan, 184
  relationship with Canada, 385–86
  shipping, 414
  shipping protection, 420
  social insurance for maternity, 176
  white slavery, 232, 240
Great Depression, 340–41, 417–19
Great Dismal Swamp, North Carolina-Virginia border, 379–80
Great War, 272, 309
Greene, Julie, 12–16, 432
Group of 8 (G8) summit, 9
Grupo Democrático, 93, 100n.48
Guatemala
  beauty pageant, 153–54
  black immigration, 283
  Civil Register, 147
  fearing radical influence, 154–55
  indigenous rebellion concerns, 154
  Liberal Revolution of 1871, 153
  maternity standards, 176
  Mexican depictions of, 139–40
  Mexicans as "problems," 146
  national celebrations, 153–54
  seasonal migration, 25
  1934 Vagrancy Law, 144, 155
Guatemalan-Mexican border
  citizenship, 137–38
  coffee economy, 143–44
  competition for jobs, 150
  crossing, 143
  disease carriers, 146
  establishing ineffective border (1931–1934), 138–41
  formal crossings, 141
  immigrants and deportation, 148–49
  labor migrations, 141–46
  national identity, 137
  nationality, 136–38
  problem of uncontrolled border, 157, 162n.67
  smuggling, 136, 142–43
  transnational labor migration, 136
  witchcraft, 146
Guatemalans
  citizenship and mandatory labor, 156
  "de facto Mexicans," 140
  deportation from Mexico, 148–49
  labor migration to Mexico, 141–46
  Mexican nationals, 150
  Mexico as escape for, 144–45
  nationalism, 152–56
  use as slur, 149
Guérin-Gonzales, Camille, 215–18, 432
Guerrero, Vincente, 365
Guthrie, Robert Storrie, 414–15

Haarbleicher, André, 416–17
Hackett, Nelson, 370
Hahamovitch, Cindy, 356
Haiti, slave revolt, 295
Haitian Revolution, 49
Haitians, migration to Cuba, 269
Halleck, Horace, 378
Hamilton Nine Hour League, 397
Hansen, Marcus Lee, 42–43
Happy, Jesse, 369
Hardie, Keir, 19, 317
Hartley, E. R., 297, 303–4, 310
Harwood, John, 317
Havana, Cuba, 59, 60, 78n.9, 177
Haymarket struggle, May Day, 296
Head, Sir Francis Bond, 369–70
Hennequin, M., 237
Henson, Josiah, 378
Hernández, Crisanto, 142–43
Hernandez, Nicholas M., 343, 344, 346–47
Hickey, Patrick, 309
Hill, Joe, 233
Hill-Tout, Charles, 119, 120
Hipwood, Charles, 414
historiography, military revolution, 52
Hochschild, Arlie, 166
Hoerder, Dirk, 33–37, 432

Hoffnung-Garskof, Jesse, 137
Hollingsworth, Anthony, 367
Holly, James T., 374
Homestead Act, 400
Home to Harlem, McKay, 411
Hondagneu-Sotelo, Pierrette, 164
Honduras, black immigration, 283
Hopkins, A. G., 6
Horton, James, 371
Horton, Lois, 371
Hosmer, Brian, 104, 111
Hotchkiss, David, 378
Hours of Work and Manning Convention, 418–19
House Committee on Immigration and Naturalization, 282
The House of Bondage, Kauffman, 237
Housewives Committee, 194, 195
Houston, Sam, 366
Howells, William Dean, 390
How Europe Underdeveloped Africa, Rodney, 23
Huffington, Arianna, 207
Hughes, Langston, 411
Human Rights at Work, American labor, 357
human trafficking
　Braun investigating, 225–27
　investigating immigrant prostitutes, 232–35
　mobility, 224–25
　shift to sex trafficking, 241n.4
　slavery and, 222
　white slavery and, 222–24
Hungarian Republican Club, 226
Hungary, 229–31
Hunt, DeVere, 391
Hunter, Hiram, 313, 314
Hunter v. City of Pittsburgh, municipal home rule, 321
Hutar, Patricia, 202
Hutchison, Elizabeth Quay, 173–74
Hydro-Quebec, creation, 299

Hylton, Enoch, 279–80
Hyndman, H. M., 19
Hynes, James, 384

Iacovetta, Franca, 42
illegal immigrants, labor rights, 31n.17
Illinois Labor Alliance, Chicago, 298, 347
Immigrant Reform Control Act (IRCA), 27
immigrants
　communities of yesterday and today, 44
　distinctions from migrants and refugees, 40
　identities and practices, 41–42
　labor in Chicago industries, 331
　rights, 40–41
Immigrants' Protective League, Chicago, 338
immigration. *See also* Bracero Program
　Caribbean republics banning black, 283
　control, 215–18
　global labor migration, 356
　Mexicans to U.S., 245
　new workers, 26
　non-Native, 126
　policies, 40
　racial problems in U.S., 280–84
　transnational history, 217–18
Immigration Abuses: Glimpses of Hungary and Hungarians, Braun, 231–32
Immigration Acts, 331
immigration restrictions
　Asian immigrants, 267, 273–74
　Caribbean migration in late 19th/early 20th centuries, 268–73
　destabilization of British rule, 284–88
　interwar United States, 273–80
　1924 Johnson-Reed Act, 267–68
　returning stowaways, 284
　Spanish American republics, 280–84

imperialism, supernational processes, 18
imperial labor, 50–51
imperial protection, British crown, 286–88
imperial ties, binding migrants, 271–73
Independent Labour Party (ILP)
   Hartley, 303
   Manchester, England, 316–19
   socialism, 297
Independent Political Labour League (IPLL), 311–12
India, 76, 205
Indian Act, female autonomy, 124
Indians at Work, Knight, 104
Indian Seamen's Union, 416
indigenous labor
   agriculture, 114
   Canadian history, 127n.5
   commercial fishing, 114–15
   culture, 111
   Guatamalans, 137
   mid-19th-century British North America, 109–26
   Mi'kmaq in British Columbia (B.C.), 110–11, 124–25
   Mi'kmaw people in Nova Scotia, 109–10
   Native and non-Native workers, 125–26
   Squamish in B. C., 110–11, 124–25
indigenous people
   extinction or assimilation, 117
   Guatamalans, 148
   labor systems, 103–6
   non-Native workers and, 125–26
   workers in racial context, 107n.6
indigenous women, 41
industrialization
   Alemán and Mexico, 87
   First World conditions, 28
   supernational processes, 18
Industrial Revolution, 20, 296
Industrial Workers of the World (IWW), 309

Institutional Revolutionary Party, 247, 254, 349
international feminists, gatherings, 165–66
International Human Rights Day, 357
internationalism
   labor, 355–60
   local democracy, 307–10
   maritime labor, 424–25
   proletarian, 295
International Labor Organization (ILO)
   Convention No. 3, 171, 174, 176, 178, 181, 185, 187
   conventions before World War II, 175–78
   global labor, 357–60
   labor feminists, 165
   maritime standards, 409–25
   maternity, 171–73
   revising ILO convention, 181–83
International Metalworkers' Federation (IMF), 92
International Monetary Fund (IMF), 165, 166
International Planned Parenthood Federation, 199
"International Seamen's Code," 413
international socialism, 8
International Typographical Union, 359
International Women's Year (IWY), 194–210
   alienation from feminism, 196, 210n.5
   goals, 197
   liberation, 195
   policy recommendations, 208–10
   reproductive-labor issues, 198–99
   strategies and struggles, 199–208
International Worker's League, Chicago, 298, 347
International Working Men's Association, 296
Islam, 8
Italy, Group of 8 (G8) summit, 9

Jackson, Andrew, 376
Jackson, Edmund, 379–80
Jalisco. *See also* Bracero Program
    bracero quotas, 253–55
    change for braceros, 259–61
    emigration history, 255–56
    migrants for Bracero Program, 252–61
    Valles region, 254–55, 258
    veteran braceros, 256–58
Jamaica
    1924 Johnson-Reed Act, 275–76
    Kingston's *Daily Gleaner*, 269, 275, 276–78
    nationalism and globalization, 218
    visa distribution, 279
    worker migration to Cuba, 268–69
James, C. L. R., *The Black Jacobins*, 23
James, William, 332
James, Winifred, 272
Japanese emigration, 274, 280, 284
Jean, George Edward, 113, 116
Jeffers, Clayton Lloyd Alexander, 285–86, 288
Jewish white slavery, 238, 239
Jim Crow procedures, "Negro" race, 268, 274
Johnson, Jack, 363
Johnson, Tom, 319–21
Johnson-Reed Act (1924)
    extended families, 279–80
    quota system, 218, 275–76
    race and culture, 275–76, 289
    race-based restrictions, 267–68, 273
Joint Indian Reserve Commission, 119
Jones, Samuel, 320, 321
Jones, William, 284
Joppke, Christian, 40–41
Jordan, June, 272–73
José Zepeda, Juan, 260
Joseph, Mathias, 122
Journal of Negro History, Porter, 380
A Journey through Texas, Olmstead, 366–67

Jowett, F. W., 297
Juarez, Benito, 334

Kabeer, Naila, 197
Kalinowska, Polish delegate, 181
Kant, Immanuel, 332
Karl, Terry, natural resources, 24
Kauffman, Reginald, *The House of Bondage*, 237
Keefe, Daniel, demoralization of Braun, 237–38, 239
Kennedy, James, Czechoslovakia, 41
Kerr-Ritchie, Jeffrey R.
    biography, 432–33
    citizen advocacy, 357
    fugitive slaves, 363–81
    slavery, 358
"Khalassi watch," use of whip, 415
kidnappings, Front de Libération du Québec (FLQ), 300
King, Hendrick, 57
King of England, 285–86, 288
Kirk, Neville, 18–21, 433
Klein, Jennifer, 164
Knack, Martha, *Native Americans and Wage Labor*, 104
Knight, Rolf, *Indians at Work*, 104
Knights of Labor, 226, 309
Kopf, Benjamin, Ford, 82
Kuri, Prudencia, Peru, 206

labor
    coerced and free, 24
    free, 25
    free vs. unfree, 69–74
    internationalism, 355–60
    recruitment and immigration control, 215–18
    skilled craftsmen, 69, 79–80n.38
labor and empire, 49–53
labor contracts, Guatemala, 144–45
labor feminists. *See also* feminism
    conventions before World War II, 175–78

labor feminists (*Continued*)
  in and outside United States, 178–81
  International Labor Organization (ILO), 171–75
  revising ILO convention, 181–83
labor history
  Australia, 22n.6
  feminism and reproductive labor, 163–67
  free workers, 25
  local, national and transnational lives, 39–40
  nation-state boundaries, 12
  New Zealand, 22n.6
  transnational, 18–21
  as world history, 23–28
labor market
  all-women's road-construction crew, 202
  editorial cartoon, 208
  emancipating women, 200–202
  incorporating women, 209
  migrants, 36
  productive labor, 202
labor migration
  Bracero Program, 248
  control, 215–18
  global, 356
  human cargo, 49–50
labor movement
  British world, 19
  Chicago, 298
  groups, 164
Labor Party, municipal politics, 306–7
labor politics, transnational, 295–300
labor rebellions, British Caribbeans, 286–87
labor systems, indigenous peoples and, 103–6
La Follette Act (1915), U.S., 421
Langer, William, 174, 185, 186
language skills
  Mexicans learning English, 338–39
  retaining Spanish, 338–39, 340
  transnationalism, 20–21

Laparra López, Everardo, 153
LaPietra report, 13, 16n.2
Laporte, Pierre, 300
Lascars, 414, 415
Latimer, Murray, 184
Latin America
  nursing breaks, 177
  transnationalism, 11n.27
  U.S. restricting immigration from, 281
Latin American Labor History Conference, 210n.1
Latin American women, feminism, 165–66
Laughlin, Harry, 280, 281–82
La Villa factory, Ford in Mexico City, 82, 84–89
Lévesque, René, 299
Leacock, Eleanor, 123
League of Nations, International Labor Organization, 412–13
Lenihan, James, 121
Lenin, domestic labor, 196
Lenroot, Katherine, 180
lesbians, feminist, 207
Lesotho, all-women's road-construction crew, 202
Liberal, Mondragon defending revolution, 341
Liberal Revolution of 1871, Guatemala, 153
Liberation Theology, 26
The Liberty Bell, black community, 379–80
Lichtenstein, Alex, 49–53, 433
Lichtenstein, Nelson, 355–60, 433
Liga de Obreros y Campesinos, Ford workers, 86
Linebaugh, Peter, 295
Littlefield, Alice, *Native Americans and Wage Labor*, 104
Livingstone, Elaine, 198
López, Francisca, 142
López, Gerardo, 254

López, Marcelo, 146
local democracy, 307–10
Lockhart, Daniel, 367
Lombardo Toledano, Vicente, 86, 87–88
London County Council (LCC), 306–8
longshoremen, Squamish men, 110–11, 120, 125
Looking Backward, Bellamy, 309
Lord Jim, Conrad novel, 410
Loyalists, 112–13, 115
Lubin, Isador, 418
Luce, Henry, 81, 98n.3
Lundy, Benjamin, 365
Lutz, John, 111, 124
Luxemburg, Rosa, 295
Lux en Umbra, Masonic lodge, 333, 334
Lytle, H. W., *From Dance Hall to White Slavery*, 235
Lytle Hernández, Kelly, 217

Maben, William, 318, 319
Macarthur, Mary, 175
McBriar, Alan, 307
McCombs, James, 311, 312
McCreery, David, 144
McCullough, J. A., 311
MacDonald, Margaret, 19
MacDonald, Ramsey, 307
Macdonald, Sir John A., 387, 394, 396, 397, 400
McGrath, William L., 171–72, 186, 187
McGuinness, Aims, 15
McHenry, Jerry, 367
McKay, Claude, 411–12
McKay, Eric, 279–80
McKeown, Adam, 36
McKinley, William, 420
McReynolds, Samuel Davis, 417
Madero, Francisco I., 337
Magnussen, Warren, 305, 307
The Making of the English Working Class, Thompson, 23
Mallon, Florencia, 25

Manchester, England, municipal politics, 316–19
Manila, Spanish trade, 76
Mann, Thomas, 91
Mann, Tom, 19, 297, 310, 317
Mann Act, prostitution, 240, 241
maquiladora industry
    out-migration, 27, 29n.9
    U.S.-Mexican border, 261
Marcus Braun Affair, 229–31, 238
maritime standards
    citizenship, 422–23
    internationalism, 424–25
    International Labor Organization (ILO), 409–25
    melting pot of American identity, 423–24
    opponents to regulation, 419–20
    protection, 420–22
    workforce, 360
maritime work
    Asian seamen, 415–16
    black labour, 414–15
    conditions, pay and routines, 412
    detailing standards, 413–14
    discrimination, 421–24
    global standards, 416–19
    Hours of Work and Manning Convention, 418–19
    Royal Indian Marines, 415
    subsidy program for U.S. shipbuilders, 421–22
    themes of sea writers, 410–12
Marte de Barrios, Licelot, 200
martial labor
    bondage, 76–77
    labor relations, 80n.52
Martin, James S., 391
Marx, Karl
    Capital, 61, 78n.17
    consolidation of capital, 65
    primitive accumulation, 295
    servitude of labourer, 69
    worker unity, 356

Marxists, struggle with feminists, 195–96, 197
Masaryk, Tomá, 41
Mason, James M., 371
Mason, Walter J., 186
Masonic lodge, Lux en Umbra, 333, 334
maternity convention, 171, 173
maternity leave
    British Women's Trade Union League, 175
    Chile, 173
    Convention No. 3, 171, 174, 176, 178, 181, 185, 187
    government workers, 185–86
    Great Britain, 176
    labor feminists in and outside U.S., 178–81
    Maternity Protection Convention, 175
    neglected models, 183–85
    Railroad Retirement Board, 183–85
    Rhode Island, 183–85
    Second Labor Conference of American States, 177
    teachers, 181
    U.S. women, 171–73
    wage contributions, 176–77
Matory, Lorand, 7–8
Mayan villagers, seasonal migration, 25
May Day, 296, 300, 317
\Mazarello, A. M., 415, 427n.27
Medina, Aurora, 257
Meixueiro, S. G., 335
Merchant Marine Act (1936), 420
Mexican autoworkers
    Detroit experiences, 85–86
    unionism, 53, 92–97
    violence and repression, 96–97
Mexican Blue Cross
    Chicago liberals, 333–34, 335
    nationalism, 335–36
Mexican Civic Committee, 349
mexicanidad, definition, 147, 148
Mexican immigrants, U.S. restricting, 280
Mexican Institute for Social Security, 196
Mexican labor force, U.S. meatpacking industry, 26–27
Mexican Martyrs, Front, 348
Mexican migrants, Chicago's labor movement, 298
Mexican nationalists, alliance with U.S., 298
Mexican Popular Front
    Chicago section, 343
    internal debate, 344–45
    transnational organization, 342
Mexican radicals
    Chicago, 346–47
    education, 344
    immigration to U.S., 343
Mexican Revolution
    creating nationalism, 146–50
    liberal beliefs, 329, 331–32
    reforms to benefit Mexicans, 156
    state formation after, 138
Mexico. *See also* Bracero Program; Guatemalan-Mexican border
    abolition law and slavery, 365–66
    agrarian radicalism from, to Guatemala, 155–56
    agricultural training, 202
    "American Century," 81
    automobile industry, 83–84
    Big Three automaker investments, 83
    black immigration, 283
    Bracero Program, 217, 245–47
    criteria for citizenship, 147–48
    escape for Guatemalan workers, 144–45
    farm workers to Canada, 40
    Fordist revolution, 84
    Ford Motor Company, 52–53
    Ford's Breech visiting, 81–82
    fugitive settlements, 376, 378–79
    fugitive slaves from Texas, 365–67

Guatemalans "infiltrating," 139–40
indigenous culture, 104
industries moving to, 26
Institutional Revolutionary Party, 247
1924 Johnson-Reed Act, 275
making Mexico's "American Way," 89–90
maternity standards, 176
nationalism through revolution, 146–50
nationality of Guatemalans in, 140–41
social reforms, 331–32
tension with U.S. and fugitives, 365
unionism of automakers, 92–97
U.S. treaties for fugitives, 368–72
workers experiencing border, 141–46

Mexico: The Paper of the Homeland
endorsing liberal groups, 334, 335
learning English, 338
Mondragon and Miranda, 333
nationalism, 336–37
Rembao's "The Swallows of Becker," 339

Mexico City
American century, 98
Antara Polanco, 97
benefits to automakers, 89–90
Ford negotiating with, 98n.6
Ford's La Villa factory, 82, 84–89
1968 Summer Olympic Games, 261

migrant farmworkers, Bracero Program, 246–47

migrants. *See also* Caribbean migrants
access to Mexican, 274
communities of yesterday and today, 44
dependence on food resources, 36
distinctions from immigrants and refugees, 40
experiences and identities from homelands, 26
moving glocally, 36–37
"pledge allegiance" to new, 39

term, 350n.1
textile factories, 35–36
UN Convention on the Protection of the Rights of Migrant Workers, 41
U.S. Senate's Dillingham Commission, 36
wages and conditions, 26

migration
Afro-Caribbeans, 217–18
Bracero Program, 217
circulation of goods, 270–71
economics and, 37
Guatemalan-Mexican border, 141–46
impact of "homeland," 42–43
Nations Unbound, 39
regional socialization, 34
U.S-Canada, 42–43
workers, 20

Mi'kmaq
British Columbia, 110–11, 124–25
Cape Breton Island, Nova Scotia, 112–13
cod fishery, 129–30n.29
contact with Europeans, 112, 129n.23
economic basis of Squamish and, 122–23
fishing, 115–16, 130n.34
gender relations, 123–24
interaction with non-Natives, 112, 129n.23
mobility, 117
petitions, 131n.39
potato rot, 129n.27
Potletek, 113

Mi'kmaw people
agriculture, 114
hunting, 115
Nova Scotia, 109–10, 125
St. Anne's Day celebration, 116

military history
Britain and Seven Years' War, 58–59
recruits enlisting for adventure, 67–68

military labor
  eighteenth century British, 51
  freeing the war worker, 66–69
  free vs. unfree, 69–74
  Seven Years' War, 57–77
  transition to capitalism, 62–63
  white and black, in Caribbean campaign, 61
military revolution
  Britain waging war, 68
  fiscal-military state, 63–66
  historiography, 52
  militarism and colonialism, 66
  primitive accumulation, 61–63
Miller, Frieda
  financing methods, 182
  International Labor Organization delegate, 175, 178
  motherhood contribution to welfare, 185–86
  social policy, 180
  social security disability, 193n.91
  Women's Bureau, 172, 174
Mills, Walter Thomas, 309
Mintz, Sidney, 50
Miranda, F. Patron, 330, 333
Missler, Frank, 227–30
mobility
  human trafficking, 224–25
  Mi'kmaq, 117
Mohawk, ship disaster, 420
Monckton, Robert, 60
Mondragon, Julian Xavier
  discrimination of Mexican children, 339–40
  Liberal, 341
  Mexican-centric paper, 330, 331, 333
  national self-esteem, 337
Montefiore, Dora, 19
Moody, Sewell, 119
Mora, Jesus, 337
Moreno, Fidencio, 343
Mormons, fugitives, 363

Morris, William, 307
Morro Castle, ship disaster, 420
Mosely, Solomon, 369, 370
Mother's Aid programs, 197
Motor Carrier Act (1935), 420
movable type. *See* Toronto printers
Municipal Labour Representation Committee, 313
municipal politics
  Broken Hill, New South Wales, 314–16
  Christchurch, New Zealand, 310–14
  cities and nation-states, 304–7
  Manchester, England, 316–19
  municipal reform triangle, Detroit, Cleveland, and Toledo, 319–21, 322
municipal socialism
  Hartley, 303–4
  United States, 320
Murray, James, 59
Murray-Wagner-Dingell, social security, 180
Mutiny Act, court-martials, 58

Nadasen, Premilla, 163–67, 433
NAFTA (North American Free Trade Agreement), 3, 9n.1
Narrative of Life and Adventures of Henry Bibb, an American Slave, Bibb, 373
National Health Service, Britain, 176–77
National Industrial Recovery Act, 417
nationalism
  British, and Canadian patriotism, 385–86
  "Buy American!" 28
  Guatemalan experiences of, 152–56
  Marcus Braun, 227–28
  Mexico creating, 146–50
  women's rights, 186
nationality
  Cárdenas government, 149–50
  citizenship, 157–58
  coffee growers claiming Mexican, 150–52
  definitions, 149, 157

Guatemalan, 154
Guatemalan-Mexican border, 136–38
Guatemalans in Mexico, 140–41
transnational social fields, 137
National Labor Relations Act, 428n.38
National Maritime Union (NMU), Boyer, 423–24, 430n.69
national origins, term, 274
National Sailors' and Firemen's Union, standard setting, 413
National Selective Service Act, maternity, 186
National Typographical Union
 expansion into British North America, 390–91
 U.S.-based, 384, 386, 389
National Vigilance Association, white slavery, 232, 234
National Women's Party (NWP), 174
nation-state
 boundaries, 12
 measuring importance, 40–41
 municipal politics, 304–7, 323n.5
 role in transnational and global histories, 27
 transnational history, 13–14
 Trouillot, 7
Nations Unbound, Basch, Schiller and Blanc, 39
Native Americans and Wage Labor, Littlefield and Knack, 104
Needham, George, 317–18
Nelson, Barbara, 197
Nelson, Donald, 87
Nervo, Amado Ruiz de, 334–35
networks, migrants, 36
Newberry Conference on Labor History, 21n.4, 210n.1
New Deal
 labor standards, 417, 428n.38
 Roosevelt, 172
 United States, 27

New International Economic Order (NIEO), 198
New Jersey State Chamber of Commerce, 184
"New Law of Migration," Mexican President Calles, 138–41
New South Wales, municipal governance, 314–16
newspapers
 Caribbean migrants, 271
 El Universal Ilustrado, 330, 331, 333
 fugitive battles, 371
 Mexico: The Paper of the Homeland, 333–39
 New York Times, 230–31
 Ontario workman, 392
 Toronto Globe, 373
 Washington Post, 208
New World
 Breech, 83
 Old and, migrants, 277
New York City
 Caribbean migration to, 269–70
 Fifth Avenue, 97
 Puerto Ricans to, 25
New York Times, Braun scandal, 230–31
New Zealand
 egalitarianism, 21–22n.5
 labor history, 22n.6
 labor movement, 19
 Social Democrats in Christchurch, 310–14
Ngai, Mae, 273, 356
Nicaragua, black immigration, 283
Nolan-Ferrell, Catherine, 105, 106, 136–58, 433
nongovernmental organization (NGO), 196, 198, 357
Noon, Faroz Khan, 416
North America
 fugitive slaves across, 363–81
 immigrant prostitutes, 224
 Toronto printers and U.S., 387–93

North American Convention of Colored People, Toronto meeting, 374, 375
North Canterbury Labour Representation Committee, coalition, 313
A Northside View of Slavery, Drew, 377
Nova Scotia
    Mi'kmaq, 112–13
    Mi'kmaw peoples, 109–10, 125
Nye, Richard, strike committee, 396

O'Connor Parker, Julia, 180
Ohio Valley, Braddock's failed expedition, 58, 66
Ojala, Eric, 201
Okoth-Ogendo, Opinya, 206
Olcott, Jocelyn, 165, 194–210, 433–34
Old World Britain, labor movement migrants from, 19
Olmstead, Frederick Law, 366–67, 379
O'Neill, Colleen, 103–6, 111, 434
O'Neill, Eugene, 410–11
O'Neill, Guillermo Baquero, 340
Ontario Workman
    British nation, 396
    Canadian labor law, 397–98
    Canadian patriotism, 399–401
    nationalism, 394–95
    printers' newspaper, 392
Organization of American Historians, LaPietra report, 13, 16n.2
Orientalism, Said, 24
Ortiz, Fernando, 34
Ottawa, politics, 300
Owens, John, 57

Packinghouse Workers Organizing Committee, Chicago, 298, 347–48
Pallares, Natalio Vazquez, 348–49
Palme, Olaf, 199
Palmer, Bryan D., 295–300, 434
Pan-African Association, 272
Panama, 176, 283

Panama Canal
    Caribbean workers, 50
    construction, 13
    migration at completion of, 268–270
    women in, Zone, 14, 17n.6
Pankhurst, Emmeline, 317
Parenteau, Bill, 111
Paris, Champs-Elysées, 97
Parker, Geoffrey, 63
Parnaby, Andrew, 105, 106, 109–26, 434
Parques Polanco, 97
Parrenas, Rhacel, 166
Partido Acción Nacional, 95
Partido Liberal Mexicano, 249
patriarchal logic, labor authority, 70–72, 80n.52
patriotism
    American Dream, 28
    British nationalism and Canadian, 385–86
Paull, Andrew, 120
Pease, William and Jane, 370
Peck, Gunther
    biography, 434
    contract workers, 216–17
    migration, 218
    "white slavery," 216, 221–41
Pedraza, Jose, 344–45
Pennington, James W. C., 374
People's University, Vasconcelos, 332
Pérez, Isabel, 146
Perkins, Frances, 418
Pingree, Hazen, 320, 321
Pinta, Dolores, 180
Piore, Michael, 25, 26
Planters, 112–13, 115
planters
    anti-Guatemalan discourse, 152
    coffee growers, 150–52
    requesting government support, 151–52
Plunkitt, George Washington, 320
Polish Insurrection, 296

politics
    gender differences, 207
    local democracy, 307–10
    transnational labor, 295–300
Pope, James, 357
Population Conference, domestic labor, 204–5
Porter, Kenneth, *Journal of Negro History*, 380
Portes, Alejandro, 43
potlatch, 119–20, 123, 124
Powderly, Terence, 226, 232, 233
pregnant workers. *See also* women
    post-World War II, 173–74
    United States, 182
Press Act of 1704, 67
primitive accumulation
    capital, 68
    global capitalism, 295
    military option, 61–63
    producer and production, 69
Printer, New York publication, 391
printers. *See* Toronto printers
Progressive Era
    antislavery language, 236
    Detroit, Toledo and Cleveland, 322
    white slavery and human trafficking, 222–23
Progressive reform, *The Survey*, 418
Progressives, 307, 308
proletarian internationalism, 295
pronatalism, women's rights, 186
prostitutes. *See also* white slavery
    Braun investigating immigrant, 232–35
    contract labor to, 233–37
    feminist, 207
    feminization of white slavery, 240
    immigrant, in North America, 224
    Jewish, 238–39
    Mann Act, 240, 241
    opposition, 235
    white slavery changing to, 233

Protection of Mothers and Children and the Rights of Women, 181
Puerto Rico
    Dominicans to, 25, 29–30n.10
    homeworkers, 177
Putnam, Lara, 217–18, 267–89, 434–35

Quebec, 59, 299, 300
Queen Victoria, 394
Quiet Revolution, Quebec, 299
quota system
    immigrants from Europe, 274
    1924 Johnson-Reed Act, 218, 275–76

race restrictions, 1924 Johnson-Reed Act, 267–68, 273
racial discrimination
    Mexican children, 339–40
    shipping, 423–24
Raibmon, Paige, 104
Railroad Retirement Act, maternity, 175, 184–85
Ramos, Domingo, 281
Rand, Silas T., 117
Ratzlaff, Carl J., 418
RCA, moving to Mexico, 26
recruitment, labor, and immigration control, 215–18
Rediker, Marcus, 51, 295
Refugee's Home Society (RHS), 378
regulations, maritime labor, 416–19
Reid, John, 125
Rembao, Alberto, "The Swallows of Becker," 339
Remes, Jacob, 358–59, 384–402, 435
reproductive labor
    concept, 210n.5
    demands, 199
    divide between productive and, 207, 214n.62
    domestic labor, 198–99
    feminism and, 163–67

reproductive labor (*Continued*)
  socialization, 203–4
  tribune organizers, 202
  women's emancipation, 209–10
resistance, Bracero Program, 251, 264n.30
responsible parenthood, domestic labor, 204–5, 212n.49
Reuther, Victor, 92, 93, 96–97
Reuther, Walter, 90, 92
revisionism, Bernstein, 308
Revolution, slaves in British army, 78n.15
Revolutionary War, slaves, 365
Reynosa, María, 205, 206
Rhode Island
  Cash Compensation Act, 183–84, 185
  cash disability program, 174
Rhuberry, Fraine, 82, 88
Riga, L., 41
Riley, Isaac, 377–78
Roberts, Michael, 63
Rodney, Walter, *How Europe Underdeveloped Africa*, 23
Rodriguez, Maria, 257
Roediger, David, 27
Romo, Francisco, 259
Romo, Lupe, 257–58
Roosevelt, Franklin D.
  domestic reform, 417–18
  marine legislation, 420
  New Deal, 172, 350, 417
Roosevelt, Theodore
  Braun, 230, 232
  Hungarian Republic Club, 226
  international prostitutes, 233
Rosal, Lic. Vicente J., 145
Rosales, Jose, 349
Rosemblatt, Karin, 178
Ross, R. S., *Barrier Truth*, 316
Roth, Joseph, 347
Royal Commission on Indian Affairs, Tom, 117

Rufino Barrios, Justo, 153–54
Russell, Earl, 397
Ryan, James, 397–98

Said, Edward, 24, 28
St. Anne's Day celebration, 116, 123
Salazar, Javier, 258, 259
Salvation Army, 271, 313
Sánchez del Castillo, Raúl, 93
Sandos, James, 253, 264n.33
Sangster, Joan, 435
Santino, Augusto César, 28
Sargent, Frank, 229, 231, 236
Sassen, Saskia, 15, 17n.7
Satzewich, Vic, 39–45, 435
scandal, Marcus Braun Affair, 229–31
Scandinavian Workers Congresses, 310
Schiller, Nina Glick, *Nations Unbound*, 39
Schmitz, Eugene, 320
schoolteachers, assimilation, 160n.40
Schopenhauer, Arthur, 332
seamen, labor standards, 360
seasonal labor. *See also* Bracero Program
  braceros, 246
  Mayan villagers in Guatemala, 25
Seattle World Trade Organization (WTO), protests, 9, 11n.29
Second Decade for Development, 197, 200
Second Labor Conference of American States, 177
Seminole Indians, black settlements, 376
Seminole Wars, first and second, 365
Serang, A. K., 425, 430n.72
Serang, Mohamed, 425
servant
  labor types, 72–74
  term, 71
Service Employees International Union (SEIU), 164
Seven Years' War
  Americas as one theatre, 75–76

global scale, 76
key victories, 75
Mi'kmaq autonomy, 125
military labor, 57–77
sex trafficking, shift from human trafficking, 241n.4
sexual division, labor, 204
sexuality, women's, 207
Shadd, Mary Ann, 373
Shadrach case, Wilkins, 367, 371, 373
Shanly, Frank, 398
shipbuilders, subsidy program for U.S., 421–22
ships. *See also* maritime standards
  human cargo, 49
  sailors, 360
Shukla, Sandhya, 8, 11n.25, 13
Simons, Marlise, 205
Sinarquistas, Mexico, 253
Sindicato Rojo de Trabajadores de Ford, 86
single tax, 309, 319, 320
Sipilä, Helvi, 203
skilled craftsmen, labor, 69, 79–80n.38
slavery
  antislavery mobilization, 372–76
  coercions, 223–24
  feminization, 225
  human trafficking and, 222
  labor form, 69–70
  nineteenth century states, 358
  Thirteenth Amendment, 221–22, 356–57
  unfree labor relationships, 221–22
  Universal Declaration of Human Rights, 356, 357
slaves. *See also* fugitive slaves
  human cargo, 49
  service in British army, 78n.15
Smith, Adam, 420
smuggling, Guatemalan-Mexican border, 136, 142–43
Snodgrass, Michael, 217, 218, 245–61, 435

social democrats
  Christchurch, New Zealand, 310–14
  German, 308
social insurance, wage contributions, 176–77
socialism
  Broken Hill, New South Wales, 314–16
  Christchurch, New Zealand, 310–14
  cities and nation-states, 304–7
  Detroit, Cleveland, and Toledo, 319–21, 322
  international, 8
  local democracy in practice, 307–10
  Manchester, England, 316–19
socialist education
  blue-collar workers, 343–44
  Cardenas administration, 342–43
  radical politics, 348–49
Socialist Party, coalition, 313
social reproduction
  care work, 163, 164
  concept, 210n.5
  labor feminists, 164–65
Social Security (1939), 184
Social Security Act (1935), 173, 428n.38
Sociedad Feminil Mexicana, women's association, 335
Society of Independent Mexican Laborers, 334
soldiers
  death in Havana, 78n.9
  empire building, 74–77
  freeing war worker, 66–69
  Herculean labors, 62–63
  imperial authority, 51
  labor types, 72–74
  military labor, 70–74
  mundane labor, 74–75
  pensions, 79n.38
  wage and responsibility, 59–60
  winning empire for Britain, 60–61
Somavia, Juan, 187
Sombart, Werner, 320

South Africa, labor movement, 19
South Carolina, slaves, 364
Soviet Union, 4, 215, 295, 419
Spain, Manila's return to, 76
Spanish-American War, seamen, 420
Spanish Civil War, 346–47, 348
Spanish colony
   fugitives seeking refuge in, 364
   terminating slavery, 365
Spanish language
   Chicago schools, 343–44
   Front enrolling Mexican children, 345–46
   sustaining migrant's skills, 338–39, 340
Sproat, Gilbert Malcolm, 119
Squamish
   economic basis of Mi'kmaq and, 122–23
   employment options, 119
   household gardens, 121
   longshoremen in British Columbia, 110–11, 125
   small-scale agriculture, 120–21
   wage labor, 119–20
   women, 121, 124
Stamp, Edward, Squamish, 119
Stassinopoulos, Arianna, 207
state building, military revolution and, 64–65
Statute of Artificers, 71
Stead, William, 232, 235
Steel Workers Organizing Committee, 298, 347
Steinfeld, Robert, 52, 70–72
Steiwer, Frederick, 423
Stern, Steve, *dependencia* approach, 24
Stoler, Anne, 5
Storts, Peter, 57
Stromquist, Shelton, 297, 303–22, 435
Struggle, Juan Uribe, 343
sugar plantations, worker migrations to, 268–69

The Survey, Progressive reform, 418
Sutton, J. E., 318
Sweden, Scandinavian Workers Congresses, 310
Sydenham Gospel Mission, Christchurch, New Zealand, 313

Taft-Hartley Act, 87
Talamentes, A., 338–39
Taylor, Paul, 252
Taylor, T. E., 312–13
Téllez Girón, Benjamin, 88
Tereshkova, Valentina, 200
Texas, fugitive slaves to Mexico, 365–67
textile factories, migrants, 35–36
textile production, 27, 35
Thane, Pat, 308
Third World
   economic security, 200
   funding extravagance in First World, 28
   material security, 208
   working people, 23
Thirteenth Amendment, 221–22, 356–57
Thomas, Albert, 413
Thomas, Deborah, 218
Thompson, Claude, 310
Thompson, E. P., 23, 297
Thorn, "Jimmy," Independent Labour Party, 310, 311, 314
Tillett, Ben
   dockworker leader, 306, 309, 314
   labor movement, 19
   Labour party, 317
   speaking tour, 297
Tinkham, George H., 417
Tinsley, James, 375, 376
Tinsman, Heidi, 8, 11n.25, 13
The Tocsin, Broken Hill's labor government, 315
Toledo, municipal reform triangle, 319–21, 322

Toluca plants, G.M. and Chrysler, 93–94
Tom, Cheakamus, 117–19
Toronto Globe, 373
Toronto Ladies' Association for the Relief of Destitute Colored Fugitives, 373
Toronto printers
  British imperial nation, 393–98
  and England, 393–98
  freedom of movement, 389–90
  labor history, 358–59
  labor issues, 392–93
  National Typographical Union (NTU), 384, 386
  North American working class, 387–93
  Toronto Typographical Union (TTU), 384–87
  tramping printers, 387–89
  traveling, by city, 387–90
  and United States, 387–93
Toronto Trades Assembly (TTA), 400–401
Toronto Typographical Union
  Toronto's printers, 384–87
  travel and distance, 388–89
Torres Bodet, Jaime, 248, 249–50
Tough, Frank, 111
Tracie, U. J., 391
Trades and Labour Council, 311–12, 313
Trade Unions Act, passage, 387, 400
Trafficking Victims Protection Act of 2000 (TVPA), 221–22
transcultural
  term, 33
  transregional and, 33–37
translocal, term, 10–11n.20
transnational
  labor history, 12–13, 18–21
  labor migration, 215–18
  refugee movements, 34
  reintroduction of term, 34
  relationship between nations and, 15
  supply chains, 356
  term, 6, 7, 8, 10–11n.20, 12, 13
  Tyrell's definition, 14
transnational history
  aboriginal labor history, 111–112
  central ideas, 13
  discussions, 16n.1
  fall of Soviet Union, 4
  listening and learning, 16
  place of nation-state, 13–14
  project, 6, 15–16
  public policy, 3
  role of nation-state, 27
transnationalism
  globalization, 7
  Latin American reflections, 11n.27
  migrations, 37–38n.4
transnational labor, 136, 295–300
transregional, and transcultural, 33–37
Traven, B., 411
The Treasure of the Sierra Madre, Traven, 411
Treaty of Detroit in 1950, 89
Treaty of Washington, 387, 396
Tresckow, Jans von, 238, 239
Trevino, Eliud Garcia, 335, 336
Trouillot, Michel-Rolph, 5, 7
Truett, Samuel, 14–15
Truman administration
  Point Four international program, 52
  Truman Doctrine, 82
  visit to Mexico, 82
Typographical Unions of Great Britain, 393
Tyrell, Ian, 14

Ubico, Jorge, 142, 153–54
Ukrainian Canadian workers, identities, 41
Underground Railroad, 368, 372
Unión General de Obreros y Campesinos, Lombardo Toledano, 87–88

United Automobile Workers (UAW), Mexican autoworkers, 53, 92–97
United Auto Workers (UAW)
   Free World Labor Defense Fund, 94
   working-class, 89, 90
United Electrical Workers (UE), 180
United Farm Workers, 261
United Fruit Company, 268–69, 283
United Kingdom, women and world problems, 198
United Nations Commission on the Status of Women, 165
United Nations Convention on the Protection of the Rights of Migrant Workers, 41
United States
   anti-Vietnam War movement, 215
   automobile industry, 83–84
   Bracero Program, 217, 245–47
   Caribbean migration to, 269–70
   Cold War alliance, 28
   Congress passing Foran Act, 226
   description of Guatemalans in Mexico, 140
   exceptionalism, 172–73, 187
   Family and Medical Leave Act (1993), 187
   feminization of white slavery, 236–37, 240
   fugitive slaves to Canada, 367–68
   global political economy, 9
   homeworkers, 177
   immigrants of African ancestry, 278
   imperialist capitalism, 342
   indentures and factory workers, 223
   indigenous culture, 104
   industrial restructuring, 27
   International Labor Organization (ILO) convention, 171–75, 181–83
   1924 Johnson-Reed Act, 267–68, 273, 275–80
   labor feminists, 174–75, 178–81
   labor movement, 19
   limiting Japanese emigration, 274
   Marcus Braun affair, 230–31
   Mexican immigration to, 245
   migration restriction in interwar, 273–80
   quota and numerical cap in 1921, 274
   racial immigration problems, 280–84
   reluctance to ratify, 45n.11
   self-governing power of cities, 305–6
   tension with Mexico and fugitives, 365
   Toronto printers and, 387–93
   Trafficking Victims Protection Act of 2000 (TVPA), 221–22
   treaties with Mexico and Canada, 368–72
   U.S-Canada relations, 42–43
   white slavery definition, 232
   women, 14
   women and world problems, 198
United States Senate's Dillingham Commission, 36
UNITE-HERE, 164
Unity Committee, coalition, 313
Universal Declaration of Human Rights, 356, 357
Universal Negro Improvement Association (U.N.I.A.), 272
University Club, Breech's speech, 84, 85
University of Chicago, Chicago Front, 343
Uribe, Juan, *Struggle*, 343
Uruguay, maternity, 176
U.S. Bureau of Investigations, 225, 227, 234
U.S. Immigration and Customs Enforcement, 358
U.S. meatpacking industry, Mexican labor force, 26–27
U.S. Women's Bureau, maternity protection, 171

Vagrancy Law (1934), Guatemala, 144, 155
Vallíeres, Pierre, 299
Vancouver, George, 118
Vasconcelos, Jose, 332
Veenhoven, Ruut, 206
Vega, Jose R., 336
Velásquez, Juan, 141–42
Venegas, Henrique, 343, 344
Venezuela, 176, 283
Vietnam War, 215, 363
Villa, Pancho, 363
Vines, D. F., 415
violence
  globalization, 31n.17
  Mexican autoworkers, 96–97
visas, British Empire, 278–79
Voice of the Fugitive, Bibb, 373–76

wages
  capitalist sector, 26
  farm workers, 262n.7
  Squamish men and women, 119–20
wages-for-housework campaign, 204
Walpole, Horace, 59
Walrond, Eric, 270
war
  artisans of, 69–74
  Ford converting production, 86
  freeing war worker, 66–69
  jingoism, 68
  labor of soldiers, 62–63
  military revolution, 62
  War Labor Board, 179
  War Measures Act, 300
  War of 1812, 365
Ward, Samuel, 365, 367, 373
Washbrook, Sarah, 144
Washington, George, 58
Washington Labor Conference (1919), 414
Washington Post, editorial cartoon, 208
Way, Peter, 51, 57–77, 436

Weaver, James, 222
Webb, Beatrice, 297, 306, 309
Webb, Sidney, 297, 306–7, 309
Webster-Ashburton Treaty (1842), 370
Weinstein, Barbara, 24, 178
welfare system
  American exceptionalism, 172–73
  decline of, 166–67
  U.S. and women, 172–73
  women's inclusion, 163
Wellstone, Paul, 222
West Indian Emancipation Day, 373
Whetton, Nathan, 256
White, Richard, 111
whiteness, transnational study, 21, 22n.8
White Niggers of America, Canadian New Left manifesto, 299
white slavery. *See also* prostitutes
  Braun's Jewish, report, 239
  Braun's reputation, 238–39
  coercions, 223–24
  contract labor to prostitutes, 233–37
  contract workers, 216
  feminization, 236–37, 240–41
  growing panic, 237
  human trafficking and, 222–24
  Jewish prostitutes, 238–39
  language of, 223, 232–33, 236
  Marcus Braun affair, 229–31, 238
  nationalization of, 240–41
  prostitutes, 233
  redefinition, 232
Whitlock, Brand, 321
Wicken, William, 125
Wilberforce, fugitive settlement, 377
Wilkes, Robert, 398
Wilkins, Fred, 367, 371, 373
William, Henry Sylvester, 272
William, Lee G., 246
Williams, Eric, 23, 28
Williams, J. S., 392
Wilson, Havelock, 413
Wilson, Woodrow, 41, 412–13

Winant, John, 175
Winks, Robin, 367
Witt, Peter, 319
Witton, Henry, 399–400
women
  British Caribbean immigrants, 270
  domestic labor, 163
  equal pay, 186
  global feminist networks, 174
  history, 5
  international feminism, 163–67
  Panama Canal Zone, 14, 17n.6
  reproductive labor, 163–67
  Squamish, 121, 124
  Third World, 30n.16
  Toronto union, 389–90, 404n.22
  U.S. welfare state, 172–73
Women in Development (WID), 197
Women's Bureau
  Civil Service Commission, 186
  maternity protection, 171–72, 182
  United Electrical Workers (UE), 180
  weakness, 173
  women's rights, 179
Women's Institute, 313
women's labor
  all-women's road-construction crew, 202
  articulation and disarticulation, 30n.16
  commodification, 200
  editorial cartoon, 208
  emancipation, 202, 209–10, 214n.69
  family structure and household labor, 205–6
  mothers, 178–79
  U.S. in post–World War II, 173–74
  wages-for-housework campaign, 204
  women's rights vs. men's, 173
  Yale University study, 202
women's rights, 166, 173
working-class identities, 27, 240, 244n.47

working-class mobilizations, 14–15
working-class politics, 304
working-class struggles, 297–300
World, emigration from Jamaica to U.S., 275–76
World Bank, 165, 166
world history, 3–9, 12–16, 23–28
World Plan of Action, domestic labor, 198, 205, 209
World Population Conference (1974), 204–6
World Social Forum (WSF), slogan, 10n.4
World War I
  Chicago industries, 349
  death toll, 178
  global labor migration before, 356
  labor movement, 19, 320
  production demands, 331
World War II
  displaced persons to Canada after, 40
  international conventions before, 175–78
  U.S.-Mexico border after, 83
Wright, Jabez, 315
Wrigley, E. A., 68, 69
Wu, Chau Chit, 416

Young, Robert, 111
Young, Ruth, 180
Young Men's Christian Association (YMCA), 338
Young Women's Christian Association (YWCA), 198

Zaalberg, C. J. P., 419
Zaragoza, Ignacio, 336
Zavala, Manolo, 259
Zinsser, Judith, 200
Zionism, 209, 238–39
Zolberg, Artistide, 275
Zuno de Echeverría, María Esther, 199, 207